The Art
of Teaching
Reading

The Art of Teaching Reading

Lucy McCormick Calkins

Teachers College, Columbia University

Photography by Peter Cunningham

New York San Francisco Boston
London Toronto Sydney Tokyo Singapore Madrid
Mexico City Munich Paris Cape Town Hong Kong Montreal

Publisher: Priscilla McGeehon
Acquisitions Editor: Aurora Martinez-Ramos
Supplements Editor: Jennifer Ackerman
Production Manager: Ellen MacElree
Project Coordination, Text Design, and Electronic Page Makeup: Electronic
Publishing Services Inc., N.Y.C.
Cover Design Manager: Nancy Danahy
Cover Photo: Peter Cunningham
Senior Print Buyer: Dennis S. Para
Printer and Binder: The Maple-Vail Book Manufacturing Group
Cover Printer: The Lehigh Press, Inc.

For permission to use copyrighted material, grateful acknowledgment is made to the
copyright holders on p. 575, which are hereby made part of this copyright page.

Library of Congress Cataloging-in-Publication Data

Calkins, Lucy McCormick.
    The art of teaching reading / Lucy McCormick Calkins.-- 1st ed.
        p.cm.
    Includes bibliographical references and index.
    ISBN 0-321-08059-9
    1. Reading (Elementary)--United States. 2. Group reading--United States. I. Title.

    LB1573 .C185 2001
    372.41'6--dc21

                                                                    00-041211

Please visit our website at http://www.awl.com

ISBN 0-321- 08059-9

1 2 3 4 5 6 7 8 9 10–MA–03 02 01 00

To my youngest son Evan
the social activist in our family,
who knows that reading, writing,
listening, and talking
are ways to build a better world,
and who uses words to right injustices,
to rally around causes,
and to create communities.

Contents

Acknowledgments

This book has grown up among the teachers, principals, teacher educators, and children in the Teachers College Reading and Writing Project's two hundred schools. It is the child of that entire, incomparable community. For fifteen years, Project members have read, taught, recorded, studied, reformed, apprenticed ourselves to mentors, invited critiques, and drafted and revised the ideas that now fill these pages. I am grateful to each educator and each child—and there are thousands—who has asked a probing question, offered an idea, shared a story, developed a rubric, or collected work that now lives in this book.

Our work in reading over all these years and in all these schools exists because of the generous and continuous funding of the Joseph E. Seagram and Sons Foundation. One year, Seagram helped us study and support whole-school systemic reform in reading. Another year, they allowed us to launch a study of struggling readers. Still another time their funds helped us support teachers in becoming mentors to the Project community. Patsy Glazer, vice president of public affairs, has functioned as guide and advisor throughout all these years. Always, Seagram has been ready to support us in the difficult work of outgrowing ourselves. We are honored and humbled by their continued generosity and hope this book is a testament to them.

Research suggests that we grow strong according to the number of nurturing relationships in our childhoods; the child who has the chance to grow up with a grandparent, neighbor, pastor, music teacher, coach, and scout leader, for example, garners the strength of all those individuals. If a book, like a child, gathers strength from the number of relationships that have nurtured its formative years, *The Art of Teaching Reading* is blessed indeed.

When I began writing the book, I asked Kathy Collins to join me as a research associate to help me extend, revise, and live into our best ideas for teaching reading in the primary grades. Kathy is the wisest, most principled teacher of primary children that I've ever known, and I wanted to learn and to let my readers learn at her side, from her teaching and from her students. Readers who know young children well will see that Kathy's greatest gift is that she, too, knows young readers well, and her responsiveness to them makes her teaching sparkle with humor, insight, and originality. Kathy's ability to talk to children (and teachers of children) in ways they can hear, shines through this book and especially through the primary chapters of *The Art of Teaching Reading*.

It is hard to find words which convey the gratitude I feel toward Kathleen Tolan, who is regarded by everyone in our community as the lead staff developer in reading. A remarkable number of the brilliant teachers in these chapters have relied on Kathleen as their mentor, as I have. Kathleen opens trails-of-thought for us all to travel as she probes, questions, invents, and explores, and I'm very grateful.

The Art of Teaching Reading brings to the page the thinking and curriculum development work of our Reading Think Tank. This group of about twenty-five brilliant educators has met together over the past decade. We convene for weekend retreats and frequent study groups, and we are constantly conducting classroom research. We plan and lead an extraordinary summer institute together. I'm grateful to everyone who is or has been a member of this Think Tank.

Randy Bomer, now a professor at Indiana University's School of Education, was co-director of the Project when we began this work. Many of its bravest aspects can be attributed to the seminal thinking Randy and I did together at the very start. His thinking is so woven into the fabric of all that my colleagues and I think, do, and imagine, it is difficult to tell where we leave off and he begins. Countless phrases in this book were his first, and I thank him for his words, his wisdom, and his friendship.

Others, too, deserve special mention. Donna Santman, a former Project colleague who is now teaching at I.S. 89 in Manhattan, has taken our team's best thinking far and then farther. Kathy Doyle, who has played a star role in most of my books, is back again as a key player in this one. Kim Tarpinian (Glen Head School, New York), Sharon Hill (The Manhattan New School, Manhattan), Ginny Lockwood and Teresa Caccavale (P.S. 116, Manhattan), Lisa Ripperger, Liz Phillips, Hannah Schneewind, and Renee Dinnerstein (P.S. 321, Brooklyn), Erica Leif and Mary Chiarella (P.S. 199, Manhattan), and Gillan White and Cathy Grimes, (Wooster School, Danbury, Connecticut) in particular have allowed me to learn alongside their teaching. I am grateful to Laurie Pessah, Katherine Bomer, Alexa Stott, Mary Ann Colbert, Mark Hardy, Annemarie Powers, Pam Allyn, and Rory Freed-Cohen, all colleagues at the Project, for sharing their reading work with me.

How grateful I am to Gaby Layden for her wisdom and experience in working with struggling readers, for her extraordinary work with the elements of story, and for teaching me with the same clarity and generosity that characterizes all her teacher-education work.

I couldn't have written this book without Lynn Holcomb's wise, informed, and kind help, especially her knowledge of leveling books and assessing young readers. Isoke Nia, director of research at the Project, pioneered the idea of units of study and generated important new thinking around elements of story.

Lydia Bellino, contributing author of *Raising Lifelong Learners* and principal of Goosehill Elementary in Cold Spring Harbor, New York, has for two decades been the person I call on for help when I'm embarking on new chapters in writing and learning. Lydia's knowledge of reading and of schools is deep and wide, and I rely on her good sense.

Because *The Art of Teaching Reading* posed enormous writing challenges for me, I asked Kate Montgomery, co-author of *Dear Exile* and a former Project researcher, to become my writing companion through the final weeks of revisions. Kate helped me find simple structures beneath complex details and build bridges for readers. Kate knows the book as no one else does, and I have savored her companionship and trusted her judgment.

Beth Neville and my assistant, Susan Forrest, have worked side-by-side with me to produce the pages and manage this book project. Each has endured more sleepless nights for the book than I can bear to imagine, and their zealous dedication to excellence leaves me breathless. Susan is my third hand in all I do, and I can't imagine doing any of it without her.

Many reading researchers have come to Teachers College, visited our classrooms, and helped us grow our ideas about teaching reading. We are especially indebted to Marie Clay, whose ideas are foundational to our work and to all work in the teaching of reading, and yet who visits our classrooms with humility, warmth, and receptivity. Marie is a hero to us and we salute her. We thank David Booth, Pat Cunningham, Beverly Falk, Jerry Harste, Ellin Keene, Steven Krashen, Tony Petrosky, Kathy Short, Frank Smith, Elizabeth Sulzby, and Sandra Wilde for joining us in study groups and for lifting the level of our thinking in crucial ways. Elizabeth Sulzby read chapters in manuscript form and helped me in ways I especially cherish. We've benefited enormously from a yearlong course of study with Gay Su Pinnell. Marc Tucker, president and CEO of the National Center on Education in the Economy, and Lauren Resnick, director of the Learning Research and Development Center and professor at the University of Pittsburgh, brought me into the center of their work with standards and put me into conversations about teaching reading and school reform that helped me widen and extend my own knowledge. I'm grateful for these opportunities and for their interest and generous support.

Every day I count my blessings over the opportunity to work within the New York City public schools. My work benefits from the wise leadership of Peter Heaney (Senior Assistant to the Chief Executive in the Division of

Instructional Support), Judith Rizzo (Deputy Chancellor for Instruction), and Bill Casey (Chief Executive for Program Development and Dissemination). I work side-by-side with many of the world's most brilliant principals and other school leaders. I am especially grateful to Liz Phillips (Principal, P.S. 321, Brooklyn), Anna Marie Carrillo (Principal, P.S. 116, Manhattan), Carmen Farina (Principal, P.S. 6, Manhattan), Gary Goldstein (Principal, P.S. 199, District 3), Ella Urdang (Principal, Smith School, Tenafly, New Jersey), Pat Romandetto and Lesley Gordon (Superintendent and Deputy Superintendent, District 3), Frank DeStefano (Superintendent, District 15), Laura Kotch (Director of Elementary School Initiative, District 10, the Bronx), Irma Zardoya (Superintendent, District 10, the Bronx), Claire McIntee (Superintendent, District 26), and Barbara Schneider (Project Coordinator, District 2).

Lois Bridges, who edited earlier books of mine, gave me early and wonderful help, and I am eternally grateful. What a privilege it has been to have Susan Meigs as my developmental editor. She has combed through each sentence and, like the greatest of teachers, helped me in ways that afterwards seem invisible. Although she has added, adjusted, and reworked sentences in every paragraph of the manuscript, when I reread the pages I hear not her voice but my own, and it is all the more resonant because of Susan's talents and time. In every future book I write, I will include a clause in my contract that I must have Linda Howe as my copy editor. My book was blessed indeed to have her close attention.

Ginny Blanford, senior editor at Longman, has overseen this book's journey. I thank her for her patience, guidance, and for setting a steady course. Aurora Martinez has devoted great care to this project. It has been a pleasure to work with Todd Tedesco at Electronic Publishing Services and I thank him for his humor and hard work. I value Tim Stookesberry's warm enthusiasm. The entire team at Addison Wesley Longman has welcomed me into their fold, and I appreciate their support. Peter Cunningham, my wonderful photographer, tiptoed on table tops and slid along the floor in order to capture the beauty of our young readers.

It is not easy to add a project of this dimension to all I already do. This has only been possible because of the enormous support I have received on all fronts. For years, Laurie Roddy gave heart and soul to the Project, and I thank her. I am more grateful than words could ever say to Laurie Pessah, codirector of the Project, and Beth Neville, assistant director of the Project, for their grace and guidance at the Project's helm. And most of all, I thank my dearest friend and strongest supporter, John Skorpen, and our two beloved sons, who fill our lives with the deepest form of peace and pleasure.

LUCY McCORMICK CALKINS

The Art
of Teaching
Reading

Building a Place for Reading   I

Iremember the morning my younger son, Evan, climbed aboard the school bus and headed off to kindergarten and the big wide world. I safety-pinned a tag onto his chest containing his name and bus route.

These words are my tag, safety-pinned onto the chest of this book. Before it heads out into the big wide world, I hope to name what I've tried to do and chart the route along which the book has traveled.

"In *The Art of Teaching Reading,* I've tried to convey my vision for the whole of teaching reading," I write. Then my mouth goes dry. I feel panicked and small. I can see authorities in the world looking down at me, their faces big, like those of Sendak's wild things, asking, "Who are *you* to have a comprehensive approach to teaching reading? What evidence do you garner, what people do you cite, what theories do you establish that entitle *you* to author a comprehensive approach to teaching reading?"

For a moment, I'm ready to throw in the towel, to admit that the job is too big, too contentious, and too desperately important for me to be worthy of it. But then I think, what I've done is what every teacher needs to do. Each one of us *must,* in our classroom, author a comprehensive approach to teaching reading. We *all* feel those faces looking down at us asking, "What right have *you* to compose a vision for teaching reading?" and we all feel small, panicked, and inadequate to the job. Too often, we *do* throw in the towel. "You're right," we say. "Just tell me what to do and I'll do it." Desperate not to leave anything undone, we race our children through everything ever recommended: leveled books, phonemic awareness, cueing systems, literature circles, shared reading, theme studies, accountable talk, literature logs, guided reading, word studies, author studies, writing workshop, inference and interpretation questions, running records, interactive writing … the sheer quantity leaves us breathless.

The problem is that if our teaching is to be an art, we need an organizing vision that brings together all of these separate components into something graceful and vital and significant. It is not the number of good ideas that turns our work into art, but the selection, balance, coherence and design of those ideas.

Artists know this. Artistry does not come from the *quantity* of red and yellow paint or from the *amount* of clay or marble but from the organizing *vision* that shapes the use of these materials. It comes from a sense of priority and purpose (Calkins, 1994). That sense of priority and purpose must come from a teacher who authors a vision for teaching. If our teaching is to be an art, we need to do more than compile materials and methods; we also need to infuse them with a sense of priority and vision, passion and grace.

Sometimes in our hurry to please everyone, to do everything we've ever been told to do, we leave out one thing: ourselves. Yet the truth is that what we bring to children will always be ourselves. In the end, the teaching of reading happens in small intimate moments when we pull our chairs alongside a child who is reading or struggling to read. Nicole's finger bobs along under the print as she reads a few words. Suddenly she stops, her finger frozen in the air, her eyes wide with anxiety. We wait. "I don't know what this says," Nicole whispers, her voice strained. The teaching of reading is about the infinite complexity of moments like these. "What can I do that will help her the most?" we think, and we ask this again and again in all the millions of moments that constitute our teaching. We don't bring a reading program to these moments. What we bring are all the conversations about reading we've ever had, and all our beliefs and willingness to learn from a child.

I worry when I see bureaucrats, policy makers, and legislators trying to script our every move in classrooms and to control our every decision by putting us in a stranglehold of standardized testing. I understand these policy makers. They have come to realize that our planet's well-being depends on

whether all of us can work together to enfranchise all our children as full citizens in the world of literacy, and they want to get in on the action. But sometimes what they seem to be saying is that the job of teaching reading is too big and too important to be left in teachers' hands. I don't worry that they'll succeed in teacher-proofing the profession or controlling our classrooms, but I do worry that if too many big faces loom down on us asking, "Who are *you* to schedule your day?" and "What gives *you* the authority to choose books for your classroom?" we will lose faith in our own abilities to be decision-makers. And if we're not decision-makers and curricular designers, if we allow our language arts instruction to be so externally controlled that we feel as if we are simply managing someone else's program, then why study the teaching of reading? When control is taken out of teachers' hands, what is the motivation for us to join study groups, to visit each other's classrooms, to pore over student work with our colleagues, to read professional literature?

I worry that the learning landscape for us, as teachers, is in jeopardy. When a teacher goes to her administrator and says, "I'm rethinking my approach to teaching *writing.* I want to pilot some new ideas," chances are the administrator will respond, "With my blessing." Is this why 35,000 teachers attend institutes every summer on the teaching of writing? Yet sometimes it seems teachers have been taught that it's not safe to be learners in the field of teaching reading. Is this why the learning landscape in the field of reading is so different? When a teacher says, "I want to pilot some new approaches to teaching reading," principals are apt to respond, "Are you *certain* it'll work? What evidence do you have? I'm not convinced...."

In order to be powerful learners of our craft, in order to make our teaching better, we need to feel uncertain and to experience disequilibrium. In order to be powerful learners, we need to be off-balance, tilted forward, ready to be affected by other people's ideas, ready to be surprised and changed by our children. The Pulitzer-prize winning writer Donald Murray once gave important advice to those of us in the field of writing. He said, "If you know how to confer with young writers—watch out. If you know how to help kids revise and edit—watch out. If you know how to teach kids the qualities of good writing—watch out. Watch out lest we suffer hardening of the ideologies. Watch out lest we lose the pioneer spirit which has made this field a great one."

The field of reading needs teachers who will be the architects of a new world in which every teacher engages in a lifetime of study on the teaching of reading. The answer to raising standards and holding our profession accountable, to insuring that every child becomes a strong reader and writer, lies not in teacher-proofing the profession but in teacher-education. We raise standards and improve the teaching of reading in our schools by giving teachers real conversations-in-the-air that can become internalized conversations-in-the-mind, informing us as we live in the moment-to-moment complexity of our craft. But if we're going to be involved in those learning conversations, we need to know that we have not only the authority but also the responsibility to author—to co-author, really—a comprehensive vision for teaching reading. If our teaching is to be an art, we need to know we can draw from all we know and believe and see in order to create something beautiful.

When I write that this book represents *my* vision for the teaching of reading, I'm not being entirely accurate. What this book represents is the vision of several hundred teachers, principals, and teacher educators who have worked over two decades to help the largest, most complex school district in the nation meet the challenge of giving *all* children the literacy education they deserve. We're not there yet. Not only are there still schools across New York City in which readers are dying on the vine, also the teaching in the classrooms I describe and the thinking about teaching in this book are very much works in progress. We have much territory yet to explore. We are especially aware that we need to do more with nonfiction reading and with responding to the needs of second language learners. But the schools and classrooms this book describes are vibrant and alive, a testimony to the real world practicality of these ideas. Readers in these schools score extraordinarily well on standardized tests and more importantly, they choose to read. These schools already function as teaching resources for the country. Thousands of educators visit these classrooms each year and also visit scores of other, similar Teachers College Reading and Writing Project classrooms, which I haven't described. Visitors come away heartened by the extraordinary teaching and learning they see. Across the country, people watch videotapes, read classroom vignettes about New Primary Literacy Standards, and see informed standards enacted in scenes from these and similar classrooms.

The Art of Teaching Reading holds the thinking not only of the immediate network that constitutes the Teachers College Reading and Writing Project community but also of the larger network of researchers, scholars, and teachers upon whose shoulders we stand. Each of the tenets in our approach to teaching reading is one that lives in the wider world.

We Regard the Independent Reading Workshop as a Central Part of the Reading Curriculum and Teach Actively into It

My hunch is that if I approached each of you and asked, "What are you really after in the teaching of reading?" you'd answer as I do, "I want my kids to be lifelong readers." Sometimes I think we say these words—"I want my kids to be lifelong readers"—without realizing they are among the most important an educator can ever utter. When we say, "My goal is lifelong reading," what we are saying is, "You can hold me accountable for my students bringing books on trips, reading over vacations and asking for magazine subscriptions for birthday presents." We are saying, "You can judge my teaching by whether my students initiate reading in their own lives, whether they weave books into their lives with the people they know and the passions they feel." These are not small goals.

Sometimes I think we say, "I want my kids to compose lives in which reading matters." But then, because we will not be there twenty years from now to see if they have a stack of books beside their bed or a manual open beside their computer, we teach toward smaller goals. Sometimes I think we hold students accountable for reading a particular passage or for doing a particular assignment, but we do not hold them accountable for living richly literate lives.

Like you, I cannot imagine anything in all the world more important than helping kids live lives in which reading and writing matter. I want children to collect, trade, talk over, and live by books. I want children to carry poems in their pockets, to cry with Jess when he finds out that his friend Leslie has drowned, to explore the Alaskan wilderness, and to stand, feeling small under the vastness of the Milky Way. I want our children's heroes to include the wise and loving spider Charlotte, spinning her web to save the life of Wilbur, and Mary and Colin, taming the wild animals, the rose bushes, and each other in their "secret garden."

There is, of course, no one best way to mentor children into becoming lifelong readers. My colleagues and I are convinced, however, that one of the simplest, clearest ways to do this is to embrace the age-old and widely held belief that children benefit from daily opportunities to read books they choose for themselves for their own purposes and pleasures (Krashen, Atwell, 1987; Cambourne, 1988; Harste, Burke and Short, 1996; Holdaway, 1979; Smith, 1985; Meek, 1988). Because I enter each new school year saying, "In this one fleeting school year, I want to be sure my students learn to author richly literate lives for themselves," this means that for me, the independent reading workshop cannot simply be a way to keep kids busy while I collect milk money and permission slips. The independent reading workshop—a term I will discuss in chapters to come—provides that opportunity for mentoring children in the project of composing a literate life, for teaching children to choose just-right books and to monitor for sense, to carry books between home and school, to not have a lonely reading life, to read a second book by an author in a different way because they've read the first, to have and develop ideas from books. The independent reading workshop is the closest we come to seeing how kids author their own reading lives. If we're not teaching into our children's independent reading lives—if we're not drawing from and giving to those lives, how can we be certain our teaching is affecting them at all?

Our image of the reading workshop grows out of larger beliefs about learning in general and about language-learning in particular. We believe that learning involves the same process, whether it happens in school or out of school; the ways a person learns to ride a bike, follow a map to a destination, or watch the sky for signs of a storm all involve processes that are vital to a child's progress in learning to read (Moffett and Wagner, 1992). Always, we succeed as learners because we want to learn so badly, we pick ourselves up and try again when we stumble. Always, we picture the whole of what we are after and persist at the subroutines because we see ourselves as the kind of people who can do this work (Mayher, 1987). If we are doing the hard work of approximating, we benefit from having teachers who observe and respond to what we are trying to do (Smith, 1973, p. 195).

Teaching reading, then, begins with helping children to want the life of a reader and to envision that life for themselves. It is important for the child just learning to ride a bike to see others riding with vigor, joy, and power. "I want that for myself," the child says. In a reading workshop, children watch each other swapping books, gossiping about characters, reading favorite passages aloud to friends, or searching for information on a hobby, and they say, "I want that for myself." Learners are willing and able to work on the particular parts of becoming stronger readers because they see the big picture of a literate life, they value it, and they consider this life as doable and worth doing.

My image of the independent reading workshop has also been influenced by my own work and that of my colleagues in the teaching of writing. Just as young writers deserve time to work on their own important writing projects every day, enough choice of topic and audience that they can often write for their own purposes, and instruction to help them raise the level of what they are doing, so, too, young readers deserve the same kinds of opportunities and instruction. Their most important project is to compose a richly literate life.

We Believe That Teaching Begins with Listening, with Respecting the Intelligence in Our Students' Efforts

Two decades ago, Don Graves taught me a lesson that has stayed with me ever since. We'd visited a classroom together to collect data on children as writers, but they were not writing that day. Instead, they were copying math problems out of their math books. I walked the aisles, waiting for data to appear. There was nothing to be seen so I leaned against the radiator at the back of the classroom, keeping a weary eye out for someone to do something so I could record it in my notebook. But no, the children just kept copying out math problems. Finally, I signaled Don, who'd meanwhile been scurrying around the room, and we left.

Before I could let out a quiet groan, Don said, "What a gold mine! Wasn't it amazing! How do you suppose that kid up front could write with a two-inch-long pencil? And that guy with the golf ball eraser on the end of his pen? Zowie." In his enthusiasm, he didn't notice my silence. "Wasn't it something the way some kids had desks down around their knees, chairs so high, desks so low, and the other kids, on their low little chairs, reaching up to desks that towered over them …"

I had learned a lesson. Denny Taylor has since remarked, "There is never a time when I pull my chair alongside a child and a miracle doesn't appear." Her words are pinned to my bulletin board. Teaching begins with seeing the significance and intelligence of what children are doing—and almost doing. Teaching means watching children through the lens of "Zowie! What a gold mine!"

In the field of reading, there is a rich tradition of respectful observation of the learner. Long before I began my work with Don Graves, Ken Goodman had already begun to teach teachers to watch children as they read, attending especially to any departures they made from the actual words of the text, and to regard these departures—or *miscues,* as he called them—as a gold mine (Goodman, 1965). Because errors are not made randomly and because each error is partly right, an error provides us a window onto the mental processes a learner uses. A pattern of errors can especially inform our teaching of young readers.

Many people have devised ways to record and study oral reading errors. Whether a teacher uses miscue analysis (Goodman, Watson and Burke, 1987) or running records (Clay 1993), it is important to understand the strategies and sources of information readers rely upon as they read. "Reading acquisition involves learning to use all the redundant sources of information in texts to problem-solve the meanings" (Clay, 1991, p. 14). A reader can problem-solve a text by attending to segments of print and their corresponding sound segments (some would say this reader is relying on the graphophonic cueing system; others say this child is relying on visual features of language). Readers can also focus on the way the syntax or grammar of our language allows us to combine words into sentences which "sound right." As a reader proceeds through a text, if a reader encounters difficulty, he or she considers what "kind of word" would fit into this sentence. Some people would say this reader has relied upon the syntactical cueing system. (Others say this reader has relied on structure cues.) Finally, and most importantly, readers can also focus on the meaning of what they are reading. When a reader uses meaning to hypothesize what an enigmatic word might be, the reader has predicted and must check this hypothesis against the print. When a reader monitors for sense as he or she reads and self-corrects a miscue because it didn't make sense with the text or the reader's knowledge of the world, this reader has self-corrected for meaning and done so by relying on meaning cues. As a reader works with and integrates these three and other kinds of information, the reader "creates a network of competencies which power subsequent independent literacy learning … learning generates further learning" (Clay, introduction, 1991).

Readers learn from reading itself, especially if they integrate information from all three sources of information (and use all three cueing systems). But learners also benefit from instruction. The instruction that will help learners most is grounded in observations that acknowledge what they are already doing. Jerome Bruner (1978) describes the teacher's role as "scaffolding"; Michael Halliday (1975) speaks of it as "tracking"; L. S. Vygotsky (1978) talks about working in the child's "zone of proximal development"; and Marie Clay (1985) speaks of the importance of sensitive observation accompanying each stage of teaching. Each of these researchers uses a different metaphor to suggest that teachers provide temporary support to enable a child to work in ways that are a step beyond what the child could do independently. "What the child can do in cooperation today he can do alone tomorrow. Therefore the only good kind of instruction is that which marches ahead of development and leads it; it must be aimed not so much at the ripe as at the ripening functions" (Vygotsky, 1962, p. 104).

Teachers Need to Understand and Demonstrate the Qualities of Good Reading and Help Students Grow Toward These Qualities

The research for this book began fifteen years ago when my colleagues and I realized that just as we had benefited from drafting and revising our own writing and then bringing an insider's perspective on writing into our classrooms, so, too, we needed to bring an insider's perspective on reading into our classrooms. In schools across New York City and the surrounding suburbs, we soon formed almost one hundred adult reading groups. Our schools were filled with conversations about Toni Morrison, Eudora Welty, and Wallace Stegner. For several years, the teacher-leaders of these reading clubs met to study the conditions that we, as adults, need in order to grow as readers. We also studied the qualities of good reading, just as years earlier we had studied the qualities of good writing. We studied with graduate-level literature professors and read research on proficient readers (Gordon and Pearson, 1983; Anderson and Pearson, 1984), and we apprenticed ourselves to mentor-readers within our own community. From all of this, we developed a firsthand understanding of terms that had once seemed enigmatic to many of us: *interpretation, intertextuality, critique, synthesis,* and *envisionment.* We had for a long while known what these terms meant in textbooks and reading programs, but now we came to understand more deeply what they could mean in our lives and in our students' lives.

The talking, writing, reading, questioning, and learning we did alongside Toni Morrison's *Beloved,* Anne Tyler's *Dinner at the Homesick Restaurant,* and Lawrence Thornton's *Imagining Argentina* are deeply ingrained in everything we have done since. Over and over in our teaching, we draw on the resources of our own reading lives. We test new ideas for teaching against the question, "Would I do that in my own reading life?"

In classrooms, we try to identify what our children are already doing in the name of proficient reading and to imagine what is possible. "What is growth in reading once you can read?" we ask. We look at our children's work in response groups and ask, "How do we hope these conversations will change over the course of a year, of a child's school career?" We look at what our children are doing in the name of prediction, for example, and ask, "How could we help our students journey toward a richer sense of what it means to predict as they read?" If our students predict by pausing at the end of a chapter to guess how their book will end and then, when they reach the book's final page, saying, "I was (or wasn't) right," we can help them predict responsively at moments such as when the hero fingers the blade of the knife. We can help them consider, "What does my knowledge of other texts like this one (or of situations, places and people in the world like these) lead me to expect?" We can help readers not only set up expectations but revise these continually in the light of new information. In similar ways, we can support other lines of growth in our young readers. In their important book, *Mosaic of Thought,* Ellin Keene and Susan Zimmermann suggest ways to support readers use sensory images to enhance comprehension, infer, connect the known to the new, determine importance, ask questions, and synthesize (1997, Keene and Zimmermann). We've considered other lines of growth as well, including some which are less apt to be listed in the canon of reading skills. How do we help readers develop stamina? Weave reading projects and purposes into their lives? Not have lonely reading lives? Notice when a text turns a corner? Take notes on non-fiction texts which are useful to them? Grow ideas in response to their reading? Talk about books in ways that help them think about books? Live differently because they are readers?

Our research into the qualities of good reading has influenced not only our work with intermediate students but also our work with beginning readers. Recently, I met with a group of educational leaders from major cities across the United States. I suggested we first compile an agenda of our concerns and questions. One person began. "My issue is teaching comprehension, starting in grade 3." The next person said "Ditto." It was almost unanimous. Everyone in that room was concerned over how to do more to teach students the thinking work of reading, starting in the intermediate grades.

"Why locate comprehension instruction in the intermediate grades?" I asked. "Isn't reading *always* about thinking?" Almost forty years ago, in his now classic *The Process of Education,* Jerome Bruner (1963) suggested that

> Experience over the past decade points to the fact that our schools may be wasting precious years by postponing the teaching of many important subjects on the ground that they were too difficult.... The foundations of any subject may be taught to anybody at any age in some form. (p.76)

If we want to help all our children think deeply about texts and live comfortably in the world of ideas, then won't we want to introduce children to this habit of mind from the very start? As Bruner goes on to argue, the basic ideas that lie at the heart of, and give form to, life and literature are as simple as they are powerful.

> There is nothing more central to a discipline than its way of thinking. There is nothing more important in its teaching than to provide the child with the earliest opportunity to learn that way of thinking—the forms of connection, the attitudes, hopes, jokes and frustrations that go with it. In a word, the best introduction to a subject is the subject itself. At the very first breath, the young learner should, we think, be given the chance to solve problems, to conjecture, to quarrel as these are done at the heart of the discipline. (p. 76)

In our work, we have approached kindergarten and first-grade children expecting that they can question, synthesize, and interpret. We believe that if children grow up *always* seeing reading as thinking guided by print, we won't have problems with comprehension starting in grade 3.

We Believe Reading Is Social, and That Children Learn to Read Best Within a Richly and Rigorously Interactive Community

I want children to know what it is to open a good book and be opened by that good book. "Great literature, if we read it well," Donald Hall has said, "opens us up to the world and makes us more sensitive to it, as if we acquired eyes that could see through things and ears that could hear smaller sounds." We read the page and suddenly, chapter by chapter, our lives unfold. It is all utterly meaningful. We read *Charlotte's Web* and watch as Wilbur the pig comes to realize that "friendship is one of the most satisfying things in the world," and we grow to understand that Charlotte's generosity has been as good for her as it has been for Wilbur: "By helping you perhaps I was trying to lift my life a little. Anyone's life can stand a little of that." Although it is powerful to read this at home alone, it is exponentially more powerful to put this story smack in the middle of the heartaches and hopes of our own friendships. Robert Coles, in *The Call of Stories,* writes of the power he found in bringing literature into the hospital, into the midst of disease and vulnerability, life and death. "It's one thing to read Tillie Olsen or Ralph Ellison or William Carlos Williams in a literature course; it's another to read them now. I've never thought of stories or a novel as a help in figuring out how to get through a day. But now, when you're coming back from the work we do in a clinic and you pick up these stories, you feel as if the author knows you personally." For children, reading literature with friends in the classroom has the same power. Here, amid friendships that form and dissolve, invitations to birthday parties that come or do not come, clothes that are in or out of fashion, and parents who attend or do not attend the school play, here children are working out their life and death issues.

Reading literature within a classroom community is powerful because literature can help us escape the boundaries of ourselves. We feel less alone when we understand that our pain and joy are shared. Nelson Mandela has said that what kept him alive in his imprisonment were all the messages and names and memories scrawled and scratched into the walls of his tiny cell. When I think of the violence and the economic, social, and racial rifts in the world today, I know that we need to read great literature together to help us live shoulder-to-shoulder on this earth. Kafka has said, "Reading is an ax to break the frozen sea within us," but reading can also be an ax to break the frozen sea *between* us. By reading, we cross the boundaries of time and space, we read the words and live in the worlds of people centuries ago, of people in faraway lands or in castes not touching our own. By reading, we can walk city streets and stand in fields of wheat, we can live inside skin that is black, brown, or white, we can see through ancient eyes or through the eyes of a child. We can read of people utterly different from ourselves and find kinship with them.

We need to read and talk back to books in the social world of the classroom for these personal and interpersonal reasons, but we also need to do this together for intellectual reasons. When we teach comprehension, much of what we teach is a depth of listening, understanding, and response. Part of teaching comprehension, then, is making a place for astute and active listening. If we want children to listen to an author, won't we also want children to listen to each other, to link their ideas with those of their classmates? If we want children to determine what is and what isn't important in an author's words, won't we want them to listen to each other and be able to say, "Are you saying that …" If we want children to empathize with characters in books, won't we want them to hear each other's ideas and perspectives and see these worlds and texts through each other's eyes?

Lauren Resnick (1999), Director of the Institute for Learning at the University of Pittsburgh, points out that the talk that makes students learn is "accountable" talk. "Students need to listen—really listen—to one another…. This means that students should use what others say in their discourse. In unaccountable discourse, students' statements rarely connect to one another; one speaks, and then another speaks, but the second never builds on the first … . In accountable discourse, students take one another's remarks seriously and respond directly to them: using a statement as evidence supporting a proposition; refuting a statement by offering evidence to the contrary; concurring with a statement by offering supporting evidence…. If students are to learn from each other, they cannot simply make bald assertions. They must be able to back up their statements with evidence". Readers, like listeners, need to engage in accountable discourse.

Vygotsky has helped us realize that by encouraging students to interact with others, we give them frames for thinking alone. If others repeatedly say to us, "So what do you think this is really, really about?" we will soon ask their questions of ourselves. The conversations we have "in the air," then become conversations we have in our own minds.

It is important to give our students the words that will help them read actively, but it is even more important to invite them to become active readers. If we want children to read with wide-awake minds, then we need to invite them to live this way in the dailiness of our classrooms. Teaching reading, then, is rather like teaching living.

Co-Authoring a Literate Community in the Classroom

1

Every summer our family spends three weeks in a lakeside cabin in northern Michigan. While we are there, we catch grasshoppers in the meadow, sail clear around Fox Island, and look for crayfish at the farthest edge of the sand bar. But for my sons, none of this compares to the magic of their tree fort.

Built between the boughs of a giant fir tree leaning out over the lake, the fort is little more than a platform of logs strapped together. But to Miles and Evan, the fort is a castle in the sky. All winter long, they dream about it and design the next summer's additions. Of course, as they tell stories of the fort there is another story: the story of the people who live there together. They each have jobs and titles. Peter, whose mother allows him to play with squirt guns, is Chief of Defense. Charlotte, the only girl, is Chief Spymaster. Evan, who loves the idea of a harbor below the fort and has tied his homemade raft out onto a buoy, is Director of Transportation. And Miles, as Chief Engineer, plots and envisions next summer's new dimensions.

I listen to my children talk about their fort and I think, "This is a metaphor for curriculum in the reading and writing workshop." In our classrooms, what we're doing—not just in September but all year long—is building a fort, a clubhouse for readers and writers. And we're helping children assume positions of responsibility and influence in the literate communities of their classrooms.

The curriculum that matters is the world we make, the identities we fashion, the habits we form, the roles we assume. To a very large extent, the curriculum in a reading workshop is life together as citizens in a richly literate community. It's the stuff we do in the fort, the dreams we fashion, the contraptions we build, the projects we tackle … and the way all of this changes us forever.

Jerry Harste, professor of education at Indiana University and co-author of *Creating Classrooms for Authors and Inquirers* (1996), was wise when he said, "I see curriculum as creating in the classroom the kind of world we believe in and then inviting children to role play their way into being the readers, writers and learners we want them to be." Of course, teachers don't create the literate world alone. We don't set the stage and then open the curtains to invite children to assume the roles of the learners we want them to be. Instead, our students join us in building tree forts for literacy, and as they do so, they grow into identities as readers and writers. In the classroom we make a place for listening and collaboration. Our beliefs about teaching and about literacy infuse all that we do in this place.

Making a Place for Reading at School and at Home: Children Help Co-Author the Rituals and Tools of the Classroom Community

In the independent reading workshop more than anywhere else, we help our children build richly literate lives. We begin the year by learning about their reading lives outside of school. Then we invite them to join us in fashioning even richer reading lives by working together within the classroom.

"Reading and writing will be at the heart of everything in our classroom this year," Kathy Collins, a teacher at P.S. 321 in Brooklyn, told her big-eyed first graders at the start of their first morning meeting to launch their independent reading workshop. "We need to make this a classroom where reading is so, so special," she continued. "I'm wondering if anyone has a book at home that is an absolute favorite?"

Hands shot up. "I do …" "I've got the best book …"

'Wait a minute. Do you think you'd be willing to bring your special book to our classroom tomorrow?" Kathy asked over the commotion.

The next morning, as the kids unpacked and rushed to show Kathy their choices, she began having mixed feelings about her idea. "They certainly didn't bring in Faith Ringgold *Tar Beach!*" Kathy said, recalling the ambivalence she'd felt showcasing *The Little Mermaid* and *Titanic* and books that beeped and bopped.

These books may not have been Kathy's idea of great children's literature, but they did come into the room layered with life stories. Josh, holding up his cross-section book of automobiles and trains announced, "My dad reads it to me." That was all Josh planned to say. He was done. A flurry of hands popped up as the circle of children clamored onto knees and waved frantically, pleading, "Call-on-me, call-on-me!"

But Kathy's attention remained steadfastly fastened on Josh. With one hand, she quelled the appeals as if to say, "Wait, I'm listening to Josh. Listen with me." Looking into Josh's face, Kathy said, "You read with your dad? That is *so cool.*"

Josh nodded, "He reads to me, but last night he was tired. We just laid on my bed and went through the pictures."

"Don't you love it when someone reads with you?" Kathy asked. "And in bed! That's the best! I'm just like you Josh. I can't fall asleep without a story. I was like that as a kid and I'm like that as a grown-up. I need to read before I can sleep."

Soon the room was full of talk about bedtime stories and read-aloud times. "After my baby brother goes to sleep, my mom sometimes reads to me," Marissa said.

"You and Josh are alike in that way. You both have parents who read aloud to you. That is so neat."

"My grandma reads the Bible and then she puts a little piece of paper in it to save her place," Cheltzie said.

"Wait a minute!" Rohan blurted out. "My mom does the *exact* same thing. She folds up a Kleenex and uses it for a bookmark." From all corners of the room children compared notes on bookmarks.

"My grandma gave me one you can buy at the store. Wanna see it?" Emma said, and raced off to dig through her backpack, producing a laminated kitten-bookmark with pink silk tassel.

"You can use a Popsicle stick," Meon added.

"Wow," Kathy said. "Maybe we should all save Popsicle sticks. Then we could use them as bookmarks, the way Meon suggested, or we can use Kleenex. Or if anyone has a birthday coming up, they can ask for a bookmark from the store, like Emma's. Because we're going to be doing tons of reading this year and you are right: readers need ways to mark our places in books." When we and our children work together to bring the tools, traditions, rituals, and landmarks of literacy into our classroom, we are deeply engaged in the project called Making a Place for Reading in our schools and in our lives.

The reading lessons are giant ones. Whether made from Kleenex or from a Popsicle stick, bookmarks have everything to do with making a commitment to stay with a book and to carry books back and forth between home and school, and this work is not at all inconsequential. Likewise, what could be more important work for readers than to talk together about the times and places for reading throughout their day? We help children develop identities as avid readers by inviting them to join us in building the habits and the places for reading.

The next day, after attendance, Diana took her place at the front of the morning circle. The children grew quiet. "This is *Bambi* and there's a movie to go with it," Diana announced, as she held up her book for all to see.

For a moment, Kathy respectfully turned the pages of the book. Then she said to the class, "When Diana showed this book to me yesterday, I asked her when she gets to read it. So she drew a picture of herself reading *Bambi*."

Diana turned ceremoniously so that the entire circle of classmates could see her drawing. "It's me, in the car with my seatbelt on. When my mom drives me to school, I read *Bambi*."

Kathy didn't ask "Who wants to go next and share their book?" Instead, she and the class launched into a giant conversation about the reading places in their own lives. "You have given me an idea!" Kathy said to Diana, and she drew a quick sketch of herself reading. "Here I am," she said. "I'm on my bed, with books and newspapers all around and sunshine pouring in the window. Can you see the smile on my face? This is the best!" Soon the entire class had followed Diana's lead and drawn a picture of themselves reading. Now the classroom was full of stories of bedside tables piled high with books, reading lamps, and flashlights, pillow barricades to keep little sisters away, and even a reading fort in the bathtub with the shower curtain pulled for privacy.

"Diana, you got this whole conversation going and now everyone of us is going home and fixing up reading nooks for ourselves," Kathy said.

It was not an accident that Kathy's children talked during their first week of school about bookmarks and reading nooks. In a far section of New York City, Teresa Caccavale's second graders were admiring Charlene's book bag. The class then decided that because they were going to be the kind of readers who brought books with them everywhere and who carried books between home and school, they needed a special book bag like Charlene's. A few grandmothers signed on, and before long, the children in Teresa's second grade each had a beautiful corduroy book bag with a drawstring cord. They also each had a ritual of carrying their books between home and school.

The teachers in these classrooms are key members of the Teachers College Reading and Writing Project's Reading Think-Tank. For more than fifteen years, members of this think-tank have worked together to rethink, deepen, revise, and extend our ideas about teaching reading and to share these ideas with the others who have studied with us. Although our classrooms vary tremendously, because we teach and revise our teaching together our diverse classrooms demonstrate a commitment to shared goals. And one of our most important goals is taking to heart the challenge of helping young people compose a life in which reading matters. Because we want children to build literate lives for themselves, we are not the sole authors of the literate worlds of our classrooms. We co-author those worlds.

Children are great world builders. Their eyes sparkle when we ask them, "How should the chairs go, the time go, the books go, the celebrations go so that our reading and writing matter this year? Let's draw on all we know about our best reading and writing experiences and make them happen here—only better." Children love to make lists, to sketch plans, to drape plaid blankets between chairs and sofa, to build cathedrals with stained-glass windows. They are not only making worlds, they are making themselves. In our classrooms too, children fashion identities and role-play their way into them.

Learning to Be Affected by the Words of Others

When Josh held up his cross-section book of automobiles and trains and announced, "My dad reads it to me," neither Josh nor his classmates expected his words to matter. Other children responded to Josh's comment by raising their own hands. This isn't unusual. In many classrooms, kids talk as if no one is listening. After reading a book with our students, we ask, "What did you think of the ending?"

"Weird," one child says.

"So-so," another says.

For both children, intonation alone suggests, "That's that. The book's ending is weird. The ending is so-so." End of conversation.

Often children talk as if they don't expect anyone to probe further, to request elaboration, to ask an extending question. The child who responds to the book's ending by saying "Weird" doesn't expect a listener to say, "What would you have anticipated from a more normal ending?," nor does she expect her teacher to ask the class, "Do others agree? Disagree? Let's talk about this."

Children talk in snatches of thought, not passages of thought, because no one is listening. This is true in school as well as at home.

Recent research shows that parents talk with their children an average of ten minutes a day. "How was school?" they ask. "Fine," children respond, and that is that. Few parents invite more detail. Children return to their television, Walkman, CD player, video game, or computer. "Our children," Bill Moyers says, "are being raised by appliances."

When children learn to listen to each other and to be affected by each other's words, this has everything to do with the teaching of reading. For the most part, the problem in America is not simply that children cannot decode words but that children do not respond to words by creating movies in their minds or worlds of response in their lives. If words and stories and ideas do not engage children's minds or make a difference in children's lives, how can we expect our students to think and to live well in response to books?

When Josh showed his classmates the cross-section book he and his father read together, Kathy knew that according to teaching protocol, the conversation needed to move on to another child. But if we want to teach reading, the challenge is nothing less than creating a counterculture in which words matter. Paulo Freire says, "Reading is not walking on words, but grasping the soul of them." If we want children to know what it is to take in the words and thoughts and stories of another person and to let those words leave a lasting mark, then we need to mentor children to become citizens in a listening community.

In order to co-author the literate world of the classroom with children, we ask them about times when reading has worked in their lives. We listen intently to what they say and work from their ideas. We let children's words affect us. In doing so, we model the inner listening that is at the heart of reading.

If we want our students to give weight and meaning to words, we need to listen to their words with an even keener ear and to look at them with an even keener eye. When Kathy hears Josh say, of his cross-sections book, "My dad reads it to me," or Meon say, of a Popsicle stick, "You can use it as a bookmark," she hears not only the words but the values behind them. In Josh's statement she hears the importance of sharing reading, of making it a part of relationships and talk. In Meon's she hears the value of commitment to a book, of going back to it even when your current chunk of reading time has run out. With this kind of observation and listening, we can teach not over or around but *into* our students' emerging intentions.

We Adopt Mentor Readers and Become Mentor Readers for Each Other

On the second day of school, Principal Liz Phillips stopped by Kathy's classroom. "Can you stay a minute?" asked Kathy. "We were talking about all the kinds of reading we do in our lives. Could you list for us the reading you've been doing lately?"

Before long, Liz had spread the contents of her book bag onto the floor and was chronicling the story behind each artifact of her reading life. "This," said Liz, holding up a tattered piece of yellow legal-size, paper, "is a list of books I'm thinking about for the next meeting of my reading club. We have met one night each month for the last twenty-one years; we have snacks together and then talk for hours about a book. For the next meeting, we're all supposed to bring some ideas for the next book, so these are some I'm thinking about." Then Liz held up a book. "This is a new book I haven't read yet. I just saw it at the bookstore, and I remembered that my good friend Eileen told me that she loved it. And," she continued, "here are some menus that my daughter gave me to help decide what food to serve at her wedding." Before long, she'd also told about:

- A phone message on a pink message slip from the office at P.S. 321
- An article from *The New York Times* that she planned to copy for all the teachers
- A book about teaching that she's reading for a study group at the Project
- A poem written for her by a second grader
- Information about a conference on New Standards she'll soon attend

Liz, Kathy, and the children pulled ideas from all these data. Clearly, Liz wasn't just a book reader. She read lots of different kinds of texts. And a lot of her reading grew out of her life projects and interests, and she has lots of reading friends. Kathy suggested that for homework, her children look through their own book bags, shelves, or closets and think about how reading fits into *their* lives. "Bring in a few items that together give us a picture of you as a reader."

Later in the year we mentor children in the mind work of proficient readers, but early in the year, it is more important to help children understand that their reading lives are their own, to choose and to shape. We mentor children first in the habits of living like a proficient reader, encouraging them to assume these habits and this role.

The Social World of Readers

Often children see reading as a lonely and isolating activity. They prefer the sociability of watching television, videos, and movies to what they see as the stark loneliness of reading. "Reading is spooky," one middle school child said. "Sometimes when I'm reading, I lose touch."

As Nancie Atwell points out in her important book, *In the Middle,* if we are going to help children grow up loving reading, we must turn reading into a companionable activity. When John Goodlad researched American classrooms for *A Place Called School,* he asked children "What's the one best thing about school?" Thirty-two percent responded, "My friends, sports, activities," and sixty-two percent, "Mixing and meeting with others." If we want our children to love reading, we need to be sure they see it as a companionable thing to do.

When Rohan heard that Cheltzie's grandmother leaves a little piece of paper in the Bible to save her place, he could hardly contain his excitement. A tremendous sense of comradeship can grow as children swap the techniques and tricks of their literate lives.

In Kathy Doyle's fifth-grade classroom in New Jersey, (yes, this is a second Kathy and because both play key roles in this book, I'll distinguish them by using surnames when necessary) children gathered in a circle on the second day of school, each holding a book they considered to be a landmark in their own history as a reader. Each child said something about his or her book and then Kathy Doyle asked, "What conversations could you imagine having with someone in the circle?"

"I like the same book as Nicholas. We could talk more."

"I hate poetry so I'd like to see what Emily sees in it."

Then Kathy Doyle said, "Find a partner, and have one of those book talks." After only ten minutes of book talk, the children were full of plans for their future reading relationships.

"Me and Dorene realized we *adore* the same kinds of books."

"Miles is going to bring his *Dune* books in for me to read."

"I entirely forgot about the Amber Brown books till this reminded me."

Frank Smith argues that the big purpose of school is to ensure that every child is given full membership in the club of literacy. Literacy must be a social activity. We talk, dress, and think like the people with whom we associate. We identify with the communities we join, the company we keep. Smith says, "If you ask 'Who am I?' the answer is not to be found in the mirror, but in the company you keep." It is important then for us to help our children know that every one of us is a member of the club of readers.

Words That Change the World

Developing a Classroom Library

2

At a recent author celebration at P.S. 95—a school for eighteen hundred children in the South Bronx—nine-year-old John stood and read, "When I was little, my father bought clothes for me. Then he left without a word. Now I'm all grown up with no father. I feel like a piece of paper, used and thrown away." Marisol, dressed in her Holy Communion finery, read:

> I'm the kind of kid who never had a birthday party. I live with my aunt. She cooks macaroni for me and tells me to get going and where have I been? She doesn't think about my birthday. I went back to the Dominican Republic and my baby stepsister, she's big now, and they gave her a party. No one could tell I never had one.
>
> Soon I will be ten. I pretend there will be a party and the kids will come, and we'll play "duck, duck, goose" and we'll listen to the radio and there'll be a pink cake, "To Marisol." But then my dream ends. I'm the kind of kid who never had a birthday party.

A week later, Marisol turned ten, and all the children, their parents, their teacher, and Pam Allyn, my colleague and their staff developer, gave her a big party in the park. Balloons hung from the trees, there were gifts, and the children played "duck, duck, goose" and listened to the radio. And there was a huge pink cake. On it were the words "To Marisol. For all the birthday parties you never had."

Marisol is no longer the kind of kid who never had a birthday party. Later, the class talked about how it was *words* that had made the difference. The words of Marisol's memoir gave them the idea. They talked about how words can be the blueprint for something as big as a birthday party or a nation. They talked about the words that people put onto paper—words like the Declaration of Independence and the Constitution—that have changed the world forever. It wasn't just Marisol who was changed that day. Every child in that classroom had learned something about the power of words.

When children come to us in September, they do not always come cherishing words. We see this in the poem, grimy with footprints, crumpled on the floor, in the book, layered with sneakers and frisbees on the floor of the coat closet; in the child who finishes her writing and without even glancing at it, hands it to us saying, "I'm done. What should I do next?" We hold the paper, the words, and the child, who has put herself on the line and who doesn't so much as glance back to see what she has said. We want to tell her that what she should do next is to live differently because she has words. She needs to listen to those words—to them and through them and under them.

We watch another child reading the final page of a book. We know by heart what he will find there, and we smile in anticipation of his response. The child's eyes move steadily through the words and then he snaps the book shut and shoves it to the side. "I'm done. What should I do now?" How do we say, "You should live differently forever." How, in September, do we begin to create a world in which words matter? To do this we need to consider.

- Putting literacy at the heart of our schools
- Building classroom libraries
- Matching books to readers
- Organizing our libraries to support purposeful book choice
- Using book reviews to support intentional book choice

Putting Literacy at the Heart of our Schools

Six years ago, when Carmen Farina became principal at P.S. 6 in Manhattan, her first priority was to create bottom-line standards for kindness and respect across the entire school community. She wanted to do this without casting aspersions ("I heard you say this" or "I saw you do that"). And so Carmen bought and wrapped a beautiful hardcover copy of Kevin Henkes' picturebook, *Chrysanthemum,* for each of her staff members. At the first faculty meeting, each staff member was given a gorgeously wrapped package and a long, personal letter from Carmen explaining why she'd chosen this particular book.

Carmen read the book aloud, and the school community talked long and deeply about the little acts of kindness they could do for each other and for children, and about ways they'd been bruised by words. "Sticks and stones *can* break our bones, but it's words that can really hurt us," they said. "And what about our children?" the teachers asked as they resolved to create a bottom-line of absolute dignity and respect throughout their school.

Carmen asked her teachers to share their copies of *Chrysanthemum* with their children during the next few days, and soon the whole school had heard the story of this child, taunted because her name was different, and the whole school was deeply involved in a conversation about ways they, too, can feel marginalized for being different.

That was six years ago, and since then not a month has gone by without the 38 professionals at P.S. 6 receiving a carefully chosen book and a long letter from their principal, explaining why this was her choice for the Book-of-the-Month. Each month, all 986 children in the school listen to the Book-of-the-Month and have grand conversations about it. Fifth graders and kindergarteners alike at P.S. 6 can recite these beloved lines from *The Jester Has Lost His Jingle:*

> Laughter is like a seedling
> Waiting patiently to sprout
> All it takes is just a push
> To make it pop right out

And when the school community gathers together, Carmen can say to her children, "I've watched so many of you acting like some of our heroes, with Ruby Bridges' courage to stand up for what's right and with Miss Rumphius' commitment to making the world a more beautiful place." Every child at P.S. 6 understands Carmen's literary references and more importantly, they understand that literature can help you live your life.

More than forty other principals across New York City have followed Carmen's example, giving their teachers each a carefully chosen Book-of-the-Month. Some principals have asked Carmen to alert them of her book choices but she tells them, "You need to listen to the pulse of your school, to find a book that can help you with your own questions and hurts and needs and dreams." In each school, the Book-of-the-Month arrives accompanied by a letter from the principal. In the letter with Toni Morrison's *The Big Box*, Carmen asked teachers to pay extra attention to the importance of supporting children's varied and diverse strengths and she vowed to do this for her staff as well. "In this time of standards, we need to do all we can to not be put in a box and standardized," she wrote. "Do we allow students freedom to be themselves? Certainly there needs to be structure and expectations, but within this structure, there needs to be a conscious effort not to require all children to act the same, think the same, or enjoy the same things … to not all be "put in a box." Carmen ended her letter by celebrating the diverse strengths of her staff "to Sheila Brown, for being a four-star listener, often on the same issue for disparate constituencies; Phyllis Bethel, you sing, you dance, you inspire; Dawn Falcone's passion for math is contagious, as is her patience and tact in explaining it to colleagues and students."

"The books have given us at P.S. 6 a shared language; we refer to characters from books as if they live among us, and books truly are touchstones for us," Carmen says. "_____ helped us think through our responses to bullying, Keselman and Montserrat's *The Gift* was the perfect book for the winter holidays because it reminded parents that the gifts our children treasure most are those that can't be bought."

Meanwhile, of course, the Book of the Month conveys other messages. Every child in the school knows that the leader of their school is a Book Person. Parents write Carmen suggesting candidate books: "When I read this one, I thought of you," a mother wrote. "Our class thinks you should consider this book for the Book of the Month and here's why," some first graders recently wrote. And because Carmen has given herself this job, she becomes even more a book person. "I try to find books no one has yet found," she says. "And I confess I'm always ordering books to review and perusing the shelves of bookstores and libraries."

The Book of the Month is just one of many ways in which schools wave the flag of literacy from their flagpole. At P.S. 116, children can opt to eat lunch at the Magic School Bus or the Paula Danzinger table. At P.S. 321, the first Friday of each month is Parents-as-Reading Partners day: parents are invited to linger in their child's classroom for the independent reading workshop. Every older child at P.S. 321 has a younger reading buddy, and the two classrooms (the mentors and the mentees) go on several field trips together and do a shared thematic study. Rituals such as these make a powerful statement. "We are Book People," they convey.

Building Classroom Libraries

Once a month, I meet with a group of about one hundred and twenty New York City principals. Because we are each working to turn whole schools into richly literate communities, we talk a lot about a Bill of Rights for All Children.

Many of the principals in this study group have gathered their teachers together to establish bottom-line conditions that will exist in all the classrooms across the school. In most of these schools, every child at every grade level is given at least half an hour each day in school to read books of his or her own choosing, books the child can read with fluency and understanding. Every child also carries books between home and school and reads more at home every evening.

The most urgent problem is the tragic lack of books. "If you are a teacher and you have no classroom library," David Booth told hundreds of teachers who'd gathered for one of our summer institutes, "sell your shoes. Wrap newspaper around your feet. People will see you, shake their heads, and say, 'Ah! There goes a teacher.'" I love how this anecdote reveals the dedication of teachers, but it is troubling to think of the lengths to which we must go in order to acquire books. Yet simply providing children with more books can double the amount of reading they do (Krashen, 1993; Cleary, 1939; Bissett, 1969; Houle and Montmargreth, 1989). Few of us question that books are staples in a learner's diet. How can it be, then, that every classroom in America doesn't have a rich library? Why are so many teachers put in the awkward position of spending hundreds of their own dollars on books? Why are we forced to hoard points from our children's book club purchases?

The book crisis has escalated because of four trends. First, the understandable pressure to equip every classroom and every school library with computers has had a direct and devastating impact on libraries. Libraries are now called media centers, which means that the budget for technology drains the budget for books. At a meeting of IBM executives Steve Krashen tried to explain the tug-of-war elementary school educators face when they need to decide between funding classroom libraries and purchasing computers. The IBM executives were mystified. "How could there be any question?" they wondered. "*Of course* the priority needs to be books. If you have a fifth grader who is an avid reader and you put that child and a friend beside a computer, they'll learn the computer in a day." Too often kids *aren't* avid readers—and the first solution needs to be to provide them with the books they need.

Then, too, the push to establish guided-reading book rooms filled with multiple copies of leveled books has also had devastating consequences for classroom lending libraries. I've seen reading specialists pick through classroom libraries, pulling out all multiple copies of books so they can be sequestered in a book room. I'm all for schools that have adequate lending libraries taking the next step to provide lean, carefully chosen guided reading bookrooms, but it is troubling if a child's only access to books is through the keyhole of guided-reading groups.

Sometimes when classroom library shelves are especially lean, book monies have gone to support whole-class or small-group book sets, which are closeted away until the appointed moment when children will be asked to read them. This isn't necessary. Good literature, by definition, deserves to be read and reread. If you and I, as teachers, can read Carol Fenner's *Yolanda's Genius* year after year and wipe away the tears each time, our children, too, can discover the power of revisiting a beloved book. In many Project schools, whole-class sets of books have now been dispensed among many classroom libraries, available for circulation. We round up the multiple copies when we need to do so.

Of course, neither technology, guided reading, nor whole-class novels are the whole reason for depleted classroom libraries. The problem is also one of the profession's mistrust of teachers: vast amounts of money are invested each year in teacher-proof programs that detail the texts we are to teach, the lessons we are to give, the groups we are to organize. One study (Jachym, Allington, Broikov, 1989) found consumables in the teaching of reading cost at least $90 per pupil and often well over $100 per pupil each year. This means that thousands and thousands of dollars are spent on kits, teachers' guides, laminated charts, and workbooks that prescribe our every move.

Schools that belong to the Teachers College Reading and Writing Project have made it a major priority to provision classrooms with adequate lending libraries. We've built up classroom libraries in several ways:

- In every grant the school writes, teachers include a request for books. If funding is available for art, we create curriculum in which children study the art of beautiful picture books and read about artists. If funding is available for steering children away from violence, our pathway to that goal will include the best of children's literature.

- We have no pride when it comes to asking for help in acquiring books. Our students ask local merchants to donate books related to a topic they're researching, promising to put a bookplate inside the cover to acknowledge the donor. We ask parents of older children if they'd be willing to donate the books their son or daughter has outgrown. We hold book sales, bingo games, and dance festivals, with proceeds going toward purchasing books.

- We let parents know that the gifts teachers value most are books. Some principals even send home copies of teacher's wish lists. We consult book reviews in *The New Advocate, The Horn Book, Bulletin of the Center for Children's Books, Language Arts* and *The Reading Teacher* for recommendations.

- When teachers retire or leave a school, principals offer to buy their libraries.

- Some schools have a display in which they thank donors, and in this way, inform potential donors about the possibility of supporting education in this way.

- Children and teachers write letters to publishers asking for extra review copies of books or donations from their overstocks.

But most important, we build up classroom libraries by knowing the books we have well and cherishing them. Although it is vitally important to provide our children with the libraries they deserve, it is also true that through all the generations, we hear stories of children who have learned to read by reading and rereading a single volume—perhaps the Bible or as in Speare's *The Sign of the Beaver,* Defoe's *Robinson Crusoe.* Sometimes I think we'd be better off if it wasn't just beginning readers who read books over and over but all of us. We find more in books if we give more to them and approach them as treasures.

On the first day of school this year, after watching her children browse through and explore their beautiful library, Kathy Collins said to her first graders, "I can see you are already Story Lovers. I watched you guys come into this room today and so many of you went straight to the *books!* You guys are just like me." Over the next few days there was lots of talk about the preciousness of books. "The reason we meet here in the library at the start of every day, and often during the day," Kathy said, "is that it's a really important place. See how the bookshelves are all around the carpet, on three sides of us. We're wrapped in books! We are so lucky to have a library like this in our classroom. It's our greatest treasure." The truth, of course, is that the children's greatest treasure was their teacher and her contagious love of books.

Matching Books to Readers

Even those of us with classroom libraries often don't have the libraries we need to support the real readers in our rooms. In almost every classroom, the shelves are full of books that are far too difficult for our children. If a child sits holding a Lloyd Alexander book, her eyes skimming over the words, yet she comes away from it with no grasp of the plot line and no images in her mind's eye, then this reading experience has been destructive to that child. When a child's expectations for a reading experience are so low that alarm bells don't sound in her mind when a book doesn't make sense, we face a major problem.

Perhaps the problem is that we've stocked our library shelves with the books we *wish* our children could read. A mother, who is also a teacher, came up to me during a break in a talk I was giving. "Oh, please Lucy, would you help me. My daughter Lara is in third grade and she's reading MacLachlan's *Sarah, Plain and Tall.* She is supposed to read it at home, so she reads part of it, then I read the whole thing to her and she tape-records my reading, and she listens to that again and rereads the chapter while listening to the tape, and after all that, she still can't answer the questions."

Mystified, I asked, "Why do you do all this—with you reading the book to her and so forth?"

"Because it is way too hard for her," the parent said. "She just started to read. She can read *Little Bear* but not this book."

"Then tell her to read *Little Bear,*" I responded.

"Oh, no," the anxious mother said. "The teacher said it's not at her grade level. She said *Sarah, Plain and Tall* is a good book for third graders."

"Not if the third grader can't read it!" I responded, barely able to contain my vexation over the damage that is being done to this young reader.

Lara's predicament is shared by countless others. Because her teacher doesn't want Lara, as a third grader, to be the kind of reader who can only read books at the level of *Little Bear,* Lara is denied the opportunity to read at all and instead spends hours each night pretending to be the kind of reader she is not (yet). The problem is that children don't get to be stronger readers by holding heavier books. If the books are inaccessible to the child, holding a heavy book does no more for a child's reading than holding a cinder block. I am especially alarmed because the readers who are at risk are so often the ones holding books they cannot read. The lower a child's proficiency level (and therefore, the more urgent the child's need to spend time reading comprehensible texts), the less likely it is that the child will actually have opportunities to read extended text on his or her own (Allington, 1980). Instead, in classrooms in which children have especially dire needs, they either do ditto sheets and exercises, or the teacher walks whole groups of children through a story together, the children bobbing their fingers along the text to accompany the teacher's reading. What they eventually do with these inappropriate texts may *look* like reading, but it is in fact something quite different.

Underlying this practice is the widely held assumption that we are holding children to high standards if we ensure that they are reading books "on grade level" (whether or not they can make sense of those books). I have actually heard administrators tell teachers, in the name of higher standards, "I don't want to see any children languishing with books below their grade levels." But there is nothing rigorous about a child stabbing away at texts that he or she can't begin to read. Always, we need to ensure that all children are reading with comprehension.

Organizing Our Libraries to Support Purposeful Book Choice

The organization of the classroom library will change over the course of the school year in support of changing curricular goals. Early in the year, when we induct a new group of readers into the norms of our classrooms and urgently want to get each reader onto a course of reading lots of books he or she can understand, we sometimes go so far as to ask readers to choose from a limited set of books. These books will tend to be easy ones we know well (which allows us to reach readers more easily). This starter library may highlight books in series. Kathy Short, co-author of *Creating Classrooms for Authors and Inquiries* (1996), has helped us realize that it can be easier for children to read several books from within the same series than to hop between separate books, because each new book in a series contains the same characters and the same general characteristics as other books in that series. Reading the second or third book in a series is rather like rereading a familiar book, and this means that reading within a series can often give the reader extra support. Books within *some* series, of course, are only loosely related to each other. The first indication of this fact will be the book's cover, which might say "Created by" rather than 'Written by,' which suggests an array of authors across the series. For example, the first *Boxcar* books (written in the 1950s), weren't mysteries at all and their language for today's reader is dated, with references to horses and buggies and so forth. All of this changes in later *Boxcar* books. It is crucial that we take the time to read at least a couple of titles in each of the series our children are reading. Because I've read *The Magic Treehouse* books, I know that full comprehension requires reading through the series *in order* (otherwise children will discover that the lost librarian reappears and then is lost again, that scrolls are suddenly and inexplicably the objects of a quest, and so on).

Although early in the year we tend to highlight easy books, books in a series, and books we know, later we will shine a spotlight on different areas of emphasis within the curriculum. Each of those areas of emphasis will affect the classroom library. Perhaps for a time we'll highlight nonfiction books or books in which there is complex movement through time. Kim Tarpinian, a fourth-grade teacher and a member of our Reading Think-Tank, saw that some of her fourth graders loved Laura Ingalls Wilder's *The Little House* books, so she gathered a shelf full of similar titles and labeled it "Cousins to *The Little House* books." Kim also has a shelf of "prequels" and sequels to her read-aloud books, and the waiting list for these books is always long. Because the characters are familiar, children can read these books even if they are a notch above their reading level, and so, stretch themselves in important ways. Last year, Kim's library even included a shelf for "Sad, Depressing Books that Make You Cry and Cry." When Kim noted a few children reading computer manuals, she decided to promote more of this kind of reading. One way was to set up a "Computer Manuals" shelf and to prominently display manuals cover side out. When Kim worried that her children seemed to be involved in a competitive race toward harder and longer books, she deliberately highlighted the shorter and easier books, which then stood a better chance of gaining social currency. Like most teachers in our community, she had soon set up other shelves as well, based on students' reading patterns: "Light Sports Books," "Bruce Books," "Historical Fiction about Girls," "Last Year's Favorites," and "Books That Have Matching Movies." Kim's students draft and revise memoir, poetry, and picture books in the writing workshop, so they also have shelves and baskets full of these genres.

Obviously, children need to be able to take books out of the classroom library and carry them between home and school. Taking books home each night is especially important for readers who struggle to make it through a chapter book. To help these readers make continual progress through a text, we ensure that they read the same book at home and at school instead of switching between several texts.

In the classrooms I know best, teachers and children have carefully thought about a system for checking books out of the classroom library and returning them to their proper places. In some rooms, each child turns four book-size pieces of cardboard into name plaques. When the child removes a book from a bookshelf, basket, or a display area, he or she leaves one of these cardboard nameplates in the book's stead as a placeholder. Then, when it comes time to return the book, the child replaces the book and removes the nameplate. In other classrooms, children signout books on a clipboard and cross off their names when they return them. Some teachers ask children and their parents to sign contracts promising that if they lose a book, they'll contribute five dollars toward the cost of new books.

Using Book Reviews to Support Intentional Book Choice

I have come to believe that if we give children the opportunity to choose their own books but they simply pull books at random off library shelves, then we've gained nothing. Giving children the opportunity to choose their own books is of no special benefit until we also help children become purposeful readers with intentions and social networks that steer their reading choices.

Of course, when *we* go to the library or the bookstore, our selections are guided by the reviews we have read or heard. Children are less apt to have other people's reviews in mind when they look over a collection of books. One way teachers can provide some of this supportive context for book choice is to encourage children to share their opinions about books they've read. In many of our classrooms, children leave a brief review inside the front cover. These can be as short as a Post-it saying, "If you are a girl and love horses, you'll love this" or "Starts slow but gets great, great, great." But the most important part of these message exchanges is the signature itself. The signature says, "I traveled this way" or "Read this book and think of me." It suggests, "Let's have a book talk."

Most teachers agree that it is also helpful to develop rituals to promote great books. At the start of the year, it is the teachers who tend to give the promotional talks, both as a way to engender enthusiasm for books and as a way to model these book talks. In most of our classrooms, children soon take over the job.

Every Friday in Kim's classroom, four children take a turn recommending a book to their classmates. These students have thought about the form and purpose of book promotions and generally agree that it helps to describe the kind of reader who might like a particular book. "If you liked Sandra Belton's *Ernestine and Amanda,* you are the kind of reader who might like this book," one child said recently. Another counseled, "If you are having a hard time staying with your reading and keep giving up on books, and if you want a really quick book that you can't put down, then you could try Alice Mead's *Junebug.*" In their book recommendations, children even give advice about reading a particular book: "Pay close attention to the cover and the chapter titles because *everything* turns out to be important." "This is part of a series but you can skip about, reading them in no special order, because it makes no difference." Sometimes children mention that they have left a few Post-its at key passages. One Post-it warned, "Read the next page closely because there is a twist," and another cautioned, "The part ahead was confusing to me. Watch out." Another child wrote "Alert! Time jumps backwards." In many of their book reviews, children read an excerpt aloud. This, of course, gives them a reason to practice reading aloud smoothly, and it also helps prospective readers anticipate the voice of a book.

Promotional book talks are a formal means of supporting what happens informally all the time. Books take on social currency. They are the talk of the town. Children tell each other, "You gotta read my book. It's so cool." In order to support this sort of social energy around books, and in order to teach children to talk well about their independent books, it's important to have duplicate copies of many titles. This keeps the waiting lists reasonable, allows friends to read a book together, and helps books gather social momentum. Alan Purves has said, "It takes two to read a book" and for us and our children, it is true that the books we have shared are the most important ones in our lives.

A Swim

Toad and Frog
went down to the river.
"What a day for a swim," said Frog.
"Yes," said Toad.
"I will go behind these rocks
and put on my bathing suit."
"I don't wear a bathing suit,"
said Toad.

That certainly was a fast run.

But her feet got tangled up,
and she fell smack on her bottom.

control

bounced

Ongoing Structures in the Reading Curriculum II

Once upon a time I believed that the solution to teaching reading lay in the independent reading workshop. I celebrated the importance of children reading books of their own choice for their own purposes, and the power of one-to-one conferring. I wanted to devote our days and our years to independent reading.

Then I came to understand the exquisite intimacy and power of reading aloud, and of using the experience of that shared read-aloud as a time to mentor young readers in the qualities of good reading. Suddenly I wanted to redo our schedule to give gigantic blocks of time to reading aloud.

Then I discovered the power of response groups. We named these groups book clubs, and for a time we were so enthralled with this one structure that the term book clubs became an abbreviated way for New York City to refer to our work in the teaching of reading.

Next came our researching guided reading groups and strategy lessons and our new appreciation for the close access they gave us to the minds of young readers as they traveled along contours of particular texts. What a thrill to feel I was teaching reading-as-it-happened.

But then we delved deep into word study and found that when we invested our time in helping children puzzle over the patterns in words, we were enabling them as readers in visible, exponential ways. We took this word work into the writing workshop and found that all our work with children's writing could do double-duty for us in ways we'd never dreamed possible.

Finally, over time, I have learned that each of these (and other) structures for teaching reading has special powers and particular limitations. Each structure is suited to certain jobs in the reading curriculum. When children spend time in independent reading, for example, they have the opportunity to compose reading lives for themselves and to be coached in the big work of living like a reader. This is marvelous—but it's limited, too, because it's hard to mentor children in the thinking processes of reading if we aren't traveling with them, side by side, through a shared text and because big and deep responses to texts require time to probe and talk. On the other hand, when we gather with our children to talk about a shared read-aloud book, we can show them ways to think about texts because we're thinking with them, but when we're teaching children as a group, it's hard to coach them as individuals.

What this means is that when we plan the structures of our reading curriculum, we are defining what reading will mean in our classroom and in our children's lives. As Randy Bomer reminds us in *Time for Meaning,* the decision about how we spend our time in the reading curriculum is not a detail. Time, after all, is life. It's all we have.

As we make decisions about scheduling the various components of a reading curriculum, it is important to bear in mind the value of being consistent. When I was a new teacher, I thought that in order to teach the processes of reading or writing I needed a creative lesson plan. Time in my classroom was a kaleidoscope of readers' theater, response groups, reading projects, writing in the style of an author, word work, and inference questions. I felt very creative, and rightly so. My days were full of planning and innovating. But meanwhile, my children could not develop their own rhythms and strategies because they were controlled by mine. They could not plan because they never knew what tomorrow would hold. I eventually came to realize, as I wrote in *The Art of Teaching Writing,* that "the most creative environments in our society are not the kaleidoscopic environments in which everything is always changing and complex. They are instead, the predictable and consistent ones—the scholar's library, the researcher's laboratory, the artist's studio. Each of these environments is deliberately kept *predictable* and *simple* because the work at hand and the changing interactions around that work are so unpredictable and complex" (p. 32).

When a child knows there will be time in school for talking with a reading partner, that child can plan for these conversations. "Let's meet tomorrow and figure out if all the places in this book are on the map at the front of it." When the structures are predictable, we, as teachers, can observe today's work and coach toward tomorrow's. "When you two talk tomorrow, remember what we said today about keeping the book open and referring to it often."

Many teachers are coming to believe that a full literacy curriculum usually includes most or many of the component structures I list here and develop further in the chapters of Section II:

- *Reading aloud:* A teacher will read aloud novels, picturebooks, poems, editorials, essays, announcements, summaries, and letters. Over the course of each day, teachers read aloud several different times and for several different purposes. Children will also join into shared readings, which may be aloud or may be silent, and these, too, will vary according to their purpose.

- *Reading workshop:* For about an hour a day, children work in a reading workshop that is structured parallel to the writing workshop. Each day's workshop includes:

    Independent reading: Children need at least thirty minutes a day to read books they can read, preferably of their own choosing. This reading will be silent, save for emergent and beginning readers, and mostly solitary. Emergent and beginning readers may not be able to sustain reading for thirty minutes, but they will read for longer periods of time if they read first alone and then with partners who can read similar books. All children also benefit from talking with partners about their books.

    Minilesson: For five to fifteen minutes, we teach the whole class of children something we hope they'll use in their independent reading lives. To make it more likely that what we demonstrate "takes hold," we often ask children to practice the strategy while they are still gathered for the minilesson. They do this with either their independent reading book or a shared text that has been duplicated, enlarged, or read aloud. The topics of minilessons build on each other so that across a sequence of days we teach a line of work.

    Conferring and coaching: As we move among our readers during the reading workshop, we confer with them individually, in their partnerships, or in small groups.

    Guided reading and strategy lessons: In a guided reading group, we gather together a small group of readers who are able to read similar

texts with support. We select a text which will be somewhat challenging, introduce the text to the group, observe and coach readers as they read it side-by-side, and then follow this work with a teaching point. In a strategy lesson, we again work with a small (although sometimes a large) group of readers and we usually have a shared text. We teach a strategy, usually by demonstrating it and then we scaffold readers as they try that strategy, helping them become increasingly independent with it. Later, we observe to see whether the tool we taught has become part of each reader's ongoing repertoire. Strategy lessons are rather like small-group minilessons in the middle of the reading workshop.

- *Classroom lending library:* Many of us believe that the classroom library needs shelves, bins, or other points of access that support book choice. Books will be clustered by topic, author, series, and sometimes by level of difficulty. We recommend there be *at least* twenty books per child in a lending library and exponentially more for K–2 children, who read smaller books.

- *Assessment:* Teachers are engaged in a continuous process of identifying what children can do or almost do. We use running records or miscue analyses, error analyses of writing, reading observations, and interviews to monitor the habits and strategies readers demonstrate and to understand their partially developed theories. We do this so that we can support and extend children's strengths, move them to slightly harder texts, and hold ourselves and our students accountable for reaching clear and explicit goals.

- *Work with struggling readers:* Teachers are also constantly engaged in work to support children who display, in various ways, difficulties with print, meaning, and fluency. We use a range of strategies to ensure that these children—and the schools they attend— discover ways to reach their literacy goals.

- *Phonics and word work:* Teachers support students as they work with word recognition, word building, word solving, and spelling patterns. This word work will also be woven into shared reading, interactive writing, the writing workshop and independent reading.

- *Book talks about the read-aloud:* At least one of the read-aloud episodes will be extended by a book talk, which will probably involve the whole class talking together and may also involve small groups or partners talking together about the read-aloud book. Children will also engage in book talks about texts they read independently.

- *Centers and book clubs:* By teaching children to talk well about books, we teach them to think as they read. In small groups, which some might refer to as literature circles but we call centers or book clubs, children deepen their ideas and their responses to texts. Meanwhile children practice and benefit from the talk strategies we have taught them during the whole-class read-aloud. We usually think of centers as a primary structure and book clubs as an upper-grade structure (I discuss both in Section III).

- *Writing workshop:* Children spend an hour a day invested in their own writing. Children draft, revise, and edit their writing. They incorporate help from mentor authors, writing partners, and conferences with their teacher. In a writing workshop, children may engage in a genre study on *writing literary essays,* which I describe in Section IV. (For further exploration of writing workshops, see Calkins, 1994.)

The components I cite are described often in the current literature. Where my list varies from others, the differences reflect at least three orientations. First, I am describing curricular elements of a *K–8* reading curriculum, and therefore, shared reading and interactive writing have not been given the attention they may receive in lists geared specifically toward K–2 reading classrooms. Second, my colleagues and I place an especially high priority on helping children develop higher-level comprehension skills, and this is reflected in our emphasis on the read-aloud, centers and books clubs (which could be called literature circles or response groups), and partnerships. For us, centers are not ways to keep children busy while the teacher leads guided-reading groups, nor are they directed largely toward word work. Finally, although we regard reading and writing as tools that can be used in social studies and science-related investigations, we resist the idea of merging most of our language arts instruction into theme-investigations. We do not want all our reading or writing to be in the service of thematic studies.

We have enormous respect for others who decide differently and incorporate their language arts curriculum into studies of immigration, The Civil War, and so forth, but we try to spotlight reading and writing in and of themselves. We value aesthetic reading for its own sake and think it is important to have time each day to highlight the habits and strategies of proficient reading, and to consciously reach toward ways of growing stronger as readers and writers.

How do all these components fit together into a day or a week? There is no one answer. Teachers structure their time differently. It may help to peek in on two classrooms, on two schedules. These schedules, however, are not meant as templates. They simply show how two teachers have structured their days. These teachers each devote approximately two-and-a-half hours a day to reading and writing instruction (separate from the reading and writing they do in social studies, math, and the like). If a teacher has only an hour and a half to devote to language arts, other choices will need to be made. In any case, we will all need to find our own ways to structure our time and priorities.

FIRST GRADE

8:20–8:30	Unpack, jobs, sign in
8:30–8:45	Songs, picturebook or poems, shared reading of the day's schedule, alphabet work with names, etc.
8:45–9:45	Writing workshop including a minilesson, writing, partnerships, use of the word wall to support spelling of high frequency words, and a brief sharing
9:45–10:15	Choice (dramatic play, blocks, alphabet center, art, etc.)
10:15–10:30	Word work
10:30–10:45	Shared reading or interactive writing (which may include more word work)
10:45–11:45	Reading workshop, including minilessons, private and then partner reading or alternatively, minilessons, private reading time, centers; either way, conferring, guided reading, and strategy lessons occur simultaneously
11:45–12:30	Lunch and recess
12:30–1:15	Thematic studies (social studies/science/health). May include interactive writing; will include reading-aloud.
1:15–1:55	Special (dance, science, art)
1:55–2:45	Math
2:45–3:10	Read-aloud and book talk

8:20–8:30	Unpack, jobs, homework buddies
8:30–9:00	Morning meeting, including reading aloud, current events, and word work/spelling
9:00–10:00	Reading workshop: (minilesson (ten minutes), private reading (35 minutes)/partner reading (ten minutes), final share (five minutes) *or* minilesson (ten minutes), private reading (twenty minutes), centers or book clubs (thirty minutes). Within either time frame, as children read and work with partners, teachers lead guided reading groups or strategy lessons and confer.
10:00–11:00	Writing workshop
11:00–12:00	Math
12:00–12:45	Lunch and recess
12:45–1:30	Special (gym, art, music)
1:30–2:40	Thematic studies (science and social studies), usually including some reading aloud, and often including some reading and writing
2:40–3:10	Read-aloud chapter book and book talk

Any compilation of the components in someone else's reading curriculum will always seem overwhelming. You may find it vexing that areas you consider a priority or a mandate in your teaching aren't priorities in these teachers' schedules. You may see the emphasis these teachers placed on one component and say, "I couldn't possibly do that." The problem with writing a book is that it is a one-sided conversation. If I could hear your responses, I'd surely reassure you that although I'm passionately invested in these components of a reading workshop, I know there are many paths to similar goals. And I know we each must tailor what we do to fit the contexts in which we work, the needs of children and parents, the constraints imposed by standardized tests and district mandates, and above all our beliefs. If the big-picture vision I describe is one you could not possibly implement, I trust that you'll nevertheless rummage among these ideas as one rummages through an attic trunk of stuff, some of which fits and some of which doesn't.

Reading Aloud 3

How important it is to teach children to lose themselves in the dream of the story. We want our children to gulp down stories—to thunder across the finish line at the Kentucky Derby or live alone in a thatched hut and work at the mill. When you and I were young, we hid fugitives in a secret room under the floorboards, we fell in love, we dreamed a dream, we carried a secret too terrible for words. Novelist John Gardner, in *The Art of Fiction,* describes reading this way:

> It creates for us a kind of dream, a rich and vivid play in the mind. We read a few words at the beginning of the book or the particular story and suddenly we find ourselves seeing not words on a page but a train moving through Russia, an old Italian crying, or a farmhouse battered by rain. We read on—dream on—not passively but actively, worrying about the choices the characters have to make, listening in panic for some sound behind the fictional door, exalting in characters' successes, bemoaning their failures. In great fiction, the dream engages us heart and soul; we not only respond to imaginary things—sights, sounds, smells—as though they were real, we respond to fictional problems as though they were real: we sympathize, think, and judge.

Our strongest readers open a book and find themselves on a train moving through Russia or listening in panic for some sound behind the fictional door. But when other children read they are not on that train, they are not listening behind fictional doors. They are thinking instead about short vowels and "Whew, what a long paragraph" and "How many more pages are there?" and "What's Pedro doing by the window?" How do we help all children become passionately engaged in the world of the story? How do we help them know what it is to lose themselves in the drama of a story? Reading aloud to children is part of the answer.

Reading Aloud to Children Matters

When you and I were young, we used toothpicks and raisins to turn potatoes into people. Our fingers smelled of potatoes, but we didn't care. Now, children buy plastic potatoes and plastic eyebrows for the ready-made eyebrow holes. When you and I were young, we turned Playdough into families of rabbits, each with a name and a story. Now Playdough comes with a machine. All you need to do is to crank the lever and out comes perfectly formed hearts and spaghettis. The difference between play then and now matters. It is not inconsequential whether or not a child learns to transform a row of wooden blocks into the ramp on a pirate ship. It is not a small thing that children learn to walk in the shoes of story characters, to live in other worlds, to smell seaside roses from their city apartment, to breathe mountain air while they sit at a desk tucked in the far corner of the classroom. We teach all this by reading aloud. How can we make reading aloud an even bigger priority for ourselves and our children?

Renée Dinnerstein, a kindergarten teacher, recently realized that with all the new classroom pressures, she needed to put a special halo around reading aloud, so she had created a variation on the tooth fairy. Kindergarteners at P.S. 321 sometimes come into their classroom and find that, lo and behold, the Book Fairy has been there, leaving a lavishly wrapped package bound up in ribbons and lace. Gifts like these turn ordinary days into celebrations of literacy. Once, when Renée and her children had been totally immersed in an alphabet study, the Book Fairy produced three alphabet books. For days afterwards the children continued to remark on the extraordinary coincidence; the Book Fairy brought alphabet books *just when* they were studying alphabet books. How perfect!

In Kim Tarpinian's classroom, they celebrate each child's birthday by having that child choose an excerpt from a book Kim has already read aloud to the class. This means that September birthday children can choose from only a very few books, but by the time summer birthdays roll around, children are choosing from over twenty novels. There is always great anticipation around these selections. Kim rereads the excerpt aloud and the birthday child talks about why this excerpt matters especially. Kim always writes a birthday wish for the child inside the book's cover, and that book, with the child's birthday wish inscribed, remains in the class library, a reminder of the significance this book has played in a child's life. As the closing ritual on the final day of the school year, each child again chooses a favorite passage from one of the read-alouds. Before the final day of school, each child practices reading his or her passage aloud beautifully, and during the final moments of the last day, each child reads an excerpt to the class. Kim and her children end the year carrying with them the voices and words of these beloved books. These children are lucky indeed to have, in Mem Fox's words, the "constant good fortune of hearing great literature beautifully delivered into the ear and from there into the heart and from the heart into the bones."

Reading aloud is so important, I have often proposed to Teachers College that we never place a student teacher in the classroom of a teacher who doesn't read aloud each day. In the teaching of reading, there are only a handful of things that everyone agrees are essential. Perhaps the most important of these is the fact that children need to listen to the best of children's literature read aloud to them. After evaluating ten thousand research studies, the U.S. Department of Education's Commission on Reading issued a report, *Becoming a Nation of Readers* (1985), which goes so far as to state that "The single most important activity for building the knowledge required for eventual success in reading is reading aloud to children." (Anderson, Hiebert, Scott and Wilkinson, 1985, p. 23). The study found "conclusive evidence" supporting reading aloud in the home and in the classroom, and it claimed that adults need to read aloud to children not just when children can't yet read on their own, but throughout *all* the grades.

We read aloud many times and for many purposes. If we are predictable about this, our students can anticipate not only *that* we'll read aloud but also the roles we hope they will take on during each of these read-aloud times:

- We read aloud to start the day.
- We read aloud within reading and writing minilessons.
- We read aloud in support of the social studies and science curriculum.
- We read aloud in support of whole-class book studies.
- We read aloud to help children talk and think about texts.

Reading Aloud to Start the Day

Ralph Peterson, author of *Life in a Crowded Place* (1992), suggests that we respond to the challenges of our elbow-to-elbow classroom living by using ceremony, ritual, and celebration to create learning communities. One important part of building a classroom community is finding ways to cross the threshold, ways to mark the classroom as a world apart. Although time to put away backpacks, check in with homework buddies, and perform classroom jobs is important, it is also necessary to have a ritual that starts the day. In many classrooms, the morning read-aloud convenes the community and acts as almost a blessing on the day. There may be a song or a choral reading of a familiar poem that serves as an incantation. Perhaps children recite together the Shel Silverstein poem "Invitation" that begins:

> If you are a dreamer, come in
> If you are a dreamer, come in
> If you are a dreamer, a wisher, a liar
> come in
> come in.

Perhaps we join together in a choral reading of Eloise Greenfield's "Things":

> Went to the corner
> Walked in the store
> Bought me some candy
> Ain't got it no more
> Ain't got it no more.
>
> Went to the beach
> Lay down on the shore
> Built me a sandhouse
> Ain't got it no more
> Ain't got it no more.
>
> Went to the kitchen
> Lay down on the floor
> Made me a poem
> Still got it.
> Still got it.

In any case, we are soon reading aloud a poem or a picturebook. We often choose a text that can act like a lantern, lighting our way. We might read Byrd Baylor's *I'm in Charge of Celebrations,* in which a girl from the Southwestern desert says, "Sometimes people ask me, 'Aren't you lonely out there with just the desert around you?'" It is a question that can be asked of all of us. "Aren't you lonely out there with just your desk and your papers?" "Aren't you lonely out there with just your street, your apartment, your bunk bed?" Baylor's heroine responds in astonishment,

> I guess they mean
> The beargrass
> And the yuccas
> And the cactus
> And the rocks.
>
> I guess they mean
> The deep ravines
> And the hawk nests
> In the cliffs
> And the coyote trails
> That wind
> Across the hills.
>
> *"Lonely?"*
> I can't help
> Laughing
> When they ask me
> That.
> I always look at them …
> Surprised.
> And I say,
> "How could I be lonely?
> I'm the one in charge of celebrations."

For our opening read-aloud we select poems and picturebooks that make us all laugh and fall in love with words. Above all, we read favorites. Of course we read texts our students have written and texts *we* have written, and we reread often. Our goal, as the poet Julius Lester says, is for the literature to "link our souls like pearls on a string, bringing us together in a shared and luminous humanity." This read-aloud time tends to last only five minutes or so. We don't stop to clap out the syllables in compound words, preteach vocabulary, or elicit children's predictions. We simply get out of the way of the text and let the words work their magic. We heed Cynthia Rylant's wise advice: "Read to them," she says. "Take their breath away. Read with the same feeling in your throat as when you first see the ocean after driving hours and hours to get there. Close the final page of the book with the same reverence you feel when you kiss your sleeping child at night. Be quiet. Don't talk the experience to death. Shut up and let these kids feel and think. Teach your children to be moved."

Reading Aloud Within Reading and Writing Minilessons

In the minilesson before our *writing* workshop, we will often return to texts we've introduced during the morning read-aloud (or during a later read-aloud of a chapter), this time to study passages we love, to talk about what the author has done, and to consider the effect the author was hoping to create. We will probably not reread the book in its entirety for this discussion. If Baylor's *I'm in Charge of Celebrations,* for example, had a big effect on students, we may refer to it when we study how some authors use a list structure in their texts and notice that it lists times when she used her writer's notebook to record magical moments. We may liken this book to Rylant's *When I was Young in the Mountains* and discuss the different choices Rylant and Baylor have made.

In the minilesson before our *reading* workshop, we may also return to the text we introduced during the morning read-aloud. When we revisit books, we show readers the richness that is there in literature for those who have the eyes to see. "This morning, I want to talk about the scientific language some authors weave into their texts," we might say. "I bet that this morning when you heard me read 'I guess they mean the *bear grass* and the *yuccas*,' some of you weren't certain what those scientific terms meant. Listen again while I read a couple of sections from *I'm in Charge of Celebrations* and pay attention to what you do when you hear (or read) words you don't know." Later in the year we might refer to *I'm in Charge of Celebrations* again, this time as part of a mini-lesson on author studies. "When I begin to read an unfamiliar book by an author, I first remember what I know about that author, and use that knowledge to anticipate how this new book might go," I say. "From knowing *I'm in Charge of Celebrations,* what can we expect we might find in this new Baylor book?" Several weeks later, we might return to study on overhead transparency of one page from *I'm in Charge of Celebrations* as part of an inquiry about learning to read aloud smoothly, paying special attention to punctuation.

Reading Aloud in Support of the Social Studies and Science Curriculum

It's terribly important for children to listen to nonfiction texts read aloud. If our children are going to comprehend and write news articles, essays, how-to texts, directions, arguments, and proclamations, they need to develop an ear for the rhythms and structures used in these genres. These texts also open new worlds to youngsters. We cannot take all our children on field trips to see fish ladders bypassing the giant dams of the Snake River or to stand under the massive ruins of Rome. But we can give our children the words that will take them to new worlds, launch new investigations, and introduce new concepts. Oftentimes our upper-elementary children will encounter difficulties on standard-

"Close your eyes, listen, and picture this ..."

ized reading tests not because they can't read the words or recall a passage but because they don't know the difference between a continent and a country, a century and a decade, a species and a gender.

Toward the end of this book, I discuss the special challenges and opportunities involved in reading—and reading aloud—non-fiction texts, but for now, let me suggest that we need to appreciate the extraordinary cognitive demands that listening to nonfiction texts can place on our students. The answer is not to search high and low for fictional texts that carry bits of factual information, because it is crucial for children to hear a wide variety of texts read aloud. It would be wiser to support our students as they grow to be stronger listeners to nonfiction texts. We do this by:

- Reading aloud nonfiction books that support our students' interests and hobbies as well as our curriculum.
- Reading aloud very simple, accessible books to introduce a subject, only later moving to more complex texts on that subject.
- Giving children more information early on so they are in a better position to learn more: it helps to watch the movie or make the field trip or hear the overview of a subject *before* reading a nonfiction text on that topic.

- Actively modeling our own learning process by pulling back from a text and saying, "Wait a minute! So far, he's said birds migrate in four ways [we list them]. *Now* it looks as if he's on a new topic of how he can research bird migration, or at least I think he is…. Yes, look, I was right. He says here …"

- Activating our children's minds by asking them to talk to partners:

  "Let's look at this diagram. Tell your partner what you notice."

  "Wait. Let's review what we've said so far. Go back over it with your partner, starting with …"

  "What I often try to do when I read nonfiction like this is to pause and think, 'What's surprising me so far?' Try that with your partner."

- Read aloud pieces of nonfiction texts, such as headlines from the newspaper, the opening paragraphs of magazine articles, intriguing passages from books. It's not always necessary to read entire nonfiction texts.

Reading Aloud in Support of Whole-Class Book Studies: Teaching the Qualities of Good Reading

We also read aloud to demonstrate to our children and to mentor them in the habits, values, and strategies of proficient readers, and to help them experience the bounties of thoughtful, reflective reading. When I taught fifth and sixth grade, my students and I sometimes read a chapter book together. I'd assign a chapter or two each evening, and in school we'd "walk through the text together" (as this was called), defining and finding examples of literary techniques, such as foreshadowing and personification, and noticing symbolic meanings. Only now, in retrospect, do I realize it was educational malpractice to *require* that my struggling readers fake their way through a book they could not read. How could I justify asking struggling readers to do the very thing they should no longer do: struggle along with very little comprehension? But there were other problems as well; the time lapse between when children read the text at home and when all of us responded to it in class meant that I could only deal with the remnants of their reading. Granted, because this work was done with the whole class, there were always a few children who could answer my questions, carry the conversation, and delude me into believing that this was effective reading instruction. All too often my strongest readers provided an abridged oral version of the story and the book talk became a discussion of summaries of the book rather than the book itself. But something is wrong when we spend time, day after day, valiantly trying to lead book talks about texts only a few children can remember.

I have since come to believe that working together around the whole-class read-aloud text is a much better way to achieve the goals I was aiming toward back then. Instead of assigning the class to read a chapter or two of Taylor's *Roll of Thunder, Hear my Cry* each night and then discussing it every day at school, we now read the book aloud and weave discussions into read-aloud times. Our discussion often occurs at selected moments during the read-aloud, in the midst of the rich, vivid drama-in-the-mind that happens as children listen to a text. We often help students actively generate meaning as we progress through the text. When a class of children listens together to the best of children's literature read aloud, they experience the potency of truly responsive reading. Readers gasp at the scary parts, feel a growing suspense as the plot thickens, say "hmmm" when a new character or a new twist in the plot emerges out of nowhere. We teach thoughtful, responsive reading by gasping at the scary parts ourselves, shuddering visibly and aloud in ways that invite children to shudder with us. When we laugh at the funny parts and weep at the sad parts, we are teaching comprehension.

To create a forum for literary study, it helps to have a few copies of the read-aloud text or a class set of excerpts from the text. We do not want children to follow along in the print as we read aloud. Instead, we bring out the multiple copies later to lift the quality of the longer book talks. At these times children can work in clusters for a few minutes and refer to the text as they prepare for the book talks. Then, with the book or excerpt in hand, they can cite specific passages and check the text when needed.

I held up a picture book—*Gorilla,* by Anthony Browne—and said to John Fletcher's third graders, "I've got a favorite book to read today." I heard squeals of delight. Pleased, I asked, "What are you thinking?"

"*Willy The Wimp!*" Julius said, referring to the Anthony Browne book his class had read, reread, and studied two weeks earlier.

"You're right!" I confirmed. "So guys, think about what you know about Anthony Browne, think about what *Willy the Wimp* might lead you to expect, and let's look over this new book like you always do." I looked at the cover and thought for a long time. "Hmmm," I said, but I did not yet so much as glance at the children. Instead, I turned to the title page and studied the picture of a little girl writing a book about gorillas. Finally I turned to page one and thoughtfully read aloud:

> Hannah loved gorillas. She read books about gorillas, she watched gorillas on television, and she drew pictures of gorillas. But she had never seen a real gorilla.
>
> Her father didn't have time to take her to see one at the zoo. He didn't have time for anything.

By now, children were bursting to talk. "Turn to your read-aloud partners," I said, "and talk over your noticings and expectations."

The room buzzed. Soon I called the group back into a shared discussion, and for the next twenty minutes we discussed the cover and first page of *Gorilla*. During our conversation, these ideas emerged:

- Anthony Browne writes a lot about gorillas. *Willy the Wimp* was a gorilla; now a character in this new book, Hannah, also loves gorillas.
- The father in *Gorilla* resembles the father in *Piggybook* (Browne). Many authors have characters who resurface from book to book.
- The *main* characters are different in *Gorilla* (Hannah) and in *Willy the Wimp* (Willy), but both books begin by showing a character who has one very strong character trait. Hannah is obsessed with gorillas; Willy acts like a wimp.
- In *Willy the Wimp,* Willy tries to stop being a wimp. Will Hannah try to stop being obsessed with gorillas? Will she try to get her father to have time to take her to see a gorilla?
- *Willy the Wimp* is mostly about just one character, Willy. *Gorilla* might also be about Hannah's father.
- In *Gorilla,* on page one, we learn not only about Hannah but also about her father. He is always too busy for Hannah.
- The start of *Willy the Wimp* is like the start of Mario's [a student] story. Mario's story was about the day he got his first bike, but he rewrote it to start with a buildup, saying that every day, for a very long time, he'd longed for a bike. The class named the revision strategy the "*Every day, one day strategy.*" Was Anthony Browne using the same strategy? *Every day* Hannah wanted to see a gorilla, *one day* she gets to?

For John Fletcher's third graders, this one conversation became what in our community we call "a touchstone conversation." Kathleen Tolan has helped us realize that just as there are books we refer to often, there can also be book talks that set the standards in our classrooms. Later in the year, John and I would often say to his children:

- "Study the beginning of this book like we studied the lead to *Gorilla*."
- "Remember how we noticed the kind of work Browne was doing in his opening pages when he used the strategy of writing about *everyday* in Hannah's life, and then wrote about *one day*? What kind of thing do you see *this* author doing at the start of the text?"
- "Remember how it paid off to spend a very long time thinking about one page in *Gorilla*? Plan on pausing at least once in your book to *really study* just that one page."
- "Remember how Mario and Anthony Browne's stories both followed the *Every day I wanted, one day it happened pattern*? Could there be a pattern to the book you're reading?"

When we read aloud, we can mentor children in the thinking processes that are common among proficient readers. The read-aloud gives us opportunities to work with youngsters as apprentices, demonstrating the tools of thoughtful, skilled readers and inviting children to try these out. When we read aloud, we help youngsters join us in thinking "What do I know about this kind of text and this topic that can help me anticipate how this new text might go?" We help readers to pause and think, "What decisions has the author made here and why might he have made them? Do I know other authors (in this classroom or in the world of literature) who've made a similar decision?" As we read aloud with children, we help them experience all the strategies of effective reading. We do the print-work, the phrasing, and the punctuating for children, deciding who is talking to whom and what their intonation will be, so that children's minds are more able to anticipate, infer, connect, question, and monitor for sense.

We will want to explicitly mentor children in the mind-work of reading. Although there are millions of texts, there are only a limited number of strategies that good readers use over and over in various combinations. We notice, develop theories, recall, predict, question, infer, synthesize, interpret, and make connections of all sorts. We do this when we are five years old and when we are fifty, whether we listen to texts read aloud or read those texts silently, and whether the texts are poems, our own drafts, manuals, or novels. After reading aloud four or five pages of a chapter book in our class, we may pause. "Okay. So wait a minute. I want to make sure I have things straight in this story. (Don't you do that—pause early in the book to be sure you've got it straight?) So this book is about ..." By now, children will probably chip in, adding to the synopsis of the book. Alternatively, we may find that as we read aloud we lose traction and are merely mouthing the words. We might say to the kids, "Wait, I'm reading the words without having my mind on them. Do you ever do that? Let me reread that section. Is that what you guys do, too, when this happens to you?"

If I'm reading a mystery and spot a clue, I'll dramatize the discovery: "Wait! This sentence might be a clue," I'll say. I'll pause, look at the kids and whisper "Listen," and reread the passage. "Tell each other what you're thinking!" If I simply adore the words an author has used I might say as an aside, "Check out Kevin Henkes's description! Just listen to this," and then reread, savoring every word. I may want to show the children that I often "sneak a peek at" the upcoming text. I may give voice to the predictions I hope children are making. Talking almost as if I were a youngster, I might pause in my reading to say, "Wait a minute, wait! I'm getting a strange feeling about this. I'm starting to wonder *what* might be going on?" The kids, listening, join in and generate their own predictions and theories. These, of course, deserve to be developed. I may decide to linger: "Say more about that" and "What makes you think that? Can you take us to the sections of the text that make you feel this way?" Or, I may simply read on, with bated breath.

As effective as it can be to say what we are thinking or invite children to talk in the midst of listening to a text, we need to avoid pausing to discuss a text so often that we overwhelm the story. Although I've described many ways to demonstrate the habits of proficient readers, the single most important habit we need to model is engagement in the text.

Reading Aloud Can Help Children Talk and Think about Texts

Oddly enough, many students will listen to a text and have nothing to say. But when these same students talk about television shows or movies, they don't need conversational starters or webs. Something is drastically wrong, then, when our students are silenced by texts. I suspect this is often the result of problematic instruction. For too long, children have read literature and then faced a barrage of questions, each with one right answer. Recently I heard a teacher hold up Arnold Lobel's book, *Frog and Toad*, and say to a group of children, "Frog and Toad are friends who are what, class?" I know the book well but I didn't have a clue about what the teacher expected the class to say. One boy piped in, "Friendly? Frog and Toad are friends who are *friendly?*" The child's intonation alone showed that he was asking, "Is this the answer you want?"

But no, the teacher was looking for another word to fill in the blank in her sentence. She repeated her question. "*Frog and Toad* is about friends who are what, class?"

"Adventurous?" a child suggested, and although I cheered his ingenuity and knowledge of the story, the teacher continued to scan the room looking for raised hands and the right answer. Now she produced a clue. "It starts with a 'd.'"

I wracked my mind. "Frog and Toad are, what?" I thought, "Damp?"

No one ventured another guess, so the teacher completed her own sentence. "Are Frog and Toad *different,* class?" she asked, and proceeded to deliver her predetermined lesson on multiculturalism. Frog is green and Toad is brown, but they are, after all, still friends.

Douglas Barnes (1993), in his important article "Supporting Exploratory Talk for Learning," reports that most of the questions asked by the teachers he observed were strictly factual and required little or no ability to sustain sequential thinking. Even more discouraging was Barnes's observation on the effect of such questions on students' participation in lessons: they were mainly offering single word replies, and the questions they asked were for reassurance rather than expressions of lively curiosity.

To help our children think, talk, and eventually write well about texts, we must make a dramatic break from the habit of grilling them with known-answer questions. I do not know why it is ingrained in us as teachers to pepper children with oral, workbooklike, fill-in-the-blank questions. We want to say, "Let's talk about the reasons children made fun of Crow Boy," but because we are accustomed to the conversational pattern that dominates classrooms, we say, "Did the children in this book like Crow Boy? Did they make fun of him?" A child answers. If this isn't the answer we were looking for, we restate the question. Another child answers. Again, this isn't the answer we wanted. Now there is silence. We try giving part of the answer we want (Cazden, 1988; Mehan, 1979). Why is it so inconceivable that we

In the midst of reading aloud, Ginny Lockwood has asked her children to say-something to their partners.

should simply say to our children, "Could we talk about the reactions the children in this book had to Crow Boy?" and then back out of the conversation, leaving space for them to comment and elaborate on each other's comments without acting as Masters of Ceremonies? In helping classrooms of children learn to converse together, the easiest step is to use "say-some-things," a strategy we learned from Kathy Short, Carolyn Burke and Jerry Harste's book, *Creating Classrooms for Authors and Inquirers* (1996). We tend to read aloud and to pause at "talk-worthy" spots.

At first, we simply encourage children to talk to anyone who is sitting nearby. After a few weeks, we assign children to sit beside the same read-aloud partner each day. Long-term read-aloud partners allow children to say things like, "You know how yesterday you said such and such? Well, it's happening still," or, "It's the same as before!" Children practice getting in and out of talk positions quickly, so that before long, we can pause at a key section of the text and look out at our children, who note our signal and get knee-to-knee with their partner. The room erupts in conversation. After a few minutes, we simply resume reading (beginning with a paragraph of overlap as the voices subside).

I recently watched Alexa Stott, a teacher at P.S. 199 in Manhattan, pause in the midst of Mead's *Junebug* to let her third-grade students talk in pairs. "What I do during say-something times is crawl around, listening and often sparking ideas that children later feed back to the group," Alexa explained. Listening in on a partnership that didn't seem particularly animated, Alexa asked, "So, what do you think about Jolita giving Junebug those bottles?"

"Weird," Jorge nodded, getting aboard Alexa's train of thought. "It's like she likes him and then she doesn't."

"It's her friends, they are stronger than she is, they make her do things," Joey added.

"So, do you think Jolita might be feeling two ways: that she loves Junebug but wants to go along with her friends?" Alexa asked. Alexa was, of course, deliberately planting ideas that would help her children discover the essential elements of the book. "I confess," Alexa says, "I often talk with one set of partners in a voice that is just loud enough so that another set sitting nearby on the rug will hear me too. Sometimes I think they listen all the more intensely because they are eavesdropping."

How important is reading aloud? Critically important. "Don't you ever want kids to just lie back and let the words flow over them … to just listen?" people sometimes ask about the read-aloud. But I have to admit that I don't really see the read-aloud in this dreamy, sleepy sort of way. Too often children consider the read-aloud as a time to doze, dream, fiddle, and snack. I see the read-aloud as the heart of our reading instruction time, and I want kids' full attention to be on what we do together.

The Independent Reading Workshop 4

For years now, I have squeezed into crowded sessions at national conferences to hear authors tell the stories of their lives and their craft. I've loved knowing that while he was writing *Make Way for Ducklings,* Robert McCloskey kept ducks in his Greenwich Village apartment, that E. B. White wrote drafts of *Charlotte's Web* sitting on a bale of hay in a barn watching a spider at work, and that Karla Kuskin found the idea for her picturebook, *The Philharmonic Gets Dressed,* when her daughter was given a doll for her birthday and immediately proceeded to lift up the doll's skirts to check out her underpants. "All of a sudden, I remembered my childhood fixation with underpants. I remembered twirling around on the fence at recess and my classmates chanting, 'I see London, I see France, I see Karla's underpants.' The idea for a picturebook was born."

Stories like these are not just cute author anecdotes, they are revolutionary, because they help us realize that writing isn't simply desk work, it is also life work. Writing is not just a matter of making lists and drafting entries and turning details into drafts, it is also a matter of keeping ducks in a city apartment, of watching a shaft of sunlight turn a bale of hay into gold, of remembering recess games and taunts. When we teach writing, we teach young people to live differently because they write (Calkins with Harwayne, 1991).

How good it would be if we could, at national conferences, squeeze into crowded sessions and hear the stories of great *readers.* Most of us and most of our students do not have great readers who function as mentors in our lives. If we thought of teaching reading as apprenticing ourselves to great readers, the teaching methods we use would change in radical ways.

I do not think these great readers would tell us that they write compare-and-contrast essays or answer someone else's questions at the end of each chapter or make collections of figurative language. Instead, these great readers would tell us about bringing their reading to the people and passions and places of their lives. They'd tell about packing two suitcases when they leave on a trip, one for clothes and the other for books. They'd show us book reviews folded into billfolds and describe piles of books on bedside tables and cite the reading friends who keep them company. These reading stories would not just be cute reader anecdotes. They'd be revolutionary. They'd help us see that, because they read, readers live differently. They'd help us see that reading is not just a little thing we do with black marks on the page, it's a big thing we do with our whole lives.

The Structure of the Reading Workshop

In the reading workshop, as in the writing workshop, it is important to maintain a simple, predictable structure because it is the work children do that will be changing and complex. *How* we structure the reading workshop is up to each of us. The important thing is *that* we structure this time, and that we do so in ways our students can anticipate. Those of us coming from a writing workshop background may find it helpful to structure the reading workshop in ways which parallel our writing workshops, so that our children learn to work productively inside the two structures at the same time. Whatever we decide, the structures of a reading workshop must be predictable. If I ask children, "How does your reading workshop generally go in this classroom?" I hope they can answer. If a child says, "First we listen to a chapter of the read-aloud, then afterwards we talk," I know this child will listen to the read-aloud anticipating the conversation she'll soon have. If a child says, "We get free-choice reading time every morning," this means she can turn the lights off at night, saving the final chapter of a novel to complete in school.

Most of us begin the reading workshop with a minilesson followed by reading time (which is when we confer, lead guided reading groups, and do strategy lessons). After reading alone, our children meet with partners and have conversations which are often guided by us. Then we gather the class together for a sharing. Some teachers follow a somewhat different structure but always, our workshops are highly structured and predictable. Readers can be more planful, purposeful, and full of initiative if they work within a predicable, consistent structure.

The Minilesson

The reading workshop, like the writing workshop, usually begins with the class gathering on the carpet for a minilesson in which we teach a strategy readers can use not only in the independent reading workshop but also in their reading lives. Minilessons generally explore one topic for a week or two (reading with expression, thinking about characters, making time for reading in one's life). Although minilessons are primarily a forum for teaching youngsters strategies they can use in their independent reading, they also give us an opportunity to shape the values of our classroom community.

In minilessons we teach children to value reading. In millions of ways, we celebrate reading. We wear our love of reading on our sleeves. "I want reading, this year, to be the best experience you've ever had in your life," Daria Rigney said at the beginning of a minilesson. The day before, a couple of her fifth graders had seemed to fritter away a few moments of reading time, and Daria wanted to be clear that doing this was incomprehensible to her. "If you are not cherishing reading time, we need to talk about that," she said, "I don't want us to waste one precious moment of the reading workshop." Once I watched Daria gather her students around her for a minilesson and say, "I want to talk about any dazzling reading experiences you've been having."

Nell responded, "I read *Catherine Called Birdy* this weekend. I read in my loft bed with a flashlight, and I just blocked out everything else in my head so I could really feel I was in those times, you know, olden times, no electricity."

Nodding, affirming every word, Daria echoed Nell's sentiments. "Don't you just love it when you are so close to a book that you feel you are part of it?" Whether she realizes it or not, Daria is teaching her children. The teacher who announces to her students, "I'm going to quiz you at the end of every chapter of this book, because otherwise I know you won't read it," is also teaching powerful lessons, as is the teacher who says, "No talking during reading because it's never about your books." Now Daria turned to the rest of the class. "What else has been dazzling you lately?"

Kevin said, "I started *Bud, Not Buddy.* Stephen told me about it and its so neat! There's different words and it's historical."

"So you are dazzled by reading a different kind of book," Daria confirmed. "One where the language is rich and delicious. How about you, Sue? We know what a rich reading life you have."

Listening to Daria, I couldn't help but notice the ways in which she supports her kids' progress toward becoming avid readers. When Kevin described *Bud, Not Buddy* by saying, "There's different words," Daria nodded, acting as if she was simply affirming what he had said, and proceeded to expand on his comment. "You are dazzled by reading a different kind of book, one where the language is rich and delicious." Daria's enthusiasm sweeps Kevin along, teaching not only strategies but also values. The language Daria uses to convey these values is as important as the activities she models within the minilessons.

Reading Time

After the reading minilesson, children go to private "reading nooks" or to their desks to read alone, usually for thirty to forty minutes. This—actual reading time—is the most important part of the reading workshop. When we teach reading, we are teaching children to do something. Children can't learn to swim without swimming, to write without writing, to sing without singing, or to read without reading. If all we did in the independent reading workshop was to create a structure to ensure that every child spent extended time engaged in reading appropriate texts, we would have supported readers more efficiently and more effectively than we could through any elaborate plan, beautiful ditto sheet, or brilliant lecture.

Children learn to read by reading, and they aren't doing enough reading. A U.S. Department of Education longitudinal study of almost 25,000 eighth graders found that students watched television an average of 21.2 hours a week but spent a mere 1.9 hours a week outside school reading, and that included homework. When literate fifth graders were monitored to determine how they spent their free time, 90 percent devoted less than 1 percent of their time to reading. In contrast, they spend 33 percent of their time watching television (Trelease, 1995).

It is no small goal, then, to give our students long stretches of time each day to read the books they are able to read. Anyone familiar with American classrooms knows that long stretches of time for reading are quite rare. Only 40 percent of fourth-grade classrooms have anything resembling an independent reading workshop. It reminds me of when my son Miles was in first grade. He studied food and found to his amazement that there was no chocolate in chocolate jimmies and no chicken in packaged chicken soup. Sometimes it seems that there is no reading in reading classrooms. We can see this not only in the statistics but also in the materials. I recently learned of a 98-page teachers guide to accompany Ruth Krauss' 99-word book, *The Carrot Seed*. Frank Smith tells about one very short story, "Rico and the Red Pony," in which he found seven "literal comprehension" questions, five "interpretive thinking" questions, five "critical thinking" questions, and three "creative thinking" questions. There were more questions than words in the story. Many American children run through this kind of pedagogical treadmill day after day (Smith, 1995, p. 4).

In his book *Time for Meaning,* Randy Bomer, the former co-director of our Project who is currently professor of education at Indiana University, tells of a day he gathered language arts teachers together and asked, "What topics are you expected to teach?" As each teacher called out one thing or another, Randy wrote the topic on the chalkboard: poetry, punctuation, debate, parts of speech, fables, word processing, media studies, the cueing systems, revision, myths, note-taking, author studies, summarizing, predicting, memoir, using a table of contents, reading with expression, character studies … "As the flood of items slowed to a trickle," Randy writes, "a pall of hopelessness settled over the room, and rightly so." We need more time with our students. But time is life. How could there be more time? "What we really mean when we say, 'time is the problem,'" Randy says, "is that it's hard to choose and control what we do with the time we have. What we do with time is what we do with our lives. When we are unable to spend time on what we most value, it is because we have not found a clarity of purpose" (p. 2).

If our goal is to help children compose richly literate lives, then we need to give them time each day to do just that. The independent reading workshop needs to be as central to the teaching of reading as the writing workshop is to the teaching of writing. Too often, we suggest our children "carry on" with their reading while we catch up on paperwork, tutor a student, meet with a small group, or resolve a recess issue. But why do these things draw us away from reading rather than from any other part of our day? When we're not fully invested in the independent reading workshop, what message does this convey to our students? Why would we collect milk money or teach one guided-reading lesson after another during the independent reading workshop? Our kids are busy composing reading lives before our eyes and we're missing the show—and it's the greatest show on earth!

Independent reading is far from the entire reading curriculum, but what children do during independent reading should affect, and be affected by, the entire curriculum. Too often in the teaching of reading, the separate components of the reading curriculum exist independently of each other. Young children gather on the carpet to chime along as the teacher points to the words of "If you give a mouse a cookie, he's going to ask for a [Post-it] of milk." The youngsters draw on several strategies to guess the word masked by the Post-it and develop a repertoire of ways to respond when they encounter Post-its masking words in texts. But do these children understand how to use these strategies in their independent reading lives, where there are no Post-its over words? Independent reading needs to be scaffolded, to use Jerome Bruner's term, and supported by read-alouds, book talks about shared texts, explicit instruction in skills and strategies, interactive writing, guided reading and other small-group reading instruction, and the writing workshop.

Teachers of beginning or emergent readers may be having a hard time imagining a classroom filled with first graders carrying on as readers because, as these teachers say, "They can't—you know—*read.*" It's a curious thing, but it is rare for a teacher to tell me her children can't carry on as *writers.* In the writing workshop, we accept and teach into our children's approximations of writing. In Chapter 13, I describe how we sometimes shorten the reading workshop for kindergarten and early first-grade children (adding more time for interactive writing, shared reading, word work, and so forth), and I explain that we expect children to approximate reading if they cannot yet read print, and that we find many ways to scaffold both their emergent readings and their early work with little books. I hope this book shows how important it is to give children at every proficiency level time to read on their own.

The Tools That Support Reading Time: Bookshelves: Following the minilesson, when children head off to read, they carry what we call their "bookshelves" with them, sturdy baggies or plastic 9x12-inch magazine boxes. Each bookshelf holds the books the child is reading and the child's reading tools—bookmarks, a reading conference record sheet, and a log of books read. In first grade, children may have as many as ten tiny books, usually all at a roughly similar level, in their bookshelf collection. Meanwhile, a fifth grader who is reading chapter books may have just two. The contents of the bookshelves might include:

- a reading log in which readers list the titles of the books they've read, the dates they began and finished reading those books, the time they spent reading, and so on.
- a clipboard-sized white board with accompanying pen for interactive writing sessions, guided reading, or word work.
- one or more short texts (perhaps an editorial, a short story, a poem) that may be used for small-group work (perhaps for guided reading).
- a bag for carrying a book or two between home and school.

- a laminated alphabet chart and/or a copy of the high frequency words that class has studied and posted alphabetically on the word wall.
- magazines or newspapers for nonfiction reading.
- a note from the teacher left the previous evening recommending a title or challenging the reader to read more each night.
- a record of conferences, conference suggestions, and skills taught.
- bookmarks.
- a timer the child can use when reading with a partner to determine when to read and when to put the book down to talk.

We're wildly enthusiastic about these bookshelves because, frankly, they have managerial as well as instructional advantages. Our primary children tend to have a set day when the entire class, or a smaller group, of them "go to the library" in their classroom. In Ginny Lockwood's first grade at P.S. 116 in Manhattan, for example, children regard Monday mornings as "shopping time." Ginny typically gives her children a pep talk about choosing books, and then she and the children return last week's books and refill their bins with new books. Of course, a child may go to the library on another day, but the recurring ritual of the Monday morning book exchange helps teachers keep books circulating through children's lives. We want to be certain that beginning readers often have new texts in their hands, for those texts bring with them opportunities to do new problem-solving work. Our upper-grade children do not generally have an established library time but go when they need new books and select several books during any one visit.

Because children have a bunch of books "on deck," when they finish one book, they immediately begin the next, without roaming around the classroom. Before we had bookshelves, beginning readers especially seemed to spend a great deal of time running back and forth to the library to return finished books and select new ones. The classroom library began to have all the problems that the stairwell used to have when I taught in an urban high school, becoming not only the social hub but also the place for arguments and congestion. The bookshelves changed this by supporting engagement in sustained reading.

The bookshelves certainly help us with management, but they also help us with assessment. When we draw our chairs alongside children to observe as they read, we can, with a glance, see if today's book is representative of what that child has been reading. Does this reader seem to choose humorous light books consistently? Might we want to nudge him to widen his repertoire? We can also look over bookshelves once the day is over, reviewing what particular

children have been reading and making note of the conversations we want to have. Sometimes we leave "book gifts"—a book by a favorite author or an article about a series the child is reading—in the child's bookshelf.

Children do not, of course, make all the decisions about what they will read. As I explain in later chapters, we teach children to choose "just right" books, steering them to read mostly those books they can handle with ease. We also teach children how to ratchet up to work with books that are a notch too difficult for them and how to get extra support from a parent, a friend or from us if they want to read particularly challenging texts.

The Structures That Support Reading Time: Reading Nooks: Along with bookshelves, there is a second structure that helps enormously during the reading time portion of our reading workshops: reading nooks. We support classroom management and stamina when we ask readers to find a private reading place for themselves. Usually we introduce the idea gradually. At the start of the year, all children read at their desks. Some children profit from always reading at their desks, especially those who are still shaky at tracking print and need their books to lie steady on the desk. After a few weeks we're apt to suggest to five or six readers that they might each carefully select a nook somewhere in the classroom that might become that child's private reading space. We don't call these nooks isolation zones, but they function as such. "Put your name on a Post-it and leave it to mark your space. We'll see if that space works for you. Are you able to work on your reading there?" Sometimes teachers describe a reading place as "a cozy, comfortable corner to curl up in." I prefer to describe reading nooks as places to do your best work. (And I would definitely *not* expect children to do their best work in the far corner of the coat closet.) Eventually, half the class may be reading at their desks (with empty seats beside them, which allows us to pull in easily to confer), while others each have a long-term "reading nook."

Meanwhile, we let children know that what they are doing—finding places in their lives for reading—is part of making a reading life. Children soon come to school with stories of how they brought lamps into closets and turned them into reading places. Conversations like these are not only about making places for reading, they are also about establishing the ritual of reading before one goes to sleep, on Saturday mornings in bed, and often during the day.

Teaching During Independent Reading

During independent reading, teachers confer with children individually and in partnerships. A teacher may also gather a cluster of children together for a strategy lesson around a shared text. Sometimes the strategy lesson incorporates the various books children are already reading (this might be a repeat of the minilesson). A teacher may also gather a small group for a guided-reading session in which the teacher introduces a new and shared book, supports the children's progress through that book, and watches for a teaching point to emerge.

The content for this instruction will come from two sources. First, the teachers will each have approached their year with a curricular calendar containing units-of-study, which they envision embarking on as a classroom community during the year. That is, although many of the structures of the reading workshop will remain steady, the class will usually be "on-about" a shared inquiry or unit. Just as children in a writing workshop might focus on writing poetry for a while and then memoir, children in the reading workshop might focus on having book talks for awhile and then on reading nonfiction. (I discuss this in Sections III and IV.) Sometimes, the content of a teacher's instruction during independent reading grows out of that teacher's particular focus during that period. If a class of second graders has been doing a lot of nonfiction reading, the teacher may work with small groups to help them read, attending not only to surprising details but also to the author's main ideas.

Then, too, when we confer, we also draw on our knowledge of each child as a reader and a person. As I discuss in Chapters 8 and 9, we do formal and informal assessments often and develop instructional plans based on these and on our knowledge of how readers develop. We may approach one conference or strategy lesson already knowing that this child is a gist reader, recalling only the barest bones of texts, and another conference already knowing that this child reads as if in a cocoon, shut off from everything but the world of the story.

Partnerships in Support of Independent Reading

When most of us imagine a reader, we envision a solitary someone curled up with a book, but the truth is that reading and writing are always embedded in talk with others. In her book, *On Being Literate,* Margaret Meek writes,

> When we think of "a reader" we may have a romantic vision of someone sitting alone, reading a book, silently, with enough leisure to read at length without interruption, the kind of reading busy people say they wish they had more time to do. The fact is, readers read wherever and whenever they can, often together … as we read we turn the monologue of the book into a dialogue (1991 p. 33).

Margaret Meek asked teachers to write their reading histories. In looking them over she found that these narratives were not tales of solitary journeys. "I used to believe that reading was a solitary activity and literacy a cloistered virtue pursued at school…. Now I know reading as a fully social activity," she writes. "We were always in dialogue with others—those who taught us to read, those for whom we wrote, who lent us books, shaped our preferences, encouraged us, forbade us even" (p. 234).

The books that matter in our lives are the books we have discussed. "It takes two to read a book," Alan Purves has said, and it is true in my life that the books I remember most are those I have shared. If I simply ask people, "What are you reading in your independent reading life today?" and then, "Is there something social behind this book? Was it recommended by someone? Is it part of a conversation with someone?," it soon becomes clear that our so-called "independent" reading lives are not independent after all.

Interestingly enough, although most upper-elementary and middle school classrooms put great emphasis on teacher-supported book talks about teacher-chosen books, children are rarely encouraged to talk about the texts they read independently. If book talks are so integral to our teacher-sponsored curriculum, why wouldn't we want to do everything possible to be sure that students initiated book talks in their independent reading lives?

It is by talking about books that children learn to conduct a dialogue in their minds, to think about books even when they read alone. In our reading workshops, partnerships support talking, and therefore thinking about texts.

Partnerships in Primary Classrooms: When our children read with a partner, they are reading with someone who likes to read the same kinds of books. This means that reading partnerships are roughly ability-based, although we don't label them as such. This is especially true in the primary grades. Because readers actually process print together, the partners need to be able to read the same books. If one child is a much stronger reader than the other, the stronger reader tends to do most of the work (and get most of the practice).

When children have spent as much time as possible reading alone and their stamina seems strained, we give them a second wind by suggesting that it's time for them to read with partners. When K–2 partners meet, one child typically chooses a book she has already read from her bookshelf. Then the two readers look over the book together. Because this book "belongs" to one of the partners, the book's "owner" will do what amounts to a book introduction for her partner. Then the partners decide how they'll read the book. Once children can read books on the level of Rylant's *Henry and Mudge* series or Lobel's *Frog and Toad* series, we encourage them to read books silently to themselves. Now their partnerships resemble those of upper-grade readers. Until then, however, children tend to read aloud by following one of these formats:

- Choral reading, holding one copy of the book between the two readers
- Taking turns (with books that contain just a line or two on a page, we encourage readers to alternate after a few pages rather than a single page because this helps them get into the swing of a text before they swap)
- Echo reading (one child reads a chunk of pages and the other rereads "to make it smooth")
- Taking Parts ("You be Frog, I'll be Toad.") This is often done in the second reading of a text, and only some texts lend themselves to this.

- "I'll read a book to you (and you help if I get stuck) and then we'll talk about it. Then you read one to me."

If the teacher has made a big point of insisting that children not jump in quickly to help each other past every difficulty, they learn to wait for their partner "to have a go," piping in with help only after the partner solicits support. Frequently, one partner will say to another, "Let's look at the picture." "Could it be…?" Of course, sometimes the child who knows the troublesome word simply produces it. Because these readers also have lots of opportunities to read on their own, we do not worry a great deal over the times when children produce the correct words for each other.

"The division between private and partnership reading supports my kids' stamina as readers," Kathy Collins says. "At the start of the year in my first grade, private reading time lasts only ten minutes before the children begin to fray around the edges. We work toward half an hour of sustained private reading each day, but it takes time."

When children read books alone during private reading time, they eventually learn to note, with a bookmark or Post-it, sections they want to talk about later with their partners. (I discuss this in more detail in Chapter 15.) When partners meet together, we usually ask them to read through the book together first and then return to the book to talk about the marked pages.

Teachers who have visited our primary classrooms sometimes find that when they try to replicate what they have seen, the structures don't necessarily work for them. The truth is that these structures don't always work for us, either. We may spend several weeks demonstrating to children the tiniest ways in which good partners work together.

"What a great partner I have!" Renee Dinnerstein said, bringing out her book and putting it between herself and her student teacher. At this point, Renee took a brief step back from the role-play and, in a stage whisper said to the audience of children, "Now watch how I look at my partner while we talk." Then the reenactment continued. Details such as the importance of sitting side by side, of having only one copy of the book, and of holding it between the two partners aren't details at all when it comes to primary partnerships. But the good news is that children are amenable to instruction.

Partnerships Between Proficient Readers: Partnerships vary not with age but with reading proficiency. It's not always the case that *all* upper-grade readers are proficient readers or that all first graders are beginning readers. If fifth graders are beginning readers, their partnerships will be very much like the ones I've just described. On the other hand, if first graders are reading early chapter books, these readers need to read silently, and they probably need more support in comprehension than in reading the words on the page. A good rule of thumb is that once a child is reading books at the level of Rylant's popular *Henry and Mudge* series, it is probably not wise to ask that child to read aloud frequently, because it leads to subvocalizations, to excessive worry about accuracy, and to a concern with performance rather than comprehension.

Sometimes children seem so pleased with their facility at processing print that they roll along through sentences and pages without anything registering. A troubling number of readers read without giving close and thoughtful attention to the text. These readers may become adept at disguising the fact that they don't recall the texts by producing flowery talk. "It really made me feel I was there," they say, but when pressed, they can sometimes offer very little detail about the world of the story. If we want readers to hold themselves accountable for coming away from a text with a more detailed sense of what that text holds, one way to do this is to encourage those in upper-grade partnerships to reminisce over and retell the sections of books they've just read. Being able to retell a text is not sufficient for true comprehension, but it is a place to start. Within a very short while, partners will also begin to talk in other ways about books.

When our upper-grade children meet in partnerships to talk about books, there will be times when it is beneficial if both members of the partnership are progressing at the same time through the same book. There will be many other times, however, when this is less necessary.

Management During the Independent Reading Workshop

A reading workshop requires strong classroom management. Many teachers worry that a classroom of children won't be engaged enough in their reading to allow us, as teachers, to work with individuals and small groups. We've found that individual bookshelves, reading nooks, and partially leveled libraries (described later) help enormously, because these structures make it more likely that children sustain interest in a book or in several books. Here are some other strategies teachers have successfully used to manage reading workshops:

- In some workshops, teachers expect that if children have conferred with or met with them during the preceding day, they remain on the rug

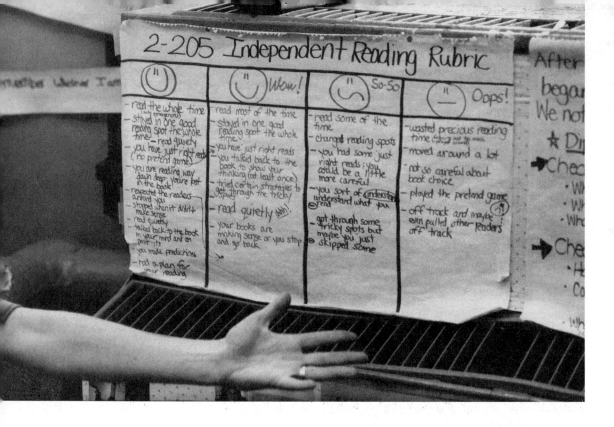

after the minilesson for a quick check-in ritual that holds them accountable for doing whatever they were directed to do.

- If children feel they are stuck and need the teacher, rather than remaining in their seats, where they tend to be restless and cause trouble, they are asked to join the teacher and quietly listen in on his or her conferences or strategy lessons until the teacher can turn his or her attention to the child.

- If children interrupt the teacher during a conference or a strategy lesson, the teacher acts astonished. "Couldn't you see I was reading with so-and-so?". When the child states his or her issue or question ("My book is too hard," "I ran out of Post-its," "Daniel is too loud so I can't concentrate"), the teacher is apt to say, "How could you solve the problem on your own?" and in this way help the child act independently.

- If a class of children seems unable to sustain a focus on reading for forty minutes, we sometimes divide reading time into sections. We may, for example, begin with twenty minutes during which children do their independent reading, followed by partnership time. Then there may be a second reading time, this one devoted to a particular kind of reading. In some classrooms, children use this time to reread familiar books aloud in partnerships to practice fluency and phrasing. In other classrooms, children use this time to read nonfiction or picture books.

In the end, the best thing we can do to nourish and energize our students' independent reading lives is to nourish and energize our own. We need to make the time to burrow under the covers and read that tantalizing book gathering dust on the nightstand, to read the newspaper, to track down the picturebook we adored when we were six, to order the new Oprah book everyone is raving about, or the new Pulitzer Prize winner or that latest sleazy beach book. We need to do this because, by reading, we layer our experience and develop greater breadth and depth to draw on in our teaching. But we need to do this most of all, because when we love reading, when we ourselves draw power and strength and peace from reading, we educate our students' imagination about what their own world of reading can be.

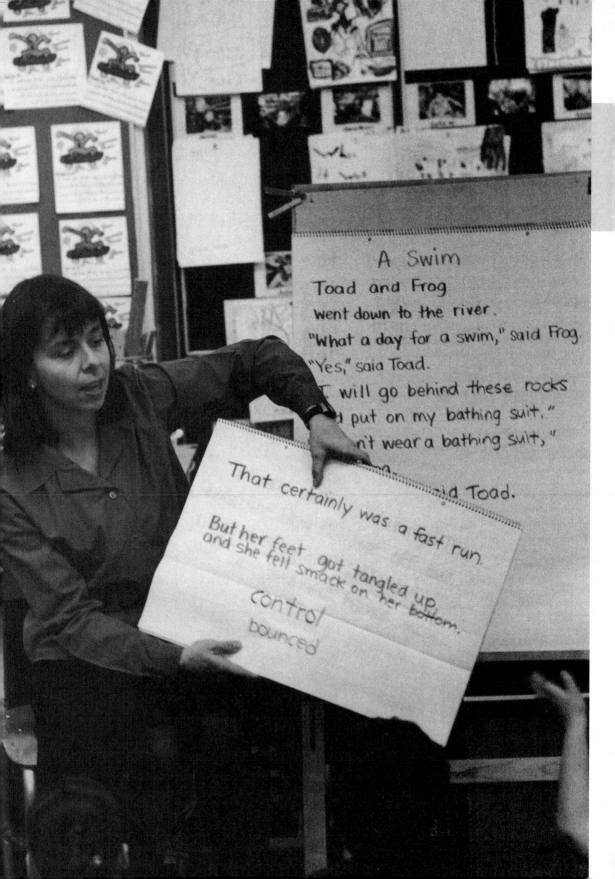

Minilessons 5

Whether we realize it or not, each of us, in our classrooms, authors a world and a story. In C. S. Lewis's *The Lion, the Witch, and the Wardrobe,* Lucy enters a strange closet. She pushes past the coats and suddenly feels cold air on her face. Something prickly sweeps against her arm, and she sees that she is standing among pine trees in snow. Ahead, a light gleams golden, a lamppost at the edge of the forest. In the opening pages of his novel, C. S. Lewis builds a world with its own seasons and thresholds.

As teachers, the stories we author begin anew each September when a new group of children cross our threshold. Soon they are sitting in a circle, perhaps around a candle and a book, and we're telling them about a writer who can change their lives if they listen. Yes, authoring the world of a literate classroom begins as any story begins: at a time, in a place, and because characters step across the threshold. "Let's hurry so we don't miss one precious moment of reading time," we say. And we tell our children about other readers and writers who've gone before them, who have made and read literature in this same place. We invite our children to become passionate readers and writers. We give them a new land with its own history and its holy places. We give them lampposts to light their way, and we give them the troubles that launch us on journeys.

Standing in the snow, Lucy hears the jingle of bells from the evil Snow Queen's sleigh. Before long, her little brother, Edmund, will step into that sleigh, lured by the taste of candy, and Lucy and the others will begin a long journey to rescue him and the kingdom of Narnia.

In every story and every curriculum, there will be the jingle of emerging difficulties and this jingle will launch a journey. In the story of our classrooms as in any story, one thing is certain: There will be trouble. On the final day of our reading institute, I looked out at the hundreds of teachers sitting with their notebooks full of teaching ideas, book lists, and recommended strategies. And I said to those teachers, "I have one last thing to tell you. When you go back to your classrooms to try out these ideas, *they won't work*. There will be trouble."

And it's true. We'll shelve books carefully into categories, "light sports books" or "Beverly Cleary books," and children will return them in any old order. We'll suggest that readers mark the sections they'd like to talk about, and soon books will be wallpapered with Post-its. We'll pull up next to reading partners and find that both children are talking simultaneously. Readers will blithely abandon books. Book talks will detour into jokes about last night's baseball game or today's lunch menu.

The important thing to realize is that in our classrooms, as in any story, trouble can galvanize us to set off on a journey. Trouble can lead us to climb every mountain, ford every stream, and follow every rainbow till we find our dream. As teachers, instead of scurrying about to hide or patch things that aren't working, we are wise to gather our class together and make a big deal out of the trouble. "I've realized that sometimes in this class we start a book, it looks good, and then it gets slow or confusing so we dump it. And we start another book, and *it* looks good, and then"—here, children will chime in— "*it* gets slow, and we dump *it*." When we gather the classroom community together in solidarity around shared trouble, when we look from person to person and all agree, "Yeah, I've had that trouble," it can be a life-giving moment in our curriculum.

In books, authors give us new worlds with their holy places, their heroes, and their history. And authors also give us trouble, the sound of the evil Snow Queen's sleigh bells. Soon we have a mission. Often, before the characters set off on that mission, they are given gifts: Lucy is given a vial of liquid that heals wounds; her brother, Peter, is given a magic sword and shield. In our classrooms, teachers identify and name problems. We define the mission. And then, after we've identified the mission, after we've met in solidarity around the mission, *sometimes* we can give our children a gift. Pulling the class in to listen with intensity, we say, "I have one thought that might help with this problem. Listen up."

Minilessons are the best forum teachers have for pulling the classroom community together to take on a problem. Minilessons, then, power our curriculum. It is through minilessons that we imbue the consistent, highly structured routines of our workshop with a sense of high drama. *Every day* we launch the school morning with song and with a read-aloud. *Every day* we pursue an inquiry into spellings and words. *Every day* students gather on the carpet for a minilesson and disperse to read privately in reading nooks and then to talk or read with reading partners. But *one day,* when we gather on the carpet, the teacher says, "Readers, I really need your attention. All weekend I've been thinking about the reading we're doing together and there's one thing that concerns me...."

Perhaps in Monday's minilesson, we call our children's attention to the fact that many of us aren't getting enough reading done in school or at home. We could let the discussion snowball to get lots of voices talking about the challenges of making time and space for reading. Then we could suggest a possible solution, perhaps one we use in our own lives, and say, "What if some of you give this a go and see if it helps." We could ask readers to turn and tell their partners how they'll weave this strategy into their lives. The next day we gather the class together and say, "Joline had another good idea about how to get more time for reading" and recruit children who are also willing to try out this second solution to the problem. Soon the whole class has begun to work on the issue, and new problems and possible responses emerge.

The minilesson is not a free-standing structure. Instead, the topic of the minilesson weaves its way into much of the community's reading work. If our minilessons are about making more time for reading, partners will be asked for perhaps that week and the next to keep track of the amount of reading they're doing. For these two weeks, children know they must talk with their partners not only about *what* they are reading but also about *how much* and *how long* they are reading. Generally the minilessons and the classroom structures reinforce each other in this fashion, and together they galvanize the classroom community to work together to solve a problem or meet a challenge.

Early in the school year, for example, we might have strings of minilessons that scaffold work around some of these problems:

- How can we choose "just right" books?
- How can we sustain our reading for a longer time?
- How can we make more time for reading in our lives?
- How can we tackle tricky words?
- What are some ways reading partners can support each other? (or, How can we be good reading friends for each other?)
- How can we read in ways that help us talk about texts?

These topics don't come from a "manual of minilessons" but from our own observations of readers. "What is the one issue I could bring to the forefront that might take us the farthest?" we ask as we think over the reading workshop and the particular readers with whom we work. Because we've traveled this route with other readers, we have a game plan in mind, and we anticipate some of the issues we'll confront (I discuss these in great detail in Section III). But it is also important for us to keep in mind that every year, the particular needs and strengths of a new classroom full of students will call for new directions.

The challenge in planning minilessons is not only to identify topics to address and content to convey, it is also to consider "*How* will I teach this content in ways that make a lasting impact?" In thinking about minilessons, most of our attention tends to be directed to *designing the method* rather than *choosing the content.* It's easy to decide to teach envisionment or note-taking or fluency in a minilesson, but it's another thing altogether to design a five- or ten-minute-long intervention that might make a lasting difference in the lives of our students. In this chapter, I want to focus on the methods we use to craft effective minilessons.

The Architecture of a Minilesson

In a study group on minilessons (which included Carl Anderson, Isoke Nia, Teresa Caccavale, Grace Chough, and me), we realized that the minilessons that work well in our reading and writing workshops tend to have a similar structure or architecture. Each of the five components, however, is tiny, and the entire minilesson lasts between five to fifteen minutes.

- Our minilessons begin with the *connection.* Usually we, as teachers, talk about how this topic fits with the work we've been doing together and about how it fits with our students' lives as readers and writers. We give an overview of what is to come.

- Next we *teach* students something we'd like them to try. We usually do this by demonstrating or telling them about a technique or retelling and reenacting something we've seen others do. Sometimes a child helps us do the teaching part of a minilesson.

- Then we usually give all our children an opportunity to "try it" or "have a go." Although this *active involvement* phase may involve children working alone, they often turn to their partners to try something out orally, practice a strategy for a moment, or plan what they might do later.

- We *link* the minilessons to the ongoing work of today's workshop and the students' lives as readers and writers.
- At the end of the hour-long workshop, we often gather students together to *follow-up* on the minilesson.

I recently began a minilesson by gathering first graders on the carpet and saying to them, "You know how we've been coming up with ways to have good book talks? Well, yesterday Jane and Dillon came up with another way. I want to tell you about their method for having book talks because the rest of us may want to follow their example." This was the connection phase of my minilesson.

To *teach,* I first retold an episode I'd seen. "Yesterday Jane and Dillon were reading this book, *Oh, no!*" I held it up. "And when they finished it, they didn't just put it away and start a new book. Instead I saw them doing something neat." In an aside to the class I said, "You watch, I'll be like them. See if you can notice what they did." Becoming six-year-old Jane, I reenacted what she had done when she finished reading *Oh No!* I paused for a moment

at the end of the book and then returned to the pages I'd just read, lingering especially at one page. I said (as if to my partner), "Remember, this was the funny page! They got paint all over!" Then, turning to the next page, I also looked it over and smiled, "Oh yeah, here's where she gets bike oil on her dress!" I continued to reminisce about the text for a minute or two longer. Then I paused, switched out of the character of a child, and asked the class, "So what did you see?"

Jane herself was the first to speak, "There were some funny things that happened in *Oh No!* and we just wanted to talk about them again."

Nodding, I said, "So, after you were done reading, you went back to the good parts and remembered them?" Instead of saying, "You went back to the page on which she'd spilled oil all over herself" or even "You went back to the funny parts." I described what these girls did in more generic terms to make their strategy transferable. I didn't want today's lesson to be about the book *Oh No!* or even about recalling the funny parts in a text. "I remember when I watched you guys, Jane and Dillon, you told me you were reminding yourself of the story. I repeated their phrase, savoring it.

"*Reminding yourself of the story.* What a great thing to do when you've finished with a book."

"Yeah," Jane said. "It's like we're remembering what happened in the story and talking about it."

From across the circle, John popped in, "That's like vacation pictures."

"What?" I asked.

John continued, "Like when you go on vacation and you look at the pictures and talk about them even if your vacation was from before."

"It does sound like that doesn't it?" (Although several children had participated in this discussion, I would not regard this as the active involvement phase of the minilesson, because most children were simply watching and listening.) Now I repeated some of what the children had said. "When readers finish a book, they like to go back through the book and talk about it, like vacation pictures, reminding each other of the cool things: the surprises, the places, whatever … and the best part is that you are all so lucky! You've each got a partner so you can do this."

Knowing it was time for *active involvement,* I suggested that we practice Jane and Dillon's strategy by looking back on the picturebook we'd read aloud the day before. Opening Judith Viorst's *The Tenth Good Thing About Barney,* I showed the children the first page and said, "Why don't you remind yourselves of the story." After each child talked with a partner for a moment, I turned to the next page and this continues. We did not talk as a group because to me the important thing was to give children a feel for looking back over a book with a friend.

By then, it was time for us to read. Pausing for a moment to be certain I had everyone's attention, I did a very simple *link.* I simply said, "Today I want you to try what Jane and Dillon did. Whenever you finish a book, flip back through it to remind yourselves of the story, and when you next meet with your partners, talk about those stories. I'll be coming around to admire your work." Forty minutes later we convened on the carpet for a brief share session. To *follow-up* the minilesson, I had asked two children to demonstrate the way they had used Jane and Dillon's strategy that day, and I asked every child to do this again that night at home. In the pages that follow, we'll examine the five components of minilessons more closely.

The Connection

To start a minilesson, we take a minute to draw students into what we'll be saying. This is the "Listen up" phase. We try to establish eye contact with our students (in the fullest sense of the word). We want them to feel that we've been thinking about them and their work and that we have one crucial problem to address or one strategy to teach today. We tell students what we'll teach and how it fits in with their ongoing work. We may begin by saying, "I've been thinking about you readers" or "I stayed late last night in the classroom rereading your work" or "I watched some of you struggling yesterday with...."

Perhaps because they think of this part of the minilesson as the "motivation" phase, some teachers mistakenly teach with leading questions. "Yesterday, we said that readers do what?" or "What were we working on yesterday?" or "What are some ways to have good book talks?" Launching minilessons with a series of questions introduces lots of problems. We are often looking for a particular answer, and yet children can't read our minds enough to produce that answer. Instead, their responses take us way off track and turn a straight, clean minilesson into a conversational swamp. At the beginning of a minilesson, it is important to establish the direction and momentum for the day. It's difficult to do this if all our sentences are designed to elicit the answers we want from our students.

Although there are times in the school day for real conversations, in a minilesson we are often trying to convey information, and I don't generally recommend masking this fact. In one class I watched recently, a child was trying to answer the "What did we talk about yesterday, class?" question, but what she recalled was only a minor part of the previous day's lesson. "We talked about Barney," she said, "and my sister's cat is named Barney." A few hands shot up, and the teacher called on Matt. "*My* cat's name is Whisper," he said and proceeded to describe his cat. By this time the children were already restless and confused.

What I would suggest is that we refrain from asking questions at this point in the minilesson, and that we avoid spending half the minilesson reviewing yesterday's work. This is the time to move on, and a very quick summary of yesterday's point is enough.

THE CONNECTION

WE DON'T BEGIN LIKE THIS	WE TEND TO BEGIN LIKE THIS
What did we talk about yesterday?	Yesterday we talked about ...

Who knows what good readers do when they … (get oriented to a new story, etc.)

When good readers begin reading a story, we already know that in the opening pages, we'll learn a few key things. It helps to remember to be on the look-out for answers to questions. Yesterday, we said readers are asking "Who?" Today we'll think about another question readers are asking.

Yesterday we talked about, what? No, not the story's ending. No, not the donuts. It begins with a [K] sound. We talked about what? Yes, characters! And today we're going to talk about *setting*. When we read a book, there is such a thing as *setting*. Who knows what setting is?

We've been thinking in this class about how the traditional elements of story can help us read, and specifically about how, when we read books, it helps to think about the *characters* in the book, to be sure we know their names and can describe their traits. Today we're going to focus on a second element in traditional stories—the *setting*. Thinking about the setting of a story will help us remember and retell stories and understand them too. I'm going to show you *how* to pay attention to setting and *why* this will help.

The Teaching Phase

Once we have made the connection, we try to teach our students a strategy or a habit we hope they will use often when they read. The challenge is to convey information in a way that leaves a lasting impression on our students. If we teach a technique but no one uses it that day or another day, then our teaching has been a waste of precious time.

In a minilesson, we find it efficient to use these same few teaching methods over and over whether we are teaching readers how to use the index in a nonfiction book or showing how punctuation acts as a road sign, we often use these methods:

- The teacher tells students about a strategy.
- The teacher demonstrates a strategy and helps students label what the teacher has done.
- A certain number of readers employ the strategy while others observe, research, and name what they see.
- Students read (or do something else) in a particular way and spy on themselves, then discuss in pairs what they saw themselves doing.
- The teacher tells about or reenacts what other students have done, and the strategies the readers used are given names.
- Readers look at records from work they've done and name what they see.

One method that is especially helpful when we want to teach students a new strategy is to tell the class, as I did with *Oh No!*, what we saw one of their classmates doing. "Let me tell you what I saw Tony doing" we say (even if the secret truth is that we may have nudged Tony to use the strategy in the first place). "I'm wondering if some of you want to try Tony's strategy?" Students are sometimes more eager to take on techniques that have social currency. Then, too, we often tell students about a strategy we use in our own reading or about a tip a teacher once gave us.

It is especially powerful if, instead of *telling* students about a strategy we use, we actually *demonstrate* that strategy. This often means reading a text publicly while the class watches. In a first grade classroom, we might, for example, pretend to be six years old. "Watch what I do to get ready to read," we might say, and then look through the book, talking aloud about what we see in the pictures. We often follow this role-play by turning to the class and saying, "Talk in partners about what you noticed me doing;" or by saying, for example, "Did you notice that I wondered what *kind of book* this would be? Readers do that a lot." We might then list a few of the things we or the children noticed on a chart titled, for example, "What Good Readers Do to Get Ready to Read."

Similarly, we may demonstrate a strategy we'd like readers to use. For example, if I want to encourage fifth graders to scan their textbooks, noticing the bold headings and speculating how the chapter will be laid out, I'd be apt to make an overhead (or copies) of selected pages and to think-aloud as I do this sort of strategic reading with the excerpt. Then I might walk the whole class through similar work, and ask partners to try it together, and finally encourage readers to use this strategy in their lives (including during independent reading).

As an alternative to us reading publically, role-playing or telling children about effective reading strategies, we sometimes ask the whole class to observe a reader, or a team of readers, in order to research what they are doing. We are apt to do a play-by-play commentary. When first graders Dan and Jorge came to the front of the circle and demonstrated to the class how they work in a partnership, their teacher, Lisa Ripperger, said, "Let's watch how Dan and Jorge settle into their partnership reading. Oh, look. Isn't it perfect how they're sitting so close together so they both can see the pages? See how quickly they have chosen the book they're going to read together." After a moment, Lisa added, "Look, do you see them talking? I bet they're planning how to read the book together. Let's listen." After waiting a moment to let Dan and Jorge follow on cue, Lisa commented, "Yep, there they go, I hear them reading. They've decided to read the words together chorally." Then, turning to the group, Lisa said, "Can any of you imagine getting started with your partner in that same amazing way that Dan and Jorge have shown us?"

Whether we're charting "What Good Partners Can Do to Work Together" or "What Good Readers Do to Get Ready to Read," a predictable problem can present itself. When we call on children for their responses, a child will provide us with an idea that doesn't make sense. Sometimes, out of our worry about hurting a child's feelings, we back ourselves into a corner, charting responses that make no sense. But we don't do children any favors if we don't give honest responses to some of their off-the-wall comments. We need to be ready to say something like, "How does that fit?" or "I'm not sure that readers actually do that. What do the rest of you think?" or "Isn't that a lot like what Ashley has already said?"

At times during the teaching phase of a minilesson, we may *gather* information from the class rather than *giving* it. We still need to avoid asking known-answer questions ("What does a good reader do to get ready to read?"). I'd far rather ask a real question: "I've told you all to look a book over before you read, but so often you just begin reading without looking at it. What do you think we could do to help you remember to look the book over before you start reading the print?" Or alternatively, we might say, "Will you talk this issue over with your partner, and then let's bring our ideas together" or "Will you talk this over as a group and let me listen in on your talk?" This way we are able to take notes on their talk and can then bring forth only the particular points we want to highlight from their discussion. "So, let me comment on three things you mentioned," we can say.

THE TEACHING PHASE

INSTEAD OF DOING THIS:	WE TEND TO DO THIS:
Teacher: "When we read stories, there is such a thing as a *setting.* Has anyone ever heard that word before? Holly: Where it takes place? Anna: You get a picture from where it is? Teacher: (calls on Carl) Carl: I don't know. Teacher: Open your book, Carl. See how it says, we went to the river? That's what, class? Children: Setting? Teacher: Yes, the setting is a farm in Alabama. What do you know about Alabama?	Teacher: The setting of a story is the *when* and the *where.* Sometimes a reader can skip past the setting, and all of a sudden a lot of things don't make sense. So pretend I am reading a book and it is set in Colonial America in 1790, but I don't notice that. And then I read (pretends to be reading a text) "We were going to the store. I'd never been on such a trip before and I couldn't sleep I was so excited." I might think, "Whaaat? Why had she never been to the store until now?" But of course, if I remember this is Colonial America, then I am thinking …" You need to notice the setting of a story and to carry it with you always, in your reader's backpack, and it'll explain a lot of other things that happen.

The Active Involvement Phase

The fact that we, as teachers, say something has very little to do with whether our children learn it. Telling is not teaching. If we want our minilessons to stand a chance of making a lasting impression on our students, it's wise to nudge students to "have a go" or to "try it" as they sit together on the carpet.

Granted, by doing a two-minute-long exercise our students aren't truly learning a strategy; they'll only really understand it when they use it for their own important purposes. But asking students to try a strategy briefly makes a bigger impression than our words alone and may break through their resistance.

Trish Lyons, first-grade teacher in Tenafly, New Jersey, told her children about watching two boys reading a non-fiction caterpillar book. They hadn't read the book cover to cover, front to back, as they read stories. Instead they'd use the subtitles, indexes, and so forth to skip from one category to another, related one. "So get with your partners," Trish said, "and I'm going to give you each a nonfiction book on flowers [their science unit]. Will you and your partner look it over and see how this book is arranged? Does it have subtitles? An index? What are its parts?"

Although it is common for us to ask children to use the strategy we've highlighted with one of the books from their own bookshelf bins, sometimes texts with particular characteristics are required (characters using dialogue, punctuation that acts as intriguing road signals, texts with compound words, texts by an author we know well), in which case we might pass out books or copies of a page or enlarge a page by using the overhead projector. Alternatively, we may just say, "Continue reading from your book bin and use this strategy if it makes sense to do so. We'll talk in a few minutes about whether you were able to use the strategy."

When we nudge children to take a strategy we've demonstrated and use it with their own chosen texts, we turn an approach that at first seemed lodged in a particular text into a more universal one. When readers have transferred a strategy from one text to another, they see that it can be used with yet other texts.

I recently watched Teresa Caccavale talk to her second graders about how she surveyed the *New York Times* that morning, dipping into the headlines and reading the opening paragraphs of several articles before settling on one to read. Then she passed out copies of the *Scholastic Newspaper* her class subscribed to and suggested that everyone try the same process of skimming before they settled into reading one story.

Another time, I watched a teacher help her first graders read a page from *The Hungry Giant,* paying attention to making the giant's voice loud and real. Then the class read a page from *"Will You Be My Mother?"* taking care to make the lost, orphaned lamb's voice sound small and pleading. Finally, the teacher passed out a pile of selected books and asked children to begin reading the books in pairs, trying to speak the voices in ways that reflected the characters.

I have three important pieces of advice for this stage of active involvement. First, *all* children should be active. Calling on only a few children in a whole-class discussion is a far cry from what we imagine as active involvement.

Second, this stage should take no more than five minutes *at the most*. Children will probably not complete their work. The point is to get children's feet wet so they are willing to use this strategy later. Finally, readers will usually not report back to the whole-group on the work they did with their partners because if each reader reports on what he or she found—or tried or learned—the minilesson will, guaranteed, become a *maxi*-lesson.

THE ACTIVE INVOLVEMENT PHASE

INSTEAD OF DOING THIS:	WE TEND TO DO THIS:
"So it is important to know the *setting* of a book. What was the setting from *The Homecoming*, John?" "Sarah, tell us the setting for *Roll of Thunder, Hear My Cry?*"	Would you get with your partner? I'm going to continue reading. As you listen carry with you an awareness of the setting—Colonial America, in 1790, perhaps in a Massachusetts colony. When I pause, talk to your partner about how your knowledge of the setting informs your understanding: "At the store, Pa bought me a piece of penny candy. I wrapped it in my handkerchief, planning to eat it on Christmas Day. We stayed overnight in the town and prepared for the long journey home."

The Link

The link is the "off you go" phase of the minilesson. It can be as simple as saying to kids, "Okay, let's bring our bookshelf bins to our reading places and get started." If we don't help students transfer what they have learned to their own independent reading, our teaching amounts to nothing more than footprints in the sand. Yet if each minilesson ends with an assignment ("Today I'd like you to …"), we risk turning the reading workshop into a traditional classroom: we dole out a daily assignment and our students do as they are told. Although sometimes we'll ask all students to use what they've learned from the minilesson, at other times, we'll say, "Add this strategy to your repertoire and use it when it furthers your purposes."

The Link to Children's Ongoing Reading

If our message is "Do this today" we might say	If our message is "Add this to your repertoire and use it when it fits your purposes," we might say
• "Get started while you are still here in the meeting area."	• "Can I have a few volunteers who will use this strategy today? Will you three plan to bring what you do to the share meeting?"
• "Tell your partner how you'll start doing this."	
• "Write this assignment in your reading log."	
• "Raise your hand if you know how to start doing this." "Okay, off you go. The rest of you, stay and I'll help you."	• "If you do this, come and get me (or sign up on the chart, or bring your work to the meeting)."
• Ten minutes into the workshop, we ask children to pause briefly and reflect with their partner. "How is (or isn't) the strategy working for you?"	• "Would you take a few minutes to look over the work you did yesterday? How many of you think you can use what we talked about in your work today?"
• In conferences, we follow up on the minilesson: "Show me some evidence that you are doing the work we talked about today" or "Walk me through how you've done what I asked you to do."	• In conferences, we help children reach their own goals which are often unrelated to that day's minilesson. "Could you use any of the strategies we talked about recently to help with this?"
• In guided reading and strategy lessons, we help all children work through difficulties they might be having in using the strategy taught in the minilesson.	• In guided reading and strategy lessons, we teach readers according to their own unique needs in ways that are probably not linked to the minilesson.
• Ask partners to show each other how they used the strategies we taught in the minilesson and discuss it.	• Expect partners to work in ongoing ways that reflect their goals and priorities.

We're more apt to insist that there be a carryover between a particular minilesson and that day's reading workshop if:

- the minilesson suggests a way of thinking rather than a concrete activity. If we want children to envision as they read, this goal is abstract enough that it helps for them to try it immediately. If we are suggesting a more concrete activity such as when we say, "When you finish a book you loved, you may choose another by the same author," this suggestion doesn't as easily vaporize in a wisp of thought.
- the minilesson suggests a strategy every reader is well-advised to do almost all the time, such as taking a moment to recall what we've already read before reading more.
- the minilesson occurs early in a string-of-minilessons when our goal is to help all our children develop a repertoire of strategies for dealing with a particular issue. Later we'll expect children to be able to choose from all these strategies, using the one best suited to a specific instance.

The Follow-Up

We reinforce and extend the minilesson at the end of the day's workshop by gathering all the students together in a share meeting. Teachers may ask questions: "Who tried what we talked about today? How did it work for you? Did it work in different ways for others?" Alternatively, two or three children who followed up on the minilesson might be asked to talk about or demonstrate what they did, or the teacher might describe the good work they did and invite others to follow their example. Instead of convening as a whole class, children may meet with a partner to talk about the work each child did today and to plan for tomorrow. The minilesson is meant as explicit, direct instruction but as Randy Bomer reminds us, "If students don't make sense of and use what was taught, the teaching wasn't explicit, regardless of how definitive the teaching may seem in the teacher's minds or words" (Bomer, 1998).

Putting the Pieces Together: Looking at Two Minilessons

Susana Gonzalez leaned close to her kindergarten children and, speaking in the whispering voice she uses when she's saying something truly urgent, Susana said, "I've been noticing that you've been doing a lot of good reading together—with each other and by yourselves. And I see you guys doing lots of neat stuff when you come to hard parts. I thought we'd gather what you all do onto a giant list." (This was "The Connection.") "What do you do when you come to a word you don't know?" Then Susana said, "I'll be a first grader. Watch with your partner what I do when I get to hard parts." Susana read just two sentences from an enlarged text, then children talked in partners about the strategies she used. Susana called for a few suggestions.

Hands flew up in the air. "You look for parts you *do* know."

"You chunk it!"

"You figure it out and say it."

"Anything else?"

Pharoh said, "You could act it out." This didn't make a whole lot of sense and Susana acted confused and asked for clarification. Pharoh seemed stymied. "Can anyone help Pharoh?" Susana asked.

"You can look at the pictures," Clyde said. Susana asked for elaboration. "How will the pictures help?"

"They tell about the words. You see what's happening in the picture. You look at the picture to see what's happening and the words match it."

Susana meanwhile, had scribed the suggestions onto chart paper titled, "What We Do When We Come to Hard Parts." Rereading the list, with the class chiming in, she said, "So, you do *all* these things …" thus ending the second component of the minilesson. Moving into the Active Involvement stage, she brought out a big book version of Numeroff's *If You Give a Mouse a Cookie* and said, "Let's try it with this book." Then she said, "To make certain there are some hard-words for all of us, I've masked a few words with post-its. Let's really notice what we do when we come to those hard words.

Soon the class was chiming along together. "If you give the mouse a cookie," everyone read, "He's going to ask for a *post-it* of milk."

"Cup?"

"Glass?"

"Drink?"

Susana highlighted the strategy her children used to generate these responses. "I saw some of you rereading and thinking. I saw you, Summer, looking at the picture. I saw you, David, guessing and reading on to the next part." Soon she peeled the post-it away. "It is also important to look at the letters, isn't it?" she said. "What do you notice about this word?" Soon the class resumed reading, and repeated the same strategic work for two other post-its. Instead of finishing the big book, Susana soon said, "You guys had so many strategies you used when you come to tough words—and we pretended the post-its were tough words. (She reread the list of strategies) Let's try these strategies in other books now." Soon her children were dispersed about the room reading independently.

The next day's minilesson began similarly with more work with *If You Give a Mouse a Cookie,* but this time Susana said, "You are getting so good at using strategies when you come to difficulty. Let's try this with new books." Get hip-to-hip with your partners and try reading the book I give you, making sure to use all your strategies when you come to difficulty." Within a second, Susana's children were sitting hip-to-hip with their partners, and she was passing out books. Susana did a bit of shuffling as she passed out the books, clearly in an effort to match books with readers. The room erupted as all thirty children began reading their books with their partners. After three minutes, some had finished reading. "Can I stop you," Susana said to the others, quieting them. "I saw you using *so* many strategies! I saw … (and again, she reiterated the list, this time attaching children's names to each strategy.) We're going to head off to independent reading today and I have a hunch you're going to meet up with some hard parts. Try these strategies, okay, and remember them because we'll talk about them later."

Erica Leif began her minilesson by saying to her fifth graders, "When we talked yesterday about ourselves as readers, we talked about needing balance in our reading lives. We talked about how Nick and Jonathan use their own hobbies and interests to drive their nonfiction reading. And I started thinking about my own life, and how I as a reader go about feeding my reading life." Then Erica said, "I realized that one thing I do is I ask questions, and then I try to answer them in my reading life (the connection)."

Erica pulled out her white board and wrote on it with red marker: "Hedge funds and Mutual funds."

Then she said, "There are things called hedge funds and mutual funds. They have to do with money and the stock market. I realized that I am going through life, not knowing about these things. Other people in my life know about these things. So I decided that I wanted to know what this stuff was all about. I read a *New York Times* article, but I only got a little bit out of it."

"So I decided that I am going to take on this question of what *is* a hedge fund, and I am going to read *The New York Times* business section. I usually skip that section but I am going to read it to start this investigation. I am also going to ask my friend who works for the hedge fund about the basics. If I start reading all this stuff before I know anything at all, it's like getting the blender going without much in it, you know? I need more information before I can understand these articles. I am also going to ask my brother what magazine I could read. I am not going to get a year's subscription, but I might buy an issue or two at the newsstand and read it."

"As readers and thinkers we have questions all the time. Sometimes they fly through our lives and we let them go. Today, we're going to catch some. Will you, right now, open your notebooks and as you think back over your life last week and even last month, write down a few questions you've had that you might want to explore further. Choose one, and with your partner, plan out what you could read to help you explore this question."

After about five minutes, Erica said, "It's exciting to come up with plans to pursue a haunting question, isn't it? (This ended the active engagement phase.) Will you continue to think today about whether you have a question that could send you on a reading investigation and begin to gather the texts you'll need? We'll revisit this topic tomorrow." (This was the link.) Erica set a timer to ring in half an hour and she and her children dispersed.

Minilessons may not be as powerful as Peter's magic sword and shield, or as potent as Lucy's vial of healing liquid, but they may be the best forum teachers have for pulling the classroom community together to take on a problem. They are a gift of sorts, a resource to draw on. With careful attention to the architecture of our lessons and an assertive responsiveness to our children's needs and goals, minilessons can turn classrooms into places where magic happens.

Coaching and Conferring with Readers

6

Throughout the world, teachers of writing come alongside youngsters as they write and confer with them in ways they hope will help this day with this draft as well as another day with another draft. We listen as children respond to what they have written and tell us their intentions, and we intervene to demonstrate and extend the strategies and concepts our youngsters use. Teacher-student conferences are so important in the writing workshop that the workshop itself is sometimes referred to as "the conference method of teaching writing."

Perhaps because we worked first in the field of writing, my colleagues and I have made a special effort to explore ways in which teachers of *readers* can likewise pull alongside our youngsters as they read and confer in ways that help them today and tomorrow. It has been surprising to realize that over the last two decades hundreds and thousands of pages have been published about the importance of conferences in the teaching of writing, but that much less attention has been given to conferences in the teaching of reading. It's intriguing also to realize that in the field of *writing,* conferring well means that the conference acts as a lever to raise the level of that student's writing long afterward. Conferring well doesn't mean writing well during the conference. Instead, it means that the conference has a lasting effect. In the field of *reading,* however, there has generally been *no assumption* that our work with individuals, or with small groups of readers, will be judged as successful on the basis of whether or not those interactions raise the level of what our students do afterward. Instead, success is based on whether students read well during the interaction. If a teacher's interaction with a *writer* is meant to alter all the work the student does after the interaction is over, then why wouldn't a teacher's interactions with a *reader* also be directed towards altering how a student reads after the interaction is over?

There are several possible explanations. If a teacher doubts that a class of children can carry on reading while he or she works with individual readers, it makes sense to give up the dream of working with individuals in ways that might have a lasting effect on their reading. Although granted, kindergarten and first-grade teachers have reason to question whether their children can carry on independently as readers, it is worth noticing that beginning writers often work industriously and independently. Why would this be impossible for beginning *readers?*

Perhaps we doubt that reading is as amenable to instruction as writing is. Although we can imagine conferring effectively by using the concreteness of writing, it may be harder to imagine conferring effectively about an activity as elusive as reading, especially once children read silently to themselves. Then, too, we probably believe that it's more reasonable to tell a writer, "Write with more detail" then it is to tell a reader, "Read so that you grasp more detail." We may even believe that writing strategies can be discussed, chosen, and implemented, but that reading strategies must develop naturally and less self-consciously, that for readers, strategies grow from repeated, scaffolded experiences rather than from conversations.

Conferring with young writers *is* different from conferring with young readers, yet I am convinced that we *cannot* give up on the belief that conferring with individual readers can lift them to new levels in the reading they do tomorrow.

I find it helpful to classify reading conferences. We can *confer with* a reader following the research-decide-teach structure integral to our writing conferences. We can also *coach* into a child's reading, and we can be a *partner* to a child who is reading. Often we'll do a combination of these three things.

Conferring with Readers: Research, Decide, Teach

Conferring with young readers (as with young writers) first involves *research* in order to learn where the child is as a reader and understand the child's intention, then *deciding* what we should teach, and then *teaching* in a way that can influence what that child does on another day with another book.

In conferring with a reader, I begin by recalling whatever I already know about this reader. My hope is to enter every conference with a theory of the reader and a tentative instructional plan already in mind. For example, from across the room I notice Pedro and recall that in our last conference, he read in a staccato word-by-word fashion and had lots of difficulty with words. At the time, I asked him to read easier books and specifically directed him to the *Little Soup* books by Robert Newton Peck. Now as I approach him, I see that Pedro has been reading *Little Soup's Birthday*. He and his partner, Matt, are talking about the book. I pull my chair alongside the two boys. They keep talking. That's because I've established a procedure: when I join students, they carry on as if I weren't there. Otherwise, we can't do the assessment we need to do. Even if a first glance has already given me plenty to say to a reader in a conference and I don't need to watch, I still make a point of withholding comments for a minute and letting children carry on a bit longer. I do this so children learn they should not stop what they're doing and look expectantly at me.

Now I listen as Pedro retells *Little Soup's Birthday* to Matt. "It was about this kid, and this other kid has a birthday, and they live on a farm," Pedro is saying to Matt. "And he gives him a squashed toad."

"Gross. He likes weird junk," Matt responds. "And he has a sister."

For a moment there is silence. "It's snowing on their farm," Pedro adds, and again the boys are quiet.

The moment I hear Pedro retell the story by referring to the main character as "this kid," I have a possible teaching point in my mind. Although I'm often tempted to jump at the first teaching point that comes on the horizon, I've learned to wait. Pedro and Matt continue to retell the chapters they've read, and after listening for a few minutes I have even more possible directions in mind for the next part of this conference. I stop their talk and ask, "How's it going?" then follow-up with, "Can you tell me what you two have been working on as readers and as partners?" I want to learn about their assessment of this conversation and their intentions for these talks.

Pedro points out that he's been reading easier books and it works. The books feel smooth. I nod, affirming the direction of his work. "Our talks are just so-so," he adds, and I am pleased that he sees this. Then I weigh the teaching options.

- I could suggest to Pedro and Matt that they continue to read books that make sense but stop to retell the story every fifteen minutes rather than every thirty to forty minutes. The boys seem to be at risk of missing a great deal of the meaning of the text.
- I could encourage Pedro and Matt to do a more chronological retelling for a time, one that would hug the shore of the text more closely. It

might even help them to turn the pages of the book and summarize them ("This was the part about …").

- I could teach Pedro and Matt that retellings of a story should contain many of the elements of a story and help them use a list of story elements (characters, setting, plot, movement through time, change) to structure their retelling, which now seems "all over the place." Because I hadn't taught the elements of story, this might be too ambitious for this conference.

- I could listen to them read the text aloud and do a more informed assessment of their reading.

I wonder which option will have the greatest payoff for these readers and decide to suggest a more chronological retelling. "Pedro and Matt," I say. "I want to congratulate you on working to make sense out of books. That is so smart. And you are right to pick books that'll help you with this project. So congratulations." For a moment they bask in my approval. They aren't surprised, however, when I say more. "I want to work with you today on the *retelling* part of what I saw, as a next step. What I noticed about you two today is that when you went to talk over the book, you sort of swiped at it, saying stuff you could remember about *Little Soup's Birthday.*" Then I reread the transcription I'd made as they spoke, highlighting the hop-around-and-make-points nature of their book talk.

I typically begin this phase of my conferences this way, noticing and supporting readers' intentions and the direction of their work. Then I often name for readers what I saw them doing. Sometimes I'll ask, "Do you do this often?" But this time I carry on. "Would you two try, whenever you get together to talk about your reading for the next few weeks, to do a retelling that looks more like this," and I proceed to demonstrate how I'd do a chronological retelling of their book. Demonstrations usually convey more than instructions. In conferences, as in the teaching phase of a minilesson, I try to demonstrate something that is very possible for children to do. For example, in this instance I look back and scan the pages as I narrate their general content.

Next I say, "How about if you get started with this while I watch?" This of course is reminiscent of the active involvement part of a minilesson, and it is the richest part of a conference. I watch them working in this new way and coach into what they do. It is clear to me that Matt considers it to be cheating to look at the text as he retells it, so he tries valiantly to keep his eyes from flicking toward the page. I intervene, "It's smart to glance at the page for help, Matt. I do that, too." If I stay in this conference a while, this prompt will become more efficient. That is, another time, I can simply tap on the page of the book as a reminder for Matt to use it as a resource. I end this research-decide-teach conference by asking the boys to record the plan to do this kind of retelling whenever they meet in their reading partnership.

Researching and Deciding: The First Two Components of a Research-Decide-Teach Conference

I often begin a conference by watching for a minute from afar, where I can see things that are invisible once I move in closer. Does the reader seem engaged with the text? How does the reader interact with others? With space? Is the reader using his finger? A bookmark under the words? Subvocalizing? Since I expect the reader to continue working while I watch, if a child who is reading turns toward me and automatically begins to read aloud when I pull my chair alongside her, I'll say, "Just continue reading the way you were before I came." Later, I may ask, "Will you read a bit aloud," but I don't want children to do this the instant I draw close or I can't assess their ongoing reading. Often as I sit at a table to the side of one reader, I am in fact observing all the readers around me. I'm deciding which reader needs some help, and I'm watching to see if anything I see suggests a direction I could take in a conference. As I sit in the midst of these readers, I'm also apt to look at my notes to jog my memory about the earlier interactions I've had with them. I may read the page over one reader's shoulder. Eventually, I intervene. For a more proficient reader, I tap her arm and say, "Can I stop you?" If it is an emergent or a beginning reader, I'm apt to let her finish the book first and then say, "Can we talk?"

There is no magic list of questions to ask readers during these brief interviews, but I'm likely to begin with one of these:

- "How's it going? What's up with your reading lately?"
- "Last time we talked about … What's happened for you since?"
- "I saw you stop and do some work on this page. What was going on?"
- "How'd you like this book? Were there some tricky parts?"
- "Wow! Your reading is changing! Do you feel how different it is?"
- "What were you going to do next?"
- "I was just watching you and I noticed you were … Can you talk to me about that?"
- "How's reading been for you lately? Has it been a really good time for you as a reader or a so-so time?"
- "What new work have you been doing lately as a reader?"

- "So if this was New Year's and you were resolving to do and be more in reading, what might your new resolutions be?"

No matter what question I ask, some readers launch into a long retelling of their books. As the child talks, I often find myself looking for ways to steer him away from the text and back to his reading life. I *can* learn a lot from hearing all the details of a text (especially if I know it well enough to note what the reader has and hasn't attended to, and if I'm ready to listen keenly, trying to construct the text out of what the reader says) but usually I find I can't yet focus on this sort of detail. I need a bigger context first. To switch the conversation away from a blow-by-blow account of the plot, I'm apt to say, "What a story! I'm glad to hear about it, but when I conference with you, I'm also hoping to learn about the work you are doing now as a reader," and then I again ask one of the questions listed on the previous page.

With emergent and beginning readers, I observe more and interview less. Sometimes I ask these readers to show me how they do certain things. In order to learn about a whole range of activities, I might say, "Show me."

- Show me how you choose a book.
- Show me how you get started with a book.
- Show me how you and your partner read together.
- Show me what you do when you reach the end of a book.
- Show me how your reading changes when you read a really hard text like this one.
- Show me how you two talk about a book.

Of course, what a reader does when on exhibition *may not* be what that same reader does regularly, but at the very least we're given a glimpse into what children believe we want them to do, and this alone is valuable.

It is misleading to suggest that the direction of a conference comes only from observing readers, because the truth is, our research itself usually has a direction or an angle of vision. When we watch and interview young readers, what we notice about them as readers comes from the questions we ask and the features to which we attend. The direction of our research is shaped by our whole-class emphasis, our knowledge of how readers grow, and our knowledge of this particular reader. At different times during the year, the changing emphasis of our whole-class teaching will influence what we look for during the research phase. For example, as I describe in Section III, early in the year my priorities might be to match readers with books, to encourage reading that makes sense, and to develop stamina. I'm apt to use conferences to check on whether readers are making sense of a book. "Would you read aloud a bit?" I'll ask. Then I ask questions. "I don't know this book very well. Can you tell me what's going on?" Quickly, I learn whether or not this reader is making sense of the text. Then, too, if I'm trying to rally the class around the challenge of reading more, I'm apt to ask, "When did you start the book?" and to look for evidence of the reader's rate of progression through the text. That is, what I attend to in a conference often grows out of the whole-class emphasis at the time.

The questions I have in my mind as I observe and interview a particular reader also derive from my hunch about this child's reading level. With a child who is reading an early chapter book, I already know that I need to keep my eyes open for certain clues. Is the reader:

- carrying the book between home and school and maintaining momentum through it?
- figuring out who is talking, especially if the text doesn't regularly spell this out by saying, for example, "said Bill."
- dealing with sections of the text that contain more exposition? These tend to be in large, chunky paragraphs, which are harder to read than the more airy sections of dialogue.
- keeping the characters straight, especially if there are many?
- following the plot, especially if time doesn't move along chronologically?
- determining who is the narrator of the story?
- pointing at the text or subvocalizing (in which case I may want to tell them it is time for them to graduate from using these strategies)?
- recalling the earlier chapters as he or she reads a later one. Can the reader accumulate the text?

Teaching: The Third Component of a Research-Decide-Teach Conference

As I said earlier, I often begin the teaching phase of a conference by telling the reader what I've noticed. "I notice that you are reading nonfiction and that's great, but the *way you are reading* seems pretty much the same whether it's fiction or nonfiction, and I want to suggest that you'd be wise to read a book like this somewhat differently than you read narratives." As I mentioned earlier, the teaching section of a conference includes all the components of a minilesson. I begin my conferences with "the connection," in which I tell the child what I want to talk about, why it seems important, and how it fits into the things we've been doing together. Next I teach. I give information. I offer a bit of advice. I demonstrate what I hope the child will do. I suggest a strategy other readers use. It is tempting to end the conference here, but if I'm the only one who is active during the teaching part of a conference (as in a minilesson), the chances are great that the reader's behavior will remain unaffected. Instead, I often try to get the reader to start using the new strategy right then and there, and I coach the reader toward this, as I did when Matt and Pedro began to retell *Little Soup's Birthday* while I watched. Finally, I need to record the conference so that the reader and I both realize that we now have an agreement. At the end of a conference, I say to the child, "So tell me what you are going to do," and then at least one of us writes down the plan. The plan can be noted in the child's reading log or in my record book. What matters is that this record informs the reader as he or she continues to work, and informs our next conference. I expect a reader to take the conference seriously and to do what we agree upon.

Some teachers find that if they want conferences to have a lasting effect on a reader, one conference should set the direction for future ones. It helps to expect that particular conferences will yield "personal goals" and that other conferences will address the reader's progress toward these goals. In Kim Tarpinian's fourth grade, for example, readers know they will have conferences that yield personal goals and these conferences will direct their reading lives for that month. Kim's students draw on plans generated in conferences to write up their monthly goals. These goals are sent home to parents, and they provide a direction for future conferences. The children know that before the month is over, they will be expected to provide evidence of serious work toward their goal. Last October, these were some of her students' goals:

- Try out different times during the day for reading so that *somehow* I carve out more reading time. Try before dinner, or on the trip to lessons.
- Make plans for my reading life. Become a collector of book recommendations and become more hooked into books.
- Try to read *all* of Gary Paulsen's novels and talk with Peter about what I notice in them.
- Give myself a retelling test often so I make sure I'm understanding the book. Use Post-its to mark the major new parts of the story.

- Reread last year's read-alouds and try to see things I didn't see before, and that way try to be a deeper reader.

In Donna Santman's sixth-grade class, the goals were a little different. In November, these were some of her students' goals or personal reading projects:

- I want to read to know more stuff (like learning about cell structure, because I think it's cool).
- I am trying to read so I *do* something. First I'll read a chess book so I can be ready for a tournament.
- My family traveled to Wyoming this summer so I am reading books about the West.
- I am trying to find the "big stuff" in books, not just what happens.
- I am trying to talk about my books and grow intellectually.
- I am trying to read the type of books I have always rejected and that's why I am reading fantasy and poetry.
- I am trying to only read books I adore and then to write like the authors I love.

Putting the Components Together:
A Research-Decide-Teach-Conference

Erica Leif stops alongside ten-year-old Pedra, who is reading *US Daily News*. Erica watches for a moment and then asks, "Why'd you decide to open the paper to this part?"

"Well," Pedra responded, "sometimes I see the Rosie O'Donnell show, so I am interested in this." Pedra gestured toward the page in front of her and especially toward the photograph of Rosie O'Donnell.

"Were you just flipping through the paper and you spotted her?"

"Yeah."

"Is there a huge article on her or what?" Erica asked, glancing at the page, which appeared to contain lots of tidbits of gossip and news on celebrities.

"No, it's not a whole part, it's just a few lines."

For a few seconds, Erica scanned the page. "I'm the same as you," she said. "When I'm flipping through the newspaper and a photograph of someone catches my eye, I read the caption and then sometimes the whole section. But I'm wondering, do you have *any* plans when you get to the newspaper, any sections you always read?" Pedra shook her head, "No." She added, "I didn't used to look at the paper, but now I do. I just look and see …"

The two readers continued to look at the page together, and I suspect Erica was mulling over whether she knew enough to steer Pedra's reading life. Obviously Erica decided she did, because she shifted now into a teaching mode. She gestured toward the heading at the top of the page, and the two of them together sounded out the unusual names of the authors. "It looks like this might be an ongoing spread by these two authors," Erica said. "Do you think if you open the paper tomorrow, you'll find a section by these guys?" Pedra was uncertain.

"I asked," Erica said, "because now that you are reading the newspaper, you might want to do what newspaper readers often do. Many of us have columns we look for, that we know will be coming, and we turn right to them. If these guys *did* write again tomorrow, do you have any idea what kind of thing they'd write about? I mean, if you scan through the paper, what sorts of things would you expect these two particular reporters to focus on usually?"

"Like, the personal life?" Pedra asked.

"I think so," Erica said. "And famous people—it's *their* personal lives, right?" Then Erica said, "I like it when there are structures in a paper I can count on. It'd be cool tomorrow to test out whether this section is continued. Or wait! You could do it now! To test our theory, you could get *yesterday's* paper—we have it—and see if this section was there, and if so, how it was the same or different."

Pedra raced toward the newspaper bin. "If it's everyday, I'll read it every-day. Like my dad reads the sports section," she said.

"When you come back," Erica inserted, "Write down your plan—to find a column or two you can follow every day." Alone for a moment, Erica recorded her own notes on the conference.

Coaching Readers

When we coach readers, we act rather like a running coach acts, running alongside the athlete, interjecting brief bits of advice: "Today, remember to breathe from your stomach." As we jog side by side, the coach watches us. We strain up the hill and our breathing becomes shallow. "Stomach," our coach says. We are tired and our breathing becomes faster. "Breathe deep."

Similarly, when we coach a reader, we read along with the reader, watch-ing that reader move across the terrain of the text. Our first interjection may need to be a bit longer than the ones that follow. Instead of "Breathe from your stomach," we might say, "You're skipping past the tricky words. Stay with them a bit, work on them." Then as the reader reads along, we watch. "Oops," we say when the reader garbles or skips past a difficult word. Next time we may just point at the word or say "Stay with it." Next time we may watch the reader catch herself and go back to make a second try. "Nice," we say.

A coaching conference can begin with the same kind of observation I described earlier in this chapter. But my assessment may *not* have been part of this day's conference. Perhaps I recently did running records on the reader, and I have an instructional plan in mind for my work with her. If last week I learned she needs work on envisioning while she reads, or on maintaining flu-ency and phrasing, or on cross-checking the print with the meaning in a text, chances are these will still be issues for her today and they'll be issues in almost any text she reads. So the research part of a conference can be a brief oppor-tunity to learn how the student is progressing in an area of concern.

Then again, sometimes the difficulty I'll want to address comes not from an assessment of the reader but from an assessment of the text. If a child is read-ing historic fiction set in Colonial America, I might direct the child to pause often, to envision, for example, the scene and setting of the Jamestown settle-ment. Instead of simply assigning this, however, I may want to be sure my words have real traction. So I say, "Get started now, and I'll read the text, too, along-side you [we're each reading silently]. Let's you and I pause often to tell each other what we're seeing." I'll watch the child's eyes and keep pace with his progress through the text. Where the story refers to Sarah, the character, taking her first two-day-long trip to the store, I say, "So I'm picturing Sarah probably going on horseback, or in a carriage, and I can see her getting up really early and they ride for hours through the woods on a wide trail maybe, because I don't think there are paved roads." We continue to read, and at another key spot, I pause again and say, "What are *you* picturing?" Later we read on and I simply say, "Let's stop and envision." I may not expect the child to continue articulating what he envisions, but I give time for him to make a mental movie. Later, I again say, "Are you picturing it?" and we pause, think, and read on.

In coaching, we intervene as lightly as we can while readers continue to move through the text. We can say a bit more with proficient and experienced readers than we can with beginning readers, but always the goal is to intervene just enough to scaffold the reading work we hope will happen. The goal of coaching is partly to help readers develop unconscious habits. If we always teach readers by asking them to stop and have long, reflective conversations about reading, we defeat our purpose, because talking about over deliberate reading strategies is not reading.

If a five-year-old is in the midst of a repetitive book trying to read a page that says, "The elephant drinks water," and he pauses before the word *elephant,* I don't want to call his reading to a halt and have a big conversation about the strategies he might use when he comes to a tricky part. If I do that, the child's hold on the pattern in this book will surely fall apart. I'm far more apt to simply tap the drawing of the elephant, calling the child's attention to the strategy he needs—looking at the pictures—in order to proceed. In this way, I encourage him to keep going. "I don't think young children need to be able to *talk about* sources of information," Marie Clay said to us. "They simply need to *use them.*"

When I *coach* a reader, I'm trying to have that reader walk-the-walk. I don't worry whether the reader can talk-the-talk. Although I use coaching especially when working with beginning readers who still need to develop a felt-sense of moving through a text, if I want to get at the mind-work of more experienced reading, I'm also apt to coach proficient readers. That is, whereas a research-decide-teach conference works very well if we're thinking about the reader's life habits, if my goal is for a reader to envision what's happening as she reads, or to pay attention to what the author seems to highlight especially, or to keep track of who is doing the talking in a dialogue, or to notice when an author "turns a corner," simply *assigning* this sort of mind work makes the conference too nebulous to have a concrete and substantial effect. It is reasonable to tell—to assign—a reader to talk over the amount of reading she is doing and/or to deliberately decide to make more time for reading. It is possible for a reader to simply resolve to mark with Post-its places to talk about with a partner, or to keep a list of book recommendations, or to begin reading more diverse texts, or to read green dot books, or to stop more often to retell a book.

If ten-year-old Brian is reading a book that's a bit hard for him and I want to be sure he is thinking as he reads, I whisper "Where are you?" when I pull alongside him. Brian points to the section of the page he is reading. Now I read beside him, keeping my eyes aligned with his. The character does something, and I point at the line and mutter, "Weird." A paragraph later, the plot takes a new turn, "What the heck?" I say. Now we are again reading silently. Brian turns the page, and we continue. Halfway down the page, the plot thickens and Brian remarks on it. "Huh?" he whispers, touching the part of the text he's just read. This continues for a few more minutes. Before I leave, I say, "I love the way you are talking back to the text in your mind. Would it help to jot Post-it notes talking back to the text?" and soon he has jotted this goal into his reading log.

I join six-year-old Marigold as she reads. She holds the book above her desk unsteadily and reads in a slow, staccato fashion. "Can you put it here," I say, as I place the book on the desk in front of her. "For now, try having your book steady on the desk." Then I look at her face, signaling her to carry on with her reading. She reads a few lines, still in a slow, staccato fashion, and I interject, "Can you put your words together, say them quickly?" I fluently restate what she has just read hoping to demonstrate what I mean by putting words together quickly. I know this will be my longest intervention. Now as Marigold continues to read, every few lines I interject "Say it quickly," or I simply repeat the line she's just read with fluency, nudging her to reread it that way. I don't think giving her a speech about fluency will help. I think she needs to feel it. Before I get up to leave, I say, "Will you reread the book a few times and practice reading it as if you are talking? Do that with most of what you read for a bit, okay?"

When I coach young readers in this way, I aim not only to intervene efficiently and lightly so that they continue processing extended text, but also to coach toward one major goal over and over so that they aren't being pulled in five directions at once. If I'm working toward fluency, I may just give the child a difficult word. This gets complicated when we are coaching emergent or beginning readers who often need help above all in integrating information from several sources—from meaning, syntax, and print because in those instances we can't coach toward only one goal because several are important at once.

I do not find coaching easy. The child sits beside me, reading or gesturing toward reading, and everything happens at a terrifying rate. My instinct is to intervene in a million different ways toward one goal: so that the text the child produces is correct. My instinct is to help a child break long words into chunks, to adjust the child's punctuation by intervening to reread portions "with expression," to nudge readers to "try that word again" to correct any mispronunciations. All of this might be defensible if I were always going to be beside the child as he or she reads. But in the end, children need to read as best they can, without our presence to hold them up. Conferring is about helping learners become independent. I can help learners become more independent if I steer them to work on manageable endeavors that are within their reach and if, bit by bit, I coach and nudge them, I model and demonstrate ways to develop the thinking muscles and habits they'll need to read well.

It helps to have some quick prompts in mind to give a reader a structure or scaffold. I've learned many of these prompts by watching Reading Recovery teachers as they work with children, and some by watching Gay Su Pinnell as she works with children.

If the reader needs help with one-to-one matching:
- Use your finger.

- Point under the word.

- Did it match? Did you have any words left over? Was it just enough words? Try it again.

- Try it again. Read it with your finger and be sure it matches.

If the reader is inactive and passive:
- (wait, and wait some more)

- Hmmm. What could you do? (The child responds.) Okay, try that now.

- You might try rereading. Try that now.

If the reader needs help in dealing with difficult words:
- Why did you pause?

- Back up, try it again, and get your mouth ready.

- What would make sense there?

- Would (I supply the word.) make sense? Does it sound right? Check it.

- Do you know any part of that word? Okay, let's back up and try it again.

- Does that sound (look) right? What *could* that be? Does that make sense?

- Can you go back, turn your brain on higher, and try it again?

- Let's think about the story. (We talk about it.) Okay, now let's back up, read it again, and get our mouths ready.

- What can you do to figure this out?

If the reader isn't self-correcting:
- Check it. Does that sound right? (fit there? make sense?)
- Does that make sense? Try it again.
- Does that look right?
- Was there a tricky part?
- Can you go back and try this again? You almost got it, but not quite.
- I notice you seem unsure. What are you noticing? That's smart.
- What? Does that make sense? (sound right?) Could that be right?

If the reader isn't reading with fluency:
- Can you put your words together, say it quickly?
- Say it as if you're talking.
- Look at me. Say it to me as if we're talking. (The reader does.) Try to read like that.
- Try it like this (I say it quickly and with fluency).
- Can you read it again and help me really feel what is happening in the story?

If the reader isn't thinking about the text:
- Sometimes the picture can help us think about the story.
- So let's review. What's happening now?
- What are you thinking?
- Geez, he's mean (funny, etc.,) isn't he?
- Oh no! What do you suppose will happen next?
- Whaaat? Does that make sense?
- Huh? Let's go back …
- Check the picture. Does it make sense?

Proficient Partner Conferences

I love to play tennis with people who are better than I am because the strength and directness of their shots sets me up to play better than I would otherwise. Similarly, when a child reads with us as his mentor partner, we can raise the level of what that child would do alone. The power of the proficient partner conference comes from our enacting, in a partnership with the child, the kind of work she could be doing. In the back and forth of our work with this child, we shift between demonstrating the kind of reading we hope this child is stretching toward, allowing her to join us at this level, then again showing her the sort of reading work we hope she is stretching toward, and then again allowing her to participate. Because the example we set needs to be, in Vygotsky's phrase, within the child's "zone of proximal development," this conference, like others, relies upon our first observing the child as a reader. Drawing on this knowledge, we position our participation in the partnership so that we're one step ahead of her.

If Jose isn't reading with intonation, we can say, "Why don't I read a page, then you read a page," or "How about if I read Frog's lines and you read Toad's lines?" The child will most often rise to the occasion, taking his cues on how to read from the parts we have just read to him. If a child doesn't seem to be empathizing with any characters except the protagonist, we can be a partner who keeps showing feelings about the secondary characters. "I can really understand that little brother! He must feel so jealous! He's acting annoying, but I know just how it feels when the older brother gets all the attention, don't you?" and later, "His mother must really wonder what he's doing all the time when he never tells her anything. I would be so puzzled and worried, wouldn't you?" Oftentimes, the child will eventually join in, offering speculation on the emotions of the book's other characters. If children seem to talk only briefly and perfunctorily in their partnership, I might draw on a class list of "Ways to Talk More" to say, "Can you tell me more about that?" or "Could you show me an example of that?"

Sometimes, the role of a proficient reading partner can be filled by another student. Although we generally put matched partners together, sometimes we will decide that a particular child needs more time reading with a proficient partner than we alone can provide. We might, for a time, link two children together, the one acting as a particularly proficient partner for the other. Eli tends to read very quickly, taking in all the print but not spending sufficient time spinning out the meaning and the implications in the stories he reads. Jabbar, on the other hand, pauses constantly, thinking over everything and wondering what it all could mean, sometimes to the extent that he loses the thread of the story and then loses interest in the book. Together they can read and talk over their shared book for several weeks, Eli pushing Jabbar to read more quickly and to take in more text at a time, Jabbar encouraging Eli to spend longer puzzling through the implications and revelations in the story.

Coaching and conferring take courage. It's not easy to pull up alongside a perfectly happy, thoroughly engaged reader and interrupt, "Could you tell me how your reading has been going?" This is especially true if we are new at conferring and aren't at all sure what to research or decide, say or teach. The student turns trusting eyes to us, and we feel exposed in their gaze. "Am I doing more harm than good? At least she was reading before!" we think to ourselves. But we musn't be too timid to try. Our wisdom, our experience, and our teaching are too valuable to run untapped within us. Just as each book, well read, makes children better readers, each conference, well taught, makes us better teachers. Our children deserve our bravest selves.

Teaching Readers Within a Leveled Classroom Library 7

When we talk about independent reading and the importance of children choosing books, we necessarily bump up against the question: Choosing from what? For years I was against any notion of leveling or arranging by reading level our classroom libraries. I didn't want them turned into the SRA reading kits of my childhood, with green readers plugging away at the bottom rung of the reading rat race while purple readers strutted above them. I abhor the idea of structuring libraries to support one-upsmanship and competition.

I had other reasons for being against leveled libraries. I argued that the difficulty level of a text isn't a fixed, static thing; instead, the difficulty of a text varies in relation to the reader's background knowledge, interest, and familiarity with the genre and subject. Then, too, I felt certain that because life is not leveled, it is important for readers to learn to find appropriate texts for themselves, and to monitor as they read, asking themselves. "Is this book right for me?"

Several years ago, Jerome Harste visited us. Talking about the importance of professional inquiry, Jerry said "You must always assume that one of the pillars of your thinking is dead wrong." At the time, I wrote down Jerry's advice and tacked it on my bulletin board. Little did I dream that within a year I'd feel convinced that my opposition to a leveled library was "the pillar of my own thinking" that was dead wrong. I am now convinced that most teachers are well advised to level about a third of the books in their classroom libraries.

The turning point for me came one May day when I visited the classrooms of six teachers from our Leadership Project. These teachers were each apprenticing to be a mentor teacher for us in the teaching of reading, and they each knew how essential it is that readers read the books they can read with comprehension and relative ease. In one classroom after another, I marveled at the wonderful tone and values and at the overlay of literate conversations. But when I pulled in close to listen to children as they actually read their independent reading books aloud to me, an alarming number of children stuttered their way through sentences that seemed almost impenetrable. Often I watched as readers let all sense of the story break down. In classroom after classroom, I said to the teacher, "What's up with that child's book choice? The book seems too hard." And in classroom after classroom, these smart, dedicated, knowledgeable teachers said to me, "I've talked to that child fifty times this year about choosing appropriate books." As I walked away from the day, I couldn't help but think, "Who are the slow learners here, the children or us?"

Imagine all the work those teachers *could not* do with youngsters because their every interaction during reading time dealt with the issue of book choice! Imagine all the growing and all the thinking those readers could *not do* because their days were spent reading at frustration level.

With great trepidation then, my colleagues and I began several years ago to slowly make our way into the terrain of leveled books. Our goal has been to reap the advantages and avoid the risks. We know there is a thin line between leveling books and leveling children, and we've been resolute in our determination to avoid the latter. We've tried especially to avoid the well-documented risks of classifying readers into long-term ability-based reading groups. Ability-based reading groups are equally problematic whether children are explicitly named "great readers" and "bad readers" or "green dot readers" and "purple dot readers" (Pierce, 1993, p. 99). We have also tried to steer clear of an inappropriate emphasis on accuracy. If children are matched with books on the basis of accuracy counts only, we know this might put too much emphasis on reading as calling out words and not enough emphasis on reading as understanding. We want to match readers with books while still allowing children to make the miscues good readers make when they read for comprehension.

Now, after several years of developing and refining our work, we are quite enthusiastic about the ways in which leveled lending libraries have enabled our students to grow as readers. This does not mean I now believe that all uses of leveled libraries are helpful. I do not. But I have come to believe that, like so many other structures, leveled libraries can be used in ways that enable or in ways that limit.

The Big Picture: How Book Levels
Work in Our Classrooms

In most of our classrooms, we put dots representing the book's level on about a third of our books. We hold off putting dots on some to encourage children to make their own decisions about whether these books seem just right for them. If we've put a dot on two *Junie B. Jones* books, we may deliberately leave another two books in that series unleveled, in this way scaffolding the children's act of judging against the template of the books they know. There is no substantial difference between the books we level and those we don't, but we're less apt to level the books that readers of all levels study, such as the Eyewitness Series of nonfiction books.

Once we've assigned books to levels—and I'll talk more about how we do this later in this chapter—we select a few representative books from each level to be our assessment books for that level. We keep these books out of classroom circulation, using them as tools for a very informal sort of assessment. If I have six leveled bins in my classroom, each representing progressively more challenging texts, I'll have at least two sets of six assessment books that are matched to these six levels. I use my observations of children reading these assessment books or more informal observations of children's successes or difficulties with their independent reading books to steer them toward "just right" books.

I can imagine some teachers' protests. Yes, it is true that readers profit from reading a range of books and sometimes need the opportunity to struggle and persevere. And yes, the level of difficulty a book poses will vary depending on the reader's background with this kind of book. And yes again, the truth is that *I* can't always recall the details of the novel I'm reading; does this mean my books are beyond my reach and should be kept from me? I understand these and other arguments against book leveling, but my experience in classrooms has convinced me that a judicious and flexible system for pointing children toward a fairly broad range of texts can help them develop an internalized, felt sense of what reading should feel like. I think too many children have become so accustomed to reading at frustration level, they don't even know what they are missing. This is a big enough concern for me that I'm willing to swallow my own doubts about leveled libraries and systems for matching kids to book levels, and proceed cautiously forward.

Earlier, I mentioned that we observe children reading either our assessment books or their own book choices in order to determine a level that seems right for them. How can one tell? First and most important, we notice if children are reading with engagement and responsiveness. If a child laughs at the funny parts or brings the book to recess in order to continue reading, we have a pretty good indication that this is a just-right book. But I also recommend asking a child to read aloud and listening to the child's phrasing and fluency. Does this *sound* like language? Can I tell from intonation or side comments or our book talk that this reader is making sense? It is also worthwhile to notice the child's miscues and to roughly calculate whether the child is reading with at least 90 percent accuracy. There is nothing magic about these figures. There *are* times when a child's accuracy is below 90 percent and the reading experience nevertheless seems to be valuable. Substitutions of *a* for *the* and *in* for *at* will probably not affect meaning, and some children have a higher tolerance for word-level errors than others. Nevertheless, error rate is not a bad indication of difficulty if we use it cautiously. Marie Clay (1997) suggests that an error rate of one in twenty words suggests an easy text and an error rate between one in twenty and one in ten suggests an instructional level or a learning text. An error rate of greater than one in ten suggests a hard text. (p. 21). In general, we are wise to recall Marie Clay's caution that when children read below 90 percent accuracy, the supportive context of meaning tends to fall away.

When I find a child reading a book that seems "just right," I'm apt to say, "This book really fits you, doesn't it?" And I'll tell this reader, "There's a whole basket of books at just about this level of difficulty at the end of the bookshelf. Look for the green dots and you'll know which books have a good chance of being about right for you." If we begin the year emphasizing reading just-right or even easy books, most children eventually become accustomed to reading fluently and with understanding, and soon they are making wise book choices, unconstrained by assigned levels. We still keep an eye on this and are ready to hold a reader to a particular course when this feels necessary, but it is also exciting for a reader who has a palpable sense of what reading should feel like to venture toward more difficult texts. Marie Clay says it this way: "... at the heart of the learning process there must be the opportunity for the child to use a gradient of difficulty in texts by which he can pull himself up by his bootstraps: texts which allow him to practice and develop the full range of strategies which he does control, and by problem-solving new challenges, reach out beyond that present control (1991, p. 215).

At the start of the year, when we're especially determined to firmly and decisively move readers toward just-right books, we tend to highlight the leveled bins in the classroom library. The countertop of our library, for example, may feature these bins, each coded with a colored dot. We'll still organize books by topic and author: within a "Basketball Bin," for example, half the books may have a variety of leveled dots and the others are left for readers to assess for themselves.

At the start of the year, we talk up the value of picking books to read in which we feel strong as readers. We steer kindergarten, first and second graders' book choices more firmly and spend less time talking with them about how to choose just-right books, because we're wary of too much metacognitive talk at these levels. But with all our readers, we talk up the importance of reading books that make sense. We role-play how reading feels when it's too hard, hoping to show children that it's not a good thing to be stymied by every fifth word. The language we use in this work is very important.

WE TRY NOT TO SAY:	WE TEND TO SAY:
Don't read this book because it is too hard for you.	Find books that make you feel strong as a reader.
You can't read that. It's too hard.	Put that book aside for now. You'll probably be able to read it by January. For now, your reading muscles will grow best if you read green dot books.
Is this book beyond your level? Then put it down. You need to stay within your level.	Is this book sort of a confusing one? Then put it aside for now. You want to read books that make lots of sense.
You are a green-level reader (or you are in the green group). You can't read blue dot books.	For now, why don't you read books with a green dot on them. I think they'll make you feel strong as a reader (or they'll be a smooth read for you).
You and Bob are both in the Level Two reading group so you'd be good partners.	You and Bob like to read the same kinds of books so you'll be good partners.

Let me be clear about this. We are not forming leveled groups. We do not speak of children as the green readers, and it would be rare for us to convene all green dot readers. We certainly don't envision that children reading green dot books will all move in unison on a specific day to the next level. We have no requirements for what every child who is reading a green dot book must do. We would *never*, for example, say, "You must read twenty green dot books

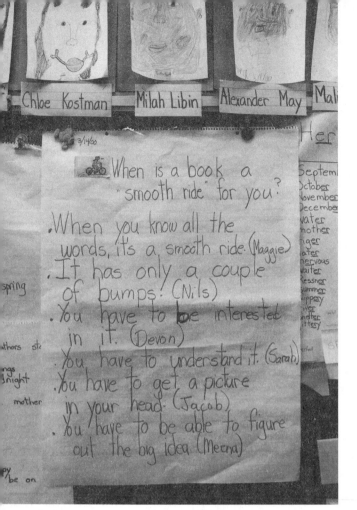

before you can move to blue dot books," nor would we say or imply that readers must pass a test before they can move to more difficult books.

Children will want to follow their friends or their interests to books in higher levels, and I'm hesitant to make any blanket statement about whether or not this is okay. It certainly is *not* okay if that worry about social acceptance regularly leads a child to attempt books she cannot read with comprehension and relative ease. The answer to this lies in changing the social climate and the mores in our classrooms. It helps to find and talk up "quick reads," to bring in a new series of especially accessible books and expect that even our strongest and most experienced readers will want to choose them. It also helps to read aloud the books we're trying to promote and to do promotional book talks that do not emphasize the fact that these books are easier. In these ways we may succeed in luring children toward easier books. If I can't entice children toward these books, I am willing to tell a reader straight out that for now he needs to read a particular level of book in order to become stronger as a reader. We don't help matters any by allowing children to pretend to read books they can't read. In fact, after we help a child abandon a difficult text in favor of a more appropriate one, we've been known to unabashedly tell the class about the smart, brave work this reader has done.

Designing and Adapting a Leveling System

The current conversation about book levels grows out of a long and divided history. Americans have long tried to quantify factors that make for difficulty in texts. Historically, these attempts to assign levels of difficulty to texts have been grouped together under the term "readability." Basals have been written to match predetermined readability formulas, which took into account a limited number of factors such as word difficulty, word frequency, word length, and sentence length. The Dick and Jane books of my childhood and many controlled vocabulary books since then were written to fit the characteristics of early readability levels, and the texts are as odd as they are—"Come Dick! Come Jane! Come, come, come!"—because the

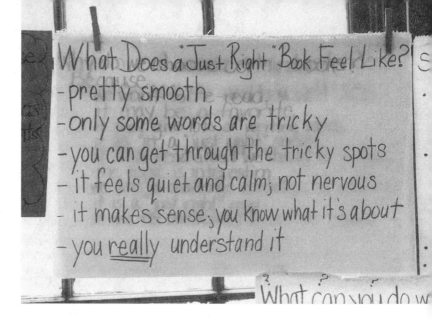

goal was to conform to a formula, using short choppy sentences and regular one-syllable words rather than language that made sense, was interesting, and sounded like the language children speak fluently. (Cullinan and Fitzgerald, 1984). Many researchers have found that students read and comprehend literature storybooks with greater success than they have with books which have the controlled vocabularies which fit these old understandings of factors contributing to text difficulty, (Rhodes, 1979; Bussis et. al. 1985).

When Marie Clay and Barbara Watson came to Ohio State in 1984, they brought an absolutely different understanding of factors which create text difficulty and of levels with them from New Zealand. At that time, the Ready to Read series of books was foundational to all New Zealand classrooms. Teachers across New Zealand knew Ready to Read books so well that they had an intuitive, tacit understanding of what challenges particular Ready to Read texts were likely to present to readers and of the indicators they could watch for to suggest readers were ready for new challenges. They tended to describe other books in reference to these touchstone texts, and so Marie Clay and Reading Recovery teachers began to think about American books in similar ways.

It was Barbara Peterson (1988) who first examined how real readers in authentic classroom contexts actually experienced these levels of text complexity. This research was groundbreaking in its attention not only to texts but also to readers and the learning they do at various text levels. Since then, Gay Su Pinnell and Irene Fountas (1996, 1999) have created broader categories of book levels for use in guided reading groups, and these categories are now being combined and brought into many classroom lending libraries.

When Peterson first did her research, there were very few of what we now call "little books." These have since mushroomed. They have often been written-to-order with predetermined, but new, descriptors in mind. Authors of "little books" tend to keep in mind that beginning readers can use high frequency words to anchor their progress through a line of print. When we know that readers "draw on a variety of resources to support their reading and understanding of the author's message, we can supply those resources. Barbara Peterson (1988) found that factors such as the match between the illustrations and text, and the predictability of language patterns and story episodes influenced the quality of reading in ways not accounted for by readability formulas which stress the number of letters and syllables in words and words in a sentence. When Reading Recovery teachers began their work toward the levels we have today, people were quite relaxed about them. If many Reading Recovery teachers felt a book needed to be moved up or down, it was moved. Levels were regarded as approximations, and decisions about a books' level of difficulty belonged in the hands of teachers.

Finding Our Own Way

For me to feel comfortable in this realm of leveled books, I needed a guide. My husband travels the world looking for whitewater rivers to paddle. When John journeys to particularly remote places, he goes with a tour guide who can warn him of the waterfalls and hydraulic holes. Lynn Holcomb was one of the early Reading Recovery teachers in our region, and she's since helped Scholastic and the Wright Group level their books. Now a staff member at the Teachers College Reading and Writing Project, Lynn has functioned as my guide. Above all, she has demystified published book levels and the gradients of difficulty for us, and helped us feel at home in this human and fallible system.

I have a better sense now of just how fallible many published leveling systems are, because a dozen of Project teachers I work with do freelance work as levelers for publishers. These teachers don't have access to some special scientific formula. They are simply good teachers who devote a Saturday to being trained and then are regularly given several hundred books to categorize by levels. Determining a book's level is approximate, messy work and it is tricky because every reader in the world is different and will find particular texts easy and particular ones difficult for reasons that are hers and hers alone. Kids born and bred in the city may have trouble with the simple word "silo." Kids who live on a farm may be confused by passages about subways. The reasons reader experience difficulty are far more numerous, complicated and human than any over-arching system can accommodate.

My point isn't to devalue book levels, because in fact I've found them to be extraordinarily helpful. But it is crucial that we, as teachers, do not accept book levels as if they are endorsed by a Higher Authority. Levels are only approximations of gradients of difficulty. It's crucial to understand that if a book seems misplaced in one level, we can move it to another level. In Project schools, children as well as teachers regularly question the placement of a particular book in one leveled bin or another. The important thing is that we trust ourselves and our children more than we trust published levels, and also that the challenge to level books lures us to read *more* (not less) children's literature and to talk *more* (not less) about books with our colleagues and our children. If we find that book levels distance us from books and silence our voices, then the levels are doing more harm than good.

How valuable it has been to have shoulders to stand upon in our efforts to level our K–2 classroom libraries. Like everyone else, my colleagues and I have made efforts to coordinate published lists of book levels. Many publications and publishers have charts that roughly correlate Reading Recovery levels, guided-reading levels, and levels from an assessment known as *The Developmental Reading Assessment* (DRA). Although the Reading Recovery system assigns numbers to levels and other systems assign letters, it isn't at all hard to decide how levels from one list mesh with levels from another list. What *is* hard, impossible even, is to correlate levels that have been established by readability formulas or the Lexile formula (which tend to be based on formulaic counts of syllables per word and words per sentence) with the levels one finds in *Guided Reading* or Reading Recovery, which are based on studying the sources of information books provide for readers.

Sometimes teachers assume that because a published list divides books into a certain number of categories, this must be the number of categories which we bring to our classroom. This is far from the truth! The Reading Recovery scale, for example, was designed to scaffold readers who are failing to thrive, and for this reason, Reading Recovery levels provide a series of very small steps. Dividing books into so many bins, each representing a very small step forward, doesn't pose a risk for Reading Recovery children. They won't end up lingering too long at any one of these levels because they are guided by a vigilant teacher who is always ready to advance the child to the next level. Because the leveled libraries that I'm describing support independent reading, however, the teacher will not always be at a child's elbow to move that child along from one level to the next. If the levels are too discrete, there is a risk that children will languish at one level for too long while they wait for us to move them along to new challenges. Another risk is that children may not have the diverse range of books they need and want as readers. Even the Guided Reading levels, which are less discrete than the Reading Recovery levels, were designed with a particular function in mind. These books are meant to be introduced in guided-reading sessions, and again, a vigilant teacher makes book choices for children, and does so by giving special attention to the importance of moving children along toward books that will stretch them.

In designing levels for a classroom lending library rather than for Reading Recovery or guided reading, we need to realize that children will be making choices without us necessarily being at their side, and we need to give them room to read books that are a bit easier one day and a bit harder another day. It is helpful, therefore, to have less discrete divisions in a classroom lending library, with approximately two guided reading levels within one bin. We often use a plus-sign to convey to children which books in any one bin will be especially challenging so they can choose or shy away from these books.

Among Project classrooms, we use a system of levels that we speak of as Groups, and each of the emergent and beginning reader Groups contains several Guided Reading levels and even more of the very discrete Reading Recovery levels.* Staff members of the Teachers College Reading and Writing Project have worked in a think tank led by Lynn Holcomb to create these Groups and they can be found in the appendix. Within each of the these Groups, we have listed several assessment books we keep out of our classroom libraries, and we have also named benchmark books. The latter are well-known books we use as a shorthand way to refer to the level. For example, many Reading Recovery teachers in America regard *Pat's New Puppy* as a benchmark for their Level 7 (our Group 3) books. Because of the challenges in this text, the book has come to be trusted as litmus paper, signifying which children are and are not ready for the challenges of other similar books. If a child can read *Pat's New Puppy* with ease, this has become a signal that they'll fare well with a whole set of other Reading Recovery Level 7 books. We've chosen benchmarks for each of our Groups.

Many thousands of books have not been leveled by a publisher yet. This is just as well, because it means that teachers in a school need to make their own decisions. In Colonial America, people used to gather together for barn-raisings and quilting bees. In Project schools, we gather for Leveling Parties.

---

* I discuss leveling books for more proficient readers later.

Somehow the endeavor becomes vastly more manageable when it is a shared one. We rope in everyone and anyone—high school students, parents, para-professionals, principals—and set to work categorizing books.

When working with books for emergent and early readers, there are so many resources the that work is almost clerical at first. We grab a book, and then use references—the Reading Recovery leveling list, publishers' levels, the levels from *Guided Reading* and *Matching Books to Readers*—to slot the book into its bin. After a bit, we pause to review these bins and decide which to combine to create a classroom lending library. By this time, we tend to have six or so books in a bin, and we find that this gives us a sense of the books at that particular level so we can begin to make decisions on books that have not been previously leveled. We rarely feel absolutely certain, but our rule of thumb is that when we're not certain, we put a book in the higher level (which means it's more likely to be too easy than too hard).

Usually we soon notice that our library has large gaps. I recently worked with some first-grade teachers in a nearby suburb who found, through the process of leveling their books, that they had almost no books easier than Level 20 (which is generally thought of as early second grade) in any of their first-grade classrooms! No wonder their children were having a hard time sustaining an independent reading workshop. The Director of Reading in a large urban district in the Midwest recently told me that when she arrived in the district, she inherited a basal in which the preprimer contained only two stories which were easier than Level 15. When the first rungs in the ladder of difficulty have been sawed off, no wonder some children find it difficult to progress.

Once we've tentatively leveled books, the work really begins. We now take books to our children and begin adjusting the categories so they "ring true" for our readers, and using the categories to inform our teaching.

Thinking About the Features of a Particular Book Level (Group One): An Example of How Levels Can Affect Teaching

As we work with children and leveled books, we think about the features of particular books, cull out descriptions of levels, and anticipate the reading work children will tend to do at these levels. I cannot put the descriptions of all our Groups into this book, but let's look at Group One books and readers as a case in point. We describe our Group One books (which generally corresponds to Reading Recovery Levels 1 and 2 and *Guided Reading* levels A and B) like this:

- *The font is large and clear,* even in the captions. A Group One book will tend to have black letters against a white background.

- *There is exaggerated spacing between words and letters.* In some books, we find that publishers have enlarged the print size but have not adjusted the spacing accordingly. The exaggerated size of the font, if spaces are not equally exaggerated, can create difficulties for readers who are still learning to distinguish between one word and the next. Group One readers rely on the spaces between words to signify the end of one word and the beginning of another. These readers need to read the spaces as well as the words. While working with Group One books, a reader travels the journey from regarding words as black blobs on white paper to noticing some features of words.

- *There is usually a single word, phrase, or simple sentence on a page, and the text is patterned and predictable.* In the book *I Can Read,* once a child knows the title (which is ideally read to a Group One reader) it is not hard for the child to read "I can read the newspaper," "I can read the cereal box." A Group One reader, for example, is regarded as a preconventional reader because this child relies on the illustrations (which support the meaning) and the sounds of language (or syntax) and not on graphophonics (word/letter) cues to read a sentence such as, "I can read the newspaper." The reason that the number of letters or syllables in the word *newspaper* is not the primary means of determining the gradient of difficulty of *I Can Read* is that Group One readers won't yet have the skills to work with print in a word such as *newspaper,* they will instead use picture cues and the meaning of the sentence to form their hypothesis.

Often we find books that seem to belong to Group One but do not use common language structures. This is especially apt to happen with these books, because they've usually been written on demand to match a formula. Sometimes authors were so intent on using high frequency words as a pattern that they sacrificed the normal sounds of language. We recently found a text, for example, in which the repeating sentence was, "Come, come here. Come, come here." Children enter school with a strong sense of how language tends to go, and Group One readers rely on that strength. The sentences children hear don't tend to go, "Come,

come here." Because of this unusual language structure, we moved that book out of Group One in our libraries.

- *Two or three anchor words (sight words) are usually used on each page,* and often these come first, providing readers a way into the text. A Group One book *may* be a labeling book containing one illustrated word on a page (such as Mom, Dad, sister, cat) but it tends to be easier for a child to read "I see my Mom. I see my Dad. I see my sister. I see my cat …" because the repetitive sight words give the reader an easy way into each new page.

- *The words are highly supported by illustrations.* No one would expect a Group One reader to word-solve the word *newspaper.* We would, however, expect a child at this level to look at the picture and at the text and to "read" "I can read the newspaper." When we are assigning levels to books, sometimes we *think* the illustrations provide strong support because once *we've* read the print, it seems to us that the picture matches the print. But it's not always the case that the picture alone is enough to help a child read the print. For example, in *The Fox on the Box* (which actually is an end-of-Group-Two book) one page says, "The fox played on the box." The accompanying picture shows a fox standing on top of the box. *If* a child *could read the print* then it would be easy for that child to look at the picture and confirm that yes, indeed, the picture shows the fox playing on top of the box. But if that child couldn't read the word *played* in the first place, what in the picture could possibly tell such a reader that the unfamiliar word was *played?*

Once we've described and studied books in a certain level, it's helpful to begin to think about the kind of reading work readers at that level will probably be doing. A child who is working with Group One books, for example, is likely to need us to help her locate known words (*I, the*) and to use these words as anchors, pinning down her one-to-one matches between what she says and the blob of letters representing a word. "I," the child will say (if this is a known word to her), pointing to the first word on the page that says, "I can read the newspaper." Now the child moves on to read the next word, *can.* Again, if this is a known word, the child will read, "I can …," and although she has never seen the word *read,* she's heard the title of the book, and her progress along the line of known words has anchored her reading so that she can match the letters *read* with the oral reproduction of "read." Luckily, the next word is a familiar one, *the,* and she knows her matching efforts are on track. She uses the picture to guess at the final word, *newspaper.* She will be pointing to the correct string of letters (*newspaper*) because the known words at the start of the sentence got her off to a strong start matching spoken and written words. Because the reader of Group One books does not yet have consistent control of one-to-one matching, this child will sometimes continue orally "reading" words even though her pointing finger has reached the end of the line. Typically, her finger will hover at the end of the line of print as she continues to say words from the sentence. "Did you run out of words?" we'll say to this Group One reader. "Go back and try again." Perhaps this time the child will point correctly. "Did it match?," we'll ask. "Did it come out just right? Try it again!" We ask questions such as these when the child's pointing is right and not simply when it is wrong.

Group One readers will tend to be ready to move to Group Two books once they can read one-syllable words with one-to-one correspondence. I am convinced that a Group One reader need not necessarily read Group One books *with total accuracy* before moving on to Group Two books. The child can move to these less supportive books when the requisite concepts are under control. Recently, Lynn Holcomb and I listened as a child read the Group One book *I Paint*. One page shows a child painting stripes onto a snake. The print said, "I paint stripes." The child pointed to the words and read, "I paint *snakes*." Although the child had substituted *snakes* for *stripes*, she had, nevertheless, demonstrated the competencies necessary for us to move her to Group Two books, and these more challenging books will be better suited to teaching her to check her hypothesized text against the actual print, looking all the way across words. The child showed us a command of one-to-one matching, she generated words that made sense, she matched the picture and the print, she generated text that sounded syntactically right, and she may have even checked her wise hypothesis—*snakes*—against the initial consonant. If we are looking to see whether this reader seems ready to take on new challenges, I think the answer is yes.

This description of a Group One reader really describes only how such a reader processes text. I've said nothing about the reader's attitudes as a reader, her sense of herself as a reader, her ability to think or talk in response to texts, her life habits in relation to books, and so forth. All of these are important dimensions of a reader. But it is a reader's ability to process print especially that allows a teacher to match a particular reader with a particular level of text difficulty.

Levels in the Upper-Elementary Grades

Upper-elementary teachers face an especially challenging job. This is partly because there are no published lists of book levels for the upper grades with the same credibility as the Reading Recovery levels (or the levels derived from their lists). There are and will continue to be published lists that attempt to level books for upper-elementary readers, but it is important to keep in mind that these categories have not been field-tested like the Reading Recovery categories or those that stand on the shoulders of Reading Recovery's work. It is also important to keep in mind that most chapter books can be read at a wide variety of levels. When a teacher evaluates the complexities in a book, is that teacher considering the challenges inherent in getting through the print enough to comment generally about a text or is the teacher evaluating the difficulties inherent in grasping the significance and nuance of the text? MacLachlan's novella, *Baby*, could conceivably be grouped with books the level of Dahl's

Matilda, but because the book has depths worth exploring, I'd instead regard it as a challenging book for many proficient middle school readers.

A grant from Alan Levenstein has established a Books for Children Project within the Teachers College Reading and Writing Project community. Each week this project brings fifty of our mentor teachers together in small groups to work toward the challenge of providing New York City children with the classroom libraries they deserve. As part of this Books for Children Project, a group of teachers led by Kathleen Tolan and Anne Marie Powers have begun to develop and use a gradient of difficulty with our upper-elementary level books (see the Appendix). These still tentative levels have been helpful to us, especially in defining some of the features that make for difficulty in chapter books, because knowing this allows us to anticipate the ways particular books will tax our readers and to tailor our teaching not only to the child but also to the book. These are some of the features that make for difficulty in books:

- Books with self-contained episodic chapters are easier than cumulative books in which the plot unfolds across a sequence of chapters.
- Books with a lot of dialogue are easier than books with a lot of exposition. This is especially true if the dialogue is free standing rather than embedded into paragraphs. Inexperienced readers sometimes get bogged down in the descriptive details.
- In the most accessible chapter books, line breaks show phrasing and all sentences stop at the end of each page. There are double spaces between the lines.
- As books become more challenging, they begin to include compound sentences.
- As books become more complex, background knowledge is required. Readers may need to know about dinosaurs, museums, or soccer.
- When there is one or perhaps two characters that move the story along, the story is easier to follow than if there are multiple central characters.
- Books with characters that stay the same, or are static or flat, are less challenging than books that contain complex, dynamic characters.
- As books become more and more reliant on figurative language, literary voice, and humor, difficulty increases.

Earlier, I wrote that I have needed a guide through the complex terrain of leveled books. But I am not the only one who needs a guide. Our children need one as well. The best guide, of course, is a knowledgeable teacher who can sit at a child's side, hear the child's interests and tastes, know the child's strengths, and steer that individual to the right book at the right moment. But we're not always there for each child at each juncture. Our children need guides they can carry with them as they negotiate their own pathways. Just as a trail guide lets prospective hikers anticipate the gradient of difficulty among trails, and the black diamond signs on my map of the ski mountain warn me of moguls and ice, a leveling system can help young readers find their way to books they can handle with assurance and finesse. The levels can also signal them, "Look alert. This will be a challenge," and help all of us gear ourselves up for anticipated difficulties.

Bringing Reading Assessment into the Very Real World of Classroom Teaching

8

Assessment is the thinking teacher's mind work. Assessment is the stance that allows us to learn from our students and thus to teach them. Assessment is the compass with which we find our bearings and chart our course, and the map on which we do this.* Assessment is also the thinking *student's* mind work. It is the student's growing awareness of what it means to do good work, and his or her own sense of progress and goals and next steps. Clear goals and honest, frequent assessment, including self-assessment, allow students to become managers and authors of their own learning lives.

As I begin this chapter, I want to say to my readers, "Put down this book. Take a detour. Read Marie Clay's *An Observation Survey of Early Literacy Achievement* (1993), read Peter Johnston's *Knowing Literacy* (1997), and Sandra Wilde's *Miscue Analysis Made Easy: Building on Student Strengths* (2000). Read Chapter 6 of Connie Weaver's *Reading Process and Practice* and Chapter 5 of Goodman's *On Reading*, and study Barro et al., *The Primary Language Record*. Then observe readers with your colleagues alongside you and with these researchers perched on your shoulder helping you to say, "Look!" and "Why?" and "I wonder" and "Could it be that …."

Instead of being able to take a sabbatical in order to become strong assessors, the preservice students and the teachers with whom I work find themselves learning the tools and schemas for assessing readers while doing thousands of other things. A teacher once explained this by saying, "Have you ever tried to change the tire on your car while driving along a mountain road? That's what

---

* In this chapter I am talking about ongoing classroom assessment rather than about preparation for standardized reading tests, a subject I address in detail in *A Teacher's Guide to Standardized Reading Tests: Knowledge Is Power* (Calkins, Montgomery, Santman, Heinemann, 1998).

it's like trying to assess your readers in the midst of classroom teaching." This chapter, then, will not be about ideal methods of assessment. Books like those I've mentioned earlier address that topic well. Instead, I hope to offer guidance to teachers who are finding it difficult to fit assessment into the very real world of classroom teaching.

In some classrooms, I have seen instruction grind to a halt for a month or two while teachers try to administer required assessments. Because it is especially important—and especially difficult—to assess children well at the start of the year, I strongly urge schools to support two days of one-to-one appointments between all teachers and all children before the first day of school. I also think schools need to consider developing a gradient of assessment expectations for teachers. A first-year teacher in a crowded city classroom may need help in determining which assessments are especially critical. As teachers, we sometimes collect endless data but then find little support or time to use the data to inform our teaching. I advise, therefore, starting with a lean, economical system of assessment and then moving heaven and earth to be certain that this assessment affects teaching and learning. So, I've been asking myself, "What is the bottom rung of reading assessment? What assessments are so necessary, they should be required of every teacher?" It seems to me that every teacher must accomplish these goals, and develop methods of assessment to do so.

- We need an efficient means of quickly and roughly matching readers with books so that the class is engaged in productive work from the first week of school on and we can begin to assess individuals more closely.
- We need to understand and support our children's habits, values, and self perceptions as readers.
- We need to understand the strategies and sources of information individual readers use and don't use, and we need to tailor our instruction to each child's reading strengths and needs.
- We need to take early note of (and then to understand, teach, and track the progress of) children who are failing to thrive.
- We need to hold our teaching accountable (and receive the necessary feedback) as we work toward clear and public goals.
- If we do all this, we will achieve a classroom system of assessment that forces us to develop multilevel teaching plans.

Even these minimal goals are ambitious. But once we have experienced the efficiency and power of linking assessment and teaching, we are on the road toward a lifetime of learning.

We Need an Efficient Means of Quickly and Roughly Matching Readers with Books

Before we can begin to assess children, they need to be engaged in productive reading work. A prerequisite to assessment, then, is finding a quick, economical system for steering children toward books they can understand. As I discuss in Chapter 7, if we assess children early in the year, and if we've leveled even just 30 percent of the classroom library in accordance with the levels of our assessment texts, we can tell a student, "For now, it looks as if your reading will be strong if you read books with a green dot on them." Matching children with books enables us to ensure that children are spending long chunks of time each day reading comprehensible texts. This alone contributes enormously to a reader's growth.

I suggest that within the first week of school, we match all children with books, even if we need to do this very approximately, and that we do this knowing we will later move toward the deeper assessments that will teach us how to coach each individual child. Approximate information about our children as readers can be put to immediate use. If we know that Beverly Cleary's books are right for a large percentage of our class, this knowledge will inform our decisions about the promotional book talks we give, the books we highlight on our library shelves, and the author studies we sponsor. Knowledge of each child's just-right books also allows us to set up roughly well-matched partnerships and guided-reading groups. This will also mean that from the very start of the year, we have some idea of which children require special support.

There is no one way to go about matching children with books. We can simply ask children to select books that are easy for them to understand and then watch for indications of engagement or disengagement, following up on the latter by asking these children to read passages aloud and talk about those passages. If books have been leveled, this will give us a peek into the child's ability to handle books at particular levels. Alternatively, we can use either a published assessment or our own ladder of assessment books to roughly match books and readers, but if we do this, we need to be certain that these books are correlated with the levels in our classroom library so we can quickly use what we learn to inform our practice.

I never used to suggest that we assess readers using a preselected set of assessment texts because I knew using preselected texts meant contrived contexts for assessment, and because it is important to assess readers as they read self-chosen books for real purposes. But I've recently become convinced that there is something quite powerful about watching the way several children handle the same text (as long as that text is roughly appropriate for

	Aaron	Adrian	Allison	Ambrese	Calvin	Christine	Co...
What kind of reader are you right now?							
What kind of reader do you want to become?							
What do you plan to do to become that kind of reader?							
How did this plan help you grow as a reader? Be specific!							
What is your next goal? What is your next plan?							
What texts will finish your fiction standard?							

each of them). When several children each read aloud a page from *Little Soup's Birthday,* we soon notice that only *some* of these readers inflect their voices to convey their recognition that the mother must call Soup three times before he responds. Only *some* children learn that this is *not* Soup's birthday but his friend's.

Once a child is proficient enough to read silently, we generally suggest that the child read the first few pages of the assessment book silently and alone, so they can get acclimated to the book before reading the next page or two aloud to us. The beginning of a book is always especially challenging, and what a reader does farther into the text is more revealing. We might duplicate the third page of the book to use as a record of the child's reading and then as the child reads, mark copies of the text with codes to convey what each reader does with that page. Although it is important to study the strategies and cueing systems each reader uses (I'll discuss these later), my first expectation is that within the initial two weeks of school, every teacher is certain that every child is reading with understanding.

People have different views of the criteria a teacher might use to match children with books. Various reading assessments have popularized the idea that a child has an independent, an instructional, and a frustration reading level. According to many scales, children must read 95 percent of words accurately for a book to be at a child's independent reading level and 90 to 94 percent accuracy translates into a child's instructional level. Neither of these hard and fast figures allows for the fact that errors vary in quality as well as quantity. In general, I'd recommend that we watch whether a child can read the book with 90 percent accuracy and talk in detail about the text.

We Need to Understand and Support Our Children's Habits, Values, and Self-Perceptions as Readers

During the first days of school, as we move among youngsters and begin to understand them as readers, it is absolutely crucial that in our minds we are not asking *only* "Where do you, as a reader, fit into my ladder of books?" Even if we don't say it, children can read us astutely. If every conversation with every child is all about weighing and measuring that child's place within our leveled libraries, we end up teaching lessons we never intended to teach: that we are mostly interested in weighing and judging them as readers, that all our conversations about their reading are an effort to line children up according to whether they are better or worse readers.

It is crucial that we look at our kids with other questions in mind from the very start. We need to ask, "What wonderful things have particular children invented to support themselves as readers?" and "What unique features of my children as readers could I spotlight and celebrate?" Does one child adore nonfiction books and another read aloud to her brother and still another make book jackets for her books? Children should immediately and always sense our interest in the wholeness of each of them as a reader. Individuals will benefit enormously if we spotlight ways particular children can mentor the rest of us.

Then, too, we need to ask these big questions when we assess our children, because the questions help *us* remember that we're teaching children not simply to get through print but to compose richly literate lives. If we want to be sure that we teach in ways that say "Reading is not just a little thing one does with black marks on a page, it is also a big thing one does with a whole life," then we need to be sure we are assessing the big picture of children's literate lives.

If Daria Rigney had simply pulled her chair close to Adam and recorded his miscues as he read his Matt Christopher book, she might have decided the book was too easy for him. "I figured I needed to know *why* he was reading *this* author," Daria said. "So I interviewed him."

"I love Matt Christopher," Adam told his teacher. "I've read all sixty of his books. I always find out when a new one is coming out and I get it that day." Adam went on, "Last year, I decided I needed to communicate with Matt Christopher. We wrote letters to authors in third grade, and I didn't want to write to his publisher like we did then, because I knew they'd just send me the form letter to join his fan club. So I decided I needed to figure out where he lived." To do this, Adam reread many of his books, noticing their settings and other clues. "I figured out the place where I thought he lived from the geography of his books and then got the area code for that area and checked on the internet ... now we talk on the phone all the time," Adam explained. Without an interview, Daria might well have pushed Adam out of these books into harder ones instead of supporting and building on the incredible reading project he had embarked upon.

One of the most powerful things we can do, early in the year, is to generate conversations among our children about their readerly lives. In individual conferences or in whole-group talks, we can ask questions about their reading habits. It is wise to plan on asking one or two questions only and then "unpacking" children's responses with follow-up comments: "Can you give me an example of that?" or "So walk me through that. How would it go?" Here are some effective starter questions:

- What should I (we) know about you as a reader?
- With whom do you share your reading?
- When has reading really worked for you in your life? Tell me (us) about that time. When has reading really *not* been a good thing for you in your life?
- What are some neat things you do with reading at home?
- Can you walk me (us) through a day and tell about the reading you generally do?

How powerful it can be to involve the whole class in an inquiry about what we are each like as readers. After our children have made timelines of their own histories as readers or drawn pictures of themselves as readers, or brought their favorite books to school as we saw Kathy Collins's children doing, we may interview one reader publicly, asking the rest of the class to listen to the details of this child's reading life and think, "How am I like this reader? How am I different?" This will lead to talks about readers' lives, values, habits. When we discover that one child has turned a bedroom closet into a reading nook, we can ask all children to talk about the places they read.

Then, too, once we've talked about our lives as readers, we can easily ask children to plan for their reading lives, and to make resolutions. Last June, Kathy Collins's firstgraders talked in partners about the reading they'd done all year, and then wrote their resolutions for their summer reading. these are a few of their goals:

What are your goals for reading over the summer?

I'm perbel gonae be tired
When I come back from camp
So I might as well get out a book.

What are your goals for reading over the summer?

In My Spair time of reading I will
try to read 25 books.

What are your goals for reading over the summer?

I am going to make a schedule
and add reading in 3 places in the
morning, after noon and night.

We assess in part because this makes our teaching alive. How important it is to learn about where and when children read at home, about children's perception of themselves as readers and their quirks, tastes, histories, worries, attitudes, and hopes. Working in this fashion, teachers have helped communities of children talk and think about the pressure to read harder books, the joys of using local libraries, and a million other aspects of being a reader in the world today. If we are in touch with the details of many readers' lives, the whole fabric of our teaching will sparkle with the stories and voices of particular children.

We Need to Understand the Strategies and Sources of Information Readers Use and Don't Use

It is essential that we do more complete assessments for at least a range of our readers and for all our struggling readers. Although it is important to assess all our readers, this is not a wise way to proceed if it means that we race through these assessments and then have no time to develop instructional plans for any of these children. Assessing readers cannot mean merely collecting data. We need to understand the patterns in our readers' behaviors and the logic behind what they are doing so that the moment-to-moment decisions we make can be informed by our understanding of individuals as readers.

It is particularly important that we assess every struggling reader, because the more challenged the reader is, the more idiosyncratic that reader's strategies are likely to be. Struggling readers tend to represent extremes; two struggling readers are apt to be very different from each other. These readers often do not make equal use of all their cueing systems (or sources of information). It's as if these readers are sitting on two-legged rather than three-legged stools—that's why they struggle in the first place. One child will have one leg missing from his stool, another child will have a different leg missing; one child will use very little graphophonic information, relying mostly on a sense of story to create texts, while another struggling reader will be overreliant on graphophonics, neglecting meaning and her own understanding of how texts tend to go as he struggles through letter-sound work.

For all children, but especially these struggling and beginning readers, assessment and instruction must become aligned so that we tailor our interventions to the child, and scaffold and celebrate even the smallest steps. We need to ask, "What indications will we look for to tell us if our teaching is working?" and we need to adjust our interventions when we don't see the expected progress.

In order to gain a more complete portrait of our students as readers, teachers will probably want to use running records, an informal reading inventory, or a miscue analysis to analyze the strategies each student relies upon as he or she reads. We will also want to interview and observe readers and study samples of their writing.

Running Records

The running record, a tool for coding and analyzing reading behaviors, was designed by Marie Clay to be used by teachers often and with a range of texts. The most important belief underlying both running records and miscue analysis, which I describe briefly later, is that when readers produce an oral reading that differs from the text, these "miscues" (as the departures from the text are called) reveal how readers are using sources of information available to them. If a child picks up a text that says, "I jump on my bike and ride away," and reads "I *hop* on my bike and ride away," we know this child is hooked into the meaning and syntax of the sentence and may have substituted one word for another. The child may have done this because she is envisioning the text in her mind's eye and her character jumps onto the bike in a hopping sort of way. We'd say this child draws on the *semantics* (or meaning of the text) and the *syntax* (the sentence structure). If another child read the same sentence "I jomed on my bike and ride away," and if this child shows no distress over not making sense or sounding right, we'd have to conclude that at least in this instance, the child has relied on graphophonics but not much on meaning or the structure of English. The two children need to be on very different courses as readers. The first child doesn't appear from this one sentence of work to be having difficulties, but we may want to work with that child to be certain she *can* read word perfectly when asked to do so. The second child seems to need work to support comprehension. Studying a reader's miscues helps us to construct a portrait of the sources of information that the reader tends to draw on in reading. In Chapter 9, I address some of the ways our instruction can vary, depending on what we see children doing as readers.

The system of taking running records has been streamlined so that we can do running records often, without needing advance planning or special arrangements. In order to conduct a running record, we simply sit alongside a child as he or she reads a book. Usually, we do running records with a book the child has read only once or a book that is unfamiliar to the reader, in which case we often read the title and give a brief book introduction ("This is called *Dan, Dan, the Flying Man.* The flying man flies over things and he gets caught"). If the text is just a little difficult, the running records show what the child does when he or she encounters difficulty.

We don't usually tape-record the child's reading (unless we're studying how to become more proficient at running records and use this way to check ourselves), and we don't generally code the child's reading behaviors onto a typed copy of the text (although when we *can* do this, it's very helpful). We use universally accepted codes to record what the child does as he or she reads. In the running records that follow, I have numbered each miscue (see running record at right) and analyzed each numbered miscue, looking especially at the sources of information he has probably drawn upon in each.

① Roy has miscued, reading *in* as *I*. When we take a running record, we represent miscues in the way shown, writing the child's version above the line and the actual words of the text below the line. The codes here show that Roy monitored his reading, so that after miscuing, he backed up and reread the text, this time self-correcting. The SC indicates he read *correctly*.

It is interesting to surmise why Roy produced *I* instead of *in*. The two are graphically similar. Or perhaps he read the first page as a complete question, "What would you like?" and was starting to answer the question "I (like …)", which would suggest that he has a strong sense of the structure of language. Clearly, when he rereads from the beginning he is using the syntax or structure of the sentence to help himself.

② Roy again miscued on the first word of the line. He tried *what* and *will* before self-correcting. We can surmise from our hypothesis (above) that he is using his knowledge of how sentences and books tend to go. He probably expected this to be a repetitive book. "What would you like in your sandwich? What would you like…." Both of Roy's miscues are visually similar to the actual word (they begin with *w*). The fact that Roy knew his miscue wasn't right, even without reading on, and that he self-corrected, suggests that he

What Would You Like?
Wright Group

"What would you like   ✓ ✓ ✓ ✓ ✓

in your sandwich?" $\frac{I}{in}$ R   sc① ✓ ✓

"Would you like a spider?" $\frac{What/will}{would}$ sc② ✓ ✓ ✓ ✓

"No I wouldn't!"   ✓ ✓ $\frac{won't}{wouldn't}$ ③

"Would you like a mouse?"   ✓ ✓ ✓ ✓

"No I wouldn't!"   ✓ ✓ $\frac{won't}{wouldn't}$ ④

"Would you like a grasshopper?" ✓ ✓ ✓ ✓ $\frac{green\ cricket}{grasshopper}$ ⑤

"No I wouldn't!"   ✓ ✓ ✓

"Would you like a fat worm?" ✓ ✓ ✓ ✓ $\frac{—}{fat}$ ⑥ ✓

"No I wouldn't!"   ✓ ✓ $\frac{won't}{wouldn't}$ ④

"Would you like peanut butter?" ✓ ✓ ✓ some ✓ ✓ R ⑦

"Yes I would!"   ✓ ✓ $\frac{want}{would}$ ⑧

" I like peanut butter."   ✓ ✓ ✓ ✓

is attending to letters at the middle and end of words. He may have gotten the word *would* from the title.

③ Here, Roy substitutes a visually similar word that makes sense to the entire story but doesn't necessarily sound syntactically right. People will probably have different views about this miscue, but I'm comfortable thinking the reader has looked at the picture and thought, "Would I eat a spider?" and then, "No way would I eat a spider," and said, "No, I won't" rather than "No, I wouldn't." He may be using meaning and visual cues more than syntax here. However, Roy holds onto the pattern he's established throughout the rest of the book, substituting *won't* for *wouldn't,* which signifies that he *is* using syntax, in that he maintains a unified pattern throughout the text.

④ Roy is continuing his substitution throughout the book. Some people would count each reoccurrence as an error. For reasons I explain below, I've only counted this as a single error. Notice I've coded the same miscue as ④ later.

⑤ *Green cricket* is a great substitution for *grasshopper,* even though one could argue that *green cricket* is two words and *grasshopper,* one. Roy used visual graphophonic meaning (the picture) and syntax to substitute one insect name for another. Some people would argue that because green cricket is two words, this substitution should count as two errors. I would regard it as one error, but this is a judgement call.

⑥ Roy's omission of the word *fat* fits with the pattern of language earlier. In the preceding questions, there was no adjective before the noun, and Roy may predict that this line will follow the pattern of the others. We can say he used meaning and syntax to generate this miscue because it makes sense and sounds right.

⑦ Roy uses syntax to invent a word that sounds right, then goes back and self-corrects using visual cues.

⑧ This is an interesting error that doesn't fit with the rest of the reading because it isn't syntactically strong. Substituting *want* for *would* is a visually (graphophonically) based miscue, and up to the error it could sound syntactically strong, but if Roy was relying on syntax, he would have had to read, "Yes, I want *it.*" As it is, this miscue doesn't make sense or sound right.

Roy was able to retell the story well, even surmising that the character who asked the questions was the grandpa. Roy told me, "The Grandpa asked the boy what he wanted on the sandwich and the boy didn't want all those other things. He wanted peanut butter."

So what do I make of this running record? Roy's accuracy level could be calculated in different ways depending on whether we choose to count each substitution of *won't* for *wouldn't* as an error, or to regard all of these as one combined error. I would regard this as one error because Roy kept the pattern (syntax) throughout the story. If he had wavered at all or shown any indication that he noticed something wrong but didn't self-correct, I'd have regarded each reoccurence as an error and his accuracy rate would have been lower. My judgement in this instance is just that—a judgement call—and some other informed people instead opt to tabulate each reoccurence as a miscue. Depending on how we score this, we could conceivably conclude that Roy is reading at 87 percent accuracy and that the text might be too hard for him. If we count the reoccuring use of won't for wouldn't as *one* error, however, he is reading at a 93 percent accuracy rate. There is a 1:3 self correction rate which is good. This means Roy self-corrected one out of every three errors. A closer look at the work he is doing, the information he is drawing upon, and his hold on meaning suggests to me that he seems to be effectively reading a well-chosen text. In this instance, even if I'd scored his reading in such a way as to give him an 87 percent accuracy rate, I probably wouldn't follow the rule of thumb that suggests children generally need to read with 90 to 95 percent accuracy, but I'd keep a close eye on this reader.

The truly important thing, of course, is that we take the time to look over the running records and see what the child has done. During a recent visit with us, Marie Clay said she often suggests that teachers write a ten-line summary of what they've learned from a running record, responding to the question, "Where is this child as a reader?" and this is wise advice.

Informal Reading Inventories

In informal reading inventories, children read from a graded series of passages. Often teachers estimate a child's approximate level and then check this estimate by asking the reader to read aloud from a list of words designed to match the level of the passage. Assessing reading using word lists has some limitations because good readers use the meaning and syntax of language in order to read, and both aspects are missing when a child reads a list of words. But some teachers find it helpful to peek at what a child does with words in isolation because this spotlights a child's ability to instantly recognize words or features of words and to take words apart. If the child has some success with the word list, the child moves on to the passage itself. The child may be asked to read the passage silently and then aloud, and then to retell the passage or answer questions about it. The teacher meanwhile records both the child's miscues and the retelling; later, the miscues are translated into an accuracy count. The accuracy count plus the child's retelling determine whether this graded passage is at the children's independent, instructional, or frustration level.

Compared to running records, informal reading inventories (IRIs) have disadvantages and advantages. Whereas teachers can do running records of a child's ongoing reading of texts that child has chosen for real purposes and is reading within a social context, IRIs run the risk of seeming a bit more like a test. On the other hand, children are reading extended passages in the company of an observing teacher who takes note of what a child can do and of a child's strategies. This is not like a standardized test. Some people appreciate the fact that the IRIs are packaged to make them easy (charts turn miscue counts into accuracy levels, for example, and comprehension questions are provided). And one strong advantage of informal reading inventories is that they *appear* to provide objective and standardized assessments. If parents doubt our informal assessments about the appropriate books for a given child, we can show them the child's performance on the *Qualitative Reading Inventory* 3 (Addison Wesley Longman, 1997) or the Developmental Reading Assessment. If superintendents want an objective tool for tracking children's progress as readers, we can sometimes persuade the system to adopt these instruments rather than relying on multiple-choice, norm-referenced tests.

Miscue Analysis

Ken Goodman, the researcher who developed miscue analysis, has documented that all readers miscue and that the difference between skilled, proficient readers and poor readers has less to do with the number of miscues (this will vary in relation to the difficulty-level of the text) than with the nature of the miscues (*Findings of Research in Miscue Analysis: Classroom Implications,* 1976). Strong readers read efficiently and aim to construct meaning from what they read. As part of this process, strong readers make miscues. For example, very strong readers tend to make miscues that involve switching one function word with another (they might read "I went down *to* the dock" when the text says "*by* the dock"). A miscue such as this can be thought of as a good miscue because it preserves the meaning of the text. As Sandra Wilde, author of *Miscue Analysis Made Easy* (2000), recently pointed out to my colleagues and me, if readers want to make a word-perfect performance of the text, they need to slow their reading down and focus on words as ends rather than as means to an end. Teachers who use miscue analyses believe it would be counterproductive for readers to be so focused on reproducing an exact word-perfect match of a text that they self-corrected a good miscue.

Miscue analysis was originally developed for use by researchers. Each miscue analysis required a great many hours. For years, teachers have gotten the message that although there are short-cut ways to use this tool, it is important to study the tool in its detail first, learning to use it as it was designed. As a result, miscue analysis has not been as widely incorporated into the teacher's repertoire of assessment tools as it should be. Yetta Goodman and Carolyn Burke made miscue analysis more accessible in their *Reading Miscue Inventory* Manual and Sandra Wilde's *Miscue Analysis Made Easy* (2000), a brief book that attempts to put a version of miscue analysis (Procedure III) into the hands of teachers, provides even more help for the classroom teacher. I refer readers to these books.

In order to do a Procedure III miscue analysis, a teacher selects a text challenging enough for the reader that he or she makes some miscues. Often this means selecting a text we think *will be easy for the child one year from now.* We use passages that contain about 500 words (or more) and are complete in themselves rather than excerpts. The child is given the original text (the book), while we sit beside the child with a tape-recorder and our own copy of the text. "I'm trying to learn what readers do when they read. Would you read this, and if you get stuck, do whatever you'd do if I wasn't here. After you are done reading, we'll talk about what you've read."

In a miscue analysis, teachers do not introduce the text or ask a child to reread a familiar text. Both practices occur frequently in running records, but running records are predicated on the belief that most of the time, readers should be reading at a 90 percent accuracy level. In miscue analysis, the reader's accuracy level is less important. What *is* important is the pattern of strategies a reader uses when he or she encounters difficulty. In order to glimpse what readers would do in silent, independent reading, the teacher doing a miscue analysis does not supply words for children who encounter difficulty. In contrast, in running records, if a child has been stymied by a word for twenty seconds, we supply the word and record a T (for told) in our records in order to preserve fluent reading, but it is probably accurate to say that fluency in reading is more prized by those who choose running records as their assessment tool than by those who choose miscue analysis.

During the reading session in a miscue analysis, the researcher or teacher marks what a reader does by using codes similar to those used during running records. An audiotape is made for backup in case we miss certain parts. Then we ask children to pretend we've never read the text and tell us everything about it. We don't ask questions until the reader has finished the initial retelling, and we're careful to avoid gesturing in ways that confirm or challenge the retelling. After the reader has retold the text, we use probes to uncover more about what they do and don't understand. Sandra Wilde recommends that teachers ask "What else can you tell me about so and so?" or "So and so was in the story. Who else was in the story?" We might also ask "What else happened in the story?" and, if necessary, probe further by asking "What happened after that?" (*Miscue Analysis Made Easy*, 2000).

When the child has left, we set to work. Before much time goes by, we record general comments, perhaps noting the child's fluency, intonation, and engagement and our general impressions about the strategies revealed in child's miscues. Then we select a section from the middle of the text and analyze, by coding, what the child has done and the logic she has used. The section needs to include twenty-five miscues, so we estimate the portion of the text which we'll code. We number each sentence on our copy of the text, and then read the miscues (with the reader's corrections if there were any) in each sentence, asking ourselves three questions: "Does it sound like an English sentence?" If so, beside the first sentence we record a Y (for yes, the sentence does sounds like an English sentence). Next we ask "Does it make sense?" and again record a Y or N alongside the other code. If the answers to the first two questions are yes, then we ask the third: "Was the meaning changed?" (if it was not, we mark an N for no). The three answers together—a code of YYN— are a sign of a reader making good miscues. Although the reader miscued, the resulting sentence sounded like English, made sense, and didn't change the original meaning. It could still have been visually or graphophonically dramatically off, it could even be a completely different word or phrase, but a sentence coded YYN is regarded as a good miscue.

Of course, it is also important to understand the extent to which readers draw on visual or graphophonic information, and so we also look at the single-word substitutions readers have made, including those that have been corrected, and assess whether the word readers produced visually matched the word on the page. We code each substitution to indicate whether the

RUNNING RECORDS, INFORMAL READING INVENTORIES, AND MISCUE ANALYSIS

	RUNNING RECORDS	IRI	MISCUE ANALYSIS
RECORDING	• Tick marks on blank sheet	• Recorded on typed copy of text	• Recorded on a copy of the actual text
SCORING AND ANALYSIS	• Substitutions, omissions, insertions are scored as errors and analyzed based on semantic, syntactic, and/or visual cues • Self-corrections are not errors • Accuracy rate is determined by number of words/number of errors • Errors are analyzed as if the child read up to and including the error	• Little analysis of cues used other than whether or not there was a meaning change • Accuracy score determined to place within a range of frustration level, instructional level, independent level • Errors/miscues are simply counted up and not necessarily analyzed much	• Miscues coded according to whether sentence still sounds okay, whether it makes sense, and whether the meaning changes • Miscues are analyzed within their entire sentence • Miscues also coded based on high/medium/low visual similarity • Although accuracy scores are often calculated, emphasis is on quality, not quantity, of miscues. "Good miscues" are not regarded as problems
RETELLING	• Usually includes retelling component	• Most recent ones include retelling	• Always includes retelling
READERS	• Beginning readers whose strategy use is still evident during reading, usually K–2	• Most IRIs were used for readers who could read a page of text without picture support, therefore, at least mid-first grade or higher	• Especially effective in grades 2–8, and even higher if used as *Retrospective Miscue Analysis* where kids analyze their own reading

continued

	RUNNING RECORDS	IRI	MISCUE ANALYSIS
TEXT TYPE AND SIZE	• Generally 100 words or less • Real book or text with illustrations of some sort • Whenever possible using a meaning "chunk" of text	• Graded passages often taken from textbooks or other basals	• Whole and authentic text • 25–50 sentences are coded from middle of text
TEXT INTRODUCTIONS	• Teacher often reads title and gives a book introduction. Some teachers use running records on second reading only	• Title and introduction • Possibly some work on building background knowledge prior to reading	• Teachers never do an introduction. The goal is to get as close a peek as possible into the processes children use when reading independently. The point is not to see whether readers read at a certain accuracy rate but to understand the strategies readers use to construct meaning
TEACHER ASSISTANCE	• Because reading ultimately needs to be an independent endeavor, teachers refrain from assisting a child who is stuck during a running record. We learn from exactly what the child in difficulty does. However, if the child is totally stumped and enough wait time has passed, the teacher would give the word and record as a *told*	• Wait time, no prompting, told-error	• Teachers avoid telling children what the text says (even if the child is totally stumped). The goal is to understand what the reader would do without assistance. We know errors may compile, lowering the accuracy rate, but this rate isn't our focus. Instead, we're studying readers' strategies in the face of difficulty.

continued

	RUNNING RECORDS	IRI	MISCUE ANALYSIS
DEPTH OF ANALYSIS	• Accuracy • Cues used or not used • Looking for patterns over time • Approximate level	• Accuracy • Meaningful miscues or not • Comprehension score • Broad grade level assigned	• Use of semantic, syntactic, graphophonic cues • Overall understanding of text • Retelling

visual similarities were high, medium, or none. Usually, if two of the three parts of a word (the beginning, the middle and the end) are similar, as when a reader says *break* for *bread,* we'd assess this miscue as having high graphic similarities. We also assess substitutions of one-, two- or three-letter "function" words for another (*to* for *in*) as having high graphic similarities. Better readers tend to have fewer graphic similarities in their miscues because these are generally meaning based.

Finally, we examine the ways the miscues compare with the retelling. If the retelling has been accurate and detailed, we'd be much less concerned about a relatively large number of miscues that don't follow the YYN pattern. If the retelling has been scanty, even if the reader made few miscues, we'd want to explore the reader's comprehension further. Does the reader comprehend better when reading silently? When reading texts that differ from this one? When listening to a read-aloud?

We need to do these assessments so as to guide all our teaching, and especially, so that we take note of, understand and teach children who are failing to thrive. This work is so critical that I devote most of the next chapter to it.

We Need to Hold Our Teaching Accountable (and Receive the Necessary Feedback) as We Work Toward Clear and Public Goals

Our assessment system should provide us, as teacher, with a constant source of feedback on our progress toward our goals. It is too easy to become lulled into believing that by suggesting, mentioning, or assigning readers to do something, we've accomplished the job of teaching. We may *tell* readers that it is important to read a lot both in school and at home, but teaching means more than telling. It means finding ways to track our children's progress through books, and pulling our chair alongside Yassir to say, "I'm so puzzled, Yassir. In class today, you've read 13 pages already. Yet at home last night you only read 4 pages, and none the evening before. What's going on?" We may learn that Yassir forgets to bring his book home, or that he sleeps in the same room as his two brothers and this makes bedtime reading a challenge. We and Yassir soon are wrestling to devise solutions to these problems. *This* is teaching.

It is crucial, then, that we, as teachers, ask ourselves, "What is it my children should know or be able to do as a result of our work together?" and then ask, "How will I collect evidence often of each child's progress?" And it is especially crucial that we realize that when a child isn't doing all that we hoped she would do, this information needs to alter our teaching because our job is to climb every mountain and ford every stream in order to teach children.

Throughout the year, then, we will draw imaginary lines in the sand, saying, "This is the day to really notice which of my children seems engaged (and which do not seem engaged) in their reading," or "I am going to ask everyone to jot a summary of the read-aloud, just to see how many seem to understand the gist of the story," or "I am going to see what my kids do when I ask each one to read the words off the word wall" or "I'm going to interview children on their favorite authors." I recommend that teachers at different grade levels identify certain observable signs of reading progress and look for them across the grade or across a group of readers, and that we sometimes systematically collect data according to these indicators and bring what we learn to meetings and study groups with our colleagues and to curricular planning groups. In the first week of October, every first-grade teacher might observe her class during independent reading to notice which children do and do not seem to have a sense of one-to-one matching on one-syllable words in texts at their level. And it is crucial to understand that when we do these informal assessments, we are assessing ourselves and our teaching as much as we are assessing our children.

Our assessment system should provide us with a constant source of feedback on our progress toward our goals. If I talk to readers about the value of thinking between their reading of one nonfiction book on one subject and another and then watch to see whether they are actually doing this work, I may need to confront the limitations of my teaching and deepen my work.

Our teaching will be more powerful when we hold ourselves accountable for having a real effect on our students' work.

Using Our Assessment System to Develop Multilevel Teaching Plans

Instead of teaching in a whole-class fashion to a hypothetical average student, we need to take into account the range of development within our classrooms, designing a curriculum that meets all our children where they are and takes each child further. Our classroom-based system of assessment should wreak havoc with any instructional plan that doesn't allow us the elasticity and breadth necessary to teach the full range of readers. Our assessments should nudge us, as teachers, to look at all our children and their work, and to look at ourselves and our work.

Supporting Readers Who Struggle with Meaning, Print, or Fluency **9**

Randy Bomer drew his chair close to listen as John read aloud. After making his way haltingly down the page, John came to an abrupt stop. He didn't know the next word. John put his finger under the word, then winced and stared up at the ceiling. Watching, Randy intervened. "You know, John, you're probably not going to figure that word out by looking up at the ceiling. I'd look at the word."

John, his gaze still fixed on the ceiling, responded, "Sometimes God tells me the word."

We don't usually turn to God for help with our reading. But on the other hand, we all know what it's like to struggle with a new skill, wishing help would fall from heaven. Struggling readers are no different, whether they are struggling because they are only just learning to read, because they have just moved to a new and more difficult phase of reading, or because they are somehow off track. In this chapter we will explore six aspects of working with students as they encounter new stages of difficulty in reading:

- Ways to study and plan for a reader who is having difficulty
- Some general principles for working with struggling readers
- Helping readers who need support turning their attention toward meaning
- Helping readers who struggle especially with print
- Helping readers who need help reading with fluency
- Helping inexperienced readers
- Helping whole schools that struggle with a great many struggling readers

Ways to Study and Plan for a Reader who is Having Difficulty

Gaby Layden, the resident expert among my staff on struggling readers, and I recently worked together with a group of teachers observing several readers who were having various difficulties. "Let's all just watch and jot down exactly what we see these readers doing," we said. The teachers' observations were not very different from those other teachers have often shared with us. Here are some examples:

> He couldn't sound out *captain.*
>
> He doesn't use the letter sounds.
>
> She reads with no understanding—you can tell.
>
> She doesn't know vocabulary.
>
> He doesn't know his word endings.
>
> She never finishes a book.

We listed their observations on chart paper. I sat looking at the list, trying to think how staff development work might proceed from this place. I glanced to my side, where Gaby had laid *her* list of observations. I saw a starting place. I asked the teachers to try to figure out why the observations they had made and those Gaby had made were so different. What had she been aiming to do that was different from what they had been aiming to do?

THE TEACHERS' OBSERVATIONS	GABY'S OBSERVATIONS
He couldn't sound out captain. He doesn't use the letter sounds.	He uses a fair bank of sight words to read with some accuracy, but when he gets stuck on a word, he seems not to be doing anything. He gets to the start of it and seems to just sit there.
She reads with no understanding—you can tell.	When she encountered difficulty with a word, she substituted a word that was the same part of speech and began with the same sound, but it made no sense and she read on, not bothered by this.

She doesn't know vocabulary.	She miscues on *attention* (attenty-on) and *completes* (complĕtes). Showed moderate visual matching but the approximated version didn't seem to ring any bells. Vocabulary?
He doesn't know word endings.	Although he could word-solve most words, he deleted endings and paid little attention to the tenses of words. His reading was also word-by-word. Fluency?
She never finishes a book.	The reader seemed to take a break at the end of every paragraph.

Looking from one set of observations to the other—Gaby's and the teachers—I was reminded of something Marie Clay told me: early on, her students will often focus on what a reader can't do. "I tell them, goodness! You can't teach from that." I found myself coming to a new understanding of her adage "You need to teach from their strengths." While it is certainly true that it would be hard to plan instruction based on the observation that "He couldn't sound out 'captain,'" the issue may not be the teachers' focus on the problems children encountered (Gaby had done this as well) as much as their response to those problems. When Gaby watched a child struggle to decipher the word *completes* and noticed that even after deciphering the word, she didn't recognize it, Gaby regarded the child as a reader with strengths as well as limitations. Although this might be a child who has a vocabulary problem, this is also a child who handled the print-work of reading with some finesse. The teachers' observations summed up the child's difficulties in reading as error, as wrong. Whereas the teachers said, "She reads with no understanding—you can tell," Gaby said "She substituted a word that was the same part of speech and began with the same sounds; it made no sense but she read on, not bothered by this."

Gaby's detailed descriptions of what readers actually did when they read acknowledge the fact that even when a person is wrong, that person is also often partly right. That day, we all realized again the importance of looking directly at what children really do and of approaching their goof-ups not as errors, as black holes of wrongness, but as miscues, as evidence that they're putting undue weight on one strategy, or holding onto old advice that is no longer appropriate for them, or not balancing the cueing systems. Instead of "He couldn't sound out *captain*," Gaby had said, "He uses a fair bank of sight words to read with some accuracy but when he gets stuck on a word, he seems to not be doing anything." This kind of thinking gives us a window on the child's logic, theory of reading, and repertoire of strategies.

We worked that day to turn our observations and all the other information we had on these children, such as running records and writing samples, into instructional plans. It would have been easy to say, "I need to work with this child for a couple of weeks before I can make plans" but we believe it is important to venture forth, positing tentative theories and making instructional plans, even without all the evidence in. Having a tentative theory about a reader allows us to watch more actively, to confirm or change our hypotheses. Even if we've done only a single running record or watched a struggling reader for only ten minutes, we step back to ask ourselves, "So, what could be going on here?" Gathering data alone is not enough. Equal time must be spent analyzing and theorizing from these data. Then, too, all of those who will be working with the struggling reader must work collaboratively to form a shared instructional plan and then must proceed in sync with that plan.

We began with Jake, a fourth grader, who was reading a *Nate, the Great* book, a book we often see in second-grade classrooms. Jake hadn't encountered difficulties with the words of the text, but he did not seem engaged by them either. He read in a rapid monotone and on several occasions, he read right past end punctuation without thinking that anything was wrong. While reading silently, he didn't seem to make a lot of progress, since his attention wandered often from the book. He'd read, pause, read. His teacher told us that because she knew *Nate the Great* was "below grade level" for Jake and she sensed his lack of interest, she'd tried offering him harder books but that Jake had stabbed at the words and his sentences hadn't even sounded like English. This reaffirmed for us his continuing at this level for now, although clearly we want him to read a lot, to get practice, and become a stronger reader.

In building a portrait of a child as a reader, it is always crucial to look at the child's writing. Jake's writing didn't surprise us. He spelled fairly conventionally but used little punctuation and his style rambled among topics. The draft made sentence-level sense but didn't hang together in a coherent or structured way. This affirmed for us that he probably wasn't having trouble with the graphophonic cueing system—he was spelling reasonably—but that he probably was having some difficulty interpreting punctuation, paragraphs, and the structures of texts.

We could have safely surmised that Jake would profit from work on reading punctuation. Yet the question is not "What could I teach this child" but "Of all the things I could teach this child, what feels most fundamental? What will enable the most progress?" We weren't sure Jake was actively interpreting and making meaning as he read and for us that came first. We headed back to the classroom and pulled Jake to the side. We told him we didn't know his book well and could he tell us about it? Jake retold the story: "They were looking for the note and it was torn and they were trying to find, you know, where it was and what after that." Over time I've learned to listen very attentively when children retell a book. It is easy to get lulled into accepting retellings that, in fact, make no sense. Jake did have something to say about the text and wove fragments of information from the book into his comments. It would be easy to buy into this as a reasonable retelling, but it was pretty confusing. Was the problem in his retelling or in his reading of the book? At this point Gaby told Jake that when she retells a story, she says who the characters are, and where and when the story takes place, and what the main events are, and how much time passes from the start of the story on. Gaby jotted down a list as she spoke. "Can you tell us about your *Nate, the Great* book again and this time follow these guidelines?" she asked, slipping him the list of story elements. To our astonishment, her intervention worked. Jake said, "Well, Nate is a kid who acts as a detective, and he got a phone call from Rosamund, who is his friend, in the middle of the night, and she was saying she lost a note and Nate said he'd go help her find it." The change in Jake's retelling was impressive enough that we felt sure it would help him to keep an eye out for these story elements as he read and to continue retelling with these story elements in mind. Chapter 22 describes this work with story elements in more detail. Although Jake seemed capable of building meaning, he was disengaged and we hoped that challenging him to keep an eye on story elements and then asking him to retell the story with a partner using these elements might involve him more.

Meanwhile, we figured he had enough control over the meaning of what he was reading that it made sense for us to nudge him to attend to missed punctuation. We headed back to the classroom to work with Jake.

When Project teachers, reading specialists, and staff developers work together to develop shared instructional plans for struggling readers, we find it valuable to try out parts of these instructional plans in each other's company. Instead of simply talking about what we hope to do, we actually work a little with the child. This accomplishes all sorts of goals. We learn more about our readers and are able to collaboratively refine our plans for readers based on what we learn. We develop more of a shared repertoire of ways to work with a particular reader, and other readers as well. We use each other as members of a think-tank, coming together around a child who needs us to understand him and each other. Sometimes teams of us work with a few shared individuals as case studies, and regard our collaboration as a form of professional development, and sometimes we do this with all people who will work with all the struggling readers in a school as an extension of the process of identifying and working with children who have special needs.

Some General Principles for Working with Struggling Readers

When readers struggle—either because they have reached a new, more difficult stage of reading or because they are somehow off-track—a few guiding principles tend to help.

- It is crucial that everyone working with a particular child agree on instructional plans. More than others, struggling readers need coherence across the day. They cannot be reading different books or be pulled in different directions by the resource room teacher, the classroom teacher, and the after school tutor.

- Almost without exception, if the child is struggling for an unreasonably long period of time, she is trying to read books that are too difficult for her. This is an emergency. We do kids no favors if we allow them to continue trying to read texts that are too hard. Giving a child books that are just one notch easier but still challenging won't help if the child still can't process them fluently and with understanding. Although we may think that tinkering with levels is more kind than dramatically moving the child down to where she can read fluently, the truth is that it isn't wise to be so worried about hurting a child's ego that we let her persist in reading books which are too hard for her. Moving a child down one notch (but not down to a just-right level) will mean the child gains none of the extraordinary benefits that come when at last reading makes sense. We must firmly put our long-time strugglers onto books they can read easily. This is the only way the child can feel how reading is supposed to go.

- These readers need extra time for reading but tend to receive just the opposite. We do them a disservice if we keep them busy and engaged in reading-related activities instead of structuring time before school, in school, and after school so they can read, read, read.

- We need to coach these readers up close. We will usually be trying to get rid of outgrown or dysfunctional behaviors and to build new habits. To do this, we need to be right in there as they read, asking them to pull a finger away, watching their eyes, gesturing toward the picture to cue them to look at it and think. This kind of teaching can't happen across a physical distance. This is side-by-side work.

- When a reader stops, we need to give her time to do some work, to be active. If she miscues, we need to let her keep going, to run into difficulty, and (we hope) to self-correct. If we jump in to correct every miscue, we don't allow her to monitor for meaning or to initiate self-correcting herself, both of which are of paramount importance. As important as it is to give a reader time to do her own work, it is also important to give her control of her own books. We need to guard vigilantly against the tendency to hold the book for her, to point for her, turn the page for her, and chunk words for her.

- Writing can be a very powerful way to teach reading skills, especially for struggling readers who need to become more resourceful word solvers. If there is an after-school or summer school program for vulnerable readers, writing needs to be a priority.

- We sometimes inadvertently accommodate children's weaknesses by lowering our expectations when they encounter difficulty. If other children are expected to write each night and are kept in from recess or get a phone call home if they don't do the assigned writing, we need to be sure that struggling readers are also kept in from recess and are getting those phone calls home.

- Too often struggling readers stop expecting school language to make sense to them. Yet if children don't comprehend what is said to them or read aloud to them and don't ask for clarification, they probably won't comprehend written texts. One place to start, then, is to help children get meaning from oral language. It is important to teach struggling readers to listen in whole-class meetings so they learn how to attend to language.

- Working with a colleague or two will usually help teachers see more ways to intervene with struggling learners. Putting into words our image of exactly what the student is already doing can enrich our understanding of how that child learns. If we can join together to watch a student at work, we will certainly see more ways to help that child.

- Vacations tend to take a great toll on struggling readers. Children often lose a huge amount of ground during summer vacation, so it is wise to provide some form of summer reading support.

Although all children learn and all readers struggle in their own individual ways, sometimes their learning styles and struggles have similarities. Narrowing the arena of their struggle can usually help us begin to devise an instructional plan for children at vulnerable points in their development.

Helping Readers Who Need Support Turning Their Attention Toward Meaning

Children Who Don't Seem to Notice Whether the Text They Generate Makes Sense

Within the category of children who struggle with meaning is the child who doesn't yet monitor for sense or self-correct when he reads. These children will generate a nonsense word, or an incorrect word, or a word that is the wrong part of speech and continue as if nothing is wrong. This behavior is often a sign of bigger problems: if a child doesn't monitor for sense, then even if he has strategies for dealing with difficulty he will never access those strategies because he first needs to experience what is happening as difficulty. Although the problem reveals itself because the reader doesn't monitor for sense, this reader is also failing to listen for a text to *sound* right. Children who ignore meaning (semantics) usually ignore syntax as well.

This struggling reader probably needs to be reading easier books so he isn't producing Swiss cheese texts, whose giant holes make purposeful reading impossible. When we can, we'll join him in previewing a text before he reads. Together we'll read the title, flip through the pictures, and get a conversation going about what the book might contain. What's probably going to happen? How might this story go? In this way we'll help to "activate the semantic—or meaning making—cueing system" (Y. Goodman), and we ensure that the child is poised to expect the text to make sense.

Above all, we'll help this reader expect words to convey meaning. As he reads, we'll occasionally say, "Does that make sense?" It will be especially important that, even when a sentence *does* make sense and sound right, we still ask, "Does that make sense? Does that sound right?" because monitoring for sense is important, not only when words hover on the edge of nonsense, but always.

If the reader miscues and produces nonsense, and shows no awareness of this, we might say, "What?" or "Huh? That makes no sense! Let's reread." When he resumes reading and again produces a miscue that doesn't make sense, we'll watch for even the slightest hint that the problem is registering. We'll nurse this hint of uncertainty. "Why did you pause?" we'll ask. "That's so smart! What are you thinking?" And when he goes back to try again, we'll support the gesture to self-correct whether or not it yields a right answer.

Children Who Can Read the Words But Can't Retell the Story

Within the broad category of children who struggle with meaning, there will also be children who read the words beautifully but can't retell any part of the story (save for describing the pictures). If we persistently nudge these children to talk about the text, they tend to reread part of it aloud. These readers often focus on reading as a performance or an accomplishment. "I read the whole book," the child will announce, but when we ask her what she liked about the book, she has nothing to say. This child reads books as if she is collecting trophies but doesn't seem to find any meaning as she reads.

In many ways, our response to this reader resembles our response to the first. We'll help the child read easier books and we'll do book-orientations to help her anticipate how books will go. But we'll do more: we'll not only help the child monitor for sense, we'll also work to be sure she constructs sense. We'll sit side by her side reading silently, and we'll talk back to the text frequently. When the child and I read, for example, that the character has stepped on a loose board in the attic, I'll lock eyes with the reader and say "Oh, no," and if we read on and find that the character has headed safely back downstairs, I'll say "Whew!" or "I'm so relieved. Now what about her brother?" When we resume reading, I'll look to see if she reacts to the text as we encounter it. After we read a part that seems remarkable, I may look at the reader as if saying, "What do you think of *that?*" In this way, I'll try to help the reader read responsively.

We'll also instruct the child to pause often to ask herself, "Wait a minute. What has this book said so far?" and to retell the book. Again, we'll probably have to do this for her as we sit alongside her, trying to invite the child to come along with us in reminiscing about the story. This child not only needs to retell the story, she also needs to read anticipating that she'll be retelling soon.

Children Who Can Talk About Any One Page but Don't Generate a Coherent Sense of the Story

There will also be some children who can talk about a page they've just read but don't seem to accumulate any coherent overall sense of the story. They understand individual sentences, but they don't construct a larger text from them in a cohesive way. If they try to retell the text, they do so in disconnected fragments. These children often do the same thing when they write, using phrases and fragments that don't come together to make sense. Sometimes they disguise this problem by presenting their writing as a poem.

We are wise to do a book introduction for these children so they have the big picture and get a sense of how it feels when the small pieces of a story hang together. We'll say, "The big brother does all these mean things to the little brother. Let's read and find out some of the mean things he did," and then later, "Wasn't Peter mean to his brother? Could you believe the way he …" and, "What else did he do that was mean? Let's look back and remember." Of course, we won't always be there to introduce these children to every book they encounter so we'll also teach children to give themselves a book introduction. "If your friend read the book, ask him to tell you about it," we suggest. "At the very least, look over the book before you read it. What does it seem to be about? What does it lead you to expect?" These children also benefit enormously from talking about their reading with a partner, from retelling yesterday's reading before they begin today's, and from knowing as they read that they'll be retelling.

With these readers, I might use a strategy developed by Caroline Burke and Yetta Goodman (1980) called "schema story." It can be helpful to give a child a story text that has been cut up into separate paragraphs. The child works at piecing the text together, relying on his sense of how stories tend to go. Usually reading activities like this make me a bit squeamish, because they are so different from reading as we do it in our own lives, but I suspect that this activity would be a good fit for this particular kind of struggling reader.

Readers Who Need Support with Vocabulary

Some children within the broad category of readers who struggle with meaning clearly need to build a larger vocabulary. They can often pronounce a close approximation of the word on the page, but they don't hit on the exact word because it is unfamiliar to them. These may be second language learners or children who don't yet have a lot of book experience. Either way, they'll profit enormously from read-alouds, book talks, book orientations, and book introductions geared toward rehearsing and talking about some of the words and concepts in a book. These readers need to be encouraged to hang on to meaning when they meet an unknown word: they should try to pronounce the unknown word and replace it with a synonym that works in the sentence. In this way, they will gradually build up a web of words related to the unknown word. These readers will profit more from extensive reading than from vocabulary drills because reading is an extraordinarily potent way to learn vocabulary even when the unknown words aren't taught directly. Nagy, Herman, and Anderson (1985) have demonstrated that children pick up word meanings ten times faster through reading than through intensive vocabulary instruction.

These children need to realize that it is okay to take a stab at unfamiliar words and figure out an approximate meaning from the context. This is how we all learn new vocabulary from texts. They also need to know that if they can't construct a meaningful sentence, they can ask a partner or a teacher for help. They do not need to write the unknown word down or look it up in the dictionary unless they want to do so. When children are asked to research every unfamiliar word, this can focus their attention more on the words they *don't* know rather than on the words they do know. This isn't helpful or necessary. Readers who hold tight to meaning learn vocabulary words through reading, conversations, and life experiences of all sorts.

Helping Readers Who Struggle Especially with Print

Readers Who Become Passive in the Face of Difficulty

Some beginning readers (and off-track older readers) will read along until they come to a difficult word and then stop, frozen and at a loss. At most, these readers might appeal for help, but they generally become inactive in the face of difficulty. They may know quite a few words, but they don't seem to be able to generalize from what they know. As writers, they tend to spell conservatively and rarely try to approximate words they don't already know how to spell.

It helps to sit alongside a child like this and face the difficulties with her. If she reads "I fed the ____" but freezes at the start of the word *giraffe,* we'll first wait, signaling to the reader that we're not going to jump right in and help. If the student is still at a loss, we say, "Hmm, what could you do?" Again we are signaling, "It's your responsibility." If this still doesn't prompt the reader to do anything, we are apt to say, "You could try looking at the first letter and checking your picture. Try that."

The reader needs to know that we expect her to *try something*. We will prompt her to use a particular strategy if necessary, but we won't do the reading work for her. We might, in the end, say, "What *could* it say?" and then, thinking aloud, muse, "Should we reread?" But we will then wait for the child to reread "I fed the _____." "Let's look at the first letter." In the end, we might say, "Could it be *giraffe?*" and see if she nods. "How do you know? Check that it's *giraffe,*" we say, and wait for her to actually do so.

Another time when we sit with this reader, we'll look to see if she is active *in any way,* and whether or not her activity yields anything helpful, we'll support her efforts. "I saw you glance at the picture! I loved the way you did that. Did you also glance at the *b* at the start of the word? You did? Hurrah!" Over time, we'll work to teach this reader a whole repertoire of strategies. We will also help this child as a writer to be a more resourceful word solver as she grapples with unfamiliar words when she writes. We'll want her to use the words she knows to help her tackle the words she doesn't know. We want her to understand that if she knows the word *and,* this can help her with *animal* and *ant* and *sand.*

Readers Who Read, Letter-by-Letter

Other struggling readers will tackle difficult words by stuttering their way, letter by letter, through them. If the book says "I gave the man a *dime* for the candy" and the child is stuck on *dime,* he will be apt to proceed like this: "/dah/ /yh/ /mah/ /ehh/." In working with this child, I would do lots of work with meaning to balance the printwork ("What *could* that be? What word might go there?"). I might say, "Think about the story. What might you be giving to the man?" Even if the coin was shown in the picture, I might avoid saying, "Look at the picture," because I don't want to set up an expectation that there will always be a one-to-one match between words and pictures. That won't be true beyond an early level book. I might go so far as to say, "*Sometimes* the pictures can help you make sense of a word."

In order to help this child access the sounds as well as the meaning of language as support for print work, I might suggest, "Reread the sentence and get your mouth ready for the word." Children won't know what this means unless we demonstrate by rereading and making the initial sound. I might also demonstrate the way to chunk sounds. "___*i-m-e.* I've seen that before. Could it be *ime?* Would that work? /D/ /ime/?" I might nudge the child to look at the strings of letters in a word and ask, "Is there a part of this word I already know?" and "Have I seen any part of this word in another word?" Because breaking a word that you can't read into syllables is always hit or miss. I'd want the child to get used to trying words one way, then another. When working with this child, teachers need to remember that there is research (Adams, 1990; Moustafa, 1998) showing that readers profit from solving new words by using the spelling patterns in familiar words. Rather than sound out a word such as *pike* in a letter-by-letter, left-to-right fashion, readers access known patterns (*ike,* as in *like*) and figure out the unfamiliar word by analogy. Another time of the day, this reader might profit from Cunningham's *Making Words* activity in which a teacher asks her children to each write a spelling pattern such as *old* on his or her white board. "Now add one letter to make *sold,*" the teacher says. "Now change one letter to make *told*" (Cunningham, 1995). This child would surely benefit from spelling pattern work and from encouragement to use the words he knows to read the words he doesn't know. Most of all, children who need help chunking words and working with word endings, prefixes, rimes, blends, and so forth will profit from a writing workshop.

Children Who Need More Knowledge of Letters, Sounds, and Words

Sometimes we find children who struggle with reading because of a sheer lack of knowledge about print and words. In general, children who are well on their way as readers tend to know at least ten to twenty words by sight and produce them easily as readers and writers by the end of kindergarten, and close to a hundred sight words by the end of first grade (Stanovich, K. E. 1991). This is not an instructional goal. We don't need to teach high frequency words. The point is that the child who is reading and writing a lot will repeatedly encounter certain words and develop automaticity with them. If children don't seem to have developed automaticity with a bank of words or word chunks or to know blends, diphthongs, letters, sounds, and word chunks, the place to help them learn all this is in the writing workshop. As children write, they actively use this information. By using sight words, word endings, blends, and diphthongs when they write, children come to feel comfortable enough with print and familiar enough with letter sounds to use them when they read.

Children Who Need Support with Fluency and Phrasing

Every one of us reads metrically: we may say, "Once upon a time / there was a girl / named Alice" or "Once upon a time there was a girl named Alice," or one may pause after each word. When a reader makes exaggerated pauses between short oral phrases, this interferes with comprehension. It becomes a bigger problem when the reader moves into texts that contain complex sentences. A child who has problems with fluency and phrasing often reflects the accumulated experience of reading at frustration level. Our first intervention will be to make certain that this child is on a steady course of books he can read with ease. The most helpful will be easy books with long sentences that sound like normal language and contain lots of high frequency words. Some accessible books contain only a brief fragment of text on each page; these texts obviously can't provide ideal support for fluency.

Even after they've moved to easy books, these readers may continue to read with staccato phrasing because it has become a habit; the child thinks this is how reading should sound. We'll want to coach this reader using the fluency prompts listed on page 115. We'll also support fluency by helping the child think about the meaning of the story. "How would you say that—'Close the door right now'—to someone?" we'll say. "Look at me. Tell *me* to close the door right now. Say it to me." We may also say the phrase ourselves, smoothly and with natural intonation, asking the child to echo us.

By the time children have begun reading early chapter books, coaching for fluency may involve helping them take in more of a sentence with their eyes. As they start the sentence, readers need to already have some idea of where it is going. If readers use a pointing finger or a bookmark as a guide, this can interfere with fluency and phrasing. Gay Su Pinnell has suggested to me that when children can read books at about Level C (according to the Guided Reading Levels), they won't usually need to use a finger to point unless they encounter difficulty. And very few children benefit from moving bookmarks slowly, line by line, down the page. If a bookmark *is* to serve a beneficial purpose, it is wiser for readers to use it to portion off half the page rather than to move the bookmark down the sentences. The most helpful portion to cover (and remove from sight) is that which the reader has already read.

Bookmarks, then, are more helpful if they *follow* rather than *lead* the reader. Strong readers tend to scan ahead of the words they are reading. It is not advisable for bookmarks to take away the opportunity for readers to look ahead.

Work on fluency need not occur in one-to-one conferences only but may also become part of a whole-class study. Readers can choose some lines they love in their books and practice reading them smoothly and with meaning—such as this one from Mem Fox's *Wilfrid Gordon McDonald Partridge:*

> And the two of them smiled and smiled because
> Miss Nancy's memory had been found again, by a small boy, who wasn't
> very old either.

Above all, we support fluency and phrasing by giving children many opportunities to hear beautiful texts read aloud—and read well.

Helping Inexperienced Readers

Some children will have no particular problems—as long as they are reading very easy books. A fifth grader who began to read late or who hasn't spent much time reading, for example, may still be reading the very earliest series books. Yet, although she can read *The Magic Treehouse* books with only a little difficulty, when she reads books that are "on her grade level," her reading falls apart. If we push her to read harder books, she has trouble understanding them.

This child needs to keep reading *The Magic Treehouse* books. She needs to spend a lot of time reading so that eventually, we *can* move her along to harder books. Before school, during school, after school, and before bed, she needs to read. And with practice, she'll get stronger. We can move her up a notch at a time by doing guided reading with her: introduce the book, help her understand the gist of it, and prepare her for the difficulties the book will pose. We would be foolish to push her along so that she is reading at frustration level.

Helping Whole-Schools which Struggle with a Great Many Struggling Readers

So far, I have focused on assessing and teaching *individual* struggling readers. But the problem of struggling readers requires a different response if we are talking about *whole schools* filled with struggling readers. In these instances, our approach needs to proceed on several fronts at the same time. Struggling readers often come to school from home situations that would challenge the best of us, and these schools are almost invariably heart-wrenchingly lacking in resources. Although the problems of whole schools filled with struggling readers are complex, the first step toward improving reading generally seems clear. The place to begin is to ensure that bottom-line opportunities to learn reading and writing are available for all children. Children will not learn to read easily if schools don't have books that match their reading abilities and provide extended time during the school day to read, and if children aren't able to work and progress at their own levels. Teachers need to read aloud several times a day. Children need lots of opportunities to learn about written language by writing and they need lots of opportunities to use language purposefully by talking and working in collaboration with each other.

Schools filled with struggling readers, like struggling readers themselves, are similar in only one sense: they all struggle. And these schools, like these readers, each struggle in their own unique way. Struggling schools, like struggling readers, do not benefit from a one-size-fits-all intervention. Instead, whether we are talking about struggling schools or struggling readers, we need to begin with intelligent and respectful assessment. Although something obviously isn't working in these schools, there is often a great deal that *is* partially right amid other conditions that are, in the end, not right. All too often, I see people regarding struggling schools, like struggling readers, as black holes of error and consequently people devise instructional plans for these schools that essentially bulldoze away all that *was* good in the school. None of us as individuals or institutions can get better without people recognizing what we *can* do and without building on our strengths.

What is required, then, is that the wisest, and most experienced team of assessors spend extended time working in collaboration with the teachers, children and the principal. They need to study the struggling school in some detail in order to develop an instructional plan that builds on the strengths and addresses the needs of the learner-school.

If we are going to reverse the trends in a struggling school and help that school to begin to make steady, positive progress, we need to be sure it has goals that are achievable, concrete, and within the school's "zone of proximal development." A school can set its sights on having all children reading texts they can read for forty-five minutes a day, and on all teachers receiving side-by-side support in the moment-to-moment-complexities of teaching reading. These goals will *probably* result in higher scores on even norm-referenced, multiple-choice tests, but schools won't move forward on the learning journey easily if they are told that their one and only goal is to have scores rise dramatically. In the end, this goal will seem out of a school's direct control. Struggling schools, like struggling learners, need above all to feel that they *can* regain control, that they can actively work in ways that will make a difference.

Guided Reading and Strategy Lessons 10

Guided reading can make a special contribution to the overall constellation of a reading curriculum. How powerful it is to guide the journey of a small group of similar readers over the terrain of a text we know well, one with its own particular bumps and challenges that we have chosen with these readers in mind. But like independent reading, reading aloud, conferring, book clubs, and everything else, guided reading is not all things. I become concerned when I see teachers trying to lead several guided reading groups a day and doing so at the expense of other learning structures that also have contributions to make. The strategy lesson is an alternate learning structure; similar but distinct from guided reading, the strategy lesson has important contributions to make.

What is Guided Reading?

In order to understand all the variations of guided reading one sees in schools, it's important to understand that the term means very different things to different people. My colleagues and I have recently spent about twenty days in a small study group with Gay Su Pinnell, co-author of *Guided Reading,* and so our understanding of this structure is very deriva-tive, based largely on her work and we are grateful for her guidance. For some others, however, guided reading is a term that has deep roots in basal reading programs. For example, in their textbook *Direct Instruction Read-ing,* Carnine, Silbert and Kameenui suggest that guided reading means a teacher selects a text for a leveled homogeneous group of readers, then the teacher determines "the critical content" that students will need in order to master the text and preteaches that content (unknown vocabulary, difficult to decode words, unique graphics, or the structure of the passage) and then asks children to read, stopping at a certain point for follow-up activities such as answering questions (Carnine, Silbert, Kameenui, 1997). In the name of guided reading, some teachers have all members of the class discuss, read and discuss again one of two texts, one "at grade level and one below grade level" (Cunningham, 2000). These interpretations of guided reading differ from ours, which is based more on the work of Pinnell and Fountas.

When I lead a guided reading group, I ask two or three sets of reading partners to join me at a table or on the carpet in our classroom library. The children will all be reading at a particular level of text difficulty (perhaps they are blue-dot readers). I may know beforehand that these particular children need work on similar issues (perhaps fluency), or that the books they've begun to read, like *Rosie's Walk* and *Cookie's Week,* tend to have long, winding sentences that span many pages and put new demands on their phrasing and fluency. Or I may simply know I haven't checked in with these readers for a while and want to see where they are in their reading.

I give each child a copy of the text I have chosen. If these readers have been reading blue dot books, I will either choose a blue dot text or a book that is a bit harder. Once I've given out the books, I usually do a three- or four-minute book introduction, which includes a summary of the book and a discussion of key concepts and new vocabulary words. This is also a time for me to walk children through some tricky parts. I might say something like, "Open your books to page 7. Here the mouse is very unhappy and he talks in an unusual way. He *grumbles.*" Then I might involve the children a bit by saying, for example, "What letters would you expect to find at the start of that word *grumbles?*" and "Can you find that tricky word on the page? Point to it. Read it. Yes, the mouse *grumbles,* doesn't he?" If I'd wanted to help with *grumbles* in a lighter, less supportive way I would simply have mentioned it in passing.

After the introduction, when it is time for the children to read the text, my expectation is that they'll read as they sit around me in a circle or semicircle, and that each child will read all the way through without pausing. If the text is a longer one, we read it over several days, so I set a stopping point partway through it. Children read either silently or aloud to themselves, depending on what they usually do as readers, but they do not read in unison, chiming along together. If they begin to do this, I ask them not to and turn their bodies a bit so that they are less oriented to the circle and less apt to do so. I meanwhile move from one child to the next, listening to each child read and lightly coaching that child. If the child is reading silently, she generally knows she should read aloud when I draw near; sometimes I signal the child by tapping on her shoulder.

If a child runs into a problem while moving through the text, I first watch to see whether he is active and strategic in the face of this difficulty. I might say, "Check the picture" or "What would make sense?" or "Could it be _____?" and provide the correct word. We provide this help because we want children to continue processing extended text. If there are too many difficulties, it means we have chosen the wrong book or have not introduced it well, and therefore we just take over and read the text aloud to that child. "Do you want me to take a turn?"

If some children finish early, we are apt to ask them to reread the text, this time silently (or without using their finger), or we might ask them to find their favorite pages. Either way once everyone is finished reading we have a very brief book talk. "How did you like that story? It was sad, wasn't it? Darnel, what was your favorite page? Joline? These conversations are not what I think of as real book talks. Talk during guided-reading sessions tends to go child to teacher to next child with very little discussion between the children themselves. Each child tends to say his or her piece, without much elaboration. Of course, this needn't be the case, but I don't recommend trying to turn guided-reading groups into response groups, literature circles, or book clubs. The guided-reading structure can't be all things, and one thing it is not (in my eyes) is an ideal time for probing into a text or for developing new ideas about the text.

After a miniature "conversation" about the book, we make a "teaching point." In about a third of the guided-reading lessons I observed Gay Su Pinnell lead, she asked the readers, "What was the tricky part?" or "Where did you do some good reading work?" and they revisited the section. Alternatively, the teacher may take children to a section of the text that she identified as one which presented difficulties. Often the teaching point involves revisiting a page on which several children have encountered difficulties with a word. In this case we are apt to pull out a white board, and write the word on it, and then work with similar words. Always, if a word or a punctuation mark is isolated from the text and addressed separately (as when it's written on a white board), before the lesson is over children will be asked to reread the page on which that word occurs. In this way, the isolated bit is put back into the context of the extended text. Perhaps the child had read, "Mom is *gardening*" when in fact the text said, "Mom is *planting*." The lesson, then, might support what the child is doing right in the reading: "You were right to notice that mom is doing something in the garden. *Gardening* was a good guess. It fits into the sentence. But look, the word on the paper starts with a *pl...*" This lesson might go on to ask, "If the text had said, 'Mom is [and the teacher writes] *digging,*' what would it have said? I like the way you are looking at the *d* and making a /d/ sound." When children have read the book, discussed it briefly, and worked on a related lesson or two, the guided-reading session is over. Children don't go onto work with flashcards or do related art activities. They may take the book back to their seats and reread it, or they may put it with a collection of other books they want to reread several times over the following days.

FOR US, GUIDED READING IS NOT ...	FOR US, GUIDED READING IS ...
Initiated by an introduction in which the teacher elicits the text from children by means of dozens of questions. Whether these questions are part of a shared picture walk or supported predictions, they can overwhelm the book and bring out lots of oral narratives that divert attention from the book.	Initiated by an introduction in which the teacher gives an overview of the text and takes children to particular pages that might pose some difficulties.
A time for children to reread texts they have already read as a whole class during shared reading.	A time for children's first readings of an unfamiliar and usually a challenging text, supported by the teacher's introduction.
A time for round-robin reading or choral reading.	A time for all the members of a small group, holding their own copies of the text, to read the text quietly and simultaneously, and usually in its entirety.
Stop-and-go reading, with children stopping after bits of reading so the teacher can focus their work for the next few pages with prompts, such as "Read and find out *why* Andrew was mad."	Reading an entire text without stopping. A child who finishes the text may reread it or return to find a favorite page while others finish.

Done with long-term ability-based groups.	Done with short-term, transient, ability-based groups.
20–40 minutes of group work.	10–15 minutes of group work.
Followed by word cards, sentence strips, hangman games, dittos, and activities.	Followed by a teaching point that usually addresses "a tricky part." The teacher may do some work on a white board or with magnetic letters, but other than this, there tend not to be many accompanying teaching tools.

Our Purpose in Guided Reading

I find guided reading is especially effective with emergent and beginning readers (and with struggling readers who read at these levels) who are still learning to take both meaning and print into account and to cross-check these two sources of information. Teaching an early reader to think about what the text might say and then to look at the print to check or revise that guess works well if the child's predictions are remotely accurate. Once children know many sight words, their assumptions about the text tend to be so, but before this happens, teachers have limited choices. If the child sees a picture of a mother driving and thinks "The lady is going to work" instead of "Mom is driving," it won't be easy for him to learn to look at the picture, think about the story, and match his predictions against the print—to use all these sources of information to say what is on the page. How can we help this child maneuver successfully through this text? We can hope that if he is one of two readers working together, one of them will recognize the word *Mom* and find a way into the text. Or we can read the text with the child first, in a shared reading, so that his independent work is a reread. We can sit with the child and help him through each page (at least until the book's pattern becomes clear to him). Or we can work with the child in a guided-reading session, using an introduction to scaffold the first read through of the text. It is at this point in a child's reading career that guided reading is most helpful. And the good news is that these readers are reading *very* short books, so guided-reading sessions can be brief.

Guided reading is also useful when we want to help any group of children move up a notch to books that are a bit harder for them than those they've been reading. When I want readers to try challenging books, I work with the group every other day for a week or two, giving them a running start on an author or a series they will then continue reading on their own.

Finally, guided reading is very effective when we're trying to ensure that proficient readers construct an integrated, comprehensive understanding of a text. Often proficient readers are able to pronounce all the words in a text and to recall a collection of details about the text, and they think that this is what it means to comprehend a text. In guided reading sessions, by introducing the text and sometimes by positioning children to read in a way which will be fruitful "you'll see the girl gets into a series of predicaments until finally she invents a way to solve her problem", we can help proficient readers develop a felt-sense for what it can mean to comprehend a text.

Issues Teachers Face When We Do Guided Reading

A teacher who decides to begin doing guided-reading work faces at least these four tasks:

- Building a library for guided-reading work
- Becoming familiar with the text
- Doing book introductions well
- Managing the rest of the class

Building a Library for Guided-Reading Work

When we have decided to try our hand at guided reading, the first issue we often face is that of securing the necessary materials. Unfortunately, when a school decides to incorporate guided reading into its reading curriculum, reading specialists sometimes go into classrooms, round up all multiple copies of books, and move them into a guided-reading book room. But why deplete classroom libraries in order to support a new structure?

A better solution is for schools to buy more of the necessary books. If we need to organize bake sales and paper drives or book fairs or to scour the streets looking for merchants who will support the cause, then by all means we must do so. I recommend a lean, trim guided-reading collection that concentrates on multiple copies at the very earliest levels, where books are short and guided reading is especially important. Most of us keep six copies of each guided-reading book in a small plastic bag and the various bags for a particular level of reader in one bin. Once children are proficient readers, most of our guided-reading work involves short texts, such as short stories, poems, articles from the newspaper, and excerpts from larger books.

Becoming Familiar with the Text

Guided reading works best if the teacher is able to use the same texts over and over. If we glance over a text and then try to lead a guided-reading group through that text, we're in for trouble. It is critical to study a text beforehand in order to imagine the difficulties it will probably pose for readers. If we have worked with many different readers on the same text, this helps us anticipate what the tricky parts in this particular text will be. If previous readers were stymied by a particular section, then we know that when we introduce the text to new readers, we will either want to say, "Turn to page 9 ..." or we'll deliberately leave this particular difficulty for readers to encounter themselves. Now our observations during the session will have a focus.

Doing Book Introductions Well

One of the most striking things we learned in watching Gay Su Pinnell's guided-reading sessions was that we needed to rethink our book introductions. Because we had read descriptions of book introductions suggesting that they were "picture walks" and "conversations," and because we had watched published guided-reading videos that showed teachers asking as many as fifty leading questions within a six-minute introduction, we had come to believe that book introductions were long, winding chats that happened as teacher and children journeyed through the pages of text in a picture walk. Too often, however, this approach ended up being more confusing than clarifying.

Gay Su Pinnell joined my colleagues and I in watching a second-grade teacher introduce the book *Souvenirs*. The teacher had a pile of the books on the floor behind her. She looked out at the circle of second graders around her and said, "Today we're going to read a story about the things people bring back from trips, called what readers?" The children were silent, and the teacher answered her own question. "Souvenirs. Who has been on a trip and brought back something really special?"

Amber piped in, "When I was in kindergarten, I went on a trip and I got a pumpkin."

"What did you do with the pumpkin?"

"I cut out eyes, a nose …," Amber said.

"You can have pumpkins for Halloween," Michael added.

"We had a Halloween parade," a third child said, and began to describe the school's Halloween parade.

"Today we will read about Miss Marvel, and she went on a trip and she brought back souvenirs for special people." Holding up the cover picture, the teacher asked, "What does it look as if Miss Marvel is doing here?"

It looked to me as if she was planning her trip around the world. Michael produced the expected response. "She is looking at a map."

"What might she want to know?"

"Where she lives," Amber said, "Cause I live on 142nd Street and my gramma looks at a map on the subway."

The introduction to *Souvenirs* continued in this fashion for over twenty minutes, during which the teacher asked the guided-reading group ninety-three questions. In trying to answer the teacher's questions, the children generated alter-stories not just of pumpkin carving and Halloween parades but also of people going to the movies, Princess Diana (there was a double-decker bus from England in one picture), and Virginia Beach.

By now we have watched Gay Su Pinnell do a score of book introductions for guided-reading groups and many others as she has worked with individual children. Whether the child is a kindergartner reading a very simple caption book or a third grader reading *Amber Brown,* in her introductions, Gay always seems to begin with a few sentences in which she conveys the main gist of the text in a way that gives readers the background knowledge they need to understand the text's concepts. If a child in the story plays T-ball or has a paper route or draws straws or says "Not on your life" or adds buttermilk to a recipe, some children might be perplexed. The book introduction gives them the background knowledge they need to understand the story. In working with a few third graders struggling through *Amber Brown Sees Red,* Gay began by asking the children if they understood the expression "sees red." They didn't, so Gay said, "This book has unusual language. When it says 'sees red,' it reminds me of a bullfight, and they wave a red flag to get the bull really upset. So *Amber Brown Sees Red* means she is really angry." Then Gay explained. "She is mad because her best friend has moved away and her mom is engaged to a guy she doesn't like."

Marcellus added, "And when her mom was planning a honeymoon, she was upset because she wouldn't get to go."

Gay asked, "What do you think she is most upset about?"

"That her mom will marry Max and she and Max won't get along."

Gay added, "Also there is a section about her dad. She thought the problems would be over when her parents divorced but the problems didn't end, did they? So when it says *Amber Brown Sees Red,* it's all inside her."

I need to stress that these book introductions are not as easy as they may seem. Lisa Ripperger and I worked together to produce videotapes of ourselves leading guided reading groups (for our course with Gay). I started with Robert Kraus's book *Whose Mouse Are You?* The book opens with the words, 'Whose mouse are you?'" and a picture of a lonely mouse. "Nobody's mouse." Turning the page, we find "Where is your mother?" and then, "Inside the cat." I sat with the text thinking, "What do I say?" I didn't think I could tell these six-year-olds that a distant narrator was asking the protagonist questions! In the end, my book introduction began, "In this story, *the book* asks the mouse some questions. The book asks, "Whose mouse are you?" I got through the first half of the book but gave up entirely on the entire text. Once my colleagues and I went through a whole stack of books searching for one we could introduce! When I told Gay, she asked us to bring out the books we'd discarded as too difficult for introductions. One was called *Twins.* This is the text:

> My sister and I are twins. We look the same.
> We have the same hair. Look at our hair.
> We have the same eyes. Look at our eyes.
> We have the same smile. Look at our smile.
> But we do different things. I like books. She likes soccer.
> We eat different things. I like bananas. She likes apples.
> We wear different things. I like pants. She likes dresses.
> We look the same, but we are different.

Gay read through the book, thought for a minute or two, and then launched into an introduction. Because it was for us, it's not exactly the book introduction she would have given in a classroom setting.

"The book I have for you is about two sisters. They are special sisters. They are twins. That's sisters, but they are born on the same day! Do you know any twins? Well, twins are alike in some ways. Sometimes they dress alike. Sometimes they do things the same and sometimes they are different. This book is all about what they do that is the same and that is different." (Opening to the first page she shows it to us.) "There they are—two sisters. Do they look the same? There are things about them that look the same." (Now she is talking as she turns the pages.) "Look at their hair. It's kind of the same. Look at the way they smile."

Now Gay turns to the page in which the book takes a major turn. Showing this page, she says, "But these twins also do some things that are different. That's a long word, *different*. Can you find it? What might some of the different things be? See the soccer ball. Do you think they *both* like soccer? Or do they like different things?"

Teachers who find book introductions difficult will be heartened by Marie Clay's chapter "Introducing Storybooks to Young Readers" in *By Different Paths to Common Outcomes* (1998). She begins by saying that "introducing new texts that young school children are going to read demands great skill." I agree. But I think we can get on the right track if we prepare by thinking about the book's story elements, that is, the plot, setting, characters, movement through time and the changes, or in the case of non-narratives, about the book's patterns. An introduction generally sets up a frame for the whole story and often talks about the ending, but it does not paraphrase every page. The question we need to ask ourselves is, "How can I set up a frame to help children think about the whole book?" Rather than immediately opening the book and doing a picture walk for readers, it's often wiser to begin talking with the book closed, opening it only when we are halfway through the introduction. Although kids should feel they are active and involved, this is not the time for real discussion. As Marie Clay says, "The teacher says the topic, title and characters with minimal interaction, as too much talk confuses the purposes and distracts from the focus of the story" (p. 174).

When Gay led a guided-reading group with five of Lisa Ripperger's first graders, I transcribed her book introduction:

> *Gay:* Today we're going to read, *Good Night, Little Kitten*. It is about a little kitten who doesn't want to go to bed. You know, when kids don't want to go to bed, they have all the things they say so they can stay up later. In this book, Little Kitten says lots of these things to his parents. And you know what Mama says, "You must." That's what happens in this book. Turn to the title page. It says, *Good Night, Little Kitten*. Turn to the next page. Look what's happening.
>
> *Kids:* The mom is talking to the kitten.
>
> *Gay:* Yes and it says *Good Night, Little Kitten*. Go to page 8. (Page 8 has a picture of the kitten in his playroom.) No wonder this kitten doesn't want to go to bed. Look at all the toys he has! Let's turn to page 12. Here, he doesn't want to go to bed and he says, "I want to stay up!" Let's go to page 14. Someone else is talking here. (This is a picture of the father cat. The text says Papa Cat, but Gay doesn't tell children this.)

Kids: Daddy!

Gay: Could be. Let's see if there is anything else I want to show you. (She and the kids turn the pages.) The parents are getting really impatient with Little Kitten.

Kids: They are talking about him. (They weren't; they were talking *to* him.)

Gay: Maybe *about* him, maybe *to* him. What kinds of things do kids say when they don't want to go to bed? Do they say, "I'm not tired" like Little Kitten says here (turning page)? And what does the mother say? "You *must.*" What I want you to do is to look at the very last page.

Kids: Maybe he woke up his mom and …

Gay: (Gay helps the children with a word or two on this page.) Think in your mind about what really happened in this story. Let's turn to the front, to the title page, and let's read this (the title) together.

Everyone: *Good Night, Little Kitten.*

Gay: Very softly to yourself, would you read this whole book? Don't try to read it with anyone.

Guided-reading introductions are such an important component of guided reading that Gay has gone so far as to suggest, "Eighty percent of guided reading is the introduction." In talking about ways to save time, she suggests that conceivably (although not ideally) we might simply give a book introduction and then leave children to read and discuss the text while we move on to work with other readers. In New Zealand, book introductions are a regular feature of classroom instruction even when teachers are conferring with individuals or partners.

Managing the Rest of the Class

If the first challenge the guided-reading teacher faces involve securing and knowing the texts we'll be using and the next is learning to provide clear, supportive introductions, the biggest challenge is the issue of the other children. What does the rest of the class do while we lead guided-reading groups? This is less of a problem when we lead one guided-reading group a day instead of aiming to lead three or four (as some teachers do), and it is even less of a problem when we streamline book introductions and eliminate extension activities involving word cards, sentence slips, or dittos. That is, it is reasonable for a teacher to work with a group for ten or even fifteen minutes and less reasonable for a teacher to work regularly with several groups for twenty to thirty minutes each.

But the issue of the other children remains. Some teachers respond by setting up various centers to keep kids occupied and at least somewhat productive. Sometimes clusters of children are given a sequence of activities to complete during a morning while the teacher leads one guided reading group after another. But I worry if the activities contain a lot of drawing (Paste this poem, into your poem book. Circle the *ow* words. Draw a picture to accompany the poem) and copying (Sort these long *a* word cards into piles according to how the long *a* sound is spelled, then copy all the cards into an *ay* and an *ai* list), and I worry when these centers contain an unambitious form of writing (Draw a picture. Write a caption to accompany the picture). Obviously, it is rare for children to sustain rigorous work in centers if a teacher isn't investing her attention into those centers. If children *do* work independently each day in centers involving phonics, independent reading or writing, how are they being instructed in these vitally important components of a balanced reading curriculum? And finally, if children rotate among center-activities during reading time, when do they get the long blocks of time they need to read, read, read?

In our classrooms, primary teachers tend to lead one guided-reading group during a morning reading time. (Upper grade teachers are more apt to lead strategy lessons—which I describe later—but they also lead guided-reading groups.) Many teachers have other times in the day (before school, after school, etc.) when they meet with readers needing special support and it's common for some of this time to be invested into guided reading.

When we do lead a guided reading group, we find it helps if other children continue to do the work we have directly, explicitly taught them to do. For us, this means other children are usually reading independently or in partners. Sometimes all children are working in small response groups which we refer to as book clubs or corners. Certain moments lend themselves to guided-reading groups:

- After a minilesson, when children disperse with books to their independent reading, some teachers keep four to six readers with them and lead a guided-reading lesson.
- Once private or partner reading time is well under way, we might signal two or three sets of partners to join us in the library corner for a guided-reading session.
- When groups of children have formed "reading centers" or "book clubs" (see Section III), we work with these groups as if they were guided-reading groups. The children tend to be ability matched, and they'll already be doing some shared reading. If a group of children in a reading center has chosen to study Fox, the character in Edward Marshall's *Fox*

series, for instance, we may do a guided-reading session to launch these children into this series. If a book club is reading Gary Paulsen's *Hatchet* together, we might bring in an article about the author and do a guided-reading session around this article.

- Most of us find ways to give extra time to our struggling readers before school, during lunch, or after school. In this work, guided reading is a staple.
- We sometimes do guided-reading work using short nonfiction texts from the social studies or science curriculum.

Strategy Lessons: An Alternative to Guided Reading

When my intention is to help a group of readers develop more skill in using a particular reading strategy, I'm apt to pull the readers together for fifteen minutes of work, usually around a shared text I've selected for the purpose. In a strategy lesson (Y. Goodman and Burke, 1985), I first tell readers what I want to teach, connecting the lesson to their ongoing work (the connection). Then I generally use my own reading or a child's reading to demonstrate a strategy proficient readers use (the teaching). Then I ask readers to try using the strategy while I'm there to observe and scaffold and coach into what they do (active involvement with support). They are often doing reading work they cannot necessarily yet do on their own. Then I make a *second* teaching point based on what I've seen, and send them off to continue this work in their independent reading (the link). I ask them to continue using this strategy, and to plan to meet again the next day or the day after. The next day, we begin the strategy lesson with a time to share and discuss their efforts to incorporate the strategy into their ongoing work (the follow-up) and then I tell them what I've noticed and what I want to teach (the connection) ... and the cycle continues.

In my eyes, these strategy lessons are much like minilessons. Just as I avoid "pop around" minilessons that mention one strategy one day and an entirely different one the next day, I try to follow a single line of thought during and between strategy lessons. Perhaps I'm working with youngsters who are reading early chapter books, like *Pinky and Rex,* and I find they are stymied by the specialized vocabulary. They can read familiar, one-syllable regular words they meet repeatedly but are less well equipped when it comes

to *goalie, pennant,* and *referee* or *medieval, joust,* and *armor.* With these read-ers, I might begin a strategy lesson with a little lesson instead of, or in addi-tion to, an introduction.

I recently told a group of readers that when they were younger they had done picture walks to anticipate how the plot of their book might go, but that lately I had noticed that they didn't tend to look over books much before they started to read. "In a way, this makes sense, because there aren't as many pic-tures any more, are there?" I said. "And the pictures don't spell out the plot of the story." But then I explained that the pictures can signal when a book has a special theme or setting. "Knowing the special theme or setting can help you with hard words in the text," I said. To illustrate my point, I showed chil-dren a book about getting dogs ready for a dog show, "Just looking through this book, I can see it may contain words like grooming, shears, and sham-poo," I said. I asked the group of readers to look through a couple of books and try to discern from the pictures whether the books had specialized top-ics. One was about soccer, another about dinosaurs, and another, about sum-mer camp. "When you look over a book and see that it's about a special topic,"

I said, "it helps to think, 'So what particular words are there, related to this topic, that I can expect to meet in this book?' You may need to go to someone who knows about the topic—dinosaurs or medieval times or soccer—to get help." Because our particular *Pinky and Rex* book focused on soccer, we brainstormed the soccer words they might expect to encounter and then read a few pages in the book to see whether this word work helped. "Stop when you get to page 9," I said, "and look back. Mark any of the words that caused you difficulty as you read with a Post-it note. Then we'll talk about them."

During that day's strategy-lesson, my coaching focused on helping children use their knowledge of books' subjects to work with difficult words; the teaching point at the end of that day's session took this further. The group ended with children pulling out their independent reading books to see if any of these books used a specialized vocabulary. At the beginning of the next day's strategy lesson, I asked, "So did any of you use that strategy during your independent reading?" The children said the problem was that their independent reading books had no pictures to lean on during their previews. "That's exactly what I thought we'd work on today," I said, passing out multiple copies of a short story about an astronaut (although I didn't tell them this was the topic). "This text has no pictures either. Would you work in partners to see if you can still use the strategy of imagining some of the topic-specific vocabulary words you might meet?" I said.

Strategy lessons can feel almost like miniature reading workshops with small groups. In any one strategy lesson there is time for the minilesson, the reading time, the coaching and the share session. In both guided reading and strategy lessons, we explicitly teach a small group of readers. Because the teaching point in guided-reading sessions tends to arise from a difficulty readers encounter as they read the text, the teaching point in guided reading often gives readers strategies for dealing with difficulties as they read a text. I have not often seen teachers use guided reading to teach a reader to envision the world of a text, to build ideas relating one text to another, to take notes which reflect the reader's understanding of the big ideas in a nonfiction article. In our classrooms, teachers are more apt to use strategy lessons rather than guided-reading sessions as the forum for teaching higher-level comprehension skills. I have recently led strategy lessons sessions to support children's work with the following:

- *Making inferences about characters.* The text may not *say* that a character was inventive, but as readers we're expected to make inferences about the character's personality based on what the character does.

- *Summarizing and accumulating.* If the text tells about a series of hardships a character endures, the reader needs to be able to retell these hardships in all their detail but also to take a step back and say, "For the first half of the story, the character is faced with one challenge after another and each time, his wits help him escape at the last moment!" Readers need to be able to see the big picture of what's happening in the text.

- *Understanding that what a character says may not be true.* We need to realize that the narrator's comments represent one person's point of view and not an objective truth. When a big brother calls his baby sister "greedy" because she plays with his toys, readers aren't meant to accept *as fact* that the baby sister is greedy. When the fox tells the Gingerbread Man to climb up on his nose and ride safely there, readers are expected to know that the fox isn't necessarily trustworthy.

Even with beginning readers, we often choose to lead strategy lessons rather than guided-reading sessions. That is, we organize small group work for the purpose of coaching readers in a particular strategy. Especially when working with beginning readers on strategies for dealing with the tricky parts in a text, there can be a thin line between guided reading and strategy lessons. When Kathy Collins wanted to help a group of children use the beginning letters of a word to figure out the word, she chose a PM Starter book, *Looking Down,* a level C book, because it followed a pattern but with word changes on each page. The pictures were a bit ambiguous, so she knew the children would need to rely on sources of information other than the pictures and the book's pattern to figure out the words. Looking over the book, she anticipated some of the difficulties her children might encounter just as she would do to prepare for guided reading. For example, the first page said, "I can see my mom. She is cleaning the car." Kathy knew *cleaning* could be ambiguous. Would children read *washing?* The next pages said, "I can see my dad. He is digging in the garden. I can see my sister. She is reading a book." Kathy wondered what her children would do with the word *garden.* Would they lean on the picture only and read the word as *dirt?* Kathy gathered the group around her and began introducing the book as if this were a guided-reading lesson. "The title of this book is *Looking Down.* It is about a girl who sits in a tree and watches the things the people in her family are doing."

"It is like she is spying," Daniel said.

"Yeah, kind of," Kathy said, as she opened to the first page. Kathy had chosen this page as a context for teaching the strategy of today's small group work. "Let's take a look at this picture. What do you notice?"

"The girl is looking down at her mom," Sabrina said.

"Her mom is washing the car," Langston added.

"You know, that's what I thought was going on too, until I looked at the words. I started to read it like this: I can see my mom. She is washing (pause) …"

"Hey, that can't be washing," Daniel and Angelika said simultaneously.

"That is what I thought. Washing starts with a *w* and this word doesn't. So I had to back up and try again. She is /cl//cl/ cleaning the car. Does *cleaning* work?" (Kathy has separated off all the consonants before the vowel, calling this the beginning-of-the-word. We do this so as to support children's inclination to separate words by onset and rime as in f/ew, tr/y, b/ack.)

"Yeah," all the children said.

"You know, when you read, you have to pay close attention to the first few letters of the word. Sometimes you might think the word is one thing, like *washing*, but when you look closely at the word it really has to be something else, like *cleaning*. Can you do that?"

The kids were confident that they could. Kathy handed out the books and moved among them, stopping alongside each of the readers as they read in low whispers. She got to Daniel as he read, "I see my dad. He is digging the dirt." He paused for a second before he turned that page. Kathy pointed to *garden*. "Could that word be *dirt*?" she asked, keeping her eyes on the page.

"Oopsie," Daniel said. "*Dirt* starts with another letter."

"Yeah, let's back up. He is digging in the …"

"He is digging the /g/ /gar/ garden." Daniel read this time.

"I was on this page [I can see my sister. She is reading a book.]" Angelika said to Kathy, "I thought it was her mom again, but this word isn't *mom,* so I said *sister* and it was *sister.*"

"Angelika, wow. You looked at the picture but you also looked really hard at the word too. It helped."

"Yeah, because it says, 'I can see my sister, not my mom. She is reading a book.'"

"Great job. Keep going."

Langston, meanwhile, seemed stuck. He was looking hard at the page about the grandfather, which read, "I can see my grandfather. He is sweeping the path." Then he added, "I'm stuck here on this word," pointing to the word *path*. Kathy looked at the word and waited until he said more.

"I think it is *sidewalk* but it can't be because it starts with a *p* and *sidewalk* is a long word," Langston told Kathy.

"Nice thinking, Langston. Let's try something else. /PPPaaa/ how about *path?* Would that work?" Kathy asked.

"He is sweeping the path." Langston reads, "Yep, that is *path,* for sure."

When the group reassembled, Kathy said, "I can't believe how much you guys used that strategy of looking at the beginning of the word. On this page, Daniel thought it was going to say *dirt,* but he knew it couldn't be *dirt* ..."

"It is *garden,*" they all said, except Sabrina, who said she'd thought it said *ground.*

"Great guess, Sabrina. *Garden* and *ground* both start with *g,* but *ground* starts with *gr* together to make the /gr/ sound. This is like /gar/ not /gr/." Kathy wrote *garden* and *ground* on the dry erase board. "When you are reading on your own, I want you to be sure that you don't use just the picture to help you. Today, keep focused on the word too and notice the beginning of it. Take this book home tonight and read it to a grown-up. Tomorrow we'll talk again about whether you are using the letters to help you read, okay." Kathy sent them off with a copy of *Looking Down.*

The Choice Between Strategy Lessons and Guided Reading

Just as a doctor, architect, or mechanic reaches for a particular tool to accomplish a particular purpose, teachers of reading also make choices among available tools. My colleagues and I find that frequently we choose between leading a guided-reading group and leading a strategy lesson (Goodman and Burke, 1985). The two structures are similar but they have important differences.

OUR GUIDED READING GROUPS	OUR STRATEGY LESSONS
We gather a group of children who are able to read about the same level of text.	We gather a group of children who would benefit from help with a similar strategy and can do some work (easily or only with our support) with the shared text we've chosen. If we're teaching a strategy such as note-taking, the text might be somewhat challenging for some children and easy for others, but they can all read it and all need help with note-taking.

The group of readers usually works with a challenging text. The group reads one challenging text today, another one tomorrow.

A text is chosen because it allows children to develop and practice a strategy. If the strategy involves reading with expression, for example, the text might well be an easy one. That is, the difficulties might not center around word-solving through a difficult text, but might instead involve doing challenging work with an easy text. The relationship between one strategy lesson and the next is more apt to involve students working with increasing independence and sophistication rather than them necessarily working with texts of increasing difficulty.

The guided-reading session begins with the teacher giving a book introduction, overviewing the text, and then helping children with unfamiliar vocabulary words.

A teacher may or may not opt to do a book introduction and to use new vocabulary words in ways which help readers with them, depending both on whether the text is challenging enough to require this and depending on the point of the lesson. Children may, for example, be rereading a familiar text, in which case a book introduction would be unnecessary, or they may be studying ways to orient themselves to an unfamiliar text. A strategy lesson begins then, not with a book introduction, but with the teacher naming the strategy and then teaching (often through a brief demonstration) and then inviting children to try the strategy. Strategy lessons resemble minilessons.

(continued)

The teacher observes children reading in the midst of the guided-reading session and develops a teaching point out of what she sees.

The teacher enters a strategy lesson having already decided on "a teaching point" (although we call it "a strategy"). The initial assessment doesn't happen in the group but before it. Teachers observe readers in independent reading, book clubs, guided-reading sessions, etc. and in more formal assessments, and organize series of strategy lessons with a goal in mind.

The teacher doesn't mention the teaching point until the final minutes of the guided reading session. The "teaching point" is taught through discussion, brief work on a white board, and references back to the problematic part of the text. After the teaching point has been made, the guided reading session is over. There may not be opportunities to watch how readers use the teaching point as they read.

The teacher *begins* the strategy lesson by making "a teaching point," then demonstrates it and scaffolds children to use the strategy and then watches them as they use the strategy, coaching into what they do, and then makes one more additional teaching point based on what the teacher sees. The next day's strategy lesson builds upon today's just as a string of minilessons build upon each other.

Variations on Strategy Lessons

There are two important variations on the strategy lessons I have described. First, sometimes our strategy lessons do not require that each child sets aside his or her independent reading in order to work with a shared text. For example, if I see several third graders pointing as they read their chapter books, I might call them together and tell them what I noticed, suggest they have probably graduated from needing to point at the words as they read, and ask them to resume reading their independent books, this time without using their fingers as place holders. I would watch, intervene when I saw a finger slide back onto the page or a child began to subvocalize rather than point, and after a few minutes I would ask the readers to talk about how it had felt to read without pointing. Before long, the group would disperse. In a similar way, if I led a strategy lesson designed to help readers orient themselves to a text before they read it or to generate predictions as they read, I might ask them to practice the strategy using their own independent reading books.

Another common variation on strategy lessons is that sometimes our minilessons are whole-class strategy lessons. I recently led a whole-class strategy lesson designed to encourage students to read diagrams and charts in their nonfiction texts. For the month, these fourth graders had been asked to read nonfiction books of their choice during independent reading time. I used an overhead projector to enlarge one nonfiction text, thought aloud as I read, and then invited students to name and reflect on the strategies they saw me using. Then I asked students to continue reading the text, working in partners with one of them reading and thinking aloud as they had seen me do and the other partner researching the reader's strategies. Soon I had sent children back to their independent nonfiction reading with instruction to pay special attention to the charts in their books.

That day as I moved among the readers, it was clear to me that some of them needed additional support if they were going to read the charts and diagrams in their texts. Soon I had gathered a small group of similar readers together for some small group work with a text I had chosen. I began this work with an introduction and a preview of the challenging words and concepts in the upcoming text. Then I talked about and modeled and invited children to join me in reading a diagram. Was I leading a guided reading group, a strategy lesson, or a hybrid of the two? Sometimes I am not certain where to draw the line between one configuration and the next. I end up shrugging my shoulders. "Oh well. *Whatever* it is, it is good teaching." And that, of course, is the point.

Phonics and Word Study in the Primary Grades

11

It was the fourth day of kindergarten and already Renée Dinnerstein's children knew they were at the center of life in Room 239. The children's names filled the "Welcome Easel" inside the doorway; they turned plastic tubs into personal cubbies, milk cartons into private mailboxes, and best of all, folders into their own writing portfolios. On the "Proud Wall" their names proclaimed their ownership of drawings, photographs, and maps. By now, the children had taken attendance with their names and played chant games with their names and sung songs with their names. It was time to begin a yearlong (and life-long) love affair with letters, sounds, and words, and for Renée, there was no question but that the most intimate and celebratory place to begin was with a study of names.

Teaching Letters to Kindergarteners Using Words That Matter

Drawing from the work of Pat Cunningham (1995), Renée began her "star-names" unit by gathering her children in a circle and giving each child a tagboard name sign. "I'm going to give you each a very special word. When you get your word, read it to yourself, then to your neighbor," Renée said. A minute later, interrupting the buzz, she said, "Hold up your beautiful name signs." Renée held her own name sign under her chin and looked out at the circle of children, who followed her lead. "Let's admire them!" Then, acting as if she was almost one of the kids, Renée said, "Wait a minute! Your name,

197

Victoria, is soooo long! So's Evanna's name! You are right. Her's is long too," Renée said, and soon Evanna, Victoria, and their names were standing together beside Renée. The room buzzed with children pointing to and counting the letters in *Victoria* and *Evanna.* "Mine's little!" Nils said, and now the class marveled that yes, indeed, Nils had a much shorter name than did Evanna or Victoria. Renée then asked her whole class to divide up into little clusters and to look at each other's names and talk for a few minutes about whatever they noticed. Before long, Renée had collected all the name signs "for a very special reason."

The next day the star-name ritual began in earnest. As the children watched with bated breath, Renée drew one name from the basket (Renée readily confesses that she secretly peeks into in the basket and makes a point of not drawing out an especially irregular name like Chloe or Phonicia until much later in the unit). Renée held up the name she'd drawn and each of the children looked at it thinking, "Is that me?"

"Look, it starts with a *J*. /J/" Renée said, pointing to the *J* in *Jacob.* "Will the *J* children stand up?" Among New York City school children, *J* seems to be the first initial of choice. Soon Juniper, Jordy, Jazmine, John, James, and Jacob had all popped to their feet. "This name starts with a *J,*" Renée said, referring to the name card she had drawn that day. "So it could be *J*uniper, or *J*ordy, or *J*azmine, or *J*ohn, or *J*ames, *but* it says …"

By this time, Jacob was very sure of himself. "Jacob!" he announced, finishing his teacher's sentence, and Renée nodded, "It does say *Jacob.*"

"Jacob, can you come up and sit in our special star-name chair?" As Renée wrote *Jacob* across a purple construction paper star, she said the letters aloud, and some children joined in. Before long, these kindergarten children will join Renée in saying the letters of the star-name as she writes them, but for now, this simple ritual poses serious challenges. She pinned the star bearing Jacob's name onto him like a medal of honor, one he wore all day long.

"Let's read this name," Renée said, and as she pointed to the name on the star, the class chorally read, "Jacob." Renée then pointed to the name on the tagboard she'd drawn from the bag and the class again read "Jacob." Soon the class had clapped the name (two-claps for the two syllables) and counted the letters (five) and said the names of the letters and gathered observations about the letters. On this first day, one child noticed that the *c* was almost like the *o,* only with a piece missing. Tara pointed to the *a* in Jacob. That was the extent of her remarks until Renée elicited from her the observation that she and Jacob both had an *a* in their names.

Although these observations were simple ones, for these kindergartners this is important work. Once children know even the *names* of letters, they will already know a lot about the sounds letters make. As the days go by, the ritual of noticing things about the letters in the star-names will become more elaborate. A list of all the children's names hangs on the wall near Renée in the meeting area, and before long Renée might respond to Tara's efforts to highlight the *a* in Jacob by saying "What other names have an *a* in them? Can you hear the /a/ sound? Let's say the names, *Jācob, Āmy, Jāmes.* But *Tara* sounds different, doesn't it? So the *a* makes different sounds."

Back on the rug, once the children had noticed a few features of the name *Jacob,* Renée took the large tagboard name sign and cut the letters up, handing one letter to each of five children who popped to their feet and stood proudly holding them in a jumbled line. From left to right, the letters read *cobJa.* "How does it look?" Renée asked. "Jacob, go back and see what you think." Jacob backed up, eyed the lineup, and said, "It's no good."

Pretending to protest, Renée pointed to the correctly written name on her chart paper and said, "Why not? Don't we have a J?"

The *J* child, fourth in the lineup, waved her letter.

"An *a?*" The *a* child followed suit.

"They are all messed up," Jacob said. Soon a helper had jumped to her feet, and with constant glances toward the name on the easel, she steered her friends and their letters into the proper order. Jacob, still standing at the far edge of the circle, eyed the configuration and gave it his nod of approval.

"Are we ready to read it?" Renée asked, and she led the class in what sounded (and felt) rather like a cheerleading cheer. "One, two, three: *Jacob!!!*" The class read the name—and gave their cheer—again and again. By their third cheer, the children holding the letters were so caught up in the spirit of things that they hoisted the letters high in a celebratory way while the room rang with the name *Jacob!*

The next step in the star-names routine was for the class to interview the star. In Renée's class, she and the children always asked the child the same two questions. (This approach eliminated the usual twenty minutes of stalling and pondering as each child thought, "Hmmm, what should I ask?") Because the questions are routine and the answers accumulate, Renée is able to put together a class Big Book with a structure predictable enough to make great early reading material. Jacob was asked, "Do you have any pets?" and "What do you like to draw?" The class watched as Renée recorded his answers on a chart tablet: Jacob has a hamster. Jacob likes to draw his brother.

Next she said, "We're going to go off and draw Jacob. Take a close look at him. What details will you add to your drawing?"

Back at their tables, the children made drawings of Jacob and wrote his name and their own on their pictures. (Renée did not correct their backward and lopsided letters because the class was learning the gist of words and letters rather than perfecting the formation of any one letter.) After a few minutes, she collected the papers. Later that day, Renée put them inside two covers, along with Jacob's answers to the survey, and stapled the pile together to be sent home with the star. "I'm going to read it when I go to sleep!" Jacob said, and Renée smiled to think of the happy dreams he'd have after reading his own name, twenty-six times.

With variations, this ritual is repeated every day for the first few weeks of school in many kindergarten and first-grade classrooms. When a teacher is able to think on her feet in response to what her youngsters notice and wonder about, the work grows in complexity each day. Someone spies an *m* in *Raymond* and in *Carmen.* By mistake (or perhaps not exactly by mistake), the *P* in *Pat* flutters to the floor. John sees the remaining letters and reads, almost to himself, "at." "Guys! Listen to what John just did," the teacher announces, and soon John is up on his feet pointing to the letters 'at' as he reads them.

"At?" the teacher repeats, astonished by John's discovery. "As in '*That* is amazing?' Does Pat have an 'at' in her name?" Before long, the class is gleefully finding other words that contain the sound in Pat's name, such as *mat, sat, Patrick, patty-cake,* and *pattern.*

This star-names work is worthy of being at the heart of a kindergarten phonics unit and perhaps also of an early first-grade phonics unit. There are other equally important approaches to word study, but let me cite some of the reasons I'm enthusiastic about this one, brought to life by Renée Dinnerstein and hundreds of other brilliant teachers like her.

This star-name work beautifully illustrates the importance of helping children develop familiarity with a growing bank of "very important words." There are no words which are more important or closer-to-home than children's own names, and so a name study is a logical place to begin when teaching children about grapho-phonics. But the important thing about Renée's work with star names is not only that she begins in a place of familiarity, with words that have as much meaning as possible for children, but also that the tone of Renée's phonics work, like the tone of all her teaching, invites children to bring their energy, ideas, and lives into the inquiry.

I want school to say to children, "Welcome. Come in. You can feel at home here. Bring your life and your ideas and your energy to this place. We are going to have a blast here, exploring lots of totally cool things together. One of the neatest things we'll explore here will be letters and words. Pull in. Look at this word. Don't you love it?" Because I want this message to be heard loud and clear, by every child, I want letters and words to be a cause for our celebration, exploration, invention, talk, and laughter, and I want letters and words to be all about community. Although there will also be more individualized phonics work, and phonics will certainly be incorporated into ongoing reading and writing, I think it is important for the community to pull together around a shared exploration into print.

As this chapter proceeds, we will explore other tenets of phonics instruction. Children need opportunities to construct their own understandings of sound-letter correspondences and of spelling patterns. These understandings will develop best when the learning students do as they write also becomes a resource for them as they read.

After we consider ways of helping kindergarteners construct an understanding of phonics and after we watch kindergarteners use and extend this knowledge as they write, we'll consider how these tenets play out in first-grade classrooms. The discussion of first grade will, of course, be relevant to some kindergarteners and vice versa.

Providing Opportunities for Kindergarteners to Construct their Understandings of Phonics

In their word-study time, Renée and her kindergarteners progressed from star-names to a giant ABC exploration project. Renée actually set the stage by placing a great premium at the start of the year on science explorations. In September, Renée put a number of wild and wonderful science objects (nests and ant farms and rocks) on an Explorations Table and taught her children to observe these treasures with explorers' eyes, to record their observations in detailed drawings, and to talk with each other about patterns they saw and questions they had. Then, after five or six weeks of star-names work, Renée put away the science objects and told her children, "We'll have to think about something *really* fascinating to study next." A few days later, Renée brought an idea to the kids. "What if we did an alphabet exploration?" Of course, the idea felt irresistible and awesome. "What could we put out on the table," she mused, "if we were studying the alphabet?"

One child had an ABC puzzle at home that he was willing to bring to school. Another child offered to contribute an alphabet stamp and a stamp pad. Several children suggested that the magnetic letters from the math center could be moved to the alphabet exploration table. "Wait!" Renée said, as if carried along by their excitement. "I have some alphabet stencils at home that my daughter used to use. Do you suppose we could include those?" Over the next couple of days, children brought in sponge letters, an old family typewriter, and a Junior Scrabble game.

Of course, the class could have admired all of the objects in the display without learning much and the collection could end up making no difference in their minds, so the next part of the inquiry was to gather children together around the question, "Can we research the alphabet like we researched birds' nests and ant farms?" Because Renée's children had recorded what they saw in their science investigations and made little books of their drawings, they quickly invented the idea of making books full of their observations on the alphabet. With prompting from Renée, a small group was soon using stencils, stamps, and drawings to collect ways to write A's, B's, and C's. They wrote a cursive *C* and a decorative curling *C* and an italic *C*. Many children made name books, giving one page to each letter in their name and lots of pictures (and some writing) of words beginning with that particular letter. Another child made a collection on one page of letters with tails, on another page of letters with tunnels, and on yet another page of letters with bumps. Still another child drew pictures of all the *m* words she could collect. Someone else turned alphabet letters into animals by adding feet and feathers.

At first this ABC investigation was a project the whole class undertook together. It felt like a mini-workshop, with time up front each day for children to learn about the interesting things they could do with the letters or to talk about a particular sound-letter correspondence. Then Renée provided time for everyone to work within small groups, each dedicated to a particular enterprise. One group wrote name books, another sorted letters into categories such as letters with tails and letters with bumps, others made alphabet books, or used magnetic or spongy letters and paint to make names and other words. Renée's alphabet study offered opportunities for her class to be inventive within the system of the alphabet. They created things to do and made discoveries along the way. Amber and Paul noticed that the letters *a* and *g* can look differently sometimes. When Jazmine and Lisa were making kids' names out of scrabble letters, they realized that nobody had *q* in their name but lots of kids names began with *j*. They decided to check to see if this was true in other kindergarten classes.

Later, the ABC exploration became one activity among many during exploration time in Renée's classroom. While some children did dramatic reenactments of *The Three Little Pigs* and some painted pictures, others explored the alphabet. Since she often has a paraprofessional or a parent involved during exploration time (choice time) in her classroom, either Renée or another adult often joined the alphabet work. The presence of an adult can bring out wonderful discussions about letters, sounds, words, and language; but just messing about with the alphabet is also marvelous for children. In this fashion, Renée moved between whole-class and small-group investigations, and taught her children that they could pore over words and letters with the same curiosity and awe they brought to their investigations of ants and worms.

This ABC study illustrates a core belief in our work with phonics and word study: children need opportunities to actively construct a knowledge of phonics. We teach children not only about a particular system—the alphabet—but also about how they can invent ways to explore this system. This work generates discoveries that spill into many other parts of the day. We want children to see print everywhere: we want them to notice the initials on our briefcase and then to consider what their own initials are; we want them to tell Marisol that her *M* is like the golden arched *M* at McDonald's and to see that the *S* in Sam's name is also on a red stop sign outside the school.

People often ask whether there is a preferred sequence for learning letters, and the answer is that the easiest letter to learn is the first initial of your first name! In general, I'd teach by immersion in the alphabet rather than by covering each letter in sequence, but if I did take the whole class into a study of a few letters (and it makes sense to do this, knowing children will soon see and learn letters from every corner of the world) and I had to pick one letter to teach first, it would be *M*. *M* meets all the qualifications. The name of the letter contains its sound (unlike, for example, a *W*). We can stretch out the *M* sound without necessarily making sounds that don't belong to that letter (if you try to stretch out a *K* or a *T,* for example, you find yourself saying vowels, not the consonant itself). The upper- and lowercase *M* are almost the same. The golden arches remind us all that an *M* makes the sound at the start of McDonald's! And best of all, once a child knows the *M,* that child can write some of the biggest messages of his or her life: *Mom* and *me!* Learning the alphabet means accumulating a remarkable network of knowledge about particular letters. A letter has a shape and a name, it makes a sound or two, it can appear in different ways (upper- or lowercase, cursive or print), and it can be found alone or surrounded by other letters in a word.

For Renée and the other teachers with whom I work, alphabet or word-work centers do not replace independent reading, and it would be highly unusual for children to work independently in alphabet or word centers while teachers led one reading group after another. It is also important to note that Renée does not spend time each day carefully detailing an intricate series of activities with phonics. Instead, she teaches her children a few generic things they can do over and over with letters, and then the children themselves invent and improvise from these activities. But most of all, they talk about and notice and categorize and combine and draw and write with letters.

There is nothing sacrosanct about either the star-names or the ABC explorations I've described. After completing a cycle of star-names work, Renée could, for example, have followed Pat Cunningham's advice and gathered food labels (a Cheerios box, the label from a milk carton) and led children through a sequence of work with food labels that paralleled the earlier work with children's names. Alternatively, children could have studied the environmental print in their classroom and school. When working with the names of children, the names of food, or the words in their world, any of these words would be complicated material indeed if the challenge was for five-year-olds to learn to spell these words accurately, but this early work is not yet about learning to spell. It is, rather, designed to immerse children in discussions of words, letters, letter-names, etc. and to help children begin to recognize these words when they occur in meaningful contexts. Although a five year old child won't know about the 'ch' blend in Cheerios, she *can* 'read' the label on a Cheerios box, and with support, she can learn to see the label as containing letters which can be discussed. The features of these letters can be noticed. The letters can be copied. Each letter can be named, too, and counted. There is a beat to the word Cheerios—(Cheer-i-os)—that which can be felt. As children say these words, and as they name and notice features of the letters, they are developing knowledge which will be foundational to their later work as readers and writers. More than this, they are learning that everywhere they turn, their world is filled with print that is meaningful and worthy of study and attention.

It is not an accident that both the star-names work and the environmental word work brings children to print which is contextualized into meaningful material. In a kindergarten classroom, we would not hurry to divorce the milk label from its carton, or to take words out of the context of a beloved poem in order to list them alphabetically on a word wall. For at least the first few months of kindergarten, we'd sit the Cheerios box on the chalk tray and read its label but would not ask children to read from even a short list of sight-vocabulary words. If we wanted to teach our children a sight-vocabulary word like Mom (and this is a good one because its meaning is concrete and real for children), we'd showcase the word first as it's found *within* a page of "Mom is cooking, Mom is driving …."

Many teachers want to teach a few high frequency words to kinder-garteners. We tend to do this by first reading aloud a beloved book over and over. The stories and poems children read with special pleasure will yield words worth coming to know well. Cheryl Tyler's kindergartners loved one page, above all, from Joy Cowley's book, *Mrs. Wishy Washy.* With squeals of joy these children read and reenacted the page on which Mrs. Wishy Washy orders the muddy animals into the bath. These children loved "'Into the tub you go,' she said," and they kept a duplicated copy of the page close by when they wrote, using it as a personalized bank of known words. Many educators hang the whole-class collection of known words onto a giant chart and refer to that chart as a word wall. These alphabetic listing of the high frequency words that a class of children are expected to know are a mainstay in many first, second and third grade classrooms but kindergarten teachers often prefer to keep these words contextualized. Cheryl, for example, didn't remove the words *into, the, tub, you,* etc. from the beloved page of *Mrs. Wishy Washy,* hanging those words alpha-betically on the wall under the appropriate alphabet letter. Instead, she hung the page of the book, illustrations and all, onto the wall.

Helping Children Become Word Solvers as Readers by Helping them Become Word Solvers as Writers

Always, we want children to know that letters give us word power. So alongside direct work with the alphabet, children need to be putting this knowledge to use as they write. "We're all of us writers," I told Renée's kindergartners one mid-September day. "Every day in this classroom, we'll put onto the page the things we do and love and wonder about." To demonstrate, I drew a picture of my dog, Tucker, on chart paper at the easel. Then, as if the idea had just dawned on me as I drew Tucker, I said, "Tucker got lost in the woods" and I added a tree to the paper. "I had to look for her," I said and added myself to the paper. "Now I'd better write *Tucker,*" I said, and as the class watched, I repeated the name to myself quietly, listening to the sounds. "Tucker, Tucker, /T/-ucker." I isolated the /T/ sound, and the children watching me knew I was thinking, "So how do I write /T/?" By this time, children will often intervene to suggest that I write the letter *T,* but on this day they were quiet. I glanced over at the list of children's names on the wall and said, "Wait a minute! /T/ucker /T/omas! The same. I'm going to write a *T.*" Then I said, "But it's *not* Tomas. I gotta put down some more letters." Before long (with reference to Robert's name) I'd written *Tkr.* Next I labeled the picture of myself, writing *me.*

Teachers will need to decide whether on this, the first day of a kindergarten writing workshop, they feel it necessary to fill in all the letters of a word. I left *Tucker* as *Tkr* (using lowercase letters except for the first, because lowercase is what children will find in the books they read and it's what I hope they'll use when they write), because I wanted to demonstrate the process of listening to and recording the sounds I hear in a word. After stretching out *Tucker* and recording the sounds, I moved on to other items in my drawing, saying *me* and *sun* slowly, putting onto the paper the sounds the children probably heard. Then I said, "Today, all of you can draw a picture of whatever you like to do or whatever you know about, and then *you* can write."

As I moved among the children, I helped some of them produce print to label their pictures and I encouraged them to help each other. Soon children were saying things like, "Grass. How do you spell /gr?/" Sometimes children's collaborative efforts led to misspellings, but if they said a word slowly, isolating chunks of it such as the gr blend, matched the sound to letters, recorded the letters, reread what they'd written, voiced the remainder of the word and again said the next chunk slowly, they will have done a lot that is right.

Some children will not yet have had enough experience with written language, or with making rhyming words and stretching words out and hearing sounds at the beginnings or ends of words to be able to isolate, hear, and record sounds in the words they want to write. In time, the whole-class work with star-names and the interactive writing and shared reading will give these children more resources to draw upon. It will also be helpful for these children to be in a writing workshop in which their peers are listening to and talking about the sounds they hear in words. Meanwhile, of course, writing is also about constructing good stories. We'll probably begin by asking children to draw and perhaps label one picture, then we'll help children say more about what they've drawn and add onto the picture. Soon we'll help them say enough that they need to staple more pages onto their initial paper. Within a week, kindergarteners will usually approach writing expecting to make a book. Even if they aren't yet writing words, they'll learn a lot about story structures and language, and about how books go front to back, top to bottom from doing this. By early October, I'd want all my kindergartners to use what they know about the alphabet to label their drawings. Soon I'd put a list of class names (together with class portraits) inside each child's writing folder so children could use them as a reference in figuring out the spelling of *Tucker* from what they know about *Tomas*.

Once Renée's children had worked for a few months with letter names, Renée gave them each an alphabet chart to keep near them as they wrote. This became a text for shared reading. They'd chime along together reading "A, apple …" We often divide this chart into three sections so it appears less overwhelming.

As we confer with youngsters during the daily writing workshop, we help them use the alphabet chart as a resource. First we help the child hear a sound in a word. "So this is your mom?" we say, pointing to the child's picture. "Can you say that slowly, stretching it out?"

"Mmoooomm," the child says.

"What sound do you hear first?" we ask, and soon the child is looking on her alphabet chart for the letter that makes an /m/ sound. "Try the middle section of your chart," we say.

All of this—even the challenge to stretch the word *Mom* out, saying it slowly—is a critical part of phonics education. Researchers emphasize how important it is for children to develop phonemic awareness in kindergarten. Many children need practice and help in hearing an /m/ at the start and the /o/ in the middle of *mom*. A five-year-old once asked Martha Horn, "How do you spell Santa?" Martha helped the child say the word slowly, listening for the sounds. "Sssaaanta, Sssannta," the child said.

"What sounds do you hear?" Martha asked. Cocking her head slightly, and repeating "Ssssanta," the little girl said, "I hear, 'ho ho ho!'"

As kindergarten children continue to draw and write each day in the writing workshop, they begin to use not only initial and final consonants but also a smattering of vowels in order to represent the sounds they hear in words. Samples of children's writing provide dramatic evidence of what a child knows and can do with sound-letter correspondence, spelling patterns, sight words, and inflectional endings. Jose's piece of writing, for example, shows that he has a good sense of the top-to-bottom, left-to-right orientation and that, for the most part, he leaves spaces between words (below).

When I learned how to walk I walked off the couch. I to say, how I doing?

Jose has command of some high frequency words (*I, how, do*) and is almost there with some others (*th* for *the, sey* for *say*). He hypothesizes that words have consonants and a vowel and can generally discern the placement of each. He isn't afraid to write words he probably hasn't seen in print (*cowt* for *couch*). He is beginning to use word endings, although he uses the *t* he hears rather than *-ed* for walk*ed,* and separates the *-ing* from the base word in *doing.*

Sometimes when we look at samples of children's writing, we find it hard to discern the logic behind their approximated spellings. When my son Evan was in second grade, his spelling of long words was alarmingly chaotic. It wasn't until I watched him as he spelled *ridiculous* that I realized what his problem was. *"Ridiculous,"* he said, and quickly wrote the primary sounds he heard in the whole word (r-i-k-u-l-s). Realizing he needed more letters, Evan again said the whole word, "ridiculous, ridiculous," and now added more letters onto the word until the spelling looked like this: "rikulsdicos." Starting in kindergarten, we need to show children the step-by-step process of breaking a word into constituent parts, writing the letters for one part, rereading these, saying the next part, and then recording the letters for that part.

Although Evan had difficulty because he didn't segment long, complex words, when children read, they sometimes have quite the opposite problem.

Some children try to read by sounding out words letter by letter. If a child wants to read *train,* instead of chunking the word into /tr/ and /ain/, she may attempt to sound out /t/ /r/ /a/ /i/ /n/. Voicing the /t/ in isolation from the whole word and moving in a left-to-right sequence, she ends up voicing /tah/ for /t/ and /rah/ for /r/ and is consequently left trying to blend tah-rah-ah-ih-nah together into a word. It's important to show children that we solve words by relying on a range of flexible strategies. First we rely on meaning: "The boy rode the (*something*) to the city." We know that the problematic word represents a kind of transportation. Next, we usually try to recognize the word or parts of the word. Later in this chapter I'll show ways in which we help children use spelling patterns or word chunks as they read and write. For now, it is enough to say that if we don't have a visual memory for the word, we often have it for a chunk of the word (in *train* we've seen *rain,* in *routine* we've seen *tine*). It is important for a reader to ask, "What do I know that can help me with this word?" We also rely on our knowledge of the meanings of words (*electric, electricity* and *electrician* are spelled similarly despite their different sounds because of their shared meaning base). The English language is not phonemically regular; an overreliance on phonics is a common trademark of poor spellers and word solvers. Phonetic spellers may spell *action* as *aksion* and *always* as *allways.*

During the daily writing workshop, children are totally involved in work with sound-letter correspondences. How ironic (and sad) it is when schools are so frantic to support early reading that they bypass the writing workshop altogether! Along with many other researchers, Dombey and Moustafa point out that "In most classrooms, learning to write is today a basic way in which children learn about letter-sound relationships and about the varied ways in which the spelling patterns of English relate to its sound patterns" (p. 3). In the writing workshop, children stretch words out, isolate chunks of sounds, relate the sounds in one word to the sounds in another word, and search their memories, the alphabet chart, and the word wall to match sounds with letters. Once they've encoded a chunk of sounds into print, they reread what they've written thus far and continue supplying more of the needed letters. The writing workshop could almost be retitled "The Phonics Workshop" except that, of course, so much else is being accomplished as well.

In addition to the writing workshop (and I should add, totally separate from the writing workshop), we also work with kindergarten and first-grade children in very brief interactive writing sessions. These may be part of a thematic study (or social studies) or part of general life in the classroom. "Today, class, I thought we'd write *labels* for different parts of our room," I recently said to a group of kindergarten children. "What should we say here?" I asked, pointing to the paints. "Paints!" the children announced in unison. "Okay," I said. "So let's say that word to ourselves like writers do," and I turned to rehearse the writing we'd soon do on a large piece of oaktag. "Paints," I said, again and ran my hand from left to right as if anticipating how the word would go. "Paints," I said, with the class joining in. "Sarah, where will we start the writing?" As Sarah got to her feet to point to the upper left-hand corner of the paper, I said to the class, "Point to where we'll start our writing." I involved Sarah and the rest of the class in the question of "where will we begin the word" only because I knew this was still an issue for almost a third of these children. Weeks from now, most of these children will not need us to talk about where we begin a piece of writing.

Now I repeated the word *paints* with children chiming in as I did. "Paints. What sound do you hear first?" Hands rose. "James, can you help us?" To the rest of the class I said, "Tell your partner a child's name that starts the same as /*p*/aints." While the children muttered "Peter," I quickly repeated to James, who was now at the easel reaching for the marker pen, *"Paints."* He said, "It's like Peter,*"* and I asked, "Can you point to Peter's name?" The list of names is always hung prominently beside the easel. James pointed correctly and wrote the *p* in *paints*. As James returned to his seat, I said to the class, "Let's read what we have so far." We read /p/ and just as we all said the upcoming sound /$\bar{a}$/, I gestured for Arial to help us. As she started to write, I said to her, "Uppercase or lowercase?" as a reminder. Now I looked at the class and we again reread in unison: p$\bar{a}$. This time I simply added the next two letters so that the word said *pain* and recruited the class to help with the *t* sound, asking children to "write" the letter with their fingers on the carpet while John came to the easel. John made an uppercase *T* and I told him it was partly right and asked for someone to help. With correcting tape, we trimmed the T into a lowercase letter. In a similar manner, we added the final *s*. This kind of interactive writing produces a correct text. Gay Su Pinnell, Andrea McCarrier and Irene Fountas (1999), believe that this allows the text to better serve as reading material for the class. Often the teacher writes portions of words (as I did with *paint*) and also whole words that aren't yet within the children's scope. Once children are more proficient as writers, the teacher will no longer fill in the challenging parts of the text, but will instead write down only the easy parts, doing so without any discussion in order to move things quickly along. On any given day I might label two areas of the classroom or write the first two sentences in a thank-you letter. "Dear Jim, Thank you for the cake. We loved it." Two sentences of interactive writing generally contain more little lessons than children are likely to retain, so I recommend keeping interactive writing sessions under ten minutes in length.

In First Grade, Many of the Words that Matter Most are High Frequency Words

It is important to realize that roughly fifty percent of all the words children encounter as readers and writers can be found on a list of the one hundred most frequently used words. Furthermore, many researchers believe that children who are thriving as readers and writers at the end of first grade usually seem to "just know" most of these one hundred high frequency words. Strong first grade readers recognize these words easily when they encounter them in texts and spell many (but fewer) of them with automaticity (New Standards, 2000). It is also worth noting that when children are learning to read, the fact that they know some high frequency words can anchor the child's work with a line of print, allowing the child to get footholds as she moves along turning print into meaning. Also, researchers have shown that children's knowledge of how to read common words accounts for 95 percent of the unusual words they are able to say correctly (Moustafa, 1995).

I do not think the claims I've just made are particularly debatable. But the implications all this has for instruction *are* debatable. Some people will argue that teachers need to use flash cards or other activities to drill children on high frequency words so they come to know these instantly, anywhere, by sight. Others argue that these words are called high frequency words because they occur especially frequently in the natural texts we encounter as readers and writers, and they argue that first graders who thrive as readers and writers come to know high frequency words because these children use these words often as readers and writers of them. These people will suggest that we teach high-frequency words on an as-needed basis when we see individuals or the whole class struggling to read or spell a word.

I find the second position more theoretically sound. We know children learn language best when using it for real purposes. We know words, for example, are easier to read when they occur in a story than in a list (Goodman, 1965). Why not let children learn these high frequency words as they encounter them in texts that are funny or sad or otherwise, memorable?

Many of us have witnessed first grade classrooms, however, in which the class did shared readings of favorite books and poems, and wrote their own stories, and everyone *expected* that children would come to recognize and eventually to spell high frequency words, when in fact this didn't happen. Many of us, then, guard against this by spending a small amount of time— no more than ten minutes a day—convening the whole class around a very small number of high frequency words.

Usually, this instruction centers around the development of what is called a word wall. Teachers see that children—especially first or second graders—have been using certain high frequency words as readers and writers and decide that with extra attention, children could soon develop automaticity with these words. They call attention to these words (a few at a time) and then post them alphabetically on the wall to be used as a growing resource when children read and write. When high frequency words are introduced and posted, some teachers say, "From this day on, you are accountable for recognizing this word when you read it and for spelling it correctly when you write it." It is probably unrealistic to think we could introduce a high frequency word to a whole class of children one day, practicing it for a few minutes, and from that day on expect members of the class to always spell the word correctly. But if we add a word to the word wall and say, "From this day on, take an extra few minutes needed to spell the word correctly," children would *then* have repeated and note-worthy encounters with the word, and many nudges to alter their approximated spellings so these become more conventional. That is, if I was to teach high frequency words and then post them on the word wall, I'd still expect the real learning would come not from the five or ten minutes I had spent teaching the word but from children encountering that word repeatedly in the midst of their ongoing reading and writing, and using the word wall as a tool to help them recall and use conventional spellings.

I'd begin first grade with a minimal list of words because my first efforts would be to help children value knowing a few words very well. I might early on ask my first graders whether there are some words they just know, words they can read and spell by heart. In one minilesson I said, "You know, there are certain words we just know, like our names. You can read your name anywhere, whether it's big or teeny, and you can spell it with your eyes closed. Are there any words you know that are like that?" Soon the class compiled a short list of about seven high frequency words, like *I, me, mom, go,* that many of the children already knew. We put them in alphabetical order on what would be the word wall. Each week, we add another few words to the word wall.

One day, Lisa Ripperger wrote *every* on the dry erase board. "I've chosen this word because we need to write it everyday," she said. "Everyone, take a close look. What do you notice? Take a few seconds to think about it." Lisa had already given these instructions several times a week, each time with a different word and so her children were adept and efficient at this.

Daniel said, "My mom's name is Eve and it's in the beginning."

"It has vowels." Chelsea said. Lisa asked her to be more specific. "It starts with an *e* and has an *e* inside."

"I see *very* inside of it," added Jesse, "and there's *ever* too." As children shared these observations, Lisa underlined the part of the word described, like the *eve* in *every,* and covered parts, like the first *e,* when Jesse noticed *very.*

"You know what I see?" Lisa asked the class. "I see that sneaky *-er* inside, the *er* that makes /er/ like in Novemb*er,* lett*er,* moth*er ....*" The class started to reel off other words with *-er,* so Lisa told them, "If you notice something else or have other thoughts about this word, tell your partner." As the class did this, a couple of children got up to pass out dry erase boards, and markers, and napkins to each child in preparation for later work spelling *every.*

"Okay, let's get ready to learn this word, so that when we write it or read it, we'll know it by heart." Lisa said, "Look at the word. Everyone. Okay, close your eyes. Who can spell it with their eyes closed?" Lisa called on about eight children who each said, "E-v-e-r-y." The benefit of one child after another spelling the word is that each successive child spells it faster and faster. "Everyone else, spell it out loud," Lisa said to the whole class. A chorus of twenty-five kids spelled *every,* most of them still with their eyes closed. "Okay, let's get ready," Lisa said, "Get your markers out. Eyes this way. Look at the word." The children were clearly used to this routine.

"Say the word."

"Every!!!"

"Spell the word."

"E-v-e-r-y!"

"Okay, write the word!" and Lisa erased the word on her dry erase board. The children immediately wrote the word and held up their own boards to show it.

Meanwhile, Lisa had joined the class, and she too had written *every* on her board. Showing the class her spelling, she said, "Okay, check the word." The children confirmed their spelling by looking at Lisa's word and then their own.

"Clean your boards. Now let's look at the word again."

The class repeated this procedure about three times in very quick succession. Altogether, this part of the lesson took four minutes.

Some words lend themselves to more study, in which case it's necessary to extend the lesson. In the case of *every,* Lisa wanted the children to know about other words in the *every* word family. "You know, boys and girls, *every* has a word family, so if you know *every,* you can also read and write other words. The class listed *everywhere, everybody, everyone,* and *everything.*

Other frequently used words, such as *said,* don't lend themselves to this type of extension. Yet words like *every* and *each* can teach children a huge

amount about spelling patterns. When Lisa's class studied *each* together, they learned that if you can spell and read *each* you can use what you know to spell *teach, beach, reach, peach, teacher,* and so forth.

These are other ways we can help children increase their word power and gain more control over sight words:

- Pause in the midst of the writing workshop to remind writers that they are expected to spell the words on the word wall correctly as well as any others they "just know." We tell children, "Work with your partner. Will the two of you go back and look over your writing and be *sure* you've spelled those words perfectly?"

- If we add new words to the word wall each Monday, we can send home a new cumulative copy of the word wall with the newly added words highlighted. "Use this as your portable word wall," we can tell children, "because once a word is on the word wall you are expected to spell it correctly."

- Ask children to write one of the words (for example, *in, yes, she, or, because, where, again*) in tiny, tiny letters before they go to gym. Or perhaps ask children to write one of these words in huge letters in the sky before they leave at the end of the day, or to whisper the spelling to three friends, or to hide the spelling in a secret place inside their drawing, or to carry the spelling in their pocket, or to teach it to a friend.

- Ask a child to reread his previous writing to see if there are places that can be revised using the sight words (or a particular word) the writer now knows.

- Sit beside a reader and remind her that she already knows one or two of the high frequency words that will appear in the story she will be reading. "You'll find that word *she* again on this page," we'll say. "Can you see it now? Point to it. That's right. Remember, whenever you see *s-h-e,* it says *she.*" We may even say, "Let's glance ahead in the book and see if we see that word again. Yep, there it is! Look at that! And what does it say? Yes, *she.* Whenever you see *s-h-e,* it says *she.*"

Like Renée's star-name work, this spelling work begins by using what students know and encounter constantly in their lives. Equally important, the learning doesn't end when the lesson is over because children learn a self-generating system that allows them to keep learning.

Providing Each First Grader with Opportunities to Construct an Understanding of Spelling Patterns

Once children have begun to know a small collection of words well, it's easy to move to the next step: what they know can give them word power. One thing leads to another, in much the same way that Renée's star-name study led to the children's independent alphabet investigations during the ABC study. For Lisa Ripperger, Kathy Collins, and their first graders, then, their direct-study of words generally includes five or ten minutes of work with a new high frequency word and also five or ten minutes of time exploring spelling patterns and ways to use these as they read and write. Once children know a handful of high frequency words, they will know other words which contain the same high-utility chunks. Lisa, therefore said to her class, "Let's star these words on our work wall—*at* and *like*—because they are words which can give us word power."

About half of the 110 high frequency words contain high utility patterns. Both Pat Cunningham and Diane Snowball encourage teachers to star or sticker some of these generative words. We can then list the words, for example, that *at* helps us spell. But readers and writers are rarely called upon to generate lists of 'at' words. It may be more helpful, then, to follow Cunningham's advice and say to children, "If Evan knows *at*, and he wants to write, which words will *at* help him to spell? 'I sat at the dentist's for a long time?' How will *at* help him to write, 'I lay my sleeping bag out flat and roll it up.'

In Kathy Collins' class, this study began when she noticed Emerson writing a piece about his new bike. During the morning meeting, Kathy said, "You guys, guess what? Today Emerson did the coolest thing. He was writing, *I rode my bike,* but he got stuck on the word *bike.* This is the cool part. I saw him do this." Kathy wrote "I rode my b" and stopped. "Bike," Kathy (playing the part of Emerson) muttered to herself. "Bike." Then as we watched, the idea dawned. "Wait a minute! *Bike—like.*" With a quick glance toward the word wall, Kathy (still playing the part of Emerson) completed the word.

Kathy turned back to the class. "You see! Emerson had word power. He knew *like* and that gave him the power to know *bike.*"

Conor called out, "*Hike,* too."

"Wait a minute!" Kathy said, practically falling out of her seat in excitement. She wrote on chart paper:

like

bike

hike

"Three words out of one, that really is word power," Kathy said as she looked over the list. Of course, by now every child was searching through his or her memory bank trying to add another word to the list. "You know what, if you think of another *-ike* word, put it on a Post-it and stick it to the list. By the end of the day, there was a Post-it that said, "Mike" and one that said "sike" on the list.

Kathy told her class that they would all be working hard like Emerson to get word power. For the next couple of weeks, Kathy spent ten minutes a day working on building word power through work with onsets and rimes. The onset is the initial part of a syllable formed by one or more consonants, and the rime is the vowel and the letters following it. In *Beginning to Read,* Marilyn Adams (1990) lists thirty-seven rimes that make up roughly five hundred primary level words. Kathy's plan was not to teach each one but rather to make her students aware of this system of word building. The very next day, Kathy said, "You know I realized this morning that -*at* can give us lots of word power, kind of how -*ike* helped us with *bike* and *like* and *hike*. If you know -*at,* you also know *cat*." Kathy wrote both words on a narrow strip of chart paper. Her list began like this:

-at

cat

"*Rat,* too," said Abigail.
"Okay, let's add *rat*. How would I spell it?" Kathy asked.
"*R-a-t,*" exclaimed a bunch of kids.
There was a clamor as kids called out all kinds of -*at* words. Together, the class complied a list:

-at

cat

rat

sat

hat

bat

mat

"Wow, you guys. Check this out. I bet there are even more than this. If you think of any, write them on a Post-it and add your word to the list."

By the end of the day, a few Post-its had been stuck to the strip. Right before packing to go home, Kathy told the class that they were great word finders for adding *fat, pat,* and *that* to the list.

Kathy deliberately started with -*at*. The word *cat* is familiar to most children, and she felt that it would be a comfortable way to bring all learners aboard. After a couple of days of doing this as a whole class, Kathy's class had made strip-lists for -*ot, -in, -un, -ate*. Each day, Kathy turned her students loose for five minutes to do more of this work. "Today, will you and your reading partner find as many words for -*op* as you can? Okay, get started," she'd say, and the classroom would become a beehive of energy. Kathy provided each set of partners with a strip of lined paper on which they could record their words. She walked around saying, "Oh, wow, Tina and Django have found ten words so far!" or "Hmmm, Molly and Ben have found this great word [*plop*] that is actually like a sound effect. I wonder if anyone else got that word?"

The children would scramble to figure out as many words as they could, and then they'd meet with sets of partners to compare lists. Debates would rage over whether a particular word was a real word or a nonsense word. "*Blop* could be a name for something, you know!" Emma said to the partners across the table when they told her *blop* didn't count because it was a nonsense word.

Soon, children were adding words to their lists that had the particular rime inside the word, such as *chopper, popcorn,* and *operation.* The concepts of blends and digraphs naturally arose as well. When children composed their lists, they treated blends as if they were more valuable. "Wow, Ray and Talia made *str*ing! What a blend, *s-t-r,* /str/. Did anyone else use a blend?"

"We did. We got *br*ing!" said Tina breathlessly.

"Yeah, and we made *th*ing!" added Raul.

Throughout this work, Kathy and her children stopped to admire the fact that one simple word could give them such power to read and write so many other words. The children began to suggest word families to study. Ryan, the resident chess expert of Room 1-206, approached Kathy with this bit of teaching advice. "You know," he said, "a good spelling pattern for the other kids to study would be *-ook.*"

"Why's that, Ryan?" Kathy asked, barely containing her smile.

"Well, I'm working on a story about chess, and I couldn't spell *rook.* Then I knew, because I thought of *book* and it helped me because I just changed the *b* to *r.*"

"What word power, Ryan."

"Yeah, you can make *book, look, took,* too." he added.

"What about *shook,* Ms. Collins?" asked Erik, who had been listening in.

"You guys may be on to something," Kathy said, as she got up to move on to other children. As she left, they took a few more seconds to think of other words together.

Just as there was nothing sacrosanct about Renée's use of an ABC inquiry, there is also nothing sacrosanct about the way Kathy has helped her children think about spelling patterns and about the fact that whatever they know gives them power to tackle what they do not know. Pat Cunningham's books, for example, contain a host of other ways to introduce children to these concepts. Children can sit with white boards and follow their teacher's directions. "Write *at.*" After they do this and read it, "Now add one letter to turn *at* into *rat.*" After children read the new word, "Change one letter to turn *rat* into *pat.*" Alternatively children can be given little cardboard letters and do this or similar work not by writing but by moving their letters into and out of different configurations.

Teachers will need to decide how they can design phonics work which reflects their beliefs about how children learn best. Children take on different roles in Kathy's phonics work, for example, than in classrooms based on different beliefs about language and learning. In Kathy's classroom, children initiate an inquiry into the phonics in their world and they collaborate to discover patterns. During word study time, the room is filled with "I have an idea …" or "Wait, let's try …" or "How does this fit the pattern …?" Children work on related but not necessarily identical work and they talk often with a partner. The tone and relationships of word study time matches that of every other time in the day.

There may be reasons for a teacher to design phonics activities that are less collaborative and less responsive to student initiative than other parts of their day. One skilled teacher I know met with such difficulty managing a particularly difficult group of third graders that she came to the decision that she could not give her children a full day of choices and opportunities to collaborate. Her children were used to being told exactly what to do and when to do it, and they were accustomed to doing everything under teacher's watchful eye. At least for a time, this teacher taught reading, writing, and math in one way but then deliberately (yet reluctantly) designed her word study work to represent old-school education.

In either case, it is important that word study work is as predictable and simple as possible. I'd caution against using a white board one day, partnerships another day, and cardboard letters a third day. When every day requires different directions and materials and tasks, more time is spent on choreography than on thinking about the patterns one finds in words. When the routine is simple and consistent, attention can be placed not on the complex ever-changing directions, but on the work itself and the grand ideas children have as they work together with the patterns of our language.

Just as Renée's ABC study allowed children opportunities to invent and explore the alphabet, Kathy's work with onsets and rimes provided her students the chance to make sense of the system of word building through predictable whole-class structures and independent work time. This again, illustrates a second core belief about phonics and word study: when children have the chance to explore and make sense of the systems within our language, they inevitably make discoveries and connections. They also learn how to be learners and have access to a way of learning that is available to them always.

We Can Help First Graders Be Word Solvers as Readers by Helping Them Be Word Solvers as Writers

In first grade, the word-study work includes not only sight words and spelling patterns but also helps children use both as readers and writers. We do minilessons that teach children strategies they can use when they encounter difficulty in their reading. Chapter 14 discusses these in detail. In one such minilesson, Kathy wrote this sentence on the easel: "The python wraps itself around its prey." Now she said, "Yesterday I was watching Raul as he read. He was reading a book on snakes and when he got to this sentence [on the easel] I saw him stop. He was stuck on the word *wraps*. There was no picture to give him a clue, so he had to focus on what would make sense and think about what he knew about the word. Raul was so smart because he remembered that *writing* starts with *wr-* and makes the /r/ sound, so he tried that. /rrr/aps—'wraps!' he said. He used his word power. Today, when you're reading and you get to a tricky part, try to figure it out with your word power." For a week or so, Kathy shared examples of children who had used what they knew about words to help them read. It's important to note that Kathy's intention in this minilesson was not to teach the *wr* blend but to teach an idea that extends itself beyond a particular letter combination. Kathy's class may spend a couple of weeks focusing on how the work they are doing in word studies helps them with their reading.

Word work is also lodged in the writing workshop. First graders begin the year in the writing workshop by drawing something they know and care about and then writing an accompanying caption. If I were doing a minilesson about Tucker in Lisa Ripperger's first grade, I would draw Tucker and think aloud about what I might say. "I could write, 'I love Tucker,'" I'd muse, then shake that thought away. "No, I've got to be detailed." I might go back and add a top knot of fur to my drawing of Tucker's head; as I did so, I would say to myself, "I love Tucker's top knot of fur" and begin isolating the words as I wrote them. Before I began, however, I might ask children, "will you research the strategies I use to spell these words and we'll talk about them later."

"*I*," I'd say; "I know that one." Then, moving on through the sentence, I'd say "*love.* I know that word." Then I'd back up, run my finger under the words I'd written so far, and read, "I-love-_____." Now I'd voice the word Tucker and mutter, "Where have I seen that word written?"

Although I've described a lot of methods for supporting a study into words and word-chunks, it's wise for a teacher to select only a few strategies to use over and over. We try to be sure that our word-study work, like our reading and writing workshops, is deliberately kept simple and predictable so that the thinking and the insights can be changing and complex. We want children to be able to anticipate and count on how whole-class and small-group word study will go so that instead of always waiting on the teacher's new instructions ("Today we're going to cover the word with beans," "Today we're going to find 5 objects that start with an S." "Today we're going to try to make new words out of the letters in Victoria's name"), our children can be full of initiative and plans. When the rituals and routines of word study work are deliberately kept simple and predictable, children can become inventors, choreographers, explorers ("Wait a minute! Tori's name is inside Victoria's name! Maybe there are parts of other people's names *inside* names!").

The importance of consistency became clear to me when I picked up my son Evan after his first visit to a particular friend's house. Evan said to me, "Mom, his toys are *nothing* like mine."

"How so?" I asked, expecting to hear that his friend had the toys that are off limits to my son. But Evan had something different in mind.

"His toys are one-time toys. Mine are over-and-over toys," Evan said. "Like, he has board games. You take them out, play them, lose, and then you go on. You do the puzzle, it's done, then you go on. *We* have Legos and micromachines and blocks. You do 'em over and over, on and on, changing it." Evan and Miles *do* return to their Legos over and over to create worlds with historical backdrops, compose identities for their characters, and spin out elaborate plot lines. Now, when I think about Renée's and Kathy's and other teachers' work with children's names, high frequency words, and spelling patterns, I know there is power in the over-and-over nature of this kind of study and in the way the curriculum is deliberately kept simple and predictable so that the children's thinking is highlighted. Children's ideas and observations about the letters in their names are the main event, as is their growing ability to put this knowledge to real use. And these ideas become more layered and complex as their thinking grows, day by day.

A Curriculum of Talk 12

Twenty-three first graders gathered close as their principal, Lydia Bellino, read Barbour's *Little Nino's Pizzeria* aloud to the class. The children listened raptly to the story of a little boy, Nino, who helps in his father's popular pizza shop. Then some men in suits descend on the restaurant and shortly thereafter Nino's father closes up the shop. Nino's father becomes the manager of a chain restaurant where Nino is not welcome. At the end of the book, the father reconsiders his decision, reopens the old place, and renames it Nino's Pizzeria in honor of his son, who again helps out.

As Lydia read, she paused from time to time and looked quizzically at the book, then at the children. With each pause, Lydia invited the children to do a "say-something" to the whole group. She didn't ask particular questions. Instead she looked at the text and at the children in a way that signaled, "Hmm. I'm just thinking about this text. How about you? What are you thinking?" When Lydia paused on one particular page, a little girl with a tiny face and huge brown eyes walked silently up to the book and pointed to a heart shape carved out of the wood headboard in a small cradle, tucked into the far corner of the family's living room. Lydia looked at the heart, the cradle, and the sleeping baby. "There is a little baby sister!" Lydia said. "You know something, as many times as I've read this book, I've never noticed that little sister!"

"Same with me!" a little girl with pigtails announced. "My father only talks to my brother."

"Yeah," a third child added. "And in the book he names his shop after the boy, not the girl."

"He doesn't talk to the mother either."

"Same in my family. The boys try to rule."

"He should have talked to the mother. She would've told him not to buy the fancy pizza place."

"My father's the same way. He ignores me because I'm the girl and I'm the youngest."

At this point, the teacher, who had been sitting on the side, approached Lydia. Shaking her head in dismay, she whispered, "Don't they know it's just a story!"

Later, Lydia and I recalled the teacher's words. "It's just a story," the teacher had said, implying, "Why get so worked up over a story? Let it go." But isn't the propensity to tell stories and to rethink stories a fundamental part of being human? Early peoples told stories that explained the earth and accounted for the sun, the stars, and the rain. Over the generations, parents have gathered their youngsters close and told them the stories of their lives. What is religion or science or history but the effort to take stories and imbue them with meaning? Much of our lifework is about taking the moments of our lives and asking, "Why did it happen this way? Could it have been otherwise? How does this moment connect to others? What does this mean to the world? To me?"

Helping children think about texts is as essential to the teaching of reading as it is to the whole of our lives, and the most powerful way to teach this kind of thinking is through book talks based on read-aloud books. We teach children to think with and between and against texts by helping them say aloud, in conversations with us and with others, the thoughts they will eventually be able to develop without the interaction of conversation. The great Russian psychologist Lev Vygotsky helped us realize that by giving our students practice in talking with others, we give them frames for thinking on their own. If others repeatedly say to us, "So what are you thinking about this?" or "What in the text makes you say this? Where's your evidence?" then we, as readers, begin to ask these questions of ourselves.

In schools, talk is sometimes valued and sometimes avoided, but—and this is surprising—talk is rarely taught. It is rare to hear teachers discuss their efforts to teach students to talk well. Yet talk, like reading and writing, is a major motor—I could even say *the* major motor—of intellectual development.

In Teachers College Reading and Writing Project classrooms, from the first day of school on, teachers at every grade level (kindergarten through eighth grade) read books aloud and deliberately structure opportunities to talk about them, so that children learn to think, talk, and write thoughtfully in response to literature. In a sense, these read-alouds become units of study.

In September, as I mentioned in Chapter 3, we'll read especially accessible texts, modeling and supporting engagement and responsiveness. Over time, we'll help children talk about the read-aloud book in increasingly sophisticated ways, and as I show in later chapters, we also help readers talk, and eventually think and write, about their independent reading books.

This "talk-curriculum," as I call it, begins with whole-class book talks about the read-aloud, and moves students toward talking about the books they read independently. Over time we'll nudge students along several other continuums as well:

At first ...	Later ...
students talk about the texts we read aloud.	students talk about the texts they read independently.
students' talk is scaffolded by us, as teachers.	students' talk is student-led.
students talk about the texts they've just heard or read in school.	students talk about the texts they read at home.
the thinking happens primarily through talk.	the thinking and idea-building happens through talking and writing.
reading is interspersed with talk (often after every few pages).	the talk comes after a larger chunk of reading or at the end of the text. This means readers do more synthesizing and summarizing.
the talk continuously roams among many assorted points.	the talk eventually lingers over, probes, and develops an extended idea or two.

Some teachers may decide to move students along only one of these continuums, but it remains essential that at every grade level we teach toward independence. Even kindergarten children can learn to talk as partners about books without a teacher leading the conversation. In this chapter, I'll suggest ways to support students and lift the level of talk (and therefore of comprehension) in classroom communities. I will describe several phases of teaching, including:

• Getting students started talking and writing in response to the read-aloud text.

- Talking to *develop* rather than to report on ideas.
- Structuring and framing book talks so students learn to focus and develop their talk.
- Teaching the class to lead and then assess today's talk and aspire toward tomorrow's.
- Keeping book talks rooted in the text.

Getting Students Started Talking and Writing in Response to the Read-Aloud Text

At one time I assumed that if I read an accessible text aloud really well, all my students would understand it, but I've come to realize this hope is far from the truth. Many of us find that when we pause at talk-worthy spots, some children don't have much to say. To talk about a read-aloud children must first listen and build the world of the story in their minds. Some children aren't accustomed to listening or reading with wide-awake minds.

Recently, my colleague Donna Santman worked as a staff developer helping Nancy Bezzone's thirty-six fourth graders learn what a read-aloud book-talk session could be. Donna read a little bit and then said, "Tell the person beside you what you are thinking." The room erupted into talking. After a few minutes Donna said, "So what did you think?" We don't always feel it is necessary for partners to report back to the teacher, but in this instance, Donna wanted to gauge the extent to which the students' brains were turned 'on.' Donna called on Nadine, who sat on the fringes of the circle and seemed less than tuned-in to the conversation. This child had nothing to share. When Donna asked, "What's in your brain about this story?" Nadine shrugged, giggled a little, and said, "Nothing, really."

Immediately, from all corners of the classroom, children thrust their hands into the air, making "call on me" pleas. It would have been all too easy for Donna to simply shift her attention to the children who *had* been listening to the read-aloud. But if talk of standards means anything at all, it means that Donna, and each of us, must hold ourselves accountable not only to assigning work (or, in this instance, to asking "what are you thinking?") but also to enabling all children to do the work. If Donna had simply shifted her glance to the "call on me" children, how would she be teaching Nadine and others like her?

"You know, the same thing happens to me sometimes, Nadine," Donna said. "Sometimes if I go into another teacher's classroom and try to listen to her reading aloud, my mind sort of listens without *really listening*, and soon

I'm off, daydreaming about what I'll do after school or whatever. Does this happen to anyone else here?"

Predictably, now that Donna had made dozing and dreaming during the read-aloud an acceptable thing to do, a dozen hands went up. "Is that right?" Donna asked. "It happens to you, too, Francis? Tell us about it."

Soon four or five children had vividly described their process of listening and yet not listening to the read-aloud. "This is important," Donna said, "It is so important that we share with the community what's going on in our minds," and of course she was right. There are probably children in all our classes who spend read-aloud time dozing, admiring their teacher's legs, or watching a bird in the tree outside the window, and once these children have dozed off and missed a part of the read-aloud, it's not always easy for them to reconnect with the text. If children are struggling over the challenge of making a movie in their minds as they listen to us reading a text aloud, how much more will they struggle when they read the print themselves.

Then, too, there will be children who may not doze and drift during the read-aloud yet still find themselves not understanding or following the text. We desperately need to teach children that mental sirens should go off when a text doesn't make sense. For too many of them, reading is only about getting across and through each line of words. They need to understand what it

feels like to "get" the book and to expect this fullness of meaning. If the read-aloud book doesn't make sense, if the pieces aren't fitting together, if the progression doesn't seem logical, then children need to say, "I don't get it." We can demonstrate by monitoring our own attention to the text and noting those places where we lose the meaning as we read aloud. "Wait," we'll say. "I've got to reread this." We also need to teach children—as Donna has been doing—what it means to listen actively and alertly, and to say "Huh?" when they are confused.

Once Donna had told her read-aloud group that she was glad they were talking about this problem and that it really matters that kids listen with their minds turned on, the group was deep into an inquiry on listening and reading with wide-awake minds. "Let me tell you what I do, sometimes, when I'm in another teacher's classroom and I have a hard time concentrating. I sit as close to her as I can, like this (and Donna acted out what she does), and I watch her mouth as she reads. Can I ask those of you who are having some trouble staying with the read-aloud story to try that for a start, and we'll talk about whether it helps. And that means, for all of us, no lying down during read-aloud, no braiding each other's hair. We need to be alert. The other thing is, I want you, Francis and Jeremy, Nadine and Yassir, to plan on saying something when I ask 'What are you thinking?' So be ready. Listen in a way that makes you have something to say back to the text."

For the next three or four days, Donna and this class of children worked on being sure that everyone was following the text and picturing what was happening. Every day Donna stopped in the midst of a chapter and said, "I can just see it in my mind. Tell the person beside you what *you* are seeing." Sometimes Donna would end this three-minute-long talk time by noting aloud the scenes in her mind. More often, she ended partner talk simply by resuming reading, backing up to reread a paragraph or two as a way of reclaiming her position in the text.

Obviously there is nothing sacrosanct about Donna's particular suggestions. One could imagine the class generating their own list of *Ways to Listen so We Can Talk Back to a Text*. My list might include any two or three of the following ways to generate more talk (and therefore more thought) in response to texts:

- Stop to think and talk often during the reading so we get into the habit of thinking back in response to what we see and hear. For example, we can look at just the cover and the title of a book and already talk in pairs about what we are thinking. We can read or listen to a paragraph and pause again to talk about what we are thinking. We wouldn't want to continue reading in such small chunks for long, but doing this early in a book can be helpful. If we begin early to spin images and theories off a text, then we can revise and extend them through continued reading. An early response to a book sets a reader up for continued responses.

- Sometimes simply repeating what is said in the text will launch a chain of thought. We might hear the title and say to our partner, "So, this book is called *Amber in the Mountains*" hoping that repeating the text will lead us to think and say something more.

- One way to mobilize thought is to have a few "starter phrases" to get ourselves responding or saying something back to a text. Any of these phrases (not all of them!) might be a good place to start:

  - I noticed …
  - One thing I pictured was …
  - It reminded me of …
  - I like the part in which … (or I didn't like …)
  - I wonder why …

- What would have happened if …
- I was surprised to see …
- I didn't understand …
- It wasn't fair when …
- My idea changed when …

- Some readers find it easier to sketch what they are thinking and only afterward to talk about it. We might suggest that students listen knowing there will be time for a quick sketch of whatever they are thinking or envisioning. Then we can suggest that students talk in pairs about their sketches.
- Sometimes we're more able to think about a book if we jot down a few specifics as we read the book or hear it read.
- Sometimes it is easier to think about a text if we first make certain we have the facts straight. After reading the opening section, we may want to pause and look back in order to get things straight. Who are the characters? What do we know about them? Where does this story occur? Is there a main problem the characters are wrestling with?
- It helps to mobilize our thoughts if we recall yesterday's reading before we listen to today's section of the text. This can also help readers build upon and extend their first thoughts.

After a few weeks of weaving these say-something interludes into the read-aloud, we might invite children to jot notes rather than to talk during these interludes. Early in the reading we find it helpful to generate ideas about the book, and the best way to do this is with talk. For the first few chapters of the book we still call for say-somethings. Then, midway into one of these partnership say-somethings, we will ask readers to open their reading logs and jot down what's on their mind. "Let's finish the talk on the page," we'll say. Then, after our fingers fly for a few minutes, we might say, "Who has a jotted note that will spark a good conversation?"

In this way, we hope to show children that readers write about their reading because writing helps them think more deeply and generates good conversations. I'm careful to stress that this writing *is not about recording the conversations we have already had, but about pushing these conversations further,* sparking future conversations.

This distinction is important, because one of the challenges in teaching children to talk (and write) well about books is to get them to see that talking and writing about books are ways to grow as well as to share ideas. (I discuss this in more detail in Chapters 18 and 24.)

Talking to Develop Rather Than to Report on Ideas

Fifteen years ago, when the Teachers College Reading and Writing Project first ventured into the terrain of teaching reading, we met weekly in small groups to talk about adult literature. We read Marquez's *Love in the Time of Cholera,* Allende's *In the House of the Spirits,* Kennedy's *Ironweed,* and thirty other novels that year, and we learned to talk well about them. I'll never forget our first lesson. We'd asked Anthony Petrosky, author of *Fact, Artifacts, and Counterfacts* (1986), to help us think about what it means to form a community of readers. Tony suggested that a few of us carry on a book talk in front of the larger group. A bunch of us sat together in the middle of a large room to talk for twenty minutes about *White Noise,* by Don Delillo. We were all, officially or unofficially, Project leaders, and we were pleased to strut our stuff in front of Tony and the others. Talking together about *White Noise,* we each wove our best thinking into the conversation, moving gracefully (we hoped) between one person's views and another's.

Later, critiquing the conversation, Tony said, "You were reporting on ideas you already had, but you weren't growing ideas through your talk. When no one talks back to anyone, when no one calls anyone on what they've just said, the conversation just cruises along on autopilot, all at a level of generalization and superficiality. That is what I sensed was happening today." To think that he'd described our book talk as full of generalizations and superficiality! We were dejected but also delighted, of course, because Tony led us to realize that this Book Club Project would be as demanding as any Outward Bound journey. "There was a lot of reporting," he said. "You laid out your ideas. But you didn't talk together. If I'm leading a group and after ten minutes I still don't hear people talking back to each other, I perspire."

Tony nudged us that day to think about how a group leader can push members to talk back to each other. He offered comments like, "Randy, what you said seems to me to contradict what Ellen said. Could you two resolve that?" Tony also showed us how a group leader could help members think about ways to develop a fleeting observation into a full-fledged reading of a text. "How does that observation fit with the whole of this text?" or "Could you use that comment to say something about the book as a whole?" We watched how these sentences alone can make a gigantic difference in a book talk. We were off and running!

Tony's challenge proved a major one. We wrestled for months before we really began to understand what he had been saying. I later realized that for several months my own book club followed the same course Tony had observed during our Delillo conversation. I don't know why it took me months to see that we had fallen into the exact pattern Tony observed when we discussed *White Noise.* I think our focus at first was so much on establishing rituals for the group and on having smart things to contribute to the group, that we didn't even remember Tony's wise critique. Instead, during those first months, our focus was on the fact that we were each expected to arrive at meetings with some ideas to add to the conversation. Before a book club meeting, I'd review my underlined passages and marginalia and try to enter the room with a few good ideas, like cards to play, in my pocket.

After a few months, when we looked at videotapes and studied our book talks, it became clear that a typical conversation would involve one of us "playing a card." Shirley might, for example, note the Christ-metaphor in the text. Then Katherine would lay *her* card on the table, tying it loosely to the first idea. "What you say about the metaphor, that reminds me. The ending was odd, wasn't it? I never dreamt it would end like that." Then Randy would lay out a card, "And the writing style, too! It's an odd memoir because the author's a journalist, so it has more facts and figures than most memoir."

Our book club talks usually began with people "laying out cards" or reporting on the ideas they had formed before the meeting. Sometimes (but rarely, I confess, until we become conscious of the pattern), after mucking about in the ideas in front of us, one of us would say, "So, what are we on about? What's on the table that we could consider staying with for a while?" It was as if we were asking, "Which card should we talk more about? Which card should we play?" The group would establish a focus and, for as long as possible, talk, think, jot, reread, and talk some more around that focus. As one idea led us to the next, the focus would change. First one person, then another would follow the same line of inquiry. Instead of reporting on ideas we already had, we would develop and refine ideas in the company of each other. What a palpable difference there was in the room whenever this happened! We'd find ourselves leaning forward; we'd build on what each of us had said, we'd think in collaboration with each other.

Our students usually begin as we did, initially using whole-group conversations as a forum for reporting their ideas. One child lays out her thought;

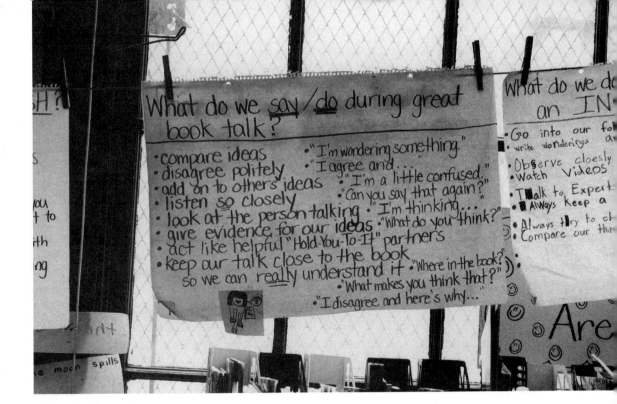

the next lays out another, only tangentially related idea. The conversation hops from one underdeveloped idea to the next as readers comment on the ending, the funny part, the character, the author's style but no one extends or challenges anyone else's ideas.

"I thought it was funny," one child will say.

"Yeah," another child will add. "The baby was so cute!"

"I didn't think they should have gone home at the end," yet a third child will say. The conversation continues in this fashion, without anyone elaborating on anything.

My colleagues and I have come to believe that one of the most important ways to lift the level of children's book talks (and our own) is to steer the conversation so that after some important, rich time for laying-out-one's-cards, people talk for a long time about one idea, pursuing one line of inquiry together. The mark of a good book talk is that instead of speaking in "sentences-of-thought," to use Mina P. Shaughnessy's term (1979), readers speak in paragraphs- or essays-of-thought. The mark of a good book talk is that people are not just reporting on ideas they've already had; they are, instead, generating ideas together.

Structuring and Framing Book Talks so Students Learn to Focus and Develop Their Talk

We help students focus and develop their book talks in a number of ways. Sometimes we frame different parts of the conversation so children get a feel for what it can be like to "lay out their cards," talk from those cards, choose a focus, and pursue a topic as a class. I recently watched Ginny Lockwood do this with her second graders.

"Let's take a few minutes to share the ideas and questions we have about this book that might generate big conversations," she said. "Can we lay some of them out?"

Several children made suggestions and Ginny repeated their ideas, embellishing them a bit. She wrote each idea on a giant Post-it note and stuck them on her chart paper. Then she asked, "So, among these possibilities, are there ideas you think we could stay with for a while?"

Soon the class selected a focus. Ginny repeated it, musing over the idea in a way that invited the others to do so. "Can anyone say more about this idea?" she asked. "Andre, do you agree with what Yassir just said? Can you tell us your ideas?" Andre made a vague comment. Ginny repeated it, showing great interest and helped Andre elaborate. Repeating what he said as if she was mulling it over, Ginny then looked out at her class, as if asking, "What do you think?" The class was silent so Ginny said, "I'm just wondering if I can think of any examples of this in the text. . . ." Soon Sara had added an example.

As the conversation gathered momentum, there were still times when children chimed in with unrelated topics. "I'm confused," Ginny said on several occasions, "Does that fit with what we were talking about?" When the answer was no, Ginny said, "Could you save it then, because we're talking about *this* for now."

Ginny jotted notes as the talk unrolled. On several occasions she said, "Let's rethink what we've said so far." Then she went over the conversation, identifying the conversational moves children had made and summarizing their content: "Yassir *opened the conversation* with a big idea. He wondered why . . . . Andre *added to* this and *we asked for more detail* and so Andre *extended his first thought,* saying . . . .Then Sara and Francis each *found examples* in the text itself." Ginny framed the conversation so that her students participated in a focused book talk. Eventually, the class will begin shaping their own conversation in the ways Ginny has taught them and will become less reliant on her leadership.

In similar ways, Mark Litner structured the book talk about Gary Paulsen's *Monument* among his fourth graders.

Mark: Could one of you *get us started* with what we've read so far in *Monu-ment?* An idea that could *spark a conversation?*

Melissa: Well, I don't know why the town needs a monument.

Mark: (Ponders Melissa's comment publicly.) Hmmm … You don't know *why* the town needs a monument?! What a thought … Who can speak to that?

Jason: Why's Rocky so mad?

Mark: Jason, hold your question. Melissa has already *put a question on the table,* so let's all think about it. Melissa, tell us again what you are wondering?

Melissa: *Why* they need it, the monument?

Mark: (To class) Should we ask her to *say more?* Aren't you wondering what she's thinking? Could someone *ask Melissa to explain?*

Mario: Explain.

Mark: Mario, do you mean you are interested in what Melissa said and want to hear more? Because I'm not sure you showed the interest in ways that'd make *me* want to say more.

Mario: (To Melissa) When you said why does the town need a monument, isn't it 'cause the dead guys from the war?

Lorena: I think they want to be more famous, like, known for something.

Lila: 'Cause the book says no one goes to Bolton unless you are on the way somewhere.

Pedro: And all it has is grain elevators.

Mark: So Melissa *started us off* with the question of why does Bolton need a monument anyhow, and Mario *added* his idea that a monument would honor the dead from the war. Lorena *countered,* suggesting the monument is a way to make the town famous. Lila *gave us evidence from the text* when she remembered that Paulsen described the town as a place no one would go unless you are passing through, and Pedro *added* that the town has little more than grain elevators. So I'm going to suggest you talk to your partner about two things. Would you respond to Melissa's question about why Bolton needs a monument? Do we have anyone who disagrees with what we are saying so far?

(The room is filled with the buzz of many conversations.)

Rose: I don't think they need one.

(Silence.)

Mark: Does anyone have *a follow-up question* for Rose?

Mario: *Why?* Why don't you think they need one?

Rose: They probably just heard about that Vietnam wall and they thought it'd be cool or something, but they're just trying to be cool.

Mark: So we have two different points of view. Lorena and Lila and Pedro think the town needs this monument so the town becomes someplace and has an identity. It sounds like you three think it's healthy for a little farm town to want a monument. And Rose, am I hearing you right that you think the town's wrong about needing a monument? What about the rest of you?

Sometimes after scaffolding conversations in this firm, decisive way, a teacher may want to go back and comment on ways in which the children did well. "I love the way we really stayed with Melissa's question, all talking together about it," the teacher might say. "I want to compliment Rose on having the courage to say 'I see it differently,' because that really got us into a great talk, and sometimes it's hard to go against the flow of opinion like that."

After leading book talks like this for a few weeks, teachers will probably want to pull back from this role and give children more rein. If we want students to initiate and lead their own discussions about books—and everything else—throughout their own lives, they need to learn to carry out their own book-talks. We may continue to start whole-group conversations by asking children to turn to their say-something partners to get their thoughts going on a topic; then, while partners talk, we may listen in to try to hear something we could use to spark the whole-group talk. The teacher might say, "Hannah has something to say to start us in a conversation," and then steer the group toward extending that one comment. "Who can add onto or develop what Hannah has said?" By this time, however, we'll want to stand back and let children go on without us.

Teaching the Class to Lead and Then Assess Today's Talk and Aspire Toward Tomorrow's

If we have had a leading role in a book conversation and then pull back, there will be trouble. Students may talk over each other, fight for the floor, get very loud, even insult each other. When all this starts to happen, I suggest that teachers just sit there and let it happen. I wouldn't advise stepping in to resolve things. Although I *might* try to record as much of this chaos as I could without stopping or slowing down the conversation, I'd let the problems happen. The deeper and bigger the problem is, the easier it will be to get students to commit themselves to fixing it. After about twenty minutes (which may well feel like an eternity), I'm apt to say, "Let's pause and reflect on the conversation. How did it go?"

I can ask this knowing full well that the class will be in an uproar over the problems of the day. "How could we make things better?" I can ask, and steer the group into a discussion about what they think might conceivably make a difference.

Eventually children will begin to talk about how they felt during the conversation. As teachers, we need to be prepared to delve into the problems, because by identifying a problem and gathering momentum around it, we create a context for good problem-solving work. Jeffrey—big, sweet, smart Jeffrey—surprised his teacher, Kathleen Tolan, and me by saying that some kids in the fifth grade class made him feel unsafe during book talks. Jeffrey was a beloved member of Kathleen's class, which was as close-knit and trusting a community as I'd ever seen. How could it be that Jeffrey didn't feel safe? He was tall, weighed probably well over 150 pounds, and was clearly a leader. It would have been easy for Kathleen to brush his worries aside and reassure him. Instead, she asked Jeffrey to tell her more. When he hesitated to talk to the entire class, Kathleen asked him to meet with her after school.

Jeffrey said the voices in the group made him feel unsafe; they came at his ideas quickly and loudly. "They pound at me," he said. He told Kathleen that sometimes even her voice frightened him. The conversation broadened to include his fear on the playground and in the boy's bathroom. Because he's big, people expect him to intervene when others fight. That scares him, so on the playground people call him names. "The classroom—it's safe here, but not all the way safe," Jeffrey said.

The next day, in a class meeting, Kathleen opened the issue up, and Jeffery repeated much of what he'd said the evening before. Kathleen said she suspected that others felt as Jeffery did. One by one, a few children spoke about their fears of being judged and of times during book talks when their opinions had been stepped on. "Some people intimidate us so we step down in the book talks," Ashley said.

"But that's not true!" smart, passionate DeVoia said. "*I'm* who you're talking about. *I* do what you say. *My* voice gets loud and I bang on the table, but I don't want to intimidate you. I'm just excited."

Soon the children were deeply involved in an inquiry on talk and how to bring out quiet voices. "Why don't we just study ourselves today," Kathleen said, "and notice whatever we can about the roles we each play." The class proceeded to listen to the read-aloud, to sit in silence for a moment, and then to have a book talk, only this time, after the book talk, Kathleen said, "Why don't we take a moment and each jot some notes about the role we played in today's book talk." Students first shared these jottings with partners, and then Kathleen opened the issue up for the whole class to discuss.

"When I said, 'Journey's a weird name for a boy,' and then Galen jumped in to add, 'It'd be weird for a girl, too,' *I* was going to say that. I just didn't have time to finish before he broke in," Tony said, and the class talked for a bit about how it often felt to them as if the next person was stepping on their heels.

"So does it make sense for us to take as our goal that we give a little circle of silence around people's comments in case they have more to say?" Kathleen asked. Within ten minutes, the class had settled on three plans for the next day's book talk. The next morning Kathleen began by saying, "Today, before I read the next chapter of Patricia MacLachlan's *Journey*, let's review your plans for today's book talk." Then she asked them to keep an eye on how things went so they could talk about it later.

Afterwards, Diana, a quiet student, said, "I realized I didn't talk." The class was startled by her statement. "You didn't know that?" they said.

Diana's eyes protested, and, with Kathleen's urging, she said, "I *feel like* I'm participating." It soon became clear that a few of the children felt as if they were actively participating because they listened keenly, taking in everything and watching the conversational ball as it moved back and forth across the classroom. Diana, for example, would turn her body all the way around to listen to Sydney and then to listen to DeVoia. And she'd remember exactly what each person had said.

In time, Diana, Angela, John, and the other, quieter students realized that in order to take time to formulate ideas they could contribute to the group, they almost had to stop listening long enough to get their own thoughts going and to hold one idea in mind. "Try it," the class suggested. "After you get an idea, say it over to yourself while you try to get into the talk."

The next problem, predictably, was that the quiet children had a hard time inserting their voices into the conversation. Often by the time there was space enough to interject their point, their original comment was no longer relevant. The group made several suggestions. One was for the quiet voices to start the conversation, speaking first each day. Tony also noticed that John tended to lean forward and act agitated whenever he had something to say. Soon the whole class was on the alert watching John's body language. They learned to say, "John, do you want to add anything?"

Meanwhile, DeVoia wanted help in knowing when she got carried away and talked too much. She knew that Kathleen and the class mostly valued her willingness to think and talk back to the texts, but everyone acknowledged that from time to time DeVoia and a few other children needed a little reining in. "Give me a sign," DeVoia said to the other kids, and soon the class had a pact that if anyone was dominating for too long, another child might touch his or her lips in a way that meant "Be careful about talking too much." The class also knew that if an outspoken student and a quiet student started to speak at the same time, the outspoken student needed to be the one to back down.

It's important to notice how this group of children identified the problem: they wanted everyone to feel safe in the conversation. Kathleen helped to define the issue in this way rather than "Some people talk too much and some don't talk at all." In the name of wrestling with problems, it's easy to inadvertently stir class members up to feel indignant toward each other, and it's especially easy to generate resentment toward some of the more dominant voices in a book talk. This can present a real problem because, especially at the start of the year, we need our outspoken students to function as leaders. If they learn that when they are passionate, strong-willed, and talkative in response to a book, their classmates are sure to become judgmental and claim they're "hogging time," it will teach all class members that it is risky to get deeply involved in a book talk. Also, when we silence the strong voices in a community, we risk taking the engine out of our group's conversation and settling for conversations that are dispassionate, disengaged, perfunctory, and polite. Although we do not want the same handful of children to dominate day after day, we also do not want conversations to be even-keeled, with every child participating equally each day. We want to create communities in which students feel strongly in response to books and bring those strong responses to the group. We want a community in which every student takes responsibility for thinking, "How can *I* be a more helpful member of this conversation?"

Here are some ways to help students reflect on their book talks:

- Some of us sometimes record discussions on chart paper as they occur, and others take notes in our spiral notebooks and type transcripts up to distribute or to turn into overhead transparencies. Some teachers video or audiotape discussion so the class can analyze it later.

- Enact a "rewind" in the discussion so that children think more about it. If the discussion grinds to a halt, or if it jumps all over the place instead of staying with an idea—or if it is especially grounded in the text and deserves to be celebrated, we may use our notes to recall an earlier juncture in the discussion, repeat the comments children had said then, and suggest the class resume talking from that earlier point on.

- Look back on a discussion in order to assess it according to a student-designed rubric. If the class is working on a conversation goal (such as disagreeing with each other with respect, letting the quieter voices speak first, building on each other's ideas), the class profits from a rubric that makes these goals public. Written records of whole-class discussions allow us to reflect on progress toward goals, but even without transcripts, children think back on a talk and assess it according to a clear goal.

- Once a book or a section of a book is completed, it can be helpful to look back over the book as a whole and the class' work with this book. The class can ask, "What have we done together with this book that we can do again with another book? That we could do even better next time? That we could do with our own independent reading?"

Hannah Schneewind asked her second graders to join her in rereading a transcript of their book talk. The children noticed that one child claimed that a character was mean. No one had asked him to elaborate. "How could we have helped Francis say more about his idea?" Hannah asked. The class discussed this for a bit, and then Hannah pointed out that comments often go by without being developed. Soon the class had put together a repertoire of responses they could use to enlarge on each other's ideas:

- I agree with what you are saying because …
- What you just said matches what was in my mind because …
- Why did you say that? Can you show me how you got that idea?
- Could you say more?
- Could you give an example?
- I'm not sure I understand what you are saying. Could you say it in another way?
- I hear what you are saying but I see it differently …

Other classes have listed phrases to help children "piggyback" on each other's ideas. It may seem unnatural to give children phrases like these to promote what should be natural conversations, but these phrases are only important for a fleeting period of time.

- I'd like to add on to what David said.
- I have an example of what you just said.
- Another thing that goes with that is …
- I see a connection between what you said and what we were talking about earlier.
- So, are you saying …
- I agree with the part about …
- Going back to what you said …
- If what you said is true, isn't it also true that …
- Is one example of that the part on page 13, when …
- That's true, but …

The *method* both Kathleen and her students and Hannah and her students used to improve their book talk is one we use often and for many reasons. The class identifies a problem, brainstorms ideas for dealing with it, puts those ideas into action by altering what they do, reflects on whether things got better or not and why, and generates new and related concerns. We use variations on this same method to create most strings of minilessons and units of study in our reading and writing workshops.

Of course, the ways we extend what someone else has said in a book talk are also the ways we can extend our own and each other's thinking and writing. If I am asked to think or write about a book, I will tend to generate one blurb, one thought. The challenge is to say more, to move from "a sentence of thought" to "a passage of thought." Interestingly enough, in the writing workshop, as in our book talks, we teach students to generate observations and ideas and then to review them to find "a seed idea to develop." We then teach writers to linger with this idea for a while, letting more ideas accumulate. Of course, in the writing workshop, children react with anxiety when we suggest that they take a week to develop their seed ideas, writing for several days about inner-tubing along the creek, building a home for their guinea pig, or their anxieties inside the elevator. "I already said it all," children tell us in the writing workshop. Similarly, in book talks, children resist the idea of talking for a long time about one person's comment. In both disciplines, this becomes a teaching moment. We will make a big deal of it if a writer *does* linger with a particular topic, especially if, as a result, the writer develops new details and insights. A piece that was originally about inner-tubing becomes an essay on courage in the face of physical and emotional challenges; a story about a guinea pig provides a window into a father-son relationship. Similarly, a book talk about Grandpa's irritating habit of constantly taking photographs in MacLachlan's *Journey* can develop into an exploration of Grandpa's motives for taking pictures.

Keeping Book Talks Rooted in the Text

If we let children talk together about their books and do not intervene, another predictable problem will arise: the book will evaporate from the book talk. I recently listened to some students talk about Wilson Rawls' *Where the Red Fern Grows*. The conversation began with the recognition that the two hounds, Big Dan and Little Annie, are different from each other but that they really love each other. "My dogs follow each other everywhere," one child said. Another added that his dog chases cats. After a flurry of dog-chasing-cat stories, the conversation turned to the fact that one child had no pets.

Throughout all this, the teacher nodded happily, and finally, when talk had subsided, said, "So we've talked a lot about the big idea of 'Relationships between Animals,'" and she wrote that on chart paper. "I love the way you found a big theme!" I was flabbergasted—it may have been a great *talk,* but how could it have been a great *book talk* about *Where the Red Fern Grows?*

I don't think this teacher is alone in her appreciation of conversations such as this one, which spin off from books into children's lives, or in her appreciation of book talks that address "big ideas," such as sibling rivalry, loyalty between pets and people, or the need for forgiveness. Many teachers seem to expect that a good book talk begins with a comment about a book and then spins off to one of life's "big issues." For me, however, red lights flash when there is no book in the book talk (as I'll discuss in more detail in Chapter 25). I'm all for personal connections and conversations, but I expect them to be deeply embedded in the text. And if a book talk is going to begin with the observation that Old Dan and Little Annie are different, I'd expect to hear excerpts read aloud to show the particulars of the differences. I'd expect us to pore over sections of the text that show similarities despite the differences. For this to have been a good *book talk,* in my opinion, the children's books should have been out and open, and their claims supported and explored with evidence from the text.

Conversations in which readers make predictions, like conversations about "big issues," can either take readers away from the text or bring them back. Teachers regularly ask children, "What do you think will happen next?" Yet how rare it is for a teacher to say, "Walk us through your rationale. What makes you suspect that will happen next?" How rare it is for the teacher to say, "Show us the grounds for your prediction." It is even rarer for students to hold *each other* accountable by saying, "I don't get why you think *that* will happen. Can you show me evidence?" or "I don't think I see it that way. Look on page 9. . . ."

Of course, not only predictions but *any* response needs to be grounded in the text. If a first grader announces that Sal, in Robert McCloskey's *Blueberries for Sal,* is very brave, I would hope that another child or a teacher, listening to this theory, would say, "Show us what you mean" or "What gives you that idea?"

When young readers discover that they will be called upon to ground their ideas in specific textual references, it becomes important for them to find a way to record their observations and ideas as they read. In Chapter 18, I'll discuss ways in which children use Post-its, bookmarks, or page numbers jotted on charts to help them quickly locate sections of the text that support their claims. Almost all children will insist that they are blessed with perfect memories and can recall any idea and any textual reference without needing to record anything at all. The truth is, however, that all of us benefit from jotting down our fleeting impressions so that we can later look back on our own ideas and develop them, just as we also help our companions in a book talk develop *their* early impressions into full-fledged theories. Then, too, if we don't mark certain passages as we read, we waste a great deal of time looking for textual references whenever we need to substantiate claims.

The expectation that students will be able to ground what they say in the text is a big part of what Lauren Resnick, director of the Learning Institute at the University of Pittsburgh, means by "accountable talk." The habit of asking for evidence is also one of the "Habits of Mind" upon which Ted Sizer's Coalition of Essential Schools is based. As I will explain in Chapter 24, the ability to make a point and defend it with examples is the crux of what many students are asked to do when they write literary criticism. In these essays, students are expected to say, "Here is what I think about this text and here's why." And, of course, in our own lives we are usually best served by judgments and decisions based not on guesswork or hearsay, but on our own well-considered evidence.

Teachers who want to help students ground their ideas in the text can do so by giving students time to prepare for a book talk by marking those sections of the text they plan to refer to or by reviewing their notes. We can also watch for times when children's eyes flick back to the texts they are holding as they talk, and we can applaud this, "I just saw you glance at the text. Can you tell us what you were noticing?" Children sometimes think it is cheating to look back at a text to buttress their ideas, and we need to show them that just the opposite is true. We can help children develop the habit of turning to specific sections of the text by encouraging them to ask each other for evidence of their claims. We can transcribe and replay the conversation, looking for places in which there could have been specific references to the text. Half the class can be asked to observe the other half discussing a text. The young researchers can notice especially whether the book talk was truly grounded in the text. Either way, if the teacher wants to suggest that as learners we look back on what we have done and make "New Year's Resolutions," the class might generate a list of comments they could use to hold each other more accountable to the text:

- Show me what you mean.
- What makes you say that?
- What were you reading when you thought of that?
- Will you find the part of the book that makes you say that?
- Is one example of what you are saying on page 93?
- Can we look at the book together and see what it says?
- I'm not sure I agree, because look on page 126?

We can help children develop the habit of turning to specific sections of the text by encouraging them to ask each other for evidence of their claims.

Grounding one's claims in specific textual references is also important in a book talk because it allows a group of people to think together. The habit of saying, "This is what I think and here's why" allows others to weigh our conclusions in the light of our evidence. When we say, "One example is on page 16," this not only allows us to prove our point, it also invites others to join our line of thinking and to inspire us with more ideas.

Of course, when one child cites a particular passage as evidence, others may not look at that passage expecting to have more ideas. Children's minds may not be turned on when they hear Randalio say, "Old Dan and Little Annie are totally different because, listen to this scene where Little Annie gets trapped in the river." We want to say to the class, "Let's all of us look at the section Randalio is citing. Will you talk in twos (or jot) about what *you* see as similarities and differences in the ways the two dogs handle this emergency." Then, after five minutes, we might say, "So, Randalio has given us his interpretation of this scene. Who sees it differently?"

In discussing how to help children base their talk in the text, I'm also discussing how to cultivating a climate of debate, of questioning, of multiple interpretations. In order for this to be life-giving (and it can be just that), children need to think about how to disagree with each other in ways that allow the other person to hear what they're saying. This comes down to the etiquette of disagreement. If a friend pounces on an idea saying "I totally disagree" or "You're wrong," most of us will feel angry and defensive. What a difference if our friend prefaces her comment with "I see what you are saying, but I think differently about it" or "I get your point, but I wonder if you could also say …" or "I had a different idea about this" or "I partly agree and partly disagree with you because …"

All the polite talk in the world, however, is of little help as long as children cling to the idea that the purpose of a book talk is to tell others what they think and to win over other people's support for *their* idea. It is very important, then, to stress that one goal of a book talk is to open our ideas to those of others, which will often refine or alter our original ideas.

"How many of you changed your mind or got new ideas in today's book talk?" we can ask, and when six hands go up, we can congratulate those children. "Hurrah for you," we say. Then we can turn to the other members and suggest that next time, if they really listen, they, too, may find themselves with new ideas as the book talk unfolds. Listen to what Ilisa Samplin, a fifth grader from Joanna Cohen Merrick's classroom, says about how book talks changed for her once they became opportunities to think new thoughts:

<u>Reflection Sheet</u>
Ilisa Samplin
        June 10

   When I came into this
classroom, I was at a
stage when I loved to
read and thought I
knew everything about
reading, but I really
didn't. I had conversations
in class with my friends
about books, but they
were "right there"
converations. What I
mean when I say that
is we talked about the
stuff that was written
right there in the book
so there was almost no
point to the conversations
because we already knew
that information from
the book.

   I also used to hate
post-its. I just read
books but didn't really
"acknowledge" them. I
didn't talk about all of
them and may not have
understood or liked every
part. I only knew my
own opinions. I didn't
have too many

conversations, so I
didn't know what other
people's feelings or thoughts
were. I wasn't able to
<u>compare</u> to new things.
I couldn't <u>agree</u> or <u>disagree</u>
or <u>add more</u> to what anyone
said. It was like I took
the book out of a hole,
read it and then locked it
back into the hole and
erased it completely from
my mind. I never dug it up
or thought about it again.
Now I wish I would have
dug them up and I thought
of maybe digging them out
sometime.

   I just read but didn't
work or talk about the
books I "<u>read</u>": I think
the word read means a lot.

   You have only read a book
when you tear it till the
pieces won't give anymore.
You have to take a book
and know it so that you
could tell the story, but
not only tell the story, to
live and dig under the story.
I didn't really <u>read</u> my books
last year or the years before
that. I just kind of
<u>held them.</u>

somos el Barco
Barco, Somos el mar
en ti, Tu navegas en mi
the boat. We are the sea
in you, You sail in m...
...ream sings it to the river
...river sings it to the sea
...sea sings it to the boat
...that carries you and me

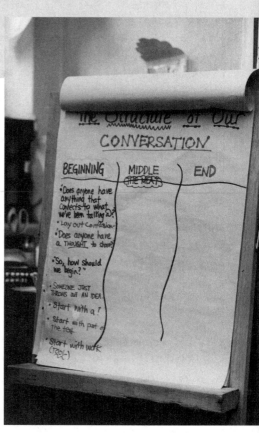

The Structure of Our
CONVERSATION

BEGINNING | MIDDLE (THE MEAT) | END

• Does anyone have
  anything that
  connects to what
  we've been talking ab?

• Lay out confusion

• Does anyone have
  a THOUGHT to share?

• "So, how should
  we begin?"

• Someone just
  throws out an idea.

• Start with a !

• Start with part of
  the text

• Start with work
  (TRS...)

Units of Study
in a Reading Workshop

III

In this section, I lay out one possible curriculum for the September, October, November, December, and January of a K–1 reading classroom and a 2–8 reading classroom. I do this knowing that there is a world of difference between the grade levels I've grouped together and that there is no one best plan for a curriculum in the teaching of reading. What I am presenting is one community's most recent vision of a curricular calendar, and it is totally open to revision. I describe the way our year tends to unfold not because I hope you will *follow* these descriptions, but because I hope you will learn from them as any of us learn from visits to the classrooms of other teachers and to the lab sites of other thought-collectives.

In the following chapters I hope to make the case that as teachers, we need to be planful in our teaching not only in terms of the ongoing structures (see Section II) but also in terms of our changing units of study or inquiries. As we have found, units of study tap into an enormous energy source in our students and in ourselves.

Across the nation, many teachers have found it beneficial to plan their *writing* workshops by thinking about structures (minilessons, partnerships, author celebrations) that last and by thinking about the units (writing poetry, memoirs, editorials, mentoring ourselves to authors) that change. In our classrooms, my colleagues and I have found it equally helpful to think of units of study within the *reading* curriculum.

Some people may be puzzled by the idea of "units of study" in a reading workshop, perhaps because the term suggests a rigid, top-down scope and sequence curriculum such as one finds in textbooks and published programs. I trust that in the following chapters readers will see that my understanding of units of study is very different. It is different first and foremost because these units are created by a network of teachers and children and marked with their imprint. Often, when a teacher or a child devises a new tool or a new technique, the news travels like wildfire from classroom to classroom. The language and methods and ideas within a unit of study are *shared,* which is totally different from being *imposed.*

I visited a large city recently to learn about the extraordinary effort under way to bring balanced literacy into every classroom in every school. I saw charts showing how several parallel staff development projects were working toward this goal. It was an elegant plan, yet something was missing. The arrows all seemed to be one-directional, to go from the staff development organizations *down* to the schools and classrooms. In New York City, by contrast, the arrows on such projects go every which way. We are all learning from each other, and teachers and principals across the city are known for particular contributions to our growing and shared image of a literacy curriculum. It may be accurate to say that we tend to learn the ongoing structures, such as those I described in Section II, not from individual teachers or principals but from researchers, books, thought collectives, and sometimes, staff developers. In our community, clusters of teachers become famous for the units of study they create. Usually these units begin with a cluster of us, but then we all join into the drafting and revision process of curriculum development. Rather than representing an imposed, top-down structure, our units of study invite invention and discovery. (Notice that although here I lay out a sequence of units of study we are currently creating, adopting, and adapting, in Section IV I mess up that one line of units by suggesting others that could just as well replace them.)

Sometimes when people learn about our units of study, they become concerned, not that these represent curriculum that is imposed on teachers but that they represent curriculum that is imposed on children. Some teachers are surprised to discover that we believe so much in planning. "Don't you want your teaching to emerge in response to kids?" they ask. They want to get it straight. "Do you believe in planned, whole-class units of study or do you believe in teaching that is responsive to the particular children in a classroom?" My answer is "Both." I *do* want teaching to be child-centered and responsive, and yet I also believe we benefit from anticipating possible areas of emphasis that our entire classroom community can rally around.

As important as it is to assess readers and design small group and individual interventions which move each child toward our goals for that child, we need to not lose sight of the tremendous power in a community of learners exploring strategies together. And although it is important for each reader to read the particular book he or she can read, most reading skills are multilevel; readers can *all* work on book orientations, on asking critical questions of a text, on being resourceful word-solvers or on thinking between texts. Teachers need to think, "Out of the whole world of reading, what habits and values do I want to be sure to develop in all my students?" and to realize that sometime we will want our teaching to be angled so as to help each member of the classroom community join into a whole-class shared inquiry that supports every reader.

In an earlier chapter we heard Cheltze announcing, "My Grandma reads the Bible and then she puts a little piece of paper in it to save her place." Her teacher, Kathy Collins, responded, "Does she? She uses a bookmark? I do that!" Soon an entire class of first graders had jumped onto the bookmark bandwagon. Before the conversation was over, every member of the class had resolved to be the kind of reader who uses popsicle sticks, Kleenex, and anything else he or she can find as bookmarks. This was responsive teaching, and yet it was not as spontaneous as it might appear. It wasn't serendipity that led Cheltze to talk about her reading habits, nor was it a spur-of-the-moment decision that led her teacher to celebrate the bookmark. Kathy begins the school year knowing that she will draw on a wide array of ways to get children talking about their reading lives and that she'll demonstrate her own reading habits. Kathy didn't know that Cheltze's grandmother used Kleenex as a bookmark, but she knew her September teaching would be geared to helping children develop reading tools, habits, and identities. She knew she'd want to use children's ideas in order to "coauthor"—with them—a literate world inside the classroom. Kathy's curricular planning allowed her to support Cheltze's bookmark strategy as a whole-community inquiry without risking that her instruction would become helter-skelter.

But if Kathy's class is listening to Steven Kellogg's *The Island of the Skog,* the story of a boatload of mice that discover a fearful monster dwelling on their island, and Peter wonders if the monster will turn out to be the giant creature he met in *The Mysterious Tadpole,* should a mental "Minilesson alert!"

light bulb flash in Kathy's mind? She *could* stop everything and call the children's attention to Peter's wise expectation that the two Kellogg books might relate to each other: "Whenever you read one book, other books will come to mind," she could say. This, in many ways, is good teaching at its best. But if three minutes and one page later, Brianna gets stuck reading a word and wisely backs up to reread the problematic sentence, should "Minilesson alert!" again flash in Kathy's mind? In our efforts to be responsive, we can end up lurching first in one direction, then in another, and fail to scaffold the community's continued work toward any one goal. My colleagues and I find it more helpful to anticipate some of the directions we'll support, at least the beginning of the year in our reading and writing workshops.

Finally, I would add that of course we develop and revise our curricular plans by taking into account our children's needs and also the goals or standards that we and our community have adopted. To form a curricular calendar, we ask, "What is it I want my children to know and be able to do as readers by the end of our year or our two years together? By the end of fourth grade? By the end of eighth grade?" Then we need to think, "What needs to be in place *now* in order for this to happen?" If we dream that our children will be able to converse intelligently about books, simply assigning this goal is not enough. We also need to structure our children's progress toward this goal. To do this, we need to demystify the goal: "What *exactly* do I mean when I say I want my students to talk intelligently about books?" Perhaps we decide that among other things, children need to refer back to the text in their book talk. The next question becomes "What needs to be in place in order for *this* to happen?" Soon we realize that if all children are going to be able to refer to specific passages in their reading by January (a reachable goal for all children working at all levels), they need to read books they understand in September. We not only need to be sure we build the foundation, we also need to communicate these goals clearly and support children's early efforts toward them. Eventually we pull away and collect evidence about what children do independently and then return to teach and develop the curriculum further in response to the needs and interests we see. This is how curriculum development happens in our community.

The first four chapters in this section discuss units of study in our kindergarten and first-grade classrooms, although Chapter 13 focuses more on the big question "What does a reading workshop look like when many children can't yet read?" than on an opening-of-the-year unit of study. This one chapter is out of step with the others, then, but I hope it is nevertheless helpful. After four chapters which focus on units of study in the fall and early winter of K-1 reading classrooms, I shift and focus on four units of study for classrooms in grades 2–8. Second grade teachers especially will need to draw from both sets of chapters. It's important to read the chapters for a particular grade level in sequence and to imagine a school year unfolding sequentially. As you read, you'll see that each chapter addresses a wide span of ages and I trust you'll bear with me on this.

September in a K–1 Reading Workshop 13

Kathy Collins and I intended to spend a long August morning in her classroom planning for September in her first grade reading workshop. But then Anna's mother came by. "I've been through here every day," she said to Kathy, "hoping to catch you. I wanted to be sure you knew from the start to phone me *the minute* anything goes wrong." With a worried smile she added, "After all, this year's the biggie." She might just as well have said, "After all, this year is going to make or break my daughter." Raymond and his mom came next, poking their heads around the doorway, and for a while Kathy tried to lure bashful Raymond into a conversation. Eventually he drifted off to the dormant hermit crab and his mother seized the chance to whisper, "He is so awfully nervous about first grade, learning to read and all. He has a fourth-grade brother, so he knows what to expect. He knows where he's supposed to end up, but not the path. It makes him terribly anxious."

Anna's and Raymond's mothers aren't alone in believing that first grade will be a make-it-or-break-it year for their children. The growing recognition that children profit from (and even need) early success as readers has led schools to decrease class sizes in kindergarten and first grade, to provide more support personnel for this crucial time, and to add professional development opportunities for primary teachers. All this comes at a high cost, however, because the new focus on early literacy has sometimes created a hyperactive, highly pressured, and highly regimented curriculum that can work at cross-purposes to our hopes.

Like Raymond, Kathy approaches the new school year profoundly aware of everyone's expectations. She knows full well that she is expected to bring each of her children across the great divide from *emergent* to *conventional* reading, and the responsibility is enormous.

It seemed significant therefore to have both Raymond's and Anna's mothers intrude on what was to have been an indulgently long, relaxed, and private planning fest. I saw the anxious strain in their eyes, heard the edge in their voices, and knew I was glimpsing the pressures that invade the dreams and plans of all primary teachers. As I listened to the anxiety in these parents' voices, I remembered what a third-grade student wrote about his memories of first grade: "Oh, those were the good old days! We did not have so much work back then, but now I am growing big and I am jammed full of work." His memoir ended with "Sometimes I wish time flies back to first grade. I was so smart back then."

I suspect that most of today's primary-level teachers, like that third grader, think with nostalgia about the good ol' days when our children weren't "so jammed full of work," when our youngsters came to school and felt smart.

Establishing the Conditions for Language Learning

In between the interruptions, Kathy and I talked about what a priority it would be for her this year that Raymond, Anna, and every other child who comes to her class feel smart. Although it is always vital that our teaching begins where the child is and takes the child where he or she can go, this is nowhere more important than in kindergarten, because the most important ingredient for success in school is engagement. When Marie Clay (March 2000) said, "Even in the reading programs I despise, 80% of children get there," she went on, "I can only chalk this up to the active, constructive mind of the child at work." My hunch is that when children *don't* "get there" it tends to be because their active, constructive minds never get going in school, and therefore stories, ideas, words, letters, and sounds go past them. The greatest risk is *not* that a child will have a knowledge gap, but that the child will learn passivity and disengagement in the face of school and of written language.

This chapter will consider how we build a place in our classrooms that supports all our children as readers, especially before they can read conventionally. *The chapter, then, focuses more on kindergarten (especially the first half of kindergarten) and the earliest weeks of first grade, but it has implications for all we do in the primary grades.*

How can we create a classroom context in which emergent readers do what they can do, and actively read in ways which become self-extending (Clay 1991)?

With all of today's pressures, we can keep our eyes so fixed on our destination that we forget how utterly worthless the trip is if the children aren't with us. In our hurry to cover the curriculum, we can deluge children with charts, rubrics, and lists of spelling patterns until their eyes glaze over.

When we post thirty high frequency words on a word wall that is used by only six high-achieving students, we are teaching lessons to young readers but not the lessons we intended to teach. We are teaching a great many children that print isn't for them, that words make sense only to someone else, that the code is confusing and overwhelming, that reading is hard. Is it any surprise that in many primary classrooms, a contingent of children becomes passive in the face of print? Is it any surprise that these children give up on the little black marks that swarm across the wall, the page, the school day?

Instead of thirty words, we'd be wiser to slow down, to post just three or four words on the word wall at the start of the year and be sure that every child develops a concept of, for example, the stability of words. Before we get too frantic over whether our children have developed automaticity with lots of words, we need to be certain that they understand that every time they see *M-o-m*, it will say *Mom*. *M-o-m* might be on a name tag (in which case it says *Mom*) or it might be on a Valentine (in which case it says *Mom*) or it might be in the middle of a story … a story about—Mom! We can put these letters—*M-o-m*—on paper, other people will see them, and presto, they'll say, "Mom." My point is first, that we're wise to slow our instruction down just a bit to be certain that what we are teaching is actually being used by our learners. My larger point is that our teaching is always *conceptual*. We may *think* we are teaching item knowledge (such as a sight word), but children are meanwhile also developing concepts of print, of story, of written language, and of themselves as readers and writers.

Sometimes teachers mistakenly think that what comes first in a primary reading curriculum is the letter *A* (then *B*), the little words—articles and prepositions—such as *a, the,* and *in,* and the earliest of leveled books. These well-intentioned teachers set out to teach these items by every means possible, including dittos, flash cards, and "Repeat after me" drills. These teachers are *not* wrong to value letters, sounds, and words. Yes, it *is* crucial for kindergarten children to develop some knowledge of these. The mistake instead is thinking that these items in and of themselves constitute the foundation of literacy and that they can be taught as effectively with flashcards as with stories. Because beginning readers are forming concepts of what a *letter* means and what a *word* means and how they work in the world even as they learn a particular letter or word, the context in which learners meet these items needs to convey true, helpful messages about language.

We are teaching concepts of literacy even when we don't realize it. If we put four words onto flash cards and flick these in front of a five-year-old, we are *perhaps* teaching these four words as items, but we are *definitely* teaching the child that building words with letters is nothing like building castles with blocks. The child is learning that written language is not something you do with friends. The child is learning to feel out of control as a reader, for the control is literally in someone else's hands. The child is learning to expect print to be confusing and intimidating. Is it any wonder this child grows up accepting confusion in texts and not monitoring for sense?

When we plan for September in a primary reading workshop, we need to think, "How can my instruction further my children's concept development?" These are some of the concepts that enable children to become strong readers and writers:

- Children need to learn about when and why people read and write. Long before they are skilled word solvers, they can learn to initiate approximate versions of reading and writing for their own important purposes and to regard both as sources of pleasure, learning, and relationships.

- Children are developing concepts of school and of themselves as students. It is crucial for them to learn to be active, constructive, and engaged learners. They may learn this first in the block corner; then we can help them transfer this sense of themselves and of school to the domain of print.

- Children will develop concepts of language. It is fundamental for them to talk with each other and with us in sustained narratives, so that language doesn't just label or report what's happening in the here and now ("That's my truck. Boom. Move!") but also creates imagined worlds, actions, and ideas ("Yesterday I made a garage and then Bobby …").

- Children need to develop a concept of genre and to internalize a felt sense of the registers and structures of different genres so they can, for example, pick up a storybook and expect to find characters and a sequence of events. If a child sees a cat on one page of a story book and a dog on the next, we hope that child will put these together and anticipate that the dog might chase the cat. We hope the child will expect a recipe book to sound differently than a story, and to follow a different and yet equally predictable structure.

- Children need to learn the concept of sound-letter correspondences. Generally, children who are off to a strong start as readers and writers know many or even most letter names by the end of one year in full-day kindergarten, and they know also many accompanying sounds. They also understand letter stability (whatever the print font, an *M* is still an *M*) and are beginning to understand that letters combine to make chunks and words.

- Children need to develop an understanding of words so that if they are asked to break a sentence ("My friend Mary likes to draw ducks") into little parts, they will divide it not only into "My friend Mary" and "likes to draw ducks" but also into separate words (Sulzby, 2000). Children need to understand that in sentences and stories, each glob of letters on the page is one word. They will learn this first in their own writing. Once children develop this initial sense of words, we can help them to point with one-to-one matching. Children will eventually profit from learning to count on and use their knowledge of a few sight words to anchor their one-to-one matchings.

- Children need to develop print-specific directionality, to learn that most English writing is "read" from front to back, top to bottom, and left to right, unless the text has been arranged in a playful manner.

How do we design a curriculum that helps all our children come to school and feel smart and also gives children experience in working with print and stories that allows them to slowly consolidate the network of relationships involved in reading and writing? How, especially, do we teach big concepts—such as what different genres are like and why people read and write—when our children can't yet read conventionally?

For both kindergarten and first-grade children we begin the year by creating a particular kind of learning environment, one characterized by the conditions for language learning described by Cambourne (1993) in *The Whole Story*. Cambourne argues that if we study the conditions within which children learn oral language (virtually all children painlessly accomplish this stunningly complex learning), we can ascertain the conditions that will support all literacy learning. Researchers have pointed out recently that learning to read is not the same as learning to talk, but there are many conditions that support all forms of language learning. Cambourne argues that these conditions include (p. 33):

Immersion: Learners need to be saturated with the kind of texts they are expected to read and write.

Demonstration: Learners need repeated demonstrations of what we hope they will soon do, although they will only attend to self-selected aspects and actions, organizing and integrating these into their literary knowledge.

Engagement: If a child is not engaged, all the demonstrations and immersion opportunities in the world will amount to nothing. Learners won't engage with a demonstration unless they see the action as doable and worth doing.

Expectations: In subtle ways, we convey to students our confidence that they have the ability to participate in the literacy event and to master the strategies. We help children trust that their efforts will be celebrated.

Responsibility: Learners need to make decisions about how and what aspects of a learning task they'll learn.

Use: Learners need time to use and practice literacy for the learner's own purposes.

Approximation: Learners must be free to approximate and make mistakes.

Response: It's important for learners to receive nonthreatening responses from us and for these responses to scaffold their continued engagement. (p. 33)

What Are Emergent Readers Doing in a Reading Workshop If They Can't (Yet) Read Conventionally?

It is helpful for us to think about how Cambourne's conditions translate into practice by considering, for a moment, the kindergarten *writing* workshop. Teachers across the world gather children together and convey faith (or *expectation*) by telling them, "You are all writers" and "Today we are going to write stories." The teacher turns to the easel to say, "I'm going to write about cooking bacon this morning, because the grease splashed up and burned my hand," and soon she is *demonstrating* the process of writing. She draws herself standing by the stove. "That's me," she says, and repeats, "me" while recording an *m.* "Me," she says again, reading what she's written and preparing to write more. Soon children choose markers, pens, and paper and decide what they will draw and write. They're on their way, *approximating* and receiving *responses.* "That's your Dad?" we say, "How would I know? You need to write 'Dad.' Say it slowly with me … What sounds do you hear at the beginning of the word?"

At the start of the school year, our kindergarten and first-grade *reading* workshops tend to parallel our primary writing workshops. We may gather children together and with all the trust *(expectation)* in the world, we say, "You are all readers. Today I'm going to read Paul Galdone's *The Three Billy Goats Gruff* to you, like I did yesterday, and then you can read it and other books with each other." Soon after children have heard us reread the familiar tale of *The Three Billy Goats Gruff,* they disperse with their own copy of this book or other familiar storybooks in hand and reread these books to each other.

"But … they can't read," you may think, and that's probably mostly true. At the start of kindergarten, most of our readers can only approximate reading, just as most of our writers can only approximate writing. But children need opportunities to approximate reading, if this is what they can do, because children learn any language—the reading of it, the writing of it, and the speaking of it—by approximation. They'll learn by being *immersed* in written language, by seeing us and their classmates *demonstrate* what seems doable and worth doing, but their *engagement* comes in part because we convey the *expectation* that they can do this. They learn by *use,* by practice, and by our informed *responses,* which help them do with our support what they can soon do independently (Vygotsky, 1962).

When children head off to read, we'll follow, ready to learn from and assist their approximations of reading. For the first few months of kindergarten and for some children at the start of first grade, reading a book may not yet mean reading the words. Instead, many readers will probably turn the pages and generate their own text to accompany the print.

When it was time for reading, five-year-old Nicole made a beeline for the books displayed in wicker baskets on a shelf called Old Favorites. I credit Elizabeth Sulzby with teaching my colleagues and me to highlight multiple copies of these returnable storybooks. Sulzby's Kindergarten Literature Program (KLP) has informed our work. I describe this in more detail later in the chapter. One basket contained six copies of Tomie DePaola's *Strega Nona,* another contained multiple copies of Virginia Lee Burton's *Mike Mulligan and His*

Steam Shovel. Nicole bypassed these and reached instead for Esphyr Slobodkina's *Caps for Sale* and Don Freeman's *A Pocket for Corduroy.* All the books on the Old Favorites shelf (some teachers use Sulzby's term and call this the KLP shelf) are ones her teacher had read aloud five or six times, so Nicole wasted not a moment before she was snuggling against a pillow reading. Lydia Bellino, her principal, pulled in to listen to and transcribe Nicole's reading of *Caps for Sale.*

The book begins:

> Once there was a peddler who sold caps.
> But he was not like an ordinary peddler,
> carrying his wares on his back.
> He carried them on top of his head.
>
> He walked up and down the streets
> holding himself very straight so as not to upset his caps.
> As he went along he called,
> "Caps! Caps for sale! Fifty cents a cap!'

Nicole looked at the first picture, then at the words, and this is the story as she "read" it that morning:

> Once upon a time there was a man who had caps for sale.
>
> He said, "Caps for sale. Caps for sale," but nobody wanted some caps.
>
> And then he went on the bridge and said, "Caps for sale," but nobody wanted them. Everybody was in their houses.
>
> And then he got sad.
>
> Then he found a tree and he took a rest.
>
> Then the monkeys tooked his caps.
>
> Then he woke up.
> He wanted to check if his caps were there.
> Only one cap was there.
>
> And then he feeled if his caps were there.
> It wasn't there.
>
> He looked on the north side of the tree and then he looked um, uh, to the other side of the tree,...
>
> Then he looked up
> And he saw the monkeys wearing his caps.
>> A red cap,
>> And then a gray cap,

And then a blue cap.
And then a black cap,
And a gold cap.

Nicole continued in a similar manner, looking at the print and "reading" the story.

As Margaret Spencer (1988) points out and Nicole illustrates, "Favorite story books apparently teach far more than we have understood." Marie Clay (1991) agrees. From hearing favorite storybooks read over and over and from being invited to read them as best they can, children learn, she says, "the structure of plots, anticipation of events, memory for what happened from a previous reading, and the ways in which language is used to create the effects of surprise, climax and humor" (p. 80). Elizabeth Sulzby has taken this work a step further and helped us understand the journey a child takes from emergent reading to conventional reading, and to anticipate, see, and support signs of growth in oral and written language development. And how much there is to see in a child who reads emergently! I love the literary rhythms in Nicole's rendition of *Caps for Sale*:

He wanted to check if his caps were there.
Only one cap was there.

And then he felt if his caps were there.
It wasn't there.

I can feel the suspense growing in Nicole's version of this story, as the man looked "on the north side of the tree and then he looked um, uh, to the other side of the tree…. Then he looked up"

Nearby, Amaury was scanning his brightly colored, oversized picturebook. It was not one his teacher had read aloud. On each page, there was a picture of a group of animals. Backing up to the start of the book, Amaury's gaze shifted from the picture to the print, then back to the picture, and finally, touching the print as he said each word, he began to read. Amaury improvised the text in the following way:

THE TEXT SAID:	AMAURY READ:
Here are all the animals Walking in a row	Once upon a time they walked to the forest.
Now they are all going home Let's see where they go	(skips pages)

There are monkeys in the jungle	3 little monkeys in the woods
There are hippos by the pool	(spoken in rhythm)
	2 little hippos in the water
There are tigers in the grasslands	4 little tigers in the field
And lions keeping cool	(skips the page)
There are crocodiles in the river	2 little alligators in the swamp
There are elephants on the plain	(counts: 1, 2, 3, 4, 5, 6, 7, 8)
	8 little elephants in the meadow
There are giraffes so high they touch the sky	3 little giraffes eating the leaves in the tree
And toads out in the rain.	(counts: 1, 2, 3, 4, 5, 6, 7, 8, 9, 10, 11)
	11 little frogs in the rainy day.

When I first began teaching, I would probably have watched Amaury's reading and concluded that it was nowhere and all wrong. Because Amaury's oral rendition of the book didn't match the print, I would have despaired. "He's *still* not reading," I'd have said. For the next few weeks, I would probably have continued to watch him: "Not reading. Not reading," and "Still not reading." Then one day (especially if Amaury was meanwhile in a writing workshop), seemingly out of the blue, Amaury would have opened a predictable patterned text and read it with some accuracy. Astonished, I'd have said, "What do you know! Suddenly—out of nowhere—he's reading!" I might even have used Amaury's out-of-the-blue breakthrough as evidence that you can't really *teach* reading, that it just clicks (or it doesn't). And I would have been all wrong. Amaury's growth as a reader was right there before my eyes all along, but when I was new to teaching I had eyes for one aspect of reading only—sound-letter correspondences—so I would have discounted the skills and progress and conceptual work he'd been showing me. Now, after taking lessons from emergent readers, I can watch Amaury's accomplished work with this text and celebrate his strengths. Because of the skills he demonstrates, I can look forward with optimism to the work he needs to do with sound-letter correspondences and print.

Amaury already knows

- That books are interesting and worth attending to closely. If we pay close attention to the pages of a book, we can find and construct meaning out of what is on those pages.
- That the language of books is different from the language we speak. In this instance, Amaury shows that he expects patterned, rhythmic language as well as literary turns of phrase ("Once upon a time they walked to the forest").
- That picture and print go together to make one coherent meaning. Readers must look closely at the picture and think about what the picture might be saying but then look at the print to read the black marks on the page. At an earlier stage, Amaury would have ignored the print and "read" only the pictures. Now he at least shows that he knows the story is in the print.
- That when we read the black marks on the page, we read from front cover to back cover in order, first the left-hand page, then the right-hand page, our eyes moving from left to right and from top to bottom. This spatial orientation marks a big accomplishment.
- That the utterances we say need to be segmented to roughly match the graphic units on the page (each bit that we say is represented by a block of print surrounded by white space).
- That texts come in different genre, and that some books have a pattern, a "way they go," and reading the text involves figuring out the pattern for a particular text.

Amaury's approximation of the text convinced Randy Bomer, who was working with him, that he'd be wise to look at Amaury's writing to see if his invented spellings might indicate that Amaury would profit enormously now from focusing on the correspondence between utterances and words, and between letters and sounds. Does he read his own writing with one-to-one matching, pointing somewhat correctly at the print which represent the words he says? The evidence may suggest that Amaury can be brought quickly into conventional reading.

It is absolutely crucial for kindergarten and first-grade teachers to realize, as Marie Clay (1991) says, that "*attention to the formal properties of print and correspondence with sound segments is the final step in a progression, not the entry*

point to understanding what written language is." She goes on to explain, "Many conceptual shifts about the nature of written language have to occur before the child begins to use the alphabetic principle of letter-sound relationships which is often considered to be the beginning of reading" (p. 33). Amaury, like Nicole, is certainly well on his way toward being ready to flourish as a conventional reader. Other children, however, will need more support.

Meanwhile Crystal read a poem by Prince Redcloud. She held the paper, and said the words aloud:

Close the barbecue
Close the sun
Close the homerun games we won.

Close the picnic,
Close the pool,
Close the summer,

Open School.

Crystal, like Amaury and Nicole, is an emergent reader. She would not have been able to read this poem save for the fact that she's heard it many, many times and joined into whole-class shared readings of the poem.

Shared reading is a method developed by Donald Holdaway (1979) to bring the strengths of a parent reading to a child sitting on his or her lap into the classroom. If a father, for example, reads and rereads a book to his child, pointing at the words as he reads them, the child follows the print and chimes in where she can. Parent and child may pause to respond to the story, to talk about the print. "Look Pat. It says *Pat* the bunny! That's your name." Teachers can create a similar reading experience by using big books or other texts that have been enlarged (perhaps a poem or a song on chart paper) and a pointer. Children develop the identity of being one who reads from shared reading.

On the first day of school, Crystal's teacher, Teresa Cascavale, had hung a laminated copy of Prince Redcloud's poem from her easel at the front of the meeting area, and as families came into the room that first morning, many of them stood in front of the poem and read it. Teresa later read the poem aloud. When she'd finished, Hershal shot up his hand. "It rhymes," he said and soon the class was listening again and again as Teresa read it aloud, and working in partnerships to collect rhymes: cool-pool-school, sun-won.

"My kindergarten teacher put a line under the words that rhymed," Jessie said, and so of course Teresa borrowed the idea to Jesse's delight. Then Teresa asked, "Do you want to read it with me?"

Teresa was soon making a "yucky face" over the clamor of discordant voices that ensued. "The poem sounds messy when we all read it differently. Let's start again and stick together so it sounds good." After two or three tries, the class read it somewhat in unison, with Teresa pointing under the words as they read. During that day, they read the poem twelve times. By the second day of school, the class had begun reading the poem in creative ways, first with one side of the room reading one stanza, the other side, the next stanza, then with hand motions. The next day the class made word substitutions, then they masked words and guessed which word had been masked. That night children each took a copy of the poem home, underlining rhyming words, finding a word from the poem they wanted to learn forever, and drawing an accompanying picture. After all this, Crystal sits among her classmates. Like Amaury and Nicole, she cannot yet read conventionally but she is a confident and happy emergent reader, and is developing skills which will soon make her, like her classmates, ready to read conventionally. When Crystal reads this familiar poem, she reads it in a nearly word-perfect fashion. To an observer, it might *seem* that she's a conventional reader, but she still has a distance to travel. Her work with Prince Redcloud's poem can teach her important lessons about learning to read. She is tracking print, reading it top-to-bottom and left-to-right. She is developing a sense for words, letters, and white space. She may become familiar with one or two words. All of this, like the lessons Amaury and Nicole are learning, is invaluable.

What Are We Aiming Toward When We Teach Emergent Readers?: Should We Hurry All Kids Straight Toward Conventional Reading?

When children read emergently (or pretend to read), as many of them are apt to do at the start of kindergarten and even at the start of first grade, teachers have several choices. We can do everything possible to hasten them away from this sort of reading, so that at all costs, when children in our classrooms "read," what they produce matches or nearly matches the words on the page. If children don't yet have the requisite knowledge to read conventionally, a teacher can nevertheless get them to do something that *looks like* conventional reading if we give them highly patterned, repetitive, simple texts, if we read these books to them first (or give the books such weighty introductions that we might just as well have read the book to the child first), and if we keep children rereading the same text over and over. Although the work Crystal has done with "Close the barbecue/Close the sun" is very valuable, I worry when I see some teachers valuing emergent readings only if they produce correct texts. I worry when I find that more and more of today's primary teachers feel so pressured to push four- and five-year-olds toward always producing word-perfect reading *and do so in ways that reduce the richness and complexity of all their reading.* For these children, reading becomes merely pointing a finger under memorized and repetitive texts.

If in looking over a kindergarten or early first-grade classroom, we see some children talking and thinking about a giraffe book and other children chanting their way through memorized texts, many teachers are apt to put a special premium on the readings that result in accurate reproductions of the text at hand. Some teachers are apt to place more value on the child's accurate rereading (for the twentieth time) of "Brown bear, brown bear, what do you see? I see a brown bear looking at me. Red bird, red bird, what do you see?" or "Close the barbecue, Close the sun," than on what the child does as she constructs her own new text to accompany pictures in a familiar or unfamiliar book. The problem is that, although a child may accurately reproduce "Brown bear, brown bear," or "Close the barbecue," this may not necessarily mean that the child is remotely well on the way toward conventional reading (which is why Level 2 or B books are regarded as preconventional levels). Such children may not know how stories tend to go or that texts make sense or that readers ask themselves, "Does this sound right?" and match what they say to the letters on the page. Such children may not have a sense that book language is different from ordinary language, or of what a word is or of sound-letter correspondences. If we work at it long enough, children can produce the correct text, but this does *not necessarily* mean they are reading conventionally. It will be important to pull our chairs alongside our readers to really see what they are doing as they read.

I would suggest that we look again at the issue of what is "rigorous and challenging" and realize that constructing a coherent story characterized by story elements, a story that matches the pictures in a text, can be an even more demanding and exciting intellectual enterprise than chanting one's way through "I see the cow. I see the pig...."

Of course, it is also important for emergent and beginning readers to have lots of opportunities to read and reread simple and memorable patterned texts. Children love to join together like a choir, reading rhythmic, familiar poems, songs and Big Books while someone—the teacher or a child—draws a pointer along under the accompanying print. In early kindergarten, for most of our children, this shared reading will not yet be a time to teach letters and sight words. If children aren't yet labeling their own drawings with invented spellings, they won't tend to notice the double b's in *rabbit!* When most of our children are emergent readers, they can nevertheless learn extraordinarily powerful lessons from shared reading. They can learn that books are read left-to-right, cover-to-cover, that one page connects with the next, and each page is read top-to-bottom; they can learn that the little black marks on a page hold meaning, that the pictures accompany the print, that books have a special song and flow and rhythm. They can learn what it feels like to read just as a child whose bike has training wheels can learn what it feels like to ride bikes.

As long as our focus, as teachers, is not on particular letters or words, it's not a big problem if the text we use for shared reading is much more challenging than the simple books these children will soon be able to read. Later (or at other times in the day) we may want shared reading to provide a forum for teaching children high frequency words (perhaps *I* and *see*) or letters (m) or spelling patterns (at, cat, sat). For reasons I describe later in this chapter, the texts we use for shared reading will need to provide much more support for beginning readers if we're using them to teach the printwork of reading. Either way, however, when we read and reread enlarged texts with our children, they soon have these texts "under their belt" and during reading time, children will reread these texts. This is important and worthwhile reading work for a kindergarten or early first-grade child, but the fact that the resulting renditions of a text are often word-perfect does not mean however, that this intellectual work with these texts represents a more sophisticated intellectual accomplishment than a child's emergent reading of a long, complex story book.

What About the Start of the First-Grade Year?

I want to go a step further and say that I think first-grade teachers would also be wise to anticipate that during the first two or three weeks of first grade, a good many of their children will do richer versions of the emergent readings we expect to see in kindergarten as well as chanting their way through memorized texts and probably also working with words in some little books. Why don't I immediately, once children cross the first grade threshold, move every child who does not always read conventionally toward this goal (taking them immediately away from making up stories in familiar books, toward working with words in the "little books")? These are some of my reasons:

- I don't think it makes sense for children to walk across the threshold into our first-grade classrooms and be immediately told, "This is altogether different from kindergarten." We want children to bring all they know from kindergarten into first grade, including their sense of themselves as individuals who knows things and can do things. Why would we teach children that school involves one thing in kindergarten and something utterly different in first grades? It makes much more sense to plan for continuities.

- If children learned to construct stories that sound literary and that match the pictures in kindergarten, I will want to signal to them to "Continue to think in these ways as you read," because it will provide crucial support for the print work they'll be doing soon.

- We want children to draw on all sources of information as they read. Across our curriculum, we will want to be sure that various components of the school day support a child's development with each of these sources of information. In September, within interactive writing, shared reading, the writing workshop, and word study time, we will spotlight the print work of reading. The independent reading workshop and the read-aloud can remind children that reading is about making sense and that written texts sound like language—like book language, in fact. Soon, independent reading will, like shared reading, be a time to work with print as well as with meaning. Rather than put children into leveled little books the instant they enter first grade, we first need to remind them of a bigger message: language is about making meaning and your brains need to *think* as you read.

- It is important that children can function purposefully, joyfully, and independently in the reading workshop while I do the assessing, coaching, and guiding necessary to help more children progress toward reading conventionally. If I ask too much of children too early, some will react by becoming dependent and cautious. It's wiser to get the room functioning smoothly before raising the ante.

- Before I can help children read conventionally, I need to assess them carefully so that I can offer support that is tailored to them. It may require a few weeks to do the assessment and instructional planning necessary to move all of a first-grade class toward reading words.

Anticipating the Texts Our Children Will Read and Their Ways of Reading Them

During the entire kindergarten year and the first weeks of first grade, we will welcome children into the full range of wonderful literature and expect them to find meaning and pleasure in these stories. Our library will contain

- Environmental print (labels, charts, class news, songs, print on food labels, names under each other's photographs, etc.).

- Poems and songs we've read and reread, some written on chart paper (including, ideally, some texts from the previous year and also functional print, such as the class theme song). Some functional texts will serve also as sources of shared reading (the alphabet chart, the name board, the daily schedule).

- Highly predictable, heavily scaffolded texts such as the "little books." Many of these will be leveled once the second unit of study begins (see Chapter 14).

- Big Books that have been read and reread in shared reading can be propped up on the easel or laid out on the carpet and reread individually.

- Nonfiction books, magazines, pamphlets, and maps related to whole-class and individual inquiries and to areas of interest in the classroom.

- The best of children's literature categorized in all sort of ways, such as by author, topic, last-year's favorites, theme.

- Children's published writing.

- Other books for beginning readers (some of these will and some will not be leveled).

I expect that children will be reading in a wide range of ways.

- Some will read conventionally, others will be emergent readers. All children will be readers.
- Some will narrate stories to accompany the pictures in complex storybooks they've read repeatedly (such as *Caps for Sale*).
- Some will chime along, reading the words in familiar patterned books such as Bill Martin's *Brown Bear, Brown Bear* or Joy Cowley's *Mrs. Wishy Washy* or in poems such as "Close the barbecue, Close the sun …." They'll also do this with songs the class comes to know by heart.
- They will all reread their own writing and the writing of their friends.
- They'll do dramatic play within the pages of books, speaking in the voices of characters and supplying sound effects.
- They'll make up stories, lists, and poems to accompany the pictures in unfamiliar texts from wide-ranging genres.
- They'll study books in order to learn. These may be nonfiction books about giraffes or waterfalls or *any* books. Children might study illustrations in which parent-animals watch their youngsters performing in a school play and try to match each parent-animal to a child-animal.
- They'll read and use the print in the classroom (labels, purposeful writing, the daily schedule).

Conferring That Supports Emergent Readers

We begin encouraging children to read from the very first moment they flow into the classroom. The blocks are often tidily wedged into their bin, the math manipulatives shelved, and Hermy the hermit crab is, as always, tucked into his shell. Children often settle like Monarch butterflies in the nooks and corners of the library, where books abound, open and enticing, beckoning to them. Some children will search for trusted, familiar stories and "reread" these old favorites, others will be conventional readers and begin using all the cueing systems to read books that are at a level of difficulty they can handle; and still others may read the Westminster Dog Show catalog, choosing among all the varieties of dogs.

In all our classrooms we tend to begin the independent reading workshop in September by laying out our bounties and saying, "Go at it!" Then we watch to see what the children will do. The worrisome truth, however, is that texts *won't* beckon to all our children. At the start of the year, there will be children who would just as soon sit idly on the library carpet as read. When I approached five-year-old Sam, he was flipping through short stack of books as if none had much to offer. One of the books he had pushed aside was Steven Kellogg's *Can I Keep Him?* "Oh, I *love* this book," I said, fetching it from the discard pile. "Can we read it together?" I put it in Sam's hands. (Because I want readers to be active and to take ownership of reading, I try to resist my tendency to pull books out of children's hands.) Now I watched what Sam did. He flipped the book open to a page halfway through the text and then glanced this way and that.

"When I read, I like to start at the beginning," I said, "with the cover, and the title." Then I pointed to the picture, which shows a little boy fondly petting an absolutely enormous creature. The boy and the creature seem to be in the arctic regions on an iceberg. I pointed to the dominant part of the picture, the creature, as if I were just then noticing it. "Huh?" I said, and glanced into Sam's eyes as if to say, "What do you think of *that?*"

Sam said, "He's big."

"Yeah," I added, my finger moving to the boy. "It looks like that little boy likes him, doesn't it?" I will eventually want Sam to read the print, but I know that first he needs to be able to look at the picture and generate thoughts and words in response to what he sees. Many two-year-olds can do this, but sometimes our kindergarteners are so afraid and insecure in the presence of print, they look at books as if their minds were paralyzed. I'm going to want to act out a kind of reading that is very much within Sam's reach. Now I pointed to the print and said, "Oh, look, it says, 'Can I keep him?' That's the title of the book." Now I say to Sam, "I wonder what this book will be about?" as if I've just this second seen the title *Can I Keep Him?,* looked at the picture of that boy with the creature, and am now on the brink of predicting the book's contents from all these clues.

I *hope* Sam will say something, so I pause a moment for him to do so, but he is quiet. I wait for him to open the book. He sits passively, so I carry on, trying to structure Sam's experience of this book so he begins to generate an idea for how this story will go. "So that boy is patting the huge creature … and the book's title is *Can I Keep Him?* … hmm." I waited. Sam was silent. "Do you suppose *this boy* wants a pet?" Sam nods slightly. "Do you? He wants to keep this big guy?" I say, as if Sam has been the one to suggest this all along. "You think so?" Sam nods again. I act as if this has been Sam's theory (not mine). "What an idea, Sam! Let's look. Let's see if you are right." Sam opened the book to the next page. "I love the way you turn one page at a time," I comment. "That's how I read too. First the cover. Then the next page. So let's look." Now I watch where Sam's gaze falls. I don't want to take his spatial orientation for granted, and if he doesn't "read" left to right and top to bottom, I'll make a great point to scaffold this now and during the writing workshop.

Reading and Rereading Books Aloud and Inviting Emergent Readers to Do the Same

My colleagues and I trust an old-fashioned method for enticing emergent readers toward books and toward becoming active and engaged as "readers" themselves. We read to children. We read the books that represent children's literature at its best, books written by beloved authors who are trying to spin a good story, to speak the truth, and to make a book that can change the world. We read the books that children ask to hear again and again: *Koala Lou* by Mem Fox, *The Ghost-Eye Tree* by Bill Martin, *Crictor* by Tomi Ungerer, *Corduroy* by Don Freeman, *Ira Sleeps Over* by Bernard Weber, *The Runaway Bunny* by Margaret Wise Brown, and fairy tales of all sorts. We do not limit our reading to the books children will soon be able to read themselves. In homes where children flourish as readers and writers, parents read and reread beloved storybooks, and then children read these same books to their teddy bears and baby sisters. Some children point and label, "Doggy!" "Raining, raining!" Eventually, children who've heard these books often will spin tales that are so literate and textlike, we look twice to check that they haven't gone out and taught themselves to read.

Of course, it's not unusual for children who sit beside their baby brothers creating imaginative, literate-sounding renditions of cherished stories to, lo and behold, begin to read the print. Children who teach themselves to read may be the exceptions, but the journey they travel—from pointing and labeling with pictures to storylike approximations of reading to paying attention also to the print work of reading—is one that all emergent readers deserve to travel. During September's reading time in our K–1 classrooms, we read a few favorite, carefully chosen books and don't have to wait long for "Pleeeeze read it again!!" By the third or fourth reading, children listen differently, "coauthoring" the refrain with us, anticipating changes of tempo, and laughing more gleefully than ever because now they're insiders to the story. At the advice of Elizabeth Sulzby, we read these beloved books many times within even just a week or two, and then, like wise parents, leave the books out during reading time, pulling up in our own chairs to listen.

In many of our kindergarten and first-grade classrooms, then, we start the year by reading aloud the most compelling storybooks we can find. We sometimes put our own gold-seal with the words Old Favorite on these books, which we reread often. These Old Favorites are kept in special bins that, at least for now, are highlighted in the library. Some teachers go so far as to require that children start each day's reading workshop with these familiar Old Favorites. After ten or fifteen minutes of reading Old Favorites, children can then read any books they choose. In a kindergarten classroom and for the first few weeks of first grade, during this free-choice interval children choose from all the ways of reading described earlier in this chapter (see page 274).

Understanding Children's Development as Emergent Readers

Elizabeth Sulzby (1985) has developed descriptors of eleven ways of reading emergently (these aren't exactly stages because children don't progress steadily along from one to the next; instead, at any one time, children will exhibit a range of these ways of reading). These eleven levels have helped us see that children who are reading emergently present us with an extraordinarily rich instructional opportunity. In a nutshell, Sulzby's research has found that after listening to a story such as *Corduroy* read aloud four or five times over the course of two weeks, some pre-K and kindergarten children will read it in a manner one might expect of toddlers. Turning the pages, these children will produce nouns that label the objects on the page and sometimes make comments. A child at this level (Level 1) might read the first pages of *Corduroy* like this: "Bear, people … He's fat!" We can extend this by saying, "Yes, the bear is waiting on the shelf, isn't he? The people are shopping." The child's reading will soon expand to follow the action on the page. "People walking, shopping." Level 3 is a big step ahead. Sulzby calls this level of emergent reading "dialogic oral storytelling," and it's easy to understand why. "The bear is up there in the store, and look, the people are looking for him. Look, look. Here's where they are gonna find him. She's gettin' him. She gots him." Children tell a story, usually in the present tense, about what is in the picture before them.

The next big step happens when children's readings reach Levels 6 and 7. If we were to close our eyes and listen to a child's version of the story at these levels, we'd think the child was *reading,* not *telling* the story. The story may be less elaborated, but it will be much more literary. Nicole's reading of *Caps for Sale,* (see page 264) for example, sounded literary in part because she used the past tense, the usual tense for written narratives.

Marie Clay (1991), who describes stages of emergent literacy similar to Sulzby's, agrees that when children invent texts, the "transition to 'talking like a book' is a very important step in learning" (p. 78). Although Levels 6 and 7 *sound* as if the child is reading the print, it's not until Sulzby's Level 8 that the child seems to recognize that *the print holds the words*. The child might say, "I can't read it. I don't know the words." By Level 9, a child may almost rubber band parts of their reading to the print, retelling a page of the story and then seeing one of the words she has spoken on the page. "I know *he!*" the child says. Although she had previously been telling the story as a narrative, she may now go through the text, picking out known words: "he" "and" "Mom." The resulting text makes no sense, of course, but clearly this is a child who can track print, look for and find known print, and notice features of print. In another reading session, this same child might sound out long words, in a letter-by-letter, laborious fashion creating nonsense words. In yet another session, this child will return to the rich, approximated story-creation work of level seven. As Clay (1991) describes this stage, "Now there comes an important transition which takes some experience to observe. The child combines his ability to produce sentences, his half memories of the text, the picture cues to meaning, and visual cues from letters. Putting all these cues together in a sequence of actions he seems to compose his response word by word" (p. 80).

The Transition Between Emergent and Conventional Reading

We help children read conventionally by helping them read emergently—by working with phonics (see Chapter 11), by teaching actively and assertively during the writing workshop (see Calkins, 1994), by eventually helping them read the words in appropriately chosen books (see Chapter 14) and in environmental print, and by doing a great deal of shared reading with them.

It is important to realize that if we offer kindergarten children opportunities and support for emergent (or approximated) reading of wonderful storybooks, and if we simultaneously involve them deeply in a writing workshop and in lots of work with print, many children never need to plug along through every gradient of "the little books." Elizabeth Sulzby's (2000) research has shown that once children reach Level 11 in her scale of emergent reading, if these children are also using invented spellings to write in ways a literate adult can decipher *and* are able to read their own writing, attending to both meaning and print, a great many of them can switch over to reading books that are in our Groups 3 or 4 or higher, even. Books at this level would include Mercer Mayer's *Just Me and My Puppy*, William Joyce's *George Shrinks*, and John Stadler's series of books about Snail (*Snail Saves the Day, Three Cheers for Hippo!*). Other children will still benefit from working their way along, beginning with Group 1 or, more often, Group 2 books (Levels 3 and 4, C and D), but these children are less apt to be stymied and end up banging away at these books for a long time because will be ready to move from preconventional to conventional reading.

What Does Management of the Reading Workshop Look Like In Kindergarten and Early First Grade?

I've described our first unit of study by telling what children rather than teachers do in our kindergarten and very early first-grade reading workshops. This is not an accident. Especially with young children, we teach by putting particular materials into their hands, by organizing time and launching activities, by enabling them to do good work, and by watching with particular angle of vision. But we do also teach by establishing classroom routines and delivering minilessons. So what, you may ask, are the routines of a reading workshop in kindergarten and first grade?

Many of the teachers in our community begin the year in kindergarten and first grade by highlighting the Old Favorites storybooks, putting multiple copies in a featured shelf in the classrooms library. As I mentioned, some teachers even ask children to begin the reading workshop each day by rereading Old Favorites, and only then reading as they choose. (Soon we'll put children in leveled books, but not yet.) We are also apt to divide reading time into private reading time and partner reading time. Sometimes the private reading time comes first, in which case children reread Old Favorites alone, to themselves, but sometimes the partner reading time comes first, in which case children "read" Old Favorites to each other. We might ask children if they liked having grown-up, private reading time, and get them thinking together about what they could do in private reading time if they finished reading all their books (go back and reread, find another book, locate their favorite parts). We also talk up the joys of reading with a partner, demonstrate how partnerships work, and coach them into reading with partners (see Chapter 6). Early in the year, we're less concerned that partners talk over the text together as they read and more interested in having partners read books to each other, chorally, taking turns, playing parts, or doing echo reading, in which one child reads a few pages and the partner rereads these pages, working towards "a smooth read." When getting through books from start to finish is still a big deal, too much talk between the pages keeps readers commenting on the books rather than positioning themselves to construct stories, creating literary renditions of books. We don't want the partnership structure to derail children from constructing a literary work in their mind's eye. Although we'll soon teach children to read-talk-read, for now we may put more emphasis on simply reading (and this, of course, includes pretending-to-read) to and with each other.

In Kathy Collins's first grade, for the first few months of the year, all the children sit at their tables for both private and partner reading time. Kathy thinks of herself as a nooks-and-crannies sort of a teacher, one who wants her children to be comfortable and interactive as they read, so it took her a couple of years to face the fact that for her, a reading-in-nooks management system gave children too much latitude. "It sounds odd, but I feel as if I can scan the room better now because they're all sitting on the same level." Kathy says. "The kids are less apt to roll about on the floor like tumbleweeds. With one quick look, I can tell just from the way they're sitting whether they're doing book talk or Pokémon talk."

Details, like whether children should read at their tables or in nooks around the room, matter. We are only able to assess and confer with readers, lead guided reading sessions, or give strategy lessons if the other children read without constant supervision. But what about kindergarten classrooms? Do the management structures of Kathy's first grade match the needs of early kindergarten children?

I do not have an answer. Very good kindergarten teachers in our community make quite different decisions about the structures of independent reading during the autumn months of kindergarten. It seems to me that the jury is still out on whether it works better to structure reading so that all kindergarten children read alone for a bit and then meet with a long-term partner to read together, or whether it is best to have a twenty to forty minute reading time in which children shift between reading alone and reading with someone else. It also seems to me that the jury is out on whether early kindergartners benefit more from having a reading bin in which they keep one or two Old Favorite books they're rereading, some texts they know by heart, a study book or two, and so forth, or, because so many of their texts are on the walls and easels in the room, whether it's better to invite them to "graze" through their environment reading their world, reading a Big Book while lying on top of it on the carpet, then reading a song while standing before the easel, then reading the list of star-names with pointer in hand, then reading a familiar storybook or a pattern book.

Over the course of kindergarten, we will move children toward staying longer with a collection of books, a place, and a partner. But if there *is* a time for richly literate roaming around, it is early in the kindergarten year. I suspect that the most skilled and experienced kindergarten teachers may often opt for this less constrained structure early on and will be able to pull it off. Other teachers will begin the kindergarten year with the more constrained and orderly routines and structures, ones that resemble the structures we often put into place in our first-grade classrooms. I'll describe these in the section that follows. Either way, as the year moves along, all teachers will eventually set up structures to support children's transition toward conventional reading. By January, in the kindergarten classrooms connected with the Teachers College Reading and Writing Project, children are usually involved in fairly long-term partnerships with reading bins and with time for private and for partner reading.

The following management structures have been helpful to many of us:

- We may eventually organize a time each week when the whole class or a group of children "goes to the classroom library" to select some new books for the upcoming week. These books are stored in each child's reading bin.

- We may eventually have the whole class do private or partner reading first, and then switch. Some days we begin with one, and some days we begin with the other.

- We may ask children to start by reading a particular kind of book and only then to switch to a book of their choice. For a time in kindergarten and early first grade, we may ask children to begin each workshop by reading Old Favorites. When these books are separated from "look-at-and-talk-about" books and the "chant-along" books and the "construct-my-own-story-to-match-what-I-see" books, we make it more likely that children get into the habit of doing emergent readings of these Old Favorites. Later in kindergarten classrooms we tend to ask children to begin by reading the little books (Renée Dinnerstein calls these the "learning to read" books). In first grade, we will soon ask children to spend most of reading time on books from their leveled bin (or other books like these). Later, children will be given more opportunities to select books they feel are "just right" for them.

- If we are steering children to read books of a certain color or level, instead of having each child select ten individual titles, we might put plastic bags of five books each in the bins and encourage a child to select one or two bags.

- Children know where they will sit during every reading time and often sit near their partner even during private reading time. This tightens the transition between private and partner reading time. When it is time to read with their partner, they pull their chairs close together.

- Children keep all their reading tools—Post-it notes, pencils, and bookmarks—in their reading bins.

- After school, teachers add and subtract books from individual bins, leaving a gift of a new, just-right book and sometimes taking away too-hard books, leaving a note of explanation.

- Children eventually bring their book bins to the meeting area for minilessons, and during minilessons they sit beside their reading partners in assigned rug spots. This makes interactive work easier.

I've emphasized the management of primary reading workshops because I find that concerns over classroom management sometimes deter teachers from allowing children to read at all. Fairly often, I find kindergarten or first-grade teachers who, especially at the start of the year, keep their children together "safely" on the carpet, where, as we teachers put it, "they can do so much more because my arms are around them." Sending thirty very young children off to work and assuming books will hold their interest can feel very risky during these early September days. Although it is reasonable to worry over the management problems that might arise when we say "Off you go" to our readers, it is not reasonable to give in to those fears. Every reading researcher I know agrees that above all, as a bottom-line condition, every child needs extended time each day to work on his or her reading. Just as children learn to swim by swimming, they learn to read by reading.

During these first weeks of school, then, it is important for teachers to get past the juncture in their schedule that comes *after* children have listened to stories, when it is time for them to say that brave "Off you go" and send youngsters off to read.

Teaching Kids to Compose Rich Reading Lives for Themselves

Time and again, we're surprised to see that when given beautiful texts and time to read, children can work in readerly ways for long chunks of time. During the first week of reading workshop, teachers are apt to end reading time early enough to make children groan, "We have to stop already?" We're ready to use this comment to our best advantage. Gathering her children together, Kathy Collins talked about the groans she heard when reading ended on the previous day. "I know you guys are *dying* for more time to read," she said. "And I've been thinking whether there are little moments we can find during the day for reading." Kathy had glimpsed Kyle looking at a book during the early morning transitional time and wove this into the minilesson. "When I saw Kyle making a beeline for the books this morning, I thought, 'He's just like me!' because I do that, too. I squeeze in any extra moments I can find for reading. I was wondering, do any of the rest of you do like I do, and Kyle does, and find extra moments to read in the middle of your day?" Of course, children responded in a chorus of yesses. "Will you tell your partner about a time when *you* found surprising moments for reading?" Kathy said. After a few minutes, she elicited a few comments.

Danny, an emergent reader, said, "Last year I could pick reading at choice time."

"What a great idea," Kathy responded. "I know if *I* had choice time, I'd definitely choose to read."

"Or we could take books to lunch," Sammy suggested.

"Well, that's an idea. As long as we don't get any food on our precious books."

After hearing from another child or two, Kathy wrapped up the minilesson with the plea for everyone to be on the lookout for chances to read, read, read … and to bring their ideas for making reading time to tomorrow's minilesson. Later that morning, to make her point that readers squeeze time to read more dramatic, Kathy looked at the clock and said, "We have gym in ten minutes, so for now, let's just sit here and wait."

"We could read!" children responded, on cue.

"You are right! What an idea!" Kathy answered back.

Soon Kathy's kids began bringing books along whenever they knew they'd be waiting. "Today's the eye doctor," Kathy said the next morning. "So we'll be in the hall, sitting in a long line, waiting our turn. It'll be a bit dull but sometimes in life, people do have to wait." Not surprisingly, her children took the bait and before long, twenty-eight first graders sat in the school corridor and read while they waited for their eye exams. They seemed very pleased with themselves for being the ones to invent the whole wonderful plan of reading as they waited in the corridor.

"Outside of school, do you ever do this—read—when you have to wait?" Kathy asked, and soon she was listening to Ryan's report of how he actually read children's magazines while he waited at Dr. Judy's office. Of course, it turned out that other children in the class also read when they were waiting for Dr. Judy, the beloved neighborhood children's dentist, and they even discovered that others had looked through the very same magazines! They all agreed that the words had been too hard, but the pictures were great.

Other children told about bringing books with them in the car. "If my Mom runs in to get the dry cleaning or some vegetables, I'm not going to just sit there and stare!" Emily announced and everyone concurred.

"What if the worst thing happens and you forget your book?" Kathy asked. "That happened to me on the subway one day. But the good news was there was still stuff to read," and soon she was telling her students about how she ended up reading advertisements and signs. "I also peeked and read the headlines in other people's newspapers," she confessed.

During these early weeks of school, then, we talk about the fact that readers find ways to read often. We spotlight children who "read the room" while waiting for their classmates to gather, who use the print as a resource, who see cool words in the world and try to read them, who weave reading and books into play dates and sleepovers.

Reading and Choice Time

If we're trying to help children Make a Reading Life, this goal will affect not only the reading workshop but the whole day. As I've said, we'll encourage children to anticipate reading during transitional moments, when they are waiting, and the like. It will also be important to help children weave reading into their Choice-Time activities.

In every kindergarten and first-grade classroom, there needs to be time for blocks, dramatic play, and drawing. But as the year evolves, these "choice centers" (as I'll call them) will change, so that dramatic play may become The Three Little Pigs, and blocks may become The Castle Project, dress up may become making a bank. Children will soon spend at least a week together in a center and be encouraged to plan together. The curriculum for Choice-Time supports literacy in millions of ways:

- Children learn to expect that their schoolwork will be interesting. They approach school expecting to be engaged.
- Children have opportunities to spin stories and speak in the voices of characters, to make royal proclamations, "read" complex recipes, and recite incantations. They can also take the role of the narrator, creating the scene: "Pretend it's raining," they'll say. As narrator, they mark the passage of time: "Now it's the next day." In these ways they build worlds, which is, after all, part of what any reader must do.
- When children encounter difficulty (the cloth won't cover the doll's butt, the roof keeps caving in, the glue makes the wrong things stick together), we can teach them to be resourceful, flexible, and risk-taking problem solvers. They can learn to try one strategy and then another when things are difficult rather than become passive. Later, when their

difficulties involve print, we can remind children of their problem-solving prowess in other domains.

- Children can learn to use what they know to maximum advantage. If they know how to do one thing, this can help them improvise in other situations in which they are less sure about how to proceed.
- As children use literacy to open an account at the play "bank," read the flight manual for a turbo jet, order from a make-believe menu, and design road signs, they can learn why people read and write.
- When children plan their play together, they usually use sustained narratives to create imagined worlds and sequences of activities. It is enormously important that sustained language is being used to express imagined ideas.
- When children share what they have done, they are using sustained narratives in the past tense. They are constructing the story of their work, and this involves a literary use of language.

I've written this chapter as if there is widescale agreement on the underlying tenets I've proposed. I've said, "*Of course* kindergarten children need to invent their own versions of beloved stories, make and label their own block structures, take on roles within dramatic play, hear rich and beloved stories read and reread many times, spell using their best current knowledge of sound-letter correspondences, reread and revise what they've written by adding more content and more pages, reread texts they come to know by heart …." I've also said that *of course* we should expect most kindergarten children, by the end of the year, to know the names and many of the sounds of the alphabet, to read left-to-right, top-to-bottom, matching one utterance with one word, to spell representing most of the sounds they hear, to have approximately ten to twenty sight words they can read and write easily …. But the truth is that in many schools, teachers are led to believe that kindergarten teachers who choose dramatic play, early writing, blocks and reading aloud do this instead of helping children know letters, sounds, and sight words. Across America, one often hears about kindergarten children who no longer have choice time or recess because their whole day is spent on dittos, exercises, drills, and seat work. How I wish that I could somehow reach these teachers and tell them they needn't worry about choosing between helping children reenact a familiar story and helping them use words they know when they encounter new words.

In the New York City schools I know best, many of our kindergarten classrooms are videotaped and visited because they represent high literacy standards at their best. Children learn to write and read in these classrooms, but more than that, they learn to love reading and writing. During the kindergarten year, children need to learn to regard themselves as poets, actors, researchers, and songwriters. Kindergartners can learn to weave reading into play dates, choice time and recess. How important it is that kindergarten teachers who understand and value developmentally rich, early childhood classrooms become the spokespeople and mentor teachers and curriculum leaders for the new push toward literacy in the primary grades. We need to help the public form a new and more rigorous and more joyful image of what rich literacy looks, sounds, and feels like in the earliest grades.

Bringing in the Print Work of Reading

14

As teachers, sometimes we're rather like the man in the circus who gets plates spinning on the ends of long poles. We get one plate spinning, then move to the next and the next, then hurry back to the first plate to keep it spinning. In this fashion, we get one child going, then the next and the next, but we also get one *aspect of reading* going, then the next and the next.

If our initial emphasis in K–1 reading classrooms is on helping children read often and with understanding, engagement, and pleasure, at some point this emphasis will need to become broader, because we also want to move our children toward reading conventionally. We want children to use a range of strategies to read texts that have not been read to them, including thinking about the story, ("What might make sense here?") and including word recognition ("Have I seen this word before? Parts of this word?") and sound-letter correspondences. This means that in addition to helping children study the pictures and construct meaningful, coherent emergent readings of a text, we also want children to attend to the print work of reading. Starting on the first day of school, we'll support the print work of reading through word study, interactive writing, shared reading, and especially through a writing workshop. But there will come a time (and in first grade this will be before our first month of school is over) when we want to shine a curricular spotlight also onto reading the words.

How Do We Decide When to Shine a Curricular Spotlight on the Print Work of Reading?

When our whole-class teaching conveys the message that "in this classroom we'll use what we know about letters and sounds, *think about* the story, and read the words written on the page," we will propel more children to read print. Our focus will also make some children suddenly recognize that the emergent readings they've been doing all along are no longer enough. Kindergarten teachers especially will have to decide with care when it makes sense to put this sort of whole-class emphasis on reading the print. Many children enter kindergarten as four-year-olds. Even the rigorous New Primary Standards don't require children to read conventionally *by the end of kindergarten* (although many children will be doing this). For the first few months of kindergarten, I might support all kindergarten children's emergent readings, their readings of shared texts, their invented spellings, their reading of their own writing as they do it, their explorations during word-study time, their use of sight words in their writing, and their ability to talk deeply about books, and support some children as they read conventionally, but not shine a whole-class curricular spotlight on the print work of reading until somewhere between mid-November and December of the kindergarten year. This, of course, is a decision we make taking in account our particular students and also the particular context in which we teach. If a teacher decides to steer kindergarten children toward reading the words in little leveled books in October, I want to stress how important it is that this teacher maintain a parallel emphasis at some other time during the day on doing emergent readings of rich stories (Old Favorites) and of glorious new books.

If we push children who aren't yet ready to read the print to bob their fingers along as they call out the words in books we have thoroughly introduced, they can learn to do this. But I've seen many children who can hit a wall with level B (2) books, and I suspect this is because these children weren't first given the chance to develop the breadth of experience with book language, their own writing, making up stories, emergent reading, and so forth that will stand them in good stead for the long haul of becoming skilled readers. It's hard, therefore, to overemphasize the importance of a strong kindergarten and preschool program!

By the third week of first grade, most of us will probably want to move first graders toward more conventional reading (if they are not already doing this). These are some of the steps we'll take next:

- Assessing readers in order to match them to books.
- Anticipating the ways in which readers who are working with different levels of books may need different sorts of help.
- Revising the structure of the reading workshop to ensure that every child spends time reading conventionally every day.

- Highlighting the strategies readers need when they attend to print.
- Putting structures into place that support the print work of reading throughout the day.

Assessing Readers in Order to Match Them to Books

Whether this unit-of-study happens in December of kindergarten, in September of first grade, or at some other time altogether, it's necessary to prepare by assessing children in order to match them with books they're likely to be able to read successfully. We'll want to do running records of our children reading. These will be especially valuable for children who *can* read conventionally. For children who aren't yet reading conventionally, we'll need to listen to their emergent readings of familiar but not memorizable books and study their writing.

As we prepare for this unit of study, Project teachers tend to gather a few preselected assessment texts. If we do not yet know the child's reading, we rely on the child's writing to point us toward a book the child is likely to read with ease. As we pass the book along to the child, we say, "Today I have a book that I want to read with you. I'm going to read the title and tell you a little about it first [we show the book]. It's called *Max's Box*. It's about this kid named Max who loves to pretend, so he has this great box and he pretends with the box. I love it because when I was little, I pretended, too. Do you pretend? [The child responds.] Here, why don't you hold the book. [Pointing to the title, we read] *Max's Box*. Okay, go ahead. If you get really stuck on anything, try to work it out the best you can."

In earlier chapters I've discussed the importance of analyzing running records. As a child reads, we are watching and recording what the child does to process print. We are also asking ourselves:

- From the child's intonation, do I suspect she is making sense of what she reads?
- Does the child do any side talk about the *story* as he reads? "Oh, this part is funny." Does he make predictions, use information from pictures?
- Does the child seem resourceful and confident in the face of difficulties? Paralyzed and dependent?
- Does the child notice miscues? What sources of information does he rely upon? Print? Meaning? Does he self-correct? Make more attempts?

In trying to identify a child's just-right level, we err on the side of easier books.

Readers Who Are Working with Different Levels of Books May Need Different Sorts of Help

Children who have not had many opportunities to work with invented spellings within a writing workshop setting may see words as black blobs and white spaces rather than as groupings of individual letters. We will probably steer these children, at least for now, to read Group 1 (Guided Reading Levels A and B or Reading Recovery Levels 1 and 2) books. For a little while, we'll encourage them to point to the words as they read. They need to learn that one cluster of letters represents one utterance and to see that letters combine to make words. These children will profit from writing and from learning to use high frequency words to anchor their one-to-one matching as they read published books and their own writing. If the text says "I see the dog" and the child recognizes *I* and *the,* she is apt to point accurately, either the first time around or in self- correcting.

We'll soon want to help these readers "cross-check," integrating information from several sources, including the picture, the sound of the sentence, and the initial letters of words. If the child is reading a repetitive book in which every page says "Here comes the (something)" and the new page has a photograph of a motor vehicle, we'll say to this child, "What could that word be?" and direct his attention to the illustration. Then, returning to the print, we'll help the child read "Here comes the_____"; pointing at the letters *t-r-u-c-k,* we'll say, "Oh it starts with *t-r,* /tr/. So, what could it be? If the child is silent, we might say 'Could it be /tr/uck? Or /c/ar?" Assuming the child says "truck," we'll say, "How did you know?" or "Are you certain? Check it," and look to see if the child gets conformation from the letters.

Meanwhile, especially if either this year or the year before children have had a strong writing workshop and been encouraged in emergent reading, most of our readers will be further along. These *beginning* readers will probably orient themselves to books and get an idea of a book's content from looking it over. They'll know a small collection of words pretty well and will probably rely on these words. The pictures and sight words give them quick access to the patterned sections of the text, and their knowledge of letters, sounds, and word chunks will help them with simple one-syllable words. But these readers will become stymied over other, more challenging words. We can hope they will monitor their reading so they know when they are in trouble and will pause and make a second go at hard parts. They may especially need more resources for dealing with difficult words and for looking all the way across words.

Readers are bound to miscue, and so monitoring for sense and sound ("Does that sound right? Make sense? Check it") is important. Children who haven't had broad experience listening to stories or opportunities to construct their own emergent texts as they read may *not* monitor for sense, and this is cause for great concern. We'll also want to begin helping children monitor for visual accuracy (self-correcting not only because the meaning breaks down but because the print on the page doesn't match their hypothesized word). We want readers to say, "It could be *sleep* but it starts with *b*. Hmmmm."

Among our readers, we'll also find a few children who don't fit any of these categories. There may, for example, be a child who calls out a string of phonemes that together say and mean nothing. Children like this are usually the product of lopsided instruction, to which young readers are especially vulnerable. A child who calls out phonemes usually comes from a program that taught reading primarily by means of phoneme drills. If children haven't had rich experiences with shared reading, reading aloud, and emergent reading, they can develop odd ideas about what reading is. Other children will show the effects of instruction that has been lacking in the opposite way. They may have had no support in working with sound-letter correspondences. When they are asked to read the exact words in a book, they will look at the pictures and make up a story—which may be wonderfully creative but have nothing to do with the print on the page. These readers will need to focus much more on print. With all our children, we need to pay attention to which sources of information and strategies they use and which they reject.

Ensuring that Every Child Spends Time Reading Conventionally Every Day

Once we've assessed our young readers and determined that it is time to highlight the print work of reading, it will be important to revise the structures and expectations of our reading workshop. We want to ensure that every child spends time (and in first grade, I estimate this to be twenty to forty minutes a day) reading the words in books that provide enough support so that they are soon processing print in unfamiliar books. Many first-grade teachers move emergent reading to library and choice time, and to the opening moments of the school day. Kindergarten teachers will probably tell children, "Start each reading workshop by reading *these* books (we might call them something like Learning to Read books or Just-Right books), then switch to *any* book you choose. Kindergarten children who are really ready to read the words will choose to spend more time with the easy-to-read little books but children who are less ready to read conventionally will quickly run out of steam. If these latter children are not able to switch to familiar texts, books with great pictures, or to reading with an adult, their engagement in reading can peter out, which is the last thing any of us wants.

There are a number of organizational challenges for teachers who want to take children through the transition from a reading workshop which is about looking at books and reading emergently to a workshop that also focuses on reading the print in leveled books. We may work individually, saying to each child, "In first grade, it's important to spend time every day reading the words. I think you'll feel strong if you read books from this bin. Do you notice the green (or yellow or blue) dot?" We can match children with books by working one-by-one with each of our children or we can do this with clusters of children. Last September, Kathy Collins and I decided to try gathering clusters of her first graders together for the sake of efficiency. We knew that we risked creating a hierarchical feeling among reading levels, but we also knew that *any* way of matching children with books carries this risk. We decided that this year, we'd try being open about differences among readers and books. At the start of the third week of school, Kathy asked six children to join her in the class library for a quick meeting. The group sat clumped on the rug. Kathy had a basket of books in front of her. "Remember last week when I read with you all by yourselves?"

"Yeah, we read that Max book," said Daniel.

"Yeah, me too," chimed in Alex.

"Well, I realized something. I realized that you are similar as readers. Isn't that cool?"

"What's *similar* mean?" Angelika asked.

"It means alike," Sammy said.

"In this case, Angelika, it means that these days you and these other kids do some of the same kinds of reading. It also means that the same kinds of books will help you become stronger readers."

"Me and Langston were reading partners in kindergarten," said Alex.

"So you guys were kind of alike in kindergarten too?" Kathy asked. The boys looked at each other and smiled. "Well, I thought about you guys and couldn't wait to show you this bin of books. I just *know* this bin of books will be a great place for you to find books at reading time." Kathy started pulling out some books and reading the titles aloud. "I love this bin," Kathy said. "There are so many cool books."

"Hey, all these books have red dots on the covers," Sammy noticed, and Kathy turned the bin around to show children that there was also a red dot on the bin itself. She explained that the red dot meant the books were kind of the same and also that the books needed to be returned to this spot.

Soon Kathy had partnered the six children, given each child a new, more official-looking plastic "bookshelf," and shown each set of partners that their individual bookshelves would be housed on a countertop near the place where they read. Each child selected two bags from the bin, each filled with four red-dot books. The books were brief. Because these short books cannot sustain a child for long, we find that in kindergarten and first grade, we need at least one hundred books for each of the first three groups of books, and more is better. Once the children reach higher reading levels, a single book lasts longer and children move through books more slowly so the bins can contain fewer titles. In a matter of days, all Kathy's children knew where they could find just-right books, had a collection of these books in their bookshelves and a well-matched reading partner, and understood that for now, these books were to be their main fare during the reading workshop.

Some children will watch us steer other children toward particular book bins, and most of us use minilessons as a forum for shaping these children's perceptions. In one minilesson, Kathy asked, "How many of you have lost three teeth so far?" With mouths open wide, several children pointed at the gaps in their teeth and said, "Me!" "How many of you have lost only one tooth?" Again, children answered through wide-open mouths. "So we're different. Look at our different sizes," Kathy said, as she beckoned to tall, willowy Bo to stand and to tiny Adam. Waiting for conversations to subside, Kathy said, "See, we are each so different. We're different in our hair color, and we're different in how we paint trees, and we're different at handwriting, and we're different at reading too. Stand up if you *love* science books about gross animals. Okay, sit down. Now stand up if you *love* poems even more. See what I mean? We're different. And some kids read books with lots of words, and some kids are just starting to read books with words."

"We're different," Laura said in conclusion.

"And that's why we have all different kinds of books in our class. In order to become a stronger reader, it's important to find books that will help you become strong. These bins [Kathy pointed to the part of her library that now highlighted leveled bins] are really helpful when you're trying to become a stronger reader."

"I'm 'comfa-ble' with yellow books," Jacob said.

"Me too," said Charlie.

"So for you guys, right now, the yellow bin is your home base. And there are some kids who find their home base in the red bin, and there are some kids whose home base is this blue bin, or the green, or whatever. Everyone, with your eyes, just take a second to find your bin, your home base." The kids looked hard at the leveled book section to find their bin. "For the next few weeks, we're going to stick with books that will help us become stronger as readers. We're each going to have a kind of home base bin from which we'll choose books. These books will definitely help us become stronger readers because your home base bins are full of books with words you can read."

Highlighting the Strategies Readers Need When They Attend to Print

Matching children with books is only one step toward helping children engage with the words on the pages of their books. We'll also want to demonstrate (enthusiastically) the strategies that will stand our children in good stead as they try to read print. We'll do this in minilessons, shared reading, conferences, guided reading sessions, and strategy lessons. Meanwhile, we'll also be doing word-study work.

In late September, I pulled Kathy's children together for a minilesson. "Readers, we've been studying ways to figure out what the print says when we read a book, and we've listed some strategies. Let me read the list we have so far, and while I do, would you each, in your mind, think of a time when you used that strategy?" Turning to the chart on the easel beside me, I said, "We know we look at the pictures and they help us think about the story. We know we think 'What *could* it say? What would make sense?'" Continuing, I said, "We wonder what the trick or the pattern of the book might be. Are there rhyming words? Is there a pattern? Is it a list book? And we use a pointing finger—many of us do—when we are reading. When we point at a word, we look at the first letter and get our mouths ready to make that sound."

Looking at the group, I said, "You do all these things and yesterday you started doing something more. Yesterday, Zach got the idea that you can't just look at the first letter of a word, you need to look *all the way across the word!* After Zach got that idea, I looked for other readers who were doing it. And I saw that Calen was reading *Mouse Paint.*" At this point, I opened up a Big Book version of *Mouse Paint* and turned to the page in question. "When he got stuck, Calen said, 'The picture isn't helping me.'" I acted out Calen's part. I read, "They thought it was mouse paint. And he_____right in." "Calen used his pointing finger to point to the word in question, to *really* look at it, and he saw it began with a '*c.* He reread and he said, 'the mouse *somethinged* right in!' Then he whispered, 'Could it be *climbed?*' But then he did it! Calen looked *across the whole word* (and I dramatized his actions, running my finger under the word in the Big Book once, twice, three times, moving my mouth as I moved my finger and finally producing the expected word—*crawled!*) Now I reread the entire sentence inserting the word *crawled* into it. Then I continued, "After that, class, I went to Kate, and she was reading *The Haunted House.*" Again I told the story of Kate's reading up to the point at which she encountered difficulty. Because I didn't have a Big Book version of Kate's book, I'd copied an excerpt on chart paper. Acting out Kate's role, I read "I am a scary, scary owl" [the text said "*scary, spooky* owl"] and then, backing up, I used my finger as I looked all the way across the letters in the word I'd read incorrectly. Noticing that the word began *sp* not *sc,* I made the /sp/ sound. Then I darted my finger across the word several times, eventually reading *spooky* correctly. After imitating Kate, I said, "Did you see that? Kate didn't just use the first letter, she looked *all the way across the word!*"

I now turned the reading workshop toward the next phase. "Today, when you are reading, will you remember how Calen saw that the word was not *climbed* but *crawled,* and will you remember how Kate was able to read 'a scary, *spooky* owl'? Does anyone have any questions about this strategy?"

Britanny chirped in, "When you start the book, you can see if it's a rhyming book, and you can rhyme it in your head, and you can sound out the letters."

"Yes, there are so many things in books that can help you. You've got all these tools. It's your tool kit." Looking out at the children, I said, "We'll start with private reading time. Those of you sitting behind Sarah can get started."

About ten children clambered to their feet and headed to a shelf full of boxes. "I love the way these readers are getting their bookshelves and going quickly to their desk seats, not missing one moment of reading time," I said. Then I motioned for the remaining children to get started. Within a few minutes, the children were all sitting in their assigned seats with their individual bookshelves beside them, reading through their collection of books.

As Kathy and I moved among the readers, we noticed several things. First, the children were all reading. This was no small feat. It was late September, and yet children were clearly reading the words and showing lots of evidence of Kathy's teaching in the independent reading workshop and of the children's kindergarten education. Some children clearly took the time to look over a book and orient themselves to it before they began to read. Many were reading with their fingers, pointing crisply under each word as they read it. Kathy and I now taught a few of them to graduate from this phase, pointing with their eyes only, bringing out their finger only when they encountered difficulty. And today, it was evident that many children were making a point to look all the way across a word. Holding a Sunshine book about mirrors, Sara read, "See my *fingers*." Then she paused, peered at the print, and reread, correcting herself to say, "See my *face*." Watching her, I could see that the minilesson had sunk in.

The next day, Kathy's minilesson made the same point but did so in a different way. This time she said to the class, "Can you guys watch me, really spy on what I'm doing? Watch what I'm going to do now. I'm going to pretend to be six, and I've got a book I'm dying to read." For the next few minutes, Kathy read two pages from a Big Book in a way that explicitly demonstrated all the strategies the class had gathered, especially pointing at words, noticing first letters, and looking all the way across words. While she did these things, she voiced her decision to use particular strategies, muttering in a stage whisper, "Wait, wait, I've got to look all the way across" and then proceeding to do so. After a minute or two of this, Kathy asked the children to recount what they'd seen her doing as she read.

A few days later, after Alex, the class stuntman, had come in full of stories about biking up a gut-squishing hill in Prospect Park, Kathy decided that she'd help children think about selecting just-right books. Kathy began by telling the class about Alex's ride, and the class talked about how it feels when you pedal straight uphill. They agreed it isn't fun to ride uphill because you need to keep taking breaks and the bike gets wobbly. Then Kathy said, "Do any of you ever feel like that when you're *reading*? I mean, do some books ever feel like an uphill ride? Exhausting? Frustrating?" Roy's hand shot up. With his other hand, he pointed to a nonfiction text about snails in the "featured books" basket. "That book. That book is so hard for me that I get out of breath when I read it." Kathy took the snail book out of the basket and held it up. "So this book is like an uphill book for you, huh?" Most of the other children were nodding in agreement. Then she said, "Now I have a question for all of you. What happens when you ride your bike *downhill?*" The kids called out, "It's easy. You don't even have to pedal. You go so fast." "Sometimes my pedals are going so fast, I don't even have to keep my feet on them." "You don't have to do any work." Then Kathy said, "Are there any books you've read that are like that, like riding downhill? Books that are so easy for you, you don't even have to do much more work than turning the pages?" As if on cue, they called out *"In a Dark, Dark Wood!"* Kathy pulled that book out of the scary book basket and held it up. "So this is a downhill book, so easy you can just fly right through it?" "Uh-huh," they said. Then Anna said, "We should look for flat-road books, books that are a little work but not too hard so you have to put them down."

Now Kathy sent her class off to their independent reading to check if the books in their individual bookshelves were uphill, downhill, or flat-road books. "Flat-road books are great for readers to practice their reading. I want everyone to be sure they have flat-road books," Kathy said, and as she and I conferred that day, we were surprised by how immediately her children applied this metaphor to their reading. Kathy knows, of course, that readers also grow from reading books that are a bit easy and a bit hard for them, but for now her intention was to hold readers on a just-right course.

A week later, when I conferred with Stephanie, she told me, "Even when I read a flat-road book there are bumps."

"What do you mean?" I asked.

"Sometimes when I'm flying along, I get to a hard word that I don't know."

"Did it happen to you in this book?" I asked. Stephanie was reading Pat Hutchin's *My Best Friend.* She opened to the page that said "Joey likes vegetables," and pointed to the word *vegetables,* where she was stuck.

"Stephanie, can you read that to me?" I asked as I pointed to the first word in the sentence.

"Joey likes/vvv/ ...?"

I pointed to the picture.

"Joey likes peas, but it can't be peas. It starts with *v.*"

"Could it be vegetables?" I asked.

"Yep!" she said.

"Try it out," I said.

"Joey likes vegetables. Yep, it's Joey likes *vegetables!*"

That day, for the reading share time, Kathy talked with her children about how sometimes even when you have a great book that's a flat-road ride, you might hit bumps in the road, like Stephanie did. She showed the class the part of her book in which she had hit a bump. "When bike riders or rollerbladers hit bumps, they have ways to get by them. Stephanie has some ways too. She looked at the picture and said the first sound of the word in her mouth. And she came to me for help too." Kathy said, "Why don't we spend the next week or so learning about ways to get over the bumps," Kathy suggested. This was Kathy's first of a string of minilessons on "What to do when we get to hard words."

The next day, Donna Santman was visiting Kathy's class and they conferred together with Stefano and his partner Quinn, who were reading John Stadler *Hooray for Snail.* The boys were stuck on the page that says "Snail listens."

"Snail *llllooks?*" Stefano said, his eyes scanning the illustration madly.

Donna asked what he was doing, and he said that he was looking for the picture to help him. "You're not just *looking at* the picture Stefano. You're *studying* it. Let's try it together." They began to talk about what was going on. Quinn said the snail was looking at the coach because the coach was talking to him.

"It looks like the coach is yelling at him," Stefano said.

"And Snail is just listening …" Returning to the print, he read, "Snail *listens!*" Quinn smiled, victorious.

"See you guys, you didn't just look at the picture. You thought about what was going on in the story and that helped you so much."

Stefano and Quinn shared this with the class, and soon studying and talking about the pictures became one of the strategies on their "What to do when we get to hard words" chart. Kathy and her students eventually developed the following chart:

<u>Some Popular Reading Strategies in 1–206</u>

We study the picture (like Stefano and Quinn do)

We study the picture and look at the first couple of letters in the word (like Anna and Sophia do)

We can look at the beginnings and endings of words to be sure our guesses work (like Marissa and Sara do)

We can reread lines to see what would make sense (like Alex and Sophia do)

We can listen to the sound of the story to let rhyming and repeating words help us (like Afiya and Marco do)

We can think about things we already know when we read it because it can help us get the words (like Julian and Zoe do)

Children can watch us deliberately demonstrate the strategies proficient readers use to deal with the difficulties we encounter as we read, but this alone isn't enough. The important thing is that children need to begin using these strategies themselves to get over the bumps in their reading. In Kathy Collins' classroom, she went to some lengths to ensure that the strategies she demonstrated and the class listed were in fact becoming part of each child's repertoire. For a few weeks, Kathy alternated between asking children to observe *her* reading (briefly), noticing strategies she used when she came to difficulty … and asking her children to work in partners with one reader reading and dealing with difficulty, while the other first grader functioned as a researcher, recording the strategies the other used. Some of the field notes Kathy's first graders took as they documented their partner's reading strategies are on the next page.

Putting Structures into Place That Support the Print Work of Reading

It is misleading to suggest that minilessons are the primary way we help children become more skilled at reading the print in books. Young readers also need to practice these strategies. The real work of this unit in the comes as we confer with individual readers and partners, extend the length of time children can sustain their focus on reading, organize and launch guided-reading groups,

Tina
1998

Brian My Prttnr Look's at The Pikchrs
he Goos Back at searched for
dalighis.
he Goos Back to The
Lotrs. he nass
The Wrod.
he macs Sase.
It was a KaPawd
Vrod He sasd His figr
Put win The wrod

Molly 3-2-98
1. Erik looked at the Picter.
2. Erik wen't back to the cover to chek a word.
3. Erik wen't back to another Page.
4. Erik Sounden a word out.
5. Erik Said the word over and over intil he got it right.

3|2|98 Raul and Ryan.
he figerd it out Because
he Soundid it out.
he figerd it out Because
he read Sentinc
and went Back
Raul did Grate

Tina: "Brian, my partner, looks at the pictures. He goes back and searches for delicious. He goes back to the letters. He knows the word. he makes sense. It was a compound word. He used his finger, put in the word."

Molly: "1. Eric looked at the picture. 2. Eric went back to the cover to check a word. 3. Eric went back to another page. 4. Eric sounded a word out. 5. Eric said the word over and over until he got it right."

Raul and Ryan: "He figured it out because he sounded it out. He figured it out because he read the sentence and went back. Raul did great."

and continue ensuring that children are reading appropriate books. Meanwhile, we also help children develop their muscles for reading through shared reading, word study, and the writing workshop.

We'll want to be certain that if we are working with print in shared reading texts, the texts need to be matched to the reading abilities of most of our children. As I mentioned earlier, if most of our children are still learning to do one-to-one matching in books which have spacing between words, bold fonts, and only a line or two of print, for example, it would be unfair to expect these children to isolate and work with words while reading the text of the song "This

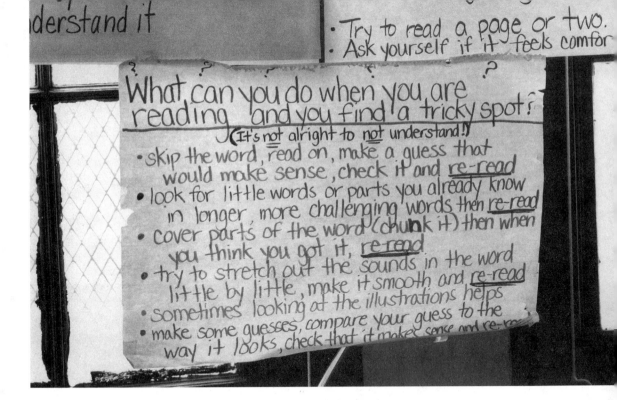

What can you do when you are reading and you find a tricky spot? (It's not alright to not understand!)
- skip the word, read on, make a guess that would make sense, check it and re-read
- look for little words or parts you already know in longer, more challenging words then re-read
- cover parts of the word (chunk it) then when you think you got it, re-read
- try to stretch out the sounds in the word little by little, make it smooth and re-read
- sometimes looking at the illustrations helps
- make some guesses, compare your guess to the way it looks, check that it makes sense and re-re

Land Is Your Land, This Land Is My Land." We could read this song with our students, pointing at the words as we read, but the point of this shared reading would not be to support children's work with print. Instead, we could hope they'd be reminded that print goes left-to-right, top to bottom. Even with a text like *Mrs. Wishy Washy,* if I wanted beginning readers to notice the features of print, I'd first read the whole book and then focus on just a single page and only then work with print, expecting my students to be with me. The words of "This Land Is Your Land" and even of many picture books will be a blur to most kindergarten and first-grade readers, and especially so because we tend to move along quickly through line after line of print during shared reading sessions, expecting children to follow the words with their eyes.

Lydia Bellino, the principal of Goose Hill Primary School, helped the kindergarten teachers in her school return each day for two weeks to a shared reading of a tiny draft of a poem from Karla Kuskin's anthology *Near the Window Tree: Poems and Notes.*

The poem went like this:

> I like bugs
> I kiss bugs
> And I give them hugs.

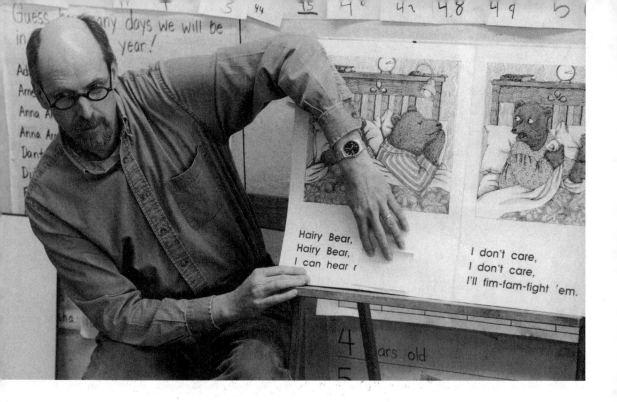

Lydia did not begin by reading the poem to the kindergarten children so they could echo-read it, copying her intonation. Instead she supported, or scaffolded, children's first encounter with the text. She began by showing children the poem, which was accompanied by a large picture of a beetle. "Let's read this," she said. She pointed to the first word. The children read *I like* and then paused. "Hmmm," Lydia said, "I'm wondering what this could say?" Then she tapped the picture, as if she was thinking before their eyes, and soon the children chimed in, "It's a bug!"

"Could this word be *bug?*" Lydia asked. "Let's try." Now she and the children looked closely at the print: "*b*-/b/—that looks like bug!" Lydia said, and pulled the pointer across /b-/ugs/ saying "bug" as she did so, hovering for a second on the *s*. A child noticed and revised *bug* to *bugs*. "So let's back up and reread," Lydia said, and before long, she and the class had noticed the repetition of *bugs* at the end of the next line and seen its similarity to the upcoming word *hugs*.

Over the next two weeks, Lydia and this group of kindergartners did these things with Kuskin's little poem:

- Lydia covered a particular word (*like, give*) with a Post-it, and the class reread the poem with one-to-one matching and determined what was under the Post-it. Lydia later gave each child a copy of the poem, and now they worked as partners, one child covering a word of his or her choice and the other child rereading and in doing so determining which word had been masked. The reader had, of course, memorized the poem but determining which word had been masked was still a challenge which required children to match the now familiar words with the actual print on the page.

- Lydia covered parts of words (like the *em* in *them*) and children again reread and determined what was masked.

- Lydia altered the poem so that it said "I like *pigs*," and "I *hate* bugs."

- Lydia and the children tried a "Now that you know *bugs*, what do you know?" analogy (*hugs, lugs, rugs, mugs*) and did this also with *like* and *give*.

- Copies of the poem were laminated. Lydia put green dots alongside the first and third lines, blue dots alongside the second line and divided the class into two sections. One section read the green-dot lines, the other the blue-dot line. Children then moved dots in different ways and read accordingly.

- A few words from the poem (like, kiss, bugs) were added to the word wall, and a copy of the text was put into every child's writing folder. As Lydia explained, "Now if you want to spell any of these words, you'll have this poem beside you."

- The class did interactive writing in order to alter the poem. "Instead of *hugs*, what could you give to bugs?" Lydia asks. "It needs to rhyme with *bugs*." Soon these bugs had been given *rugs, mugs, tugs, and jugs*. Meanwhile because the word *bug* had shown itself to be generative of many other words, Lydia starred this word on the word wall, reminding children this meant *bugs* could give them word power.

When we help children read, puzzle over, think about, and explore texts that are accessible, we are not only teaching specific lessons about words and print and reading strategies. We are also teaching children that texts can be our teachers, and that closely studying the words on a page can inform, delight, and inspire us. It's hard to imagine more important work we and our children could do together.

Talking and Thinking About Books
15
Comprehension for Young Readers

Thirtyfive years ago, Jerome Bruner (1963) suggested in his now classic book, *The Process of Education,* that "the foundations of any subject may be taught to anybody at any age in some form" (p. 12). He went on to say that the basic ideas that lie at the heart of, and give form to, life and literature are as simple as they are powerful: "To be in command of these basic ideas, to use them effectively, requires a continued deepening of one's understanding of them that comes from learning to use them in progressively more complex forms" (p. 13). If we want to help our children think deeply about texts and live comfortably in the world of ideas, won't we want to introduce them to this kind of thinking from the very start?

In Teachers College Reading and Writing Project classrooms, we put great trust in conversation as a way to support deeper comprehension. The New Primary Standards our City has adopted stress that accountable book talks are a daily essential. By the end of first grade, children are expected to be able to retell the story in the books they read independently and to compare two books by the same author, to talk about several books on the same theme, to refer to the parts of the text when defending their ideas, to politely disagree when appropriate, to ask others questions that seek elaboration and justification, and to attempt to explain why their interpretation of a book is valid. This is a tall order for six-year-olds, but living with these goals in mind makes us taller as readers and as people.

When children enter the classroom in September, it always seems ambitious to believe we can teach them to talk in these wonderful ways. In September, it is a stretch to call what the partners are doing "book conversations."

In truth, children at first make "book comments," often based on the illustrations ("He's so cute!" "Look at her furry hair!"). Their comments tend to overlap and repeat each other's. But book talks in primary classrooms are remarkably amenable to instruction, and in classroom after classroom, very young children soon begin to converse back and forth in response to books. And as children learn to *talk well* about texts, they are also learning to *think well* about texts.

This chapter looks at ways in which minilessons can highlight the importance of thinking about books. It considers how asking children to mark sections of texts with Post-its can scaffold their talk and their comprehension and how we can encourage children to listen to each other and to the texts they read.

Minilessons That Spotlight the Importance of Thinking About Texts

One Monday morning in early November, Kathy Collins said to her class, "I'm going to tell a story, and I want you to really picture it in your minds. Here goes. Imagine that you can look inside your brain, and inside your brain you see lots of little people who look just like you do, and they all have jobs. When it's math time, you have some little people, the math people, that go to work."

"Jesse must have lots of math people," Jacob said with a smile, referring to their resident six-year-old mathematician.

Kathy continued, "Now look toward the front of your brain, right behind your forehead. There are a few of these little people. Their job is reading. They are the readers."

"I see them!" said Laura.

"First graders grow really strong at figuring out the words in books, and one of the workers does just that. He or she works really hard to figure out the words. We've all been getting good at that." Kathy paused for emphasis, to be sure everyone was listening. "There is another part of reading that we need to work on in this class and that is *thinking about the story*. The worker that does this has big ideas and helps us be sure we understand what we're reading. This is the thinking-about-books worker, and we're going to *make sure* this worker, like the figuring-out-words worker, is busy when we read."

There is nothing magical about this particular metaphor as a way to help young children become more conscious of the strategies effective readers use. We try to teach metacognitive strategies with a light touch and to use concrete and accessible metaphors so that youngsters don't get lost trying to recall the name of a strategy they want to use. The focus needs to be not *on* the strategy but *through* the strategy and onto the reading. The best ways to talk about cognitive processes usually emerge out of the particulars of a classroom. Once I listened to some kids as they looked at a dinosaur book and talked about the muscles of the Tyrannosaurus Rex. "His arms are so wimpy he couldn't even wave goodbye … to a baby," Barnaby said. John, the resident dinosaur expert said, "Uh, actually, the T-Rex's arms are small cause he doesn't need to use them as much as his legs or jaws." Not surprisingly, the minilesson that day was about how readers, too, use different kinds of muscles. One muscle is the figure-out-words muscle and it's important to build that one up. But the talk-muscle is also important, and that muscle can get wimpy and weak like a T-Rex's arms if it isn't used.

Teaching children to be consciously strategic as readers can be tricky. I recently watched two second graders talking about Chris Van Allsburg's *The Polar Express*. Becca said, "I just made a text-to-self connection." Then she paused. "No, it's a text-to-someone-else connection. A text-to-sister connection."

Her partner interceded, "That's not a kind of connection. You can only make text-to-text or text-to-self connections." The two carried on about this for a few more minutes. Finally, I asked about the connection Becca had made. She said, "My sister took the train once." That was the sum total of Becca's text-to-self or text-to-sister connection. It seemed clear to me that all her efforts to pin down the connection she had made between *The Polar Express* and her life was "much ado about nothing." If anything, the long metacognitive detour had probably pulled these readers out of "the virtual dream" of the story, and broken the spell of the enchantment.

A Scaffold for Thoughtful Reading: Teaching Children to Put Post-Its Into Books, and to Talk About Them With Partners

After Kathy Collins told her children about the "little guys in their brains," she wanted to move quickly toward showing them what this meant for their reading. The easiest way to demonstrate was through the read-aloud. "We're going to spend the next couple of weeks getting good at having big thoughts, big ideas, about our books," Kathy said. "I notice many of you do this already. I'm going to show you what I mean. I'm going to read Kevin Henkes, *Chrysanthemum* and say my big ideas out loud. Listen closely and research what I do." Kathy read for a few minutes, pausing when Chrysanthemum feels bad about her name. Taking a Post-it and putting it on the page, Kathy said to Lesley (who was functioning as Kathy's partner), "Hey this reminds me of when I was little." Then she turned to the class, switched out of role, and said, "So …?"

"You put a Post-it on the page!"

"You had a big idea!"

Nodding, Kathy said, "Yes, when I got to this page I thought, 'This reminds me …' Kids used to make fun of my name, 'Collins,' because there was a TV show about a vampire named Barnabas Collins. I can guess how Chrysanthemum feels. I felt bad then, just like Chrysanthemum, and sometimes I felt sad and sometimes angry. I'm wondering if she has all those feelings mixed together too." Then Kathy said, "My thought started with my reading, and with thinking *this reminds me.*" Then Kathy said to her class, "Today, when you're reading during private time, put a Post-it on a page if you have a 'this reminds me' kind of thought, and when we meet with partners, we'll share those connections."

Sela's hand went up. "What if we don't have that kind of idea but we have a different kind?"

"Maybe you'll invent another way to think about books," Kathy replied. "You can share your kind of thought later with everyone else."

The class went off to read, Post-its in hand. Kathy and I stopped near Julia, who was reading a book from the M & M series. She had just put a Post-it on a page.

"Julia, what are you thinking here?" I asked.

"Mandy and Mimi remind me of me and my best friend," Julia said.

"How?"

"Huh?" Julia asked, startled that I was trying to extend her comment.

"I mean, *how* do they remind you of you and your friend?" I pressed.

"Well, we're, like … girls and they're girls too," Julia said.

I wasn't surprised to hear Julia making a superficial connection. I've learned to anticipate that early on, my role will be to deepen a child's first thought. "So you're saying that you and Sela are best friends like the characters in this series. I know a little about the series. Don't they get along well for a bit, then they have little fights, and then they get along again? Is that what your friendship with Sela is like?" I asked.

"Yeah," she said. "Whenever they have a little fight in this book, I know they'll make up because they're just like me and Sela."

"That's an interesting idea, Julia. Your partner will be so intrigued when you tell her about it."

Kathy and I pulled close beside Jayden, who was reading Ellen Blonder's *Noisy Breakfast.* Jayden had put a Post-it on almost every page. The book features a dog and a hamsterlike animal preparing a noisy breakfast together.

"Jayden, can I ask you about these Post-its?" Kathy said. "It looks like you've had a big idea explosion!"

Jayden smiled and went back to the first page on which he'd put his first Post-it. Doing a Post-it walk, he chronicled his thinking for us. "This reminds me of when I help my mom. This reminds me of doing the dishes." The illustrations triggered his personal responses, but he missed the point of the text altogether even though he had read it.

Noisy Breakfast	Jayden's "reading" of the text (Through Post-its)
Listen to it crack. (Illustration of dog cracking egg over a mixing bowl)	
Listen to it drop. (A hamster looks on as the dog drops an egg into a mixing bowl)	"This reminds me of when I help my mom."
Listen to them rattle. (Hamster carrying a stack of dishes to set table)	This reminds me of when I do dishes and my brother does none.
Listen to them pop. (Slices of toast popping out of toaster, hamster rushing to catch them on a plate)	This reminds me of when I am late for the bread.
Listen to it sizzle. (Hamster pouring egg into frying pan)	This reminds me of when I have eggs and I like them scrambled.
Listen to it drip. (Hamster squeezing oranges into a glass)	This reminds me of when I squeeze the juice.
Listen to them sip. (Dog and hamster drinking orange juice)	
What a noisy breakfast! (Dog and hamster eating toast)	

Kathy and I stepped away from Jayden for a moment to mull over what we were seeing. One of the distressing things about teaching is that in an effort to solve one problem we so often create new problems. A few days ago, Jayden might have read this book without envisioning anything much at all, but now, each page seemed to launch him in a different direction, distracting him from the central theme of the text itself. What a challenge it is to be on our toes, ready to respond to the surprising turns our teaching takes. Clearly we wanted to help Jayden and our other students see the difference between making a connection such as "The guy in this picture is wearing green sneakers and my uncle has green sneakers" and making the kind of connections that deepen their understanding of the text ("I can imagine how bad Henry feels when he thinks Mudge is lost. My dog ran away once too and I felt really bad.") Jayden *had* clearly learned that books sometimes make us think about our own lives. But he was not taking in the text as a coherent, unified whole, and the enterprise of Post-its probably exacerbated this problem. We decided that for a start, we'd help Jayden read and think not just at the page level but at the whole text level.

Jayden, every page in this book reminds you of something different?" Kathy asked.

"Yup, this one reminds me of when I help my mom, and this reminds me of when I have to do dishes, and this one …" Jayden was flipping through each page commenting on his Post-its.

"Can I stop you for a second, Jayden?" Kathy asked. "I'm wondering about something. It seems that this book as a whole makes you think about when you and your mom make breakfast together. All your Post-its are about that."

Jayden nodded.

Kathy turned to the cover of the book. "*Noisy Breakfast.* Hmm. It seems that the big idea of the book is that breakfast time is noisy," Kathy said as she flipped through the pages and read softly to herself.

"It's noisy when me and my mom make breakfast too."

"It is?" Kathy asked.

"Yup. We play the radio loud sometimes. My baby sister cries sometimes and we play and stuff."

"So *your* big idea is kind of like the book's big idea? This book, *Noisy Breakfast,* reminds you of how noisy it is when you and your mom make breakfast?"

"Yup."

"I wonder if you hear the same sounds as in the book, too. Do your eggs sizzle? Or do you hear different sounds?"

"My sister is so loud I can't hear the bacon or the toast," Jayden said. "So my noises aren't food ones." He took the book and began to reread it, this time asking on each page, "Do I hear *that?*"

In Kathy's class and in other Project classrooms, children soon begin to use Post-its for a whole variety of reasons that can all fit under the general umbrella of "ideas we're dying to talk about." As the class describes the reading work behind these Post-its, charts grow. Kathy's chart soon looked like this:

Readers Get Big Ideas When We Read

- This reminds me of...

- I notice that...

- I wonder why...

- This surprises me because...

- This makes me think of another book because...

During this unit of study, we tend to structure time so that children read privately for twenty to thirty minutes, flagging big ideas with Post-it notes. Then they meet with partners. In some classrooms, to put a special spotlight on book talks, children for a time aren't *reading with* partners but simply talking over ideas from their books. In other classrooms, the expectation is that one child will choose a book from his or her bookshelf and make overall comments to introduce the book if it's unfamiliar to the partner. They read the book together and only then do they *talk* about the flagged sections.

Encouraging Listening and Response for Both Are Essential to Reading

The work I've described may *sound* simple, but pulling it off with kindergartners and first-grade children is not simple. Even the fact that two readers talk about only one book (instead of carrying on parallel talk about two different books) takes some doing! But by far the biggest challenge is helping children to actually converse about the text and develop their ideas as they talk about them. The hard part has more to do with *listening* than with anything else. It is tempting to say, "Some five- and six-year-olds may be too egocentric to listen well to each other," but if we give up on teaching children to truly *listen* to each other, we may well be giving up on reading comprehension. After all, is comprehension not all about listening at length to another person's words and ideas and stories, even if this means holding back our own for a time so that the other person's thinking can occupy space in our minds? And doesn't comprehension often involve having one's own mind changed because of what another person says? Isn't it about coming to think differently because of what we've heard? If this is the case, teaching comprehension has everything to do with teaching listening.

We don't wait until November to highlight the importance of listening to each other, nor do we do this only within the reading curriculum. For many of us, whole-group meetings are our first forum for teaching listening. Alexa Stott found it helpful to teach the physical part of listening first. When it was time for whole-class conversations, Alexa's first graders, from the start of the year, configured themselves not in a cluster at her feet but in a circle around the perimeter of the rug. For a while, Alexa urged children to be sure they positioned themselves so they could listen ("Can you listen well with that person next to you? If it's hard to keep your hands off each other and listen, it can sometimes help to fold your hands in your lap to hold yourself together in that way"). Some of these issues settled down once the children had long-term rug spots and long-term talk partners. Alexa taught her children above all that when someone spoke into a whole group conversation, all heads turned to look at that person. "I wanted to teach the habit of keying in," Alexa said. "So we'd turn our heads in an almost exaggerated fashion, like rotating fans." Sometimes in the midst of a conversation, Alexa would say, "Guys, you better remind your partner of what we need to be doing," and because she'd made a big point of highlighting the importance of looking at the speaker, she didn't need to say more.

Bit by bit, Alexa raised her expectations. Soon she emphasized listening in ways that allowed you to say back what the person had said. "Class," she'd say, "When I tell you to do so, you'll need to get your coat and your clipboard, and line up at the door." Then she'd follow this with, "Danny, will you say back what I just said?" If Danny had trouble doing this, she'd say, "Who can help Danny out?" and later she'd remind children, "Next time, try to listen so you can say back what people have said."

The next step was to hold children accountable for listening to *each other* (not just to the teacher). When Lila announced that she didn't think it was right for Goldilocks to walk right into the Three Bears' house without even knocking, Alexa said, "Turn to your partner, and say back what Lila just said." When Alexa first began to ask her first graders to say back what a classmate had just said in the large-group meeting, no one could do this. It was clear to Alexa they'd never keyed into really listen to each other. For a few weeks, then, she often asked children to repeat what they'd heard—and she did this to teach the habit of listening. Soon Alexa was holding children accountable for saying back what their partners had said in partnership book talks as well as in whole-class discussions.

Of course, these are limited goals, and the instruction I'm describing probably feels a bit like listening drills. But Alexa's clear instructions and her willingness to follow up on her teaching made a palpable difference. Soon she no longer needed to ask children to say back what they'd heard. Before long, her first graders were carrying on flowing, thoughtful conversations that were dazzling. Visitors to the room would act as if they were seeing a miracle. I knew, instead, that it was the result of clear and persistent instruction.

Whether we're talking about listening or about reading, comprehension is about far more than recall. Soon Alexa was asking children not only to say back what others (and sometimes the author) had said, but also to talk and think back to what they'd heard. Like most of us, she again used whole-group work as the forum for extending what her children would later do in their partnership conversations. After reading in Clyde Robert Bulla's *The Chalk Box Kid* that Gregory was sad his uncle would be staying with them, sleeping in the extra bed in Gregory's room, Alexa gazed into space and mused quietly to no one in particular, "I wonder *why* Gregory doesn't want his uncle to stay with him."

"Well," Sara suggested, "Gregory just got his new room all to himself and he doesn't want to share it yet."

Alexa said nothing, deliberately restraining herself from making a comment. She wanted her children to begin talking back to each other. There was silence. Sela's comment hung in the air. Everyone looked at Alexa, expecting her to receive Sela's comment, but she looked at the kids. Silence. In time, Julie raised her hand and said, "I have my own room too."

Alexa nodded. She wondered if she was about to hear half a dozen children each announce that they, too, have their own rooms. Deciding to step in, she said, "Julie, are you saying you know how Gregory feels because you have your own room and you would feel similarly?"

Julie nodded. Jacob, meanwhile, whispered something to Benson. Alexa glanced at him, and I felt sure her instinct was to put a stop to the whispering because I was right with her in this. But instead, Alexa wisely tried a different tack. "What are you guys saying about the story?" she asked, exhibiting all the confidence in the world.

To Alexa's and my surprise, Jacob answered, "In the story, Gregory's uncle is going to take over his room because he's the grown-up."

"Could you say more?" Alexa asked, and later, "Does anyone want to add to this?" In this way she continued to guide the talk with a fairly heavy hand, ensuring that children responded to what others had said. After supporting talks in this sort of heavy-handed way for a while, Alexa made a transcript of one of their book talks and shared it with her class, wondering with them whether they needed *her* to be so in control of the conversation. "When you are with your partners or at home, talking with your family about books, I'm not there calling on one person or another," she said. "What if I stopped being the person to call on you during our talks?" "What if *you* decided whether your comment fit with whatever we were discussing, and whether it might take our thinking further?" Soon Alexa would simply start book conversations off and her children added to the discussion without raising their hands. This isn't a move every teacher can make, but it can have fantastic benefits.

How was our conversation? Did we listen to one voice at a time?			
Fantastic Conversation	Pretty Good Conversation	Not That Great	UGH!
One voice talked at a time.	Usually it was just one voice. A couple of times, there were interruptions.	It got kind of loud because lots of voices were going. People couldn't hear what others were saying.	Nobody listened to anybody. The teacher had to stop the conversation.

The benefits aren't immediate ones, however. For Alexa's class, the first issue was that children all spoke at once, a problem that was also common, if less dramatic, in their partnership talks. Soon the class tried to focus on listening so that when one voice started, other voices backed down. Alexa and her students created a rubric for assessing their progress toward this goal.

For about a week, Alexa's class reflected on their discussions and applied the rubric to give themselves a score. After a few consecutive "fantastic conversations," they began to notice other ways to improve their conversations. They eventually added these other characteristics of good conversations?

> One voice talked at a time.
>
> We heard from many different people.
>
> We stayed with one idea.
>
> We gave evidence from the book.

Next, children used these same criteria and other, more basic ones (look at the person while talking, be able to say back what your partner has said) to lift the level of their partnership conversations.

The Unique Features of Book Talks
Between Very Young Children

I wish I could say that once we've helped children listen and talk well during the read-aloud book talks, this transfers beautifully to the partnership conversations they have during independent reading, but the partnership talks kids have are always very much their own. As Tom Newkirk (1998) writes about children's book talk, "it eludes control, slips into unexpected territory … it's like catching a butterfly—the more firmly you hold it, the more likely you are to kill it. And why catch it at all?" (p. 4).

The most important way to teach children to talk well about books is to help them become engaged in books and give them opportunities to spend time together in the company of books. A little bit of instruction in the importance of listening and in the value of referring to texts can make a palpable difference in young children's book talks and can help children to approach their partnership talk full of big resolves (see figure on next page), *a lot of heavy-handed instruction can destroy their talks, however.*

Jeremy brought Bronwen Scarffe's *Oh No!* to his partner conversation. In this book, the main character continually makes bloopers, such as sitting on the wet paint of a park bench or squirting bicycle oil all over her clothes. To Jeremy, the really intriguing thing was that on one page, a butterfly spiraled into the air and left behind a stream of dots. The dots were meant to depict motion, but Jeremy felt sure the dots were a stream of butterfly poop, and he couldn't wait to share the discovery with Sam. The two boys took turns smelling the little stream of dots on the page and pretending this was a scratch-and-sniff book. Then Jeremy, playing off the theme of the book, looked at his hands and said, "Oh no! I have butterfly poop on me!" Taking the idea further, he began to touch other parts of the story with his poop-covered hands, each time saying, "Oh no!" After a minute or two of this, the children asked their teacher if they could go to the bathroom. "We have to wash our hands because we got butterfly poop on them," Jeremy said.

Meanwhile Lauren and Alyse were lying side-by-side, bellies down, on the carpet with a version of *The Gingerbread Man* open in front of them. Instead of talking over the book as I expected them to do, they'd assigned each other roles from the story and began acting out their roles simultaneously. Instead of taking turns, they both spoke in the voice of their character at the same time. What a duet it was! Lauren's voice rose and fell as she played the Gingerbread Man. Alyse mustered up a deep wolf voice. Page by page, they gave voice to the text. The result was a rather remarkable "Poem for Two Voices."

When Christine and Samantha met to share their books, Christine could not wait to show Samantha what she'd done. In the version she had read of *Little Red Riding Hood*, some of the pages had been wordless and so Christine had used Post-its to fill in gaps in the text. On one wordless page, for example, poor Little Red Riding Hood's legs protruded from the giant jaws of a fiercesome wolf. Christine left this page as it was wordless, turning quickly to see what came next. On a next page, Little Red Riding Hood floated serenely in the wolf's stomach. On a post-it Christine wrote, "She got her hed bak on. She is hape in the stumak." Reading her Post-it, I could almost hear her sigh with relief.

Christine's strategy caught on like wildfire in her classroom and soon many of the children were busily adding the text they felt was missing from their books. As I watched, it seemed to me that Christine had invented the perfect way to teach inference. Wasn't her project all about spelling out the messages the author implied between the lines?

Across the room, Jasmine and Noah were reading Leo Hartas' *Apartment Book* together. The book has cross-sections of apartments that look like the open side of a doll house, only with much more detail. Jasmine and Noah quickly turned to the page with a high rise building and began to play house. Their fingers were the characters.

"Oh, I hate elevators," said Jasmine, as her finger hopped up the flights of stairs.

"You're such a scaredy-cat!" Noah's right index finger said to Jasmine's finger. "*Please* take the elevator."

Jasmine's finger agreed and soon reached the ninth floor. "I'm home," Jasmine said in a lilting voice as her finger reached her apartment.

"Oopsie, I forgot my key," said Noah as his finger reached his apartment.

Meanwhile Shakeel and Erik were looking at a nonfiction book on bugs. They were starting to get noisy. Spying on them, I realized they were talking about the photographs in the book. "These pictures are gross," Shakeel said when he saw me watching. "Look at this one!"

"Wait, Shakeel, remember that hairy sticky one?" Erik asked.

"Yeah, let's find it!" They were turning pages until they finally settled on a two-page spread.

"So you guys are looking for gross bugs. What would you say makes a bug gross?" I asked.

"The hairy ones are the grossest," Shakeel answered.

"No, it's the sticky ones with the stingers. They're whacked!" Erik said. Soon the boys had invented the "brilliant" idea of rating each bug on it's relative grossness. Their plan was to award prizes for the grossest, second grossest, and third grossest bug.

Even when children's talk about books ends up being about butterfly poop or degrees of grossness, and even when the two children talk simultaneously, neither listening to the other, I think the ten or fifteen minutes a day for partnership reading and the five minutes for talking about books is precious time indeed. In our classrooms, whether we know it or not, we are always going about the business of defining who we are as a community and as individuals. Through our curricular decisions, we define what literacy means in the lives of the classroom community and in the lives of individuals. How important the lessons are that we teach when we encourage children to find ways to care about books and to share books with each other.

We are teaching children that each one of us is unique as a reader. Who but Noah would have thought that when you "bring out your reading finger," that finger can get caught up in the drama of the story, losing the key to the apartment but finding the key to engagement and envisionment with stories! And how grateful we are to Christine for inventing the idea that all of us as readers can co-author stories, using our own words to fill in the gaps.

We are teaching children that talking and writing in response to reading is a way to think, envision, puzzle over, and open up a story. Our children grow up expecting that the writing and talking they do in response to books will be fascinating, that friends will hang on their words when they respond to texts, that those words will spark grand conversations.

We are teaching children that reading is a magnificent way to be together with friends and with authors who become distant friends. We use fingers, friends, fantasies—the works—to make texts come alive. When you read you travel to intriguing places, you do cool things. Where else could you touch butterfly poop but in a story world?

Reading Centers in the K–1 Classroom

16

One of the defining features of our approach to literacy is our belief that the best way to help children grow to be thoughtful and constructive readers and writers is to invite them into a rich kind of literacy from the start. We put a premium at all grade levels on thoughtfulness and response. We expect even preschoolers to "read" in order to learn, poring over the pictures in *National Geographic*. We aim toward high literacy even for our youngest readers. We know that five- and six-year-olds can question and compare texts, talk about the big ideas in books, notice an author's techniques, integrate information from several sources, and we believe that by putting a premium on this sort of thoughtful literacy from the start, we support children's rapid progress even in the print work of reading.

Often, in the field of reading, I hear people reciting statistics about young readers. "Eighty percent of children across the world *get there*," they say. "No matter what the program, 80 percent *get there*."

"What do these statistics mean?" I've often asked myself. When people say "Eighty percent of children across the world *get there*," where is the *there?* The answer, I figure, has to be that 80 percent of children learn to translate black marks on the page into sounds, sentences, and sense.

My colleagues and I realize, however, that we would never say "Eighty percent of children across the world get there," because for us, "getting there" means not only that a child can read, but also that a child chooses to read and reads often. For us, "getting there" means that a child thinks and acts like a richly literate person, weaving texts into the relationships, projects, and causes of ones life. For us, "getting there" means that a child learns from reading and transforms information into new ideas and actions.

We are not alone in reaching toward a higher literacy. Across New York state, for example, there is growing recognition that "getting there" must mean more than it once did. Our standardized tests have been revised accordingly. They are no longer multiple choice exams, asking students to regurgitate what they've heard. At the age of nine, our students are now required to synthesize and analyze texts, to develop, articulate, and defend extensive written responses to texts.

I can't imagine anyone disagreeing, at least in theory, with the goal of a higher literacy, a literacy of thoughtfulness. But we don't yet have a shared sense of its curricular implications for the primary grades. It is very common, for example, for people to argue that young children should first learn to read and then, around the start of third grade, begin reading to learn.

A New Image of Reading Centers: The Big Picture

By the middle of the year in our primary classrooms, our children spend a good portion of reading time thinking and talking about books they've read. We refer to the curricular structure in which this thoughtful response to reading happens especially as a reading center, and to us this term suggests children who gather in small groups to read and talk about a collection of similar texts. Centers, for us, are not places but are instead groupings of children. We could have named them literature circles or response groups or book clubs.

The reading center is the component in our reading curriculum that particularly embodies our commitment to a literacy of thoughtfulness. Our version of reading centers is more like literature circles than the word-work or activity centers some teachers establish, hoping to keep children busy while they lead guided-reading groups, but as this chapter will show, our centers are not exactly like literature circles.

The Focus of Work in Reading Centers

When we launch reading centers in a K–2 classroom, we design them around a whole-class theme. For two weeks children meet with partners to read and respond to texts that are part of a whole-class focus. Small groups of readers from within the class might choose favorite authors and do author studies. In the read-aloud, the class might all study Mem Fox, and in their small groups (or centers) some readers may study Joy Cowley, Beverly Cleary or Eloise Greenfield. One reason that each small group pursues a different author is that usually no one author would offer enough breadth for everyone to find appropriately leveled books by that author. Centers need not focus on author-studies. In one first-grade classroom, the class studied poetry together, and then children worked together in groups of two, three or four on "Nursery Rhymes," "Poems to Put on Greeting Cards," "Arnold Adoff Poems," "Poems That Could be Turned into Clapping, Chanting Games," "Poems with Weird Shapes," and "Fun Poems to Read Out Loud." Typically, we might convene whole-class centers around any of the following topics:

We may organize centers around a kind of book:	We may organize centers around a genre of text:	We may organize centers around an umbrella topic:	We may organize centers around a reading goal:
• ABC books • List books • Pattern books • Wordless picture books	• Nonfiction • Poetry • Mysteries • Biographies • Fairy tales • Variations on fairy tales	• Series books • Favorite authors • Character studies • Funny books • Books that create a mood • Books about a topic of study (such as plants, space)	• Reading aloud well • Books that can help our writing (studying descriptions, dialogue, retelling an event) • Making connections between similar books • Letting texts teach us to do things (yo-yo tricks, cat's cradle, drawing horses)

The Schedule

We often spend the first few months of school helping our readers read and carry on independently in a reading workshop and then we launch reading centers in December or January. By this time, our children will have been reading just-right books alone for twenty-minute periods, flagging sections they want to talk about, and then meeting with a partner to reread and talk about these books together. Before we launch centers, we teach readers a whole repertoire of ways to talk and think about books, including, for example, looking for connections between two books, noticing and discussing sections of a book that seem remarkable, thinking about "how this book goes" or about the pattern (and breaks in pattern) in a book, imagining what a character is thinking, questioning what is going on in the story, and so on. Before we start, we are usually quite sure that most of our readers are able to monitor for sense as they read, self-correct, use several strategies to deal with difficulties, and work smoothly in partnerships.

The centers that we organize around a whole-class focus tend to last for two weeks, with members of a center meeting three or four times each week. Centers usually replace or incorporate and provide new direction for both private reading time and partnership reading time. The reading workshop still begins with a minilesson; then children alternate between reading and talking with members of their centers; finally, a share session closes the reading workshop. By second grade, reading and talking are both more separate and sustained. Children may read quietly for twenty minutes, marking pages to discuss, and only then meet with members of their center. In kindergarten and first grade, it is not unusual for centers to be very small. They often, in fact, involve only a partnership of readers (or four children who read and talk mostly in the subgroup of partnerships). By second grade, centers are often comprised of four children rather than two, a more ambitious structure but one that gives more to and asks more of participants. On the days centers do not meet, the independent reading workshop runs in the usual manner: minilesson/private reading time/partner reading time/share session.

Participants and Activities

The members of a reading center are usually matched in terms of reading ability so they can read texts together. The members of an Arnold Lobel center, for example, might be two children who were already reading together in a partnership and were also already reading *Frog and Toad* books. Then how are centers different from partnerships? It's true that the line can be a thin one. Centers give children's work a new frame and a new purpose, but the nature of their reading is not very different from what it was. If a center contains four children instead of two, this might mean that two sets of partners, each perhaps consisting of readers who can handle *Frog and Toad*, now come together to "study" Arnold Lobel. A center, then, is not radically different from either a guided reading group or a partnership. To the children, however, centers feel quite new and exciting.

Centers are not physical entities. If children are working in "character" centers, I do not expect to see one bulletin board devoted to Cam Jensen and another to Madeline. Center members usually return to the same table or patch of floor each time they meet, but the physical evidence that they form in a center is nothing more than a portable plastic book bin with a title written on it. If centers begin in December, then the bins containing leveled books are tucked below on our library shelves and the top counter is devoted to bins full of books representing readers' interests. The red dot bin subsides in importance, replaced by a basket of Pat Hutchins *Titch* books (but it is not coincidental that all the *Titch* books bear a red dot on the cover!).

When our think tank first tried the idea of centers, a group of first graders in a "Byron Barton center" would, for example, spread out across the building in search of books by Barton. By afternoon, children were lugging around giant book bins. Although the process of gathering books was thrilling and no doubt taught children great lessons, it had obvious disadvantages: it wrecked havoc in classroom libraries, because we were always importing and exporting so many subject-specific books. More important, when children collected twenty related books, they set themselves up for a week of reading, reading, reading. What we wanted, instead, was a week of reading, analyzing, comparing, and then more reading. We came to believe, therefore, that it was better to begin with two books than with twenty. If a Tomie dePaola center contains eighteen books, children simply make passing comments as they travel through their stack. We now encourage members of a Tomie dePaola center to choose two books and to read and talk between these, adding a third or even a fourth book later in the week. This is in keeping with our general belief rigor involves doing more with less.

As I mentioned earlier, if four children have formed an Arnold Lobel center and another two are studying Joy Cowley's books and yet another cluster are poring over Beverly Cleary's books, the class might meanwhile work on a whole-class study of Mem Fox. One day, we might simply read the back of one of her books in order to learn something about her and then read one of her books with this question in mind: "How does this book fit with what we know about her?" If we did this work with Mem Fox in the minilesson, children could go through the same sequence with their individual authors when they gather in centers.

Perhaps the next day we'd *reread* that same Mem Fox book, suggesting that in an author study we need to revisit texts, look closely and think hard about how the author writes. Again, children could follow suit in their centers with their own respective authors. Maybe on the third day, we'd read another Mem Fox book together on the rug, keeping the first book open and close by as we progressed through the new book and stopping often to notice similarities and differences.

Soon we'd say to children, "In your centers, will you come up with other things you think readers could do in an author study?" and soon children would be generating the ideas that all of us would then try together in our whole-class Mem Fox study. In this way, we and our children work together to generate a repertoire of strategies for reading and responding to books.

The Governing Principles of Reading Centers

We observe and then actively and assertively intervene to lift the level of what our children are doing in their centers, and we organize minilessons and strategy lessons to provide readers with strategies they seem to need. We either confer with readers in centers, work with members of a center through strategy lessons, or we regard a center as a guided-reading group. Centers are not a way to keep kids busy while we do something else. If centers are going to be worthy of our children's time and attention, they require our time and attention as well. The clearest insight into a teacher's view of reading is to see how that teacher spends her time during the reading curriculum. We think it is so important for us to help kids initiate an active, thoughtful, constructive sort of reading and to help kids think about and between texts, that we can't imagine suggesting that children simply carry on in centers while the teacher leads one small reading group after another. Nothing in the history of schooling leads us to believe that children will work really well in centers if we don't spend any time lifting the level of what happens there.

Centers are another forum for helping children do what good readers the world over do. Although it's not harmful for children to do crossword puzzles using words from books, or to play Twister or Rummy with consonant sounds and sight words, or to write new pages that could be added to a story, we prefer to have readers doing what readers everywhere do. We can ask, "Is this something *I* do in my life as a reader?" and "Do I hope children will be doing this during independent reading and at home as they read?" If the answers are yes, this activity may be a wise way to use a center. But if we don't want children to jump up to make a tray of muffins when they read the poem, "The Muffin Man" during independent reading, then we wouldn't encourage them to create play muffins out of clay during center time. Instead, in centers we help children to do what richly literate people do as they read: talk deeply about books, encounter surprising things in books, think about the craft of writing, envision the drama of a story, share responses with a friend, and pursue ideas.

The plans for our centers are "co-authored" by the children themselves. Because we regard centers as occasions for readers to do what good readers do, we think it essential that children eventually generate their own plans and ideas about what they will do within the center structure. There are many times when we start out by modeling ways of responding to texts as I did in the Mem Fox author study, but readers also invest their own ideas for strategies they can use. When we steer children through teacher-designed activities, our purpose is to give them a repertoire of possibilities to draw on when they work more independently. Once the centers are well launched, children might choose to flag

- Children must stay in the center and with other members of the center for the duration of the center cycle. They can't finish one center and drift to another.
- It helps to take a break from reading centers. After one or two cycles of centers, we return to doing more independent reading and to partnerships and this reinvigorates centers when we return to them.
- If a center has four children, they are in matched partnerships and sometimes read and talk in twos and sometimes in fours.
- Centers meet in a consistent place. This cuts down on "roaming the room."
- A center starts with just a few books. When centers start with lots of books, readers tend to try to "get through" all the books and rarely stop to talk.
- We can support struggling readers by basing our minilessons on books from their center, which elevates their texts. We read aloud at least one of their books which supports their conversations.
- Centers based in variations on a shared theme help focus everyone's work and contribute to a sense of a community of readers. Having a shared, umbrella theme gives struggling and strong readers something in common.

the funny parts of a text or make a chart comparing two books or reread and categorize a collection of memoirlike picture books, or turn familiar poems into scripts for choral reading.

The organizational structure of reading centers provides a predictable, highly structured frame within which teachers and children can do the changing and unpredictable work of following their interests, hobbies, favorite authors, and cross-curricular inquiries. Although one cycle of centers may support children in reading "list-books" in ways which help them write "list-books" and another cycle of centers may support children thinking about how characters change, *all* centers have a consistent, clear structure that is deliberately kept predictable so that children's ideas and projects can be unpredictable.

Launching Reading Centers

Renée Dinnerstein introduces centers in her kindergarten classroom with a short cycle devoted to wordless books. Starting in about mid-November, she organizes children into small groups of partners (these are her centers) and gives each partnership a wordless picturebook. Meanwhile, each day's center time begins with children convening on the carpet for what is essentially a whole-class center around different wordless book. In one minilesson last fall,

Renée reminded children about what they had decided the day before: one way to read a wordless book is to study the pages and then to act like an author, inventing your own (oral) story to accompany the sequence of pictures. "You were great at inventing stories to go with this book," Renée said, "and I was so impressed to see you later, in your centers, inventing stories to go with your own center books." Then Renée said, "Today, I was thinking we could go back and *reread* the book to find favorite pages, and we could try to *really* study these pages and to talk a long time about what we notice and think about them." Early in the year, neither the whole-class center time nor the small-group center time last more than ten or fifteen minutes, but while they last, the children are busy, engaged, and constructive. Renée meanwhile was also able to let kids do independent reading. After spending a week exploring wordless books, Renée's class returned to their old schedule of independent reading time and partnerships. After a week or two, she again scheduled a cycle of centers, and this time her kindergartners first met on the carpet for a "whole-class center" on pattern books, and then dispersed to their centers to transfer strategies they had practiced together with the read-aloud to their center reading.

After several cycles of whole-class centers, some teachers introduce "open" centers, in which clusters of children pursue their own topics of interest. Once children understand the center structure, they start to see possible centers in much of what they do. Sometimes a few of these child-initiated centers will exist concurrently with independent reading; a cluster of readers is doing something during independent reading and we call what they are doing together a center. Eventually, the work of these two or four children can serve as an example for others. During their partnership reading time, a breathless Celia and Abby approached Teresa Caccavale with four books in their hands. Abby said, "Look Mrs. Caccavale. We noticed that these four books all have a pattern that changes at the end of the book."

"Yeah," Celia added. "We were just reading along and then it changed, just like that book you read aloud to us today."

Teresa said, "You know something, I'm beginning to think that this happens a lot in books. First in my book, then you found four more. I wonder if we could find others?"

The girls nodded enthusiastically, grabbed each other's hands, and assured Teresa they could. "Yeah, we could look at those orange books 'cause it might happen in more of them," Celia said. Abby paused to add, "We can put them in a basket." Teresa asked, "What could we call the basket?" Abby answered, "We'd call it Pattern Book Basket so other kids could read them." The Pattern Book Basket soon became unwieldy because the library contained so many pattern books, especially during this early portion of the first grade year, and before long these girls were discussing other commonalties they found in their books. "A lot of these are chase books," they said, and were off with yet another inquiry.

Meanwhile, other readers may hook onto an interest during independent reading time, and soon another set of partners will commit to a shared inquiry and call what they are doing a reading center. For example, when the Scholastic newspapers arrive in the room, it contains a story about the Special Olympics. Someone announces that she has a book on that topic, or her Grammie went to the Special Olympics, or she saw them on television, and soon another center will be up and running. A child brings his comics or his baseball cards or his Pokéman cards or his Lego directions to school, and a friend is interested. He knows a kid who has a related text, and before long another center has started. Oftentimes, then, we sponsor cycles of centers that *do not* fall under a teacher-initiated theme. We help these centers emerge out of independent reading time.

When teachers have open cycles, we generally record ideas for centers (both the topic and the members) on a public planning board, and we do this as the ideas emerge, one at a time. (This way, we do not have to say on a Friday afternoon, "We'll start new centers next week. What ideas do you have?") The planning board allows us to help children generate their ideas for centers one at a time, as we confer with individuals during independent reading or at odd moments in the day. Because the planning board is constructed in a meeting with the eyes of everyone watching our every decision, we are able to engineer partnerships and topics that will work well.

During an open cycle in Kathy Collins's class, Jacob put a Post-it note on the planning board that said "NBA center—Jacob and Charlie." Kathy met with them and said, "I just wanted to check in to see what you two have in mind for your center."

Jacob said, "I just got a Michael Jordan book with pictures and Charlie's dad has basketball magazines at home, so we want to start a center on basketball." Because Jacob and Charlie were strong readers and successful partners at other times of the day, Kathy signed them up for their NBA Center. At the share time that day, she told the class of Jacob and Charlie's idea for a center and how they were planning ahead about what they would read. Alex said, "My brother has a book of rules for basketball 'cause he plays in a league. I can bring it in for you."

"I got some basketball cards in my backpack that you can borrow if you give 'em back," Johnathan added.

"Wow, you guys, you'll have lots of work to do in your center next week," Kathy said to Jacob and Charlie. They smiled at each other and slapped hands in a high-five, clearly excited about their upcoming center. "If anyone else has a great idea for a center, add it to the planning board like Charlie and Jacob."

Six-year-old Taylor was determined to make a center on cats and already had three books for it. "I want to start a center on cats because my mom said I can get a cat when my bunny, Stripes, dies," Taylor said. "I got to find out about cats so when Stripes dies I can take care of a kitty." Then Taylor said, "I want to do it with Emma because she had Rousseau, her cat, that died and so she knows stuff about cats too and about dying, too, for my dead rabbit.

When the whole class gathered, Kathy said to the children, "Taylor did the coolest thing today. She gathered a few books about cats together because she's going to get one soon."

"After Stripes dies, so maybe not *too* soon." Taylor added.

Nodding, Kathy continued, "Taylor wants to learn about cats, so she's planning to do research on them. It reminds me of when I wanted to buy a bike. I read so many magazines and books about bikes because I wanted to find the best one for me. I was doing research on bikes, like Taylor is doing on cats."

Whatever focus centers have, they help our children know that readers have reasons to read. We read to laugh out loud, to get advice, to feel less alone, to learn about new places, to walk in the shoes of people who are different from ourselves, to be reminded of other lives, to take pleasure in something lovely, and yes, to get the tears out. How good it is for children to learn, right from the start, that literacy and life go together.

Coaching and Conferring During Centers

During centers, we move among children, and as we do, we coach and confer with readers. Hannah Schneewind conferred with her first graders who were working in an author center reading Robert Kraus' *Leo the Late Bloomer*. One child had recently read *The Carrot Seed* by Ruth Krauss to his kindergarten reading partner. "Wait a minute!" he said, looking at *Leo the Late Bloomer*. "This book is practically the same as *The Carrot Seed*. In that book, the grown-ups kept saying, 'It won't come up, it won't come up.' But it did!" Soon these boys were hot on the trail of other books in which a character was a late bloomer. They began by searching their Leo-collection for other books about late bloomers, but in the end, what began as a Leo center ended as a "late bloomer" center. Oftentimes, we confer to help kids establish a sense of direction to their reading.

Next Hannah Schneewind pulled alongside Chris and Sarah. Sarah, who had brought a Russell Hoban *Frances* book in from home, continued talking to her partner as if her teacher weren't there. "This is it. It's the book I got from the library and I read it all. We should do this one first so I can kind of show you what Frances is like." She began turning the pages.

"It looks like it might be kind of funny," Chris said as he leaned over, looking at the pages that were flipping by.

"Yeah it is. Look at this! Look at how small her hand is! Look at how small. It's so cute," Sarah said pointing at the picture on a page.

"Look at her feet!" Chris said as he began pointing as well. Look at her eyeball even! Small, small, small!"

They continued browsing through six or seven pages in this manner until Sarah looked up at Chris and said, "Do you kind of have the idea?"

"Yeah," he said nodding, "let's start reading it!" Sarah began reading aloud the section where Frances hides under the kitchen sink.

"Hey," Chris interjected. "I do stuff like that."

"What?" Sarah asked.

"Hide out in places in my house," Chris explained, "like, in that part at the bottom of my bed. If there wasn't all the poison stuff under our sink, I think that would be the perfect place to hide out, you know, where Frances is."

Sarah added, "I have a perfect place in my bedroom. It can fit me and some of my stuffed animals and nobody in my house could ever find me if I hid there."

Hannah chose this moment to shift her research from observation to interview. "Can I just stop you a minute? I've been watching you for a couple minutes, and I'm amazed by some great things you're doing. I just want to check out what I noticed you doing to make sure I got it right. First, I noticed that you [looking at Sarah] kind of introduced the book to Chris by taking a picture walk. You said you wanted to show him what Frances is like."

"Well, yeah," Sarah nodded. "I read it this weekend, the whole thing, so I just wanted Chris to kind of know some stuff."

Hannah said, "That was not only really thoughtful, but it was also really smart. Whenever my friends recommend books to me, they always kind of tell me some stuff about the book so I have an idea about it. Did it help you, Chris, that Sarah did that?"

"Kind of," Chris answered, somewhat dubiously. "I knew the book might be funny."

Ignoring Chris' ambivalence, Hannah continued. "Then the next thing you did that was so great was that you stopped to talk to each other about how you are like Frances, finding hideout spaces in your own houses. Do you feel that you know Frances a little better because you have some stuff in common with her?"

"Yeah," said Chris. "'Cause we both hide out too, just like Frances."

"Yeah, especially if we're mad or something," added Sarah.

"Wow," said Hannah. "I can really see why you might want to follow Frances for a few books." Now Hannah upped the ante. "Are you going to keep that in mind as you read? Are you going to think of ways you relate to Frances?"

"I guess so," responded Sarah, not entirely certain.

Carrying on with contagious enthusiasm, Hannah said, "It'd be good to keep a record of what you find, recording the pages where you're like Frances. And you know what? Since you are both so into *Frances* books, you'll probably want to read them at home. Take a few Post-its home with you so when you read you can put Post-its on the places you want to talk about with each other. How does that sound? I think it will help you."

Chris nodded in agreement, and Hannah began writing the plan down in each of their reading logs. "I'll get some Post-its," Chris said. As Hannah began to move on toward another pair of readers, she paused and said to Sarah, "I'm going to go to some other partners now and see if they are doing anything like this. If they're not, I might tell them they should try what you two are doing."

Similarly, Axle and Mack, two first graders in Alexa Stott's classroom, came together to study *Frog and Toad* but ended up with a new focus—trying to read *Frog and Toad* aloud *really* well. "We want to make it a smooth read," Axle explained. Their efforts focused first on the challenge of reading all the words accurately. They flagged the challenging words with Post-its and worked together on them. Then they worked on making their read aloud sound better. Axle told Mack, "I think you should breathe before you go, 'said Frog,'" and Mack had a second go at the sentence. Soon they were working to make sad parts sound sad, to read more quickly, to make their voices sound like Alexa's read-aloud voice. In the end, they shifted their centers focus from *Frog and Toad* books towards working on reading aloud across a range of texts.

Children Learn a Repertoire of Ways to Respond to Texts

In centers, children learn a repertoire of ways to talk, think, and even write about books. Ideas that develop within one center are usually applicable in others. For example, in what children named as their Dead Dog center, Angel and Leo decided to categorize and rate the books they'd found about dogs that died according to a coding system in which they marked some sections as quite sad, some as really sad, and some as really, *really* sad. In doing this rating work these boys were borrowing on a response technique other children in their class and in other classes had often used. They'd heard about children who ranked picture books according to their picturesqueness and insect books according to degrees of grossness. Some children use systems of stars (one star means fair, two mean good, three mean great), to rank or categorize books; still others have adopted movie ratings (G, PG, PG-13, R, etc.) and used this scale to convey their own hierarchy.

Children also know that after readers have finished a book, readers often turn back to particular passages to talk about them. Readers know therefore, that a technique as simple as marking selected passages can support strong conversations. In a second-grade mystery center, children read David A. Adler's *Cam Jansen,* Marjorie Sharmat's *Nate the Great,* and Elizabeth Levy's *The Something Queer* books, and their agreed-upon task was to put a Post-it in *each* book at the spot where they learned what the mystery would be. There is nothing very complicated about sticking a Post-it on a page, but reading a mystery with an eye toward discovering "at what point do we know the source of mystery?" is a wise strategy indeed. I've also seen children marking

- the one page where they especially feel the author's big idea.
- a place where the main character changes.
- sections where the book reminds them of their lives.
- sections in which the book resembles another book.

- clues to unravel the mystery.
- sections which show a view of life with which the reader disagrees (or critiques).
- places where the author has done something they want to emulate.
- cool things they want to discuss.
- places that show a central conflict.
- places where the pattern in a book is broken.

It is a small step from marking sections of books to charting these sections. In many centers, kids read a book individually, marking sections that relate to their focus or their big idea. Then they get together, as Sarah and Chris will do with the *Frances* books they read on their own, to talk about the marked sections. If both children agree that yes indeed, this section is significant to the topic at hand, then they write the page number on a chart. For example, when I pulled alongside Brianna and Maxine, two first graders in a Cynthia Rylant *Henry and Mudge* center, one of the girls commented that she wondered if once the dog Mudge had gone to dog obedience school, as he did in the books, he would behave any better. "You're onto a great question," I said. "Mudge is a really big character in this book, so it is smart to ask, 'Does he change'?" Soon, with my support, the girls began poring over information on the covers of their books in order to determine whether the *Henry and Mudge* books fell into a sequence. They decided the answer was yes and lined the books up accordingly. Next they set out to reread the books before and after obedience school, marking sections in which the dog misbehaved in all the books. Later, Brianna walked Maxine through her marked pages. If both girls agreed that Mudge was indeed being bad in a particular excerpt, they wrote the book's title and page number onto the column in their chart titled "Bad Before Dog School".

Several years ago, I watched members of a kindergarten center realize that the two books they were reading were both stories of chases. Soon they were rereading the classroom's entire set of little books looking for other chase books. I was intrigued by the size of their pile and even more intrigued by the amount of reading, talking, and thinking they accomplished as they pursued their inquiry. In similar ways, I've watched children search for journey books, comparing them in intriguing ways. How long does the trip take in that book? In this one? Do they end up back home or far away? What do guys take on the journey in that book? In this one? Teachers who know something about motifs like these can help children explore issues that are fundamental to the genre. Does the character change during this journey? What difficulties are there in the journey? How does the character get past the difficulties? Later, if any of these six-year-olds major in literature at college, they'll learn again that the journey motif underlies much of literature.

In centers, children also study topics that interest them. I've watched first graders race to learn how to care for a snake (and to do so in time for Greeny, the class snake, who waited in the aquarium), and I've watched whole classes use reading centers to study flowers, pollution, dinosaurs, and other curricular topics. Often children's reading of nonfiction books begins with questions—and it would take a very skilled researcher indeed to find the answers to some of them. An easy-reader book on hamsters is not likely to tell readers how high hamsters jump, nor is an easy-reader book on spiders apt to reveal what kind of spider wove the web in Brianna's basement.

Children come to learn that in centers, they can categorize, rank, and judge books based on certain qualities. They can locate sections of texts that are noteworthy for particular reasons. They can make charts of what they see in books by listing page numbers in columns or categories. They can search for more books with similar features.

The examples of centers I've cited might be a bit misleading. When children are encouraged to invent their own ways of responding to books, they come up with lots of wonderful plans and projects, but with a fair share of problematic ideas as well. Once a group of kindergartners decided they'd compare two books. To do so, they sat across from each other, each holding a book as if it were a deck of cards. They each opened to the first page. One child scanned the page and said, "I have a *W*. Do you have a *W*?" The second child scanned his page and responded "yes." The rule was that a positive answer entitled the second child to be the one to choose the next letter. "I have an *H*. Do you?" Another time, I watched first graders doing an author study of Joy Cowley's books. Their grand conclusion was that all her books were orange!

One of the wonderful things about centers, however, is that even when children are calling out, "Do you have a W on page one?" the work they are doing has value. Searching for *w*'s is not my idea of an ideal reading project, but there is something very powerful about two five-year-old children dreaming up weird and wonderful things to do together with books.

If, as researchers say, 80 percent of our students learn to read easily, and if this *is* due to the active constructive mind of the child, of most children, then I have to believe that centers call out that active, constructive mind. Centers invite children to approach books with initiative, thoughtfulness, and joy. What more could we ask?

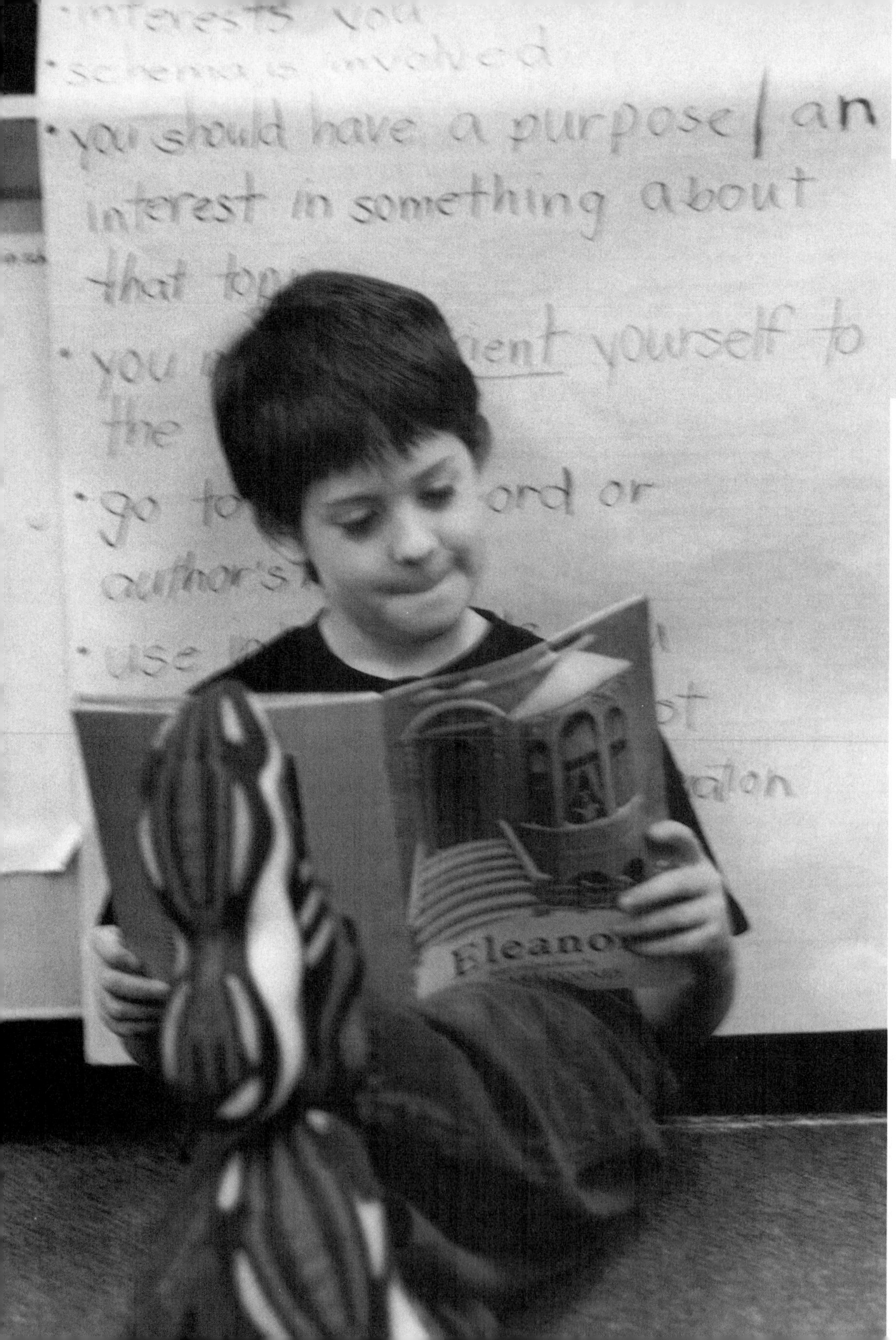

you should have a purpose/an
interest in something about

September in a 2–8 Grade Reading Workshop

17

Reading with Stamina and Comprehension

Although I know it's coming, that first red-tipped August leaf always catches me by surprise. My heart always aches with a luscious, sad pang for the endlessness of my childhood summers. But always too there is the quickening anticipation of whatever lies over the next rise. From the sighting of that first crimson edge my days turn—as a sunflower turns to the sun—toward September and the opening of school.

How I have loved those long August mornings when I busy myself in the classroom. As I drag the carpet from one corner of the classroom to another, frame it with long, low bookshelves and set out the poetry books and dried flowers. I am like a child making mansions in the spaces among the sumac bushes. This is how August lesson-planning goes. We shelve books into baskets, and dream of how we'll steer our children to the books that are just right for them. We set up the easel beside our chair at the front of the library area and envision the first poem we and our children will learn by heart.

The beginning of a new school year is worth all this and more, for an astonishing amount of instruction happens the instant children cross the threshold into the world of our classrooms. In Chapter 1, I quoted Jerry Harste: "I see curriculum as creating in the classroom the kind of world we believe in and then inviting children in to role play their way into being the readers, writers and learners we want them to be." His words are worth recalling again when we turn to the challenge of launching reading workshops in our classrooms.

Last summer, my husband John and I took our sons backpacking through the Rocky Mountains. Beforehand, we fretted over whether Miles and Evan, who sometimes whine that their feet hurt just walking through the mall, would wimp out on us. We knew it was audacious to even dream they'd shoulder huge packs and clamber up snow-capped mountain peaks. We kept our worries to ourselves, however, dressed them for their parts, and acted as if it was a matter of course that they would rise to the challenge of the Wind River Range. Miles had a compass dangling from his belt and a bandanna around his neck, while Evan carried a pocket jackknife and his own state-of-the-art water bottle. When Miles and Evan became, overnight, strong and resilient back packers, it was a reminder. We take on roles and those roles shape our destinies.

Now, in schools across the nation, children cross the threshold into our classrooms and immediately know that they are in a place where reading and writing are cherished. Most of us convey this message by reading aloud five or six times a day during these first days of school, when nothing else quite works anyway. We act as if our students will definitely, for sure, love reading and writing as we do. "Reading and writing will be at the center of life in Room 402," we say. We talk about literacy as if we couldn't imagine anyone on earth not loving words and stories and poems as we do. "Let's start the day off with a treat," we say. "Let's each take some time with our books. Don't you *love* to start the day that way?" We convey the values of the classroom when we treat reading time as such a precious commodity that not a moment can be wasted. "How can we get to the meeting area quickly and smoothly so we don't waste one precious moment of reading time?" we ask, and soon our children are helping us to work out systematic rules for classroom management, and all these rules serve our greater goal.

Although my colleagues and I assume from the start that our children all love reading as we do and trust that this assumption—in and of itself—will sweep some children along in its wake, our focus will *not* be on making certain each child's attitudes are 100 percent congruent with our optimistic expectations. There will of course be children who balk. "Aww, come on," a child will whine. "Can't we play with the computer?" The class will carefully watch our responses.

"You'd rather play on the computer than read the next chapter of *Owl in the Family*?" I ask, as if this is surprising. I may acknowledge that this child doesn't seem to like to read. "I can promise you something. This year, reading will be different for you." Meanwhile, I'll direct my efforts toward mobilizing my children to live their lives *as if* they were avid, passionate readers.

Our goals for September will include:

- Reading Easy Books with Understanding
- Reading a Lot of Books with Stamina

- Reading with Fluency
- Reading with Friends
- Celebrating Reading
- Reading in a Way That Allows Us to Retell
- Holding Readers Accountable to the Text

These are ambitious goals, and they deserve some discussion.

Reading Easy Books with Understanding

In the teaching of reading, there are a handful of goals we need to work toward with decisiveness and firm clarity, so that we can accomplish them and then move on to other goals. For example, when beginning readers have only a shaky sense that the words they say match the print on the page, it helps to be very clear that these readers need to point crisply under each word as they read. But once a child is able to point, once a child has mastered one-spoken-word-to-one-printed-word matching (at least with texts at that level of difficulty), it is equally important to help that child *stop* pointing with her finger, and instead begin using her eyes to point at words, bringing out fingers only when the text gets difficult and she needs extra help. In a similar way, I recommend that every teacher of reading begin the year by steadfastly directing children toward reading a lot of easy books, and reading these books fluently and smoothly, with clear comprehension, and at a good pace. We can feel less ambivalent about directing children toward books that are easy for them if we bear in mind that this is a temporary goal. Once all our readers develop a felt-sense of what it means to read texts with a strong, clear understanding of them, we will encourage readers to tackle texts that are a notch or two more challenging but to aim toward keeping the same tenacious hold on meaning while reading slightly harder books.

Although in the best of all worlds I might want students to begin the year reading "just-right" books, my colleagues and I know that no amount of fine-tuned matching between readers and books could ever guarantee that a particular book will make a lot of sense and be interesting to a particular reader. We therefore tend to talk up the idea that for now, at the start of the year, we'll all read easy books. We have become convinced that if we tell our students that we're going to start the year reading books that are *easy* for us, books we can zoom through, this will give many of our students the permission they need to read books that are, in fact, appropriate for them. In our work in hundreds of classrooms, we've found that a great many children begin the year reading books that represent someone else's hopes for their reading. Often these children think it's okay to produce a "Swiss cheese" version of a text with giant holes in places where the reader has mentally mumbled past. And we know that no harm will be done to our other students if they begin the year doing some light reading.

When we do promotional book talks in September and feature certain books to display, we choose easy books, often ones that are part of a series. (This way, students get involved with a sequence of books and this holds them on a course.) Our read-aloud books in September will probably be the shorter, lighter books that are easy to listen to and love, the books that will make us moan when reading-aloud time is over. We'll read these books in ways that model what it means to begin a book, to plan our passage through the book using bookmarks as goals, to read long chunks over an allotted time and short chunks in stolen moments, and to have another book waiting before we finish the first one. At the start of the year, we're apt to bring out only part of the classroom library for circulation. We often make a starter library of books that are shorter, easier, and above all, familiar to us. This gives students a feeling for moving through books at a good pace, and it helps us understand their understanding of books. Because we know the books, we can support our children's interest in them with our own knowledge and interest. We can also ask questions and interpret student responses more efficiently.

As I mentioned in Chapters 7 and 8 on teaching within a leveled library and on assessment, we sometimes begin the year featuring only the leveled part of our libraries, and we may use a ladder of leveled books to roughly match children with the levels "in which they'll feel strong as readers." Then we and the children watch for and celebrate signs of engagement, interest, and response. We cheer when Samantha's mother gives her all five books in Lynne Reid Banks' *The Indian in the Cupboard* series and when Samantha promises to share them with her friends. We delight in Evan's announcement that he read Phyllis Reynolds Naylor's *Shiloh* right through lunch, and we celebrate the way Joe sneaked a peek at his *Goosebumps* (R. L. Stine) book during an extra moment between gym and math. If we see a child chuckling in response to a book, or quickly finishing the chapter on the sly even after we've said, "Let's put our books away and come to the meeting area," or better yet, if a child walks to the meeting area with her nose still in the book (sitting down without actually tearing herself from the page), we'll cheer and we'll definitely regard all these signs of engagement as indicators that this child is reading with comprehension.

On the other hand, when we notice children whose heads are like revolving fans during independent reading, always turning this way and that way to scan the room, or when we notice children who seem to develop urinary tract infections—going to the bathroom every five minutes whenever it's time to read, we'll want to pull up a chair and say, "I don't know this book. Tell me about it." We'll probably follow that question up with, "Show me a part you love" and "Would you read that part to me?" If the section tells of Edward, kicking at a seaside rock with anger, we'll ask, "Who's Edward? Why is he so angry?" Or sometimes we'll ask a general question about how the part the child has read to us fits with the rest of the book. Alternatively, we may say to a reader who is reading a particular page. "So tell me, what's going on on this page?" and then, after hearing a bit, we might follow up with "Show me that part."

Using these quick checks, I find it relatively easy to discern whether or not a child is understanding even the books I haven't read. If I think the book is too hard, sometimes I find it helps to say, "Is this book a confusing book?" (almost as if it's the book's fault), rather than "Is this book too hard?" When I ask if the book is a confusing one, the child is apt to shrug and say, "Kind of." I take this as an admission and leap to congratulate the child: "Strong readers do just what you've done. Strong readers say, 'This book is kind of confusing. I'm going to read one that'll make a whole lot of sense to me.'"

During this "reading should make sense" unit of study, we're apt not only to confer with children but also to offer minilessons that address the topic of finding easy or just-right books. In a recent minilesson, Kathleen Tolan showed children how to give their books a "Does this book make me understand?" test. Kathleen put her bookshelf of books in front of her and asked children to watch. Then she haltingly tried one book, shook her head, set the book to the side and said, "No, I don't feel that strong as a reader with this book." She tried another book, this time reading smoothly, with expression. "*This* makes me feel strong," she said, and put the second book in a separate pile. Then Kathleen said to the students, "What did it look like when I read a confusing book?" and then "What did it look like when I read a 'just-right' book?" Soon each child, still sitting in the meeting area, was giving his or her books a reading test. "Let's find the books with no lumps or bumps," Kathleen said, using the children's words. "Let's find the books where our reading is strong and straight."

Donna Santman began the year with her middle school students by asking them to bring their most beloved books to school. Donna showed her class her well-loved copy of Judy Blume's *Are You There God? It's Me, Margaret.* The next day, Donna's students made an exhibit of their own favorite books. The class spent time simply moving around among each other's favorite books making note of them. They had brought in titles by John Steinbeck and J. R. R. Tolkien, they had brought computer books and "fine literature." The collection of books these sixth graders brought in seemed to say, "I'm sophisticated," "I'm grown up," befitting their new status as students in junior high.

"I shouldn't have been surprised that this is what the kids would show-case," Donna said, "but I wasn't ready for it. I already knew I wanted to launch the year with a unit on stamina, and that as part of that, I'd push them to read a lot of easy books. Then they all came in with fat books, the thicker the better. Yet I also had as a goal to visibly and dramatically build a curriculum in support of their intentions." Donna, like most of us in the think tank, hoped to set the tone for the school year by "leaning into" her students' hopes and goals, demonstrating to them that they would be co-authors of the curriculum, that their words and ideas mattered.

Of course, sometimes we can say, "Yes!" to what our students suggest. At other times we need to do some fast pedaling if we are going to build from what kids have said but still launch them on the course we envision. This time Donna did some fast pedaling. After she and her students studied their exhibit of books, Donna grouped her students together in small clusters and asked them to talk about three questions: "Why did you bring this particular book? Is this book typical of your reading life? Does this book represent the you you *are* or the you you want to *become*?" Soon, many of these young people were saying they'd brought in books that represented "the me I want to become in school."

Listening to these group discussions, Donna said, "You've found books that represent your futures as readers" and talked about how, when we want to grow, we sometimes take on things we can just barely handle. Donna congratulated her kids for thinking seriously about their future reading. "We're going to do that a lot in this classroom. And we're going to deliberately plan our reading lives so we each make sure we grow stronger, reaching new goals for ourselves."

Donna then brought the class around in a U-turn by suggesting that the best way for students to reach their goals might be to begin the year not by reading books that represented their future as readers but by reading the books that made them feel strong as readers now. She tried to make it a community goal that for a short time everyone would return to books that were easy for them, and that together, everyone in the class would get into the groove of reading, reading, reading.

In September, the challenge is not deciding *what* to teach but deciding what *not* to teach. When a new group of children enters our classroom, all our vows to notice and celebrate their strengths usually give way to an overwhelming sense of, "Oh my God. There is so much to teach them." Every child at every moment presents us with yet more issues that merit our attention. What a temptation it is to rush about, giving a lot of little tips and setting a lot of little goals, with no follow through on anything! We need to look at all the possible topics of instruction and say, "That can wait." The art of teaching reading is always about selection, but this is never more true than at the start of the year. In September it is important to foreground only a few goals. If we keep our teaching simple, we can see through our teaching methods and focus on the children. We need, above all, to connect with each individual in our care.

Teaching children to read books they can understand with ease will have dramatic payoffs, so this is an especially effective lesson for the September of a reading workshop. In September I also want to do everything possible to ensure that all my children are reading for longer and longer stretches of time each day, that they are making time for reading, and that they begin, continue through, and complete books at a good pace. These are not small goals.

Reading a Lot of Books with Stamina

If our goal is for children to read with increasing stamina at home and at school, it's probably wisest to work toward this goal by focusing first on the time we have together in school for reading. "Yesterday you were able to sustain reading for *fifteen minutes,*" we'll say. "For *fifteen* minutes, it felt as if everyone was hooked into his or her book. Then some of you started getting restless, so we stopped. Today, let's aim for *twenty* minutes, okay?" Some classes keep chart, recording their progress in being able to sustain their attention on their book. Sometimes each child keeps track of the number of pages he or she reads during that day's reading time in school and resolves to read an equal number of pages at home. Once it's established that every child's goal is to read at least as much at home as he or she reads in school, we can begin to extend the reading block in both places.

It is important to systematically collect data about how much students are reading and to expect and deal with the difficulties we encounter. This is important first, because the amount of time students spend reading matters more than people realize. Also, this is one of the more concrete goals I have for readers, and this is an opportunity to show students that I expect my teaching to actually affect what they do. In September, when we are showing children what it means to be members of this learning community, it is especially important to do the follow-through necessary to be *absolutely sure* that our children are not "Teflon" learners. We want to be certain that our words and our demonstrations don't simply "slide off" but instead make a palpable difference in their reading lives. We also want to be sure they see that taking our teaching seriously has payoffs for them as readers.

Some teachers talk to readers about the importance of putting a Post-it note in their book twenty pages ahead of their current place as a way to mark their goal for that day's reading. Others talk about the value of making and

living up to plans for progressing through the book. Many of us ask children to leave a trail of Post-its labeled *Monday-school, Monday-home, Tuesday-school, Tuesday-home* as they journey through a book to visually record their progress. Having readers do this for a week or two highlights the goal of reading a lot and makes stamina a tangible issue that we end up addressing in our individual conferences. Many of these concrete tools can be effective levers for a time but then they eventually need to be abandoned.

Of course, when the emphasis of our teaching is on reading longer and reading more, it becomes the topic of many minilessons. On one October morning, when I stopped by to visit Mark Hardy's class, he had just finished reading aloud a book from Jon Scieska's *Time Warp Trio* series. Although school had only been in session for three weeks, students were already on their third read-aloud. During this first "unit," Mark had selected three very short books as read-alouds. "I didn't want to start with a heavy-hitter like Lois Lowry's *The Giver,*" he said. "As long as I am encouraging them to get through shorter books at a good pace on their own, I need to use shorter, lighter books for the read-aloud, too." That day, after ten minutes of reading aloud, Mark said to the students who'd gathered on the carpet, "We'll be finishing this book soon, and I don't have anything lined up for us to read next. I've noticed this sometimes happens in your reading lives, too. You move along at a good pace until you finish a book, then your whole reading life stalls while you search for the next book. What some readers do, and I thought what we'd try, is to have 'books-in-waiting' or 'books-on-deck' so they can move from one book to the next book without losing a beat." The class went on to discuss how good readers often select books in waiting by deliberately going from one good book to another, related book. This conversation led the group to discover that there were more books in the *Time Warp Trio* series. "Today, during the reading workshop and at home, would you all think about having books-in-waiting?" Mark said.

Soon children had dispersed to their "reading nooks" and Mark and I began a quick "status of the class" check. He had jotted down the titles and the number of pages for every student's reading the day before. Now we quickly circled among the students. After this check, Mark gestured to five students to gather on the carpet. "I called you over because I've noticed you guys aren't making a lot of headway through your books," Mark said. "I wanted to show you a strategy I use to push myself to read longer chunks of a text."

In general, we let our upper-grade students know that we expect them to get through *at least* a book a week. There will be some exceptions, especially later in the year when children tackle more challenging texts, but over the years we've seen too many children reading long books, such as Sharon Creech's *Walk Two Moons,* at the rate of three pages a day. We're not convinced such a child can hold the world of that story in his or her mind for six weeks. If a child needs to read at that pace (which we doubt), we'd suggest the child tackle briefer books. We are apt to steer such a child to Ursula Le Guin's *Cat Wings* series, to Judy Blume's *Chocolate Fever,* to Doris Buchanan Smith's *A Taste of Blackberries,* to Clyde Robert Bulla's *The Chalkbox Kid,* to Jon Scieska's *Time Warp Trio* trilogy, to Karen Hesse's *Sable,* or to another similar short novel.

In Mark's classroom, the readers who weren't making a lot of visible headway in their books each had their own idiosyncratic explanations. Children who were forgetting to bring their books between home and school made a plan to remind each other about their books at the end of the school day and to phone reminders to each other every evening. Another child couldn't squeeze reading into her day. Her friends listened to her hectic schedule and suggested she might need to read on the subway between lessons and school. "If I don't get sick," she agreed. Yet another child found himself stalled because his book turned out to be complex and hard. He agreed to put the book down and to choose more carefully next time. Still another found himself reading only as a bedtime ritual and, all too often he was too tired to read.

Mark's conversation about making more time for reading was meanwhile being echoed in hundreds of other classrooms. In Linda Chen's classroom, Jeremy's Post-its indicated he'd read twenty-six pages within the forty-minute independent reading workshop in school and four pages at home that night. The Post-its made Jeremy's progress through a book visible, and his problems, which of course weren't his alone, public. Soon the class had spent a week on an inquiry into how they could make more time for reading (resulting in the chart below).

<u>Making Time for Reading</u>

- Before we read, we can look over the chapters and plan our progress through a book. "If I read three chapters a day, I'll be done by Sunday," we can say and aim for that.

- Try not to save reading for last, after all the other homework is done. If we only read in bed before falling asleep at night, often we're exhausted and do fall asleep!

- If we're in the habit of just reading little bits of a book at one sitting, we can set goals for how far to read each time. Mark a place in the book and try to read up to that point before taking a break.

- It can help to have a "break book" alongside our main book so that if we need to take a break, we can shift into a different sort of reading altogether.

- It helps to carry books with us everywhere, developing the habit of reading often.

- If we find it hard to get past the first few chapters and into the mainstream of a book, it can help to have a friend or parent read several chapters aloud, or have someone tell us about the book. If we understand the gist of the story, it's sometimes easier to get into it.

- To develop the habit of reading it helps to have one or preferably a few predictable times a day when we read.

Reading with Fluency

During our September unit of study on reading a lot of books with clarity and stamina, we also emphasize the importance of reading with fluency. Some teachers touch on this topic lightly, watching for and talking with children about the most egregious problems, such as the third grader who reads chapter books in a word-by-word way, pointing at each word as he reads. "You've graduated from pointing at the words," we tell this child. "When you were a beginning reader, you needed to do this, but now it's holding you back. Just keep your finger near and bring it out only if you encounter difficulty." During a recent visit to a fifth-grade classroom, Gay Su Pinnell whispered to me, "I'm seeing a lot of sausage-machine readers who put exaggerated pauses between words," and suggested that the problem might result from prolonged finger-pointing at words. Other children subvocalize instead of pointing, and this too can interfere with fluency.

Some teachers take the work with fluency further and make fluent reading a priority during September. Erica Leif's fifth graders, for example, had lived through a similar Reading with Stamina and Meaning unit of study during September of the preceding year, and so for her children, Erica highlighted fluency as one of the aspects of reading with clarity that poses special challenges. "I told my kids that now that we were all reading books we could *really* understand, our voices should *sound like* conversation. One day I read aloud in a minilesson while my kids followed the text on an overhead, and then we talked about what they noticed about my voice," Erica said. The children inevitably talked most about the relationship between punctuation and voice.

Erica led minilessons and strategy lessons for two weeks helping her children learn how to read sentences with periods parenthesis, and commas—and these were very proficient readers. She first used the overhead projector to display sentences from favorite picturebooks and novels. They practiced reading aloud these lines from E. B. White's *Charlotte's Web:*

> Wilbur never forgot Charlotte. Although he loved her children and grandchildren dearly, none of the new spiders ever quite took her place in his heart. She was in a class by herself. It is not often that someone comes along who is a true friend and a good writer. Charlotte was both.

They practiced reading the last lines of Mem Fox's *Koala Lou:*

> When the first stars of evening appeared in the sky, Koala Lou crept home through the dark and up into the gum-tree. Her mother was waiting for her.

Before she could say a word her mother had flung her arms around her neck and said, "Koala Lou, I DO love you! I always have, and I always will."And she hugged her for a very long time.

They also practiced reading aloud pages from William Armstrong's *Sounder*:

> "Sounder and me must be about the same age," the boy said, tugging gently at one of the coon dog's ears, and then the other. He felt the importance of the years—as a child measures age—which separated him from the younger children. he was old enough to stand out in the cold and run his finger's over sounders head.

When Erica's children met each day in their independent reading partnerships, the first thing they did was to take turns reading a section of their independent reading books aloud. "Study your partners," Erica said. "How did your partner read the comma, the dash? Was there a difference? How would *you* have read the passage?" Soon, as a class they were working on reading aloud sentences that contained many commas, or commas and semicolons, ellipses and parentheses.

One set of partners found themselves stymied by a sentence in Patricia MacLachlan's *The Facts and Fictions of Minna Pratt,* and so Erica put the sentence up on chart paper for the whole class to analyze:

> As hard as Minna tried, all she could see was her mother's room, half clean, her father in a suit, tripping over books, all of them, the lot, in danger of falling into distraction.

"What does *all of them* modify?" they asked. "Are they tripping over *all of the books, the lot?* Or is it that all of the family, the lot of them, were in danger of falling into distraction?" The class talked about the fact that sometimes sentences contain invisible punctuation. There are sometimes places in a sentence in which readers need to make half-pauses, and Erica's children felt that one of these came at the end of "all she could see" in MacLachlan's sentence. They also talked about how readers sometimes need to get to the end of the sentence before they can figure out the structure of the sentence. At first this passage seemed to contain a long list of equal items, all of which Minna saw, but a closer look suggested that some of the phrases were subordinate to others. Soon Erica's children were drawing arrows to show that "half clean" modified Minna's mother's room, "tripping over books" modified her father, and that the phrase "all of them, the lot" referred not to the books but to the family. "Why didn't she use a semicolon before 'all of them?'" one child asked, and this led them to realize that because the phrase beginning with "all of them ..." was not a complete sentence on its own, she had no option of using a semi-colon.

Readers, of course, can't take half an hour to figure out their intonation for a single sentence, but by doing some deep work with a few complex sentences, Erica's children brought a new consciousness to their work with other sentences. Soon the class had developed a rubric for assessing "Am I Using a Good Reading Voice?" On the list, the children included the importance of not overacting. "We need to read like we're *talking*," Erica said. "It's ridiculous to act like a movie star," the children added. The rubric also included the idea that as good readers, we try to push our eyes ahead to take in more of a line at a time. That way, we aren't caught off guard by a question mark or a fragment. "It's kind of like rock climbing," the kids said. "You need to look ahead to see what's next on the cliff so you can be ready."

Of course, Erica's children didn't instantly become fluent readers just because she put a spotlight on fluency. After the early weeks of school, Erica still had a few struggling readers who hadn't made the breakthrough that readers often make around second or third grade, when they begin to take in more of a sentence at a time. But at least the goal of fluency was "out there," in the community. And parents and children were beside themselves with delight. "This is having a *profound* affect," parents said to Erica at parent-student conferences. "Our child's reading is totally different. It's like night and day."

Reading with Friends

While children are growing accustomed to longer and longer stretches of reading and to reading lots of books, and to reading with fluency, we need to nourish them as readers. One of the best ways to do this is to make reading a sociable activity. Early in the year, it is crucial that we cultivate a climate of conversation and sociability around books. While we're still getting to know children, we will probably be hesitant to establish long-term reading partnerships. Instead, at the end of independent reading, we may just ask kids to sit together with a classmate and address a topic. We might, for example, sponsor very brief conversations by saying:

- Today, would you get with two or three classmates to talk about your very favorite books in the whole world.

- Today, would you talk with someone you usually don't talk with about a book that changed your life.

- Today, would you and a friend decide on a book you both know that might make a great movie. If you have time, talk about how you'd cast the characters.

- Talk to someone you don't know too well and tell that person some things you notice about yourself as a reader.
- Find a person who's reading the same kind of books you read and talk about the author's style in the book you're reading today.
- Talk with a classmate about when you tend to read and where and why.
- Recommend a book to a friend, or ask for a recommendation.

Celebrating Reading

Another way to nourish our children's growth as readers is to celebrate their progress. Just as we schedule frequent and early author celebrations in the writing workshop, so, too we hold frequent and early reading celebrations to bring new energy to our reading workshops. Donna Santman decided to mark her children's new ability to read with stamina by scheduling a reading marathon on the third Wednesday of school. Children came to school that day prepared to read for a full seventy-minute double period, and in watching how individuals fared in reaching for this goal, Donna was able to note their progress and their need for progress. Other classrooms have grand celebrations to mark their Hundred Books Day and then begin to plan for their Thousand Books Day. These are some other ways we've celebrated reading early in the year:

- Teachers encourage children to organize a day of lunch table discussions of favorite books. Lovers of *Pee Wee Scouts* books, sit at one table, and talk about the books. Lovers of *Calvin and Hobbes* bring their books and sit at another table.
- Children make beautiful bookmarks, and use them to mark a very favorite page. Children may read part of that favorite page aloud at a reader celebration or ask someone to duplicate that page for them.
- Teachers can convene a class or group of children together to make a symphony of words by having each child say a chosen word or phrase from a favorite book. "The conductor" points the baton at one child, who says her word, then at another child, then another, and so on.
- The class can take a field trip to the local library and get everyone a library card.

Reading in a Way That Allows Us to Retell

Although at first our minilessons and conferences focus on the importance of reading a lot of easy books quickly, it will soon be important to emphasize reading with understanding. At the very start of the year, we simplistically link the goal of comprehension to the goal of reading easy books, but we'll soon want to emphasize that readers must read with wide-awake minds.

The challenge is that simply exhorting children to "Think as you read!" or "Keep your minds alert!" is not enough. My colleagues and I have searched for concrete strategies for supporting basic comprehension. We considered asking children to record daily and nightly reflections on what they read, but children end up doing a lot of writing for no audience, in no genre, and with no expectation for revision. Because above all we wanted children to love reading, we were loath to ask them to do something we don't do. When most of us, as readers, finish reading a chapter, we don't write about it. We read another. But if we weren't going to insist on daily writing about reading, was there another way to encourage children to pay attention to the meaning of what they read?

We decided that at least for a few weeks we'd ask children to recall and retell the salient features of what they had read. This work began when Sharon Hill, a fourth-grade teacher at the Manhattan New School and a former Project staff member, read Katherine Paterson's *The Great Gilly Hopkins* and noticed her kids had only general, generic things to say: "She was mean," "She was selfish." When Sharon asked her students why they felt like this, hoping for evidence from the text, the kids didn't seem to grasp the specifics of the text they'd heard her read aloud. So as she read, Sharon began pausing to say, "Let's just recall what's happened so far." Then Sharon would start her children off: "I remember that Gilly's stepmother was bragging that Gilly read aloud well, and she got the idea of sending Gilly to read aloud to Mr. Randolph. So she …" and Sharon would say, "Miguel, take it from there." In this way, she tried to scaffold her students' reconstruction of the part of the story they'd just heard.

Sometimes instead of calling on one child to reconstruct the story, Sharon might say to all of them, "Could you each turn to your partner and retell it, starting from when Trotter said…?" On other days, Sharon would call on one child to start off the retelling. One day John was speaking while the class listened. Diamar heard a major omission and raised his hand, "I think *after* Gilly called the teacher racist, the next thing was…."

Sharon commented, "Thanks for *filling in*," deliberately giving a name to what Diamar had done so that later she could encourage all her students to use his strategy.

Later, as John continued, his retelling had major omissions and mixups. Sharon called for a *rewind* and again made a point of emphasizing the term. When she asked for a *rewind*, John backed up and retold a section with help from other students. In this way, the class had a second go at reconstructing this part of the book, and this time they added more detail and made the retelling more accurate. For the next few days after the read-aloud, one child would retell the text and Sharon would work with the *listeners*, nudging them to call for a *fill in* or *a rewind* when necessary.

When we want to teach our students to read in ways that allow them to retell a text, our work follows a sequence of instruction. First, we try to convey to children why retelling will be a helpful thing for them to do in their book talks. We may show them what they have tended to do (recall only a few general things from the text in no special order) and show them how replaying the text sequentially can allow them to recall and rethink what they've read. In read-aloud sessions, then we demonstrate not only *how* we recall texts in a sequential way, but also we demonstrate when and why we recall texts. We may pause at the end of a chapter and say, "Don't you love to think back over what you've read? Let's do that with this chapter. Remember, it started with, …" Then we return to the beginning of the chapter and page through it as we talk: "Oh yes! And I remember the next part. Remember how, …" We may show children that sometimes we find a story confusing and so we look back to reconstruct a sense of what's happened thus far. In these instances, *we're* doing the actual recall of the text.

Soon we'll want to bring children into the retelling of a text. We may pause to reflect on some of the read-aloud, retelling the text a little to get the process started. Then we pass the baton: "Sammy, take it from there," and help Sammy, and eventually other members of the class, retell the book, joining in as if we were one of the children. We may want them to have copies of the read-aloud text on this day (even if it means duplicating the chapter) so they can skim through it for support (or we may have decided on this day to read aloud a short story rather than the read-aloud chapter book since shorter texts tend to be easier). We continue to do this group retelling for a sequence of days. For now, we are probably just nudging students to walk through the main points chronologically, being sure the retelling makes logical sense. These retellings tend to focus on only one component of a story: plot. In Chapter 22, I show how we can help these retellings become fuller, with attention also to other story elements.

Next we often tell children, "Let's listen to the read-aloud today in ways that will help us retell." Now, when we come to turning points or significant events as we read aloud, we read with great meaning (as if we're saying "Wow. *This* is a big point to remember"). At appropriate moments we sometimes mutter, as if to ourselves, "Oh, wow. This is important." After one of these read-alouds, we again say, "Let's think back over what we've just read" and begin a retelling, but this time we encourage listeners to respond to what they hear each other doing, *filling in gaps* in what a classmate has said or calling for a *rewind,* as I described Sharon and her students doing.

Once the class has had some experience retelling the read-aloud text together in the meeting area, we nudge children to retell the read-aloud texts in more independent ways. For example, we may ask children to retell the read-aloud in partnership talks with their long-term read-aloud partners while still sitting together on the carpet. We may call attention to wise strategies children use to retell the texts (for example, skimming the pages to jog their memories).

We next ask children to retell their independent reading books with their reading partners. We encourage them to

- page through the book, retelling what's happening on each page.
- arrange with a partner to both read the same book to be sure to hold each other accountable. For example, if both partners have read Dick King-Smith's *Martin's Mice,* it's easier to check each other's retellings, saying for example, "Huh? I didn't see that in the book at all!"
- act as good partners, monitoring for sense and saying, "I don't get it," when a retelling is confusing, calling for *rewinds* and *filling in* important gaps.

Once children begin meeting regularly with their independent reading partners to retell the chapters they've just read, it will be important for us to observe how this work is going and to design minilessons, conferences, and strategy lessons to extend what we see children doing.

Holding Readers Accountable to the Text

In college and graduate school, I was taught the value of Reader Response methods of teaching reading. I learned that the meaning in a text is co-created by the reader and the author. The text may say "snowfall," but some readers envision a thick, blinding blanket of snow and others a few big flakes dancing in the air. "There is no one correct interpretation of a text," we learned. "Readers co-author the text, bringing their own images to the page so that they make (rather than decipher) meaning." I know these theories are deeply and profoundly true. But I also know that most of teaching involves working with paradox. And in teaching reading, it can be absolutely true that readers bring meaning to the page and also true that there is a meaning that skilled readers are expected to find on the page.

I agree with teachers who say, "You can't just say *anything* about a text". It's fair enough to claim that one reader will envision blinding snowfall and another, dancing flakes, but either way, precipitation falls from the sky. Too many young readers construct only the gist of a story. "That's not a big part of the story," they say if we suggest they're overlooking all the finer detail. On any one point, they may be right but it is important to work sometimes with children so they come to expect that reading involves constructing a fuller, more elaborated understanding of the text. We speak of this work as, "Holding ourselves more accountable to the text."

At some point in the year, it is extraordinarily revealing to work one-on-one with five or six readers, asking each one to read silently the same appropriately matched short text, a text we know well and come to know even better as we watch children experience it. After every two paragraphs, we quietly ask, "What are you thinking?" If we want a closer glimpse of the child's reading, we may say, "Read the next bit aloud, will you?" We do not rescue the child from his or her misconceptions but watch as the child negotiates his or her way to an understanding of the selected text.

Recently, Sharon Hill asked several of her Manhattan New School fourth graders to read a two-page story in which children organize a birthday party for their grandpa's one-hundredth birthday. In the first paragraph, the story tells about children decorating for the party, hanging signs showing the old man's many years. "Grandpa: 1889–1999," the signs read. One of Sharon's students saw this and, presumably reminded of the dates on a tombstone plaque, assumed this meant the old man had died. This was a reasonable conclusion, but the story continued for many paragraphs and the old grandpa was the featured, very much alive main character. What Sharon noticed was that this particular reader did not revise her first impression but instead went to bizarre lengths to weave together a convoluted tale in which the grandpa dies, comes back as a ghost, and so forth.

In discussing how common this is among our children, we realized that it is incredibly important for proficient fourth graders, like first graders, to

monitor for sense while they read. We'd tended to identify monitoring for sense as a strategy for beginning readers who struggle with sentence-level sense. In fact, at every level, readers need to keep an eye on whether a text is making sense and have a repertoire of strategies for dealing with difficulty. Perhaps more than any other strategy, readers—like writers—need to learn the importance of revision. As we read and live, all of us develop first impressions of people and early interpretations of events. But too many of us hold to those first impressions in the face of new evidence, and this isn't an ideal way to read or to live! Many readers can benefit from instruction in monitoring for sense and being ready to reread and revise their first understanding when meaning breaks down for some of us, this has became part of the unit, "Reading with Stamina and Meaning." For others, it is a separate unit, "Holding Oneself Accountable to the Text," which especially features whole and small group strategy lessons involving short shared texts.

Whether we incorporate this work into existing units of study or design a curricular unit specifically around the goal of helping readers to pay closer attention to meaning as they read and to have strategies for responding when meaning breaks down, either way it is crucial to teach readers to revise their first impressions as they continue to read and gather new information. Readers must constantly ask themselves, "Does my initial idea of how things are going in this text fit with what I'm now reading? Do all the other ways I'm getting information—from pictures, chapter titles, and the story structure—feed me information that fits into my idea?" Students need to become accustomed to the idea that as they retell a text, they look back at the text not just as a way to remind themselves of the story but also a way to check to ensure the text actually fits into their emerging understanding.

When we talk with children about a novel they have read, there is always so much they *could* say that we tend to notice only whether they have *some* ideas about the book. We pay attention to whatever meaning they have made and don't particularly notice the gaps in their understanding. But it is important to see the difficulties our readers encounter, because these difficulties, like the word-level ones we notice beginning readers making, can illuminate a reader's strategies and inform our instruction. Perhaps one reader confuses the pronouns *he* and *she* and consequently gets into tangles. Perhaps another reader always retells and rethinks a text beginning with what he read *last* (not first) and this makes it challenging for that reader to construct a coherent memory of the text. Diana reads John Steptoe's picturebook, *Stevie,* in which the older boy, Robert, narrates the story of how five-year-old Stevie moved in on him, "with his old crybaby self." Robert announces, "He always had his way. And he was greedy, too. Everything he sees he wants…. Man!" The point of the story is that despite Robert's tirades against little Stevie, Robert finds himself drawn into a relationship with the little guy, and when Stevie returns home, Robert fixes two bowls of cornflakes before remembering, with loneliness, that Stevie has left. It all seemed pretty straightforward to me until I watched Diana.

What a surprise it was when smart, capable Diana looked up from this book and said, "That kid Stevie is such a pain. He is really mean." Listening to her take on the story, I realized that of course it made total sense that Diana would trust what the book said. In so many words, the narrator of the book had said Stevie was greedy and a crybaby. Although I did my best to explain to Diana that she wasn't expected to *believe* Robert's comments about Stevie, that Robert's descriptions of Stevie were meant to reveal more about Robert than about Stevie, I am not at all convinced Diana followed my meaning or bought my message. But the bigger point is that I'd overlooked the complexity and the reading challenges of this seemingly simple book entirely.

Although I once regarded retelling as a "low" level form of comprehension, I've come to appreciate the complex acts of meaning-making that readers must do en route to what I once thought of as "mere recall." Later I'll talk about encouraging readers to synthesize, question and interpret texts. But it is also important to teach readers to construct meaning as they read. When I watch readers navigate a short text I know well, I am startled to see how they can pull off this thing called reading. I gasp over the complexity of the punctuation, the unclear pronoun references, the shifts in time and place, the expectations of background knowledge. "How is it these children can come away with a sense of story at all!" I marvel.

Once you really pull in close to consider children's understandings (and their misunderstandings), it quickly becomes clear that "simply" giving children time to read, texts they can understand, and conversations that hold them accountable to the text is a gigantic thing. An absolutely mind-blowing number of skills *are* needed and developed by anyone who reads with engagement and interest.

Talking and Writing to Develop Ideas **18**

The goal in teaching a balanced literacy program is not simply to balance writing with reading and comprehension with the print-work of reading. Teaching balanced literacy also means that I always begin the year knowing that I'll be "running from one side of the boat to the other," as we say in our community. Around mid-October, teachers often find that most of their children are reading lots of easy books in ways that allow them to retell those books. But comprehension involves much more than recall (as rich and complex as it is). At this point, the teachers I know often decide it's time to help youngsters respond more deeply to texts. Reading is nothing more or less than thinking, guided by print. This means that response to reading is not an added bonus or an extra-credit option. Response is what reading is all about. When teachers say to me, as they often do, "She can read *anything*. She just doesn't understand it," I reply, "Then she isn't reading." And so my colleagues and I often focus our next unit of study on talking and writing to encourage and grow ideas.

In this chapter, we will look at:

- Supporting Kids' First Responses to Reading: Using Post-its and Other Tools
- Making Post-its Matter More by Teaching Readers to Talk Longer about a Single Post-it
- The Relationship Between Writing About and Talking About Our Jotted Responses to Texts
- Writing and Graphic Organizers as Tools to Raise the Level of Talking and Thinking About Texts
- Writing to Follow Trails of Thought

Supporting Kids' First Responses to Reading: Using Post-its and Other Tools

I want children to know that good readers the world over pause as they read to gasp, weep, imagine, and remember, that readers question and talk about books with a friend. "If my friend isn't nearby when I read and if the book is mine," I tell kids, "I put a star beside parts I'm dying to talk about or underline those sections. If the book is borrowed, I sometimes stick a Post-it near that section or put a bookmark there. Later, when my friend and I meet, I don't have to search. I can open to that particular page."

We want children to realize that when they laugh aloud at a funny spot in a book, it's a good thing to mark that place so they can return to laugh again with a friend and then perhaps to reminisce about other funny parts in the book. Nine-year-old Amy scrawled "I think Gilly is pretty mean" on a Post-it note and stuck her comment onto an early page of Katherine Paterson's *The Great Gilly Hopkins*.

I saw her do this and brought the Post-it and the page to my next mini-lesson. "I want you to see the smart work Amy has done," I said. "Katherine Paterson never comes right out and *says* that Gilly is mean, but Amy watched Gilly doing a lot of things and developed a theory: 'I think Gilly is pretty mean.' Amy, I bet when you continue reading, you'll be noticing any new evidence."

As Amy continued to read, she accumulated more Post-its and log entries about Gilly: "I am shocked that she is not with her mom!" "Why would she run away like a pest! She's a weird girl!" and "She doesn't show her kindness" (see next page).

If we encourage children to think as they read and to register those thoughts by leaving a stick-on note on a particular page, a whole social culture soon develops. When they start a new book, some children pave the inside cover of their copy with small stacks of Post-its. Others wear or carry little Post-

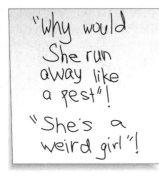

"Why would She run away like a pest"! "She's a weird girl"!

"She doesn't show her kindness"!

Gilly is changing.

it pouches. Children in several classrooms I know have adopted the rule that at the end of the book, they can each look back and choose two (and only two) Post-its that will remain in the book forever. Usually they recopy these notes, making their thoughts neater and more explicit and recording their name and the date. Their name is as important as anything else because it says, "I passed this way." When children later find Post-its left by classmates, it's as much fun for them as it is for me when I see my husband's jottings in the margins of a book we have shared. "Why on earth did he star *that* line?" I wonder, and reread the passage again. Children may also decide to move their Post-it notes from the book into their writers' notebooks or, when a child finishes with a book, she may peel all her Post-it notes off the pages and compile them into a tiny Post-it book, which she titles and saves. Such Post-it projects don't distract children from reading by involving elaborate covers, extensive writing, or papier-mâché. They simply involve reviewing, selecting, and savoring notes they've made about a book, and this is good work for readers to do. But the more lasting contribution of Post-it notes—or notes jotted in reading journals or in the margins, or highlighted texts—is that they help, as nine-year-old Amelia Fox says, "train your mind to think when you're reading."

Judith Viorst has written a poem entitled, "If I Was in Charge of the World." If *I* were in charge of the world, children across America would carry books that were furry with slips of paper and jotted notes. Because I think we absolutely must teach readers to "talk back" to texts, I'm worried. In our schools, we teach children to read, and we judge their reading according to their accuracy and their ability to retell what they have read. Both skills are fine, but clearly a good reader is more than a copy machine or a tape recorder! Do we not also want our children to grow up realizing that, as Alan Purves has said, "Books are tools to think with?"

TOOLS STUDENTS CAN USE TO HELP
THEM RESPOND TO TEXTS

TOOLS	USE
• Reading notebooks	For jottings and page numbers (these can be tiny memo books at first and move toward larger, thicker notebooks for more extended writing, book lists, goals, and notes on minilesson. Readers may also collect articles, book reviews and other short texts they've studied
• Highlighters	For marking readers' own text or duplicated copies of texts
• Fine-point writing utensils	For fitting thoughts into page margins
• Bookmarks or index cards	To mark places in the text *and* to record jottings about those places
• Post-its	To mark places in the text *and* to record jottings about those places
• Paper clips	To mark spots in books (make sure clips are plastic-coated so they don't leave rust spots on precious pages)
• Plain paper book covers	For jotting thoughts and page numbers
• Sketchbooks	For quick sketches, maps, and as graphic organizers for thoughts

Sometimes children will have a hard time developing ideas about the books they read. When a large percentage of children in one class report that they can't think of anything to say about a book, I usually find that some dynamic in the classroom is silencing children. Often what has happened is that children have come to us with their responses to books and we didn't consider their ideas "literary" enough. Surely, they could come up with something better, we thought, and we nudged them toward the ideas we wish they'd had. But nothing squelches a tender shoot of thought more quickly than this!

When Amy wrote "I think Gilly is pretty mean," she was making a passing comment, even stating the obvious. But when I gathered students together to hear that Amy had created a theory about a character and to tell them that she was now reading to gather more evidence, I gave what Amy had done a name and a place in the world. This is the kind of action I recommend in response to children's first Post-its. By saying what the reader has done, we give the strategy a name so that other readers can use it with other texts. Although Amy was thinking specifically about Gilly, I said, "Readers do what Amy has done. They notice what a character does and says, and develop theories about the character."

Ways Good Readers Respond to Books

•Good readers grow theories about characters	"I think Gilly is pretty mean" Amy, Katherine Paterson's *The Great Gilly Hopkins*
•Good readers notice, admire, and critique the way an author writes	"Right here I'm noticing how the boat is getting further and further to the end, the author slows down the story." Malika, Lois Lowry's *The Giver*
•Good readers develop a big idea about the whole book	"They're bringing pieces together to build a bridge! Maniac and some other kids like each other." Brian, Jerry Spinnelli's *Maniac McGee*
•Good readers predict	"I think Mela might never go back to the sea!" Hallie, Karen Hesse's *The Music of Dolphins*

(continued)

•Good readers walk in the shoes of a character, speaking as the character would speak	"Mela: I will leave my human thoughts on the beach and I will go home!" p. 117 Kevin, Karen Hesse's *The Music of Dolphins*
•Good readers let books remind them of their own lives	"When my dad talks to me like that, I get mad. I wonder if he's mad." Rajpal, Lois Lowry's *The Giver*
•Good readers find connections between one book and another	"Prince Horace and Sarah Ida both act mean when they are unhappy" Svenja, Sid Fleischman's *The Whipping Boy* and Clyde Bulla's *Shoeshine Girl*

By mid-October, in most of our independent reading workshops, then, after a half-hour of quiet reading, children will regularly gather with their partners to talk over their responses to the various books they've each read in school that day and at home the evening before. Sometimes teachers ask children to retell their books to each other first. Then they talk using their own and their partner's Post-it notes.

During these early months of the school year, I prefer Post-its or jotted notes to nightly journal entries in reading logs because when children fill a page with an entry that begins, "I like the part when …" and then summarize the part, they are writing for no audience except the teacher-as-evaluator, for no purpose except to prove they did the reading, with no models of good writing, and with no support for revision. Meanwhile, the child who wrote "I like the part when …" could have accomplished the same amount of *reading* work by sticking a Post-it to the page and scrawling "like it." And that child would accomplish far *more* reading work if she sat with a partner and said, "I put a Post-it on this section because I think it's really well written" and if the conversation then continued for a very long while.

Of course, there is nothing particularly crucial about Post-its in themselves. They are just stuck-on underlining, removable marginalia, or condensed journal entries. If I hope my children are jotting their thoughts onto Post-its as they read, I'll be very glad if they are accustomed to doing "say-something" conversations (Harste, Short and Burke, 1996) in the midst of our read-alouds. What is a Post-it note, stuck to an intriguing section of a text, except a recorded say-something? I like post-its because they are *self-initiated* say-somethings inserted during the flow of reading, and like say-somethings, they are concrete reminders that readers need to react and talk back to texts.

Inevitably, there will be Post-it problems. I'm not surprised when some children nearly wallpaper their books with Post-its. When we teach first graders to use exclamation marks, soon every page is full of exclamatory comments of all shapes and sizes. It is predictable that we'll need to gather readers together and point out that using five Post-its on a page is a bit extreme. "You have gone Post-it crazy," we say. "Can we try to invent some solutions to this problem?" In some classrooms children pledge to use only a certain numbers of Post-its each day. In others, before partners meet for a book talk, they promise to reread and rethink their Post-its, recycling all but the most talk-worthy ones back into their Post-it stacks.

Making Post-its Matter More by Teaching Readers to Talk Longer About a Single Post-it

At this point in the school year, children's jotted notes are placeholders for the book-talks they plan to have. A culture of Post-its—or of any other tool used in this way—becomes a culture of conversation. One reason to use Post-its is that this encourages children to have grounded conversations in which they refer back to the text often and think together about the evidence they find in the text. There is, of course, no way that a little slip of paper alone will lift the level of book talks, but the assignment to use Post-its can be a start.

Alexa Stott recently listened in as two of her third graders talked for a few minutes about their home reading. Filling their teacher in, Jack said, "We're talking about if Soup [from Robert Newton Peck's book, *Soup*] and Robert are good friends or not."

Alexa said, "That's a key question in this book. It's always important to think about the relationships between characters. But where are your tools? Your books aren't out, your logs, your Post-its."

The boys scurried to unpack their books from book bags. Neither book contained any Post-its, yet for a moment they continued to talk. Ezekiel said, "See, Richard isn't telling Soup the truth. That's not nice."

"What do you mean?" Jack asked.

"Ummmm," Ezekiel said, and began a belabored search through his copy of the book for the passage that supported his idea.

Intervening, Alexa said, "Jack, it was great the way you questioned Ezekiel, but now we're having to wait for Ezekiel to find the passage. After this, come with your ideas marked in the text so we don't have to wait ten minutes for you to ground what you are saying in particular passages."

Meanwhile, in a share meeting at the end of Mary Chiarella's reading workshop, Mary said to her students, "Today in two different conferences I saw readers coming together as partners to talk without any Post-its, jotted notes, underlined parts, or bookmarks to lean on. And in both cases, I asked the partners to take time before they talked to look back over their texts and to prepare for their conversations." Then Mary said, "I don't ask you to jot as you read because I want to you to do extra work, but because I think this work is really important."

Brad piped in, "It's hard to keep track of all the places I want to remember, so it is okay to Post-it." Then he added, "Sometimes you don't know what you want to talk about till you are *past* that part, so you have to go back to find places that gave you ideas."

Hadley added, "You can just skim. If you know what you're looking for, you don't reread everything to add Post-its."

"So it's like finding landmarks in the book," Mary concluded. "As a class, I'd like us to take on the project of going back through our reading to confirm and specify our thinking before we meet with partners."

My son Miles has always been a resister. "I can't bear to stop reading. The book is so, so good," he will moan. Miles reads volumes and with keen comprehension, so over the years, some teachers have let him off the Post-it hook. Others have said—and I'm glad for this—that Miles must vary his reading diet and habits. "You can cruise through *some* books, but you also need to read some books that require you to stop and think, to wonder and pause and talk," they've said. "If you don't want to use Post-its during your first read-through of a book, at the end of a reading time you can glance back over the pages, think, review, and jot. But you must make some notes and bring these to book talks."

For a time, I don't mind telling children who resist preparing for book talks, "You must," but if this is a persistent problem, chances are the children haven't yet seen the value of their Post-it work, and usually this is because their conversations around Post-its don't require them to reread to refer to the text. "I like this part," one child will say to a partner, and then flip to another Post-it, "This part was wacko." Next. The fact that initially there are problems with Post-it conversations shouldn't surprise anyone. Our instruction will simply need to help children become more skilled at talking among themselves about books. Teaching talk is teaching reading.

If we want children to linger over their own and each other's insights; that is, if we want children to have intriguing conversations from a single Post-it, then it helps to be explicit. When children meet with their partners, we can set aside time for them to reread all the notes they've jotted during that day's reading, thinking, "Which of these seems central to the text? Which might spark a really good conversation?" Then we can suggest that the two children talk for as long as possible off one jotted note or one Post-it put out on the table.

Meanwhile, we will also help children have long talks around the ideas they've had during the whole-class read aloud. The read-aloud session becomes a forum for teaching kids to talk and linger over their on-the-run responses to texts. In Chapter 12, I described how we made charts of phrases children could say to deepen and extend these book talks. Now, as we try to help children have grand conversations about the books they're reading independently, we can remind them of the power of phrases such as:

- Can you say more?
- I have another example of that.

- I wonder *why* the author did that.

- I'm not sure I get what you mean. Can you say it in another way?

- I see what you are saying, but ...

Talk is always a motor behind intellectual development, but I think it is uniquely important in the teaching of reading. The conversations readers have in the air become the conversations they have in their minds. We teach reading by teaching talking-about-reading and writing-about-reading.

The Relationship Between Writing About and Talking About Our Jotted Responses to Texts

Later in the year, there will be times when Post-its and other jotted notes become placeholders not only for partner conversations but also for the *internalized* conversations readers have with themselves as they *write*. Although we are wary of asking for a great deal of writing about reading early in the year, when the writing workshop has yet to gather momentum, we recognize that when our students learn to talk for a long time about the idea marked by one Post-it, this stands them in good stead when we want them to write essays in which they develop their ideas about books. As I explain in Chapter 24, when students write about texts, they tend at first to write in what Mina Shaughnessy (1977) calls "sentences of thought" rather than "passages of thought." A typical piece of writing might include one line comparing this book to another, a sentence summing up a main character, a passing comment on the author's style, and a brief prediction about the book's ending. If we want children to develop their thinking about books, to produce evidence in support of their theories, and to explore nuance and subtleties, it is crucial for them to *say more about less.* Children need to learn that they could have extended any one of their sentence-long comments about a text into an entire piece of writing.

If talking longer about a Post-it-marked passage is the perfect prelude to writing longer in response to it, then conversational prompts such as "Can you say more" or "Could you give me an example?" which we use to help children talk longer, are exactly the sort of internal prompts writers need in order to write more and more thoughtfully.

"Why don't you have kids write for a long while in response to a Post-it rather than talk in response to a post it? Why are you putting such emphasis

on *talking* about reading rather than on writing about reading? Is writing becoming a lower priority?"

As I describe in Chapter 24, there *are* many parallels between the work we're asking children to do in the writing workshop, where they write around "seed ideas," and the work they do in the reading workshop, where they talk around a single Post-it. But too much writing early in the year in the reading workshop diverts necessary writing energy away from the writing workshop. It hasn't been feasible for my own sons to do long, developed writing for their writing workshop in one evening and still have time to do long, well-developed written responses to their reading. Especially at the start of the year, we need to make choices, and for me, this isn't a hard choice to make. Good readers rarely write regularly about their reading If children learn to use Post-its or otherwise jot notes and to talk long and well about them, and if meanwhile they are learning to write well, they'll be on solid ground. And at any given time, we certainly can ask children to write instead of talk about their reading.

In a perfect world, I would postpone writing about reading until children's reading work was a notch more complex than talking for a long while about one Post-it idea, then the next. But in New York State, reading assessments are now based on children's ability to write about their reading, and so we do sometimes consolidate what children have learned to do in conversations by also asking them to do this also on the page. After children have spent a few days talking for a long while about a single Post-it passage and using conversational prompts to nudge each other to say more, we sometimes say, "Instead of meeting with your partner to talk about a Post-it, please choose a talk-worthy Post-it, put it on a clean page, and *write long* instead of *talk long* about it. Samantha and her third-grade classmates soon named this kind of "writing off a Post-it" *stretches.* This is Samantha's "stretch," a response to a book on Harriet Tubman:

> This is a shame either they live a life of hell or die trying to make it.
>
> I know not one of those masters would want be a slave. How they feel. Those slaves were brought there but not on their own will. I really call those rules and consequences threats. They are threats to the African American image. But yet they are not even looked at as part of the human Race.

Although Samantha and her third grade classmates usually jotted Post-its in response to reading, once a week they wrote longer entries. "Stretch your thoughts across the page," Samantha's teacher suggested. "Write your thoughts about Rocky (from *The Monument*)."

*for being who she is

Rocky seems almost like Sadako in a way that she's really active. Well, we don't know that yet, but I have a felling and she got her nickname, Rocky from throwing rocks when she was little. She gave up all hope on being adopted and then the authur fliped the book, like in The Invisable Thread and Number the Stars. She is also like Shea in the music of Dolphins, because she gave up hope on being adopted, and Shea gave up hope on opening up the cage inside of her.
I can sort of relate to Rocky because sometimes I want to give up, but Rocky should really have faith, hope, courage, determination, action and pride* She shouldn't look at her braced leg and her skin color and say "nobody wants me because of this," she should say "This makes me special!" If you never like yourself, and you wish you were someone else, you would never get to know yourself and how good you are. Rocky should really keep that in mind. She should look on the positive side.

Writing and Graphic Organizers as Tools to Raise the Level of Talking and Thinking About Texts

So far, I've suggested that we can help children talk well about their reading and if we're lucky, we can teach children that they can write in similar ways about texts. All this is true, but it underestimates the power of writing.

We write—we put our thinking onto the page—so we can hold onto our fleeting thoughts. When we write, we can hold our thoughts in our hand, we can put our thoughts in our pocket, and we can bring out yesterday's thoughts. When we write, we can give our thoughts to someone and combine our thoughts with someone else's thoughts, and *we can improve our thoughts.* (Wells, 1999) When we write, we can look at our thinking and ask, "What's the really big idea here?" We can say, "What patterns do I see in my ideas?" We can ask, "How are your ideas like mine?" We can notice, "Things are changing!"

Although it is powerful to ask children to select a talk-worthy Post-it and to talk (or write) for a long while about it and the section of text it highlights, the fact that children have written about a text allows them to do more than point to intriguing sections of a text and comment. Once children have written about the text, they can look at their various observations and notice patterns. They can take a passing comment and follow it up to make a theory that may encompass the whole of a book. When children are writing, they can do this work collaboratively. They can add their observations to those of their friends, or lay conflicting ideas alongside each other and try to account for the differences.

After a while in many Project classrooms, when children review what they've jotted in order to find a spark that will ignite a good conversation, they "lay out" not a single Post-it, but a cluster of related ones. And the first thing that happens in a partnership conversation is that after one reader has laid out several Post-its, the *other* partner reviews his or her notes and jottings asking, "Did *I* notice anything in the book that relates to this idea of yours?"

Almost always, both readers have marked sections of the text that touch on similar ideas, and so before they talk, they gather a pile of references. It's easy to picture two partners with a field of Post-its on the desk between them, and this sometimes happens, but removing too many Post-its from the pages they were meant to mark can cause problems. Usually, instead of literally peeling off Post-its, partners put a large blank sheet of paper between the two of them and jot page numbers or notes onto it. This may begin as an index of page references, but soon it becomes almost a graphic organizer for the conversation the partners are having. If the conversation is about ways two historic fiction books compare, children will soon have scrawled a page like this:

```
3/24/99

┌─────────────────┬─────────────────┐
│ A Balled of     │ My Brother      │
│ the Civil War   │ is dead         │
├─────────────────┼─────────────────┤
│ • Jack and Tom  │ • Sam was always│
│   grew up       │   a step ahead  │
│   together.     │   of Tim.       │
│ • Tom and Jack  │ • Tim and Sam   │
│   were always   │                 │
│   together.     │ • This book took│
│ • This book took│   place over    │
│   palce in one  │   many years.   │
│   day.          │ • In this book  │
│ • In this book  │   one stays to  │
│   one brother   │   help and one  │
│   stays for War │   departs for   │
│   and one       │   war.          │
│   deparats for  │ • Takes place in│
│   War.          │   1778.         │
│ • Takes place in│                 │
│   1851.         │                 │
└─────────────────┴─────────────────┘
```

A cluster of third graders realized that in MacLachlan's *Baby* and many of the other books they were reading, it was as if a giant tree fell in the path of their characters. The characters had a choice; they could circle around endlessly in front of the tree or confront the problem and get around it. These charts functioned as conversational props as they invented these grand theories.

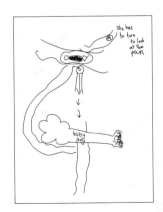

It is not hard to help a few children ground their partnership conversations in multiple references to the text or to begin using a shared sheet of paper as the basis for their talk, but we'll soon want to bring this practice to the entire classroom community. The most efficient way to do this is with either the read-aloud book or with a short shared text that children have read and then marked up on their own.

As Annemarie Powers read Sylvia Engdahl's *Enchantress from the Stars* aloud, she paused often to let children turn and jot notes (rather than turn and talk). Then she opened the conversation by saying, "Does someone have a jotting that might spark a good talk?", and the class talked. The class proceeded in this way through the opening chapters of *Enchantress from the Stars*. But then Annemarie wanted to raise the stakes a little for her fourth graders, so the next day she said, "We're near the middle of this book. Often when I reach the middle of a trail, I like to stop and look out to see where I've traveled and where I still need to go. Let's pause to do that work now, midway through this book, and midway through all our independent reading books from now on." Then Annemarie suggested that the class cluster into foursomes to review the jottings they'd made and the talks they'd had, asking, "What are some of the threads of thought we seem to be following?"

Soon Annemarie's class had decided that one of the really interesting questions for them was whether this book should be classified as fiction or as fantasy. They knew that in science fiction everything within the story must be possible within the limits of known science, and that fantasy incorporated magic, but clearly the lines between the two were blurred.

On chart paper, Annemarie began an informal chart. She recorded her students comments in abbreviated form, writing, for example, "page 1 'At the edge of the enchanted forest …'" and then the class talked at great length about how the novel's title and its opening clearly signaled that the book was fantasy. Yet soon Annemarie had also written page 13 and the words, "shields, travels to youngling planets." Again, the words were few but they served to launch a long talk about how the book's references to advanced civilizations that can harm 'youngling planets' suggest this might be science fiction. After talking through more evidence on both sides of the question, Annemarie said, "I'm going to read. When I pause, turn and talk, and let's talk first about how the new text we're hearing extends our thinking on this issue." Annemarie, of course, deliberately paused at the places in the text that fed this inquiry.

The conversations in our classrooms become deeper and richer when we use talk and writing to research a theory. The whole purpose, of course, is not to prove our point but to change our minds. Once Amy had hypothesized that Gilly seemed to be mean, she carried that theory with her, developing and revising it as she continued reading and encountering new evidence.

During the next read-aloud book, after having daily whole-class discussions throughout the first half of the book, we might again pause halfway through the book, but this time instead of settling on one idea for the whole class to follow, we may let a few main ideas crystallize and launch small groups to talk each day about one of those ideas. That is, we continue to read aloud, but now each of four small groups will listen, each thinking about their own particular line of thought.

When Gillan White's third graders reached the middle of Katherine Paterson *The Great Gilly Hopkins,* Gillan said, "I'm wondering if there are any theories you think are important in this book?" Of course everyone was bursting with theories. "Let's gather possible threads a reader could follow through the rest of the book," Gillan said, and soon the class had listed several. "So I'm wondering if a partnership would like to listen to the remaining half of *Gilly* thinking about why Gilly seems so tough?" Gillan said. After a few children had signed onto that line of inquiry, Gillan pointed to the next idea. "Do I have a group wanting to continue thinking about ways Gilly and Imogene (from Barbara Robinson's *The Best Christmas Pageant Ever*) are similar and different?" For the next week, members of each inquiry group sat on the carpet together listening to the read-aloud, pens in hand ready to jot down anything that related to their particular inquiry. After reading the chapter aloud, Gillan sent the groups off, and in corners of the room they talked and charted and talked some more. By this time, Gillan's third graders were more than ready to take this practice into the independent reading workshop.

It isn't hard for children to use charts in their partnership talks to discipline their conversation and angle their future reading. When my son Evan was in third grade, he and his partner, Jane, read the entire Frank L. Baum *Wizard of Oz* series. One day, Evan told Jane he was almost absolutely sure the Scarecrow was smart already, that he didn't *need* to go to the Wizard for brains. "Something is fishy," Evan said. "Why does the Scarecrow have to go to the Wizard for a brain if he's already got one?"

Jane wasn't so sure that the Scarecrow was smart. "He's straw, you know," she told Evan. "You can't have smart straw."

Now the two children read through the series as if they were Geiger counters. Any time the Scarecrow acted in smart (or less than smart) ways, they made note of this, and at the end of reading time when they conferred, Jane and Evan agreed: the Scarecrow was already smart.

"What about the Cowardly Lion?" Jane asked.

"He's smart, too," Evan said.

"No. Maybe the Lion is *already brave* so he doesn't need courage! And maybe the Tin Man already has a heart …" Now the two partners soon began a chart that looked like this:

> **Wizard of OZ**
>
> Scarecrow—<u>has</u> brains
> 37-"Its tedius up here…"
> 45-"if your head was stuffed youd all live in OZ and Kansas would have no one"
> 26-"
> 80 " cut down a tree to make a bridge"
>
> Lion- <u>has</u> courage
> 78- "jumped the ditch carrying Dorthy and all"
> 82-
>
> Tin Woodman—<u>has</u> heart
> 66-"we must protect Toto if he is in danger."
> 70-cried because he hurt bug
> 80-
> 96-
>
> Toto <u>has</u> ?

In the Scarecrow box on this chart, Jane and Evan listed the page numbers for those sections of the book in which the Scarecrow seemed smart. They did the same for the other characters and their character traits. This chart anchored Evan and Jane's conversations about *The Wizard of Oz* series for almost two weeks. After a time, Evan and Jane turned their attention to a giant map of Oz. They duplicated the maps inside the covers of all their Oz books and pieced them together into one central map. Each day when they met to talk over what they'd read, they'd have already marked the sections of their books that described places with Post-its and together they'd try to locate those places on their maps.

It was just luck that Evan and Jane's chart about *The Wizard of Oz* addressed one of the central themes in the book. There will be lots of times when readers pursue ideas that turn out to be tangential to a book or represent just one reader's take on a particular text. We need to expect and welcome this. The next chart Evan made after his *Wizard of Oz* work involved Karen Cushman's novel *Catherine, Called Birdy*. When Evan read *Catherine, Called Birdy* his eyes popped out as he came to a line likening her breasts to ripe peaches. "Mom," he told me, "I don't think this is a book for kids!" Evan was soon deep into an inquiry on "Is This a Book for Kids?" in which he dutifully earmarked all the sexy parts of his book and with great glee shared them with Dillon, his partner. I watched from afar, conscious that during my teenage years I'd explored a similar line of inquiry when reading *Gone with the Wind.*

The chart on the top of page 378 depicts a theory and metaphor some third graders developed about *Maniac McGee* by Jerry Spinelli. They decided that it is the story of a bridge built to link two different worlds. As they read, they sometimes sketched the progress (or disrepair) of the bridge, putting little sketches into their reader's notebook. The children talked at great length about these sketches. "Each time one person gets across the bridge," they announced, "the bridge gets stronger." It is important to notice that although the drawing looks like nothing special at all, for these readers it represents the dawning of an idea.

One day I listened to two second-grade youngsters having an extraordinary conversation as they made an EKG-like wavy line depicting the happiness and sadness of the main character in a little book called *Chato's Kitchen* by Gary Soto. It is a picturebook their teacher had previously read aloud to the class about a Latino cat, Chato, who invites his new neighbors, five mice, over so he can eat them for dinner. When they come, they surprise him by bringing their friend, the dog. Everyone has a tasty dinner, but not exactly the one Chato had been hoping for.

Maria and Angel's chart didn't look like much more than a wavy line, labeled from time to time with single words, but it anchored a good conversation.

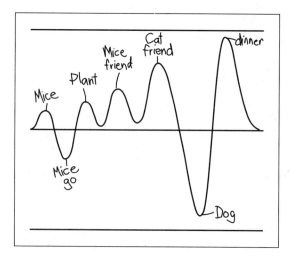

Maria:	Why did you make that last one so high? (pointing to the final bump in the chart, going off the page). He wasn't so happy then, because he was scared of the dog.
Angel:	But it's the end of the book, so it has to be the happiest part.
Maria:	But he didn't get to eat the mice that he was so hungry about!
Angel:	But everyone was eating together, and that's peace and that's the happiest part.
Maria:	I think it should be the same happy like when he invited the mice to dinner to eat them.
Angel:	But then he had just thought of it. He didn't even have time to think it was going to be so delicious like hot tortillas!
Maria:	He was thinking it would be delicious. He was dancing La bamba (shows him the page).
Angel:	Okay, it can be the same, only a little higher (he erases and amends the chart).
Maria:	This one has to be down down low down like in the earth! (pointing to when the dog came on the chart)
Angel:	They are scared like they would turn to skeletons (they both look at the page and laugh). That's the saddest part!
Maria:	The scaredest.

In David Hackenburg's fifth-grade-class, children were gathering evidence to support the theory that Jess and Leslie, in Katherine Paterson *The Bridge to Terabithia,* have a crush on each other. Other students were trying to decide if Jean Little uses fewer descriptive passages in the sections of her memoir *Little by Little* that describe her older years, when her eyesight was almost gone. Still others pored over science books trying to discover which animals were smarter, dolphins or chimpanzees. I've seen children exploring how the role of writing in Patricia MacLachlan's *Arthur, for the Very First Time* compares to the role of art in Gary Paulsen's *Monument.* How is the dog in Fred Gipson's *Old Yeller* like or unlike the dog in Farley Mowat's *The Dog Who Wouldn't Be?* In what ways has life remained the same since the times of Elizabeth George Speare's *The Witch of Blackbird Pond?*

Recently, two of Gillan White's third graders, Amelia and Samantha, reread Karen Hesse's *The Music of Dolphins,* a book their teacher had read aloud to them. At the end of each chapter, the girls met to talk over whether Mela, the heroine, was being lured more toward the dolphin or the human world. Each girl made several charts and drawings as she followed the character's tug-of-war. The next page contains some of their charts.

Charts can ignite interest and allow children to gather insights, but they can also be dead weights snuffing out any sparks of insight. The difference has to do with whether they are tools that help us reach the goal of thinking together, or whether *they* become the goal, and the conversation, merely the means to fill in the chart. The secret? Charts should be used only as long as they are helpful. They must be utterly disposable. They are a shorthand way to capture an idea, to discipline attention, and to reflect on new evidence. If readers end up charting *rather than* talking (or thinking), or if the charts take up even a fraction of the time readers spend reading and talking, this is a problem.

We encourage children to use charts, graphs, diagrams, lists of page numbers, Venn diagrams, matrixes, and anything else that helps them generate ideas together, but we do not want to see these as new forms of reading project. I am resistant to posterboards and lovely handwriting on long, elaborate charts, preferring scrawled charts. I am not at all for slow and dutiful copying of sentences from novels to serve as evidence, preferring lists of page numbers. Charts can provide a concrete focal point for collaborative talk. Two children are more apt to sustain focused talk on one idea if the idea has been written down on a chart that sits on the table between them. We expect a chart to last two or three days; by then, it usually needs to change to adapt to a new idea, or it should be sidelined.

I once watched third grade Angelo gathering evidence establishing that in *Horrible Harry*, Harry was indeed horrible. Angelo seemed to find evidence for this in every paragraph of every page. After awhile, I wondered if he hadn't established his point. Could he go on to ask himself, "So what do I wonder about now?" When I suggested he consider this, Angelo told me that he wondered if Harry was horrible as a way to get attention. With new resolve, he set out to explore whether this was the case, or whether there could be another explanation for Harry's horribleness. We need children to understand that once their hunch has been confirmed or once another intriguing idea captures their attention, it is important to move on from the first and pursue the next.

Writing to Follow Trails of Thought

Once our children have learned to develop theories around books and to read and talk with these theories under reconstruction, it can be very powerful to suggest that they use writing as a tool, not only to reflect on ideas with a friend, but also to mull over their own ideas in the company of an author. Often, our children will not only use Post-its but will also write longer entries in preparation for partnership conversations. Dori and Andrew, for example, decided when they were midway through Patricia McLachlan's *Journey* that they'd rethink the book, looking especially at the role photography plays. On the cover of Journey is an antique camera, and inside the cover, a torn photograph, showing just Journey's arm, ripped from the rest of his body. Then there is the forward. It says:

> Mama named me Journey. Journey, as if somehow she wished her restlessness on me. But it was Mama who would be gone the year that I was eleven—before spring crashed onto our hillside with explosions of mountain laurel, before summer came with the soft slap of the screen door, breathless nights, and mildew on the books. I should have known, but I didn't. My older sister Cat knew. Grandma knew, but Grandma kept it to herself. Grandfather knew and said so.
>
> Mama stood in the barn, her suitcase at her feet.
>
> "I'll send money," she said. "For Cat and Journey."
>
> "That's not good enough, Liddie," said Grandfather.
>
> "I'll be back, Journey," my mother said softly.
>
> But I looked up and saw the way the light trembled in her hair, making her look like an angel, someone not earthbound. Even in that moment she was gone.
>
> "No, son," Grandfather said to me, his voice loud in the barn. "She won't be back."
>
> And that was when I hit him.

In their partnership conversation about this book, Andrew and Dori decided to list the pages that related to photography, but soon they found they were noting every page. Andrew and Dori realized, for example, that McLachlan was writing in scenes, as if the book was a series of snapshots. Then, they realized that the scene (the snapshot) in the front of the book recurs at the end of Chapter 1, but now the light is not on Mama, who is leaving, but on Journey and his fury. As Dori and Andrew reread the book considering the role of photography, Dori wrote the entry on the left on the next page, and Andrew, the entry on the right. Both were written in preparation for their talks, and the writing in both conveys the feeling of a mind at work. How I love the halting, tentative, and explanatory tone in both entries, and the sense that these children are using writing to explore ideas.

It's a small step between the work Andrew and Dori are doing and the literary essays they'll be asked to write in middle school. My son Miles, like Andrew and Dori, drew on his experiences talking about books and charting ideas about books when, in fifth grade, he found himself in a classroom that required him to produce literary essays. One evening his assignment

2/11/92

Journey: Letter to P.M.

The camera makes Grandpa happy, makes Cat and Grandma annoyed and makes Journey change. Maybe it wouldn't have gotten any better for Journey if he didn't decid to try and see if the camera would help. If Grandfather hadn't started taking pictures at the end of the book ~~had~~ Journey would still have a problem. I think reason Grandfather started taking pictures is to get Journey to try to take pictures and to find his life from his past. I think that Journey will give away the camera, because I figure Cat went through the same thing with the father and that would prove my point about Journey being like Baseball!

Dori's entry.

Andrew's entry.

I not exactly sure how to began, but here gos nothing.
"Photography is a tool for dealing with things everyone knows about, but isn't attending to" At first ~~nobody~~ everybody in Journey knows about the problem, but doesn't attend to it I think that tells us something about how that family feels about eachother. I think in a good family if one member of the family has a problem the rest of the family should help.
Also in a way I think that this says that photography isn't to look at the people in the picture as much to look around the picture and "under neath" the picture to see what is there.

was to write about the memoir he was reading, which was Esther Hautzig's remarkable book *The Endless Steppe*. "Write how the person's character traits changed over the course of the book," the assignment said. Miles was resistant at first because he felt sure that a person's character traits are the features that do not change over time, but despite his misgivings over the assignment, he wrote an essay. Part of one draft is portrayed below:

> The story begins in 1941 in the polish town of Vilna. Esther Hautzig, the heroine of ~~the~~ Esther Hautzig's Fictional memoir, the Endless Steppe, lives an idylic life. (10 years old) Ether lives together with her extended family in a mansion enclluing ~~on~~ amazing garden. Her Father is a successful ~~well to do~~ electric Engineer. She has a summer cottage on the bank of River Wilja. ~~During~~ the school year her days are full of lessons - Piano lessons, Dancing class and trips to the library. Her problems where small ones; She fought with the librarien for grown-ups books and - She fought with her Mother for silk ~~underwear panties~~ that the other girls wore, ~~so~~ instead of her white cotton ones that her Mother made her wear. She was happy, carefree, trusting and optimistic.
>
> In the early pages of the book, you start seeing how optimistic and trusting she really is. Even when her world starts to collapse, she still acts as if her life is perfect. Because she is Jewish and this ~~is~~ taking place ~~after~~ during World War II the Russians confiscate her fathers job and her familys property, but they do not Evict her yet. It was amazing to me that instead of being pinicked and depprossed she continues to live blithfully on, Playing the garden with her cousin and happily skipping down the street to school. Things get worse and she continues to believe that her life will improve.

When the Russians come to Evict her She assumes she can take all her precious belongings as if they were headed to a hotel. When she is on her way to Siberia She is optimistic in thinking of Asia as a land full of men with long beards and Turbans and the air heavy with spices. You could say that Esther is optimistic and trusting But you could also say she is blind and that she was deluding herself. Two on one Coin. Maybe She deludes herself and acts biten. She does not see how bad things are because of the family custom to share ones joys and hide ones sorrow Maybe She hides them So well that she hides them for herself.

~~When she is freed and they move into the village~~
~~She really starts to change. She changes slowly. But, the main~~
~~change came on the news of her Grandfathers death.~~
~~The whole Family wept and when Esthers mother Mother~~
~~left Esther tried to comfort her. But, it was on~~
~~the long train ride.~~

It's a good thing when children learn how to write the essays they'll be expected to write in secondary school, but the real goal should be a richly literate life. Our hope is that when we give children tools for thinking we help them to think and read with new depth and a new sense of possibility.

Reading Projects 19

When Miles was in fifth grade, he was asked to make a coat hanger mobile to illustrate Philip Pullman's *The Golden Compass,* a diorama to accompany Esther Forbes's *Johnny Tremain,* and a game board that incorporated the elements of Gary Paulsen's *The Haymeadow.* Watching Miles at work with these projects, I began to imagine how wonderful it would be if children had a chance to pursue a different sort of book project, the kind that shapes the lives of literate people.

Annie Dillard (1987) tells of one such project in her memoir, *An American Childhood.* At the age of ten, she discovered Nicolaides' *The Natural Way to Draw.* "I was amazed there were books about things one actually did," Dillard writes.

> I had been drawing in earnest, but at random, for two years…. Now this book would ignite my fervor for conscious drawing…. For the rest of August, and all fall, this urgent, hortatory book ran my life. I tried to follow its schedules: every day, sixty-five gesture drawings, fifteen memory drawings, an hour-long contour drawing…. I outfitted an attic bedroom as a studio, and moved in. Every summer or weekend morning at eight o'clock, I taped that day's drawing schedule to a wall (p. 78).

Annie Dillard is not alone in constructing a reading project for herself. Nikos Kazantzakis in *Report to Greco,* wrote that as a child he sold all his toys to friends and purchased a set of books on the lives of the saints. "In my imagination the saints now merged with the vehement knights who set out to save

387

the world. When I read Cervantes still later, his hero, Don Quixote, seemed like a great saint and martyr" (p. 125).

I have had my own reading projects and they have brought great pleasure to my life. In high school, I read about people who felt called into leadership roles in their churches. How inspired I was by Lloyd Douglas's *The Robe,* Frederich Buechner's *The Alphabet of Grace,* and Leon Uris's *Exodus.* Later, when I lived in the English countryside and walked often on gray mornings across heath-covered moors, I bought all Thomas Hardy's books. I felt, as I read them, that I was reading my way toward a place of strength.

Thinking of how much these and other reading projects have meant in my life made it hard for me to watch my son dangling magazine photos from metal sticks. The readers I know rarely make coat hanger mobiles. Instead, they weave reading into the people, projects, and places of their lives.

By December in our upper-grade reading workshops, most of the teachers I know design a brief unit to remind children that all we've done in the reading workshop is not just schoolwork but also lifework. We don't wait until the end of the year to ask, "How will you take what you are learning in this classroom into your own ongoing reading life?" Because few questions matter more, we will return often across the remaining months of the year to this unit of study on Reading Projects. The agenda during this brief unit calls for students to work with personal direction on a project of their own choice. Sometimes we jokingly call these "Get-a-(Reading)-Life" studies. By December (if not before), we say to children, "As readers, all of us pursue purposes and projects. Your job now and always is to make a reading life for yourself."

We generally begin by teaching children about the reading projects we're pursuing in our lives. We may tell children that we've been reading about mothers and daughters, or that we've been searching for memoirs of Asian Americans, or that we've been researching mortgages because we hope to buy an apartment. And we let our children know that good readers are often "on about" particular reading interests and that often (but not always) these reading interests are shared with others.

In order to help children talk about possible reading projects, we sometimes ask them a series of questions and suggest that they talk or jot notes in response to these questions:

- What aspects of reading would you like a chance to work on for a while? Do you want to try reading books that are a notch harder? Do you want to read more nonfiction books? Do you want to get better at noticing and learning new words as you read?

- What are your interests or hobbies? How might reading support and fit into these?

- What texts have been special favorites for you? How could you do more with these texts or with other similar ones?

- What do you see as the next challenge for you as a reader? If you were to work toward a new goal in reading, what might it be?

- Imagine that you have time each day in school and again each night to do whatever reading work interests you the most. What can you imagine doing with this precious time?

Many teachers suggest that children generate several possible ideas for reading projects and then discuss these ideas with both their teachers and their parents. Then, as we talk with children, we help them weigh the advantages and disadvantages of pursuing one topic or another. We help them realize that other children share their interests. Could they collaborate on an inquiry? Josh and Brian, two of Kim Tarpinian's space enthusiasts, combined efforts to assemble a basketful of articles from *Muse* magazine, picturebooks, and poems on meteors and shooting stars. The boys began a ritual of checking the Science Times section of the *New York Times* each Tuesday for additional information. Soon they made an annotated guide to their small library so that other readers could profit from it as well.

Sarah's reading project grew out of her struggle to keep up with the reading her partners did. Deciding that if others could benefit from speed-reading courses, she could design one for herself. Sarah began to concentrate on reading smoothly and not fixating on each and every word. She logged the amount of pages she hoped to read in a sitting, compared this against the amount she actually *did* read, and monitored her progress.

Hannah and Melissa's love for the American Girl dolls led them to study the historical context of their dolls and to arrange lunchtime talks with other children in the school about the dolls and the periods they represented.

Meanwhile, a group decided to finish reading Bruce Brooks's wonderful hockey series, including *Wolf Bay Wings*, and then to read his nonfiction books. Two girls decided to continue reading about endangered animals and vowed that each day, they'd post a new and amazing statistic on a special bulletin board outside the school office. For starters, they posted the discovery that one popular kind of candy (which will go unnamed here!) with a shiny coating contains crushed beetle shells. Soon the whole school was buzzing over this fact, and the trio of readers had learned a lesson about the power of information.

Why Reading Projects?

What a payoff there is when we invest two weeks in a unit of study on reading projects! In order to understand the payoff, it's important to realize that during this unit of study children design reading projects that provide direction to the reading they do in school and at home long after the unit is over. This means that as children continue to cycle through choosing books, reading them, and responding to them, children now approach their reading with a new sense of direction. For a child, reading a book and marking parts to discuss, can represent the biggest work of that child's life—or it can be a bothersome exercise. The difference between the two has everything to do with the child's investment in the work. A brief unit of study on reading projects provides a chance to tap into our students' passions and ambitions. What a difference it makes when a child searches the world for science fiction books by the truly great science fiction writers rather than just reading *any* purple-dot book.

A second advantage of this unit of study is that because it nudges children to bring in their very individual interests, it reveals the diversity of the classroom reading community. Until now, it has sometimes seemed as if everyone in the class is reading the same sort of thing. Now one child turns to poetry and is working to make an audiotaped collection of favorite pieces. Another group of children can't stop talking about fantasy novels. Still other children combine their efforts (and their books) and create a collection of *Little Pony* books and book reviews. Part of the power of this approach is that children are no longer like or unlike each other merely because of the *level* of books they read. Now it's their hobbies and passions that give them identities as readers.

Then, too, this unit of study provides children with a chance to consolidate and practice what they have learned. During September, we may have touched on the importance of reading books aloud with fluency and phrasing, and now some children return to that work. Perhaps they were really engaged and want to go further with it, or perhaps they return to the work because we feel they need more time and more direction from us. With encouragement, we can help children design projects not only around topics, authors, or genres (the *what* of their reading) but also around the *how* of their reading. There may be children who still haven't gotten into the reading habit, and with guidance several of them can come together in a support group dedicated to making more time for reading. We may also encourage another group of children to tackle books that are a notch more difficult than those they've been reading. We may work with these readers in a guided-reading

group, providing them with a book introduction and then scaffolding their progress through the challenging text.

The Reading Project unit of study gives us, as teachers, an institutionalized opportunity to do a curricular correction. It is easier to feel comfortable establishing reading partnerships and matching readers with levels of books in September using the incomplete knowledge we can garner quickly about our readers if we can bear in mind that the Reading Project's unit of study will allow us to establish new partnerships and adjust any earlier directions we've given children about book levels.

But the most important benefit of the Reading Project is that this unit of study reminds all of us of the big goals in our teaching. Last year, the television network CBS phoned me in June to say they'd heard about the extraordinary classrooms connected to the Teachers College Reading and Writing Project and wanted to film them for the national news. CBS wanted to come the next day, which was the second to last day of the school year. I pictured the stripped down, packed up summertime rooms, the sultry June heat, the bursting anticipation of kids on the brink of vacation, and I wondered whether I wanted the whole world to see what happens in our New York City classrooms on the second-to-last day of the school year. Taking a giant leap of faith, I said, with all the serenity I could muster, "We'd love to have you. I'll phone back with the details."

Early the next morning, I waited in the fourth floor hallway of P.S. 125 in Harlem for the elevator doors to open. Out came two reporters, a producer, a co-producer, a Director of Public Relations, and an audio-technician with a microphone dangling from a fishing pole. With trepidation, I led the entire entourage down the long, green cement hallway to the doorway of Room 406. I was frankly a bit worried over what we would see of the school year. I opened the door just a crack, and quickly scanned the room. As expected, Kathleen Tolan had spent the night refilling bookshelves with books and plants, and classroom walls with framed pictures and children's masterpieces. Malika was curled into a rocking chair, nestled around a book with an empty chair to her side. I winked at Kathleen and turned to escort my entourage to that spot, but found, to my dismay, that they had already circled Shawnee, who was nei-ther reading nor writing, but pasting decals onto a little wooden box. I groaned at the thought of this scene, broadcast nationally. Then Shawnee looked up. "This is my writing box," she said. "All summer I'm going to col-lect little treasures—feathers, flower petals and stuff—and then," Shawnee pulled a notebook from her backpack, "I'll write about them."

Meanwhile Mario, clipboard in hand, bustled among his classmates ask-ing each for the titles of their favorite books. "I'm figuring out the books to read this summer," he said. "See, I'm going to have a summer book club. It'll meet in my apartment at 8:15 every morning. So far, it's me and my mind. We're going to talk over books. I'll ask, 'What's it *really* about?' and 'Do you agree?' And we'll talk it over, think it over." Then he added, "Some other kids might come too."

During the next hour, we watched Tony quoting from a magazine arti-cle on mental retardation in order to buttress a petition for his little brother to be returned to mainstream classrooms. We watched Ashley carefully arrange a set of duplicated pages, one from each of the year's twenty-one read-aloud books. "I'm going to keep them by my bed. Every day I'll read the pages and remember the books. It'll be like a bookshelf of good books." We watched children putting finishing touches on letters they'd written to publishers, trying to convince them to send any excess books along. "I only have five books but I've read them each about ten times," James wrote. "If you have poetry, that'd be good because I'm a poet too," Devoia said.

Later, in the hallway outside Room 406, the producer pulled me aside and said, "So what's the story behind classrooms like this one?" They dangled the furry, raccoon-tail microphone before me. "What these teachers know," I said, "is that as important as it is for kids to compose essays, memoirs, and responses to literature, it is even more important for them to compose lives in which reading and writing matter."

Book Clubs 20

I have always loved survival literature. I've loved learning about the Swiss Family Robinson, who salvaged what they could from the sinking ship and with it built a tree house for themselves and a civilization. I've loved learning about Gary Paulsen's character Brian, whose plane crashed into the Alaskan wilderness and who, with only a hatchet, caught fish, started a fire, and built a world. I read survival literature and I marvel at the imagination, ingenuity, and energy of people who take what they have and create a life. In the same way, I marvel at the imagination, ingenuity, and energy of good teachers. We too salvage what we can—from the homes of our childhoods, from curbside trash heaps, from school basements and family attics—and with these things, we build a world in our classrooms.

In September, children join us in constructing the reading workshop. "We need to build, in this classroom, a place where reading matters," we say to them. Soon our children are filling book bins for themselves, finding reading nooks in which they can settle into books, setting a pace for themselves as readers, developing reading friends, and co-inventing neat things to do together with books. As they build a space for reading in their lives and in their identities, this long-term project energizes the first portion of the school year. After five or six months, however, it's time for us to reach for new horizons. By then, we need to begin building the second story of the tree fort that is our reading classroom. And this time, children need more independence.

The Case for Clubs

To begin our work with reading clubs, my colleagues and I researched the small-group work that other teachers across the country were doing. It was enormously helpful to consider different configurations for small groups and to try to understand the motivations and priorities that shaped other forms of small-group work.

As my colleagues and I researched the small-group work that other teachers across the country were doing, we recognized immediately that our beliefs about reading and our hopes for book talks were consonant with those of Kathy Short (1998), Karen Smith, Kathryn Mitchell Pierce (1995), and Ralph Peterson and Maryann Eeds (1994). These teacher-researchers tend to use the term literature circles to describe their small discussion groups, and we were tempted to use their term, in recognition of our shared belief in talking as a way to compose meaning, in children generating as well as responding to questions, and in small groups as a place for listening to divergent ideas and different voices. There are, however, some noteworthy ways in which our small groups diverge from literature circles. Above all, our groups tend to be long-lasting, with a group of children reading many books together.

Many of the response groups we read about and admired formed around a particular book and disbanded after the book was completed. As adults, we had belonged to a book club for years, and it was hard for us to imagine that short-term response groups could mean as much. Our conversations about any one book were always so layered with insights from other books and other book talks that for us, a good conversation (almost by definition) was one that stood on the shoulders of many other conversations. Then, too, we valued our long-term book clubs because our shared history of talking with each other meant we read with these particular readers perched on our shoulders, helping us see texts in new ways. Because we wanted these advantages for our students, we knew our clubs would be long-lasting ones.

We also noticed that the response groups we read about were often initiated by a teacher who laid out several optional books and said to children, "Browse among these three books and then sign up to be in a group to read the book you choose." We figured that when teachers ask children to self-select among books representing very different levels of difficulty, this might be a way for teachers to avoid grouping children by ability, leaving these decisions up to the children. The resulting groups—and these were often called literature circles—tended to not be ability based. Because any one literature circle usually disbanded after the members had read and discussed one book, it wasn't a big problem if one child couldn't read the text independently and relied on a parent to read it aloud. Our groups, on the other hand, were long lasting ones and therefore it would be problematic if readers in one club were not able to read approximately the same books. Then, too, by the time book clubs were formed in our own classrooms, children knew that different classmates read books that varied in difficulty as well as in kind. We told children that they'd be gathering in book clubs, and that they could read with classmates who tended to read books that were a bit easy for them, but that it would not be okay to regularly read with classmates who chose books that were totally confusing. Then we decided that if we established long-lasting groups of readers who wanted to read together and were reading at roughly the same level, we could usually let those groups select books together.

This chapter will first talk about the nuts and bolts of reading clubs—forming them, scheduling work, guiding book choice, and deciding when children are ready for them. We'll then take a peek at a flourishing book club to give us a picture of what we can be working toward. In the final section, I discuss ways to work toward that goal, ways to lift the level of work children do in book clubs. I'll suggest that we can lift the level of children's work by using short, shared texts, and through minilessons, coaching and conferring with clubs.

The Nuts and Bolts of Book Clubs

Forming Book Clubs

"Readers," Kathy Doyle said to her fifth graders, "I've been thinking about Brian getting his Holland Lop rabbit and finding there are Holland Lop Rabbit Clubs in every county of New Jersey. The truth is, in this country there are clubs for everything. Some of you are in a chess club, a Hebrew Club, a Little League Team, a lacrosse club, a drama club. So, I wondered if we might, in this classroom, form reading clubs?"

Imagine the excitement in our classrooms when we say to kids, "You'll have to decide how your club should go. What will you name your reading club? Where will you meet? Will you read multiple copies of the same book, or different but related books? Will you meet twice a week? Three times? What will you do in your club meetings?"

Our children write us notes about the readers with whom they think they could work well. "You'll want to read with kids who like the same kind of books," we say, "and with kids who read through those similar books at a pace that matches your own." Because club members usually do read the same books and go through them together at the same pace, they need to be matched, at least somewhat, by their ability as readers. "You'll also want to think about forming a group that can work productively together," we say. Sometimes we suggest that when children are jotting recommendations to us, they consider quiet children who listen well, because the secret to good club conversations, we say, lies as much in listening as in talking. Some teachers give kids a few days to interview each other about book choices, reading pace, genre preferences, and so forth. Other teachers talk about book clubs for several weeks before they are formed and in the interval make a point of mixing and matching readers so that children are more open-minded about the possible composition of their clubs. I personally have so many agonizing memories of waiting and waiting for kids to choose me for their soccer team that if I were to return to the classroom, this phase would be over in the twinkling of an eye. Either way, our children don't have the final say in the composition of a club. We end up considering our children's requests along with our knowledge of the class as readers and people, and tinkering with names. We often have follow-up conversations: "How come you didn't ask to read with Devoia and Kawana?" We may tell a child, "I want you to be in a club in which you can feel strong as a reader. These kids tend to read books like Robert Kimmel Smith's *The War with Grandpa* and to get through them in a week. Have you considered reading instead with Niro and Sara?" Our goal is for children to feel as if the clubs are self-chosen, although of course it's never as simple as that.

In the end, we generally try to form clubs containing four members (although teachers with large classes may find that it is easier to manage six clubs with six children each, than nine clubs with four children each). If the clubs have even numbers, children can alternate between talking as partners and talking as a group. This is especially important for struggling readers, who often need close-to-the-text support as they read. When clubs fall apart, oftentimes the underlying problem is that the members are too different from each other as readers, and this shows up in tensions over book choices. If this becomes a big, long-standing problem, it is sometimes better to break a large book club into two smaller ones, even if the results is a book club with only two members.

But usually, book clubs are long-lasting. Children know they'll be together for six weeks or 12 weeks, based on our assessment of how the clubs are working. When clubs are formed, usually in February, we assume that they may last until we reach the far horizon of the school year.

When we *do* form book clubs, we try to carefully scaffold our children's first "cycle." Last January, Katherine Bomer's fourth and fifth graders formed short-term "poetry clubs," which, unbeknownst to them, were precursors to book clubs. Katherine's children found friends who read as they did, wrote to

Katherine to propose their choices for what they thought would be month-long groups, and before long were happily immersed in poetry clubs. These lasted for the month of January and supported a poetry genre study in the writing workshop. Meanwhile, children got many of the club structures under their belts. Each club had a Clubhouse (a patch of table or floor they regarded as their meeting space) and a Club Constitution (in which they vowed to do their homework, to speak courteously to each other, to let everyone speak). Each club also had a Club Portfolio containing a record of who was in attendance and who had and had not completed the homework, a brief log of conversations and assignments, and copies of the poems they'd studied. Over the month, Katherine was able to watch these short-term clubs and tinker with their membership. "Watching the beautiful work you're doing in these clubs has given me an idea. What if, instead of disbanding these clubs now that our poetry celebration is over, we make them more important than ever?!"

Mark Hardy's concern in his fifth-grade class in the Bronx was that the workmanlike, productive, on-task atmosphere he'd labored to establish in his reading workshop would be threatened once his kids went into the more sociable structure of clubs. "I didn't want to lose the productive hum we'd achieved," he said. So he decided that he'd stagger his students' introduction into clubs. During independent reading Mark suggested that two partnerships work together as a foursome. He provided this one club with a lot of support and guidance while other children carried on doing their independent reading and partnership talks. Then he pulled two other partnerships together and suggested that these four children join him in watching the first club. After they'd spent a day researching, he asked, "Do you want to try something similar?" and he provided this new club with a lot of support and guidance. After he had helped half the class carry on well in clubs, Mark pulled the whole community together to officially launch the new structure.

Meanwhile, in a number of other classrooms, all the clubs were launched at once but were, for a while, centered on the read-aloud. This avoided the problems that arise in book clubs when children forget to do the reading. As Sharon Hill read aloud to her fourth graders, she helped partners jot notes and talk about the text. Then, halfway through the book, she put sets of partners together in read-aloud clubs. Each club took an issue that had already emerged in the first half of the read-aloud book, and after each day's read-aloud, they'd disperse to far corners of the room for a ten-minute club conversation about this issue. Sharon did this sort of work for several weeks and only then suggested that clubs actually choose and read texts together.

Scheduling Work in Book Clubs

Most clubs meet for two twenty-to-thirty-minute conversations a week during the independent reading workshop. Some clubs also talk briefly at some other time, perhaps meeting as partners only. If clubs meet too often, they don't have time to gather momentum and experience an "electrical charge" around their ideas. Also, if clubs meet too often children suddenly find they have no time to read in school, which can end up meaning they lose their involvement in the book and don't read much at home either. When clubs are in session we need to help children sneak stolen moments for independent reading throughout the day. Perhaps just before lunch, we can give ten minutes over to reading. When a few children finish their math early, we can encourage them to read. Teaching children to get out their books and make time for reading in the midst of busy schedules is an important lesson and makes it less likely that book clubs will eat up all opportunities to read.

In most classrooms, club members assign themselves homework in keeping with what is expected of the whole class: usually they read the chosen book for at least half an hour a night and know they should finish a book within two weeks of starting it. Because some club members read more often and more quickly than others, these children are encouraged not to read past the assigned page (and if they do, to pretend otherwise) and to do more independent reading, maintaining a second book alongside the club book.

Their book talk continues for at least a week after they finish reading a book, and for more proficient readers, sometimes *all* their conversation comes at or towards the end of a book. This vantage point allows children to think about the book as a whole, relating parts to the entire work of art (Short, 1986).

When children are working in reading clubs, they are expected not only to read but also to write in preparation for the club discussions. Often the teacher lays out an expected length for writing-about-reading, and club members together assign themselves the topics or points of view for this writing. In many classrooms, children are expected to jot a certain number of Post-it notes or chart entries each night and to write one or two longer entries, of at least a page each, every week. They know that once (or twice) a week, they are expected to think and write at some length about an idea they had while reading. In other classrooms, club members know that on Tuesdays, for example, they are expected to write a page developing one idea in some depth.

After each club meeting, club members decide on the topic everyone will think and write about that evening, and their topic is never simply to write about the next chapter. *Perhaps* members agree that in their writing, they'll generate topics for conversation, but more often, they have had a conversation and assign themselves ways to extend or deepen that conversation. For example, if one day the group spent their reading club time talking about how *Danny, the Champion of the World* is different from other Roald Dahl books, for homework they will probably assign themselves to read the next four chapters, marking with Post-its those places where Dahl is being very un-Dahl-like. If the group ends up debating who has a worse life, Journey, who has lost his mother, or Jean Little, who in her memoir *Little by Little* describes how she lost her eyesight, children might assign themselves the job of gathering evidence to defend their positions in the debate. In Dori's group, conversation evolved into a comparison of *The Great Gilly Hopkins* and *Journey.* Dori's entry extends the conversation:

Connections between Gilly and Journey

This really is not a big thing to notice but I think they both have unusual names. And both's mother is living but they are not with them. Their lives are changing very much. Very much for Gilly because she moved three times in less then three years. I think Gilly is very rude (like our guest in our house) for a foster child. And Journey was sometimes rude to his family, like when his mother did not write the return address, when she sent the money, and he started crying. Then grandpa took a picture of him crying and Journey yelled at him; I think it wasn't really something big to yell at. And Journey doesn't seem to feel brave like Gilly after his mother left him. Gilly wants to be the boss and do things her way, and she is trying to call her mother somewhere. And tell her what is happening in her life but Journey is trying to collect money to visit his mother (if she ever tells him where she is). So, for sure, they both want to be with their mothers or parents and they want their mothers to do what other people are doing for them.

After book clubs have been established, teachers continue to frame reading time with a minilesson and a share session. Early in the work with clubs, minilessons and share sessions tend to be angled to help readers devise things to do together around books. After the minilesson, perhaps two clubs meet while everyone else reads silently. Perhaps, every club meets on two days Tuesdays and Fridays, while on other days children read independently after the minilesson. That is, some teachers choose to have every club meet at one time and others stagger club meetings, with some children read silently while others gather together in club conversations. The advantage of having every club meet simultaneously is that no one is trying to read while the room is full of talk. The advantage of staggering club conversations is that if only two or three clubs are meeting at any given time, the teacher can be more of a presence and play a more influential role in raising the level of conversations.

Guiding Book Choices

Usually the club members decide what they will read, although teachers sometimes find it helpful to direct or constrain book decisions. Karen Kapusnak, a fourth-grade teacher, decided that while she worked to get her clubs up and running, she would select the books for the clubs. A first-year teacher, Karen wanted to support her own teaching and her children's work in this way. She knew that if she chose the books particular clubs would read, she could be sure they were reading books she knew well and be more efficient and effective in guiding their work. Ultimately, Karen wants club members to have a sense of ownership and be able to let the work they do with one book lead them to unpredictable next-book choices, but her decision to control book choice for a time was a reasonable one.

There are other reasons for teachers to steer book choices. For example, if we were planning to launch a genre study on memoir in the writing workshop, a few weeks before we might ask children to make their selections from a shelf of memoirs (or memoir-ish) books. Alternatively, we might make multiple copies of short memoir excerpts and ask clubs to spend a week reading and talking about these short texts. In a recent visit to Katherine Bomer's fifth grade, I discovered that her children were reading biographies of freedom fighters. Katherine was highlighting this topic in her thematic study work and didn't have multiple copies of books, so children read whichever book they could get their hands on, swapping books with each other. Although club members were reading different books, they still had a common ground for conversation because they were each studying the life of a different freedom fighter.

I've seen teachers steer book choices in these ways:

- In your club, please choose a picturebook author (or a poet, an essayist, or a journalist) and read and talk about several texts by that same author.
- In your club, please select one of these books about immigration.
- In your club, please reread and discuss one of our read-aloud books from this year.

- In your club, please select a short book that is easy for all club members. All of us will be working on reading sections of our club books aloud with fluency and intonation and on digging deep to find more to talk and think about.

- In your club, please select an article, essay, or short story that is challenging for the group. Think about how our reading strategies can change when we read texts that are difficult for us.

- In your club, please select a book from this specific genre (mystery, memoir, biography, nonfiction, historic fiction, etc.)

- In your club, please read brochures, manuals, rule books, or directions that teach you how to do something and do that activity together as club homework.

We try to direct club discussions as little as possible because we know children will invest much more if clubs have the same allure and power as a tree fort. Mostly we encourage club members to ask, "How can we pull together to make a reading club that really works for us as readers?" We ask them to think, "When has reading worked in my life? How can we keep those conditions now that we're in clubs? What goals do I have for myself as a reader? How can gathering together with some reading friends help me reach my goals?"

Knowing When Children Are Ready for Book Clubs

When Kathy Doyle and I *first* explored the idea of book clubs over a decade ago, we launched clubs in September instead of in February, as we do now. That first year, Kathy's kids had come to her from very different reading classrooms, and she wanted to open new worlds for them right away. She wanted to give them ownership, choice, purpose, and reading relationships immediately. One day in late September, Kathy announced, "These are your clubs. You'll have to decide on what you guys want to do together as readers."

How surprised we were to see what her fifth graders did! They gathered in circles on the floor, one child at a time taking a seat on the group's one chair to read aloud to the others. The students sitting on the floor, meanwhile, followed along in their copies of the book with a finger or a bookmark. Whenever the reader paused over a difficult word, a classmate would pipe up with the correct word. In the club I watched most closely, at the end of each page, before switching readers, children would stop even if they were in mid-paragraph and go back over the page to identify all the new vocabulary words. Then they'd write these words down with the accompanying definitions!

Kathy and I watched these groups in dismay. "Why didn't these kids do what readers the world over naturally do?" we asked ourselves. "Why didn't they have the living-room conversations we each had in our reading clubs?" Yet even as we asked this, we knew these students were simply demonstrating to us what they'd been taught over the years. Reading, for them, was clearly a performance. Reading was about getting the words right. The book "talks" they'd had were round-robin, question-and-answer sessions in which they were called upon to provide one-word, fill-in-the-blank answers.

Kathy and I gathered her children together and told them that we were surprised by what they were doing together as readers. "It is so different from what we do in our adult reading clubs," we said, and we asked if they'd be willing to come to our next adult reading group to observe us, as Kathy and I had observed them. A few days later, when eight of us met with our books, twenty-five young ethnographers squeezed into the faculty room with us.

"You talked the whole time!" the kids said later, surprised that we had actually spent a whole hour talking about one part of a book. They couldn't get over the fact that we weren't reading aloud together but were instead discussing reading we had already done. "It was like you had done homework for the group," they said. "Everyone had notes about the book on papers." "You kept up a beat, talking and looking at the book and talking some more."

The reading clubs in Kathy's classroom were transformed. We've never since begun reading clubs without more preparatory work. Now, by the time we suggest that our children dream up neat things to do together as readers, we have already spent months having book conversations together. Our children have usually already learned to do these things:

- Choose "just right" books and retell them smoothly and logically, with attention, if they are stories, to plot, setting, character, tone, theme, movement through time and change.

- Generate things to talk about when they read.

- Have a conversation that goes from "laying out one's cards" to focusing on one shared issue, so that one topic is developed across several days. This requires that children talk back in response to what others say, keep open minds as they pursue (rather than perfunctorily answer) each other's questions, and have a repertoire of ways to extend what someone else says.

- Stay close to the text. This means that children choose topics of discussion that are central to the text, that they have the habit of providing and asking for specific textual references, that they keep their books open as they talk, and that they can monitor a book talk enough to say, "We should get back to the book."

- Do reading homework (reading chapters and jotting responses)

- Use Post-its or other forms of notes to prepare for, think in the midst of, and extend a conversation.

- Reflect on a conversation, identifying problems and generating other possible ways to proceed. Children are also accustomed to trying-out proposed solutions and asking, "So, did this help?"

Book Clubs vs. Reading Centers

Before we initiate book clubs, we first weigh whether to make the transition to this upper-grade model (book clubs) or whether we'd have more success working with the more primary-level model (reading centers). The two structures are variations on the same theme. Both support readers as they develop and defend ideas about a book. Both help readers think, talk, and write about a whole book and between related books. Both help children initiate, plan, and pursue their own important projects involving texts. Both structures support the development of literary skills such as interpretation, synthesis, and critique.

Some fifth-grade teachers have followed the model of reading centers rather than reading clubs, and some second-grade teachers move toward reading clubs rather than centers, but in general, we see centers as a structure for grades K–3 and clubs as a structure for grades 3–8. These are the differences as we see them:

CENTERS	CLUBS
Groups tend to stay together 1–2 weeks, then the children are reconfigured into new centers.	Groups tend to stay together 2–3 months.
Groups usually meet approximately four times a week for 30 minutes at a time.	Groups usually meet twice a week for 30–45 minutes at a time. There may also be a third brief time for checking-in.

Groups usually have four members, often two.	Groups usually have four members, sometimes six.
Children usually do all or most of the reading and writing (or charting if there is any) during the center meetings.	Children read and write at home and usually use club time to talk. When the talk turns a new corner, children may spend five minutes rereading and jotting notes in preparation for talk.
About half the talk tends to be running commentary between partners as they move through the pages or chapters of the books.	Since there are fewer times to talk, and readers tend to talk about longer sections of the text.
Children usually read shorter books they can finish in a single day. These books are clustered together because of a common author, genre, subject, or writing technique (such as use of speech balloons).	Children usually read chapter books and talk about the same books for six club meetings.

If most children are still reading very early chapter books, such as Gertrude Chandler Warner's *The Box Car Children,* Mary Pope Osborne's *The Magic Treehouse,* Louis Sachar's *The Wayside School Books,* Ruth Stiles Gannett's *My Father's Dragon,* and James Howe's *The Pinky and Rex* books, some teachers question whether these books are rich enough to support extensive conversations. We think they are, but it is also possible to suggest that children read these chapter books in an independent reading workshop, meeting for five minutes each day with a partner to work toward the basic challenges of "getting the book" and maintaining reading momentum. These children could meanwhile be involved in poetry or picturebook centers. In this way, we can build a reading curriculum that supports both the need to read extensively and the need to read intensively, thinking and talking deeply about some texts.

A Peek at a Book Club

Ten-year-old Brian held Jean Little's memoir *Little by Little.* He looked from behind his too-big spectacles at the other two boys in his club. He took a deep breath and started talking. "The last part of the second chapter in *Little by Little* reminded me of *Maniac McGee,* because a lot of people got hurt. See, in *Maniac McGee,* the way they described Grayson's death was, 'The old man was dead.'" Unsure whether his friends were following him, Brian said some more. "I read that sentence *five times over* before I got it into my head that the old man was dead. After that one sentence, I had to think a lot about it. That one sentence is really, really powerful. It's like the ultimate ending for the chapter." Brian paused and for a moment the circle was quiet. Then he added, "If I had an ending *that* powerful for my memoir, it would be real good. It gets the reader to stop and think."

Micho, the second member of the group, looked down through his shock of bangs at his copy of *Little by Little* and said, "I don't really understand the feeling you got. From *Maniac McGee,* I do, but not from *Little by Little.*"

This was a reasonable comment, because Brian had begun by comparing *Little by Little* and *Maniac McGee* but had only referred to *Maniac McGee.* Talking now about *Little by Little,* Brian elaborated: "A lot of people got hurt. The grandma wasn't about to die, but it's all happened at once. She was having the best time. Jean Little was having the best time until she lost her shoe and her father was coming home."

Sam, quietly listening until now, interrupted, "No, her father *was* home."

The two boys went back and forth for a moment about whether Jean Little's father was or was not around in that section of the book and of her life, then turned to the text for an answer. For a few minutes they flipped through the pages, looking for evidence but it was hard to find. Micho finally intervened to say, "Well, it doesn't matter." Micho turned to ask Brian, "What feeling do you get from Jean Little when she gets in the accident and all?"

Brian answered, "There was two chapters where good things happen, and she went to camp and had friends and all good stuff was happening, and then all of a sudden, she gets in an accident, and bad stuff happens. We could look at the book as good stuff, then bad stuff."

Sam jumped in on this idea. "In her whole life, she has good parts, bad parts. It starts, she had bad eyes—bad part—then she is happy—good part. Then she goes to school ... which one?"

Micho asked, "The Chinese school?"

"No," Sam said. "The 'Sight Savers' school. She loved it, right?"

"Yeah," Brian added. "They wrote big on the blackboard."

Sam had by now picked up a pen and started making a jagged line that depicted the fluctuations in Jean Little's life. He looked up to say, "Then they made her go to a different school and she had no friends."

"And then … it goes on, good to bad," Brian said and Sam nodded, still drawing.

For a moment the boys were quiet. Then Micho turned the conversation in a different direction by saying, "What you were saying is that it went from good to bad, good to bad, but I'm wondering not just how her life went, like good to bad, good to bad, but what happened to her *person?*"

"Her character traits?" Sam asked.

"Like she said, 'I don't care, I don't want friends,'" Micho said. "Later she said, 'I want friends now.' She's very demanding."

"Not really," Sam disagreed.

"Remember with the tree part," Micho insisted. "On page 37. She says, 'I do *not* have bad eyes!'"

For a while the boys talked about Jean's stubbornness and tenacity. Then they began to talk about her sensitivity. "She's sensitive at the beginning," Micho said, "Now she's learning how to write…."

"Sensitive means different things," Brian interjected. "Sensitive … she's not just sensitive, like she cries a lot. She's also sensitive, like when she loves the beauty of the orange slices, how she notices things." Soon the boys had begun charting how Jean Little was both sensitive as in "thin-skinned" and sensitive as in "writerly and wide-awake."

A week later, I returned and listened to the same book club discussing yet another memoir, Betsy Byars's *The Moon and I.* I arrived just as the club meeting was getting under way. "Since we didn't have a lot of time to talk about *The Moon and I* last time, what do you want to do today?" Sam asked. "Maybe we should read what we wrote."

"Yeah," Brian said. His reading log was opened to an entry he'd written on *The Moon and I* "I wrote 'She uses a lot of beautiful language with sounds.'"

Sam agreed, "When they have weird sounds like 'crinkle, crinkle,' I get it in my head and it stays there the whole book. Like 'crinkle' was in my head when I read the whole chapter. When she puts it a few times, you think she'll go back to it."

"She has a few sounds," Brian said, and he began skimming through the book and reading out others.

"There's a lot of sounds. She refers to her husband and goes to him for information. At the library, it was easier to ask him than to go to the reference books, and so I think they have a pretty good relationship."

Daniel, who'd been listening quietly, now laid out his card. "I think *Dogsong* and *The Moon and I* are similar because Betsy Byars really fell in love with the snake and Gary Paulsen was in love with the dogs."

Micho wasn't convinced. "Not *that* in love," he argued.

Continuing, Daniel answered, "In the beginning, they aren't. He (Paulsen) hit a dog on the nose, and she (Byars) picked up a snake and it wrapped around her arm."

Sam now jumped in with a totally separate comment. "When I was writing my memoir," he said, "I thought her (Byars's) book had lots of thoughts in it, dialogue. Mrs. Doyle says you can have dialogue at the beginning of a story. It could be, like, 'Mom, I'm home' for the start of the whole book. This book goes like that. It's sort of funny and cheerful. She always makes it cheerful."

"And she has lists in her story," Brian said. "She has lots of stuff that makes you want to read it."

Micho now jumped aboard this line of conversation. "I try to have a good variety in the things I do in my writing too. If too many people are doing one thing, I don't do that thing. It's true in our reading club too, and Mrs. Doyle says we never go with each other's ideas. That could be good because we have so many ideas and so much original ideas, but it can also be bad."

Daniel said, "Okay, let's take one eensy beensy tiny moment to write how they are the same." Daniel has persistently held onto the idea that a comparison of the two authors would help, an idea the others have overlooked.

"Who?" The boys ask, clearly having forgotten.

"Byars and Paulsen," Daniel said, as if it was obvious. This time they followed his lead. For a few minutes, the boys all jotted notes.

Then Sam broke the silence, "What have you jotted?"

"How Russell sees the animals."

"The dogs?"

"And they both want a close relationship to animals. Betsy Byars wants it to Moon, the snake, and Russell wants to get close to the dogs."

"Then the dogs barked and he got nervous and wasn't so close."

"But after that he got closer."

"It's like the steps they are taking to get closer to the animals," Sam said, picking up a sheet of paper and charting a map of the two books as steps-to-closer-relationships-with-animals. This was the second idea I'd seen him chart over the course of two days of conversations.

I decided to say nothing to this club. Instead, I smiled as I moved to another one, confident that this one was well on its way.

It is easy to listen in on an effective book club and to throw our hands up in despair, saying, "My kids could never talk like that." But of course, these boys didn't enter Kathy Doyle's fifth-grade classroom talking like this either. There is no big mystery to how children like Daniel, Brian, Sam, and Micho have learned to talk well about books. They've learned it just as they've learned how to play soccer well or to write well: through experience and instruction.

Lifting the Level of Work Children Can Do in Reading Clubs

One of the most effective ways we can help children progress toward being ready for successful book clubs is to have them meet over a few days in an early version of clubs to talk about short, shared texts. In many of our classrooms for a month before book clubs begin, children meet in these groups and talk about short stories or poems they have read in class. This time can be an extraordinarily important part of the year.

Starting in perhaps November or December, we may often have whole-class book talks surround short, shared texts rather than read-aloud books. We try to choose texts that everyone in the class can read, and we give children a bit of time to read them and mark them up. We often launch the book talk with a whole-class conversation and then, when we've established a focus-point, we ask every reader to reread the text in order to make more notes related to the focal issue that has emerged. After children reread and mark up their text in preparation for a book talk, we often suggest they talk in small groups for ten or fifteen minutes, before the whole group resumes.

Working with short texts has lots of advantages. First, everyone takes time right at the start of a discussion to read the poem, essay, picturebook or short story, and to mark the text in preparation. There is no risk, then, that someone won't have done the reading or the note-taking necessary or that they will have forgotten what they read and thought. Then, too, it is often much easier to talk about a short text than a longer one. Sometimes whole novels are so overwhelming that it is hard to know where to begin or how to pull out a single conversational thread. It is also easier to refer back to specific sections of a short text than of a long novel.

If we want to teach children particular ways of talking about texts, we find that this work with short, shared texts gives us a marvelous forum. We might, for example, want readers to

- Retell a text using the story elements. Others in the group can add to the retelling, and if children don't agree about a story element (such as the setting), they can refer back to the text.
- Spend a few minutes laying out what each reader noticed in his or her reading and then decide on one focal point for the whole-group discussion.
- Practice a particular good reading strategy. We may, for example, first lead a minilesson comparing two texts. Now, in small groups, we can ask children to read, mark up, and talk about two articles on one topic, two poems by one author.

Finally, in introducing children to reading clubs, we might give them more heavy-handed guidance during their first book. For example, we could ask clubs to progress in this way through the first book they read together:

- Spend time together looking over the book, then read for half an hour in school and keep track of the number of pages you've read. Assign nightly club homework, including reading and Post-it notes. Assign yourselves roughly the number of pages most members of the group have read during the half-hour of class reading time.
- In the club meetings, take time to look over your Post-its before talking. Each person selects two or three that go together or that seem especially significant or intriguing. The talk begins with a retelling using elements of the story (plot, setting, character etc.). Then one person lays out his or her Post-its and the group talks as long as possible about the idea on

the table, incorporating ideas from their own Post-its if they relate. Then another person lays out his or her Post-its and ideas. This continues for a few meetings.

- At the middle of the book, readers take time to look back over the book, reviewing Post-its and discussion notes, and asking, "What are some of the big issues, central mysteries, lines of inquiry or main hunches about the book we could pursue for a while?" These are shared at the next meeting and a focus is selected.

- For homework, everyone follows the one shared line of inquiry. You still collect Post-it notes but they are mostly (but not entirely) marking sections that speak to the issue on hand. You also write several long reading log entries to extend your thinking about the issue.

- In club meetings, chart and discuss evidence related to the line of inquiry. The goal is to generate new ideas, and this means the central inquiry will evolve as the book and the conversation take new turns.

- For homework, continue to pursue the line of inquiry for as long as it seems interesting. Pursue a second line of inquiry or revise the first so that it stays interesting and continues to yield insights.

- When you finish the book, select a way to linger at the end of the book (Chapter 23). After you've spent a day or two discussing the book in this way, select another way to linger at the end of the book.

Even when our concentrated work with short, shared texts is finished we continue to help children develop the skills that will be necessary for a flourishing book club. Once book clubs are up and running, we continue supporting our children's endeavors through minilessons, conferring, and share sessions.

Minilessons to Teach Children How to Work Well in Clubs

Last week I listened to Erica Leif begin a minilesson by saying, "In our study of the ways we can use retelling as part of our book-club conversations, I noticed yesterday that some of you figured out an amazing thing." Erica waited until all eyes were on her. "There were several clubs that discovered this, the club Everlasting did and so did Turbulence, and others. What happened in these clubs was that at some point in the conversation, one person retold a section of the book, and someone else disagreed with the way the retelling went. They were thinking, 'What book did *you* read?' So—and this is the coolest thing you can do in a book club—you started *going like this* (and Erica buried her head in her book and started flipping though it). You said, 'It starts ... it's on ... on page 36!' and then someone made a move to reread! So you questioned the retelling and you end up rereading for confirmation." Summing up her point, Erica said, "That's what I saw some of you doing this week, and it was so great. You can all do that. You can retell. When there is a disagreement or a mystery, someone can say, 'Let's see what it says,' and soon you will be rereading."

Putting a snippet of a book talk transcript onto the overhead projector, which Erica keeps nearby during all her minilessons, she said, "With your partner, think of *one* place in this book talk when it might have helped to crack open the text and reread it." Soon the room was buzzing. After two minutes, the class shared a few of the places they thought a group member could have initiated a reread.

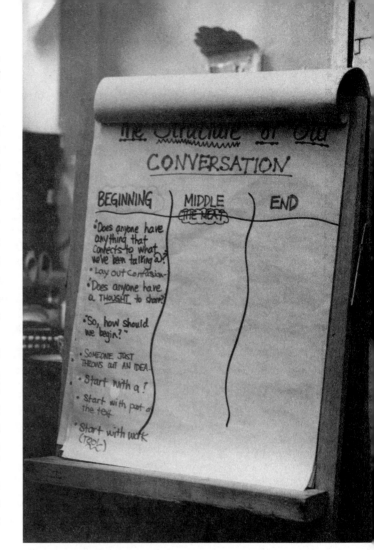

"Today, in your clubs, I want you to be sure to go back and reread part of the text out loud together at least once and preferably twice. We'll talk later about whether and how this rereading helps." At this point, Erica's fifth graders all headed to their clubhouses.

It is almost always effective when the minilesson includes a short transcript of a book talk. For example, children could reread the earlier excerpt about the ups and downs in Jean Little's life and look for an array of things:

- What are some ways to get started in a book talk?
- What kinds of questions do club members ask each other?
- How did the children get past the difficulties they encountered in the book talk?

- What predictable sections do we see in this book club transcript? (laying out many ideas, defining and settling on one to pursue, initiating a chart, raising other ideas and deciding whether or not to follow them, etc.).
- When did these children refer to the text and when *should* they have referred more to the text? What did kids say or do to prompt this?
- At what points in this transcript do charts support book talks? How could the children have done more with their charts?
- What role did each member play?

I am not suggesting that within any one day we use one transcript to make a great many points. Instead, I envision the class might spend a few days talking, for example about how important it is to monitor for sense when we talk as well as when we read. "Let's look back over yesterday's book talk, which I transcribed. I'll read it aloud and let's each listen. If you are confused by what's being said, this time let's stop the talk and say, 'Wait, I'm confused.'"

Perhaps a week later, we might be studying a different topic altogether. Perhaps we want to emphasize to our students that it can be helpful to stop a conversation in order to summarize, and in that way, to get our bearings. We might pull out the same transcript and this time use it to say, "When might we have paused to summarize? And what might we have said?" At still another time, we could look over several familiar transcripts to discover what kids do that works and doesn't work when they want to get a good talk started or to examine what we tend to do when our conversations run into difficulties. Kathleen Tolan refers to the book talk transcripts she uses as resources over and over as "touchstone transcripts."

During book club minilessons, it's also common for the teacher to arrange for one club to hold some of their meeting in front of the class. Of course, this "fishbowling" can only extend for a short time, and then we'll want to pause the book talk in order to talk about what viewers noticed. When we don't have the energy to make a transcript of a book-talk conversation, asking the class to gather around and listen to one club's conversation is a way to reflect on a live transcript. Sometimes the demonstrating club will reenact a conversation we witnessed earlier. Sometimes the club just carries on in their book talk and we watch without knowing what issues will arise. Even if we've suggested a reenactment, it's hard to predict exactly what the club will do when they are in the "fishbowl." We might have planned to show how much great talk the club is able to generate from just the cover and first page of a book, and yet now, in the spotlight of the whole class's attention, the club members might freeze. Teachers needn't worry about this, because the fishbowl structure is equally powerful whether talk goes well or does not go well.

If, for example, we'd all gathered to take note of how beautifully the club talks about the cover of C. S. Lewis's *The Voyage of the Dawn Treader* and yet the members of the club are making only vague generalizations, we could intervene with any one of these comments:

- "I wonder if the club members are going to look closely at each part of the cover illustration and talk more concretely about exactly what they see. Let's watch …."

- "Can I ask the club to freeze for a moment. Okay, class. Right now, what you see this club doing happens to us all. These guys are talking *in general* about the book, but I think their talk will get better if they focus and get very specific. Would all of you turn to the person beside you, and acting like *you're* up here, look at the cover and talk about one very specific thing you see."

- "Do you mind if I join your club? Because I was thinking about what you just said, Darnell, and that got me to look at the cover. You know what I noticed?"

- "So, class. Let's retell what the club has said so far as they've talked about the book. Who remembers how the conversation started? Yes, Darnell spoke first and he said …."

- "Okay, let's rewind this talk. Let's go back to Jocelyn saying, 'I think it's cool that they're sailing into the clouds.' This time let's linger on Jocelyn's comment, following up on what she said. Are you guys willing to do a rewind? Okay, Jocelyn, say your line again and guys, this time try to build on what she says."

I recently observed Katherine Bomer leading a minilesson with her fifth graders. Katherine spoke with passion as the children watched her closely. "Whatever the goals of your club are, you *have to make them come true.*" Katherine was silent, adding to the drama of the moment. In many of the classrooms I know best, teachers create moments like this. They want their words to be heard and felt, so they leave a space around them like the wide margins on a page. Into the silence one little boy raised his head. "But dreams *don't* come true." The way he spoke he could almost have added, "So there!"

Katherine answered, "That's true, but the type of dream we're talking about is the type you work for. We're not perfect, that's for sure. We're not aiming for perfection. We're aiming for a good club. What are you, yourself, going to do, Elisha, Lamot, Sarah, Rowan, to make your dream for your club come true?" She went on. "I'm going to help you make your dreams come true and one thing I'm going to ask is that each club becomes a 'fishbowl' club. Today we're going to have one researcher from within each club watching the club, and for today I've chosen the club member who will function as the researcher. After this, you can decide whether to continue with that person or whether to switch, and if so, how to switch. The job of the club is to do whatever you can do to make your dream for the club come true. And let me warn you that everyone in your club did the same homework last night, marking two places to talk about, and right away you'll have to do some negotiating about which of all these conversation-starters you will use."

Then Katherine read off the names of the designated researchers, asking them to meet with her, and sent the clubs off to work. "Blazing Angels, you can get started. The Open Door, off you go. Missing Pieces of Life, go. TDA, go."

Soon a group of six researchers had gathered with Katherine. She gave them each a rubric she'd created and started walking them through it, pointing out where they were to write the name of the club's book, what the phrase *duration* meant ("Look at the clock when you start researching and put the start time down. Then put the stop time down. Calculate how long you watched. That is the duration.") Katherine explained that the researchers were to fill in the left-hand column with the names of all club members, and then she read the headings along the top of the page.

Names of club members	Refers to the text for evidence	Addresses what another person has said	Asks questions of each other

"So, Beatrice, if one person said, Jane Yolen's *The Devil's Arithmetic* is time travel, and the other person said, 'I agreed with you at first but now I'm thinking she wasn't just traveling, she actually lived there,' what would you check off?" They found the column. Rohan, not understanding that the preceding comment had been an example to illustrate how the rubric worked, continued the conversation about time travel. Waiting till Rohan paused for an instant, Katherine said, "That's great, Rohan, but today, at least for part of the time, you are a researcher and that means you are invisible. You'll be dying to add your ideas about the book to the conversation, but you can't. You are invisible."

Beatrice pointed to the ghostly apparition on the cover of *The Devil's Arithmetic*. "We're like her."

"This is an important job," Katherine said. Then she motioned toward me. "See, it's exactly what Lucy is doing. She's probably dying to say something, but she's just writing everything down so she gets a lot of data."

By now the clubs were under way and the researchers scurried off to their posts. Half an hour later, the class reconvened on the carpet and the observers reported on what they'd observed. The homework for that evening was for each group to think about the data collected by the researcher in the light of the book club's goals and dreams and to come up with a plan to help the club reach their dreams. Researchers began in a report-card like fashion, reading off the names on their chart and evaluating each person's contributions that day, but Katherine suggested that they talk instead about what they noticed *in general* about the club conversations.

After one child's report, Katherine asked, "Did you notice anything that really helped the conversation?"

"They read responses they'd written in their notebooks."

"That's important," she continued, "So it really helped to refer to notes from the reading. Artifacts. This is crucial information for all of us to take note of." Listening to Katherine, I smiled to myself. What a gift she has, seeing such significance in even the littlest things her students do.

Rohan reported on his club next, relating an episode that happened during the conversation.

"Rohan," Katherine said. "I like the way you had an example, an episode, to tell us about. The other researchers may want to learn from you."

The next researcher said, "My group was good because they added their ideas onto each other's."

"Can you think of any specific examples of a time when you thought the conversation was good?" Katherine asked. "Can you give a specific incident like Rohan did? That really helped."

"No."

I wondered if Katherine would probe a bit more, but she didn't have a chance. Sarah's hand shot up, and she started talking even before Katherine acknowledged her. "The people I picked for my club don't get along well. The person may have been one of my best friends but we're not good at conversations, we've been having a lot of disagreements. Now I don't know if we are friends. I can't remember why we fought but we did. So for anybody in the future, I have advice, just give up what you think and go with the flow."

I was a little taken aback by this airing of friendship difficulties in a public forum, but Katherine simply normalized the problems, asking Sarah, "Do you think it might just be possible to have disagreements with friends, or with a good club, and still go on and be friends, and be a good club? In your life, don't you have arguments? It doesn't mean the friendship is over, does it?" Listening to Katherine, it seemed to me she was saying something very powerful about the stuff of dreams. Clubs (like other relationships) work not when they are perfect, but when we accept the difficulties with abiding generosity, not dismissing the goodness of these people and these relationships just because there are difficulties along the way.

Conferring and Coaching

In addition to the instruction provided by minilessons, we move among the clubs during club time, spending about five or ten minutes conferring with each one. Our methods of conferring with clubs are similar to our methods of conferring with individuals or partnerships.

Usually when I confer with the members of a book club, I begin by rereading my notes. I need to recall previous conferences and observations and to reflect again on the individual members. If, for example, I know that a few of the readers in The Box Car Club have habitualized a word-by-word sort of reading, then I already know that one option might be to steer this particular group toward reader's theater work. And because fluency is an issue for a few of these children, I will keep in mind that I'm looking for opportunities to increase the amount of easy reading these readers do. When I look at my notes on a specific book club, I'll notice not only the work we've done together in recent conferences but also the texts the group has been reading. If the club is reading a book significantly different from earlier books, this will inform my observations. For example, The Outsiders Club had been reading R. L. Stine's *Goosebumps* books and were now reading Paula Danziger's *Amber Brown*. This represents a real jump ahead for them. I may want to support this progress by telling them that, whereas characters in Goosebumps do not tend to grow older or to change from one book to another, this isn't true for Danziger's series. "You may want to notice how Amber changes between the books," I say. When I met with the Blue Dragon Club, I noticed from my notes that the last time, we discussed the importance of preparing for a club meeting by writing not a summary of the chapters they'd read but a focused entry on the issue they had chosen to discuss. Perhaps today I would talk to them about ending their meetings by asking, "How can we keep this conversation going in our minds tonight as we read and make notes?" and about members all writing on the same issue. If the book talk had evolved into a comparison of two books, for example, would they want to read the next chapters asking "How do these chapters compare with that other book?"

I like to research clubs (like individuals) from afar first, because the moment I draw close, the dynamics change. I always look especially for signs of engagement, because all the good things in the world can happen *around* a student, but none of them will matter if that student isn't engaged. Do the book club members look engaged? Are they leaning in close? Are their books out and open? Do they seem to be listening to each other?

Soon I will pull my chair alongside club members. I make a habit of not interrupting the conversation for at least a few minutes. If I interrupt right away, students soon learn to stop talking whenever I draw close. As the conversation unrolls, I often record it. This keeps me busy enough that I am less apt to interrupt, and it gives me the evidence I'll need when it comes time to do the teaching part of the conference. As I write, I'm gathering tentative theories about what may be going on in the conversation. Usually I'm looking at patterns in the members' talk.

Observation alone doesn't give me enough evidence to draw any very strong conclusions. It may be that, for today, children are talking about their lives without referring to the text at all. This would worry me if it was a pattern but please me if it represented a breakthrough. I need to move from observing the group to interviewing them before I feel as if I know enough to be helpful. I'm apt to say, "Can I stop you for a second?" If the club's conversation consisted of personal narratives that were only tangentially related to the book, I might simply ask, "Is your talk today typical for you?" In this instance, for example, children would probably let me know if they, too, were aware that they needed to return to the text. Sometimes I ask children to listen to me reading the transcript of their book talk and to consider what *they* notice in retrospect. If only two children had been doing most of the talking while I observed, and I wondered if this was an aberration or a pattern, I might say, "Today, while I was here, two of you did a lot of the talking. Is that how it's been going in your club lately?"

The decision phase of a conference actually occurs concurrently with the research. As we observe and talk with readers, we are developing theories about these children as individual readers and about the club as a whole. The underlying question is often "What's next for this group?" There are always a hundred possible next steps a group could take, and the challenge is to think, "What is this club *almost* doing but not quite?" or "What is the club trying to do and needing help on?" or "What is the major issue here that's keeping the club from going further?"

There are a handful of predictable issues many of us encounter over and over:

- dealing with management issues (doing homework, moving efficiently into club meetings, how to handle the situation when one child leaves to go to the bathroom, and so on)
- bringing out all the voices
- staying grounded in the text
- exploring versus answering questions, that is, avoiding premature closure.
- finding and pursuing a focus
- learning the value of disagreeing with each other and learning to do so in ways others can hear
- realizing the author made choices and asking often, "Why might the author have decided to write it *this* way?
- inserting time for rereading, jotting notes, or talking with a partner into club conversations as a way to ground the talk in the text, reenergize the conversation, and bring out more voices.
- moving between particular and general ideas; it is important for readers to shift between referring to particular sections of a text and thinking, "How can I go from this to say something about the text as a whole?"
- learning to respond or talk back to and to linger with each other's ideas
- finding opportunities to chart a conversation
- moving between one text and another
- extending today's talk by writing more about the topic of conversation as we read the next chapters
- beginning a book talk by retelling and then building upon yesterday's conversation

- book choice (does one book relate to the next? Can the group progress through the books at a reasonable rate? Are the books challenging them?)
- using advice from minilessons and conferences

After identifying the issue we want to address, in the third phase of a research-decide-teach conference we try to give club members a strategy to try or a lens for thinking about and improving their book talks. Usually, I begin this phase by telling children what I saw them doing and what I make of it.

I might, for example, say "The reason I was asking what you felt about today's conversation is that it seemed to me you had so many ideas, which was great, but having so many ideas also got your talk into trouble. You ended up jumping around a lot between one good idea and the next and the next." When I'm unsure how to speak candidly with kids about what I have noticed without making them feel defensive, guilty, or blamed, I try to remember that the very things that are problematic in book clubs—and in people too—are usually the flip side of strengths. If I am concerned because two children did all the talking and dominated the book club, the flip side is that two of the children really talked back and forth with each other, building on what the other said. The only problem is the other club members weren't a part of this. I'm apt to first support the part that is a strength, and then to show that the strength has limitations: "I loved the way you two were totally into this book, and also the way you really talked to each other. The only problem is that I'd have liked to see all four of you involved." Or, if the book club reached the end of a book and raced straight into the next book without any culminating conversation, I might celebrate the club's eagerness to read, read, read while still saying that it is important to take time to think back over a whole book before moving on. A second strategy I often use to avoid putting children on the defensive when I tell them what I've noted is to say, "I noticed you doing something that my book group does as well." I want them to understand that the problems they run into in their reading clubs are the very problems adults also encounter. I find it also helps to get children's input on what notice. If I describe a pattern I've seen, I'm apt to ask, "Does this ring true for you?" or "Is this a pattern for your group?"

Once I've named the problem I've seen and chosen what to teach, there are five directions I tend to take. I might:

- suggest a strategy for the group to try
- launch students into an inquiry to gather more information on a problem they are having

- point out something someone is already doing (or almost doing) and ask everyone to try it
- ask students to replay a conversation and try a different way of doing it
- whisper to specific students, helping them to them make a particular move in the group's conversation.

If I decide, for example, that the group would benefit from learning a different way to disagree with each other, I might *tell* the group about this and then illustrate my suggestion by perhaps reading aloud a transcript of one of their conversations and then showing how the strategy could have affected the conversation. Then, I might say, "So, will you keep talking and try to make a point of disagreeing in ways others can hear while I watch." Alternatively, if I tell them that they will be more apt to refer to the text in a book talk if they take some time after the conversation focuses on a topic to look through the book and mark specific sections with bookmarks or Post-its, I'll suggest, "What if you try that now?" Then, as all the children reopen their texts and begin to work, I might, for a moment, talk with one child to help her find specific sections that would inform the topic on hand. Once the talk is again under way, I might step in often to show children how to use the marked passages as resources: "Can you show us what part of the book gave you that idea?" "Do you have an example of that?" Before I move on to another group, I might say, "From now on, after your book club narrows in on one subtopic and plans to discuss it for a while, could you always take five minutes to look back over the text and your notes?" I record this new resolution in my records and ask the club to do so in theirs. In this way, I try to make "the new contract" very clear.

One of my recent research-decide-teach conferences was with a club of fifth graders at P.S. 166. Angela, Ricardo, and Christina, who had finished William H. Armstrong's *Sounder* the day before, had asked their teacher, Alison, if they could make a poster for the book. When Alison wondered if a poster would extend their thinking about the book and asked them why they wanted to make one, they had no answer. So Alison suggested they begin by simply having a final conversation about the book. Fifteen minutes later, she asked me to confer with them.

As I pulled close, Christina said, "I have a question for the group. What do you think it means on page 17 when it says, 'He watched his mother as she patched his father's overalls with a piece of ticking?' What is ticking?"

Ricardo, sitting across the table, answered, "I think it must be some kind of patchwork. I think poor people use older clothes to patch up the clothes they need to save, so they can keep them longer."

"I agree with Ricardo," Angela responded. "I think it is something to cover the holes. Can I say something else? I liked his mother's song that she was always singing. It was on page 39. 'You gotta walk that lonesome valley, you gotta walk it by yourself, ain't nobody gonna walk it for you.' I thought it was a nice song."

"Yeah," Ricardo agreed, "nice and sad, too. That reminds me that I wanted to say before it was over that I think this boy was a good example for people. He is a good person I think."

"And the mom and dad too," Angela added. "On page 86, why are the convicts washing stones along the edge of a pathway?"

At this point I said, "Excuse me, may I interrupt here for a moment or two? It sounds like you are bringing up loose ends, untalked-about thoughts you had. Is that what you are doing?"

Ricardo spoke first, "Yeah, we finished the book, so for homework we made a list of all the things that we had thought of to say in the group but we never said. Now we are talking about all of them."

"It is so true that there are always little hanging threads around the edges of the book. You picked up on a lot of those, didn't you!" I said.

"But you know what? This is a really special time. The time you get to talk with other readers about a whole book is so important. You have this whole work of art, this whole story inside you, and you have a group of people around you to talk about it with! In some books, the really important ones especially, you will probably want to talk about the true center of the book, what the book is *really* about, what you hope you remember about the book in twenty years, what you think the author was trying to tell you. I want you to try that today. I want you to try to leave those little threads hanging there and look at the big, center part of the book, okay?"

"Okay," Christina said.

"It's a big talk to have. How will you begin?" I asked. "How will you get ready to talk about what this story is *really* about?"

"We could write for a few minutes," suggested Christina.

Francisco added, "We could make a web of all the important things we think the book is saying."

"You mean make one all together," I asked, "or each of you make a separate one and then talk?"

They all chimed in together, "Separate."

I said, "Okay, so you are going to take some time to write. You might write a web or a paragraph, but either way, you are exploring what the book is really about. You might start the paragraph, 'For me, the big thing about this book ...' or 'I'll remember ...' or 'I think what this book is really about....' You'll want to take at least twenty minutes to really open your heart in this writing. And oftentimes when you come to the end of a book, would you try to do this sort of writing and *then* have a special kind of talk?"

A second way to teach is to engage the club in an inquiry. If, for example, I notice that group members begin to make personal connections to a book and never return to the book itself, I might tell the students that this is a problem lots of kids have. "If you could figure out some strategies for getting back to the book, that'd be so great," I might say. "Could you brainstorm some possible ideas and then try them out to see how they work?"

I recently watched a conference in which my colleague, Kate Montgomery, helped a teacher nudge her students into an inquiry. The conference began with the teacher telling Kate and me that half an hour before, the children had told her they planned to spend the whole book club meeting talking over what Jess in Katherine Paterson's *Bridge to Terabithia* meant by calling himself "the original yellow-bellied sapsucker." The children had been referring to a section of the book that read:

> Caught in the pure delight of it, Jess turned and his eyes met Leslie's. He smiled at her. What the heck? There wasn't any reason he couldn't. What was he scared of anyhow? Lord. Sometimes he acted like the original yellow-bellied sapsucker. He nodded and smiled again. She smiled back.

From across the room, we could see Ivan flick a pencil eraser and Julie braid Tillie's hair. We pulled our chairs up to listen to the group of fifth graders—Ivan, Tillie, Elizabeth, and Julie. Immediately the erasers disappeared and the braids were dropped, and everyone grabbed their books. The students quickly struck up a pose as if they were in the midst of a heated discussion. Julie said, "So, I think he meant he was a fat-bellied, woodpecker!"

Everyone laughed, a signal that they understood that Julie's comment was meant as an entry into a "we have been working hard all along" charade. Elizabeth added, "You mean a sap-sucking bird, not a woodpecking bird!"

"Right," Julie said. Then there was a long, awkward pause.

Finally Kate intervened, "Can you tell me about what's been going on in your reading club so far today?"

Tillie spoke up right away, "We wanted to know what he meant by 'yellow-bellied sapsucker,' so we went to the dictionary and looked it up and it said what it was."

"And so then we have been talking all about what he meant by that," Ivan explained, "and why he said it and different people's opinions and all that."

The others nodded hopefully.

Kate said, "You know, it's very strange that you say that is what you have been doing this whole time. I thought I saw you all with the dictionary in the first second or two of reading time, but after that it sure didn't look to me like you were talking about what Jess meant by that."

Ivan protested. "But we were ..."

Julie jumped in, "Yeah, we had a good talk."

Holding them at bay, Kate said, "Wait a minute, the point is, how can you learn from your experience if you don't even think about what your experience really is!" Then she said, "Like in the kite study you and Ms. Seitz just did in this class. Ivan, you told me your kite didn't fly at first but that you figured out a way to make it lighter, changing the tail, and then it flew. Imagine if you just pretended it flew all along! Imagine if you never really looked at it to see what the problem was because you were so busy pretending it was fine! So, you can all sit there and pretend that your kite flies, that your conversation is great, and learn nothing from it, or you can try to figure out what the problem has been so the situation will be better next time! Which is it going to be?"

The children looked sober. Elizabeth clearly spoke for everyone when she said, "We'll try to figure it out."

The others nodded. "Okay," Kate said, "that is a tough thing to do. How will you begin?"

There was a long pause. Now Kate said, "When I am trying to figure out why my kite won't fly, or why my conversation isn't going well, I first look at it very, very closely, as honestly as I can. Today and for homework, why don't you do that. Play over in your head what happened when things started to go wrong today and write down as much of it as you can remember. That way, you can look at it tonight and tomorrow to figure out what happened and to think about how you can make it better next time. And you can teach the rest of the class what you figured out!"

Instead of suggesting a strategy to try or launching students on an inquiry, we can also nudge a child to do something (or notice a child doing something) and ask the class as a whole to emulate what that one child did. If one child listens to another with a look of skepticism, I might say, "Rico, you looked as if you weren't sure you agreed with Angela. That is so smart, listening and thinking, "Do I agree," and I could tell you were dying to say to her, "I'm not sure I see it that way. Will you say more?" Then I could say, "Rico, why don't you tell her you're not so sure you agree and ask her to say more, if that's what's on your mind."

A fourth way to teach is to pause and ask the club to join us in replaying and rethinking the talk they've been having. Then we can read our transcript of the book talk. We may want to point out an area of concern, or we may want to let kids respond on their own. One way or another, reviewing transcripts of a book talk usually leads to talk about how the discussion could have been better. "So let's go back," I say, and now the group picks up the talk at an earlier juncture and has a second go at it, this time trying to improve it.

As I mentioned earlier, still another way to teach is to listen to a book talk and instead of interrupting it, simply "whisper-in" as the talk unfolds. If we'd like children to develop the habit of referring to the text more often in a book talk, instead of stopping it, we might whisper to a child, "Aren't you dying to see the part of the story she's referring to? Ask her to show you." If we repeatedly nudge a child to say, "Where do you find that?" we can, after a bit, simply glance at the child when the moment comes and the child will say, "Where do you find that in the book?" After this "show me" response has become habitual, we can say to the group, "Do you see how much better your whole book talk is now that Ronit is often saying, 'Show me'? Try to say that more often!"

It is important to notice that we are coaching one student to make a move that we hope becomes habitual, that we are not making the moves in the student's place. I don't lean over the child and say, "Where do you see that in the book?" Instead, I prompt a child so that this becomes habitual. We might prompt a child to

- ask the speaker to say more, to elaborate
- say "What?" when someone says something confusing
- summarize the conversation so far to clarify the topic at hand
- give examples to back up a theory, learning to say "For example" and to ask others for examples

All of this teaching, from launching book clubs thoughtfully, to guiding students in book choices and offering short, shared text work, minilessons, and conferences will not guarantee a trouble-free classroom of youngsters engaged in unwaveringly heady literary discussion. Book clubs, like all good teaching, are hard work. But if we, like Ivan fixing his kite, make sure to take frequent, honest looks at our methods and our students to ask ourselves, "What exactly is happening with these book clubs?" and if we take time to assess, rebuild, and rebalance our teaching of reading, our students will be on their way to a life in which it is possible to sit down with others to talk about ideas, to change minds, to hold fast to opinions, to listen, and to learn. And in today's society, isn't that worth any amount of work?

Teaching the Qualities of Good Reading

IV

When my father turned seventy-five, he began writing a memoir he called "The Log of a Long Journey." During summer vacations together in a lakeside cabin, my father would often read passages to me. After I'd put my boys to bed, we'd sit at the end of the dock, and as the sun set over the lake, we'd read and talk and read some more. Once I asked Dad why his father wasn't more present in the story. Dad had a ready answer, but apparently my question lingered.

Months later Dad came to visit. As we drove home from the airport, I asked, "How's the memoir?"

"It's finished," Dad said. "I got it professionally bound and published," he added. "Last night I sat on the living room floor and cut up paper bags to wrap copies to mail to the nine of you." Then Dad said, "But when I taped up the last box, I sat there on the floor, the box between my legs, and realized *I left out a story.*" By now, Dad was banging on the dashboard for emphasis. "Do you want to hear the story?" he asked.

Apparently each of my father's childhood summers on Cape Cod had ended with a townwide sailing race. When he was eleven, my dad skippered the winning boat, with his father acting as crew for him. The town descended around them, hoisting my dad into the sea, and he emerged like a wet cat. Then my Dad and his father walked home, my Dad's feet squishing in the sneakers. "And do you know what?!" my father said, still banging on the dashboard for emphasis, "My father said *nothing*" (wham, wham). "Not a word. Not a word about what a way to end the summer" (wham, wham). "Not a word about them heaving me into the sea."

We talked a lot that night, and when the mail truck arrived two days later, I looked for the memoir. It didn't come that day, or the next, and so months later, home for Christmas, I asked Dad about it. "Just wait," he said, his eyes twinkling.

The next morning, Dad fished a package from under the Christmas tree. It was indeed professionally bound: red leather with gold embossed letters saying *The Log of a Long Journey.*

"Open to page 96."

Puzzled, I opened to that page, and there was the sailing story. "But, but …" I sputtered, knowing this was the story he'd told me had been missing from his log.

"I added it in," Dad said. Then I read the story, and this discussion of it:

The story, as I write it, fills me with intense sadness. The most important part of the story may not be the episode itself, but the fact that I rejected it from the initial log. I didn't include it because it was just so sad. When my daughter Lucy read over an early draft of the log and asked, "Where is your father in this story?" my answer was to add him in. But now I know my father was missing from that draft of the log because he was missing from my life. For all that I was given in my childhood, one thing was missing— a father who understood and cared for me, not just in a collective sense as one of his brood, but for me as a person. What was missing was a father who understood and cared for his skinny second son. I do not remember my father giving me a single bath. I do not remember him reading to me, or coming into the shop to inspect or admire the boats I made. I do not remember camping out together, sleeping under the canvas …

I can write this now because I know that my father's role in my life helped me realize I wanted a very different role in my children's lives …

I am moved by the image of my seventy-six-year-old father, sitting on the floor of the living room putting each of nine boxes between his legs, ripping off the tape and the packaging on each box, and pulling out copies of *The Log of a Long Journey*—all professionally bound—in order to add his father to the story. I am moved by the image of that livingroom, strewn with packaging, and by the image of my dad, with his bad knees, carrying that stack of books through the Buffalo snows to the print shop.

I want to have his courage. So often in my own thinking I try to get things figured out, finished, packaged. Because our students never pass this way again, we, as teachers, decide how to teach and then we tend to act with a flourish of certainty. We bind and package our thinking and we add the embossed lettering that says, "This is done. It is accomplished."

And then we sit, the package in front of us, with the palpable sense that "I left out a story." The question is, "Do we have the courage to open the box, to mess up our thinking, and to do it over and over?" I hope we do.

The one thing that enables me to rethink my thinking over and over is that I am able to do so in the company of colleagues. This manuscript was sent out in preliminary form for review. One reader suggested I streamline the text by deleting all references to think tanks, retreats, and conversations around the Project's big table. "We don't need to know that you have adult reading groups or study groups or principal networks and we certainly don't need to distinguish one Kathy from another," the reviewer wrote. "After all, it's the methods that matter."

The methods *do* matter, and the methods that matter most are those of think tanks, retreats, conversations around the Project's big table, and shared research in each other's classrooms. The methods that matter most involve studying transcripts of our own and each other's teaching, poring over examples of student work, and attending each other's workshops, and yes, all of this *is* a method that matters very much.

Oftentimes when my colleagues and I study together we are opening possibilities for units of study. Invariably this inquiry begins with a sense of dissonance, of disequilibrium: something seems to be missing from our teaching or from our children's reading. We always skirt the issue for a bit, but then the day comes when we put a bit of data—a story or a question—in the middle of the table, and we talk and think about it as if it were a Post-it note in a shared text and we were members of a reading club.

In just this sort of way we've dug into the topics I address in the chapters of Section IV. Each of these topics has been a shared inquiry in our community, and many of us are pioneering the work I describe in this final section. Chapter 21 focuses on Nonfiction Reading, which is, of course, much more than a single unit of study. Nonfiction reading is a part and parcel of all that happens in our classrooms, and I am happy to have the opportunity to spotlight the topic. Chapter 22, "The Elements of Story," is equally foundational and very much influences the work we do even in September. And Chapter 24, "Writing About Reading," is also a thread throughout the book, but one that deserves attention on its own. My colleagues and I are fascinated by the challenges of teaching prediction, intertextuality, and envisionment; initially I planned to give each its due, but the book is too big already. In Chapters 23 and 25 I have selected just two very special qualities of good reading to describe—interpretation (which includes inference and synthesis) and personal response. I hope these chapters on two qualities of good reading help my readers imagine other units of study on qualities I do not describe.

Meanwhile, there are lots of areas we still need to explore. There are lots of stories we have left out. We have left out the story of Lydia Bellino, who intended to visit only briefly in the first-grade classroom, but who, after the children plied her with requests, chose a book from the classroom's Earth Day display and suggested they listen, asking themselves, "Do I agree?" "Do I disagree?" Then Lydia read a page or two in which two teddy bears held hands under the apple tree while birds sang and butterflies flitted. It concluded "If everyone of us does a little thing to help, the earth will always remain a beautiful place."

"Do you agree or disagree?" Lydia asked, and gestured to the children to talk in partners about their response. A moment later, Lydia asked, "What did you decide?"

"We agree!" the children chorused. Their response wasn't surprising because the book was written in platitudes that seemed self-evident.

"Hmmmm," Lydia said, puzzled. She looked at the page again as if totally stymied by their response. "That surprises me, because I disagreed."

"Whaaaat?" the children said, looking at each other big-eyed and open-mouthed. How could one disagree with the earth is a "beautiful place" and we must each do "a little thing to help"?

Then Lydia explained, "I'm *not sure* the earth is such a beautiful place," she said. "Lots of parts of the earth aren't beautiful anymore, and I'm not sure it is enough for us to just do *a little something* to keep it beautiful. I think we have to do more than that."

How does that story, and all it suggests, fit into "the box" of what I have described in the reading classroom? Isn't it important that we help children critique texts, so they grow up realizing they can understand what another person thinks and still say, "I see things differently."? Perhaps you read a glorious story about a war hero, and you know from the way it is written that you are supposed to be full of admiration and respect, but when you look at what the person in the story did, you decide that based on your values, he was not heroic but inhumane. Or you read a story in which a physically challenged person is portrayed as helpless and dependent, and you think, "I disagree." Or you read a story in which the youngest of three African sisters was the beautiful one and you see that she is lighter skinned than the others and the only one with thin lips, and you say, "I see the author's image of beauty, and I question it." You look at the beliefs implicit in the story and you say, "I disagree."

Of course, critique isn't absolutely missing from our reading workshops. Certainly Alice was reading Karen Barbour's *Nino's Pizzeria* critically when she noticed that the sister and the mother had no voice within the world of the story. And Anthony, reading E. B. White's *Charlotte's Web,* added a Post-it note to one page saying, "It's not fair Charlotte and Templeton do all the work." In his partnership talk, he explained, "Why should Wilbur get all the credit? The spider web should say "Some Spider" not "Some Pig." Yassir disagreed. "That'd be selfish," he said. "In this story, Charlotte is like a teacher or a Mom or a minister. She's not going to put up a selfish sign that says 'Some Spider.'" Marissa wondered, when she read Don Freemen's *Corduroy,* why he could only be adopted if he had all his buttons sewn on. The question, of course, was really, "Do you have to be perfect to be loveable?" and it is an important question to raise. These conversations happen in our reading workshops and we recognize their value and call attention to them.

But my colleagues and I know that if we want readers to question texts, to discuss their unspoken assumptions, to notice a particular author's angle of vision and feel empowered enough to critique the writing, we need to do more than simply support moments when readers say, "It's not fair!" or "I don't agree!" A team of us have begun to meet to think about the role critical reading plays in our lives, and we are reading Pat Shannon (1990), Carole Edelsky (1991), and Randy Bomer (1995). We will soon gather communities of students together and begin sketching out what a unit of study on critique might look like.

And there are other stories we have left out of the box. We have left out the story of Hannah Schneewind reading aloud Eleanor Estes's *One Hundred Dresses*. As Robert sat with his classmates on the carpet, listening to the story, his facial expression showed how Peggy felt as she stood by and watched her classmate Wanda being taunted. "Oh my goodness," Hannah said to the class when she saw what Robert was doing, "let me keep reading and all of you watch the way Robert's face shows what Peggy is feeling." Soon everyone was following Robert, supplying the facial expressions and gestures to match their interpretation of Peggy's mood. From time to time, Hannah paused and said, "What are you thinking right now?" or "I saw you clenching your hand in a fist. Talk to us. What are you—what is Peggy—wanting to say? What's going on in your mind?"

After Hannah had read four pages while children listened from Peggy's perspective, Hannah said, "Let's try something different. This book almost never shows us what Wanda (the poor girl who was taunted and eventually left town) is thinking and feeling. We can only surmise what is going on for Wanda. Let me reread these same pages and this time, listen as if you were Wanda. Act out *her* point of view." Again Hannah read and paused. Passing an imaginary microphone to Nicole, she asked, "What are you thinking right now?"

"I don't want to be teased," Nicole said, role-playing Wanda. "I'm nervous cause I don't know where to stand or who to sit with."

Now the microphone was passed to other students. "After school I'm going to find the owl's nest. I'll pack an apple, some water. I'll be out really late. It'll get dark. I don't care. I feel safer in the woods than here at school."

"I hate them. I could hit them all. They are as bad as the ants my mother stamps on."

"My knees show. This dress is too short. If I lean forward, I can kind of cover them. Tonight I'll make a dress deep purple and with a long skirt that hangs over the knee."

Hannah nodded, then picked up the book and read on. The next time when she paused, Hannah said, "Get with your reading partner. One of you be Wanda, one of you be the interviewer with a microphone. Wanda, please tell your partner what you are thinking right now."

If our goal is for readers to walk in the footsteps of characters, shouldering their burdens and seeing through their eyes, isn't it important that they use improvisational drama to climb inside stories? Yet we've left this "out of the box." And what about other ways of knowing? Wouldn't we be wise to think more carefully about how art can help us respond to reading?

There are many, many other avenues of inquiry that merit attention. Readers will find some units have been described in Ellin Keene and Susan Zimmerman's helpful book, *Mosaic of Thought* (Heineman, 1997). Above all, readers will want to reflect on your own reading strategies and those of the readers we admire. What is it you do as readers? How can you invite your students to join us in inquiries on these strategies? Although it is important to share this process of curriculum development with students, we need above all to gather together with a circle of colleagues. For *that* is the method that makes everything else possible.

Nonfiction Reading
The Words of Our World

21

Most of the reading I do is nonfiction reading. In the last two days, I've read Rebecca J. Lukens' (1999) *A Critical Handbook of Children's Literature*. I've read my nephew's Christmas list and decided to give him a walkie-talkie. I've read an earlier draft of this chapter. I've read the disturbing front page of today's *New York Times* reporting on the ouster of New York's capable chancellor of schools, Chancellor Rudy Crew's farewell remarks, several different reports on the action, and an editorial calling for a speedy replacement. I've read road signs, the directions for using my new CD player, and so much more.

Nonfiction reading is the primary reading fare of every teacher, researcher, and teacher-educator, and it will be the primary reading fare of each of our students. Yet ironically, the curriculum in our schools focuses on the texts and skills of reading *fiction*. When teachers read aloud, we tend to read fiction. When we lead book talks, organize response groups, or initiate author studies, our focus, almost without fail, these focus on fiction. If I were to ask teachers to list their favorite authors, the list would center on writers of fiction. And yet the texts that I read most, the texts you read most, and the texts our children will read most are nonfiction texts.

Of course, it almost isn't fair to call all nonfiction by a single label. Included under this byline is everything from books on history, science, literature, and politics to captions, headlines, brochures, recipes, directions, manuals, letters, and websites. The term *nonfiction reading* actually refers to a world of texts and purposes. Today, this world of nonfiction reading is in a state of crisis in many of our schools, and that should be of concern to us all.

The Crisis in Nonfiction Reading

In thousands of schools, the new emphasis on language arts has come at a high cost. Many urban teachers especially schedule social studies for one half-hour time block two or three afternoons a week. Science receives even shorter shrift. When there is very little time available for learning about social studies or science (or art and drama, either, for that matter), this affects not only the quantity but also the quality of the nonfiction reading students do in school. Now most of the nonfiction reading they are asked to do comes *in place of* rather than *in support of* deep studies on a subject. Miles was recently assigned a research project on evolution. He was expected to read on the topic and write about the theories of evolution, Darwin's life and times, the implications of evolution for science and religion, the political ramifications of his topic, and his own views—all in five pages and ten days! Several years ago, I decided to research guided reading. I read five or six books over and over and organized weekend-long retreats with colleagues who'd read the same books. During these retreats we took those books apart page by page, comparing and questioning them. Then there were phone calls to the authors, days in the field together in which we compared what we'd read and what we were doing with children, and then there was more reading and more conversation. How false it would have felt had I, like Miles, been expected to produce a five-page paper covering my topic after only ten days of research!

Our schools not only provide little time for nonfiction reading, they also provide few texts. Very few teachers have more than a shelf of nonfiction books in their classroom libraries. The nonfiction books we do have are outdated and hopelessly difficult. The large, glossy photographs and enlarged font disguise the difficulty of the sentences, concepts, and vocabulary from all but our children, who immediately demonstrate the fallacy of the assigned levels of many of these texts. These complex trade books pose lots of problems for young readers, but the textbooks are even more problematic.

For too many of our students, nonfiction reading has come to mean plowing through dry, impenetrable textbooks, often poorly written and dense with undigested facts. To make matters worse, schools often seem to expect that good readers will read these and other nonfiction texts as if we were electronic scanners, carrying away in our minds an exact replica of what we have read. But most of us, as teachers, know that *we* can't (or don't) meet the read-and-retain expectations we often place on students. We confide to our friends, "I don't know what's happened to my memory," as if there once was a time, back in the good-old-days, when we recalled everything we read. In truth, even very skilled nonfiction readers don't read and retain every text, and we don't aim to. If my mind held every piece of information that passed by me every day—barometer readings and baseball scores and fatalities and birthdays and news conferences and fashion headlines and humidity counts—my thoughts would be a disorderly jumble. The skilled reader of nonfiction, then, is not the person who goes through life like a scanner, retaining every text, but instead, the person who can look at texts, judge the ways they or parts of them can best contribute to a constructive learning life, and can adjust their reading strategies according to the text, the context, and the place of this day's reading within the reader's larger work.

When a skilled reader reads about, say, parrots, that person is being nothing more or less than a skilled *student* of parrots. We use the same skills whether we're learning about parrots from a pet store owner, a friend, or a book. If we are truly interested in parrots, we use these skills almost effortlessly, without knowing we're doing so. When the veterinarian tells me that if I give porkchop bones to my cockatoo, this will whittle her beak down so it won't need to be clipped, the so-called "reading" skill of cause and effect helps me understand what the veterinarian has said. When I notice that after I cover my bird's cage, she stops squawking, I've exercised the "reading" skill of sequence. Reading comprehension is not distinct from general comprehension. As James Moffett and Betty Jane Wagner (1992) have written,

> A long list of mental activities that any psychologist would consider general properties of thinking that occur in many different areas of human experience have somehow or other all been tucked under the skirts of reading. Recalling, comprehension, relating facts, making inferences, drawing conclusions, interpretation and predicting outcomes are all mental operators that go on in the head of a non-literate aborigine navigating his outrigger according to his visual processing of cues from weather, sea life, currents and the position of heavenly bodies (p. 14).

The difficult thing about nonfiction reading may not be learning to work with texts which are filled with information but instead, learning to become a learner about topics that are sometimes foreign and initially uninteresting to us. In this chapter, I will suggest that we first need to help children read nonfiction texts around their own interests, which means providing the texts and the time to do this. Then we can use various teaching methods to ratchet our children's nonfiction reading up a few levels. We will raise the level of the nonfiction reading our students do during independent reading (by getting them to do more with what they learn and to read more actively and responsively). Eventually it will also be important to use some shared texts in order to teach students to follow an author's journey of thought and to become students on subjects that may not at first be interesting or familiar to the reader.

The First Step: Helping Kids Read Nonfiction Texts About Their Interests

Although learning about subjects outside our realm of interest is an important part of any person's education, the easiest way to teach nonfiction reading is first to create opportunities for young children to read within their realms of interests. The child who is passionately interested in a particular baseball team, who is already an engaged and vested learner, will bring a level of engagement and knowledge to the newspaper's sports page that will enable the child as a nonfiction reader in dramatic ways.

If schools are going to build a curriculum that supports a lifetime of nonfiction reading, the place to begin is by encouraging children to become avid learners and to bring their interests into the classroom. If we want our children to grow up as avid readers of *words,* they need in Paolo Freire's words, to read *worlds* (Freire 1983). Annie Dillard (1987), a passionate naturalist (and a reader of words and worlds), describes her view of the universe by saying, "There must be bands of enthusiasts for everything on earth.… there is no one here but us fanatics; bird-watchers, infielders, detectives, poets, rock collectors" (p. 159). Nonfiction reading will come to life when our classrooms are filled with similar bands of enthusiasts. If children bring rock-covered barnacles and glittery stones to school, then instead of saying, "Put the stuff in your cubbies so it doesn't get lost" (where in fact such treasures do get lost), we need to make a great point of saying, "Would some of you like to study the rocks Pablo has brought in today?" By inviting children to share their inquiries and hobbies, we're cultivating a readiness for skilled nonfiction reading.

Kathy Doyle launched her work with nonfiction by asking her fifth-grade students to teach each other about their hobbies and interests. Soon the shelves and conversations in Room 106 were full of Magic and Pokémon cards, lacrosse and skateboard equipment, trail guides for ski resorts, stories of sleepovers and rules for playing poker. After a week of talking about hobbies and interests, Kathy turned the corner in her teaching and said, "I've been thinking about all the hobbies and interests we've been talking about, and here is my question: in what way could reading help us enjoy these things even more? Talk to your partner. What hobby did you share with us? Have you—or *could* you—weave reading into this interest in a way that heightens the fun of it?"

Soon Kathy called the class back together again. "I've been talking with Emily. Her interest was sleepovers, and she wasn't sure reading could make sleepovers better. But Nicole told her there were articles in magazines about things to do on sleepovers, and Jeanne suggested Emily could read mystery stories at her sleepovers." From all corners of the room there were more suggestions: "You could read joke books and get good jokes to tell at the sleepover."

"You could find a recipe for taffy, because I did that once," "You could read and tell each other's fortunes." Meanwhile Jeremy plays chess, and he told the class that reading had made a dramatic difference. He had recently read a strategy book about a play called Annihilation and tried it on his dad. "I won in three moves!" he said. "It was the first time I ever beat my dad." Brian told the class that in a magazine called *Pokémon Power* he'd read about some trading opportunities, and soon others were reporting on websites, chat rooms, magazine subscriptions, and so forth.

The good news is that we can quickly, easily, and decisively alter our students' relationship with nonfiction reading. The conversation in Kathy's class about bringing reading into hobbies lasted no more than thirty minutes, but in just that amount of time she dramatically changed her children's perceptions of nonfiction reading. How important it is to help our students understand that nonfiction reading already weaves its way into much of what we do. So many children cherish and hoard trading cards—Pokémon cards, Magic cards, baseball cards—but do they regard this as a reading project and understand that readers across the world do as they do? Some readers collect recipes, others collect book reviews, personal letters, postage stamps, books, coins, poems, newspaper articles. We collect the texts we love, we read them often, we put them in categories and try to get more, and we fall in love with a few. And most of us read other media that circles these texts. Do our children know there are magazines for Pokémon? That there is a Star Wars website? That the daily newspaper carries statistics on the players on their baseball cards? That they can go on-line to find daily news about these people? Kathy changed her students' perceptions of nonfiction reading by helping them see that they were already avid readers of nonfiction and that many of their hobbies were already reading projects.

How important it is that when we try to recruit children into a life rich in literacy, we convey to them that literacy means a life of projects, collections, actions, plans, and insider knowledge. We need to reclaim *this* reading as part of the reading life because there are many children in our care who want and need the authority and finesse that print can give them but have little interest in walking in the shoes of other characters through imagined worlds. Boys, especially, choose to read nonfiction (Barrs and Pidgeon, 1994, p. 1), and it is important to note that boys are more apt to struggle as readers than girls. Myra Barrs reports, "A long succession of reading surveys, from Jenkinson's *What Do Boys and Girls Read* in 1940 to Whitehead's *Children and Their Books* in 1977 have shown that gender is the major factor in studies of children as readers, being more strongly linked than either social class or ability or attainment with how much children read." Whitehead (1977) reports that "At all ages, girls read more than boys." Margaret Meek Spencer (1983) suggests that boys' alienation from reading may be partly attributable to the ways in which the nonfiction texts that boys choose to read are marginalized in schools: "Many boys have views of reading we never hear about because most of what they read is passed over as insignificant" (Barrs and Pidgeon, 1993 p. 61,). By making nonfiction texts more central to our classroom, we make the children who read those texts more central as well.

Nonfiction Texts That Will Support Kids' Interests

If we want children to know what it is to follow their interests into texts, we need to look again at the collection of nonfiction texts we provide for them. As I said, most classrooms have only a tiny shelf of nonfiction books, and these books invariably support the school curriculum rather than children's own interests. We need to adjust our libraries to support our students' interests, but this is a long-term proposition. The most dramatic way to put more high-interest reading material in our students' hands is to make better use of newspapers and magazines (if our students are proficient enough to read them).

The Parents' Associations at some of our schools provide each fifth or sixth grader throughout the school with a subscription to the local newspaper. Children receive the newspaper at school, read some of it first thing each morning, and are expected to bring it home each night and talk about it with members of their family.

At the start of each year, Kathy Doyle's class divides itself into four task forces. The children in two of these task forces work for a week to plan what they'll do with the newspaper. Members take on the mission of interviewing adults to learn how they tend to read the newspaper. They come away from these interviews talking about the importance of scanning and browsing. People

who read the newspaper don't give equal attention to everything we read, and this is true not only for newspaper readers but also for nonfiction readers in general. Part of what nonfiction readers do is to get an overview of a lot of texts. The children in these task forces write and post "Ideas for Newspaper Reading." For the first fifteen minutes each morning, while attendance is being taken and children are entering the room, everyone is expected to work with a partner and to use one of the ideas from the list:

- Scan the paper and get a broad sense of the main things that are happening in the world. Talk together about this.
- Find an article that addresses one of your interests and read at least the first half of it. Talk it over (include retelling) with your friend.
- Find a section in the paper that especially interests you and begin to know it well. Plan to return to this section every day for a while.
- Notice some of the author bylines that recur in the paper. Find one author whose writing and topics you especially like and plan to look for that writer tomorrow as well as today.
- Read over the headlines and opening paragraphs from a bunch of main articles and talk with your partner about what's new in the world.

- Read two related articles and sketch a Venn diagram using somewhat overlapping circles to show ways in which the articles do and do not overlap.
- Enjoy finding out what's happening in life.
- Cut out headlines that are important to this week's news and put them into your notebook.
- Read an article that looks important. Be patient if something doesn't make sense. Read it over again.

Meanwhile, the other two task forces in Kathy's classroom are responsible for helping the class become involved with magazines. These children ask classmates to contribute old magazines to the classroom and they scan through them to get a sense of what different magazines are like. On Open School Night, Kathy recruits parents who are willing to sponsor a magazine subscription for the classroom (see Appendix B for a list of recommendations). This year's parents are sponsoring twelve subscriptions. Children in the magazine groups are responsible for selecting the magazines the class will receive and communicating with parent-sponsors, and then helping the class imagine how they will dig into the magazines once they arrive.

Providing the Time for Kids' Personal Nonfiction Reading Agendas

In most of our upper-grade classrooms, students are eventually expected to read during independent reading not only from their novels but also from magazines, biographies, nonfiction books, and newspapers. When children meet with their reading partners to retell or to talk over intriguing sections of texts, they do this in the same way whether they're reading nonfiction or fiction. Some teachers worry about children picking up and reading nonfiction texts without first receiving an introduction to the text and a preview of vocabulary words. "Is it risky for kids to read those texts cold, without introductions or definitions of terms?" people ask. This is a reasonable concern, because one of the biggest problems readers encounter when they read nonfiction is the need for background information. My fifth-grade son can figure out most of the words he encounters in the *New York Times*, but oftentimes the words—such as *Security Council, General Assembly, ratification,* and so forth—mean nothing to him. One option, then, might be for Evan to read only the nonfiction texts an adult has introduced to him. Yet I have several qualms about this. First, I think it is questionable whether a three-to-five minute overview can really "give" Evan the prior knowledge he doesn't already have. Do a few sentences out of a teacher's mouth really do the job of allowing children to envision and comprehend what is outside their realm of experience? Perhaps we need to become more comfortable with the fact that all of us go through life only partially understanding some of the nonfiction we read. Is it so deeply problematic for children to read and construct a partial and incomplete understanding of a topic based on what they read? Then, too, in my eyes, allowing children to choose what they will read helps with the problem of prior knowledge, because this way, children can elect to read texts for which they *do* have some prior knowledge, even if it's simply that they have talked with a friend who read this same text and thought it was intriguing.

Some classrooms may not be ideal sites for bringing a lot of nonfiction reading into the independent reading workshop. I'm thinking especially of the classrooms in which children are already having difficulty settling down to read. If the independent reading workshop *already* has loose ends elsewhere, we may not necessarily want to encourage nonfiction reading quite yet. There is a different and louder buzz in the classroom when many children are reading nonfiction. Whereas *fiction* is designed to hook readers in to make us "lost in the story," nonfiction sometimes seems designed to make readers exclaim and comment. Whereas fiction is written to support sustained focus, nonfiction often nudges us to do more of a stop-and-go kind of reading as we move from one section of a text to another and from one text to another.

Once we have highlighted the importance of reading nonfiction texts often, our teaching will need to change accordingly. Now when we talk with children about making time in their lives for reading, we can no longer emphasize only the importance of reading before bed or of making progress through chapter books. It is equally important that as our children go about their lives, they say "yes" to reading. Yes, they take in the headlines as they pass the newspaper stand. Yes, they notice the billboard. Yes, they read the warning before the video begins. Yes, they glance at the words carved under the monument, they notice the road signs, they open up the instruction manual. If we don't support nonfiction reading, how many children will miss out on this life and be excluded from the knowledge and power that are given to those who do say "yes" to reading?

We will act as if we expect our children to read nonfiction often in their lives and to weave nonfiction into their projects and endeavors. But meanwhile, we also know that some children do not live the life of a nonfiction reader. Many children, day in and day out, do not take in the words that are on bulletin boards, road signs, brochures, and the backs of menus. For starts, the world of the classroom is full of words, and we'll want to teach kids that noticing these words can give them power. How important it is that even very young children come to see reading as a way to get places, literally and figuratively. Teachers are wise to use a daily schedule to announce that the day will include time for building pyramids out of blocks or for baking candy apples, and we will want to support the children who read these texts. "Class, I have got to tell you about a smart thing Jeremy did. He came in today and stood right here and read the schedule! He knows how today will go! I wonder if he is going to read other words in our classroom because if he does, he'll learn even more stuff. Good readers do what Jeremy does. We read our world."

We'll make a point of demonstrating the ways nonfiction texts enter our lives. We'll read aloud and preface our reading aloud with comments like, "I've got to show you this totally cool thing I read about in the newspaper. I was just looking at it quickly in the subway and my eye caught this headline" or "Last night I went out to dinner at a Chinese restaurant and on the back of the menu, they had all this information about people's horoscopes. I've got to read just a little bit of it to you! Listen to this…." When we read aloud in this way, we are demonstrating a life rich in literacy. That life is rarely filled only, or even primarily, by novels. For richly literate people, reading is like breathing. Always, wherever we are, in the midst of loving and laughing and traveling and working and eating and being with friends, always, without even choosing to do so, we inhale the words of our world. That is what it is to be a nonfiction reader.

Reading Aloud and Fact-Dropping Can Ratchet Up Our Children's Nonfiction Reading

It is not a small thing simply to invite children into the life of nonfiction reading and to provide them with texts they are likely to understand and find engaging. It isn't a small thing to create opportunities for conversations around these texts. Once our children are all reading nonfiction, our next challenge is to teach them to do this well.

Along the gradient of difficulty of nonfiction reading experiences, we begin the year at the most accessible level: reading nonfiction with engagement and success. Then, over time, the teachers in our community "raise the bar," designing experiences that ask more and more of our students, and we coach and assist students so they are eventually able to meet our rising expectations.

The first and easiest way to raise the level of our students' nonfiction reading is to read nonfiction aloud, especially *nonnarrative* nonfiction. We use the same teaching methods to support nonfiction read-alouds as those we use with novels. Because we have all listened to thousands of stories, we've developed an internal schema for story, which (as I show in Chapter 22) allows us to expect and attend to a story's important elements. When

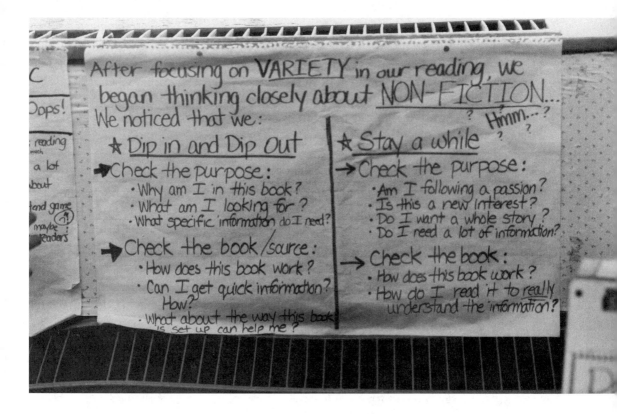

After focusing on VARIETY in our reading, we began thinking closely about NON-FICTION...
We noticed that we: ? Hmm...?
                                                                         ?   ?
★ Dip in and Dip Out   ★ Stay a while
➤ Check the purpose: ➤ Check the purpose:
  • Why am I in this book?   • Am I following a passion?
  • What am I looking for?   • Is this a new interest?
  • What specific information do I need?   • Do I want a whole story?
                                           • Do I need a lot of information?
➤ Check the book/source: ➤ Check the book:
  • How does this book work?   • How does this book work?
  • Can I get quick information?   • How do I read it to really
    How?   understand the information?
  • What about the way this book
    is set up can help me?

(left margin notes) C / Oops! / reading / a lot / about / end game / maybe / readers

we read a story and come away with a memory that includes significant elements, we do this in part because we have developed an internalized sense of the main structures and elements in a story. We approach an unfamiliar story expecting the same elements. Most of our students, however, have had few opportunities to listen to extended *nonnarrative* texts and so do not have an internalized schema for what *these* texts tend to be like. When they read nonnarrative texts, they often come away with a chaotic collection of details. They lack the "internal containers" that would lead them to *listen for* the structures and the logic of these texts. They don't necessarily have a felt sense for the fact that if a text says, "Many factors combined to make the Civil War an inevitability," what follows will be a discussion of one contributing factor and then another. Although there are ways to teach children about the structure of nonnarrative texts, the more important thing is that they develop an ear and a felt sense of what to expect in nonnarrative nonfiction texts. Some teachers help children develop an ear for nonnarrative nonfiction by asking them to listen regularly to scripted programs, such as "All Things Considered," on public radio or to watch nature programs on public television. The advantage of these programs is that the syntactic structures of the language are those of the written, not the spoken, language. When our students fill their ears with this language, they come to understand that phrases like "on the other hand" signal a counterpoint: the information that follows will contradict what has already been said; or that when the text says "one reason for this" and gives that reason, it will be followed by "another" reason; or that the word *meanwhile* signals parallel action in another setting. Although radio and television can help children become accustomed to the sounds and structures of nonfiction texts, neither takes the place of reading a lot of nonfiction texts.

As children read magazines and newspaper articles of their own choosing and carry away intriguing pieces of information, we will also want to raise expectations for this work, and there are several ways to do so. We might notice, for example, that a lot of our children seem to be reading in a sort of scan and dip way. More and more nonfiction texts-for-children contain "sound-bites" of content which support a scan-and-dip reading. Although this is one way to read nonfiction texts, we can up the ante if we suggest that children do more with the information they carry away. Donna Santman made a point of talking with her middle schoolers about the fact that well-read people often "fact drop" by weaving statistics or quotes from their reading into their conversation and writing (sometimes even when the fact or quote is not exactly relevant). For a few weeks, her youngsters gave themselves the assignment to "fact drop" at least three times each day. I overheard one student complaining after he knocked his shinbone on the desk:

"It really hurts?" a solicitous girl asked.

Wincing, the boy rubbed his leg and retorted, "Well, not as much as it hurt the Incas when they did brain surgery without any anesthesia." I smiled at this, conscious that Donna's children were taking on roles in a way that felt almost humorous to them and to those of us who watched. But all of us, as human beings, role-play our way into being the kind of people we want to be, and there was a way in which what I witnessed seemed profoundly authentic.

In Kathy Doyle's class, after several weeks of helping students browse through newspapers and magazines, dipping in here and there to read an article or part of an article, she asks for a more sustained commitment. "Find a story or a topic you want to follow across a number of days and publications," she says. When I wondered whether she secretly steers her children toward topics of global significance, she said no, the job of teaching her children to be nonfiction readers was important and ambitious enough. I think she is wise.

Using Partnership Conversations to Turn Students into More Active and Responsive Nonfiction Readers

Using partnership conversations to support nonfiction reading sounds like a simple enterprise, especially in classrooms such as ours, where talking with a partner about reading is a daily event, but the resulting mind work can be extraordinary. I recently pulled my chair alongside two first graders in Linda Chen's classroom. They'd each read a few pages of Robert A. Morris's *Dolphins* and had marked pages with Post-its. Their plan was to talk about the pages they'd read, especially the marked ones, and then continue reading. First they opened to a page that said:

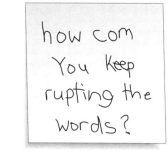

how com
You Keep
rupting the
words?

SLAP! SLAP! SLAP!
A dophin hits the water
with his tail.
That is the signal for danger.
The mother dolphin goes quickly
to her baby.

Kalie read aloud from her Post-it note: "How come you keep repeating the words?" Then Kalie said to Olivia, "I just wish I could ask the author why?"

"Maybe it's because the words are easy words so he repeats those ones," Olivia answered, and I smiled at her realization that authors of books *do* write to support young readers' progress through texts. Now they turned a few pages, until and Kalie pointed at another page she had flagged. She read part of it aloud.

Each day the calf
grows larger and larger.
He is now six months old.
He is over four feet long.

To Olivia she said, "Oh my gosh! He's bigger than me. But look, look back here," and she turned back a few pages. "Here it said,

'When the baby is born he is three feet long.'"

"Wow," Kalie said, doing the mental arithmetic to envision this growth. "They grow fast." Kalie turned to the next page. "And did you see this?" she asked and read,

"'When he is two years old, he will be as big as his mother.'"

"I can't believe it! What if two-year-old babies were as big as *their* mothers?"
"Well, most animals, when they are two; they are grown-ups."
"Not *any* animal."
"Cats are grown-ups when they are two, and dogs."
By now, the girls had talked about the pages they'd read alone and flagged, so they decided to read on together. They read the next page silently.

Sometimes the mother dolphin leaves her calf to dive for food. While she is gone, two other cows watch the baby. They help the mother dolphin care for her calf.

"Hey," Kalie said. "They're just like babysitters. Babysitter dolphins." The two laughed hysterically at this.
"Let's keep reading," Olivia said.

The baby dolphin cannot dive as deep as his mother. He can stay under water for only three minutes.

Olivia grabbed a Post-it and began to write. When Kalie leaned over to see what she was writing, Olivia said, "I'm going to ask 'Why does he have to stay under water for three minutes?'"
"He doesn't *have* to. Look. It says he *can* stay under water, not he *has* to stay under."
At this point, I moved on to listen to another set of partners talking about their nonfiction book. Yassir and Ronit were reading about penguins. The book had a photograph and a single sentence on each page. While I listened, one child read in an expressionless if accurate monotone;

When male penguins are born they are king penguins. The babies are gray and brown and fuzzy. They match the color of rocks and in this way they hide.

without pausing to comment. They turned the page as if to continue. What a difference from Kalie and Olivia! "Guys," I said, "Would you reread that page, turn your brains on to *really think,* and this time, stop to talk about what you read?" They reread the paragraph but when the time came to talk, they had no comments. "It's okay." Yassir said, and after a prolonged silence, he said, "Let's read on."

"Wait." I tried again. "When I read books like this, I like to talk about what surprises me. So, let's think," and I turned back to the text as if I was just now considering its contents. Slowly I repeated the peculiar sentence, "When male penguins are born, they are called *king penguins?*"

This time Ronit jumped in to say, "How come? Are *all* boys kings?"

"Yeah!" I said. "They must have a lot of kings!" Then, thinking some more, I added, "Are the girl penguins *queens?*" Then I said, "Let's read on and all of us *really think* "What surprises me here?"

It is equally beneficial for older readers of nonfiction texts to pause after every few paragraphs to reflect on the text or say, "The thing that surprises me here is…." In fourth grade my son Miles was expected for the first time to write nonfiction essays in response to his reading. When his teacher, Annemarie Powers, insisted that he pause to talk after reading every few pages on Westward Expansion in his American history text, he at first balked and said, "There is nothing really to say." But after a while he found that there was a lot of say. At one point Miles commented, "It wasn't Westward *Expansion* for the Iroquois! It was the opposite. It was de-expansion." This became the thesis for his essay. Later, when Annemarie again nudged Miles to talk back after every few paragraphs of a dense textbook on Ancient Greece, he looked up from one passage and said, "It's so weird that the Greeks could have had such brilliant painters and sculptors and scientists, but they couldn't invent terraces so they could farm their hills." This, too, became a thesis to an essay.

Teaching Nonfiction Readers to Follow the Author on a Journey of Thought

It was exciting to ask children to "talk back" in response to their nonfiction texts, but after listening to them we soon realized that they were using the same reading strategy over and over: they browsed through the text, picking out intriguing bits of information. Of course this can be a helpful strategy, but nonfiction readers must also try to follow an author on a journey of thought through an essay or a book chapter. Our children seemed to be over-reliant on browsing, and the assignment to respond to whatever intrigued or surprised them in the text did nothing to hold them more accountable for following the author's main argument.

Teaching Readers to Take Notes

To help children hug the shores of nonfiction, we worked in several ways to teach children to follow the main line of thought that an author puts forward. In many upper-elementary and middle school classrooms, we first began teaching children how to take notes on the main ideas in a nonfiction text. We began by reading aloud and helped students take notes on short, well-written essays, editorials, and feature articles in which the author emphasized a big idea and presented information to support and elaborate on it. The first time I did this with children, I projected an essay onto the wall and told the class of seventh graders to watch closely as I took notes. "Whether we are historians or biologists, lawyers or entomologists," I said, "much of the time when we read to learn about something, *we take notes*. Watch me take notes, and then we'll talk about what you see." I turned my attention to the text, a chapter on Victorian England from Joy Hakim's series, *A History of US,* read the first paragraph aloud to myself. Then I paused. "So this is mainly about ..." I said, and recorded a phrase. I continued in this fashion for a few more minutes, making an informal outline that used bigger letters, underlining, and indenting to show ordinate and subordinate categories. As I learned from Jacques Barzun's (1970) *The Modern Researcher,* in an outline it generally helps to use sentences instead of labels, so I wrote, "The Victorian Age was a time of extreme riches and extreme poverty" not simply "The Victorian Age." As Barzun and Graft say, "If the note taken shows signs of having passed through a mind, it is a good test of its relevance and adequacy" (p. 31).

Soon the children and I talked about how, when we read and listen to nonfiction texts that aren't stories, we don't think about characters, or setting, or plot so much as about ideas which are the big, umbrella ideas and also ideas which relate to these big ideas. "We take notes to remind us of what we've read," I said. "Watch, I'll use my notes to remember the main points the text has covered so far." Then I reread the notes I had just taken and used them to reconstruct the content of the passage. After a few minutes I said, "So let's continue by taking notes *together*. I'll read on, and you tell me when to stop and write something down. Soon we were thinking about what to write and whether the new notes should be of a larger or smaller size and whether they should be indented to show subordination. "The reason we take notes is to help ourselves pay attention to and recall what the author has said," I told the children.

This work needs to continue for a number of days and we'll probably reinforce the whole group work with small group strategy lessons. If children can all read a text displayed on an overhead projector, I will soon use minilesson time to have them read perhaps the first column of a newspaper article silently and, working alone or with a partner, to jot notes on it. I might give a few children transparencies and pens, so they can take their notes on the transparencies and the class can look at and compare the points different readers felt the author was trying to make. Obviously, if students' reading levels are too varied, I'd either read the texts aloud or ask children to work together in smaller groups, each group using a text its members could understand.

When our minilessons are about note-taking, we are apt to ask children to read nonfiction for some part of that day's independent reading workshop and make a rough outline or a visual depiction of the text that they need. Then, when they meet with their partners, children use these outlines or sketches to recall what they've read. They often see that good notes are the best support for these conversations. Sometimes we suggest that partners use their notes to recall what they read *several days* earlier. When readers know they will be taking notes on a text, they use their Post-it notes differently. "If you know you'll be outlining the text, use Post-its to mark the big ideas you'll be including in your outline," I tell them. Later it will also be important to show children that readers sometimes take notes that reflect their own interests rather than notes that only mirror back what the author has written. A text may tell about the enemies, food, and lifecycle of an octopus, but if my focus is on the ways an octopus is similar to or different from an eel, my notes would reflect that interest.

In Donna Santman's seventh-grade classroom, we focused on other ways to help students take the journey the author wants readers to take. One day we gathered five students together again around one of Hakim's books from *A History of Us.* Donna began by saying, "We're going to take some of the strategies we've been using during literacy time and bring them to social studies. You know how we've tried to notice when a novel turns a corner to ask, 'What does the author want me to know or to think now?' We're going to use this same strategy as we read Joy Hakim." Then Donna asked her students children to read a two-page chapter on Francis Drake and the rise of England as a world power. Be thinking, "What are the categories or sections in this chapter? When does Joy Hakim turn a corner and begin something new? What is the whole chapter saying?" she said.

When one or two of the children reached the end of the assigned chapter, Donna asked them to look over what they had read and get ready to recall it in ways that highlight Hakim's big ideas. Once everyone had finished, Cozy volunteered to try reviewing the text out loud. Pulling in the other four readers, Donna said, "When you listen to Cozy's retelling, compare what *you* would have said to her version."

It was clear to all of us that Cozy retold in a paragraph-by-paragraph fashion. She began, "I'm seeing it was Francis Drake who was after gold, and the Spanish had already stolen it from the native Americans, and now the English wanted to steal it." Then, gesturing to the next paragraph she said, "Drake won. He didn't want to give up. He wanted as much gold as he could and he had a ship. His ship kept getting lower in the water and no one could stop him." Then, pointing farther down the page, "He went all around the world looking for gold and spices. He brought it back to the Queen in England. He was a hero in England but a villain in Spain because he'd stolen so much gold. And after Drake took the gold, the Spanish got mad. They got a bunch of ships to fight against England, and it was obvious Spain would win because they had a bigger army, but it didn't happen that way."

This was a responsible and detailed retelling of the text, but it didn't suggest what Cozy really understood about the history. She had replayed the events in chronological order but their significance was still unclear. The group talked about this. Had Cozy's decision to summarize the chapter in a paragraph-by-paragraph fashion gotten in the way of her conveying the big idea? Donna and I suggested that students try talking about the text by turning to their partners and saying, "The big idea of this chapter was...."

Our colleague Carl Anderson, who has a background in history, was with us that day, so we nudged him to do a retelling. Carl said, "I think this chapter is about one European state—England—rising over another, Spain. In the mid-1500s, Spain was the supreme nation in Europe, and the English, using their guy Drake, tried some guerrilla tactics to get ahead. One of these was to raid Spanish ships for gold. At the end of the chapter, England uses the technology of fast new boats to defeat the old, traditional Spanish navy."

The children tried to figure out what strategies Carl had used that they could adopt. Carl gave them several hints. "First," he said, "I try to fit any one chapter of history into what came before it and even into what will come next, if possible. There is usually a thread being followed. From the title of the section, I know all these chapters, taken together, are supposed to show how England became more and more powerful. I already know this is a book about *American* history and so I gather the point will be that the Colonies, surprisingly, won the Revolutionary War against the powerful nation of England. The next strategy I use is that I try to read the whole chapter and ask, 'What are the one or two things I can name that will hold all this information under that umbrella?' This is another way (like the idea of thinking of what comes before and after this) to try to get a bird's-eye view of the whole text," he said. Carl added, "I don't assume there is a big idea in each paragraph, Cozy. Some paragraphs are important but others aren't. They don't all have equal weight. You can almost read asking which are the key paragraphs? Which are less key?" Finally, Carl said, "We can read trying to determine what the *author* saw as important, or we can read against the grain, looking for what *we* believe is important. We may notice that an author summarizes the history of a nation by telling of the wars that nation fought and we can say, 'I see what this author has emphasized and I disagree. There is more to it than that.'"

Later, when Donna, Carl, and I talked over the challenges of teaching youngsters to read texts in these ways, we realized that experienced readers of history also know a number of stock concepts, patterns, and frameworks and use this knowledge to discern big patterns in the texts they are reading. In the battle between the larger but older Spanish navy and the English boats, Carl had recognized the recurring story of newer technologies rising over and surpassing the older, more traditional ones. Because this construct was already in his mind, he had recognized it in the details of this chapter. When reading fiction, children come to recognize recurring motifs. "Oh!" they say, "This is the Cinderella story all over again!" Or they realize, "Lots of books tell the story of a journey. There are always obstacles along the way in journeys." When children read a lot of history, they need to ask themselves, "What are the recurring motifs within *this* discipline?"

Teaching Readers to Determine What Is More and Less Important

Many researchers stress that in teaching children to read nonfiction, we need to help them learn to distinguish between more and less important ideas. As readers, all of us could benefit from thinking about this very demanding and interesting challenge. My suggestions for teaching children include the following:

- The challenge to "determine what is important" is also about "determining what is unimportant." This challenge also involves coming to understand how ideas are related to each other and how a text structures and presents ideas.

- Some texts will provide a better forum for learning to pick out important ideas than others. Most textbooks are notorious for "concept overload," that is, for presenting everything as if it were of equal importance. In general, the better the writing, the easier it will be to read and discern the author's main ideas (especially if the text is nonnarrative). At this point, it will also be easier to work with shorter texts, because longer texts tend to be more complex in their ideas, their substantiating details, and their structure.

- It will be important to work often with shared texts because this kind of reading is all about "holding ourselves accountable" to the text: other readers in our interpretive community can test our thinking and hold us to a fair rendition of what the text is saying. Then, too, reading a text

in the company of other readers allows us to see that the author's ideas need not be regarded as the final word on a subject. "I see what the author is saying" a reader may say, "But I question the argument because …" We need to plan to help children spend at least a few days reading, rereading, and discussing a single short text, so they learn to lift the level of their work with that text by revisiting and reconsidering it.

- When children read a number of texts about the same event, they see that different authors can put a different spin on an event and highlight different aspects. This can help them understand that history is always an exercise in interpretation and that in reading historical texts, they need to notice the author's point of view. What does one author regard as important? Another author? What do *they* regard as important?

- Once readers have read and discussed a text and constructed an understanding of its big ideas, it is helpful to *reread* it to see how the author fit the pieces of the argument together.

- When we, as teachers, introduce a text, our introduction can give readers a sense of the main ideas in a way which helps them to connect the details and see their significance. Anne Lamott writes in *Bird by Bird* (1999) that as a writer, she sometimes has ornaments but no Christmas tree. Readers can find themselves in the same position, overwhelmed by details, and the introduction can give readers the structure–the Christmas tree.

Teaching Other Skills of Nonfiction Reading

In *Insult to Intelligence,* Frank Smith (1990) describes a published reading program that asks teachers to monitor and teach each of their students as they work toward 486 goals. It is hard for me to imagine trying to teach children well while also keeping in mind hundreds and hundreds of specific goals. Lately, when I read about published programs that are being touted as vehicles for helping teachers teach nonfiction reading, it often seems to me these programs, like the one Smith described, have made the challenge of teaching even just non-fiction reading into something that requires us to juggle 486 goals. Although being a proficient reader of nonfiction surely encompasses a vast number of competencies, it's hard to teach well if we're juggling too many tiny bits and pieces.

Earlier, I quoted Carl's advice to Cozy and her classmates. Carl said that when he reads history, he tries to think, "What are the one or two things I can name that will hold all this information under that umbrella?" He doesn't assume that everything is of equal importance. He tries to read asking, "Which are the key paragraphs? Which are less key?" Carl's advice to these readers of nonfiction is also wise advice for teachers of nonfiction. We need to ask, "What are the one or two ideas I can name that will hold all this information under that umbrella?"

Above all, nonfiction readers are (or should be) especially active. We tend to respond and talk back to nonfiction texts more than to other texts, and it is helpful to encourage children to do this. They might pause and ask themselves "How does this fit with or challenge what I already know?" and "How does this fit with other texts? Why might the two texts be different? What do I make of it?" Nonfiction readers might pause to ask, "What are the big ideas this author seems to be highlighting and how do other less important ideas fit under these big ideas?" or they might think "Can I think of this text as having sections? What are the sections? Where does the author seem "to turn a corner?" What's going on in the different sections?" It is important for nonfiction readers to think, "What is surprising me as I read? What am I thinking?" Finally, nonfiction readers profit from asking, "What do I know about the author? What is the author's point of view? The author's take on things? Do I agree?"

Then, too, it is important to bear in mind that when we read nonfiction, we are usually reading to learn, and the skills of nonfiction reading are the skills of learning. If a child goes to the zoo and categorizes animals based on the kinds of feet they have, that child is in a good position when reading about animals, to categorize those animals in terms of their feet. The best way, then, to help readers become active, assertive readers of words is to first help them become active, assertive readers of worlds.

Say eyes on when your losing focus
9:15
read aloud
writers workshop
11:30
learning adventures
12:25
Wednesday
We can retell by thinking about the
ELEMENTS OF STORY
character- who are the people/animals
in the story
setting- where and when the story
happens to show
takes place over time
change- who or what changes
plot- the important events that
take place

The Elements of Story 22

It is amazing when you think about it. That William Shakespeare, four hundred years ago, could scrawl on pieces of paper and send those words, like a message in a bottle, out into the world, and that today, and even years from today, a reader can open Hamlet to read once more, "To be or not to be, that is the question."

"To completely analyze what we do when we read," wrote E. B. Huey, "would almost be the acme of psychology's achievement. For it would be to describe very many of the most intricate workings of the human mind." Anna Quindlen (1998) likens reading to rubbing two sticks together to make a fire, and the metaphor is a powerful one. How is it that we can take something as pedestrian as print on a page and make words and sentences that tell a story?

Researchers tell us that the spark of reading comes from rubbing together several cueing systems. A child follows the syntax of the sentence as it unrolls and knows from both the structure and the sense what the next word must —, then checks this expectation against the visual information carried by the printed letters of be, and voila! Ink on a page has assumed meaning.

When we read, marks on the page become not only words and sentences but also, sometimes stories. Just as the structure of sentences suggests what the next word might be, the structure of stories makes the rader anticipate that after 'Once upon a time," there will be "in a land faraway" and sense that the lad sharpening his sword in the opening scene of the book will prove to be a player in this tale.

Neither the cueing systems nor the elements of story should be the focal point of a reading curriculum. As Marie Clay reminded me, "Children don't need to *know about* the cueing systems. They just need to use them." None of us expect young readers to fill spiral notebooks with rules on graphophonics and semantics, crosschecking and monitoring for sense. For similar reasons, I find it disturbing when children spend reading time filling spiral notebooks with definitions and diagrams of protagonists and antiheroes, rising and falling action, problems and solutions. I'm convinced that a child who looks up from a good story and talks about "sequence words" or "rising action" is missing out on the good story.

Although I do not want a reading curriculum to focus on either the cueing systems or the elements of story, *teachers* benefit from knowing both. Just as our knowledge of syntax leads us to ask, "Does that sound right?" or "What *could* that word be?" so too, our knowledge of story elements in general and of characters in particular can lead us to ask, "Have you figured out who the narrator is in this story? Is the 'I' the author or a character?"

Our knowledge of story elements, like our knowledge of cueing systems, can help us assess ways in which our students do and do not tend to compose meaning, and these assessments can help us think not only about our children but also about our teaching. Young readers are vulnerable to our instruction. They attend to the cueing systems and story elements to which we attend. If many of my students tackle tricky words by narrowing in on graphophonics without asking, "What would make sense here?" I might be wise to shift the focus of my instruction toward meaning, perhaps encouraging more book orientation and book talk. And if I've decided that my children attend too much to plot and not enough to character, I *wouldn't* ask, "What do you think will happen next? Next? At the end?" Instead, I'd probably angle their predictions by asking, "How do you think this character will change over the course of the story?"

Teaching a balanced literacy curriculum should mean that over time, we help children work with and attend to all cueing systems and all elements of story. Earlier, I suggested that *if* we begin the year in grades 2–8 emphasizing reading a lot of easy books with comprehension and meeting together to retell these books, we might want to follow this work with a unit of study that focuses on thinking and talking about texts. When I suggest shifting from having students recall what the author has said to having them generate their own ideas, I am trying to "run from one side of the ship to the other." But I could also accomplish this goal by suggesting that readers focus on coming to know and care about the characters in stories, or another story element.

This chapter looks at story elements as knowledge that can inform our teaching. Attention to story elements can be woven into all we do: book promotions, conferences during independent reading, guided-reading sessions, and read-aloud work. I will go further to suggest that we might design a unit of study around all story elements or one that spotlights one element only. All of this is described in more detail by my colleague Gaby Layden in her important book, *Using Story Elements to Teach Comprehension* (Scholastic, 2001).

What Are the Elements of Story and How Can We Introduce Them to Our Children?

Last fall, my colleagues Isoke Nia and Gaby Layden investigated the ways in which an awareness of the elements of story can scaffold children's comprehension in reading and their planning in writing. The rest of my staff were research associates and teaching assistants in what turned out to be a grand and glorious inquiry. It began with an effort to distill the elements of story into their simplest and most universal forms. We hoped these elements would function as translucent lenses through which readers and writers could view the unfolding dramas in their reading and writing. Isoke and Gaby were determined not to obscure the children's view of a text with distracting, overly technical terminology. So they gathered together all the terms people use to talk about the components of story and asked themselves which were the truly essential components of *all* stories. It was crucial that their definition of story encompass the personal stories children write about a birthday party perhaps, or a play date. These stories (plus many published ones) do not necessarily contain problems and solutions, tensions and resolutions, "rising and falling action," and in any case, these terms generally fall under the broader element of plot. Usually people identify the elements of story as *character, plot, setting, theme,* and *tone.* Gaby and Isoke decided that as an organizational frame to support children's writing and comprehension of stories, the first three of these elements were the most fundamental. And they also decided that children encounter difficulty in trying to follow changes and movement through time in stories. These could be considered aspects of plot, setting, and character, but to highlight them, Isoke and Gaby decided to list them among the elements of a story. In the end, they taught children to read and write with an eye towards these elements of story:

Characters: The characters are the people or animals who would be up on stage if the story were turned into a play. We hope the characters are believable and that some of them change as the story progresses.

Setting: The setting is the time and place of the story. In talking about a story's setting, readers need to consider the overall context. The setting is

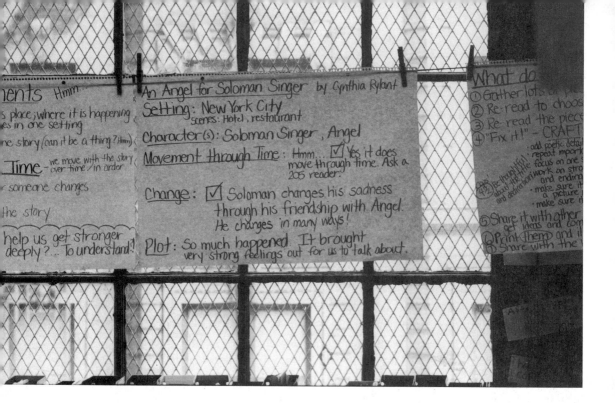

The chart in the photograph reads:

An Angel for Soloman Singer by Cynthia Rylant

Setting: New York City
    Scenes: Hotel, restaurant

Character(s): Soloman Singer, Angel

Movement through Time: Hmm... ☑ Yes it does move through time. Ask a 205 reader.

Change: ☑ Soloman changes his sadness through his friendship with Angel. He changes in many ways!

Plot: So much happened. It brought very strong feelings out for us to talk about.

(Left chart, partially visible)
...ents Hmm:
...s place; where it is happening
...es in one setting
...ne story (can it be a thing? Hmm)
Time - we move with the story - over time / in order
...r someone changes
...the story
...help us get stronger deeply? .. To understand!

(Right chart, partially visible)
What do...
① Gather lots...
② Re-read to choos...
③ Re-read the piec...
④ "Fix it!" - CRAFT
    • add poetic detai...
    • repeat import...
    • focus on one...
    • work on stro...
    • and ending
    • make sure it...
    • a picture
    • make sure...
⑤ Share it with other...
⑥ get ideas and com...
⑦ Print them and...
⑧ Share with the...

the country, state, or town, not only the scene of the action. When a character walks from one part of the house to the other, the scene changes but the setting doesn't change.

Plot: The plot is the sequence of events in the story. Writers deliberately order and highlight events to create the plot, which may not represent the actual chronological sequence of events. For example, the writer might use flashbacks to produce suspense, tension, conflict, and resolution.

Movement through time: Time always passes in a story. Writers use various techniques (the changing color of leaves, a child's eyes growing heavy, the sounds of an oncoming and then deporting train whistle, time markers, sequence words) to suggest the passage of time, which is always evident in the plot and often in the setting and the characters.

Change: In a story, there must be change. Either the characters, the setting, or the actions change. Often change is a result of a conflict and resolution, but not always.

Just as cueing systems are meant to work in synchrony with each other, so are these elements of story. If a child retelling the plot of a story says that the young man enlisted in the armed services, this event alone doesn't tell the whole story. What about the setting? Did the character live in Hawaii and enlist just after the bombing of Pearl Harbor? If the story says that the youngest son journeys from home in search of a dragon to slay, we need to know whether the setting is a time and place in which people believe in dragons. Perhaps the tradition is for sons to stay at home, to settle down near their mothers' house and grow gardens full of vegetables. It may be, then, that the real act of courage in this story has less to do with dragons than with leaving home in the first place.

Ideally, children grow up developing a felt sense for story elements. I recall a time when Miles, then four, asked if I'd play Legos with him. I agreed, and he scampered ahead of me down the steps to our basement playroom calling, "I'll set up the story." By the time I arrived at the Lego table, his play figure and mine already had distinguishing traits (a cape, a hat), names, histories, and homes. An enemy ship appeared on the horizon. Miles had instinctively relied on story elements to create a drama that would be satisfying and compelling for us both. I know this felt sense comes from years of repeated encounters with stories, but I hope that for children who have not grown up on stories, we, as teachers, can find ways to help them grow quickly into this knowledge.

When I do book promotions in order to recommend books, I am aware that a good book summary usually includes the story elements. Without drawing attention to this fact, I give an overview of the characters, settings, plot, and movement through time and change. And when the read-aloud book has grown cold and I want to retell the text, I am apt to rely on story elements again as I leaf back through the pages and say, "So, let's see. You'll remember this is the story of three farmers." If I pull alongside a child during independent reading, and I don't know the book the child is reading, I rely on what I *do* know about story elements to carry on a conversation about the book. I can safely ask questions like these that follow, knowing that if the child is comprehending the story, the questions will probably yield answers:

- What's the setting of this story? (Oh! So it's in a house ... but *where* do you suppose that house is? Do you have any clues? Is it set in modern times or in history? What makes you think that?)

- Who is the narrator of the story? What are you led to believe about the "I" in the story?

- Tell me about the main character. What kind of a person is he or she? How does the author let you know?

- How much time has passed since the opening episode in the book? Does time jump around or unroll evenly? Does time pass slowly in some places and quickly in others? Can you show me one of those places?

- I see you are reading a third book in this series! Tell me, are these characters in all seven books within the series? Do they change between the books? Do the minor characters still seem to be minor, and the major ones, major? Is the setting the same through all the books in this series?

- So what are the important changes in the story? What changes do you predict there will be?

When I work with children in conferences or guided-reading sessions, I often find it helpful to think and talk with them about the challenges particular chapter books present. I often ask myself whether it is the number of characters that pose difficulties in this book, or the movement through time, or the setting. If several children are reading historical fiction, I may gather them together for a strategy lesson to emphasize the importance of imagining the setting. If a child is reading a book with a lot of characters, I may work with readers to devise ways to keep all these people straight. If time jumps about in confusing ways, I may first walk readers through some of the places where this happens, or I may simply ask them to watch for and flag places where time jumps backwards and forwards with Post-it notes so we can talk about these places specifically.

Isoke Nia and Gaby Layden have helped my colleagues and me see that our knowledge of story elements serves as a resource we can draw upon often as we teach reading: we incorporate story elements into what we are already teaching, but we also find it fruitful to spend a few weeks teaching a unit of study that puts the elements of story into children's hands directly. I emphasize directness and simplicity here, because when teachers work for weeks to evoke from students elaborate and complex definitions of story elements, these terms can become the *content* rather than the *tools* of a reading workshop.

Gaby Layden was wise when she tried to put the elements into the hands of youngsters at P.S. 116 in Manhattan by simply saying, "I'm going to read 'A Play,' a story excerpt from Eloise Greenfield's (1979) *Childtimes,* and I want you to listen for what we call the story elements. These elements are things that go together to make *any* story. So listen for the *characters,* the *setting* (that's the where and the when), the *plot* (what happens), the *movement through time* (how things progress through time), and for *changes* that happen as the story unfolds." Afterwards, Gaby said, "Can you retell 'The Play' to your partner, including all these story elements?"

To agree upon the characters, the movement through time, and so forth, Gaby, Isoke, and the teachers and children at P.S. 116 had some talking to do. Some children were confused over what constituted a character in a story and needed to learn from Isoke that if a character talks or thinks about a distant person, that distant person is *not also a character* unless he or she makes an appearance "on the stage" of the story. Then, too, children at first thought that when a character walked from the hallway into a room, the setting changed. Isoke and Gaby explained that a story's setting is its geographical context, its place on the planet, and that what had in fact changed was the *scene*, not the *setting*. We can often deduce a lot about the setting even if we're not given a specific geographical location. We may decide that one story is set in the 1950s on a huge longhorn cattle ranch in an arid western state such as Wyoming or Utah, or that another story is set in a section of a city filled with brownstones and coffee shops.

At first, when Gaby and Isoke asked children to use the story elements to retell "A Play," most predictably turned this into a fill-in-the-blank exercise: "The characters are …," they said, "The setting is…." And so the P.S. 116 teachers challenged them to weave these elements into a fluid retelling of "A Play," a retelling that almost felt like the story itself.

Once They've Learned the Elements of Story, Children Can Use Them to Support Their Independent Reading

After this minilesson on story elements, Gaby and Isoke sent children off to do their own independent reading, encouraging these readers to think about the author's use of story elements as they read. Later, when readers met with partners, they knew that today and for the next few days they would use the story elements to retell their independent reading books. Of course, readers didn't always *know* all the elements of story in their books, since many are only revealed midway through. But they were told, "By the time you've finished the first chapter or two, you should expect to have met the characters. Know their names, their relationships to each other, and their traits. Expect also to know the story's setting." It is reasonable to ask whether it is wise for readers to consciously attend to story elements while they read. We tend to think that *for a time,* focusing on story elements probably adds new dimensions to a child's experience of stories. After all, when we read we compose our own mental text, parallel to the text on the page, and in order to be a satisfying, whole text, it must have all the story elements.

When I travel a new route, I already know approximately when I should keep an eye out for highway signs. In a similar way, it can be helpful for a reader traveling through a new text benefits from being conscious of the significant elements. If I've driven for hours and seen no signs for the Massachusetts Turnpike, I know enough to wonder if I've missed the exit. If a child has read three chapters and still hasn't any notion of the story's setting, that child would be wise to look back and see if she missed a sign. In this way, the story elements can function as a comprehension check.

Not long after Isoke and Gaby sent children off to do their independent reading, Randalio approached Gaby, book in hand. "I'm sorry to interrupt," he said, "but this time it *is* an emergency. I don't have a setting in my book." Gaby smiled at Randalio's sense that this was an emergency, thinking, "You are right. Sirens *should* be going off in your head if there is no setting." And the two of them looked back through Barbara Robinson's *The Best School Year Yet*. The author hadn't placed the drama in a specific state or town, but after a closer look, Randalio could infer a lot about the setting. He and Gaby found clues that made them guess that the setting was a small city or a big town, perhaps in Ohio or Pennsylvania, the states in which the author has lived:

- The high school has at least three floors (Imogene was locked into a third floor room), so this probably isn't a tiny rural town. On the other hand, the narrator lives in a house that has a backyard (they go there to wash tattoos off the baby), so it's unlikely that this is a major city like New York City.
- Within walking distance of the characters' homes, there is a town hall, a laundromat, a gas station, a grocery store, and enough people that crowds gather quickly at several of these places.
- The town has a welfare office.
- There is a dairy farm within range of a school field trip.
- People from South Dakota drive into town, and South Dakota is regarded as a faraway place. Children refer to Chicago as if they know it.
- There is a reference to snow, which suggests that the region has seasons.

It's not usual for readers to find that the setting in a book eludes them. It is less common for children to overlook plot. There are lots of ways, however, in which we can help children think with more sophistication about plot.

I worked with of four children who'd been reading Jerry Spinelli's *Wringer* together. I first asked them to summarize the events in the order they had occurred in *Wringer*. "Let me stop you for a moment," I interrupted. "From what you are telling me, the main character's life—Palmer's life—unfolds *differently* in fact than in the story. I mean, if you drew a line here and put the events of Palmer's life on it, in chronological order, you'd get a timeline that doesn't exactly match the sequence of events in the plot of *Wringer,* right?" We charted the events. Then I asked, "Why do you suppose the two don't match exactly? Why did Jerry Spinelli put some things that happened long ago in Wringer's life *at the end of the book?* What purpose does that changed sequence serve?" Soon the four children were each reviewing their copies of the books and their timelines, preparing for a further conversation with me on the topic.

We can help children think about plot in more complex ways.

At first we:	Later we:
• Ask children for a point-by-point retelling of the sequence of events thus far, focusing the discussion on what happened (first this happened, then this, then this), and emphasizing the sequence of events with words like *first, next,* and *then.*	• Help children summarize the main events in the book so far, highlighting the *patterns* in the actions (for example, characters get involved in one escapade after another, but always invent ingenious ways to save their skin).
• Focus on what happened.	• Focus not only on what happened but also on *why* these

The Elements of Story   467

events occurred. We emphasize the forces behind the sequence of events with phrases like *because, the reason was,* or *the main problem was.* We consider what might have brought about these events. What did the characters want? What was the central conflict?

- Talk about what happened in a text almost as if it actually happened and the text is a report on reality: "I felt sorry for him." "I hope he gets out okay."

- Emphasize that the text is the creation of the author. Authors don't *record* a story, they imagine it and create it. Our questions can reflect our knowledge that decisions behind the text are all deliberate. "Why might she have decided to start it this way?" "Why did she emphasize that one event?" "What will she have happen next?"

- Act as if the purpose of the plot is simply to show what happens.

- Talk about the plot as a vehicle for conveying ideas. How does the plot or structure of the book support its main message?

When we help students focus on the *movement through time* aspect of a plot, we're also helping them make important strides toward comprehension. When a child's understanding of a book is garbled, the problem can often be traced to an overlooked time marker: perhaps the story had a flashback to earlier events; if the reader missed it the result is confusion. Readers can help themselves by flagging an author's often subtle time markers. It is equally helpful for readers to know that, if they find that their grasp of the story is slipping, the problem may be a missed time marker. Perhaps the paragraph isn't about today's events but about the character's memories or his dreams for the future. Beginning readers know they need to monitor for sentence sense, and more intermediate readers can learn to monitor for *story* sense. Instead of rereading the *sentence* looking for a miscue, intermediate readers can reread or rescan the chapter looking for the point at which their comprehension became derailed.

Within a study of story elements, there are many ways to familiarize students with the broad themes and common central conflicts of literature. When Melanie brings me Gary Paulsen's *Hatchet* and says, "Lucy, here's *another* book about a kid having a hard time adventure outside," I can tell her that she has discovered an all-time classic conflict in literature, "person vs. nature." I can also tell her that some people classify almost all literature into the following categories:

- person vs. nature
- person vs. person
- person vs. society
- person vs. himself or herself

I could suggest to Melanie that she might want to launch an in-depth study of person vs. nature books, and I could send her off with a short list of books, including Jack London's *The Call of the Wild,* Farley Mowat's *Lost in the Barrens,* Jean Craighead George's *My Side of the Mountain,* and Gary Paulsen's *The Haymeadow.* Or, I could challenge her to search for an example of each of the four main kinds of conflict in literature. Perhaps she could think back over the books she's read and try to classify them according to these categories or to new categories she might make.

Developing a Unit of Study on Characters

In most of our classrooms, teachers and students spend a couple of weeks on a character unit of study. In first- and second-grade classrooms, this usually happens within a cycle of reading centers (see Chapter 16). Two or four readers will gather around a study of Ludwig Bemelmans' *Madeline,* and another two or four around Pat Hutchins' *Titch* or Louis Sachar's *Marvin Redpost* or Beverly Cleary's *Ramona.* During each day's minilesson, the teacher leads a whole-class character study, perhaps on Frog in Arnold Lobel's *Frog and Toad* series or on Martha in James Marshall's *George and Martha* series. During these minilessons we might tell kids, for example, that when we read books, we pay attention to what a story character does because sometimes actions give us a window into

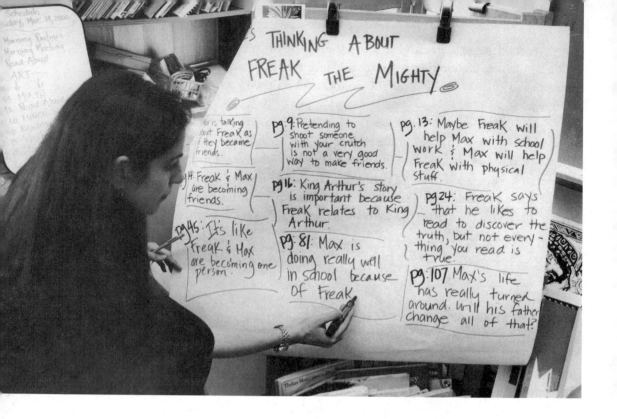

THINKING ABOUT
FREAK THE MIGHTY

... is talking about Freak as if they became friends.

pg. 9: Pretending to shoot someone with your crutch is not a very good way to make friends.

pg. 13: Maybe Freak will help Max with school work & Max will help Freak with physical stuff.

pg 4: Freak & Max are becoming friends.

pg 16: King Arthur's story is important because Freak relates to King Arthur.

pg 24: Freak says that he likes to read to discover the truth, but not everything you read is true.

pg 45: It's like Freak & Max are becoming one person.

pg. 81: Max is doing really well in school because of Freak.

pg. 107 Max's life has really turned around. Will his father change all of that?

personalities, revealing the kind of person a character is. "If you saw someone kicking a trashcan and shouting, 'Darn it all,' what would you think about that person?" I asked a group of first graders. They agreed that they'd think she was angry. "So listen to what Frog is doing in the next pages," I said, "and then I'm going to ask you to turn and talk about what kind of a guy Frog seems to be." Soon I was sending these readers to their reading centers with the assignment to read their book, pausing often to ask "What does this character's actions suggest about him or her?" Another time, a whole class will try ways of thinking about characters suggested by children instead of us as teachers: "The *Titch* group asked questions about their character. They wondered how old Titch is, and looked for clues. We could all ask questions about our characters."

Some upper-grade teachers do a fall unit of study on characters or on story elements in general, but most of us bring this unit to our book clubs (see Chapter 20). We ask members of each book club to settle on a character they'd like to study for a few weeks. Some clubs work with a character from a series of novels, such as Brian in Gary Paulsen's *Hatchet* series. Other clubs use picturebooks for their character studies. In our minilessons, we'll often read an early reader chapter book aloud. Although these books are generally written for first- and second-grade readers, they are an efficient way to highlight for upper-elementary children the strategies readers can use to think about characters across several texts. If we do a character study using the *Frog and Toad* books, in a single day we can read two of these books aloud and in the minilesson show children ways to talk between the books.

Kathleen Tolan suggested that her fifth graders look over Lobel's books observing and thinking about Toad's character, and then look again to find evidence in support of their ideas. A few of her students suggested that Frog and Toad might be a gay couple and found "evidence" when Frog sat on Toad's bed, when the two hugged each other, and most of all when Toad, at one point, "came out of the closet." Whether their theory was or wasn't correct, the process was a good lesson and one they could transfer to the more complex chapter books they were reading and discussing in their book clubs.

Readers soon learn that when studying a character, we notice details about the character and consider what traits these details reveal. The author who tells us that a character is constantly sweeping the kitchen floor might want us to infer that the character is tidy. Readers could go a step further and wonder if she is uptight or simply proud of her home? In their reading centers or book clubs, groups of children work collaboratively on charts in which they list data about a character in one column and notes about what they infer in a second column.

If readers notice patterns and generalize about how a character tends to act, they can consider why: is he just plain mean, or is he acting this way because he's been overlooked all his life? They can try to understand the motivations behind a character's actions. They can realize that "bad guys" aren't all bad, and good characters aren't perfect. They can notice, too, when a character acts "out of character." Has the character changed? If so, what might have contributed to the change?

In a whole-class character study, teachers can help children think about how characters are like us or like someone we know. Usually we'll begin with small, concrete connections. "I like chocolate ice cream, too," we'll say. But if we think and talk longer, there's often the possibility of deeper connections. "I can't eat ice cream that often. My parents say no, and they are around me all the time. In this book, she's on her own a lot. Maybe that's because it's a different country, or because the author doesn't want too many people in her story."

Sometimes teachers encourage readers to act the part of (dramatize) or to envision (draw) a particular character. I've watched as members of a book club compared sketches of a particular character and talk about how one reader's picture differs from another's. These children then referred back to the book and to their own lives for evidence that substantiated their particular view.

Amanda Hartman's P.S. 165 third graders use a variety of charts to anchor their discussions of characters. Sometimes they jot what a character does in one column, and what conclusions they draw from these actions in a second column as Ramon has done.

I've encouraged readers to think about the ways in which characters are like and unlike each other—within one book, across several books, or between a book and our own lives. Of course, even if two characters are similar, there's always more to discuss. Why are they so similar? What about them is similar? How are they different, despite these similarities? Do the authors use different techniques to depict the two similar characters?

In Hannah Schneewind's second grade, readers often talk about book characters as if they were real. How would the character like this school? What would the character play at recess? What books would the character probably be reading right now? What makes us think these things?

Of course, unless the needs of the children dictate it, we needn't study character in particular. Any element of story—classic or class-invented—can serve as the basis for a whole-class unit of study. In some classrooms, students have taken on the topic of setting, examining the obvious and subtle ways authors convey the place and time of their story. This exploration led to gloriously complicated questions about textbook-style nonfiction writing: "What is the setting in a science book, and why is it like that?" and about correspondence: "Does a letter need a setting?" In other classrooms, students have studied tone by examining works in different genres by the same author, and then bringing what they learn to their own writing. Studies of plot, conflict, movement through time, resolution, and many other story components can change the depth and caliber of both children's reading and writing.

Giving Our Students Tools and Strategies to Interpret Texts 23

I still remember my high school English teacher asking about *The Great Gatsby,* "What does the light at the end of the dock *mean?*" I remember thinking, "What do *you* mean, 'What does the light at the end of the dock mean?' It means a light, a lantern, at the end of the dock, the pier." But I knew my answer wasn't what he had in mind. So I cast about for an answer that might be symbolic enough and ventured a guess: "Heaven?"

Scanning the classroom, the teacher asked, "Any other ideas?" Another brave soul risked an answer. "Any other ideas?" Soon the room settled into silence. Opening the text, the teacher proceeded to deliver a complex discourse on its themes and symbols. I remember listening to what he said, looking down at the text before me, and thinking "How on earth did you get *that* from *this?*"

Only years later did I realize that my teacher's interpretation came not from the text but from his *Cliff Notes* on the novel. At the time, I had decided that I must not have a symbolic mind. This was sad news. I had always liked reading, writing, and drama and figured that I'd major in English someday. But my light-at-the-end-of-the-dock disability put an end to those ambitions. I took a few English courses in college, but whenever I was asked to write a literary essay, I dug through the prose of famous critics, translating their high-flown interpretations into my own words as best I could.

Now, years later, I can look back and see that my high school English teacher disenfranchised me as a reader. His message was that there is one right interpretation to the text and that I didn't have access to that it. I felt certain others were endowed with an acuity, a gift, I didn't have. Teachers often give a similar message to young writers. Many children grow up believing that *real* writers sit at their desks, quill pen in hand, and out flows brilliant, graceful prose. If these children try their own hands at writing, they are dismayed to see that their own first lines are halting and full of gaps and blunders. But in the field of writing, more and more children are discovering that even famous writers produce first drafts that are halting and full of gaps and blunders. More and more children are coming to realize that the difference between most of us and experienced authors is that these authors have more tools and are more inclined to return to their early drafts, extending, repairing, and enlivening what they have written. The implication is that we need not look at what we first put on the page and despair. Young readers need to learn a similar lesson.

I grew up believing that *real* readers took their leather-bound books in hand and read. At some point, they paused to make brilliant, perceptive comments on the dense, confusing text they were so effortlessly reading. Meanwhile, however, I always knew that when *I* looked up from reading, my ideas weren't coherent, clear, or compelling at all. Instead, I might mutter a question and point at a good part. I was certain that my first response to a text was nothing close to the interpretation my literature teacher expected. How I wish I'd been taught that even the most experienced readers can respond to a text with muttered questions, incoherent ideas, and stars up and down the margins of the page. How I wish I'd been taught that the difference between experienced readers and the rest of us is that the experts have the strategies, the tools, and the inclination to extend and deepen their first responses to a text.

Teaching synthesis and interpretation is about teaching a process, not a product. Just as we do not say to young writers, "This is how your poem should go," writing it for them, we do not say to young readers, "This text is a coming-of-age novel, showing a boy's struggle to separate from his parents. The hammer signifies all the ambivalence the boy feels." Instead, we coach our students to extend their own strategies and interpretations.

This chapter is about teaching interpretation as a process. It discusses

- Getting started by asking the right questions
- Moving our students beyond a literal understanding by opening up and digging into texts
- Interpreting a text from the vantage point of its ending.

It then visits a classroom and discusses the heart of interpreting: the interplay between the details of a text and its Big Ideas.

Getting Started by Asking the Right Questions

It is hard to help students develop their own interpretations. I recently read one of Katherine Paterson's (1989) essays in which she takes a step back from the body of her work and considers what it is she's been trying to say all along. She writes, "When I look at the books I have written, the first thing that I see is the outcast child searching for a place to stand. But the next thing that I see is the promise of such a place. Terabithia is the most obvious return to Eden in my books" (p. 112).

As I read Paterson's words and copy them down, I want to rush into classrooms and ask youngsters, "What do *you* think Katherine Paterson is really trying to say in *Bridge to Terabithia?* In *The Great Gilly Hopkins?*" And if I can rein myself in to wait the necessary three minutes, some children might mutter something, but I know that by then I will jump in and ask, "Do you think *maybe,* in all her books, Paterson has written about an outcast child who is searching for a place to stand? Could Terabithia represent Eden, the perfect place that in this world exists only in our imaginations?" My pleasure in stumbling on the *right* answer to the question "What are Paterson's books *really* about?" (after all, I have it from the horse's mouth) comes from the feeling that I'm no longer going to be so empty-handed when it comes to teaching these texts. As a teacher of reading, I long to have some old-fashioned content to deliver in an old-fashioned way to my students. How nice it is to approach my teaching confident that I have the right answer in my pocket. Now I have something concrete to say, something my students can copy into their notebooks that will stand them in good stead in the future.

But will it? What do my students gain by writing in their notebooks that *Bridge to Terabithia* is a book about an outcast child searching for a place to stand? Is it not also a book about bridges, such as the friendship between Jess and Leslie, and about how we, as human beings, deal with terrible loss? Then, too, although I have the right answer to the question, "What does the light at the end of the dock mean?" in my old notebooks, that "right answer" was not at all the right answer for me as an earnest young girl, yearning to take my love of books and plays into an English major and a career around books. It was a wrong answer for me, because it made me believe that what *I* saw in the book was worthless, that I didn't have even a starting point for an acceptable response. My high school English teacher would have given me something much more right if he had said, "When I read this book, at first I wondered why everyone makes a fuss over it. To me, it seemed like a plain, ordinary story about…. But I've been going back over it, trying to figure out if the author is trying to say something bigger. I keep returning to this scene with the light at the end of the dock, because it all changes here. And I've been wondering what the light at the end of the dock *might mean?*" If my suggestion that the light signified heaven was an outrageous and awful one, my teacher would have been so much wiser to say, "Let's play that idea out and see if it works. If the light at the end of the dock is heaven, then how do the first few chapters fit in?"

Teaching interpretation means teaching students a process that, for the rest of their lives, will yield big, thoughtful responses to texts. If we merely teach our students that *Frog and Toad* is a book about friends who are different, or that *Bridge to Terabithia* is a story of an outcast child searching for a place to stand, our goals are trivial. In the whole scheme of things, why does it matter whether a child can repeat back the teacher's interpretation of a text?

When I see colleagues clinging to teacher's guides and *Cliff Notes,* I know we hold tight to these props because too many of us were taught that we don't have symbolic minds. We were taught that our own naked, inadequate ideas about books can't be the starting point for something compelling and significant. The first step is to let go of these props and to say to kids, "I'm not sure what this book is really saying, are you?" and, "Let's go back and think more about it together." But it is also true that all responses to books are not equal, and the question remains, "What *are* the strategies good readers use to develop responsible, wise interpretations of texts?" The first interpretation strategy good readers use is to ask themselves any one or two of these questions:

- What is really important about this story?
- What does this story say about the world?
- What does this story say about my life?
- What is the point of this story for me?
- Why was it written?
- What is the story, all together, trying to tell me?
- What is this story *really* about?
- What is the story underneath the story?
- What is the moral of the story?
- What is the story's theme?
- How would I change myself if I took this story seriously?
- Does it matter if people read this story or not? Why should or shouldn't they?

Moving Our Students Beyond a Literal Understanding By Opening Up and Digging Into Texts

We as teachers tend to respond to interpretative questions in one of two ways: we reduce and package the text into a moral that could, as David Bartholomae (1986) says, "fit inside a fortune cookie" ("This is about man's struggle with man" or "Time flies"); or we are even more moralistic, saying, "She should be nicer" or "Blacks and whites should be friends." These are excellent starting points—but they are only starting points.

Now, with this encapsulated theory of what the whole text says, we can go back to the book and look at it through this particular lens. How does each part of the story fit into the larger telling of the message? We can go through the story bit by bit, checking to see if the message plays out in each of the story elements, and if it does, seeing it in all it's complexities and contradictions. Why are black people and white people not nice to each other sometimes? Why is this one particular character able to see through the prejudices around her when so many others can't? What makes some characters change? Who doesn't change, and how does that add to the message?

By working with students to view a text in light of the overall interpretation they have proposed, we can help them develop a felt sense of what it is like to open up an entirely new layer within a story. With the read-aloud or with short, shared texts, we can structure how children move toward puzzling through, playing with, and reading these layers of text. They can see that every episode takes on another, deeper meaning. If a student theorizes that his book is telling him to look at the hard side and not always take the nicest version of the truth, he might interpret in a new way a chapter in which the hero refuses a bite of cake and instead eats spoiled meat. This passage may convey the message in a new way, through metaphor. By having a character step out of the shadows, is the writer offering us another way of saying that the boy is moving away from his prejudice? As they begin to understand and practice interpretation, students can begin to ask themselves, "How do story elements like setting, characters, plot, and movement through time each contribute to a text's overall message?

Another way readers tend to respond to the interpretive questions I listed is by hiding. We say "What do you think the author is trying to say" and readers avoid the question either by simply rereading a section of the text as an answer to the question or by retelling the plot. The latter response is especially common in Teachers College Reading and Writing Project classrooms, because our emphasis on retelling at the start of the year complements the hesitation many of us tend to already feel if we are expected to replace the words of an author with our own inadequate words about a text. This is a fairly universal hesitance. It is almost as if readers don't feel that we have the authority to speak about this text, and so we hide behind the author's words and plot. While this is understandable, readers *need* to talk back to texts (by which I mean replacing the author's words with their own) and readers need to trust their own voice and their own thinking.

It is important to notice that when we, as readers, try to hold onto (and even to retell) *exactly* what the author has said, we often inadvertently *miss* what the author has said. Donna Santman tells a story about her seventh graders: "I'm reading aloud Joseph Bruchac's *The Heart of a Chief.* It's a contemporary American Indian story that takes place on a fictitious Indian reservation. In the story, there is a debate about whether or not a casino should be built, and the youngsters go to a field where they hang out often." Donna paused. "So listen, Lucy," she says to me, wanting my full attention: "The kids retell what happens in that field like this: 'There are a lot of wooden stakes. They gather the stakes into a big pile and make a bonfire and sit around it, hearing the sirens as fire trucks approach and they ask themselves if they should run or stay.'" Then Donna said, "They get the exact sequence of what happened but they totally miss what *really* happened, which was that the characters had a protest."

Minilessons and Conferences Teach Students to Move Between Details and Big Ideas

For children who are retelling the details but losing the significance of the story, we have developed a sequence of work that can help. We think of this sequence as one way to teach inference, a necessary step in interpretation. We use variations on this progression to teach readers to envision, predict, ask questions and a host of other strategies.

We enlarge and project a page or two of the text on an overheard projector or make multiple copies. Then we read aloud as the class follows the text and we pause at key sections: "So what I think is *really* going on is …" or "What I'm thinking here is that …" we say. I read aloud a page and a half of *Just Juice* by Karen Hesse. At the start of the book, the mother spreads grape jelly "so thin on the sliced white bread, you can hardly find the purple." A page later, the girl, Juice, thinks about the paper lunch bag: "Even after I've used the bag all week and it's as limp as a dishrag, I still like opening it and taking out that jelly sandwich." Reading these sections, I pause to say, "I'm getting the idea that Juice's family is really poor. That's why they don't have much jelly on their sandwiches and why they recycle brown paper bags." I may continue to do demonstrations such as this one several times as we read one page. This may involve several minilessons.

Eventually the time comes when, after I have read a section, instead of modeling the inferences I'm making, I nudge students to make their own. "So, what's *really* going on here?" I ask or "What does the author want us to realize?" I suggest children talk in pairs about these questions. After partnership conversations, I may call on several partners to bring their thoughts into the circle.

If most students can read the words of the text, I ask them to continue reading on their own. I usually mark one or two places where I think it will be particularly fruitful for readers to pause and think "What's *really* going on?" Now I ask children to read silently and to jot down their inferences about these sections. When they have finished, I ask them to talk in pairs about their inferences. Then we may go over their ideas together to construct a rich and accountable response to questions such as, "What's really going on here?" or "What does the author want us to think here?" I may repeat this work over several minilessons, and new realizations about the process emerge as the class does this work together.

Next I give readers a short text (which again assumes they can all read it) and ask them to read it with pen in hand, thinking "Where should I pause to ask 'What's *really* going on?' or to wonder 'What does the author want me to be thinking?'" I ask them to stop at least three times as they read through the text and each time, to jot what's really going on. Afterwards we talk about this in partnerships or small groups and then as a class.

Finally I ask readers to read their independent reading book and to pause to jot notes (or talk) at least a few times during that day's independent reading workshop, asking "What does the author want me to realize here?" or "What's this *really* about?" I ask readers to talk in their partnerships about these questions for the next week or two.

After working through these steps recently with a group of fourth graders, I moved about the classroom conferring with them. My goal was to help children draw inferences, synthesize, and interpret. Ryan, who just finished reading the first four chapters of Gary Paulsen's *The Cookcamp,* said, "It was a really slow beginning. Paulsen could have just cut out off the first two chapters and started when the boy got to camp."

"Why *didn't* Paulsen do that?" I responded. "What is the role this slow section plays in the story?" Then I went on, "Unless you are saying Paulsen is a bad author, you have to trust that there's a reason *why* this book starts the way it does. Will you look back and think "What *might* Paulsen want me to be thinking or feeling or realizing? What am I supposed to get out of these long, slow chapters?"

A bit later, Ryan told me he'd figured out why the beginning was lonely, long, and dull: that's how things felt to the boy who'd been sent alone on a two-day trip to a road-camp in the Canadian wilderness. "The camp wasn't much but it felt warm and like home because it came at the end of all that," he said. Later, when I told the class about Ryan's discovery, I wanted them to see that authors deliberately write in certain ways. It helps to ask why the author added a section, a character, or a flashback.

Later, Seb retold *Freckle Juice,* emphasizing that the main character kept falling out of his chair. "Why does Judy Blume have him falling out of his chair?" I asked. This was really the same question I'd asked Ryan after we discussed the lead of *The Cookcamp:* "Why might the author have written it this way?" This question reminds readers that the words in this text are deliberate and intended to accomplish an effect. Teaching interpretation means teaching readers to ask themselves "What is this author really trying to tell me?"

"I think we're supposed to know he is clumsy," Seb answered. I pressed on, as I tend to do, to ask how the character's clumsiness fit into the whole story of wanting to buy a formula for freckles. Seb wasn't sure. I suggested we reread the pages to ask "What's *really* going on?" This time, Seb and I could see that Judy Blume had made her character fall on the floor not out of clumsiness but out of desperation, trying to reach for the precious frecklejuice formula. One way to help our students develop responsible, plausible interpretations is to suggest that students pause after a section to ask "What might the author want me to be thinking?"

Interpretation also involves developing a sense of the accumulated text, seeing any one episode within the context of the entire text. Donna Santman and I gathered five of her seventh graders together and told them we wanted them to read the first page and a half of Allen Sherman's short story "A Gift of Laughter." Then we said, "Afterwards we're going to ask you to retell this story in a way that spotlights the important things." When one or two children finished reading ahead of the others, we suggested that they rehearse a retelling in their heads. Once everyone was finished, we asked Sam to retell, saying to the others, "Listen closely because we'll be rethinking Sam's retelling."

> Alan Sherman was in the living room talking to his wife about the money problems the family had when their son Robbie came out with a picture, "Daddy, Daddy, Daddy," and his father thought it was important and said, "Let me see" but when it was just a drawing, his Dad said, "Is *this* why you interrupted" and the little kid slams the door.

Then we discussed the story again, asking, "What does the author want us to get here?" and "Did Sam's retelling build up the section that was most important to the author?" Now Jory took her turn at retelling.

> In this story a man is worrying with his wife about finances, when the man hears his son yell, "Daddy" and then his son bursts into the room to show his father a picture he'd drawn. The father looks at the picture of a man who needs a shave and scoffs at it, and says, "*This* is what you thought was so important?" and the child Robbie says, "Fine, but it's your birthday on Saturday" and now the father sees his name under the picture and knows how his son feels because the father remembers a time when he was young and felt the same way.

Discussing the two versions, the children realized that Jory put more emphasis on the part that seemed important to the whole story. Later, I pointed out that we'd all bypassed the title of the story, "A Gift of Laughter," in our retellings. I raised this point not because the title seemed so important but because in helping children develop their interpretive ability, one powerful strategy they can use is to ask, "Does my interpretation of the text account for all its parts?" When readers try to account for all the elements of the text in their interpretation, the resulting revisions in their thinking can add a new layer of significance.

Interpreting a Text from the Vantage Point of Its Ending

Although readers interpret the text as they progress through it, they also construct an interpretation when they reach the end. Another way to nudge readers to interpret a text, is to ask them to do more when they reach the end.

Kathleen Tolan knew there were only six pages left in her read-aloud book, *The Giver*, by Lois Lowry. Her children also knew this would be the day they heard the book's final words, and someone said, "I don't want it to end."

"I know," Kathleen said. "So often when I see the book's last pages, I start reading really slowly, because I can't bear for the story to end." Then, pausing to be sure everyone was attentive, Kathleen said, "Today we'll be reading the end of *The Giver*, and I've been thinking about what you all do when you get to the end of a book. Who'll be finishing a book soon?" Eight hands went up. "And how many of you finished a book recently?" More hands went up. "Well, sometimes during the reading workshop, I watch you guys come to the end of a book and—watch me—this is what you do." Kathleen scanned the last page of a book and then slammed the book shut so hard that her hair blew into her face. Then she stowed the book immediately on the book shelf. "You just slam it shut. 'I'm done' you say, 'That's it!' I am always surprised, because for me, finishing a book is like reaching the top of a mountain. When I get to the end, I don't just turn around and race down the mountain. I like to linger there at the end, the top, and look back at the whole view. The whole path looks different once I reach the end. That's how it is for me with a book."

That day, Kathleen suggested that after the class heard the final words of *The Giver*, everyone in the room should sit, silent, for a moment. "Then I'll motion to you all to take fifteen minutes in our small groups. Each group can invent some way to look back to take in the whole of the book. Then try your way of looking over the terrain with *The Giver*. We'll be talking about *The Giver* for more than a week," she said, "So you'll have plenty of time to use the ways-to-linger your group invents," Kathleen said.

When Kathleen finished reading *The Giver*, the groups of children dispersed, each with a copy or two of the book. Fifteen minutes later they assembled back on the carpet. A spokesperson from the first group said her group had thought back to their favorite sections and reread one of them in light of the whole book. "We *were* going to reread the others but we got into a huge talk. So that's our plan for the next few days: we reread a part and talk about what that one tiny part has to do with the whole book. Then we'll go to another part." A second group revisited an issue the class discussed earlier, thinking about that issue now in light of the entire text. Yet a third group put *The Giver* alongside their other read-alouds from the rest of the year and talked about how it was similar and how it was different from the other books. The class recorded these and other ways to "linger and look" at the end of a book on a chart, and before children dispersed, Kathleen said, "Today and from this day on, when you reach the end of a book, find a way to linger and look at the whole book. If you invent a new way, see me so we can teach it to the whole class and add it to our chart." Soon a variation on the following chart hung on the wall of Kathleen's classroom:

Ways to Linger and Look from the Vantage Point of "The End"

- Return to a place you loved, hated, or questioned, or to places you found difficult or to places which made you angry. Reread and discuss one of those places in light of the whole text. Perhaps move to a second place and discuss it as well.

- Think about, "What is the whole book saying?" One way to think about this is to ask, "What single section best captured the author's meaning?" Another way to think is to ask, "How is the message of this book similar to (and different from) the message of (another book)?"

- How do the elements of the story each contribute to the message of the book? How does the end contribute? The beginning?

- What symbols and metaphors can you find that echo the overall messages of the book?

- Think about why the author ended it this way. When did you first suspect this might be the ending? Why— out of all possible endings— might the author have chosen this one?

- Lay some of the books you know well (which could include any of the read aloud books) next to this one. How are they similar, different?

- How might we live differently because of this book?

Kathleen's end of the book read-aloud minilesson became a ten-day project: the class returned to *The Giver* for many days, and the children agreed that their conversations were different because they took in broad stretches of text. A few days later, Julio raised a question: was it necessary to wait until the final page to look back and try to talk about the whole text? Soon a new ritual spread from classroom to classroom. In Reading and Writing Project schools everywhere, teachers began telling their students that Julio, from Harlem's P.S. 125, had come up with the idea of designating "a lookout spot" halfway through a text. As part of their procedure for launching a book, many children began marking the half-way page of their books with stickers or special bookmarks, and when they read, they planned to use their classes' "Ways to Linger and Look At" chart to inform what they did at these look-at spots as well as at the end of books.

In Chapter 18, I described a way to teach readers to develop and defend their theories about texts. Here I want to focus on a subset of this work: How can we tweak and extend the methods described earlier to help readers develop and defend their theories about the theme or message or point of a text? In her beautiful story, *Eleven*, Sandra Cisneros (1992) points out that we human beings grow like rings on a tree, one year inside the next. When you're eleven, you're also ten and nine and eight. Readers also grow like rings on a tree. When readers interpret a text in solid and compelling ways, this thinking incorporates and depends on their ability to do other kinds of thinking. When a child has a keen sense of what is important about the whole plot and of how the details reflect the big ideas, and when she has a chance to talk through her ideas, her interpretation will be the strongest.

A Peek Into a Classroom

A late spring book talk is under way in Gillan White's third-grade classroom. Gillan has been reading aloud from Patricia MacLachlan's novella *Journey*, the story of an eleven-year-old boy (Journey) who was recently abandoned by his mother. Now Journey is left with only his grandparents and his sister. He is trying to understand why his mother left him and clinging to the futile hope that she'll return soon.

On this particular day, Gillan has reached the chapter in which Journey, his sister, Cat, and his grandparents follow their newly adopted cat, Bloom, into the room where no one goes, the bedroom Mama has left behind. Soon the family will find that Bloom has had a litter of kittens in a box in the closet, and she is being, to those kittens, the mother that Journey wishes his own Mama would be. Under the kittens Journey finds family photographs that his Mama has torn into tiny fragments. He tries to piece them together, looking at the photo scraps for evidence that his mother loved him. Instead he finds scene after scene showing his mother's detachment and distance even when she was present, and showing also that his grandparents have been the real presence in his life all along.

Gillan opens *Journey* and begins to read. As she does, about one-third of the children jot down responses. This isn't a usual practice in Project third-grade classrooms (stop-and-talk is easier than stop-and-jot), but it works in this room because of the facility of these children as writers and their attentiveness to books. As Gillan reads the start of each new page, she whispers the page number. "Page 42," she says, and it is clear that her children use these whispered page numbers to anchor their jottings and notes.

When Bloom actually crosses the threshold into Mama's room, Gillan's voice slows down as if she is gazing hard at the words she has just read, as if the power of this moment in the story is so pure and miraculous she can hardly bear to let these words leave her mouth: Predictably, a child says, "Stop and jot," and now everyone is writing. After a minute or two Gillan says, "Who'd like to share?"

"Bloom had gone into Mama's room other times but no one else had," Reginald said.

Drew added, "I haven't said it yet but I am about to write, 'Cat is going to open the door for him.'" Drew and everyone else in that room knew his words were huge. Later Gillan explained to me that the image of characters shut away and people opening doors to reach them had been a major motif threading its way through many of their book talks. When the class read *The Great Gilly Hopkins,* they'd noticed people breaking through Gilly's tough skin (like that of an apple!) to reach her soft inside. When the class read Hesse's *Music of the Dolphins,* they found that Dr. Beck and others opened a door to Mela's human side. They saw that tough, orphaned Rocky in *The Monument* had walled herself off from the world, but Mick, the artist, opened a door and reached in to touch her.

Gillan let Drew's words hang in the air. Then she began to read again, slowly, making us all bristle at the majesty of this particular page in *Journey.* Soon, another child said very softly, "Stop and jot."

Two minutes later, Gillan said, "Who'd like to share?" Caroline read, "Cat is opening the door for them. They are going to learn new things about their mom." Caroline's words takes Drew's earlier comment a step further. She spells out that it is the mother who is walled away and that her children, Cat and Journey, are going to reach in and touch her as Mick touched Rocky, as Dr. Beck touched Mela. This is an interesting observation because she is suggesting they'll learn new things about the mother who is gone, and who, in the book, has always been gone.

Gillan received Caroline's comment like one receiving a gift. She restated it to herself. We could see that Gillan listened with care to Caroline's observation, and we did too, along with her.

Now Amelia spoke, her voice rising with the excitement of a dawning idea. "I think this is a metaphor for them entering the mother's world. They had never entered Mama's room *as* her world when she was here." She is very right when she says, "They never entered Mama's room." Even when their mother was alive and present, her world had been off-limits. She'd been inaccessible to her children.

I am observing silently, but in my chest I feel the same rising excitement that I hear in Amelia's voice. What these third graders were doing when they said these rather simple words was the outcome of many, many reading skills. When Caroline and Amelia spoke of this moment using the metaphor that had been so big in their discussion of Gilly, Mela, and Rocky, they were clearly doing intertextual work. They were showing how details from this text, as from the other texts, related to bigger themes. They were reaching toward a universal message for *Journey*. They saw this part of the text in relation to the whole book and noticed that at this moment, something was changing, that Journey and the others were getting closer to Mama and to the understanding of Mama they had been reaching toward all along.

Now Gillan resumed reading but read just a page. The grandfather and Journey and Cat find Bloom's babies, but they also find that this new family has been born in a box holding torn photographs of their past. This is a rich part of *Journey* and not far from the book's end. Gillan read slowly, as if her eyes and mind were wide-open, trying to take in every morsel of the text. Again, at a particularly rich passage, a child whispered, "Stop and jot." As the children wrote, Annie whispered to Gillan, "Could you reread?" The words of the story washed over them a second time. As I watched, I thought about the fact that it was now May in the school year. Earlier in the year, it wasn't the children who initiated these intervals for processing the text (and even now, the way Gillan reads aloud clearly nudges them to say, "Stop and jot"). Until recently, too, these were always "stop and *talk*" interludes.

This time Samantha shared first. She simply repeated a section of the text but even more slowly and with more meaning. "Journey *reached out for* the picture. He is becoming like Cat who *opened the shades, lifted the blanket*." To a casual listener, Samantha seems to be reiterating the text, but Gillan and I know she is saying that Cat, Journey's sister, had gone after the truth about Mama, lifting the shade and the blanket, and that Journey, who had always been more resistant to accepting the truth about his mother, now followed her example and *reached out for* the blanket. My hunch that this is what Samantha meant is confirmed when, after a moment or two of silence, she adds, "Now he can tolerate the mother too."

Joey's voice followed quickly upon Samantha's: "The box was filled with hundreds of pictures Mama has torn up. The door has opened. The door of hate." Joey's rhetoric is big, and maybe he is over his head, using the language of an interpretive conversation without exactly grounding his meaning. Gillan said, "Say more." I admired her generosity in giving him time to spin out for himself and the others what he wanted to say and was almost saying.

"His mom found the pictures—pictures of Cat and Journey—and she ripped them up because she doesn't want to see them." Joey said. "I say the door of hate because they'll learn the truth about the mom. Journey wants to know the truth about why did she leave, but now he won't want it. He'll want to take it back."

Joey was revved up now. He sat on his knees, a small nine-year-old child, his head cocked, his eyes lifted up as if he were a prayer boy. "But a door will open, a door of understanding. It will open to his grandparents, it will open to him."

As I listen to my tape recording of these words, I hear again the lilt and music in Joey's voice. I reread what I have written and wonder if the cadence is clear from these written words. I also wonder what kind of spell this book and this teacher have cast that these nine-year-olds speak in such literary ways? Their insights are remarkable, but I am equally amazed by the music of their language.

Now other children climb aboard Joey's train of thought. "Journey is sort of seeing his mother's insides," Colleen said. "Because his memories are like her insides." Gillan's response is to return to the words of *Journey*, which they have been circling throughout this talk. "Inside the box, under the bed," she rereads. I am impressed with the subtle way in which Gillan pulls the conversation (which has become more and more abstract) back to the text.

The Interplay Between the Details of a Text and the Big Idea

To me, the most striking thing about the book talk in Gillan's classroom was the way the conversation about *Journey* relied on the central metaphors that had emerged from other read-aloud books. It makes sense that if an interpretive conversation means, by definition, that readers wrestle with the universal messages in a book, there will always be a thin line between interpretation and intertextuality.

Conversation works in Gillan's classroom because her children work back and forth between the concrete details in *Journey* and the big metaphors that live in their literate community. Samantha notices that Cat *opened the shade, lifted the blanket,* and that Journey *reached out* for the torn photograph (and, Samantha suggests, for the truth he'd avoided for so long). Gillan keeps the children's focus on the text and its details. She does this by interlacing moments of interpretive conversation with a page of reading-aloud and by her own utter and absolute attention to the details of the text as she reads. She also does this by asking a child to "Say more" and by training her children to cite evidence, to ground their notes in the book's pages, and to keep their books open as they talk and make notes.

An interpretive conversation like this can happen in this class because Gillan deftly steers her third graders to focus on the details of the text *and* because the class has unearthed some of the big metaphors and themes that are played out in many of the books they read. Because conversation always moves between the specifies of the text and big interpretive meanings, children avoid over-simplifying the messages they find in books. Instead of packaging *The Great Gilly Hopkins* in a neat moralistic conclusion, "Gilly should be nicer," they talked about how Gilly is softening up, and the people who are softening her are Trotter (her foster mother) and William Ernest (her foster brother). As part of this conversation, they discuss the way Gilly, at the start of the story, has closed herself up. Perhaps her meanness is an effort to get power over people, which she may need, because as a foster child, she's never had power. Then people break through the door to her inner self. Instead of simply shoving "the message" in *The Monument* into a nutshell— "To be an artist you have to look well at things"—the children talked about how Rocky, through her relationship with the artist Mick, learns to see things as they really are, to see the insides of things and eventually, of herself. They talked about it as a learning book and also a change book. They were interested in the scenes in which Rocky's vision is fixed on the outside world, but it's not the outside world where the action is happening, it's not the outside world that is changing. It is Rocky's internal world. They also pointed out what they saw to be the turning point of the book, a scene in which Rocky looks at a little lamb carved into a gravestone and begins to cry. "I am crying but I don't cry," she says.

The interpretive work this class did was supported by Gillan's deft insistence that they move from the particulars of the text to the "big ideas" and back to the particulars. They resisted the tendency to package big ideas in clichéd phrases (Journey learned to see the truth, Sophie teaches the family to mourn, Rocky learns to see things as they really are) and instead talked long and in their own words about the ideas they found. When the class *did* want to sum up a big idea, to convey it efficiently and link it with other books and other book talks, they tended to do so through metaphor. These metaphors grew out of the books and served as shorthand reference to the long, remarkable talks the class had together. For these children, the metaphors were layered with significance.

Teaching children to synthesize and to interpret is not about books alone. Taking an overall idea and checking to see if its truth is refracted in each of its parts is an act of mind and an act of life. When a man tells himself he is living his days as the best father he can possibly be, he can, if he has the strength and the skills, look at his small words and small acts. Do they resonate with the truth of his statement? Or do they tell a different truth? If so, what underlying meaning fits? When we work with children on this thinking that is interpretation, they will know it is hard work, that no one finds the answers in the blink of an eye, but they will also know how to push their thinking further and deeper and closer to some answers. By teaching children how to interpret, we teach them how to seek meaning in what they read and how to make meaning in their lives.

Writing About Reading 24

When I was little, we turned shoeboxes into cradles for our dolls and teddy bears and turned our fantasies into story lines. Now dolls and teddy bears come with birth certificates, wedding gowns, and ready-made story lines. When I was little, we turned tree stumps on the edges of our schoolyards into pulpits, castles, and chariots. Now too many children spend recess playing Nintendo or trading Pokémon cards, buying and selling characters created by multimillion-dollar corporations.

"My greatest fear for children today," writes author James Howe (1987), "is that they are losing the capacity to play, to create a city out of blocks, to find a world in a backyard, to dream an adventure on a rainy afternoon. My greatest fear for children today is they are losing the capacity to play."

When James Howe says his greatest fear is that our children are losing the capacity to play, could it be that what our children are truly at risk of losing is the human capacity for imagination that allows us to attach meaning and significance—our minds—to the ordinary, earthly details of a tree stump, a teddy bear, a pile of wooden blocks?

Some people argue that our children need to feel more at home living in the world of *ideas,* in the realm of the intellect, and that this is what it means to live a richly literate life. But I think that literature calls us instead to think about the ordinary, the particular, a bear's missing button, a key that opens the garden gate, and a rabbit who says goodnight to a comb, a brush, and a bowl full of mush. Literacy allows us to find the life of the intellect within the details of ordinary life. As readers and writers both, we take the details—Byrd Baylor's green cloud whose parrot shape reminds us that we're in charge of celebrations and Marisol's dream of a birthday with balloons and a pink cake—and we imbue them with significance.

Teaching Writing and Teaching Readers to Write About Reading

Children often come to our classrooms bringing with them a profound disregard for the fine particles of their own lives. In the writing workshop, they protest, "I don't have a famous life," and in the reading workshop, they look up from books saying, "Not that much happens in this book. It's boring." The poet Theodore Roethke was wise when he said, "If your life doesn't seem significant enough, it's not your life that isn't significant enough, but *your response to* your life." He could have said, "If the book you are reading doesn't seem significant enough, it's probably not the book you are reading but *your response to* that book that is not significant enough." Reading and writing—like teaching—begin with learning to say. "Zowie! What a gold mine."

As teachers of readers and writers, we've learned to say, "Can you find one moment that sort of, kind of, matters and sketch it, or flag it, or point to it?" And then we help writers and readers cup their hands around that moment and find meaning in it. Alice points to the baby sister asleep in the cradle, overlooked by family members and readers alike in *Little Nino's Pizzeria,* and soon Alice and the class have taken that grain of an idea and made a pearl. They notice that the mother, like the daughter, is voiceless in the story, and they speculate about how the plot might have unfolded if the mother had had a voice in matters. They recognize instances in their own lives when boys have dominated and girls stayed in the margins. "It could have been different," they say.

"Writing is something like a seed that grows in the dark," Katherine Paterson (1981) writes, "or a grain of sand that keeps rubbing against your vitals until you find you are building a coating around it. The growth of a book takes time…. I talk, I look, I listen, I hate, I fear, I love, I weep, and somehow all of my life gets wrapped around the grain" (p. 26).

But Katherine Paterson is speaking about *writing* a book. Is Alice *writing* or is she *reading?* Does it matter? Listen to Katherine Paterson's (1981) definition of reading: "The process is the same when we read. You take that grain of sand and keep rubbing it against your vitals until you find you are building a coating around it. The reading of a book takes time…. I read, I talk, I look, I listen, I hate, I fear, I love, I weep and somehow all of my life gets wrapped around the grain" (p. 26).

Just as we don't start book clubs in September, we don't walk into our classrooms anticipating that children will understand that writing about reading involves taking an observation about the text and making a pearl of it, as Katherine Paterson describes. In September, if we *do* ask children to write in response to a book, many write pieces rather like this one, which Nicholas produced in response to Spinnelli's *Wringer:*

> *Wringer* is nothing like Spinnelli's other book. The cover is kind of strange but it gets you thinking. I don't think it's fair how they kill the pigeons—I'd let them go. I thought the kids' names were funny. The ending left you hanging, but I still like the book.

Nicholas' September writing about *Wringer* contains a string of sweeping generalizations, one after another. His writing about his summer is not very different:

> I had an okay summer. We went to the beach and had a lot of fun. We mostly did nothing. One time the hydrant exploded, and we all got wet. I watched TV every day. Some days I rode my bike. It was fun.

"Of all the ideas you might want to explore about *Wringer*," I said to Nicholas during the reading workshop, "What is the *one thing* you want to pursue?" Meanwhile in the writing workshop, I said, "Of all the ideas you want to explore about your summer, what is the *one thing* you want to pursue?"

The prospect of narrowing his topic was worrisome to Nicholas, and this was true whether he was writing about himself or his book. If his focus was too narrow, would he have anything to say? "I *could* write about the cover of *Wringer* and how it's like the story and not like it," Nicholas said, and then hurried to add, "But I don't have much to say. It'd be too short." Nicholas responded similarly when I suggested he focus on just one aspect of his summer. "We *did* find a horseshoe crab," he said, his face lighting up at the memory. Then his face fell and he thought of his blank page. "There is nothing really to say, though. That's it. We found it and we threw it in the ocean, that's all."

As readers and as writers, our students need to learn that the details of their thoughts and experiences are important. The only way to learn this is by writing and by having readers and listeners who respond deeply. "Can I see that cover to *Wringer?*" we say. "Wow. You are right. Why do you suppose it is so eerie?" "Did you *really* find a horseshoe crab? I saw one once and it was this huge brown thing. What was yours like?"

The work we, as teachers, need to do is remarkably similar whether we are teaching students to write literature or teaching them to write *about* literature. We have choices. One way to proceed is to design a curriculum in which we take children through a strategy in the writing workshop, step by step, and then take that strategy into the reading curriculum where they can use it to write literary essays about their reading. That is, as teachers of reading and writing, one option is to move our students along on parallel tracks within the two disciplines. If we had enough time in the school day, we could conceivably design a curricular plan like this:

Writing	Writing About Reading
• Children learn to see that the details of their lives are worth writing about and they jot entries in their writer's notebook often.	• Children learn to see that the details of their responses to books are worth writing about and they jot responses on Post-its and sometimes in reading logs.
• Children reread their entries, find one that matters, and take this entry as a grain of sand around which they'll pearl their writing and their lives.	• Children reread their responses, find one that matters, and take this response as a grain of sand around which they'll pearl their reading, thinking, and living.
• We listen responsively to each child's seed idea (and recruit other children to do the same). In this way, we help each child bring significance to his or her idea.	• We listen responsively to each child's seed idea (and recruit other children to do the same). In this way, we help each child bring significance to his or her ideas about books.
• We equip our students with strategies for thinking and writing more as they elaborate and develop their seed idea:	• We equip our students with strategies for thinking and writing more as they elaborate and develop their seed idea:
• Reread what you've written and ask marginal questions: "Why does this moment stand out? How does it fit with the rest of my writing?"	• Reread what you've written and ask marginal questions: "Why does this moment stand out? How does it fit with the rest of the text I'm reading?"

- Find other moments that relate to the first. How are they similar? Different?

- Ask, "What's surprising me here?"

- We help students review all the ideas they've thought about and gathered, asking "What is it I want to say and how can I say it?" We help students consider the form or structure in which they will write and envision the "kind of thing" they'll be writing. If it's a memoir, they'll want to study other examples of memoir. If it's a picturebook, they'll want to know about the possibilities within that genre.

- After students write a draft, we teach them to reread it using the conventions of the genre as a critical lens. If this is a memoir, students will want to ask themselves, "Have I created portraits of myself and others that are believable?" "Have I made a significant statement about my life?"

- Find other moments that relate to the first. How are they similar? Different?

- Ask, "What's surprising me here?"

- We help students review all the ideas they've thought about and gathered, asking "What is it I want to say and how can I say it?" We help students consider the form or structure in which they will write and envision the "kind of thing" they'll be writing. Because it's a literary essay, they'll want to study examples of essays. Teachers may need to supply examples or bring essays written by other students because published literary essays are generally far more complex than those we expect children to write.

- After students write a draft, we teach them to reread it using the conventions of the genre as a critical lens. Because this is a literary essay, students will need to ask themselves, "Have I made a statement about the text that is significant and accountable to the text?" Do I develop my thesis with evidence from the text? Do I give readers an accurate sense of the text?"

Although it makes intellectual sense to work on two fronts at one time, showing children how to write about their lives and how to use the same strategies to write about their reading, I don't know any teacher who has tried to do parallel work like this in both the writing workshop and in writing about reading. The problems are practical ones. At the start of the year, when we want to mobilize children to do this important learning within the writing workshop, the reading workshop has other priorities. There, we need to be certain that students are reading a lot, understanding what they read, and thinking and talking about books. Our readers haven't necessarily yet learned to monitor for sense as they read, to talk about books with reference to the text, or to talk and think deeply about one idea. But *if* we teach students in the reading workshop what they need to know *as readers,* and meanwhile help students in the writing workshop learn what they need to know *as writers,* within a matter of months they will probably be in a position to put the two together. In the end students find it relatively easy to write essays about their reading.

As we teach the children in our classrooms to write in the ways I've described briefly here and discuss in more depth in *The Art of Teaching Writing* (1994), we support parallel work in *talking* about books.

WRITING ABOUT READING	READING AND TALKING
•Children learn to see that the details of their lives are worth writing about and they jot entries in their writers note-books often.	•Children listen and read in ways that allow them to retell a text logically, to respond to a text, and to see their responses as worth attending to and sharing. They react through say-something responses, with Post-it notes and occasional entries in a reading log (sometimes these are 'stretches' which extend a Post-it comment.) Readers also respond to texts in partnership conversations
•Children reread their entries, find one that matters, and take this entry as a grain of sand around which they pearl their writing.	•Children select a comment or a Post-it jotting and talking for a long while about it ("One other example of this is …" This connects also to …").

- We listen responsively to each child's seed idea (and recruit other children to do the same). In this way, we help each child bring significance to his or her idea.

- We equip our students with strategies for thinking and writing more as they elaborate and develop their seed idea:

    - Reread what you've written and ask marginal questions. "Why does this moment stand out? How does it fit with the rest of my writing?"

    - Find other moments that relate to the first. How are they similar? Different?

    - Ask, "What's surprising me here?"

- We listen responsively to children's ideas (and recruit children to do the same). In this way, we help each child bring significance to his or her idea:

- Children develop a hunch or a theory, and as they continue reading, they find new evidence, which informs their developing theories. They gather and chart evidence that adds to, complicates, or challenges their initial idea and ask themselves:

    - How does this moment connect with my theory? With the book as a whole? With other moments in the story?

    - What's surprising me here?

    - Children also learn to pause at the end of the text and to talk for a while about particular sections of the text in relation to big ideas which now seem especially significant to them.

The Talking and Thinking About Reading curriculum outlined here is described in greater detail in other chapters of this book. The kind of teaching I've described throughout the whole book *does* help children look up from a text and say, "Here's what I'm thinking and here's why." This is the essential stance a reader must take in order to write a literary essay. Our teaching

in the reading workshop prepares students to draw on specific textual references to illustrate and extend their ideas, to elaborate upon their theories at some length, and to summarize texts using story elements. These are important challenges in writing about literature.

Teaching Students to Write Literary Essays

At the close of the previous chapter we listened in on Gillan White's third graders as they talked together about Patricia MacLachlan's *Journey*. Although Gillan's work with *Journey* was intended to help children talk, think, and interpret, it soon become clear to both of us that it would take only a light nudge to move her youngsters toward writing their very first literary essays.

As I mentioned earlier, once these third graders had listened to *Journey*, Gillan read Gary Paulsen's *The Monument* aloud. When the story opens, we meet a young girl named Rocky who has a bad leg. She has been at an orphanage long enough to see everyone else adopted and to steel herself from the world and from herself. In the story, Rocky is adopted and goes to live in a Kansas milltown where she befriends an artist, Mick, who's been brought to the town to make a monument. Soon Rocky has vowed to become an artist as well. She learns from Mick to see with honest eyes, and to accept the truth of what she sees.

Throughout the first half of the book, the class continued the rich book talk we glimpsed in the last chapter. Then, midway through the book, Gillan said, "We're each on our own now. I'll continue to read aloud, but I'll leave time for us to write about what I've read. We won't share our responses until we've made something of them, until we've made our own monuments." Over the next week, Gillan's children jotted notes during moments when Gillan paused, and wrote longer responses at the end of the read-aloud. Gillan would read, then close the book and say, "You can stay here on the carpet and write about *The Monument* in your reading logs. When you finish, get your writer's notebook and we'll shift to writing time." Many children ended up using most of the writing workshop to expand their respond to *The Monument.*

What children tended to do above all was to record a line or two they loved from *The Monument,* and then extend the story, writing itself, as if they were Gary Paulsen, making the in-between moments that he'd deleted from the text. They wrote mostly from Rocky's point of view, as if they were living her role inside the world of that text. Gillan and I were intrigued to see how easily and intensely the children stepped into the world of this story, and it seemed to us that their writing was not so much *about* their reading as *an extension of* their reading. Caroline, for example, scrawled this entry about the day when Rocky stood face to face with her own portrait on the wall. Caroline wrote quickly, her pen flying down the page:

> There up on the wall was me. I wanted to know me, to talk to me, the way I wanted to talk to the dancers that were gone. I remembered in the orphanage I thought I knew me but I didn't. I didn't know me until now. I never saw *me.* I might of saw a girl but I didn't see me without Mick. Without art, I wouldn't see me now. I would still see a little strange girl instead of ME!

Samantha, meanwhile, wrote as if she were Rocky, standing motionless while Mick drew her:

> "Stay there."
>
> "Okay."
>
> What is he doing? He might be drawing or writing. I wonder why he thinks the light from the sun is so special. He sees it everyday. I can't move or he'll yell, "Don't move!" and that is not fun. I am not sure why I like light so much. I like light, but not as much as Mick does. I think Mick must be religious because he praises light like it is a god or something.

Kathleen compared Rocky to Arthur, in Patricia MacLachlan's *Arthur, for the Very First Time.* In her entry, she wrote:

> Rocky is like Arthur, except Arthur is locked inside and Rocky is locked outside. Arthur uses writing to help his problem. He looks at the world through writing. He says the house where he stayed was a book, his aunt and uncle were characters and when he gets to their house, he is a new character. Arthur used to write only what he heard but now he writes what he sees. Seeing is important to Rocky too. She sees the world through drawing. She sees herself and parts of Bolton looking good in drawings and she sees her true self too, what's inside of her. She sees right past her leg-brace to her soul.

When the class reached the end of the book, Gillan asked the children to reread their reading logs and Post-its as if these were their writer's notebooks. "Find an entry or two (or a Post-it) that you wrote in response to *The Monument* that seems close to the heart of it all, and star it. I'll photocopy that entry for you, and it can be your 'seed idea.' You'll need to gather more material around it. Do any other entries you've written about the book or, earlier, about your own life, connect? If so, star them and I'll duplicate those for you as well." She also gave each child a copy of *The Monument* and suggested that they reread it on their own or have a parent read it to them. "Revisit *The Monument* with your seed idea in mind. Write more, remember more, question more. What's the real idea you are developing? Can you chart or sketch your idea? Plan to write about ten pages of entries around your seed idea." Because of the work Gillan's children had been doing all year in the writing workshop, it was not particularly surprising or new for them to be asked to write ten pages around a seed idea (see Calkins, 1994, 1991). The new part was that their seed idea was a response to a book. After about a week, Gillan asked children to reread what they'd gathered and to choose the parts they felt could be raw materials for an essay.

Giving Students an Image to Work Toward as They Write Literary Essays

Gillan wanted to give children an example of the kind of literary essays she hoped they would write. But, as we realized, there was a catch: there is no real-world genre called "writing about reading." Did we want these students to write book reviews or literary criticism or literature inspired by reading or

what? Gillan's motives were mixed. In a way, she wanted her students to emulate the essays written by our best essayists. But the essay format students are traditionally taught in school (where they write a paragraph in which they make a claim, "Here's what I think," and then illustrate, defend, and extend this claim) bears little resemblance to the form used by great essayists. The anthropologist Clifford Geertz (1983) describes an essay as a journey of thought and writes, "For making detours and going down side roads, nothing is more convenient than the essay form. Wandering into yet smaller side roads and wider detours does little harm, for progress is not expected to be relentlessly forward, but winding and improvisational, coming out where it comes out" (p. 6).

Although Gillan wanted her students to study the best available essays, she worried that their meandering form would exacerbate children's tendency to write by free association. Then, too, in the more immediate future of middle school, they'd be asked to write essays that were very different than those written by great essayists. In middle school, they'd be expected to make and defend one claim in their essays. But most of all, Gillan wanted her students to feel that writing about reading was an authentic, significant thing to do. In the end, Gillan and I constructed a hybrid version of the academic essay that combined some of the values inherent in essays while also helping students gain control over their ideas and interests.

Gillan and I suggested that children look again at an essay they already knew well, "Eleven," by Sandra Cisneros. Although "Eleven" was not written in response to literature, it could still serve as a model. Gillan's children noticed that in this essay, Cisneros had an idea she wanted to communicate, and she wrote about it in a way that helped others feel its significance for her:

What they don't understand about birthdays and what they never tell you is that when you're eleven, you're also ten, and nine, and eight, and seven, and six, and five, and four, and three, and two, and one. And when you wake up on your eleventh birthday you expect to feel eleven, but you don't.... You feel like you're still ten. And you are—underneath the year that makes you eleven. Because the way you grow old is kind of like an onion or like the rings inside a tree trunk or like my little wooden dolls that fit one inside the other, each year inside the next one. That's how being eleven years old is.

Then they noticed that in the rest of her essay, Cisneros said more about her idea. She did this by choosing a moment that captured the idea and writing well about that one moment. For example, she writes:

"Whose is this?" Mrs. Price says, and she holds the red sweater up in the air for the whole class to see. "Whose? It's been sitting in the coatroom for a month."

"Not mine," says everybody. "Not me."

"It has to belong to somebody," Mrs. Price keeps saying, but nobody can remember. It's an ugly sweater with red plastic buttons and a collar and sleeves all stretched out like you could use it for a jump rope. It's maybe a thousand years old and even if it belonged to me I wouldn't say so.

Maybe because I'm skinny, maybe because she doesn't like me, that stupid Sylvia Saldivar says, "I think it belongs to Rachel." An ugly sweater like that, all raggedy and old, but Mrs. Price believes her. Mrs. Price takes the sweater and puts it right on my desk, but when I open my mouth nothing comes out.

"That's not, I don't, you're not.... Not mine," I finally say in a little voice that was maybe me when I was four.

"Of course it's yours," Mrs. Price says, "I remember you wearing it once." Because she's older and the teacher, she's right and I'm not.

The episode continues:

But when the sick feeling goes away and I open my eyes, the red sweater's still sitting there like a big red mountain. I move the red sweater to the corner of my desk with my ruler. I move my pencil and books and eraser as far from it as possible. I even move my chair a little to the right. Not mine, not mine, not mine.

I told these children that, like Sandra Cisneros, in their essays they would have one big idea and that they might develop their idea by retelling one or two moments from the book, just as Cisneros had retold the episode about the red sweater. "You'll need to retell those moments in a way that helps readers really feel your big idea," I told them. Then, using a term from the writing workshop, I said, "You'll need to angle the retelling just as you did when you wrote your memoir." Gillan's children knew about angling narratives to make points, because in the memoir-writing workshop they'd retold episodes in ways that highlighted their themes (one child had told a fishing story to show closeness with his father, another had told about her puppy in a way that conveyed her love of animals).

Gillan's children also studied an essay about Brian, the main character in Gary Paulsen's *Hatchet,* written by Alexander, one of her former students, when he was in fifth grade at another school. Alexander had tried to develop an idea about the book, then to write about the idea in a way that would make readers see its significance, and then to elaborate on the idea by retelling incidents from *Hatchet.* This is his essay:

> I came to this new school with my own interests that had won me lots of friends at my old school, Wooster: magic cards, computers and books. I expected these new kids to quickly take up these interests, but they did not. After some days of wandering around at recess feeling like I don't belong in this new land, I have begun to realize I need to observe the ways of this place, to listen to the rules of this school. If I am going to survive here, it will happen by me listening, observing, and changing to fit in, not by staying the same and dominating.
>
> Brian, the hero of *Hatchet,* is like me in that we both know that to survive in the wild we must listen, observe, and change. I can't wait for this school to fit my interests, and Brian can't just wait for his world to welcome him. Brian and I, both, come from places where we had people we could depend on for safety. Now to survive we must change to meet our new worlds, and to do this we must listen, watch, and follow.
>
> Brian changes to fit the world of his Canadian wilderness lake. One of those changes happens on a sunny afternoon when Brian is picking raspberries. It is not long after the plane which had been flying Brian to his father crashed, and he is marooned in the wilderness. Raspberries were his

finest food. As Brian picks the raspberries, he fills his pockets of his tattered windbreaker. He eats one, then pops another into his pocket, then eats another. Brian hears a rustling and looks up to see a small mountain of brown fur slowly moving among the raspberries. The bear lifts his head up. Brian freezes, seeing the massive jaws. His mind worked frantically. Should he pick up the rock, throw it as the beast and run for the lake? Should he grab a stick and start attacking. Brian does none of these. He continues to look at the bear. Maybe he gets the idea about how the wilderness works as he looks at the bear. The bear stares straight at Brian, right in the eyes. Then cautiously the beast turns its head, and eats a raspberry, then another. Beside him, Brian slowly reaches out for a raspberry, picks it, and then puts it in his mouth. The bear and the boy are side-by-side eating berries.

In *Hatchet,* Brian not only observes and listens in order to survive, he also uses his intelligence. In the beginning of *Hatchet,* Brian is obsessed with food. He dreams of food. Whenever he moves his stomach rumbles. He longs for one juicy hamburger, convinced that he'd trade everything for one lone hamburger. On a warm summer morning Brian uses his intelligence to get food. He starts aiming his homemade bow, the fish squirms right beneath his arrow point. He releases. The arrow seems to go through the fish and yet the fish swims away, unharmed. He repeats his process with practiced caution. But this time, as he is about to release, he notices that the arrow's shaft appears as if it is broken. He pulls the arrow from the water and looks at it, and it is not cracked or spilt at all. He suddenly remembers back to an 8th grade biology class. The teacher had said something about this. Then he remembers: water bends light. That meant that the fish were not where they seemed to be, that they were above the arrow shaft. The next time he hunted he aimed below the fish. That night he ate fresh fish meat!

Brian and I live in different places, but we still learn many of the same lessons. For each of us, the important thing is that we change to fit our new worlds. But it is also important that we don't change too much. Brian needs to hold his mother and father in his mind's eye. I need to remember that my interests are still part of me.

Gillan's children set to work. They reread all the jottings, notes and entries they'd made and Gillan helped them realize that the next step was to map a plan for combining their notes into an essay. It helped them to study this plan below, written by one of Kathy Doyle's fifth graders, in preparation for an essay on Karen Hesse's *Out of the Dust:*

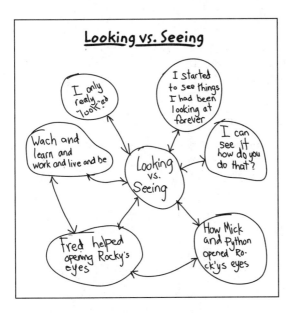

The children wrote rough drafts of their essays. This is the beginning of Amelia's draft:

THE MONUMENT

"I want to be an artest." ~~FA~~ I just said it, just like that and I tryed to hold it in but I couldn't ~~he~~ Just something about him made me wan't to stay there in that moment. To rap it up in paper and keep it in my diary and never ~~take~~ it out. I just wanted to stop ~~Har sta~~ rite there, to press the pause button on the tape of time. my tape of time diffrant then anny one's elses.

Amelia reread her writers notebook and found an entry she'd written about her last night as an eight year old and she realized that the entry fit closely with *The Monument*. She rewrote and combined the two entries, then added on them. This is the essay she eventually published:

Wrapped Up In Plastic

I lay on my warm, cuddly bed. The calendar squares are crossed out until February 8th and the next unmarked square has written in my own messy handwriting *Happy Birthday, Amelia.* My Mom walks away from my warm bed with the words held on her lips, "Goodnight my little eight year old." She shuts the door, the door of me being eight. As she closes the door it turns from wood to steel and gives a moaning sound as if it doesn't want my mom to leave. I realize this is the last night I am eight. Even if I live to be 200, I will never again be eight.

I wish I had a huge piece of saran wrap to wrap up all the feelings I have in this moment, but I don't. I could stay up all night but it won't do any good. I'm thinking, thinking, then I cry, cry, cry like Rocky. Rocky is a girl with a brace and caramel colored skin in Gary Paulsen's *The Monument*. Rocky cried looking at a book of Degas painting which Mick, her teacher, artist and friend, gave her. Looking at the picture called *The Dance Master,* Rocky cries because all of what they were was gone. Just gone. The red and blue quilt, the brown dresser, and the yellow house are here but the dancers are gone. Just gone.

On page 81, Rocky decided that she wanted to be an artist. She said it just like that, alone in her warm bed. "I want to be an artist." Rocky decided to become an artist when she realized that the dancers aren't gone. The picture called *The Dance Master* wraps them up in plastic. Like now. This piece of writing is that huge piece of saran wrap that I longed for the night before my eighth birthday. It wraps all my feelings and thoughts from the last day of me being eight in plastic. My saran wrap is writing. Rocky's saran wrap is art.

Throughout her essay, Samantha, another third grader in Gillian's c;ass. tried to show how Rocky began like a Post-it note that was all crumpled up, but slowly opened over the course of the story.

Rocky's Crumpled Paper
Rocky looked at the wall and she saw it. Paintings of everyone in the town had once covered that wall but they'd been torn down by people who did-n't like the way their paintings had looked. Her picture was the only one left hanging up, flat and unwrinkled. Throughout Gary Paulsen's *The Monu-ment*, Rocky thought she was ugly because she had caramel colored skin and

a brace on her left leg. She couldn't see that she was just like anybody else, so her insides stayed crumpled up that way … At the orphanage, books were her only friends. All the light inside of her was crumpled like a discarded wad of paper … Rocky didn't get adopted and didn't get adopted until Fred and Emma came into her life. They took her to their home in Bolton, Kansas. Although they drank, they loved her.

One day on a walk with her dog, Python, Rocky met Mick, the artist hired to make a monument for the town. His words, "Oh God, see the light?" and his actions, hands that just danced over the paper, slowly, carefully opened one corner of the wadded paper that was Rocky.

"Just draw," Mick said. Rocky looked over the town for her first drawing lesson. With Mick's power and inspiration, she drew. Just a bunch of lines, just a girl with a brace. Mick said, "I can't teach you to be an artist, you already are one." He shaded around Rocky's drawing and the picture popped off the page. Rocky could see the art, the art she had made. Now a whole side of the crumpled inside paper was open, smoother.

When they went to the graveyard for the second lesson, Rocky saw an innocent stone lamb carved into the grave of a baby who had died. She started crying, for the first time in her life. It brought back memories from being at the orphanage, helpless and lonely like the lamb. The wad of paper was almost unwrinkled all the way.

Mick gave Rocky a book, an art book by Degas. Looking through the book, Rocky cried again. So many people had left Rocky. She wanted to wrap them up in paper. The picture called *The Dance Master* was painted long ago, the dancers were dead, gone. One girl, standing to the side of the dancers with her hand to her mouth, worried, reminded Rocky of herself. She wanted to know that girl, she wanted to know herself …

When they were gathered in the courthouse to decide what monument to build, Mick hung up pictures of the people in Bolton. Everyone ripped down their drawing because they were afraid to see their true inner selves. Rocky could leave her painting up and be proud. Mick gave Rocky a monument. Art.

Joey's essay drew parallels between his relationship with his dog, Coach, and Rocky's relationship with Python, the dog that becomes her staunch companion. It began,

When I first touched my dog Coach's fur, I thought I had known his fur by heart. And after a while I got to know his face. You have to look through his outside to his inside self, and his eyes give it away. When Rocky first touched her dog Python's fur, she thought she knew his fur. She knew his face …

Caroline began her essay by writing about a friend who had moved away but left behind lessons. Then she wrote of the lessons Mick, the artist, left behind for Rocky.

> He taught a girl named Rocky to see that the insides of people are what really matters. Mick took Rocky to a grave of a girl named Claire Miller. When Rocky saw the grave with a lamb lying on its side, she remembered how lonely she had been in the orphanage … Rocky began to cry for the first time … and Mick said, "It's all right to cry. You're seeing something how it's meant to be" and Rocky drew the grave and the lamb and the loneliness.

Readers who know *The Art of Teaching Writing (1994)* and *Living Between the Lines (1991)* will recognize that Amelia, Samantha, Caroline, and Joey have written about *The Monument* using the same process they use to write about the sunshine falling on their father's shirt as it hangs on the laundry line or about finding centipedes under a rotting log. These children live with writer's notebooks at their sides. In the writing workshop, they have learned to see and above all respect the details of their lives and to jot these details down in their notebooks. The Amelia who stands at the pumpkin farm, notebook in hand, noticing that the field is dotted with orange is the same Amelia who lingers over a page in which the defiant Rocky looks at the Degas painting of dancers and weeps.

"I must write," Ann Morrow Lindbergh (1965) has said. "Writing is more than living. It is being conscious of living." When we write about our reading, everything is saturated with significance. "Writing, you see more, you hear more, feel more, think more, learn more," Don Murray (1968) has said. "It's like breathing some new kind of air," Cynthia Rylant has said. "Live in a way that lets you find poems," Naomi Nye has said.

I have always talked about this wide-awakeness and vulnerability as the "writing life." But working with Gillan's children, I came to realize that it is not only *writing* but also *reading* that makes us awake to our lives. All of us know what it is to open a good book and to be opened by a good book. We know what it is to travel through life with extra sensitivity, extra vulnerability, because by reading, we see more, hear more, feel more, think more, learn more. "It's like breathing some new kind of air," Rylant says.

The literate life is not only about reading more and writing more, it is also about living more. Anne Lamott (1995) describes writing by saying, "You can do it the way you used to clear the dinner dishes when you were thirteen or you can do it as a Japanese person would perform a tea ceremony, with a level of concentration and care in which you can lose yourself and so in which you can find yourself." But isn't this true for reading as well as writing? We can read the way we used to clear the dinner dishes when we were thirteen, and so often our children do just that. But we can also read with a level of concentration and care in which we lose ourselves and find ourselves. This is, as Katherine Paterson says, a cooperative venture. The texts we read, Paterson says, "will never be complete until a reader of whatever age takes that book and brings to it his or her own story.... It is only when the deepest sound going further from my heart meets the deepest sound coming further from yours—it is only in this encounter that the true music begins."

Personal Response 25

When Kathy Doyle's children first met in bookclubs, their conversations revealed their understanding of personal response as a strategy for reading. They read a book aloud together and paused at the end of each page to report, in a round-robin fashion, on connections they made between the book and their lives. While reading Doris Buchanon Smith's *A Taste of Blackberries,* a story in which a child dies of a bee sting, David prompted Brian, "Hasn't *anyone* died in your life?" Brian was silent. David pressed on "Is there someone in your family who *might* die? Like your grandmother? Your dog? Are you afraid because someday your grandmother *might* die?"

Brian finally responded with dubious conviction, "Yeah … *someday,* my grandmother will die." Then, his face lighting up, he said, "I once had a goldfish—two goldfish—that died!"

"See," David glowed with pleasure. "You made a connection." Surveying the other members of the book club, he said, "That's *all* of us!" Pleased that, with his prompting, each member of the book club had been able to match the main event on this page to an episode in their lives, he turned to the next page. "Let's read on."

Brian flipped over the page, muttering an aside to me as he did so, "David is our connector. If you say anything—dog food—he can make a connection between it and the book."

As I moved among the other book clubs in Kathy Doyle's classroom that day, I watched children demonstrating what it meant to them to make personal connections with a text. One group put down Dick King-Smith's *The Cuckoo Child* for a moment in order to talk about every experience they had ever had with ostriches, ducks, geese, parakeets, or parrots. They talked for twenty minutes about "birds in my life," never returning to *The Cuckoo Child*. In another conversation, David looked up from Esther Wood Brady's *Toliver's Secret,* a book about a young girl on a dangerous mission during the American Revolution, to say, "She has a green hat. My uncle has a green hat. The same!" Presto! He too had made a personal connection. In other classrooms, children told me, "We've got about twenty connections so far," as if they had been collecting trinkets on a charm bracelet. Some confessed that they had made no personal connections. "It's a fairy tale from long ago, that's why," one chile explained, totally confident that her explanation was a convincing one.

This certainly isn't personal response at its best, but it's the sort of entry point many of us are given. As teachers of young readers, we need to see what our students are gesturing toward and begin there as we take them on a learning journey. In this chapter we'll rethink the teaching that turned personal response into a trinket. Then we'll look at some students' deep, personal connections to literature and see how their teachers made those responses possible.

Rethinking the Teaching That Turned Personal Response into a Trinket

At the Teachers College Reading and Writing Project's big table, we laid out the ways in which children were responding to texts. What children were doing troubled us, especially because they seemed to be doing what they had been taught to do. How had well-intentioned teachers inadvertently suggested that responding to a text was a matching activity like the workbook exercises in which one draws lines between two columns, in this case, matching congruent details in the text and one's own life. Wouldn't the implication be that a Latino child could only 'connect' with stories about other Latino children? That boys could only connect with stories about boys?

Instead of making texts bigger, the personal responses we witnessed were making texts smaller. We were concerned that the terms "personal response" or "text-to-self connections," (Keene and Zimmerman) which should refer to huge, fundamental ways of reading, had instead been reduced to trinkets: "My goldfish died too" or "My uncle also has a green hat."

In Project think tanks and classrooms we have come to trust in this process of naming a problem, talking about it so we see it in all its looming layers, and then setting off to live with new resolve as we look for possible solutions. The more stories we told about children's modes of personal response, the more full of resolve we felt.

We tried to grapple with the question of what had gone wrong. Why did children believe, for example, that personal response happens in a round-robin way, with each reader finding a phrase in the book that matched an item in his or her life? It wasn't hard to speculate on the source of this problem. How often have we and other teachers prefaced a story with little questions: "Have *you* ever been mad at *your* parents? What did *you* do, Joe, when you were mad?"

"I went to my room and slammed the door."

"And you, Tanya. What did *you* do when *you* were mad?"

"I didn't talk to them."

"Well, this is a story about a boy who is mad at *his* father. Let's read and find out what *he* did." Most of us have also led similar conversations at the end of stories, again asking one child after another to produce a bite-sized personal response.

Our intentions have been good. We have wanted to hear briefly from as many children as possible and to welcome many voices into the circle. But when this exercise is repeated day after day, year after year, it's no surprise that children learn what we have demonstrated to them. What they are doing in the name of personal response is filling in the blanks in our sentences with a phrase or a sentence that connects the book to their lives.

In order to rethink our teaching, we recall that when we asked questions such as "Have you ever been mad at *your* parents?" before we read a story , we did this in hopes of activating the readers' prior knowledge, or schemata, of, in this case, family arguments. This way our students would anticipate what might happen (the plot) in this upcoming text. We also wanted readers to bring their own experiences to the text in ways that allowed them to envision the story and empathize with at least one of the characters. These are worthy goals, but as we have discovered, we need to teach them more explicitly.

In order to show how prior experience can serve as a resource for predicting, envisioning, and comprehending a text, we might ask *one* reader to share his or her connections to a text in some detail and then say to that reader, while the rest of the class observes, "So now why don't you read aloud in this text stopping at any section that seems to relate the story to your life in any way." If the reader pauses soon to say that the story reminds her of family arguments at home, we can help her see that the memory of those arguments can help her predict what might happen during the parental argument in this text. Then when she resumes reading, we could also show her the importance of attending to surprises or differences between her expectations and the actual text. Turning to the whole class, we can grow theories about what good readers do based on this demonstration of one reader. If we think of personal response, or text-to-self connections, as something we hope readers do *early* on in the process of reading a text, then their personal response becomes the basis for their predictions. If a story is called *The Lost Cat*, it probably helps to think, "Have I ever lost *my* cat?" because the follow-up question is, "What happened when I lost my cat that might happen in this story?" Emergent and beginning readers especially can get so focused on word solving, they forget to think about content and do not draw on their own experiences to help them anticipate what will happen. In the end, thinking about content and making life-to-text connections is an important way to support this work with print. This sort of personal response—linking one's prior experience to a text in a first encounter with that text—is inextricably linked, then, not only to envisionment but also to prediction.

How Do We Teach Students to Respond in Deep, Life-Changing Ways?

I suspect that for most of us, as for Kathy Doyle's fifth graders, the term *personal response* refers mostly to something that occurs after and as a result of our reading. When I think about personal response, for example, I remember my son Miles listening, as a nine-year-old, to me read the ending of C. S. Lewis's *Prince Caspian,* when the gentle lion of Narnia, Aslan, speaks quietly and for a long time, to the children High King Peter and High Queen Susan. We later learn that Aslan is bidding them a final farewell for they, the oldest of the four children, will never return to Narnia again. Miles, who is my older son, listened, his eyes shining. "Peter and Susan are my favorites," he said.

"Yes," I answered. "They are the oldest, like you."

Miles's face folded, tears welled. He looked up at me, eyes swimming, to say, "Why *can't* I go back to Narnia?"

I think of the childhood edition of Leon Uris' *Exodus* I found recently, with my name penned over and over inside the cover as I tried on different identities: Reverend Lucy Calkins, Dr. L. Calkins, Professor Calkins. How clearly I recall staring up at the ceiling of my third-floor bedroom, *Exodus* open on my chest, vowing that someday I, like people in that book, would have a cause and a community that circled that cause. This is personal response.

Neither Miles nor I had chosen a big idea to follow in these books. We hadn't attached Post-its or charted our developing interpretations. But we got their messages, and felt those messages in our hearts, our souls, our lives.

How do we teach this kind of deep, life-changing personal response to books? For me and my colleagues, one answer came from our work with Tony Petrosky in the adult book groups I describe briefly at the start of this book. Tony suggested that after we read a book, we name the sections of the text that stood out for us, the sections that grabbed our attention. One of us might talk about an event, another a phrase, another a moment of confusion or a big idea. After one of us talked, Tony would ask us to account for why it seemed significant. He nudged us to ask ourselves, "What do these sections have to say about the whole of the text?" and also "What do these sections have to say about me, the reader, as a person?"

Tony seemed always to want us to first see and name what was in the text, and only then to imbue those perceptions with significance. On a number of occasions, we read a poem or short story together. Then Tony would start the conversation by asking, for example, "What would you say in response to 'Living Memory?' What did you see in this? What images stand out for you?"

Three or four of us spoke, including Jean Rupp, an assistant principal, who said, "I saw that we surround ourselves with flowers, which are supposed to be for the dead but are really for the living."

"How do you feel when you see that?" Tony asked, one of his typical moves. It was a way of asking, "So?" or "Say more."

"I wonder about the sense of it. When someone dies, is it justifiable that we trick ourselves into thinking that what we're doing is for the dead, if we end up feeling better?" Jean responded.

"Where, in your life, is that coming from?" Tony prodded gently, and again this was not an unusual response. After Jean spoke for a bit about her life and the recent death of a friend, Tony nodded, "That's a tough one, isn't it. Can you say more?"

As the conversation continued, Tony used other prompts to nudge people to move between those sections of the text that bristled with significance for them and the issues in their lives which made those moments stand out:

- I'm interested. Where in your life might you be getting that from?
- So, do you connect that image in the poem with an image from your own life?

- Has something like that happened to you? Can you tell us the story? Take your time and tell us the whole story.
- How can you explain seeing it in this way? What in your life made you see it *this* way?

In our own adult reading group, my colleagues and I noticed several features of personal response:

- Personal response involves first hearing or reading a text and being affected by it.
- Personal response occurs after taking in a text. There is a sense that first you *get it,* then you respond.
- Personal response is not a low-level matching game between the text and one's own life.
- Personal response does not mean that we suddenly zoom away from the text and think only about our lives. Instead, it has everything to do with lingering over our reading and *only then* turning to our lives to ask, "What from my own life relates to this?"
- Personal response doesn't necessarily mean saying, "me too." We might notice the closeness between a parent and child in a book because our relationships were quite the opposite. The point is that what we see in a text is a result of all that we think, remember, know, and yearn for. Personal responses allow us to understand that our angle of vision grows out of all that we are.
- Personal response deepens our understanding of a text when we think, "How was my experience the same? How was my experience different?" This can lead to insights about the text and ones life, both. This conversation can be shared if the reader conveys his or her life story with enough detail that it becomes almost like a second text, and children compare texts, asking, "How are they the same? How are they different?"
- The conversation and the thinking move between particular sections of the text and particular moments of one's life, especially between the big messages and these significant moments and images. Moments from one's life and from the text ground the talk, but in the end we're using the particulars to talk about a whole text and a whole life.

The Power of Personal Response: One Classroom

Perhaps the most important way to teach personal response is to do what I did for Miles when I read *Prince Caspian*. I chose a book I love with all my heart and read it to him. "Read to them," Cynthia Rylant advises teachers,

> Read to them *The Ox Cart Man* and *The Animal Farm*, and *The Birds, and the Beasts and the Third Thing*. Take their breath away. Read these with the same feeling in your throat as when you first see the ocean after driving hours and hours to get there. Close the final page of the book with the same reverence you feel as you kiss your sleeping child good night. Be quiet. Don't talk the experience to death. Shut up and let these kids feel and think. Do this a lot. Teach them to be moved and you will be preparing them to move others.

Kathy and I chose to read Patricia MacLachlan's *Journey* aloud because we adore the book from first page to last. It gives us goosebumps. As Kathy's children pulled in close, I said only a few words. "Today I am going to read aloud the beginning of this exquisite book. I know as you hear it, it will fill you with your own memories. After I finish reading, in the silence, let's each write one vignette from our lives that connects to *Journey*." Then, with "the same reverence I feel as I kiss my sleeping child goodnight," I read aloud the foreword to the book.

> Mama named me *Journey. Journey,* as if somehow she wished her restlessness on me. But it was Mama who would be gone the year that I was eleven— before spring crashed onto our hillside with explosions of mountain laurel, before summer came with the soft slap of the screen door, breathless nights, and mildew on the books. I should have known, but I didn't. My older sister Cat knew. Grandma knew, but Grandma kept it to herself. Grandfather knew and said so.
>
> Mama stood in the barn, her suitcase at her feet. "I'll send money," she said. "For Cat and Journey."
>
> "That's not good enough, Liddie," said Grandfather.
>
> "I'll be back Journey," my mother said softly.
>
> But I looked up and saw the way the light trembled in her hair, making her look like an angel, someone not earthbound. Even in that moment she was gone.
>
> "No, son," Grandfather said to me, his voice loud in the barn. "She won't be back."
>
> And that was when I hit him.

The room was silent. Speaking almost in a whisper, I said, "Let's take a moment from our lives and put it on the page." Soon the room was full of the scratch of pens. Sitting at the front of the circle, I kept my eyes glued to the page and wrote with all my heart. At times I could hear the children shifting restlessly and was dying to give them the eagle eye, but I resisted, holding myself to a standard of total immersion in the task. After a few minutes, however, the restlessness grew. Finally I reached the bottom of my paper and looked up.

"Let me read what I've got so far," I said. The room was hushed as I read a vignette from my son's nursery school years, a vignette that related, in complex ways, to the scene from *Journey*. In my vignette, I told how Miles had entered nursery school in the middle of the year, so neither he nor I received a proper introduction to the fact that Fridays were for show-and-tell. On Miles's first Friday, everyone gathered in a circle. One child had a robot, another a spaceship. Only Miles was empty handed. But when Miles's turn came to sit in the special chair and show his item to the admiring circle, he took his place. "Ummm …" Miles said slowly, looking out at the circle. Then he fished around in his pocket and produced a little yellow thread. "I brought this thread," he said, turning so everyone could see it. "It's from my blanket." Then he began rolling it like a miniature snowball. "If you roll it, you can make a love ball." And Miles gave his love ball to Jon, who was becoming his friend.

"Would someone else read aloud what you've written?" I asked.

Silence.

I looked over the group trying to catch the eyes of a volunteer, someone I could cajole into reading aloud. Every set of eyes was lowered, glued to knees, hands, papers.

Finally, one voice piped up, "I didn't really write it that way, with the talk." Other voices murmured in assent.

I could guess what this meant. Instead of taking a moment from their own lives, one they somehow connected with the text, and putting in on the paper, they had summarized the text I'd read and their reactions to it. They had probably written *about* literature rather than *in response to* literature. And if they *had* written about a life connection, I suspected that most of them had made vague comments: "It was good. It reminded me of sad times, happy times, good times, bad times …" But I wanted the children to write what amounted to their own literature in response to this page from *Journey*, so that I could show them the power of thinking between the text and their own lives. Therefore, I said, "Let me reread this foreword from *Journey*. And I know it will make you think of moments from your lives. Take one episode from your life, one vignette that comes to mind, and write your own true story." Again,

I read the text and again I lowered my eyes and wrote, listening as I did to the scratch of pens. After about ten minutes I said, "Would you share what you've written with the person beside you?" Then I scurried about between the partners, listening to what they were saying, peeking at what they'd written.

"Let's hear someone's," I said after the partners had shared, and I gestured for Hu Ming to bring her paper and sit beside me at the front of the room.

Hu Ming looked startled when I signaled to her but began to pick her way toward the front of the circle. Meanwhile, something was clearly astir. All the children exchanged glances, put their hands over their mouths, and stared at me with big eyes. Kathy Doyle gestured at me from her position at the far side of the circle. She seemed to be muttering "No" and shaking her head furiously. Meanwhile, Hu Ming was already at the front of the circle. What was I to do? Send her back? I tried to make space for her beside me and at the same time to read Kathy's lips.

What I did not know was that Hu Ming was a selective mute, that no one in the classroom had ever heard her utter a word. Supposedly, she spoke at home, but she hadn't spoken to anyone in school and today would be no different.

Hu Ming looked at the circle of children from her place at the front of the meeting area. Everyone stared back at her. She looked at the paper, then at the group, then at me, then at the paper again. I waited. "Hu Ming," I said finally, still unaware that she was a selective mute, "Would you like it if I read your piece aloud?"

She shrugged a little, and slid her piece shyly toward me, smiling slightly as she did. I took the piece in my hands and, unsure of what I would find, began to read aloud, turning Hu Ming's words into a living voice. Hu Ming's first language is Korean and her English was still a little shaky. I read quietly, trying to say the words as she might have said them. She watched my face as I read:

> I am going to pick a scene that kind of connects to my life when I was younger and write about it. She was different. Very different. Grandma used to have a grayish white curly hair and she has a black one just like mine except hers was more curlier like Grandma's. I did not care if she had a sweet smile, younger or anything else because it would never be the same. She was here taking grandma's place. I don't care if she is a perfect step-grandmother. I won't talk to her.
>
> Anyway she is kind of a stranger. If I had to talk I would have to walk around the house calling a stranger, "Grandmother."
>
> I wish Grandma was here. Because if she was here everything will be perfect. No stranger. I hated their wedding. I had to bring a flower to grandpa and she, the stranger, gave me a sweet smile. Of course I didn't smile back. I only could not believe that grandpa was getting married

again. If grandma was here she would stop the wedding now! But she had left me and at that very moment I felt like a very small dot that nobody can see. The world she left made my heart break. Crack went the heart and all of the sudden the happiness began to just pop out and sadness began to come in.

The room was still. "What do you think?" I said, and for a moment, children talked about the power of the piece, about its effect on them. After a while I said, "Readers, we began by reading *Journey.*" With my hand, I gestured to show a line, low and parallel to the ground. "Now Hu Ming has given us another 'book,' another story," I said, and I drew a second, parallel line in the air six inches above the first. With both hands, I depicted the two texts running parallel to each other. "Hu Ming might have said to us that *Journey,*" and I motioned toward the bottom line, "reminds her of a TV show." I gestured to illustrate that the TV show would have acted as a parallel text. "Only *Journey* doesn't remind Hu Ming of a TV show, but of her own true story." I knew these children often talked between texts and related TV shows, and I wanted them to see that a personal response often led to similar sort of intertextual work. Then I added, "Can we talk *between the parallel texts,* between the story of *Journey* and the story that Hu Ming has now given us of her life?"

"Well, not really," Jocelyn said, and then, proceeding to talk between the texts, she said, "because they are completely different. *Journey* is mad and he hits his grandfather. Hu Ming isn't mad."

"Yeah," Dori added. "Hu Ming isn't mad. She just feels like a tiny dot." All of this was odd and powerful because, of course, Hu Ming was right there, silent, in the midst of this conversation about her life, her text, and the story of *Journey.* I've since concluded that the discussion was vastly enriched by Hu Ming's silent presence.

Then Lila, Hu Ming's sidekick and soul mate, said somberly and definitively, "Hu Ming's mad."

"But Hu Ming doesn't hit anyone like Journey does."

"What she does is—she doesn't talk."

The words hung in the air. Everyone's mind seemed to seize on the electric thing Lila had just said, "Hu Ming's mad ... but she doesn't hit anyone ... she just doesn't talk."

Sam gave voice to what everyone was thinking. "Hu Ming," he said, "Are you mad at us? Is that why you don't talk?"

Hu Ming, meanwhile, shrugged a little, looked at her paper, looked at me, and shrugged again. I took over and, perhaps because the intensity of that question and the ensuing silence was too much for me, I said, "What we've just done is what good readers do when they are reading together or reading alone and they make a connection to the text. The reader, like Hu Ming, takes in the whole chunk of text (the foreword from *Journey*), and lets it affect him or her. Sometimes the text fills us with reminders of our own stuff, our own lives, as it did for Hu Ming. And so we lay a bit of our own lives among the lines of the text."

To illustrate, I said, "After reading *Journey*, you'll remember that I wrote about how it reminded me of when my son took a tiny thread from his blanket and made it into a love ball." I continued, "If a group of us was talking together about *Journey*, I would need to tell about that moment with Miles in enough detail that all of us could 'read' that moment from my life like a text and then join me in and thinking between *Journey* and my memory, as we're now thinking between *Journey* and Hu Ming's memory. I might need to ask myself whether this scene in *Journey* makes me feel as if Journey has just a tiny strand to hang onto and whether Journey responds to feeling empty-handed the way Miles did or differently.

It's as if you have two related books, or a book and a TV show, that are like each other, only this time it's a book and your own parallel life. You talk *between the two texts,* your talk is like a needle and thread stitching the two texts together: How are they the same? How are they different?" I sent the children back to their reading clubs with instructions to listen to one and only one person's response ("or they'll all glob up together and lose their individual taste like different flavors of jelly beans in your stomach") and then to talk for as long as they could back and forth between the text and the episode from that one person's life.

For the next few days, Kathy's students worked on responding to texts in deeper ways, allowing the connections between the stories they read and the stories of their lives to change their understanding of both. To help them along, Kathy gave them copies of a personal response Miles had written in his fifth-grade class in response to the poem "Starlight" by Philip Levine. The poem goes like this:

> My father stands in the warm evening
> On the porch of my first house.
> I am four years old and growing tired.
> I see his head among the stars,
> The glow of his cigarette, redder
> Than the summer moon riding
> Low over the old neighborhood. We
> Are alone and he asks me if I am happy
> "Are you happy?" I cannot answer,
> I do not really understand the word,

And the voice, my fathers voice, is not
His voice, but somehow thick and choked,
A voice I have not heard before, but
Often since. He bends and passes
A thumb beneath each of my eyes.
The cigarette is gone, but I can smell
The tiredness that hangs on his breath.
He has found nothing, and he smiles
And holds my head with both his hands.
Then he lifts me to his shoulder,
And now I too am there too among the stars,
As tall as he. Are you happy? I say.
He nods in answer, Yes! Oh yes! Oh yes!
And in that new voice he says nothing,
His eyes closed up against the starlight,
As though those tiny blinking eyes
Of light might find a tall gaunt child
Holding his child up against the promises
Of autumn, until the boy slept
Never to waken in that world again.

Miles's response was this:

When I first read Philip Levine's "Starlight," it instantly reminded me of
my dad and the closeness between us. The father and the son are close in
many ways. The little boy sitting on his father's shoulders, his head resting
on his father's, looking up at the stars. His father's hand is on the other side
of the boy's head, pressing their heads together. They are close for the kid
knows his father's hands, smell and voice. He recognizes when his father's
voice is thick and choked. He knows when his father's breath smells different. They are close because they love each other. The kid imagines his
father's head is up in the stars; he imagines his father is a star. The father
loves his kid and wants to make him know his love. I think that is why he
tells the kid he is happy.

I know me and my Dad are close in many of the same ways. I can imagine writing a poem like "Starlight." I know my dad's voice, hands and smell.
But if I wrote that poem, Dad and I would not be on a porch. I would tell
of us hiking along a rocky trail, our feet stepping in unison, the sun's rays
poking through the trees and illuminating the path. "I used to come here
when I was a kid," Dad would say. Then he would spin out stories of sleeping in abandoned water towers and climbing forgotten rock buildings. Dad
never did this with his dad. He does it with us because he knows how it feels
never to walk side by side, matching your father's strides with sunlight on
your back. Dad's dad never had time for Dad. He paid no attention to him,

but Dad pays attention to us. He feels devastated when he can't play chess with me, when he doesn't have time to toss the ball around. But his eyes light up when I laugh and run up and hug him because he said yes to another expedition. Instead of closeness made up of one moment on the porch, ours is made in hours on a hiking trail. The kid remembers his father's hands holding him on his shoulders. I remember my father's hands pushing me out over a deep river on a rope swing and Dad pulling me in.

But the father in Starlight is also not close in many ways. The name even implies a distance. The boy thinks of his dad as a star, but stars are high up there and far away from others. Also, the father seems depressed and he does not tell the kid. If Dad is sad, he tells us. I feel the kid needs to know the truth. I know I would. The father tries to talk to the child but the kid does not understand. I think the father should know that it was a hard question for a four year old. When Mom asked me if I was happy, serious happy, and dug a tiny bit my brain shut down. I just looked at her, stuttering, searching for the right words. When Mom asked me how I really felt she was looking at me. In Starlight I felt that the father was looking up at the stars and dreamily asking, "Are you happy?" not really thinking about his son, but about himself and whether *he* was happy or sad.

The last line has a strange meaning. "Never to waken in that world again." This does not mean one of them died, but that the kid slept never to waken in that moment again. That moment was quick and fleeting like a butterfly, both close and distant at the same time. It is there, you see it then it is gone. I have had a moment like that with my dad, with sunlight not starlight, illuminating our path. Whether hiking to a hidden glen, lake or water tower, no hike will ever be like that one. Never again will I be a 10-year old boy, walking along a trail with sunlight on my back and my father at my side.

The students studied Miles' response and used it to help them in their responses to *Journey*. In their book clubs, the students continued to spend some of their reading club time talking about *Journey* and one or two kids' responses to those sections. Some days Kathy said, "Instead of writing down the experience *Journey* brings to mind, tell it to each other. But take your time and tell it in detail, like a story, so it can act as a parallel text, like Miles's stories about his dad." Once Kathy was convinced that students were absorbing this new, deeper way to respond to texts, personal response again became one option among many for the bookclubs in her classroom.

Several days later, David read aloud this response to *Journey:*

Moving
I walked into the dusty white room. It seemed different. It was huge and there was no carpet, chairs, tables, nothing except boxes. One of the them

said, "Albums." I opened the box and saw huge dark leather covered books. I opened one of them. The binding of it creaked. I sat on the cold wood floor and saw my old house in a colorful picture. I turn the page and there was a small trimmed picture of me at my 5th birthday. I turned more pages: cousins, places visited, houses, people, presents, birthdays. All of these, every single one of the pictures seemed like old business and I was going on to the new. I lay down on the floor and said loudly, "Hello." I heard it echo throughout the empty house. The Ryder truck pulled away. Things were not going to be the same.

After listening, Sam said, "Journey and you, David, are both looking at picture albums, but you're not looking in the same way. Journey *wanted* to think about when he was smaller, but you look and say, "These are old business. I want to move on."

Brian nodded. "Journey is afraid that his old life, when his mother was still there, is gone."

David protested, "I'm afraid too. I consider myself practically Journey." Then he added, "I put the Ryder truck into my entry and made it pull away because when I moved, it felt like my life was pulling away. When that Ryder truck pulled away, it was pulling all my stuff away from the old house. All my life and friends were crammed into the Ryder truck and it was pulling away. I was left in an empty room and had to say, 'Hello? Am I here? Is anyone there?'"

"So you and Journey *are* practically the same! You are both afraid that your old life is gone. Journey has two lives—before his mother left and after she left—and the picture album is at the center of those two lives," Brian continued.

Watching this exchange unfold and setting it alongside the whole experience with Hu Ming, left Kathy and me speechless. I thought about how, only six months earlier, David had thought that responding personally to a text meant drawing match-up lines between the details in a text and the details in a life. "My uncle has a green hat!"

What we want children to learn, above all, is that we read to become whole. We turn to stories, as Barry Lopez says, to repair a spirit in disarray. How desperate we are to make sense of our lives. "What human beings fear," Howard Becker says, "Is not growing old but growing old without things adding up." For me and for so many people I know, books are a lantern, helping us find our path in life. They give us heroes, and they give us mentors in the real work of being human, of dealing with delight, loss, anger, hope, passion, jealousy, and mystery. For many of us reading is not a way to kill time; instead reading is a way to make a life.

There are times, in mid page, when we come to a passage that brings tears to our eyes, that takes us by crazy surprise, that sends a shiver down our spine, that haunts us with a glimpse of something far beyond or far deeper (Buechner, 1999, pp. 53–54). In reading, as in life, significance and direction emerge out of the great hodgepodge. Suddenly, we're reading with heart, mind, and soul. Suddenly, everything matters too much. If we choose to listen, to let ourselves breathe that new kind of air, "page by page, year by year, chapter by chapter your own story unfolds—your life story," Buechner writes. "Things happen. People come and people go. The scene shifts. Time goes by. Time runs out." He adds, "Maybe it's all utterly meaningful.... Even the smallest events hold the greatest clues" (p. 64).

I want all children to expect something like this when they read, to watch for these responses, and to know they'll come. And when a book creates a lump in the throat and a shiver down the spine, I want readers to know they can talk, write, and live differently as a result.

We Are the Authors
of Our Lives

26

These are hard times for teachers. In rural areas, towns, and cities across the country, newspapers publish school rankings determined only by scores on norm-referenced standardized reading tests. Principals in many cities are hired with the stipulation that reading test scores must go up or their jobs will be in jeopardy. In the frenzy of this single-minded dedication to achieving higher scores, thousands of schools now have pep rallies to rev children up for standardized tests and celebrate high achievers. Some states pay children to improve their scores. In one school I visited recently, the front foyer was dominated by a display case full of Nintendo games, television sets, and toy laser guns accompanied by a sign that promised "Score Well and You'll Be Rewarded."

Because of the high stakes associated with test scores, educators often staff schools, group children, design curriculum, and provide professional development with one goal in mind: to raise scores. In some schools, teachers are expected to devote their entire language arts block to test preparation for months at a time and are told that the curriculum must match the standardized tests. When standardized tests swarm with short-answer questions, this means we can no longer teach reading using the best of children's literature and must instead fill our classrooms and our days with worksheets, exercises, and drills. In the frenzy to raise test scores, children have fewer opportunities to write essays, work collaboratively, conduct research, read wonderful literature, or talk about books.

In the midst of all this, it is difficult for us as teachers to hold on to our beliefs. Recently a teacher asked me to sign her book. I wrote, "Hold on to your dreams. Hold on for dear life." How hard it can be to remember that we are authors of our own lives. One of my most talented graduate students, a teacher with years of Peace Corps experience, found herself teaching this year in a district that prided itself on a "Balanced Literacy Approach." Literally thousands of teachers across her district were expected to follow this approach as it was scripted in the district office: twenty minutes for reading aloud; twenty minutes for interactive writing; fifteen minutes for work with the word wall, and so on. When this teacher tried to tailor the district schedule to fit her beliefs and her children's needs, she was told that no, she was to follow The District Way.

"But, but …" she said, trying to cite evidence and reasons.

Interrupting, her administrator said, "You don't know enough to question anything. Forget what you learned at graduate school. You don't know anything."

"If I don't know anything," the teacher told me, "How can they trust me with thirty-two first graders? Why am I teaching if they do not have enough trust in me to allow me to adjust what I'm doing based on what I see?" She went on to comment, "These days, it can be hard to be a smart teacher. I almost feel as if I should be stupid. Then I'd be glad to follow their scripts, whether or not they work. But I'm not stupid. And I can't be responsible for doing a good job and yet be prevented from responding to what I see my kids needing."

Some of us have tried to go along with the new mandates, but we find ourselves worn out from constantly trying to keep up, to fit in, and to take in all the different agendas other people have for us. "I'm bone-tired," a teacher told me last week, and she is not alone. I've seen a bumper sticker that says, "Give up, it hurts less," but that bumper sticker is wrong. What hurts is hollowness. Hollowness erodes our energy. Throughout our profession there's never been more talk about teacher burnout and low morale. Publishers produce teacher-proof lessons and promise that "None of your precious time will be wasted in planning." But we're not tired from our teaching or from planning our teaching. We're tired because of all the junk that gets in the way of our teaching. We yearn for the days when the whole of our lives was preparation for teaching, when every film we watched or book we read or professional conversation we had filled us with ideas to bring to our children. No, we're not tired from our teaching or from planning our teaching. We're tired because of the deep alienation we feel when our teaching is no longer ours. We're tired from going through the motions of teaching someone else's curriculum. We're tired from feeling as if there is no place in our classroom for our soul, our knowledge, or our intuitions.

So what are we to do? How can we hold onto the dreams that brought us to teaching in the first place? How can we hold on to our dreams in a world that sometimes seems to have gone berserk over "high standards" and "high stakes"?

In *A Teacher's Guide to Standardized Reading Tests: Knowledge Is Power*, I write,

> We have reached the place in this story—in the story of this book and in the story of the profession—where it's time for the music to change, for the narrator's intonation to shift, for the problem posing to be behind us. It is time to turn the page and to have the story shift. It is time to read, "One day ...," it is time for an unlikely character to step forward and to do something or to suggest something that changes everything. In this story, that character will not be the traveling minstrel, the young lad with an answer to the king's riddle, or the youngest sister emerging from her place at the hearth.
>
> In this story, we must be the characters who step forward. It is time for classroom teachers to draw our chairs up to the policy table. It is time for us to have a voice in shaping the standards and measures of assessment that so powerfully direct our profession. It is time for each of us to come out from behind our classroom door, to step forward as a major player in this drama. (Calkins, Montgomery, and Santman, 1998, p. 165)

Some of us may sputter in protest, "But ... I'm just the little guy in this." But even as we sputter, we know it is totally obvious that we need a stronger voice in establishing the policies that shape our teaching lives. We understand education because we are on the front lines.

It is not easy to gather our courage, to step forward, to speak out. In children's books, when an unlikely character—the youngest daughter, the court jester, the overlooked teacher—steps out of the shadows to turn the tide of events, this character does so by relying on his or her wits. If *we* are to make a significant contribution to educational policy, we too, need to rely on our wits.

I have found that I am less victimized by standardized tests and standards when I am more knowledgeable about them. When I am knowledgeable about standardized tests, I can challenge the conclusions that are drawn from test scores. I can plan more efficient test preparation. I can control some of the damage that test scores do to parents' perceptions of their children and children's perceptions of themselves. Then, too, when I am knowledgeable about standardized tests and standards, I am more able to determine the battles I am (and am not) willing to wage, and the causes I will (and will not) take on (Calkins, Montgomery, Santman, 1998). Each one of us needs to do the soul searching and the research necessary to define our role as advocates for our profession. "What do I believe in?" "How will my life reflect my beliefs?"

In my own work, I have chosen to speak on behalf of lean but ambitious standards that reflect our best current knowledge of children as readers and writers. Although I respect colleagues who battle against the very existence of standards, arguing that one size does not fit all, in my own life I am not convinced it is either realistic or wise to fight against the existence of standards or even against the fact that we have large-scale standardized means to assess our children's (and our own) progress toward meeting those standards. I've come to believe that for most educators, our practice *is* guided by an internalized sense of how good is good enough, and that harm is done if we never directly address the question "What are we after when we teach?" or "How do we know when we're getting there (or when we and our children are in trouble)?" I suspect, for example, that if I asked teachers "When do you envision that a child who is doing well as a reader will successfully handle books such as Beverly Cleary's *Ramona*?" many teachers would point to the juncture between third and fourth grade or to fourth grade. Yet I know of teachers who see no problem when fifth graders can just barely handle a *Pee Wee Scout* book, which is a far simpler text. When teachers hold radically different expectations for the children they teach, this is the ultimate inequity.

For several years my sons Miles and Evan studied with a piano teacher who assigned show tunes and popular music. They practiced each night, and in their lessons, their teacher sat two feet from the piano, arms folded, smiling pleasantly. He spoke cheerily to me each week, and because I know nothing about piano, I had no reason to believe my sons weren't progressing beautifully. Miles and Evan, too, were confident that they were doing everything their teacher asked, so all must be well. Then, almost by accident, my sons switched to a new teacher. Christine Shoh looked askance at their fingering, their sense of rhythm, and their ability to read music. In their lessons she pulled in close, shaping the position of their hands, adjusting their posture, and intervening often to ask them to count the beats or to redo a phrase. Watching this active, assertive teacher and seeing the extraordinary progress my sons finally made under her vigilant tutelage, I couldn't help but wonder how often in our schools children must rely on teachers who give them the academic equivalent of show tunes and popular songs and then sit two feet away, smiling pleasantly.

I think it could be helpful, then, for teachers and other educators from across a region to come together and set down, as a matter of public record, a limited number of commonly agreed upon and deeply significant goals that specify what we hope and expect children to know, understand, and be able to do at certain milestone ages. Given that many of us *have* such goals, it is only fair to make them public and open them up for discussion and reconsideration. Of course, if educators agree that we are accountable for helping all children read books at the level of *Ramona* somewhere during their fourth-grade year, then we need to give all our children the books, the time to read, the coaching, and the other necessary opportunities to learn. I'm not even against systemic and standardized ways of testing these commonly agreed upon standards, as long as test results are considered alongside other data and as long as worrisome test scores lead us to reconsider the opportunities we're giving to children and to ask whether we can give them and their teachers more opportunities to learn.

In New York City, I've worked on behalf of this vision of standards and standardized testing. As I mentioned earlier, our city has adopted the New Standards published by The National Center for Education and the Economy and The Institute of Learning at the University of Pittsburgh. I've been an active member of the committee that authored those standards, and Project classrooms are prominent in many of the videotapes illustrating the standards. Because the standards were written by a diverse group of educators representing different schools of thought, it's not surprising that I don't agree with every single aspect. On the whole, however, I think they are wise. Still, I am sorry to discover instances in which the existence of these standards has led administrators to micromanage their teachers' teaching. And I regret that teachers and children who have not yet been given opportunities to learn are held accountable to these standards.

Yet, despite the problems, these standards hold us to a course that I believe is helpful to many of us in New York City. We've adopted a standardized assessment procedure for all primary children: children read aloud from leveled books while we take and analyze running records, noting what they can do. We also ask them to retell these books. In addition, twice a year, each of our primary-level children is asked to write and revise a story while we again record what they can do. Our fourth graders are expected to read twenty-five books a year, and we hope these books are at the level of Beverly Cleary's *Ramona* or of Roald Dahl's *Matilda*. All our children are expected to write daily, often choosing their own topics and revising their work with input from classmates. Our fourth-grade statewide reading test asks students to read long texts and write essays that develop theories about what they've read. This year, scores for this test will be disaggregated in a way that will show not only how well we're doing in teaching our school population as a whole, but also how well we're teaching each racial group within our school population. I can't help thinking that if this can happen here, it can happen elsewhere.

Other states are also traveling a relatively reasonable course—teachers will want to examine standards and assessments in Rhode Island, Vermont,

Iowa, Michigan, and Hawaii—but the sad truth is that these are the exception. Mostly, as I travel the country, I see the "state-of-the standards" movement, and it is clear that all is not well. Often, the tests and the standards are capricious and damaging. In one state, first graders are expected to read and be able to spell correctly anything they can say. In another state, every fourth grader is held accountable for knowing the periodic table of chemical elements. Even when a state's standards are reasonable, they are often translated into assessment instruments that are appallingly narrow and ill-advised. Higher literacy, for example, cannot be assessed through short-answer tests that do not ask a child to read, reflect upon, critique, or write about long passages. Yet it is rare indeed for standardized tests to include complex problems and constructed responses, or to require synthesis, analysis, or interpretation.

What are we to do? First of all, I think teachers should realize that it doesn't need to be this way. It is possible to argue for standards that are leaner and more judicious, that do in fact grow out of a number of discussions and thus an emerging consensus among educators.

Then, too, I think we need to realize that not all standardized tests are equally damaging. The most damaging are norm-referenced tests, which are designed, piloted, and revised to ensure that children score along a bell curve, which means that half score below grade-level. The SAT test is an example of a norm-referenced test whose purpose is to divide teenagers so that only some are admitted to particular colleges. When a state adopts a norm-referenced test, that state, it seems to me, is trying to divide teachers and children into winners and losers. If we are testing to ensure that every child reaches his or her potential, why design a test ensuring that half of all children will fail? Our tests need to be criteria-referenced, and our hope should be that if we clearly specify the criteria for success—what it is that children should know and be able to do—eventually more and more children will do well on these tests and, more importantly, will do well as readers, writers, and learners.

We need to remember that standardized tests can only assess the achievement of higher standards if they ask students to read extended passages and respond thoughtfully to what they have read. It is worth fighting for performance assessments such as those in the National Assessment of Education Progress assessment (NAEP) or New Standards exams. Performance assessment exams are more costly than multiple-choice tests, so states resist them mightily, but one obvious solution is for states to give standardized tests *less often;* another, is for states to give these exams to a *random sampling* of students rather than to every child. Because the purpose of the NAEP test has been to document long-term trends in the teaching of reading, for example, it hasn't been important that *every* student take the test and earn a score. Therefore, this assessment has been given to only a carefully chosen sampling. In the political arena, there is a lot of rhetoric against giving tests to only a sampling of students ("We need to hold teachers accountable for educating each and every child"), but we should be able to rebut this argument. Meanwhile, the best we can do may be to argue for tests that include more performance components. Because many teachers will always teach to the test, they should be worth teaching toward.

We must also speak out for a more open system of testing and reporting scores. In too many states, we teachers barely catch a glimpse of the exams that exert such control over us and our children. We unseal the tests minutes before we distribute them, and the instant the testing session is over, they are whisked away. Months later, we receive statistical breakdowns of our students' scores, but these statistics are so remote from the test questions themselves, they mean little to us. Only if we could reread a particular question and note how a particular student answered that question could we assess the logic behind the answer and learn from what that student has done.

At the same time, if we never see the tests our students take, we are unable to protest against confusing or ambiguous questions. In one test, a question asked: "An architect's most important tools are _____"

    E Pencil and paper

    F Buildings

    G Ideas

    H Bricks

Many children selected "(E) Pencil and paper," which, according to the scores sheet, was incorrect. According to the test writer, the correct answer was "(G) Ideas" (Meier, 1991, pp. 458–459). Standardized tests are full of problematic questions such as these, but this fact is rarely brought to public attention, partly because we cannot question tests or the conclusions drawn from them when they are whisked out of our sight. As teachers, we must speak out for the right to see and study the tests and to learn from what our students do on them.

We must also insist on the full disclosure of formulas for deriving scores. If newspapers keep the index they use for arriving at a school's "index of poverty" shrouded, for example, we cannot challenge the logic behind these formulas. In New York, we learned four months too late that gigantic mistakes had been made by the publisher of our test. Thousands of children who were reported as failing the test had *not,* in fact, failed it. "Oopsie, we made a mistake," the publisher said, but by then, schools had already been taken over by the Chancellor, children had already spent their summer in summer school, and teachers and principals had already been rebuked. How many other mistakes go unnoticed because the formulae are kept from public view?

As a profession, we must also argue against the growing tendency to administer standardized tests to younger and younger children. Early childhood educational organizations unanimously agree that few useful conclusions about young children can be drawn from their performance on any one day or at any one task. And the items on a paper-and-pencil test for six-year-olds are hardly indicators of a child's true likelihood to succeed as a reader and a writer. How could these tests begin to show a child's sense of story, finesse with oral language, interest in books and in print, identity as a reader and writer, or ability to listen with comprehension?

When I say that we as teachers must take our place at the policy table and speak out on the behalf of our profession, what I am also suggesting is this: *our* literacy can change the world. When we showed children that Marisol's memoir about being the kind of kid who never had a birthday party became a blueprint for something as big as a birthday, we told children Marisol's work demonstrates that print has the power to create a new world. We extoll young people to remember that "The pen is mightier than the sword" and show them how Martin Luther King's "I Have a Dream" speech changed the course of history. But do we, as a profession, use the power of our own literacy to make a better world for ourselves and our children?

Our voices could matter very much. A magazine editor takes notice when he or she receives even five letters in response to a story. And a Washington activist tells me the rule of thumb in her work is that it takes twenty letters for a member of Congress to take notice of an issue, and a mere sixty letters to turn that issue into a priority. "Teachers constitute the largest profession on earth," she says. "Why don't they realize their collective power?"

As I write, I'm thinking of the California teachers who rallied yesterday, eight thousand strong, and won dramatically increased school funding and the right of each school community to use its own discretion over how at least these new funds will be spent. I'm rooting for the parents in a Midwestern state who have encouraged their children to boycott a state test in droves, throwing all statistical analysis into disarray. These parents argue that is it is not right to hold children to standards that most successful American citizens could not possibly meet. I'm remembering the teachers who wrote a letter to the editor recently reminding the public that when they complain because "only 60 percent of our children are reading on grade level," they need to bear in mind that "grade level" refers by definition to the level at which half of the student population reads below and half above. I celebrate teachers who use their voices and the written word to speak out on behalf of a more sane context in which to teach. Teaching reading will be a great deal easier when we raise our voices and together create the kind of contexts that support good teaching. We need to come together in the spirit of a barn-raising, but it's not a barn but a better world that we're raising, a world in which teachers can teach and students can learn.

I also celebrate the teacher who closes her classroom door and teaches according to her beliefs. In the end, the most important, most political thing we can do is to understand that each of us and each of our students travels this way but once. Our lives are ours to create. The choices we make matter more than we could dare to think. This is true for each of us, but it is especially true for those of us who teach. Day by day, minute by minute, we make decisions that shape the worlds and affect the destinies of the children in our care.

"Gather close," we say. "I want to read you a story …" And soon thirty children have explored a desolate beach along the coast of Maine and found a blue bit of sea glass, rubbed smooth, and breathed in the summer smell of seaside roses, and vowed to come back often to this place of solace. We, as teachers, make decisions that shape our lives and the lives of others, and we teach children that they, too, are called upon to create the lives they want to live.

"For homework tonight," Kathy Doyle said to her fifth graders, "and for homework every night for the rest of your lives, I hope you will find a way to build a richly literate life for yourself."

It had been a child, Andrew Lindner, who first prompted Kathy and I to reconsider what we'd asked children to do in the name of homework. "Homework isn't really *home* work," Andrew had commented one day. "Home is where the family is. Most homework is just 'later' work." Andrew's comments jolted us into realizing that if our goal was to have children weave reading and writing into the people and passions of their lives, it was a waste to make vocabulary drills, textbook questions, and syllabicating spelling words the work that families congregated around at the kitchen table. And so Kathy and I made one of the countless 'small' teaching decisions that we teachers make every day and this decision, like so many that we make, proved to be not small at all. "For homework, let's each find a way to weave the reading and writing we're doing in school into our hobbies, interests, and home lives." Soon Kathy's kids were tackling weekly assignments such as these:

- This week, strike up book conversations with people everywhere. Talk about books with grandparents, younger children, the shopkeeper, your coach. Keep a log of the conversations.

- Find ways in which reading can extend one of your hobbies or interests. Keep a record of what you read in your reading log.
- Read with a family member. Let texts spark grand conversations.
- Interview a good reader in your life. What does he or she do that you can emulate? Begin now to live differently because of the example the good reader sets for you.
- Find a reader in your life who might profit from your support. Share your love of reading with that person and record what you learn.

These assignments led to magnificent whole-class conversations and before long, Kathy and her students had decided they would each undertake a very personal project. Lila selected poems to accompany her piano songs, which led her into a study of songwriters and their songs. Brian researched landscapes and devised a plan for turning his back lawn into a nature preserve. Sam brought home a stack of electronics books from the town library, and then he and David set out to build a robot.

Lila, Brian, Sam and David are making not only poems and robots, they are also making richly literate lives. When Jean Piaget was eleven, he published his first scientific article. Piaget wrote the article, a report on the sighting of a rare bird, to impress the town librarian so she'd allow him to borrow books. Piaget's followers often cite the article as an early sign of Piaget's genius, but Seymour Papert, author of *Mindstorms,* points out that the article didn't contain any logic or language that would be surprising for an average child of eleven. Papert does, however, find enormous significance in eleven year old Piaget's project. We, as teachers, are wise to listen closely to Papert's message when he says, "I am inclined to think of the publication as being as much a cause as a consequence of Piaget's exceptional intellectual qualities."

Papert goes on to write, "What I find most impressive is not that a boy of eleven could write a report about a bird, but that this same boy of eleven took himself seriously enough to conceive and carry out this strategy for dealing with the librarian. I see in it young Jean, preparing himself to become Piaget. He was practicing taking charge of his own development, something that is necessary not only for those who want to become leading thinkers, but for all citizens of a society in which individuals have to define and redefine their roles throughout a long lifetime." Lila and Brian, Sam and David, like young Piaget and like each of us, must learn to take their lives in their own hands. Day by day, moment by moment, we make decisions about who we are and who we will be. Teaching children to compose richly literate lives is our calling as teachers of reading and writing, and this is big work indeed.

When Catherine decided to make a woodland ecosystem in an aquarium and brought a gecko and a fire-belly frog to live in it, we can look at what she's doing as playing with pets (and in fact her parents said, "It was as if she was playing with her dolls and the scaled down habitats she used to make for them, but it was much more intense). We can also see her investigations of these creatures and her stewardship of them as life work. Whole lives revolve around personal projects such as this. Perhaps because Catherine's teacher and her parents regarded her project as life work, helping her become an authority on amphibians, she went on to build a pond for toads, salamanders and butterflies and to create feeding stations for birds.

Dori and her mother formed a mother-daughter book club. Dori brought home several copies of the *Horn Book* magazine, and they used its book reviews and those in *The New York Times* to compile a reading list for their club. "We put *The Black Stallion* on our reading list because Mom read it and thought we should read it together, so I added *The Bridge to Terabithia* (it's a book to read with your mom)," Dori said. When I asked Dori what it was like to read with her mother, she said, "At the beginning of the year, my Mom thought I was becoming so independent and not needing her so much, and now, with the book club, I do. And I feel younger again and that's okay." Then Dori went on to say, "The way our club meets is she comes up and sits on my bed, and we take turns reading aloud to each other, and then we have long talks."

Andrew began reading with his little brother, Peter, who was having some trouble in his first-grade classroom. Three times a week, Andrew audiotaped sessions in which he laid out several picturebooks and Peter chose one. Then they looked the book over together and read it. In one of these sessions, Peter chose to read Mem Fox's *Night Noises*. Flipping through the pictures, he said, "There's a dog, and there's clouds …"

"There's more to the pictures than that," Andrew said. "What do you notice?"

> "Lilabee Lacy is sleeping and the dog is, too. But he's peeking," Peter said. Turning the page, he said, "Now the *dog's* sleeping!" Soon he added, "Awake, asleep, awake, asleep. Hey, it's a pattern!" Again Peter scrutinized the pages. "And he's having happy dreams, mad dreams, happy …"
>
> Duly impressed, Andrew nudged him on. "Anything else you see?"
>
> Studying the clouds in the background, Peter said, "I think I can see a face in the cloud."

The next day Andrew decided to ask his father to read and talk about the same book. Andrew had studied the strategies proficient readers use in school, and his plan was to use his dad as an exemplar to give Peter further direction. But to Andrew's surprise, his father saw less in *Night Noises* than Peter had seen. Later, when I brought Andrew's audiotape of this session home to listen to it, I heard this:

> "This is Andrew Lindner and I'm talking about the response my father and my brother gave to *Night Noises*. I think my brother was good; he was better than my father. He saw a lot in the book, and found patterns and discoveries. My father just said, 'This is good,' and 'This is bad' (even if I prompted him!). I was told adult people are taught in school to be critics and to look for the bad parts of writing, and I wonder why you do that, because you miss out on the whole story?
>
> "My dad didn't ask a single question, or find one thing to admire (and this was a good book). My brother looked and thought and listened and looked some more. And I know this tape can't show expressions, but my father was [Andrew's voice becomes languid and dull] 'Well, are we done?'— even when we'd just begun—and Peter, at every step of the way, his face was excited and he sat forward like he expected the book would be great.
>
> "Maybe the way my father reads, it's because adults, with all the things they have to do, they've lost the freedom to notice and think. Maybe they just think formally, like they are at their job."
>
> Pausing for a moment, Andrew continued, "Now Daniel did lifework with *his* parents and his *mother* did all the talking and when Daniel tried to get his *father* to talk, he just said, 'Yes, I agree.' Maybe it's just *men*—not all adults—who don't say their feelings and see a lot to admire."

Andrew was quiet for a moment. Listening to the audiotape, I could sense his mind turning over all he'd noticed. When he spoke again, it was with great earnestness:

> "But the most important thing I think I've learned from all this is that there are many different kinds of reading. There's my dad's kind, which is 'Okay, this happened and that happened …' (just what the story is about and not much else). Then there's Peter's kind and that's the kind we're doing in school. All my life, I want to do *this* kind of reading because you get a whole lot more out of any book you read, or any day you have."

I replay this audiotape again and again. How I love hearing this youngster, on the cusp of adolescence, speaking with such boyish resolve, taking his life in his hands and vowing, "All my life, I want to do *this* kind of reading." I am reminded of the film crew's visit to Kathleen Tolan's Harlem classroom, when I told the television producers, "What Kathleen knows is that as important as it is for children to compose poems, memoirs, and book reviews, it's even more important for them to compose lives in which reading and writing matter." Listening to Andrew, I know this is what he has done, and for a moment, thinking about the power of good teachers, I have goosebumps. What power—and what responsibility! Sometimes, I see teachers and I want to say, "How do you live, knowing you matter so much?"

Once we really fathom how much our teaching matters, we have no alternative but to follow Andrew's example and take our lives in our own hands. We have no alternative but to resolve, "All my life, I want to teach *this* way." We need to remember that we are the authors of our teaching selves.

Twenty years ago, when I founded the Teachers College Reading and Writing Project, a fellow named Jim was our fiscal manager. Jim seemed to adopt the Project as his family. After hours, he'd busy himself about the office, listening to classical music and doing nice things for people. He'd lay out a new blotter on my desk, wash out all our coffee cups, take a coat to the tailor's for mending.

After many years of service, Jim began to get sick. He grew thin before our eyes. No one knew what was the matter. He said he was being tested for parasites. Eventually he developed red blotches on his arms, hands, and neck, and it became clear that he had AIDS; he was the first person I knew to have the disease.

Before long, Jim left on disability. Often after our Thursday meetings at Teachers College, someone would head off to the distant parts of Brooklyn to visit him, to help him with grocery shopping or to clean his apartment. My son Evan was an infant then, and because we lived an hour in the opposite direction, I couldn't often make it on these visits. Feeling inadequate, I'd watch as people left for Brooklyn, and say, simply, "Give Jim my best."

A year later Jim entered Columbia Presbyterian Hospital, and I stopped in to visit him. It was heartbreaking to see how much he'd changed. He was so thin, his head like a skull, but still with blue blue eyes. He held my hand and looked at me with such intensity that I was embarrassed. Looking for a conversation topic, I scanned his barren hospital room. "Jim, you don't have a radio," I said. "Remember how you always listened to classical music? Can't you have a radio here?"

"Oh, I could have one," he said. "Mine got lost along the way."

Glad to finally have found something, however small, I could do to help, I said, "Jim, I'll get you a radio!"

"Oh, Lucy, that'd be great," he said. "Beethoven would be good right about now."

I left soon after that, hurrying back to the college. My plan was to get the radio the next day. I just had to write a grant first, and grade my student papers and answer some phone calls. A week later a colleague came back from a visit with Jim. "He told me about the radio," she said.

"I'm going to get to it right away," I answered, making a mental note to get the radio as soon as I'd plowed through the pile on my desk. There just were some things I had to cover, and finish, and get through, and check on first.

Then my own appendix ruptured, and I was in the hospital with tubes in my nose. The phone rang. "Jim died."

I held the receiver in my hand. All I could think was, "He never got the radio."

Now I drive past Columbia Presbyterian Hospital every day on my way to work, and every day, I see that hospital and I vow, "May I never again be the kind of person who forgets the radio."

I end with the story of Jim because in the teaching of reading, there are always so many details to plow through, to cover and finish and check, that it's only too easy to forget the radio. In the end, my wish for all of us is this: Let's hold tight to what matters most. Let's hold on for dear life.

APPENDIX A
Examples of Leveled Reading Books

Group 1 Books:
Reading Recovery Levels 1–2
Guided Reading Levels A–B
Basal Reader often used at this level: Readiness

Benchmarks:

The Farm	Literacy 2000, Rigby
Cat on the Mat	Brian Wildsmith
Time for Dinner	PM Starters, Rigby
The Birthday Cake	Sunshine, Wright Group
I Can Write	Learn to Read, Creative Teaching Press

Assessment:
DRA A–2

I Paint	Andrea Butler
The Zoo	Wonder World, Wright Group
Look at Me	PM Starters, Rigby

Group 2 Books:
Reading Recovery Levels 3–4
Guided Reading Levels C–D
Basal Reader often used at this level: Pre-primer I

Benchmarks:

Rain	Robert Kalan
Shoo!	Sunshine, Wright Group
Our Teacher, Miss Pool	Ready to Read, Richard C. Owen
The Library	Emergent, Pioneer Valley books

Assessment:

The Bus Ride	DRA 3 Little Celebrations
The Fox on the Box	Barbara Gregorich, School Zone
My Shadow	Jean Bennett

Group 3 Books:

Reading Recovery Levels 5–8
Guided Reading Levels D–E

Benchmarks:

Good Night, Little Kitten	My First Reader, Grolier Press
It Looked Like Spilt Milk	Charles Shaw, Harper & Row
I Like Books	Anthony Browne, Random House
Mrs. Wishy Washy	Storybox, Wright Group

Assessment:

Bread	Storybox, DRA 6
Get Lost, Becka	School Zone, DRA 8
Pat's New Puppy	Reading Unlimited, Celebration Press
Nick's Glasses	Ready to Read, Richard C. Owen

Group 4 Books:

Reading Recovery Levels 9–12
Guided Reading Levels F–G
DRA 10–12

Benchmarks:

Rosie's Walk	Pat Hutchins
The Carrot Seed	Ruth Krauss
Cookie's Week	Cindy Ward
Titch	Pat Hutchins

Assessment:

Are You There, Bear?	Ron Maris, DRA 10
Nicky Upstairs and Downstairs	Harriet Ziefert
The House in the Tree	Rigby PM
William's Skateboard	Sunshine, Wright Group

Group 5 Books:
Reading Recovery Levels 13–15
Guided Reading Levels H–I
DRA 14

Benchmarks:

George Shrinks	William Joyce
Little Red Hen	Brenda Parkes
Goodnight Moon	Margaret Wise Brown
Hattie and the Fox	Mem Fox

Assessment:

Who Took the Farmer's Hat?	DRA 14
The Old Man's Mitten	Bookshop Mondo
Fix It	David McPhail, The Penguin Group
Willie's Wonderful Pet	Mel Cebulash, Scholastic

Group 6 Books:
Reading Recovery Levels 16–18
Guided Reading Level J
DRA 16

Benchmarks:

Just Me and My Puppy	Mercer Mayer
The Doorbell Rang	Pat Hutchins
The Very Hungry Caterpillar	Eric Carle
Bony-Legs	Joanna Cole, Scholastic

Assessment:

Milton the Early Riser	Robert Krauss
Bear Shadow	Frank Asch

Lost David McPhail
The Blind Man and the Elephant   Karen Backstein, Scholastic

Group 7 Books:
Reading Recovery Levels 19–20
Guided Reading Levels K–L
DRA 20

Benchmarks:
George and Martha   James Marshall, Houghton Mifflin
Hill of Fire   Thomas P. Lewis, HarperCollins
Miss Nelson is Missing   Harry Allard, Houghton Mifflin

Assessment:
Peter's Pockets   Eve Rice
Uncle Elephant   Arnold Lobel
A Weekend with Wendell   Kevin Henkes

Group 8 Books:
Commander Toad	J. Yolen
Cam Jansen series	D. Adler
Flat Stanley	J. Brown
The One in the Middle Is the Green Kangaroo	J. Blume
Little Bill	B. Cosby
Pinky and Rex	J. Howe
Jigsaw Jones	J. Preller
The Seven Treasure Hunts	B. Byars
Junie B. Jones	B. Parks
Zack Files	Greenburg
Adam Joshua Capers	J. Smith
Molly's Pilgrim	M. Cohen
Freckle Juice	J. Blume
Russell Rides Again	J. Hurwitz
Pee Wee Scouts	J. Delton

Group 8 Text Characteristics:
Often has cumulative chapters
Consistent word wrap from page to page starts here
More inference is often needed

Sentences tend to be longer and compound sentences begin

Many of these books are in series

Some occasional picture support

Increased dimension of characters: often there is ambiguity and conflicting emotions

Fantasy as genre introduced

Tend to contain limited picture support

Length of text often increases, between 20 and 30 lines per page

Group 9 Books:

Marvin Redpost series	L. Sachar
Magic Tree House series	M. P. Osborne
The Littles	J. Peterson
A to Z Mysteries	R. Roy
Bailey School Kids	D. Dadey
Polk Street Kids	P. R. Giff
Ginger Brown	S. D. Wyeth
Lavender	K. Hesse

Group 9 Text Characteristics:

Literary sounding language becomes more prevalent

Sophisticated illustrations amplify feeling; they are often a part of the story

Characters tend to be more complex and dynamic

Theme (under story) tends to be used frequently

Group 10 Books:

Boxcar Children	G. C. Warner (the rewritten ones are slightly harder)
Wayside School series	L. Sachar
Sable	K. Hesse
Stories Julian Tells	A. Cameron
Amber Brown Wants Extra Credit	P. Danziger
Aldo Applesauce	J. Hurwitz
The Hundred Dresses	E. Estes
Horrible Harry series	S. Kline
My Father's Dragon	R. S. Gannett
Ramona Age 8	B. Cleary
Ballet Slippers series	P.R. Giff
Flower Girl series	K. Leverich
Gooseberry Park	C. Rylant

Group 10 Text Characteristics:

Usually contains little or no picture support
Characters tend to be older, 8, 9, 10 years old
There are often multiple dynamic characters
Often the meaning of the story relies on understanding the humor
Chapters are longer

Group 11 Books:

A Taste of Blackberries	D. B. Smith
One Day in the Tropical Rain Forest	J. C. George
Everywhere	B. Brooks
The Zebra Wall	K. Henkes
A Blossom Promise	B. Byars
Spike It!	M. Christopher
Catwings	U. LeGuin
The War with Grandpa	R. K. Smith
Encyclopedia Brown	D. Sobol
Skinnybones	B. Park

Group 11 Text Characteristics:

Global conflict introduced; could be seen as a more sophisticated
    theme to interpret
Characters become very complex, readers need to infer
No picture support
Middle school age characters and their problems
Book length is usualy over 100 pages
Characters are dependent on understanding the preceding chapter

Group 12 Books:

Einstein Anderson	S. Simon
Bunnicula	D. and J. Howe
The Neptune Adventures	S. Saunders
Time Warp Trio	J. Sciescza
Shoebag	M. James
Deenie	J. Blume
Nothing's Fair in 5th Grade	B. DeClements

| *Dunc's Doll* | G. Paulsen |
| *Spider Boy* | R. Fletcher |

Group 12 Text Characteristics:

Very complex characters

Often include technical language and sophisticated humor

Emphasis on inference; misleading language and time changes

Genres are more sophisticated; e.g., harder mystery (more clues required), complex fantasy.

Smaller print on pages, dense text

Much longer chapters, 10 to 20 pages long

Chapters are dependent on understanding the preceding chapter

Group 13 Books:

Last Summer with Maizon	J. Woodson
The Wollfbay Wings series	B. Brooks
My Daniel	P. Conrad
California Diaries	A. M. Martin
Poppy	Avi
Shiloh	P. R. Naylor
Ernestine and Amanda	S. Belton
Cousins	V. Hamilton
P.S. Longer Letter Later	J. Blume
Thin Air	D. Getz
The Gift Giver	J. Hansen
Maniac Magee	J. Spinelli

Group 13 Text Characteristics:

Background knowledge and context very important

Older children peer issues: peer pressure; real-life themes of poverty, racism, child abuse

Strong literary voice begins: point of view of narrator shifts

May have complex plot structures (e.g., circular structure of memory stories, parallel stories, and stories within stories)

Often multiple dynamic characters

APPENDIX B
Read-Aloud Book Recommendations

We've listed our favorite read-alouds for each grade level assuming teachers will recognize that each of these titles can be read aloud and appreciated by children in a wide range of grade levels.

Kindergarten

Title	*Author*
Rumble in the Jungle	G. Andrae
Fireflies	J. Brickloe
The Summer My Father Was Ten	P. Brisson
Goodnight Moon	M. W. Brown
The Runaway Bunny	M. W. Brown
The Wednesday Surprise	E. Bunting
Dad and Me	P. Catalanotto
Island Boy	B. Cooney
Short Cut	D. Crewes
Today I Feel Silly	J. Curtis
Tough Boris	M. Fox
Wilfrid Gordon McDonald Partridge	M. Fox
My Father's Dragon	R. Gannett
The Biggest Boy	K Henkes
Julius	A Johnson
Dreams	E. Keats
Jenius	P. King Smith
Leo the Late Bloomer	R. Kraus
Together	G. Lyon

Who Came Down the Road	G. Lyon
Chicka Chicka Boom Boom	B. Martin
Roxaboxxen	A. McLerran
Richard Wright and the Library Card	W. Miller
Winnie the Pooh	A. A. Milne
Uncle Ted's Barbershop	M. K. Mitchell
We Share Everything	R. Munsch
The Rainbow Fish	M. Pfhister
Tar Beach	F. Ringgold
Yo! Yes!	C. Rashka
Grandfather's Journey	A Say
Abiyoyo	P. Seeger
A Bad Case of Stripes	D. Shannon
No, David!	D. Shannon
Music for Everyone	K. Williams
A Chair for My Mother	V. Williams
Cherries and Cherry Pit	V. Williams

First Grade

Title	*Author*
Each Peach Pear Plum	J. and A. Ahlberg
Tale of the Turnip	B. Alderson
Moonbear series	F. Asch
Fudgeamania	J. Blume
Jim and the Beanstalk	R. Briggs
The Important Book	M. W. Brown
The Indoor Noisy Book	M. W. Brown
Mike Mulligan and His Steam Shovel	V. L. Burton
StellaLuna	J. Cannon
The Mouse and the Motorcyle	B. Cleary
Jim's Dog Muffin	M. Cohen
Miss Rumphius	B. Cooney
Big Mama	B. Crews
Today I Feel Silly	J. Curtis
The Art Lesson	T. dePaola
Nana Upstairs, Nana Downstairs	T. dePaola
Be Good to Eddie Lee	J. Fleming
Dear Rebecca, Winter Is Here	J. C. George

Across the Stream	M. Ginsburg
Night on Neighborhood Street	E. Greenfield
Things I Like about My Grandma	F. Haskins
Chrysanthemum	K. Henkes
Jessica	K. Henkes
Lilly's Purple Plastic Purse	K. Henkes
The Iron Man	T. Hughes
Perfect the Pig	S. Jestor
The Leaving Morning	A. Johnson
I See, You Saw	N. Karlin
Clementina's Cactus	E. Keats
Anansi and the Moss Covered Rock	E. Kimmel
The Chocolate Touch	J. F. Koller
The Philharmonic Gets Dressed	K. Kuskin
Catwings series	U. LeGuin
Hooway for Wodney Wat	H. Lester
Swimmy	L. Lionni
Uncle Jed's Barbershop	M. K. Mitchell
Piggie Pie	M. Palatini
Who's in the Shed?	P. Parkes
Applemando's Dreams	P. Polacco
Babushka's Doll	P. Pollaco
When I Was Young in the Mountains	C. Rylant
Chicken Soup with Rice	M. Sendak
Zeke Pippen	W. Steig
Alexander and the Terrible, Horrible, No Good, Very Bad Day	J. Viorst
Earrings!	J. Viorst
Ira Sleeps Over	B. Weber
Follow the Moon	S. Weeks
Noisy Nora	R. Wells
Yoko	R. Wells
Charlotte's Web	E. B. White
My Name Is Georgia	J. Winter
The Napping House	A. Wood
Crow Boy	T. Yashima
Owl Moon	J. Yolen
This Quiet Lady	C. Zolotow
Pippi Longstocking	A. Lindgreen

Second Grade

Title	Author
The Tin Heart	K. Ackerman
Life Doesn't Frighten Me	M. Angelou
The Perfect Orange	F. Aranjo
The Wizard of Oz	F. Baum
Through My Eyes	R. Bridges
Shoeshine Girl	C. Bulla
The Greedy Triangle	M. Burns
The Stories Julian Tells series	A. Cameron
Hairs-Pelitos	S. Cisneros
Double Trouble in Walla Walla	A. Clements
Second-Grade Friends	M. Cohen
Will I Have a Friend?	M. Cohen
So Much	T. Cooke
Night at the Fair	D. Crewes
When I Was Five	J Curtis
The Courage of Sarah Noble	A. Dagliesh
James and the Giant Peach	R. Dahl
Mr. Fantastic Fox	R. Dahl
Donovan's Word Jar	M. Degross
Along Came a Dog	M. DeJong
The Worry Stone	M. Dengler
26 Fairmont Ave.	T. dePaola
The Hundred Dresses	E. Estes
The Patchwork Quilt	V. Flournoy
Pierre	M. Fox
The Secret of Roan Inish	R. K. Fry
Stone Fox	Gardiner
My Mama Had a Dancing Heart	L. M. Gray
Nathaniel Talking	G. Greenfield
Amazing Grace	M. Hoffman
Good Books, Good Times	L. B. Hopkins
Bunnicula	J. Howe
Princess Furball	C. Huck
Peach and Blue	S. Kilbrone
Water Dance	T. Locker
All the Places to Love	P. MacLachlan
Through Grampa's Eyes	P. MacLachlan

Title	Author
Knots on a Counting Rope	B Martin
The Honest to Goodness Truth	P. C. McKissack
The Wise Woman and Her Secret	E. Merriam
Owl in the Family	F. Mowat
Dog Team	G. Paulsen
Solo Girl	A. Pinkney
Chicken Sunday	P. Polacco
Thank You, Mr. Falkner	P. Polacco
Piggy in the Puddle	C. Pomerantz
Tortillas and Lullabies	L. Reiser
Keep the Lights Burning, Abbie	P. Roop
Amelia and Eleanor Go for a Ride	P. Ryan
Gooseberry Park	C. Rylant
The Relatives Came	C. Rylant
El Chino	A. Say
Chocolate Fever	R. K. Smith
Somebody Loves You, Mr. Hatch	J. E. Spinelli
The Conversation Club	D. Stanley
Dominic	W. Steig
The Real Thief	W. Steig
Daddy Is a Monster Sometimes	J. Steptoe
Mufaro's Beautiful Daughters	J. Steptoe
All of a Kind Family	S. Taylor
Mary Poppins	P. L. Travers
Two Bad Ants	C. Van Allsburg
If I Were in Charge of the World	J. Viorst
Stuart Little	E. B. White
Always My Dad	S. Wyeth
The Wedding of Don Octavio	P. Zelver
A New Coat for Anna	H. Ziefert
My Grandson Lou	C. Zolotow

Third Grade

Title	*Author*
Night Crossing	K. Ackerman
Mr. Popper's Penguins	R. Atwater
Poppy	Avi
Frecklejuice	J. Blume

Superfudge	J. Blume
The Pain and The Great One	J. Blume
Everywhere	B. Brooks
Flat Stanley	J. Brown
Cheyenne Again	E. Bunting
The Most Beautiful Place in the World	A. Cameron
Verdi	J. Cannon
The Chocolate Touch	P. S. Catling
Dear Mr. Henshaw	B. Cleary
Ramona Quimby Age 8	B. Cleary
Frindle	Clements
Sadako and the Thousand Paper Cranes	E. Coerr
Molly's Pilgrim	M. Cohen
Staying Nine	P. Conrad
Matilda	R. Dahl
The BFG	R. Dahl
The Witches	R. Dahl
Not So Fast Songololo	N. Daly
An Enchanted Hair Tale	A. DeVeaux
The Morning Girl	M. Dorris
Isla	D. Dorvos
And Then There Was One	M. Facklam
April Morning	H. Fast
Soul Looks Back in Wonder	T. Feelings
The Whipping Boy	S. Fleishman
Seedfolks	P. Fleishman
Fig Pudding	R. Fletcher
The Lizard and the Sun	A. Flor Ada
Grandpa's Face	E. Greenfield
Looking for Angels	V. Gregory
Be Bop a Do Walk!	Hamanaka
Music of the Dolphins	K. Hesse
Earthquake Terror	P. Kehret
… and now Miguel	J. Krumgold
The Lion, the Witch and the Wardrobe	C. S. Lewis
Like Butter on Pancakes	J. London
In the Year of the Boar and Jackie Robinson	B. Loro
The Man Who Knew Too Much	P. Lorre

Title	Author
Number the Stars	L. Lowry
How to Be a Perfect Person in Three Days	S. Manes
Sidewalk Story	S. Mathis
The Magic Tree	G. McDermott
The Black Snowman	P. Mendez
Luv Amelia, Luv Nadia	M. Moss
Red Dust Jesse	Myers
Journey to Jo'burg	B. Naidoo
Shiloh	P. R. Naylor
The Always Prayer Shawl	S. Oberman
Mrs. Frisby and the Rats of NIMH	R. O'Brien
Junie B. Jones series	B. Parks
Skinnybones	B. Park
Rainbow Fish	M. Phister
The Best Christmas Pageant Ever	B. Robinson
An Angel for Soloman Singer	C. Rylant
Every Living Thing	C. Rylant
The Whales	C. Rylant
Baseball's Best	A. Schwarz
The True Story of the Three Little Pigs	J. Scieszka
The Cricket in Times Square	G. Seldon
My Trip to Alpha I	A. Slote
A Taste of Blackberries	D. Smith
Jelly Belly	R. K. Smith
Crash	J. Spinelli
Maniac Magee	J. Spinelli
Tooter Pepperday	J. Spinelli
The Gold Cadillac	M. Taylor
Invisible Thread	Y. Uchida
The Friendship Ring	R. Vail

Fourth Grade

Title	*Author*
Little Women	L. M. Alcott
Sounder	W. Armstrong
The Indian in the Cupboard	L. R. Banks
I'm in Charge of Celebrations	B. Baylor
The Other Way to Listen	B. Baylor

Tales of a Fourth Grade Nothing	J. Blume
The Halloween Tree	R. Bradbury
Dear Mr. Henshaw	B. Cleary
Socks	B. Cleary
The Landry News	A. Clements
My Brother Sam Is Dead	J. Collier
Talking with Artists	P. Cummings
What Jamie Saw	C. Coman
Bud, Not Buddy	C. P. Curtis
The Cat Who Ate My Gymsuit	P. Danzinger
Secret Life of Old Zeb	C. A. Deedy
Yolanda's Genius	C. Fenner
Half-a-Moon Inn	P. Fleischman
Seedfolks	P. Fleishman
Possum Magic	M. Fox
Monkey Island	P. Fox
Early Thunder	J. Fritz
Julie of the Wolves	J. C. George
My Side of the Mountain	J. C. George
The Sign of the Beaver	E. Speare
Lilly's Crossing	P. R. Giff
With Love	J. Goodall
For the Love of the Game	E. Greenfield
Come On, Rain!	K. Hesse
Just Juice	K. Hesse
Lavender	K. Hesse
Amber on the Mountain	T. Johnston
The Phantom Tollbooth	Juster
From the Mixed-up Files of *Mrs. Basil E. Frankweiler*	E. L. Konigsburg
The View from Saturday	E. L. Konigsburg
Frankenstein Moved in on the 4th Floor	E. Levy
The Lion, the Witch and the Wardrobe	C. S. Lewis
Number the Stars	L. Lowry
Dreamplace	G. Lyon
Arthur for the Very First Time	P. MacLachlan
Journey	P. MacLachlan
Sarah Plain and Tall	P. MacLachlan
What You Know First	P. MacLachlan
Emma's Journal	M. Moss

Title	Author
I Want to Be	T. Moss
Harlem	W. D. Myers
Mick Harte Was Here	B. Park
Bridge to Terebithia	K. Paterson
Flip-Flop Girl	K. Paterson
The Great Gilly Hopkins	K. Paterson
The Cookcamp	G. Paulsen
The Monument	G. Paulsen
Work Song	G. Paulsen
Freak the Mighty	R. Philbrick
Chicken Sunday	P. Polacco
Pink and Say	P. Polacco
The Empty Creel	G. Pope
My Dream of Martin Luther King	F. Ringgold
Every Living Thing	C. Rylant
Missing May	C. Rylant
The Bird House	C. Rylant
The Dreamer	C. Rylant
Van Gogh Café	C. Rylant
There's a Boy in the Girls' Bathroom	L. Sachar
Holes	L. Sacher
How Much Is a Million?	D. Schwartz
The Math Curse	J. Scieszka
Squids Will Be Squids	J. Scieszka
Tut! Tut!	J. Scieszka
Exploding Ants	J. Settel
The War with Grandpa	R. K. Smith
Sign of the Beaver	E. G. Speare
Fourth-Grade Rats	J. Spinelli
The Conversation Club	D. Stanley
The Green Book	J. P. Walsh
Tuesday	D. Weisner
Indian School	G. Whelan
From the Notebooks of Melanin Sun	J. Woodson
Letting Swift River Go	J. Yolen

Fifth Grade

Title	*Author*
Blood and Guts	L. Allison

Tuck Everlasting	J. Babbitt
No Mirrors in My Nana's House	I. Barnwell
The Summer My Father Was Ten	P. Brisson
Kids at Work	J. Browning
Hairs/Pelitos	S. Cisneros
Freedom Crossing	M. Clark
Real-Life Animal Stories	D. Cohen
Facts Speak for Themselves	B. Cole
The Goats	B. Cole
What Jamie Saw	C. Comer
Coming Home: From the Life of Langston Hughes	F. Cooper
Walk Two Moons	S. Creech
Short Cut	D. Crewes
Watsons Go to Birmingham—1963	C. P. Curtis
Catherine Called Birdy	K. Cushman
Flying Solo	R. Dahl
A Hole in the Wall	D'Angelo
Angry Aztecs	T. Deary
Ice Mummy	Du Bowster
Francie	K. English
Yolanda's Genius	C. Fenner
Bull Run	P. Fleischmann
The Life and Death of Crazy Horse	R. Freedman
The Witch of Blackbird Pond	E. George
Tarantula in My Purse	J. C. George
Frozen Man	D. Getz
My Mama Had a Dancing Heart	L. M. Gray
Childtimes	E. Greenfield
Sister	E. Greenfield
Running Out of Time	M. Haddix
The Gift Giver	J. Hansen
Yellow Bird and Me	J. Hansen
The Birthday Room	K. Henkes
Words of Stone	K. Henkes
Out of the Dust	K. Hesse
When Zachary Beaver Came to Town	K. W. Holt
A Girl Called Boy	B. Hurmence
Red Scarf Girl	J. L. Jiang
The Circuit	F. Jimenez

Regarding the Fountain	Klise
Monarchs	K. Lasky
A Wrinkle in Time	M. L'Engle
Skylark	P. MacLachlan
Baby	P. MacLachlan
Junebug	A. Mead
Felita	N. Mohr
Rachel's Journal	M. Moss
The Boys War	J. Murphy
The Great Gilly Hopkins	K. Paterson
Four Perfect Pebbles	L. Perl
Where the Red Fern Grows	W. Rawls
Forty Acres and Maybe a Mule	H. Robinet
Harry Potter	J. K. Rowling
Dog Heaven	C. Rylant
Missing May	C. Rylant
Scarecrow	C. Rylant
The Bookshop Dog	C. Rylant
Holes	L. Sachar
Call It Courage	A. Sperry
Wringer	J. Spinelli
Psychic Pets	J. Sutton
Funny You Should Ask	M. Terban
Leon's Story	I. W. Tillage
Welcome to the Green House	J. Yolen
Welcome to the Ice House	J. Yolen
You Can Yo Yo: 25 Tricks to Try	B Weber
Last Summer with Maizon	J. Woodson
Maizon Trilogy	J. Woodson
Maizon at Blue Hill	J. Woodson

Sixth and Seventh Grades

Title	*Author*
Go and Come Back	J. Abelove
Devil's Arithmetic	Avi
Nothing But the Truth	Avi
What Do Fish Have to Do with Anything?	Avi
Tuck Everlasting	N. Babbit

No Mirrors in My Nana's House	I. Barnwell
My Name Is Brian	J. Betrancourt
Vanishing	B. Brooks
Fly Away Home	E. Bunting
The Wall	E. Bunting
A Christmas Memory	T. Capote
House on Mango Street	S. Cisneros
What Jamie Saw!	C. Coman
Crazy Lady!	J. L. Conly
Walk Two Moons	S. Creech
The Watsons Go to Birmingham—1963	C. P. Curtis
Live Writing	R. Fletcher
Lily's Crossing	P. R. Giff
The Gift Giver	J. Hanson
Which Way Freedom?	J. Hanson
The Coyote Bead	G. Hausman
The Old Man and the Sea	E. Hemingway
The Birthday Room	K. Henkes
Out of the Dust	K. Hesse
The Outsiders	S. E. Hinton
Slake's Limbo	F. Hoffman
My Louisiana Sky	K. W. Holt
When Zachary Beaver Came to Town	K. W. Holt
Birthday Surprises	J. Hurwitz
Red Wall	B. Jacques
Toning the Sweep	A. Johnson
Roll of Thunder, Hear My Cry	W. Jones
Autumn Street	L. Lowry
The Giver	L. Lowry
Scorpions	W. D. Myers
Ringworld	L. Niven
Dancing on the Edge	H. Nolan
Flip-Flop Girl	K. Paterson
Jip	K. Paterson
Lyddie	K. Paterson
Soldier's Heart	G. Paulsen
A Day No Pigs Would Die	R. N. Peck
Holes	L. Sachar
The Math Course	J. Sciezska
Baseball in April and Other Stories	G. Soto

Call It Courage	A. Sperry
Looking Back	J. Spinelli
Digger	J. Stanley
Of Mice and Men	J. Steinbeck
Between Madison and Palmetto	J. Woodson
Hiroshima	L. Yep
Letting Swift River Go	J. Yolen
The Pigman	P. Zindel

APPENDIX C
Magazines for Kids

Calliope World History for Kids. Cobblestone Publishing, 7 School Road, Peterborough, NH 03458.

Cobblestone: The History Magazine for Young People. Cobblestone Publishing, 7 School Road, Peterborough, NH 03458.

3-2-1 Contact. Children's Television Workshop, Lincoln Plaza, New York, NY 10023.

Dramatics. Educational Theater Association, 3368 Central Parkway, Cincinnati, OH 45225.

Faces: People, Places and Culture. Cobblestone Publishing, 7 School Road, Peterborough, NH 03458.

Literary Cavalcade. Scholastic, 555 Broadway, New York, NY 10012.

Muse. Carus Publishing. The Cricket Magazine Group, 332 S. Michigan Avenue, Suite 2000, Chicago, IL 60604.

World Magazine. National Geographic Society, 1145 17th Street NW, Washington, DC 20056.

Ranger Rick. National Wildlife Federation, 8925 Leesberg Pike, Vienna, VA 22184.

Smithsonian. The Smithsonian Institute, 900 Jefferson Drive SW, Washington, DC 20560.

Sports Illustrated for Kids. Time Inc. Building, Rockefeller Center, New York, NY 10020.

The Weekly Reader. Scholastic, 555 Broadway, New York, NY 10012.

Time for Kids. Time Inc. Building, Rockefeller Center, New York, NY 10020.

Wildlife Conservation. The International Wildlife Park, Bronx, NY 10460.

Zillions: Consumer Reports for Kids. Consumers Union, 101 Truman Avenue, Yonkers, NY 10703.

Bibliography

Adams, M. J. *Beginning to Read: Thinking and Learning about Print.* Cambridge, MA: MIT Press, 1990.

Anderson, R. C., and P. D. Pearson. "A Schema-Theoretic View of Basic Processes in Reading." In *Handbook of Reading Research,* ed. P. D. Pearson. White Plains, NY: Longman, 1984.

Atwell, Nancie. *In the Middle: Writing, Reading, and Learning with Adolescents.* Portsmouth, NH: Boynton/Cook, 1987.

Barnes, Douglas. "Supporting Exploratory Talk for Learning." In *Cycles of Meaning: Exploring the Potential of Talk in Literary Communities,* ed. K. Pierce and C. Gilles. Portsmouth, NH: Heinemann, 1993.

Barrs, Myra, and Hilary Hester. *Using the Primary Language Record.* Greenwood Publishing Group, 1991.

Barrs, Myra, and Sue Pidgeon. *Reading the Difference: Gender and Reading in Elementary Classrooms.* York, ME: Stenhouse Publishers, 1994.

Bartholomae, David, and Anthony R. Petrosky. *Facts, Artifacts and Counterfacts: Theory and Method for a Reading and Writing Course.* Boynton/Cook Publishers, 1986.

Barzun, Jacques, with Henry F. Graff. *The Modern Researcher.* Harcourt Brace Jovanovich, 1970.

Baylor, Byrd. *I'm in Charge of Celebrations.* New York: Charles Scribner's Sons, 1988.

Bissett, D. "The Amount and Effect of Recreational Reading in Selected Fifth Grade Classes." Ph.D. diss. Syracuse University, 1969.

Bomer, Randy. *Time for Meaning: Crafting Literate Lives in Middle and High School.* Portsmouth NH: Heinemann, 1995.

Bomer, Randy. "Transactional Heat and Light: More Explicit Literacy Learning." *Language Arts* 75, no. 1:, 1998.

Bruner, Jerome S. *The Process of Education.* New York: Vintage Books, 1963.

Bussis, A. M., E. A. Chittenden, M. Amarel, and E. Klausner. *Inquiry into Meaning: An Investigation of Learning to Read.* Hillsdale, NJ: Erlbaum, 1985.

Calkins, Lucy McCormick. *The Art of Teaching Writing.* Portsmouth, NH: Heinemann, 1983.

———. *The Art of Teaching Writing.* Rev. ed. Portsmouth, NH: Heinemann, 1994.

Calkins, Lucy, Kate Montgomery, and Donna Santman, *A Teacher's Guide to Standardized Reading Tests: Knowledge Is Power.* Portsmonth, NH: Heinemann, 1998.

Calkins, Lucy, with Shelley Harwayne. *Living Between the Lines.* Portsmouth, NH: Heinemann, 1991.

Cambourne, Briane. *The Whole Story: Natural Learning and the Acquisition of Literacy in the Classroom.* Auckland, NZ: Ashton Scholastic, 1993.

Carnine, Douglas W., Jerry Silbert, and Edward J. Kameenui. *Direct Instruction Reading.* Upper Saddle River, NJ: Merrill, 1997.

Cazden, Courtney B. *Classroom Discourse: The Language of Teaching and Learning.* Portsmouth, NH: Heinemann, 1988.

Cisneros, Sandra. *Woman at Hollering Creek and Other Stories.* New York: Random House, 1992.

Clay, Marie. *Becoming Literate: The Construction of Inner Control.* Portsmouth, NH: Heinemann, 1991.

Clay, Marie. *An Observation Survey of Early Literacy Achievement.* Portsmouth, NH: Heinemann, 1993.

Clay, Marie. *By Different Paths to Common Outcomes.* York, ME: Stenhouse Publishers, 1998.

Cullinan, B., and S. Fitzgerald. "Background Information Bulletin on the Use of Readability Formulae." Notice distributed by the International Reading Association, Newark, De., and the National Council of Teachers of English, Urbana, IL, 1984.

Cunningham, Patricia. *Phonics They Use.* New York: HarperCollins, 1995.

Dillard, Annie. *An American Childhood.* New York: Harper and Row, 1987.

Dombey, Henrietta, and Margaret Moustafa. *Whole to Part Phonics.* Portsmouth, NH: Heinemann, 1998.

Engdahl, Sylvia. *Enchantress from the Stars.* New York: Macmillan. 1970.

Fountas, Irene C., and Gay Su Pinnell. *Guided Reading: Good First Teaching for All Children.* Portsmouth, NH: Heinemann, 1996.

Freire, Paulo. *Pedagogy of the Oppressed.* Continuum, 1983.

Gallagher, M., and P. D. Pearson. *The Instruction of Reading Comprehension in Contemporary Educational Psychology,* 1983.

Gardner, John. *The Art of Fiction.* New York: Random House, 1983.

Geertz, Clifford. *Local Knowledge: Further Essays in Interpretive Anthropology.* New York: Basic Books, 1983.

Goodman, Kenneth. *On Reading: A Commonsense Look at the Nature of Language and the Science of Reading.* Portsmouth, NH: Heinemann, 1996.

Goodman, Kenneth. "A Linguistic Study of Cues and Miscues in Reading." *Elementary English* 42:639–643, 1965.

Goodman, Kenneth, Dorothy Watson, and Carolyn Burke. *Reading Miscue Analysis.* New York: Richard C. Owen, 1987.

Gordon, C. J., and P. D. Pearson. *The Effects of Instruction on Metacomprehension and Inferencing on Children's Comprehension Abilities.* Tech. Rep. No. 277. Urbana, IL: University of Illinois Center for the Study of Reading, 1983.

Greenfield, Eloise, and Lessie Jones Little. *Childtimes: A Three-Generation Memoir.* NY: Thomas Y. Crowell, 1983.

Halliday, Michael A. K. *Learning How to Mean: Explorations in the Development of Language.* London: Edward Arnold, 1975.

Harste, Jerome C., Kathy G. Short, with Carolyn Burke. *Creating Classrooms for Authors and Inquirers.* Portsmouth, NH: Heinemann, 1996.

Heard, Georgia. *Awakening the Heart: Exploring Poetry in Elementary and Middle School.* Portsmouth, NH: Heinemann, 1998.

Hiebert, H., Judith A. Scott, Ian A. G. Wilkinson. *Becoming a Nation of Readers: The Report of the Commission on Reading.* Champaign-Urbana, IL: Center for the Study of Reading, 1985.

Holdaway, Donald. *The Foundations of Literacy.* Sydney, Australia: Ashton Scholastic, 1979.

Howe, James. "Reflections." *The Writing Project Quarterly Newsletter* 1, no. 3: 12, 1987.

Johnston, Peter. *Knowing Literacy: Constructive Literacy Assessment.* York, ME: Stenhouse Publishers, 1997.

Keene, Ellin, and Susan Zimmermann. *Mosaic of Thought.* Portsmouth, NH: Heinemann, 1997.

Krashen, Stephen. *The Power of Reading.* Englewood, Co.: Libraries Unlimited, 1993.

———. *Every Person a Reader: An Alternative to the California Task Force Report on Reading.* Culver City, CA: Language Education Associates, 1996.

Lamott, Anne. *Bird by Bird: Some Instructions on Writing and Life.* New York: Anchor Books/Doubleday, 1995.

Lindbergh, Anne Morrow. *A Gift from the Sea.* New York: Random House, 1965.

Lukens, Rebecca J. *A Critical Handbook of Children's Literature.* New York: Addison-Wesley, 1999.

Mayher, John S. *Uncommon Sense: Theoretical Practice in Language Education.* Portsmouth, NH: Boynton/Cook Publishers. Heinemann, 1990.

McCarrier, Andrea, Gay Su Pinnell, and Irene C. Fountas. *Interactive Writing: How Language and Literacy Come Together, K–2.* Portsmouth, NH: Heinemann, 1999.

Meek, Margaret. *How Texts Teach What Readers Learn.* Thimble Press, 1988.

———. 1993. *On Being Literate.* Portsmouth, NH: Heinemann,

Mehan, Hugh. *Learning Lessons: Social Organization in the Classroom.* Cambridge Harvard University Press, 1979.

Meier, D. "Why the Reading Tests Don't Test Reading." *Dissent:* 457–466, 1991.

Moffett, James, and Belty Jane Wagner. *Student-Centered Language Arts, K–12.* Portsmouth NH: Boynton/Cook Publishers, 1992.

Murray, Donald M. A *Writer Teaches Writing: A Practical Method of Teaching Composition.* Boston: Houghton Mifflin, 1968.

Nagy, W, P Herman, and R Anderson. "Learning Words from Context." *Reading Research Quarterly* 20: 233–253, 1985.

Paterson, Katherine. *Gates of Excellence: On Reading and Writing Books for Children.* New York: Elsevier/Nelson Books, 1981.

———. *The Spying Heart: More Thoughts on Reading and Writing Books for Children.* New York: Lodestar Books, 1989.

Peterson, Barbara. "Characteristics of Texts That Support Beginning Readers," Ph.D. diss., Ohio State University, Columbus, 1988.

Peterson, Ralph. *Life in a Crowded Place: Making a Learning Community.* Portsmouth, NH: Heinemann, 1992

Pierce, Kathryn Mitchell. "I Am a Level 3 Reader': Children's Perceptions of Themselves as Readers," *New Advocate.* 12, no. 4: 359–375, 1999.

Pierce, L., and C. Gilles, eds. *Cycles of Meaning: Exploring the Potential of Talk in Literacy Communities.* Portsmouth, NH: Heineman, 1993.

Pinnell, Gay Su, and Irene C. Fountas. *Matching Books to Readers: Using Leveled Books in Guided Reading,* K–3, 1999.

Quindlen, Anna. *How Reading Changed My Life.* New York: Ballantine Books, 1998.

Shaughnessy, Mina P. *Errors and Expectations.* New York: Oxford University Press, 1977.

Short, Kathy G. *Literacy as a Collaborative Experience.* Bloomington In.: Unpublished doctoral dissertation, Indiana University.

Smith, Frank. *Reading Without Nonsense.* 2nd ed. New York: TC Press, 1985.

———. *Insult to Intelligence: The Bureaucrat Invasion of Our Classrooms.* Portsmouth, NH: Heinemann, 1990.

Spencer, Margaret Meek. *Language and Literacy in the Primary School.* Contemporary Analysis in Education Series. Falmer Press, 1988.

Stanovich, K. E. "Word Recognition: Changing Perspectives." In *Handbook of Reading Research,* ed. R. Barr, M. C. Kamil, P. B. Mosenthal, and P. D. Pearson. (Vol. 2, 418–452. White Plains, NY: Longman, 1991.

Sulzby, Elizabeth. "Children's Emergent Reading of Favorite Storybooks: A Developmental Study." *Reading Research Quarterly* 20: 458–481, 1985.

———. 2000. An informal study group visit to The Teachers College Reading and Writing Project, January 20.

Trelease, Jim. *The Read-Aloud Handbook.* 4th ed. New York: Penguin, 1995.

Vygotsky, L. S. *Thought and Language.* Cambridge, MA: MIT Press, 1962.

———. *Mind in Society.* Cambridge, MA: Harvard University Press, 1978.

Weaver, Constance. *Reading Process and Practice: From Socio-Psycholinguistics to Whole Language.* Portsmouth, NH: Heinemann, 1994.

Wilde Sandra. *Reading Made Easy.* Portsmouth, NH: Heinemann, 2000a.

———. *Miscue Analysis Made Easy: Building on Student Strengths.* Portsmouth, NH: Heinemann, 2000b.

Zill, Nicholas, and Marianne Winglee. *Who Reads Literature?* Corbin John, MD: Seven Locks Press, 1990.

Zinsser, William, ed. *Going on Faith.* New York: Marlowe, 1999.

Jenkinson. What Do Boys and Girls Read, 1940.

Whitehead. Children and Their Books, 1977.

———. Centre for Language in Primary Education. Pembroke Publishers, 538 Hood Road, Markham, Ontario, L3R 3K9, 1994.

Qualitative Reading Inventory II (Addison, Wesley, Longman) or the Developmental Reading Inventory.

Children's Bibliography

Adler, David A. Cam Jansen series. Puffin, 1997, 1999.

Armstrong, William H. *Sounder.* Harper Juvenille, 1989.

Avery, Kristen. *Max's Box.*

Banks, Lynne Reid. The Indian in the Cupboard series. Camelot, 1999.

Barbour, Karen. *Little Nino's Pizzeria.* Harcourt, 1990.

Baum, Frank L. The Wizard of Oz series. Henry Holt, 1988.

Baylor, Byrd. *I'm in Charge of Celebrations.* Aladdin, 1995.

Belton, Sandra. *Ernestine and Amanda.* Aladdin, 1998.

Bemelmans, Ludwig. *Madeline.* Viking, 1958.

Blonder, Ellen. *Noisy Breakfast.*

Blume, Judy. *Are You There God? It's Me, Margaret.* Laurel Leaf Library, 1991.

Blume, Judy. *Chocolate Fever.*

Blume, Judy. *The Freckle Juice. The Yearling,* 1978.

Brady, Esther Wood. *Toliver's Secret.* Random House Children's Books, 1993.

Brook, Bruce. *Wolf Bay Wings.*

Brown, Margaret Wise. *The Runaway Bunny.* Harper Juvenille, 1974.

Browne, Anthony. *Gorilla.*

Browne, Anthony. *Willy the Wimp.* Dragonfly Books, 1989.

Browne, Anthony. *Piggybook.* Alfred A. Knopf, 1990.

Bruchac, Joseph. *The Heart of a Chief.* Dial Books for Young Readers, 1998.

Bulla, Clyde Robert. *The Chalk Box Kid.* Random House, 1987.

Bulla, Clyde Robert. *Shoeshine Girl.*

Burton, Virginia Lee. *Mike Mulligan and His Steam Shovel.* Econo-Clad, 1999.

Byars, Betsy. *The Moon and I.*

Carle, Eric. *The Hungry Caterpillar.* Putnam Publishing Group Juvenille, 1984.

Christelow, Eileen, Five Little Monkeys series. Houghton Mifflin, 1998.

Cleary, Beverly. Ramona series. Camelot, 1996.

Cowley, Joy. *Mrs. Wishy Washy.* Philomel, 1999.

Creech, Sharon. *Walk Two Moons.* HarperCollins Juvenille Books, 1994.

Curtis, Christopher Paul. *Bud, Not Buddy.* Delacorte Press, 1999.

Cushman, Karen. *Catherine Called Birdy.* Clarion Books, 1994.

Dahl, Roald. *Danny, The Champion of the World.* Puffin, 1998.

Dahl, Roald. *Matilda. Puffin,* 1998.

Danziger, Paula. Amber Brown series. Scholastic Trade, 1995, 1997.

DeFoe, Daniel. *Robinson Crusoe.* Dover, 1998.

Delton, Judy. Pee Wee Scouts series. Yearling Books, 2000

DePaola, Tomie. *Strega Nona.* Aladdin, 1988.

Engdahl, Sylvia Louise. *Enchantress from the Stars.*

Fenner, Carol. *Yolanda's Genius.* Econo-Clad Books, 1997, 1999.

Fleischman, Sid. *The Whipping Boy.* Troll Assoc., 1989.

Forbes, Esther. *Johnny Tremain.* Hougthon Mifflin, 1943.

Fox, Memo. *Koala Lou.* Harcourt, 1994.

Freeman, Don. *Corduroy.* Viking Press, 1985.

Freeman, Don. *A Pocket for Corduroy.* Viking Press, 1980.

Galdone, Paul. *The Three Billy Goats Gruff.* Houghton Mifflin, 1981.

Gannett, Ruth Stiles. *My Father's Dragon.* Random House Children's Pub., 1988.

George, Jean Craighead. *My Side of the Mountain.* Penguin USA, 2000.

Gipson, Fred. *Old Yeller.* Harpercollins Juvenille Books, 1956.

Greenfield, Eloise. *Childtimes: A Three-Generation Memoir.* Thomas Y. Crowell, 1987.

Greenfield, Eloise. *Honey, I Love and Other Poems. Thomas Y. Crowell, 1986.*

Gregorich, Barbara. *The Fox on the Box.* School Zone, 1993.

Hakim, Joy. *A History of US.* Oxford University Press Children's Books, 1999.

Harms, Leo. *Apartment book.*

Hautzig, Esther. *The Endless Steppe.* HarperTrophy, 1995.

Henkes, Kevin. *Chrysanthemum.* Greenwillow, 1991.

Hesse, Karen. *Just Juice.* Scholastic Paperback, 1999.

Hesse, Karen. *Sable.* Henry Holt, 1998.

Hesse, Karen. *The Music of Dolphins.* Apple, 1998.

Hoban, Russell. Frances series. HarperTrophy, 1995.

Howe, James. Pinky and Rex series. Simon & Schuster Juvenille, 1998.

Hutchins, Pat. *My Best Friend.* Greenwillow, 1993.

Hutchins, Pat. *Titch.* Aladdin, 1993.

Johnston, Tony. *Yonder.* Pied Piper, 1993.

Joyce, William. *George Shrinks.* HarperTrophy, 1987.

Kellogg, Steven. *Can I Keep Him?* Dial Books for Young Readers, 1992.

Kellogg, Steven. *The Island of the Skog.* Dial Books for Young Readers, 1993.

Kellogg, Steven. *The Mysterious Tadpole.* Pied Piper, 1993.

Keselman, Gabriela. *The Gift.*

King-Smith, Dick. *The Cuckoo Child.* Hyperion Books for Children, 1999.

King-Smith, Dick. *Martin's Mice.* Random House Children's Publishers, 1998.

Kline, Suzy. *Horrible Harry* series. *Puffin, 1998, 1999, 2000.*

Kraus, Robert. *Leo the Late Bloomer.* Haprercollins Juvenille Books, 1994.

Krauss, Ruth. *The Carrot Seed.* HarperTrophy, 1989.

Kuskin, Karla. *Near the Window Tree: Poems and Notes.*

Kuskins, Karla. *The Philharmonic Gets Dressed.* HarperTrophy, 1986.

Le Guin, Ursula. Cat Wings series.

Levy, Elizabeth. Something Queer series. Young Yearling, 1989.

Lewis, C.S. *Prince Caspian: The Return to Narnia.* Harpercollins Juvenille Books, 1994.

Lewis, C.S. *The Lion, The Witch and the Wardrobe.* Harpercollins Juvenille Books, 1994.

Lewis, C.S. *The Voyage of the Dawn Treader.* Harpercollins Juvenille Books, 1994.

Lippman, Peter. *The Haunted House.*

Little, Jean. *Little by Little.*

Lobel, Arnold. Frog and Toad series. Harpercollins Juvenille Books, 1979, 1984.

London, Jack. *The Call of the Wild.* Pocket Books, 1982.

Lowry, Lois. *The Giver.* Houghton Mifflin, 1993.

MacLachlan, Patricia. *Arthur, for the Very First Time.* HarperTrophy, 1989.

MacLachlan, Patricia. *Baby.*

MacLachlan, Patricia. *The Facts and Fictions of Minna Pratt.* HarperTrophy, 1990.

MacLachlan, Patricia. *Journey.* New York: Doubleday, 1991.

MacLachlan, Patricia. *Sarah, Plain and Tall.* HarperTrophy, 1987.

Marshall, James. George and Martha series. Houghton Mifflin, 1997.

Martin, Jr., Bill. *Brown Bear, Brown Bear, What Do You See?* Henry Holt & Co., 1992.

Martin, Jr., Bill. *The Ghost-Eye Tree.* Henry Holt & Co., 1988.

Mayer, Mercer. *Just Me and My Puppy.*

McCloskey, Robert. *Make Way for Ducklings.* Puffin, 1999.

McCloskey, Robert. *Blueberries for Sal.* Viking Press, 1976.

Mead, Alice. *Junebug.* Yearling Books, 1997.

Minarik, Else Homelund. *Little Bear.* HarperTrophy, 1978.

Morris, Robert A. *Dolphins.*

Morrison, Toni. *The Big Box.* Hyperion Books for Children, 1999.

Mowat, Farley. *Lost in the Barrens.* Bantam Books, 1985.

Mowat, Farley. *The Dog Who Wouldn't Be.* Bantam Books, 1984.

Naylor, Phyllis Reynolds. Shiloh series. Yearling Books, 1992.

Osborne, Mary Pope. The Magic Treehouse series.

Park, Barbara. *Junie B. Jones.*

Paterson, Katherine. *Bridge to Terabithia.* HarperTrophy, 1987.

Paterson, Katherine. *The Great Gilly Hopkins.* HarperTrophy, 1987.

Paulsen, Gary. *The Cookcamp.* Yearling Books, 1992.

Paulsen, Gary. *Dogsong.* Aladdin, 1995.

Paulsen, Gary. *Hatchet.* Aladdin, 1996.

Paulsen, Gary. *The Haymeadow.* Yearling Books, 1994.

Paulsen, Gary. *The Monument.* Yearling Books, 1993.

Peck, Robert Newton. Little Soup series.

Potol, Chaim. *The Chosen.* Fawcett, 1987.

Pullman, Philip. *The Golden Compass.* Alfred A. Knopf, 1996.

Rawls, Wilson. *Where the Red Fern Grows.* Bantam Books, 1984.

Ringghold, Faith. *Tar Beach.* Crown Publishers, 1991.

Robinson, Barbara. *The Best Christmas Pageant Ever.* HarperTrophy, 1988.

Robinson, Barbara. *The Best School Year Yet.* HarperTrophy, 1997.

Rylant, Cynthia. Henry and Mudge series. Aladdin Books, 1996.

Sachar, Louis. Marvin Redpost series.

Sachar, Lous. The Wayside School series.

Saltzman, David. *Jester Has Lost His Jingle.* Jester Co. Inc., 1995.

Scarffe, Bronwen. *Oh, No!*

Sharmat, Marjorie. Nate the Great series. Yearling Books, 2000.

Shaw, Charles G. *It Looked Like Spilt Milk.* HarperCollins, 1993.

Sherman, Allen. "A Gift of Laughter." Soto, G. (1991) in *Baseball in April and Other Stories.* Harcourt Brace & Co.

Slobodkina, Esphyr. *Caps for Sale: A Tale of Peddler, Some Monkeys and Their Monkey Business.* HarperTrophy, 1987.

Smith, Doris Buchanan. *A Taste of Blackberries.* Harpercollins Juvenille Books, 1992.

Smith, Robert Kimmel. *The War with Grandpa.* Yearling Books, 1984.

Soto, Gary. *Chato's Kitchen.* Putnam Publishing Group, 1995.

Speare, Elizabeth George. *The Sign of the Beaver. Yearling Books, 1994.*

Speare, Elizabeth George. The Witch of Blackbird Pond. Laurel Leaf Library, 1978.

Spinelli, Jerry. *Maniac McGee.* Little Brown & Company, 2000.

Stadler, John. *Hooray for Snail.* Thomas Y. Crowell, 1987.

Stadler, John. *Snail Saves the Day.*

Stadler, John. *Three Cheers for Hippo!*

Steptoe, John. *Stevie.* HarperTrophy, 1986.

Stine, R.L. Goosebumps series. Scholastic, 2000.

Taylor, Mildred. *Roll of Thunder, Hear My Cry.* Puffin, 1997.

Ungerer, Tomi. *Crictor.* HarperTrophy, 1983.

Van Allsburg, Chris. *The Polar Express.* Houghton Mifflin, 1985.

Viorst, Judith. *The Tenth Good Thing About Barney.* Aladdin, 1976.

Walsh, Ellen Stoll. *Mouse Paint.* Voyager Picture Books, 1995.

Warner, Gertrude Chandler. The Boxcar Children series. Albert Whitman, 1990.

Watterson, Bill. *Calvin and Hobbes.*

Weber, Bernard. *Ira Sleeps Over.* Houghton Mifflin, 1975.

White, E.B. *Charlotte's Web.* Harpercollins Children's Books, 1952.

Wilder, Laura Ingalls. *The Little House.* HarperCollins Juvenille Books, 1999.

Yahima, *Taro. Crow Boy.* Viking Press, 1976.

Yolen, Jane. *The Devil's Arithmetic.* Puffin, 1990.

Credits

Byrd Baylor: From I'M IN CHARGE OF CELEBRATIONS BY BYRD BAYLOR. ©1986 Byrd Baylor. (New York: Charles Scribner's Sons.)

Ellen Blonder: From NOISY BREAKFAST BY ELLEN BLONDER, 1994, Scholastic, Stage A, Beginning Literacy.

Lucy Calkins: Reprinted by permission of Lucy Calkins and Heinemann: THE ART OF TEACHING WRITING (Heinemann, A division of Reed Elsevier Inc., Portsmouth, NH, 1994).

Sandra Cisneros: From THE HOUSE ON MANGO STREET. © 1984 by Sandra Cisneros. Published by Vintage Books, a division of Random House, Inc., New York and in hardcover by Alfred A. Knopf in 1994. Reprinted by permission of Susan Bergholz Literary Services, New York. All rights reserved.

Joy Cowley: From WHAT WOULD YOU LIKE? by Joy Cowley. Reprinted by permission of The Wright Group, 19201 120th Avenue NE, Bothell, WA 98011 (800-523-2371)

Eloise Greenfield: "Things" from HONEY, I LOVE AND OTHER POEMS by Eloise Greenfield. 1986.(New York: HarperCollins Publishers.)

Philip Levine: "Starlight" from NEW SELECTED POEMS by Philip Levine. © 1991 by Philip Levine. Reprinted by permission of Alfred A. Knopf, a Division of Random House, Inc.

Patricia MacLachlan: From JOURNEY by Patricia MacLachlan & Illustrations by Barry Moser, ©1991 by Patricia MacLachlan, Illustrations © 1991 by Barry Moser. Used by permission of Dell Publishing, a division of Random House, Inc.

Robert A. Morris: From DOLPHIN by Robert A. Morris. 1983. (New York: HarperTrophy.)

Sarah Prince: Excerpt from TWINS by Sarah Prince.© 1999 Sundance Publishing; text ©Sarah Prince; developed by Eleanor Curtain Publishing. Reprinted by permission.

Prince Redcloud: "Now" by Prince Redcloud as appeared in THE SKY IS FULL OF SONG edited by Lee Bennett Hopkings. (New York: HarperCollins Publishers.)

Angie Sage: MONKEYS IN THE JUNGLE by Angie Sage. © 1989 by Angie Sage. (New York: Dutton Childrens Books, a division of Penguin Putnam, Inc.)

Shel Silverstein: "Invitation" by Shel Silverstein from WHERE THE SIDEWALK ENDS: THE POEMS AND DRAWINGS OF SHEL SILVERSTEIN. 1974. (New York: HarperCollins Juvenille Books.)

Index

A

ABC exploration, 201-203
Accountability, 155-157, 354-357
"Accountable talk," 15, 245-246
Accuracy rate, 122, 141, 149, 150
Active involvement phase, 84, 87, 92-94, 187
Adams, Marilyn, 218
Allyn, Pam, 27
Alphabet chart, 71, 207
Alphabet exploration, 201-203
Amber Brown Sees Red (Danziger), 182
Anchor words. *See* Sight words
Anderson, Carl, 454
Are You There God? It's Me, Margaret (Blume), 341
Arthur, for the Very First Time (MacLachlan), 379, 502
The Art of Fiction (Gardner), 49
Assessment, 44, 71, 137-157
Atwell, Nancie, 24
Author study, 325

B

Baby (MacLachlan), 133, 373
Barbour, Karen, 225
Barnes, Douglas, 61
Barrs, Myra, 442
Bartholomae, David, 479
Barzun, Jacques, 452
Baum, Frank L., 375-376
Baylor, Byrd, 52-53, 54
Beginning readers. *See also* Emergent readers; Primary grades
    assessing, 145
    bookshelves for, 71
    coaching, 112-113
    conferring, 105, 106
    guided reading for, 179
    helping comprehension of, 469
    passive, 169, 256, 257, 273
    reading time for, 70
    strategy lessons for, 190
Beginning to Read (Adams), 218

Bellino, Lydia, 225-226, 262, 301, 432
The Best School Year Yet (Robinson), 466
Bezzone, Nancy, 228
The Big Box (Morrison), 29
Bird by Bird (Lamott), 456
Blueberries for Sal (McCloskey), 244
Blume, Judy, 341, 482
Bomer, Katherine, 398-399, 402, 415-418
Bomer, Randy, 42, 69, 265
Book(s)
    difficult, 134-135
    lack of, 31-32, 438
    matching to readers, 34-36, 139-141
    putting Post-its into. *See* Post-its
    series, 36-37
Book bag, 20, 23, 70
Book choice
    for book clubs, 402-403
    struggling readers and, 120
    teaching making wise, 122
Book clubs, 41, 45, 234, 395-427. *See also* Reading centers
    book choices for, 402-403
    forming, 397-399
    lifting level of work in, 410-412
    readiness for, 403-405
    scheduling, 400-402
    vs. reading centers, 405-406
    working well in, 412-418
Book Fairy, 50
Book introduction, 75, 167, 176, 181-185, 193
Bookmarks, 19-20, 70, 171-172
Book-of-the-Month, 29-30
Book reviews, 38-39
Bookshelves, 70-72
Book talks, 225-247
    developing ideas, 233-235
    generating, 231-232
    during guided reading, 177
    leading, 238-243

about Post-its, 365-368
in primary grades, 305-319
promotional, 38-39, 340, 463
about read-alouds, 45, 57-63, 226-233
reflecting on, 241-243
rooted in text, 243-247
structuring, 236-238
Booth, David, 31
Brady, Esther Wood, 514
The Bridge to Terabithia (Paterson), 379, 477
Browne, Anthony, 57-58
Bruchac, Joseph, 480
Bruner, Jerome, 11, 13, 70, 305
Burke, Carolyn, 151, 168
By Different Paths to Common Outcomes (Clay), 184

C

Caccavale, Teresa, 20, 93, 267, 328
The Call of Stories (Coles), 14
Cambourne, Brian, 259
Can I Keep Him? (Kellogg), 273
The Carrot Seed (Krauff), 68
Catherine, Called Birdy (Cushman), 377
Centers. *See* Reading centers
Character study, 469-473
Charlotte's Web (White), 13, 347
Chato's Kitchen (Soto), 378-379
Chen, Linda, 345-346, 449
Chiarella, Mary, 366
Childtimes (Greenfield), 464
Choral reading, 52, 75
Chrysanthemum (Henkes), 28-29, 307-308
Cisneros, Sandra, 486, 504
Classroom libraries, 44
    building, 30-34
    checking books out of, 37-38
    costs of, 32-33
    for guided reading, 180-181
    leveled, 119-135
    organizing, 36-38

management during, 77-79
note-taking during, 453
in primary grades, 255-285
structure of, 66-77
in upper-elementary grades, 337-357
and writing workshops, 66
Inexperienced readers, 172. *See also* Beginning readers
Informal Reading Inventories (IRIs), 149-150, 153-155
Insult to Intelligence (Smith), 457
Interactive writing, 211-212
Intermediate readers, 469
Interpretation strategies, 475-491
asking questions, 477-478
digging into texts, 479-483
ending as vantage point, 483-486
minilessons on, 480-483
In the Middle (Atwell), 24
"Invitation" (Silverstein), 52
IRIs. *See* Informal Reading Inventories
The Island of the Skog (Kellogg), 251

J

Johnston, Tony, 348
Journey (MacLachlan), 243, 382-383, 486-489, 500, 519-523, 525-526
Just Juice (Hesse), 480-481

K

Kapusnak, Karen, 402
Keene, Ellin, 12, 435
Kellog, Steven, 251, 273
King-Smith, Dick, 513
Kline, Suzy, 381
Koala Lou (Fox), 347-348
Krashen, Steve, 32
Kraus, Robert, 183
Krauss, Ruth, 68
Kuskin, Karla, 301

L

Lamott, Anne, 456, 511
Language learning, establishing conditions for, 256-271
Layden, Gaby, 160, 461, 464-466
Leading questions, 88
Leif, Erica, 98, 110, 347-349, 412
Lester, Julius, 53
Letters
lowercase, 206
teaching, 197-205
Leveled classroom libraries, 119-135, 340

Leveling
effect on teaching, 129-133
explaining, 292-293
risks of, 126-127
Leveling system, designing, 124-129
Levenstein, Alan, 134
Levine, Philip, 523
Lewis, C. S., 81, 415, 516
Libraries. *See* Classroom libraries
Life in a Crowded Place (Peterson), 51
Lindbergh, Ann Morrow, 510
Link, 84, 87, 94-96, 187
The Lion, the Witch, and the Wardrobe (Lewis), 81
Listening
encouraging, 312-315
lack of
in classrooms, 21-22
at read-alouds, 228-229
teaching and, 9-11
Literary essays
giving students image of, 502-511
teaching writing, 500-502
Litner, Mark, 236
Little, Jean, 379, 407
Little by Little (Little), 379, 407
Little Nino's Pizzeria (Barbour), 225
Little Soup's Birthday (Peck), 103, 140
Lobel, Arnold, 61
Lockwood, Ginny, 71, 236
Long words, spelling of, 209
Lopez, Barry, 526
Lowercase letters, 206
Lowry, Lois, 484
Lyons, Trish, 93

M

MacLachlan, Patricia, 133, 243, 348, 373, 379, 382, 486, 500, 502, 519
Making Words (Cunningham), 170
Maniac McGee (Spinelli), 377
McCarrier, Andrea, 211
McCloskey, Robert, 244
Meek, Margaret, 74, 442
Mentoring, 8, 23-24, 42, 56, 59, 115-117
Minilessons, 43, 81-99
on character study, 470-473
on finding just-right books, 341
on interpretation strategies, 480-483
read-alouds within, 54
on reading print, 294-296
during reading workshops, 67-68
structure of, 84-96
on thinking about texts, 306-307

on working in book clubs, 412-418
Miscue analysis, 150-155
Miscue Analysis Made Easy (Wilde), 151
The Modern Researcher (Barzun), 452
Moffett, James, 439
Montgomery, Kate, 424-425
Monument (Paulsen), 236-238, 379, 500-502, 507-510
Morris, Robert A., 449
Morrison, Toni, 29
Mosaic of Thought (Keene and Zimmermann), 12, 435
Mowat, Farley, 379
Moyers, Bill, 29
Mrs. Wishy Washy (Cowley), 205
Murray, Donald, 6, 510
The Music of Dolphins (Hesse), 380
My Best Friend (Hutchin), 297

N

Names, study of, 197-200
Nate the Great (Sharmat and Simont), 162
Near the Window Tree: Poems and Notes (Kuskin), 301
Newkirk, Tom, 316
Newspaper articles, 442-444
conferring on reading, 110
for guided reading, 181
minilesson on reading, 93
Nia, Isoke, 461, 464-465
Nonfiction reading, 437-457
crisis in, 438-439
following author's trail of thought in, 451-456
interesting, 440-446
providing time for, 444-446
reading aloud, 54-56, 446-448
reading partners in, 444, 449-451
Note-taking, 452-455
Numeroff, Laura, 97
Nye, Naomi, 510

O

Oh, No! (Scarffe and Kent), 85
Old Yeller (Gipson), 379
On Being Literate (Meek), 74
One Hundred Dresses (Estes), 434

P

Parents-as-Reading Partners day, 30
Partners, reading. *See* Reading partners
Paterson, Katherine, 360, 375, 379, 477, 494